ENVIRONMENTAL DISCOURSES IN PUBLIC AND INTERNATIONAL LAW

This collection of essays examines the development and application of environmental laws and the relationship between public laws and international law. Notions of good governance, transparency and fairness in decision-making are analysed within the area of the law perceived as having the greatest potential to address today's global environmental concerns. International trends, such as free trade and environmental markets, are also observed to be infiltrating national laws.

Together, the essays illustrate the idea that in the context of environmental problems being dynamic and environmental changes appearing sudden, laws become difficult to design and effect. Typically, they are also devised within a conflicted setting. It is in this changeable and discordant context that environmental discourses such as precaution, justice, risk, equity, security, citizenship and markets contribute to legal responses, present legal opportunities or hinder progress.

BRAD JESSUP teaches and researches at the Australian National University across the disciplines of law and geography.

KIM RUBENSTEIN is the Director of the Centre for International and Public Law at the ANU College of Law and the inaugural Convenor of the ANU Gender Institute at the Australian National University, Canberra.

CONNECTING INTERNATIONAL LAW WITH PUBLIC LAW

This series of books flows from workshops bringing public and international lawyers and public and international policy-makers together for interdisciplinary discussion on selected topics and themes. It aims to broaden both public and international laws' understanding of how these two areas intersect. Until now, international and public law have mainly overlapped in discussions on how international law is implemented domestically. This series is unique in consciously bringing together public and international lawyers to consider and engage in each other's scholarship.

General editors

Professor Kim Rubenstein, Australian National University
Professor Thomas Pogge, Yale University

Books in the series

Incentives for Global Public Health: Patent Law and Access to Essential Medicines, edited by Thomas Pogge, Matthew Rimmer and Kim Rubenstein

Sanctions, Accountability and Governance in a Globalised World, edited by Jeremy Farrall and Kim Rubenstein

Environmental Discourses in Public and International Law, edited by Brad Jessup and Kim Rubenstein

ENVIRONMENTAL DISCOURSES IN PUBLIC AND INTERNATIONAL LAW

Edited by

BRAD JESSUP

and

KIM RUBENSTEIN

CAMBRIDGE
UNIVERSITY PRESS

CAMBRIDGE UNIVERSITY PRESS
Cambridge, New York, Melbourne, Madrid, Cape Town,
Singapore, São Paulo, Delhi, Tokyo, Mexico City

Cambridge University Press
The Edinburgh Building, Cambridge CB2 8RU, UK

Published in the United States of America by Cambridge University Press, New York

www.cambridge.org
Information on this title: www.cambridge.org/9781107019423

First published 2012

Printed in the United Kingdom at the University Press, Cambridge

A catalogue record for this publication is available from the British Library

Library of Congress Cataloguing in Publication data
Environmental discourses in public and international law / edited by Brad Jessup and Kim Rubenstein.
p. cm. – (Connecting international law with public law)
ISBN 978-1-107-01942-3 (Hardback)
1. Environmental law, International–Congresses. I. Jessup, Brad, 1978–
II. Rubenstein, Kim.
K3584.8.E578 2012
344.04′6–dc23
2011040524

ISBN 978-1-107-01942-3 Hardback

CONTENTS

CONTRIBUTORS

Editors

BRAD JESSUP is a Teaching Fellow with the Australian Centre for Environmental Law and the ANU College of Law, at the Australian National University. He has Honours degrees in law and science from Monash University and a Master's of Philosophy in geography from the University of Cambridge, and is admitted to practise in Australia. Brad teaches and researches across the disciplines of law and geography, taking critical and cross-jurisdictional approaches to his work. His Ph.D. research explores concepts of environmental and ecological justice in environmental law. Brad has also recently researched and published on the regulation of marine protected areas across jurisdictional boundaries, on public environmental law reform and transnational environmental discourses in wind energy disputes.

PROFESSOR KIM RUBENSTEIN is Professor and Director of the Centre for International and Public Law in the ANU College of Law at the Australian National University and inaugural Convenor of the ANU Gender Institute. A graduate of the University of Melbourne and Harvard University, Kim's current research projects are at the cutting edge of the intersection between public and international law. Her public law work spans constitutional and administrative law, and also includes her expertise in citizenship law. Her international law work focuses on the status of nationality. Her book, *Australian Citizenship Law in Context* (2002) represents the foundation of her continued scholarly work, looking at the disjuncture between the exclusive legal notion and the more inclusive normative understanding of citizenship.

Other contributors

DR AFSHIN AKHTARKHAVARI researches and writes on international law and politics. He is the author of *Global Governance of the Environment: Environmental Principles and Change in International Law and Politics* (2011) and co-author of *International Law: Cases and Materials with Australian Perspectives* (Cambridge University Press, 2010). Afshin is the Deputy Head of School (Academic) at Griffith Law School where he continues to work on a variety of internationalisation strategies including curricular initiatives. Afshin is preparing a book examining the nature of environmental governance through dispute settlement bodies, including investment and commercial arbitration, and other public dispute settlement bodies like the International Court of Justice, the Law of the Sea Tribunal and the Dispute Settlement of the World Trade Organization.

PROFESSOR BEN BOER is Emeritus Professor of Environmental Law in the Australian Centre for Climate and Environmental Law at the Sydney Law School. He teaches in the areas of international environmental law, Asian and Pacific environmental law and heritage law. He is co-chair of the IUCN World Commission on Protected Areas and Commission on Environmental Law Specialist Group on Protected Areas Law and Policy. Ben is a co-author, with Graeme Wiffen, of *Heritage Law in Australia* (2006) and the chief editor of *Sustainability Law after Rio* (2011). His current primary research focus is on protected areas law. He was the New Zealand Law Foundation Distinguished Visiting Fellow in 2011.

SANJA BOGOJEVIĆ is a lecturer in EU and Environmental Law at Lund University. Her doctoral research is concerned with the regulation of common resources, more precisely emissions trading schemes, and the way in which these are furthered and understood in environmental law scholarship. Sanja studied for a D.Phil. in Law at Corpus Christi College, Oxford. She has previously been appointed research visitor to the Max Planck Institute for Collective Goods in Bonn and a doctoral Hauser Global Fellow at NYU Law School.

RIVER CORDES-HOLLAND is a Ph.D. candidate at the ANU College of Law. He holds an LL.B. (Hons) and a University Medal in Law from the ANU. He has taught international law and tort law and has published on the international human rights implications of climate change and domestic regulation measures to mitigate climate change. River's Ph.D. thesis examines the notion of good international citizenship and the Australian Rudd Labor government's engagement with international climate law. River's research included a field trip to the UN Climate Change Conference in Copenhagen, 2009.

DR JAYE ELLIS is an associate professor in the Faculty of Law and School of Environment at McGill University. She teaches and conducts research in the fields of international environmental law, public international law and global environmental politics. Jaye's current research projects focus on principles of environmental law such as precaution and sustainable development and on intersections among science, law and politics. Her recent publications include 'Sustainable Development and Fragmentation in International Society' in Duncan French (ed.), *Global Justice and Sustainable Development* (2010) 57; and 'Sustainable Development as a Legal Principle: A Rhetorical Analysis' in Hélène Ruiz Fabri, Rüdiger Wolfrum and Jana Gogolin (eds.), *Selected Proceedings of the European Society of International Law*, Vol. II (2010) 642.

PROFESSOR LEE GODDEN is the Director of the Centre for Resources, Energy and Environmental Law, at Melbourne Law School, The University of Melbourne. Lee's research interests include environmental law, natural resources law, property law and indigenous peoples' land law. Engagement with the theoretical and the grounded aspects of law is a hallmark of her research, which draws on her interdisciplinary background in law and geography. Lee's current research projects include examining environmental governance under climate change with a focus on emissions trading, water law and energy regulation. Her recent publications include: *Environmental Law: Scientific, Policy and Regulatory Dimensions* (2010), co-authored with Jacqueline Peel, and the co-edited collection *Property and the Law in Energy and Natural Resources* (2010).

DR NICOLE GRAHAM is a senior lecturer with the Faculty of Law at the University of Technology Sydney. She holds a B.A. (Hons) and a University Medal in cultural studies, an LL.B. (Hons) and a Postgraduate Certificate in Higher Education from Macquarie University. Nicole received a Ph.D. in law from the University of Sydney for her dissertation 'Lawscape: Paradigm and Place in Australian Property Law'. Nicole has received awards for her teaching and has taught in law, cultural studies and environmental management programmes. Her research is concerned with the relationship between property and the environment in modern law and culture and is the subject of her book *Lawscape: Property, Environment, Law* (2011).

STEFAN GRUBER is a Ph.D. candidate at Sydney Law School at the University of Sydney. He is a legal practitioner and member of the Chamber of Lawyers, Frankfurt am Main. Stefan was educated at the Universities of Sydney, Frankfurt, Mainz, and at Harvard Law School, and holds degrees in law, philosophy and political science. His doctoral research focuses on the conservation of cultural heritage in China and explores the need for more decisive legal and political action in that area. Stefan is a member of the editorial board of the *Harvard Asia Pacific Review* and the Director of Research and Development of the Association of Pacific Rim Universities Doctoral Students Network. He has published in the areas of cultural heritage law, international environmental law, just war theory and international relations.

PROFESSOR KHENG-LIAN KOH is Emeritus Professor in the Faculty of Law at the National University of Singapore (NUS), and is the Director and one of the founders of the Asia-Pacific Centre for Environmental Law. Kheng-Lian served as the IUCN Commission on Environmental Law Regional Vice Chair for South and East Asia, and was a member of its Steering Committee from 1996 to 2004. She teaches environmental law at the NUS. Kheng-Lian has been a visiting professor at the Universidad Metropolitana de Mexico and the Richardson School of Law, Hawaii. From 1980 to 1986 she served as a legal officer in the secretariat of the United Nations Commission on International Trade Law in Vienna.

DR BETTINA LANGE is a university lecturer in law and regulation at the Centre for Socio-Legal Studies, Oxford University. A graduate of Warwick University, UK, she is currently working on a research project that examines the invocation of emotion discourses in European Union regulation of transgenic agriculture. She is also working with Dr Alexiadou, Keele University, UK, on a project that analyses the deployment of soft modes of governance, such as the Open Method of Co-ordination, for achieving convergence of education policies in the European Union. Her recent book *Implementing EU Pollution Control: Law and Integration* (2008) explores from a discourse analytical perspective the contribution of environmental 'law in action' to EU integration.

PETER LAWRENCE is a senior lecturer at the University of Tasmania Law School. Peter led a number of Australian delegations to international environment treaty negotiations during a posting to the Australian Mission to the United Nations with the Australian Department of Foreign Affairs and Trade. He has published extensively in the field of international environmental law. Peter's current research interests include climate justice and climate change and technology transfer. Peter is currently working on a book *Justice for Future Generations: Climate Change and International Law* (forthcoming). In 2011 he was an ANU visiting fellow, delivered a Wilhelm Merton Centre lecture at J. W. Goethe University of Frankfurt and a guest lecture at the Smith School of Enterprise and the Environment, University of Oxford.

DR SIMON MARSDEN is an associate professor at Flinders Law School and holds a B.A. (Hons) in Politics (York), LL.M. in Environmental Law (Aberdeen) and a Ph.D. (Tasmania). He is qualified to practise as a solicitor in England and a legal practitioner in Australia. Simon specialises in strategic and transboundary approaches to environmental impact assessment, and the relationship between legal systems. Simon's publications include: *Strategic Environmental Assessment in Australasia* (2002, edited with Stephen Dovers), *Strategic Environmental Assessment in International and European Law* (2008) and *Transboundary Environmental Impact Assessment in the European Union* (2011, edited with Timo Koivurova). Simon has worked as an academic in Ireland, England, Australia and Hong Kong and a legal adviser at the Environment Agency of England and Wales.

PROFESSOR PAUL MARTIN is the Director of the Australian Centre for Agriculture and Law at the University of New England. Paul oversees the Centre's science-informed law and policy research, with its particular emphasis on rural sustainability. Prior to this role Paul was the chair of regional catchment management organisations and of listed and private corporations. He was also a senior visiting fellow at the Australian Graduate School of Management for twenty years, responsible for a range of programmes in both law and entrepreneurship. Paul has authored books and studies on taxation, natural resources and negotiation, including *Sustainability Strategy* (2006) with Miriam Verbeek.

JULIA MAYO-RAMSAY is a barrister and solicitor of the Supreme Court of New South Wales and a Ph.D. candidate with the Institute of Marine and Ocean Studies at the University of Tasmania. Julia's Ph.D. research is focused on assessing the environmental and legal implications of climate change and climate mitigation measures on the oceans, in particular ocean fertilisation. Her other research interests include law of the sea, fisheries law and biodiversity of the oceans. Julia holds bachelor degrees in Legal and Justice Studies (Southern Cross University) and Law (University of New England), a Master's of Applied Science (Hawkesbury) and a Master's of Laws (ANU).

DR JEFFREY MCGEE is a senior lecturer in the School of Law at the University of Newcastle, Australia. He has a degree in Law from the Australian National University, a Master's degree in Environmental Studies from the University of Newcastle and a Ph.D. in Environment and Geography from Macquarie University, Sydney. Jeff teaches environmental law and public international law at the University of Newcastle. His research centres on the use of interpretative policy analysis to examine interaction between UN and non-UN agreements within the international climate regime.

PROFESSOR THOMAS POGGE is Leitner Professor of Philosophy and International Affairs at Yale, Professorial Fellow at the ANU Centre for Applied Philosophy and Public Ethics, and a research director at the Oslo University Centre for the Study of Mind in Nature. Focused on Kant and in moral and political philosophy, his publications include *Politics as Usual* (2010), *World Poverty and Human Rights* (2nd edn, 2008), *John Rawls: His Life and Theory of Justice* (2007), *Freedom from Poverty as a Human Right* (edited, 2007), and *Global Justice/Global Ethics* (co-edited, 2008). Thomas is editor for social and political philosophy for the *Stanford Encyclopedia of Philosophy* and a member of the Norwegian Academy of Science.

PROFESSOR DONALD R. ROTHWELL is Professor of International Law with the ANU College of Law at the Australian National University. His major areas of research include the law of the sea, the law of the polar regions and the application of international law within Australia. Between 2005 and 2009 he provided advice to the International Fund for Animal Welfare in their campaign to halt Japan's 'scientific' whaling programme in the Southern Ocean. His most recent book is *The International Law of the Sea* (2010) with Dr Tim Stephens.

ELIZABETH ROUGH is a Ph.D. student in the Department of Geography at the University of Cambridge. Her doctoral research examines the development of nuclear energy policy in the UK since the 1950s, with a specific focus on accounting for periods of stability and change in policy. The research for her contribution to this volume was generously funded by the Economic and Social Research Council, the Smuts Memorial Fund and the International Alliance of Research Universities.

DR MARK SHEPHEARD has research interests concerning problems of multiple and competing meaning and environmental stewardship obligations in farming. Mark's Ph.D. research at the University of New England investigated the practical implications for farming of civil duties being reinterpreted to incorporate environmental protection and sustainability obligations. Mark has received an Australian Endeavour Research Fellowship to Lincoln University in New Zealand (2010), and a visiting fellowship from the Swiss National Science Foundation to the University of Lucerne (2011). Both have been used to further his research on water stewardship obligations. Prior to his doctoral research, Mark was involved with sustainability and natural resource management research at the CSIRO and he worked for several state government natural resource management agencies.

DR TIM STEPHENS is a senior lecturer with the Sydney Law School at the University of Sydney. Tim is an international lawyer and human geographer. He holds a B.A. and LL.B. (both with Honours) from the University of Sydney, an M.Phil. in Geography from the University of Cambridge, and a Ph.D. in Law from the University of Sydney. Tim's research is focused on public international law, and in particular the law of the sea and international environmental law. His recent publications include *International Courts and Environmental Protection* (2009), the first comprehensive treatment of the role of international courts in addressing environmental disputes, and *The International Law of the Sea* (with Professor Donald R. Rothwell, 2010).

PROFESSOR ROS TAPLIN is Professor of Environmental Management and Program Director with the Institute of Sustainable Development and Architecture at Bond University. Ros has over twenty years' research and consulting experience in international and domestic environmental management and climate change policy. Her work has focused on sustainable energy, air quality, carbon reporting, environmental reporting, corporate responsibility and sustainability, new environmental policy instruments, environmental impact assessment, voluntary environmental agreements, sustainable cities and coastal management. Ros currently teaches in the environmental and carbon management programmes at Bond and her present research centres on international and domestic climate change issues.

SERIES EDITORS' PREFACE

The idea for this series began in June 2005, when Kim Rubenstein applied for the position of Professor and Director of the Centre for International and Public Law at the ANU College of Law. The Centre is recognised as the leading Australian academic centre bringing together public lawyers (constitutional and administrative law broadly, but also specific areas of government regulation) and international lawyers from around the world. Established in 1990 with its inaugural director Professor Philip Alston, the impact of the Centre and its work can be seen further at law.anu.edu.au/cipl/.

In discussing with the law faculty ideas for the Centre's direction, Kim raised the concept which underpins this series. Each volume flows from workshops bringing public and international lawyers and public and international policy experts together for interdisciplinary discussion on selected topics and themes. The workshops attract both established scholars and outstanding early scholars. At each of the workshops participants address specific questions and issues developing each other's understandings and knowledge about public and international law and policy and the links between the disciplines as they intersect with the chosen subject. These papers are discussed and reviewed at the workshop collaboratively, then after the workshop the papers are finalised for the final editing phase for the overall manuscript.

The series seeks to broaden understanding of how public law and international law intersect. Until now, international and public law have mainly overlapped in discussions on how international law is implemented domestically. While there is scholarship developing in the area of global administrative law, and some scholars have touched upon the principles relevant to both disciplines, the publications to date contain only a subset of the concept underpinning this series. It is unique in consciously bringing together public and international lawyers to consider and engage in each other's scholarship.

Beyond the first topic of sanctions, the other four topics draw from the research themes underpinning the International Alliance of Research Universities (IARU) which is made up of ANU, Berkeley, Cambridge, University of Copenhagen, ETH Zurich, National University of Singapore, Oxford, Peking University, University of Tokyo and Yale. The topics include volumes on Health (Volume 2) Environment (Volume 3), Movement of People (Volume 4) and Security (Volume 5).

The IARU has also supported the funding of participants from the IARU in some instances so that they can attend in person at ANU. This does not preclude non-IARU academics from participating, as will be seen in the rich array of participants in the first three volumes.

After the first successful workshop was complete, Professor Rubenstein contacted Professor Thomas Pogge to co-host the second workshop and in addition to doing that, he has enthusiastically joined with Professor Rubenstein as a joint series editor. His contributions to each volume are an expression of his cosmopolitan outlook, which is a theme engaged with throughout the series.

Kim Rubenstein
and
Thomas Pogge

EDITORS' PREFACE

As explained in the Series Editors' Preface, this series is a result of workshops bringing together public and international lawyers. From the second volume onwards, the topics revolve around the International Association of Research Universities (IARU) thematic research topics. When Kim Rubenstein began thinking about organising the third workshop around the theme of the environment, she was encouraged to contact her ANU colleague Brad Jessup in the Australian Centre for Environmental Law. Brad responded enthusiastically and work began to brainstorm the call for papers.

This third workshop, 'Environmental Discourses in Public and International Law', was inspired by interesting interdisciplinary work on discourse theory which enabled us to bring together a rich array of public and international lawyers with geographers and scientists and political theorists. The workshop explored how dominant environmental thought and action had been placed within public and international law, providing excellent material for the themes the series is exploring.

Our workshop took place on 13–15 August 2009 at the Australian National University. The twenty-one paper presenters and a further fourteen participants, who had read all the papers, enjoyed vigorous discussion, engaging fully with each other and the material. We were delighted that we had participants from five IARU universities: ANU, Cambridge, University of Copenhagen, National University of Singapore and Oxford.

We thank Professor Simon Bronitt, then Director of ANU's National Europe Centre, for providing us with a dynamic venue. We thank James Prest from the ANU College of Law, Tom Baxter from the University of Tasmania, and Laura Nielsen from the University of Copenhagen for presenting stimulating papers at the workshop even though they were unable to contribute to the resulting book. Tim Bonyhady, Stella Chu, Jan Cristofani, John Dryzek, Elinor Jean, Radha Govil, Alison McLennan, Rebecca Monson, Andrew Ross, Erika Techera, Fanny

Thornton, Petrina Schiavi, Hayley Stephenson and Scott Wyatt participated in discussions and we thank them for their valuable contributions to the workshop.

We are grateful to the IARU universities' support through Cambridge University for Elizabeth Rough's travel to the workshop, Oxford University for Sanja Bogojević and Bettina Lange's travel, the University of Copenhagen for Laura Nielsen's travel, National University of Singapore for Kheng-Lian Koh's travel and the ANU Vice Chancellor's Travel Fund for Jaye Ellis's participation.

The event was ably organised by the ANU College of Law Outreach and Administrative Support Team and in particular Sarah Hull. ANU law student Ali Clare worked with us reviewing the papers on style matters and we thank her and Glenda Waddell from the ANU College of Law for their assistance in putting this volume together. We also thank the sixteen anonymous reviewers whose critiques of the papers strengthened the chapters in this collection.

The staff at Cambridge University Press, especially Finola O'Sullivan, have been enthusiastic in supporting this series and Lynn Aitchison as copy-editor has been excellent.

Finally, we would like to thank our colleagues in the Centre for International and Public Law and the Australian Centre for Environmental Law in the ANU College of Law and our respective families and friends for their support and inspiration in all that we do.

Brad Jessup
and
Kim Rubenstein
January 2011

Introduction

Using discourse theory to untangle public and international environmental law

BRAD JESSUP AND KIM RUBENSTEIN

1. Introduction

The world is talking, pondering and strategising about the environment. Ever more of the environment has been identified, publicly contemplated, or designated for despoliation and resource extraction. Remote and 'wild' places like the rugged Australian Kimberley and the far reaches of North America are now subject to advanced plans for fossil fuel extraction. Environmental disasters, including fires, floods, cyclones, earthquakes and tsunami, and schemes to alleviate or prevent future human suffering from catastrophe, have occupied governmental and organisational attention. Meanwhile, concerns about environmental degradation, and in particular human-induced climate change, dominate Western media[1] and national and international politics,[2] and are connecting communities through conversation and localised action.[3] The nature, breadth and extent of global responses to climate change

[1] Indeed, the reporting of climate change in the media has become a subject of scholarly inquiry. See, e.g., *Yale Forum on Climate Change & the Media*, www.yaleclimatemediaforum.org (2010) last accessed 22 November 2010.

[2] As well as remaining politically troublesome in the national context (for example, in New Zealand, United States, Canada) climate change remains on the agenda of the G20, and the Group of 8, among other general political fora. See Parliament of Australia, Department of Parliamentary Services, Parliamentary Library, *Background Note: Climate Change Discussions and Negotiations: A Calendar*, 17 July 2009.

[3] See, e.g., Brad Jessup, 'Plural and Hybrid Environmental Values: A Discourse Analysis of the Wind Energy Conflict in Australia and the United Kingdom' (2010) 19 *Environmental Politics* 21. Philippe Sands, *Principles of International Environmental Law* (Cambridge University Press, 2nd edn, 2003) also notes that many grassroots community groups are connected through international networks.

are also points of contention between the developing and developed worlds.[4]

The discussion, arguments and posturing about the environment have sometimes led to the development of laws or legal institutions to mitigate environmental harm at the international, national or sub-national levels. Pollution control legislation, environmental assessment laws and land reservation laws have spread across public legal systems, particularly since the late 1960s. At the same time, the international community has recognised its responsibility to manage the global environment and has agreed to regulate parts of the environment, especially the atmosphere, oceans, heritage and biological diversity. As environmental economists have become more involved in environmental debates, the world also now aims to protect the environment through ecological commodification.[5]

Whether at the international, national or sub-national level, environmental laws are conventionally understood as based on accepted or agreed legal doctrines and principles[6] or as arising in response to environmental problems.[7] At international law the *Trail Smelter Arbitration*[8] represents the first adaptation of general principles into an environmental context, while the promulgation of the National Environmental Policy Act,[9] creation of the Environmental Protection Agency and the passing of the Clean Air Act in the United States in 1970 are considered an environmental law revolution within the context of a rising global environmental concern.[10] In this regard, the development of environmental laws can be considered an extension of other foundational international and public laws. Across their spectrum, these laws can also be seen as endorsing and implementing theorised environmental

[4] This was evident in the United Nations Framework Convention on Climate Change Conferences of Parties in Bali (COP13) and Copenhagen (COP15). See below Chapter 12 by River Cordes-Holland.

[5] Mark Sagoff, *The Economy of the Earth: Philosophy, Law and the Environment* (Cambridge University Press, 2nd edn, 2008). See also below Chapter 11 by Lee Godden.

[6] See, e.g., Gerard Bates, *Environmental Law in Australia* (Butterworths, Sydney, 1st edn, 1983), which more so than recent editions (for instance, the 6th edn, 2006), particularly emphasises the doctrinal bases for environmental law.

[7] See in particular Richard Lazarus, *The Making of Environmental Law* (University of Chicago Press, 2004), which characterises environmental law as a responsive instrument. Maria Lee, *EU Environmental Law: Challenges, Change and Decision-Making* (Hart Publishing, Oxford and Portland, 2005) also describes the rise of EU environmental law as reacting to social and environmental experiences in the lead-up to the 1970s.

[8] (1938 and 1941) 3 UN Rep. Int. Arb. Awards.

[9] 42 USC 4321.

[10] Lazarus, above n. 7.

principles like polluter pays, the precautionary principle and sustainable development. Additionally, environmental laws can be analysed as responding to concerns including atmospheric pollution, biodiversity loss and land degradation. Insofar as environmental laws are perceived as adoptive or responsive, the conventional view is that international law provides guidance, direction and initiative,[11] while responsibility for the implementation of laws is consigned to national governments.[12] As Hunter *et al.* argue, 'international environmental law depends for its effectiveness on proper implementation and enforcement at the national level'.[13]

This book, the third in a series connecting public and international law,[14] offers different views about the development and application of environmental laws on two important fronts. First, the chapters in this book position the development of environmental laws as being more complex than a conventional linear, principled or responsive approach. Just as environmental problems can be dynamic and environmental changes appear sudden,[15] laws can be, and often presently are, much more difficult to design and effect in the typically conflicted setting within which they are devised.[16] This is not a novel contribution. Ruhl has argued this point forcefully, critiquing the reducible, linear and predictable treatment of the environment by conventional law, and providing a complex adaptive system analysis to the law.[17] Nevertheless, although there have been efforts to deal with scientific

[11] As noted by Douglas Fisher, *Australian Environmental Law* (Lawbook Co., Sydney, 1st edn, 2003) the judiciary in particular perceive of international law in this way.

[12] Sands, above n. 3, 175 onwards.

[13] David Hunter, James Salzman and Durwood Zaelke, *International Environmental Law and Policy* (Foundation Press, New York, 2nd edn, 2002) 469.

[14] The first two volumes are Jeremy Farrall and Kim Rubenstein (eds.), *Sanctions, Accountability and Governance in a Globalised World* (Cambridge University Press, 2009) and Thomas Pogge, Matthew Rimmer and Kim Rubenstein (eds.), *Incentives for Global Public Health: Patent Law and Access to Essential Medicines* (Cambridge University Press, 2010).

[15] Hunter *et al.*, above n. 13, 23–4. Similarly there has been much scholarly discussion of environmental problems being 'wicked' following Horst Rittel and Melvin Webber, 'Dilemmas in a General Theory of Planning' (1973) 4 *Policy Sciences* 155.

[16] Dave Owen, 'Law, Environmental Dynamism, Reliability: The Rise and Fall of CALFED' (2007) *Environmental Law* 1145 illustrates this point using California's water laws as a case study.

[17] J. B. Ruhl, 'Thinking of Environmental Law as a Complex Adaptive System: How to Clean Up the Environment by Making a Mess of Environmental Law' (1997) 4 *Houston Law Review* 101.

uncertainty in law-making,[18] environmental laws are yet to shift. Invariably, when law-makers and administrators confront environmental complexity, law-making and environmental decision-making become problematic or compromised. This has been particularly evident in domestic efforts for carbon trading laws and in international negotiations over greenhouse gas emissions reduction targets, and can be seen in the legal efforts at biodiversity conservation. For example, the law has not been able to develop beyond the simple approach of species protection and habitat reservation to redress biodiversity loss.[19]

It is in this changeable and discordant setting that environmental discourses contribute to legal responses or present legal opportunities or obstacles. A discourse[20] is 'a shared way of apprehending the world. Embedded in language, it enables those who subscribe to it to interpret bits of information and put them together into coherent stories or accounts'.[21] This book argues that legal-policy decisions are not only driven by scientific discoveries, a new appreciation of theories or principles, the adaptation of legal doctrine, or an overwhelming concern about responding to impending disaster. Rather, especially when environmental problems have no simple solutions, environmental decisions may be made based on shared understandings of the problem or solutions, or motivated by dominant perceptions or interpretations of the law and the environment or influenced by coalitions who coalesce around a particular environmental discourse. While the concept of environmental discourses is more familiar to political scientists than lawyers, it resonates within the public and international law sphere – where legal outcomes are usually drawn from or amount to policy. As Blomley, a geographer and lawyer, articulates, the law has an instrumental or policy nature as well as an ideological or moral imperative.[22]

In this collection each chapter reflects on a story, interpretation or understanding of the environment, and these accounts are analysed as important influences on legal change or resistance to change. For instance, the way communities of nations, advocates, politicians and

[18] Dan Tarlock, 'The Nonequilibrium Paradigm in Ecology and the Partial Unraveling of Environmental Law' (1994) 27 *Loyola of Los Angeles Law Review* 1121.

[19] This is argued by Ruhl, above n. 17.

[20] As explained further below in section 2 of this introductory chapter.

[21] John Dryzek, *The Politics of the Earth: Environmental Discourses* (Oxford University Press, 1st edn, 1997) 8.

[22] Nicholas Blomley, 'Law and the Local State: Enforcement in Action' (1988) 13(2) *Transactions of the Institute of British Geographers* 199, 202.

individuals rationalise the need for a response or reform, or insist upon the maintenance of the status quo, and their success in realising their collective intention is relevant to the contributors' thinking.

The second viewpoint offered by this book, and the series of which it is a part, is that international and public laws are more connected and differently connected than conventionally expressed. Again, the starting point to this insight is that laws are often made and interpreted in a dynamic way, rather than always linearly or hierarchically. The relationship between international law and public domestic law is not simply one of searching for meaning or guidance from international law at the domestic level. Although examples of this relationship are given in this book, there are other synergies and connections that are also presented. International climate change negotiations, for instance, are heavily influenced by domestic policy.[23] They have become a game whereby each nation attempts to incorporate as much of their public policy into international decisions as they can. More importantly, some environmental discourses pervade both systems of law. Connecting and analysing the way they play out in each framework illuminates important lessons. The precautionary principle is one long-standing example.[24] Ellis and FitzGerald, for instance, argue that the principle emerged in both international and public law as a result of 'a combination of behaviour and belief over time'[25] expressed within a 'discourse taking place in international and domestic societies'.[26]

Many of the authors advance the Global Administrative Law Project within the frame of environmental discourses. The Global Administrative Law Project[27] has enriched an engagement with the complex ways in which the international and the public intersect, by recording public law

[23] Shardul Agrawala and Steinar Andresen, 'Indispensability and Indefensibility – The United States in the Climate Treaty Negotiations' (1999) 5(4) *Global Governance* 457.

[24] Timothy O'Riordan and James Cameron (eds.), *Interpreting the Precautionary Principle* (Earthscan, London, 1994).

[25] Jaye Ellis and Alison FitzGerald, 'The Precautionary Principle in International Law: Lessons from Fuller's Internal Morality' (2004) 49(3) *McGill Law Journal* 779, 787.

[26] Ibid. 794.

[27] See the full website of the Institute for International Law and Justice, New York University School of Law, *Global Administrative Law Project – Background* at www.iilj.org/GAL/ last accessed 6 December 2010. The website has an extensive bibliography and links to numerous articles, many of which are referred to in the various chapters throughout this book.

principles within the international arena. Concepts like justice, fairness, due process and transparency are the domain of public laws, with international laws and decision-making now being critiqued against these benchmarks of administrative law.

In contentious environmental matters the importance, and often absence, of principled governance is stark. Added to this, developments in public laws, in particular with respect to interpreting sustainable development, have contributed to new understandings about the purpose and administration of environmental laws. At both levels of law decision-makers have increasingly wider obligations of inquiry. The test of sustainable development is not only an often uncomfortable balancing of competing interests and directions,[28] but as the notion becomes entrenched in the legal systems it is now a mandatory consideration with many facets. In the jurisdiction of New South Wales in Australia sustainable development is now considered a part of the 'public interest' that must be considered in every decision affecting the environment. However, what this means will be open to interpretation and challenge at every instance.[29] Indeed, what is 'public' in 'public international law' and 'domestic public law' requires more analysis and is fleshed out in this book's focus on the issues through environmental discourses.

Further, this book illustrates how public and international law are fundamentally influenced by other disciplines, particularly environmental philosophy, environmental policy, ecological economics and international relations. Theorising about the value of the environment, and in particular of human interest in the environment, has also been responsible for significant shifts in the law, and discourses that oxygenate environmental issues and opportunities have both transcended and linked public and international laws.

[28] William Adams, *Green Development: Environment and Sustainability in the Third World* (Routledge, London and New York, 2nd edn, 2001).

[29] See, e.g., *Minister for Planning* v. *Walker* (2008) 161 LGERA 423. At para. [56] Hodgson JA, with whom Campbell JA agreed, stated:

> I do suggest that the principles of [ecological sustainable development] are likely to come to be seen as so plainly an element of the public interest, in relation to most if not all decisions, that failure to consider them will become strong evidence of failure to consider the public interest and/or to act bona fide in the exercise of powers granted to the Minister, and thus become capable of avoiding decisions.

2. Environmental discourses

An environmental discourse is a 'social construct'[30] reflecting how people interpret, give meaning to and represent the environment. As Dryzek's oft-quoted definition of an environmental discourse discloses,[31] discourses are embedded in language[32] and they provide a rallying point for people who find the interpretation of the environment within the particular discourse persuasive, convenient or satisfying. In this respect, Hajer has noted that the coalitions that subscribe to an environmental discourse do not necessarily share views and motives; rather, the coalitions are made up of a mix of people each with their own beliefs and agenda.[33] The disparate membership of environmental coalitions is made possible by the fact that discourses are usually condensed into simple, succinct and agreeable storylines. These storylines, along with other clichés, metaphors and catch phrases become ritualised, entrenched in the environmental debate and often infiltrate common language.[34] Using language and stories, coalitions engage in a struggle for discursive hegemony,[35] and in doing so the members often pragmatically adjust their interests and views to satisfy a desired outcome.[36]

Dryzek[37] argues that policy decisions about the environment reflect and respond to particular environmental discourses. Others before him had demonstrated that individual policy shifts could be attributed to dominant discourses. Hajer, for example, argued that the policy responses to acid rain in the United Kingdom and Europe were driven by, and shifted as a result in changes to, environmental discourses.[38] Litfin also analysed the negotiations that led to international laws to minimise damage to the ozone

[30] Maarten Hajer, 'Discourse Coalitions and the Institutionalization of Practice: The Case of Acid Rain in Britain' in Frank Fischer and John Forester (eds.), *The Argumentative Turn in Policy Analysis and Planning* (Duke University Press, Durham, NC, 1993) 43, 45.

[31] Dryzek, above n. 21, 8.

[32] René Kemp, 'Why Not in My Backyard? A Radical Interpretation of Public Opposition to the Deep Disposal of Radioactive Waste in the United Kingdom' (1990) 22 *Environment and Planning A* 1239, 1244, uses the phrase 'vocabularies of motive'.

[33] Maarten Hajer, *The Politics of Environmental Discourse: Ecological Modernization and the Policy Process* (Clarendon Press, Oxford, 1995).

[34] Hajer, above nn. 30 and 33.

[35] Harriet Bulkeley, 'Discourse Coalitions and the Australian Climate Change Network' (2000) 18 *Environment and Planning C: Government and Policy* 727.

[36] Yvonne Rydin, *Conflict, Consensus and Rationality in Environmental Planning: An Institutional Discourse Approach* (Oxford University Press, 2003); Karen Litfin, *Ozone Discourses: Science and Politics in Global Environmental Cooperation* (Columbia University Press, New York, 1994).

[37] Dryzek, above n. 21. [38] Hajer, above n. 33.

layer through a discursive framework.[39] More recently, Dryzek has suggested that meta-level environmental discourses, including survivalism, problem solving and sustainability have presence and power in the development of international environmental law.[40] This book extends and illustrates Dryzek's overarching contribution with an exposition of micro-level discourses occurring around specific environmental legal policy issues between public and international law.

The definition given to environmental discourses from non-legal disciplines has resonance within environmental law. In the policy-legal arena it is true that 'a shared way of apprehending the world . . . enables those who subscribe to it to interpret bits of information and put them together into coherent stories or accounts'. This is precisely what judges do. Dryzek also argues that '[e]ach discourse rests on assumptions, judgements, and contentions that provide the basic terms for analysis, debates, agreements, and disagreements'.[41] Environmental laws are promulgated dependent on a series of uncertain or arguable foundations, much like environmental discourses are curated. Further, discourses can be seen as occurring and often colouring parliamentary debates and international law fora. The case theories planned and presented by advocates in courts and tribunals make use of discourses, while community groups opposing development often adopt the tactic of devising and faithfully perpetuating a discourse to consolidate their membership into a sometimes unexpected coalition of disparate actors.[42]

3. Traversing jurisdiction

Ellis opens her chapter with the words: 'the environment is everywhere'.[43] This is an important foundation to our thinking about the environment's connection to international and public law, and the feature of the discipline of environmental law that connects international and public law. Because the environment is omnipresent, it cannot be easily confined – let alone to a jurisdiction, a state, or a legal system. Given that environmental issues occur across different scales, the environment lends itself well to regulation by both international and national law. Where the activities of all states impact

[39] Litfin, above n. 36.
[40] John Dryzek, 'Paradigms and Discourses' in Daniel Bodansky, Jutta Brunnée and Ellen Hey (eds.), *The Oxford Handbook of International Environmental Law* (Oxford University Press, 2007).
[41] Dryzek, above n. 21, 8. [42] Hajer, above n. 33.
[43] See below Chapter 5 by Jaye Ellis, 123.

on the wider environment, international law is the obvious institution to expound a legal plan. Naturally, local environmental concerns are addressed through national and sub-national laws, and as is widely and commonly understood, national laws usually give effect to international legal agreements. However, there no longer exists a neat division of responsibilities between the individual, state and the community of nations. Whereas in the past waste control and disposal were issues for local legal response, in a global world with wastes shipped far from source to disposal, an occurrence publicised by the environmental justice movement, they are now matters requiring international attention.[44] The dynamism of the atmosphere and the oceans has also meant that air and water pollution, the troubles of the 1970s that public lawyers sought to regulate,[45] are now an international dilemma pursued by climate change and ocean commons discourse coalitions and confronted through a series of international agreements.

Australia also purports to use its principal environmental law to protect places of historic interest that are in foreign lands.[46] Jurisdiction is becoming blurred, and in this instance a nationalistic discourse of 'memory'[47] is emboldening a government to transform legal boundaries. While legal principles or doctrines seldom transcend from public law systems in international law, the proliferation of international courts and tribunals[48] provides greater opportunities to introduce national understandings of environmental problems and laws couched in discursive terms. For instance, as highlighted above, arguments led by states about intergenerational equity, sustainable development and justice will necessarily be influenced by the dominant discourses to which they have been exposed.

44 David Pellow, *Resisting Global Toxics: Transnational Movements for Environmental Justice* (MIT Press, Cambridge, Mass. and London, 2007).

45 For instance, through the US Clean Water Act, 42 USC § 7401 (1970) and Federal Water Pollution Control Act, 33 USC § 1251 (1972) of the early 1970s. See Lazarus, above n. 7.

46 Section 27C(1) of the Environment Protection and Biodiversity Conservation Act 1999 (Cth) provides that:

> A person is guilty of an offence if:
> (a) the person takes an action; and
> (b) the action is taken outside the Australian jurisdiction; and
> (c) the action results or will result in a significant impact on the environment in a place; and
> (ca) the place is a Commonwealth Heritage place; and
> (d) the place is outside the Australian jurisdiction.

47 Joan Beaumont, 'Contested Transnational Heritage: The Demolition of Changi Prison, Singapore' (2009) 15 *International Journal of Heritage Studies* 294.

48 Ellen Hey, *Reflections on an International Environmental Court* (Kluwer Law International, The Hague, 2002).

Environmental law is also a conduit for the infiltration of public law principles into international law. Upon the birth of environmental law, lawyers recognised that the greatest foe of environmentalists would be the state. Struggles centred on government action, and the discipline of environmental law drew heavily on administrative law.[49] As Sive reflects, in the United States, 'the earliest group of important cases were essentially judicial reviews of administrative actions, instituted by environmental advocates'.[50] This largely remains the case. Environmental litigation is most commonly between a community of concerned people and a government. Decision-makers and their governments are challenged on the grounds of unfairness, opaqueness and improper process.

Traditionally, public law, and in particular administrative law in the domestic context, is thought of as either 'the law relating to the control of government power, the main object of which is to protect individual rights' or slightly differently as 'rules which are designed to ensure the administration effectively performs the tasks assigned to it. Yet others see the principal objective ... as ensuring governmental accountability, and fostering participation by interested parties in the decision-making process.'[51] In a global context where national government activity is becoming privatised or directed by international bargaining and organisations, and with legal recognition of human rights and the rise of a global environmental activism and a global ecological citizenry,[52] the application of principles of public law are being reconsidered much along this line.[53] As Hey explains within the context of the discourse of environmental justice:[54]

[49] David Sive, 'Some Thoughts of an Environmental Lawyer in the Wilderness of Administrative Law' (1970) 70 *Columbia Law Review* 612.

[50] David Sive, 'The Litigation Process in the Development of Environmental Law' (1995) 13 *Pace Environmental Law Review* 1, 5.

[51] Paul Craig, *Administrative Law* (Sweet & Maxwell, London, 3rd edn, 1994) 3.

[52] Andrew Dobson, *Citizenship and the Environment* (Oxford University Press, 2003).

[53] Alfred Aman Jr, 'Globalisation, Democracy and the Need for a New Administrative Law' in Michael Likosky (ed.), *Privatising Development: Transnational Law, Infrastructure and Human Rights* (Martinus Nijhoff Publishers, Leiden, 2005) 271. See also articles in the Global Administrative Law Project, such as David Dyzenhaus, 'The Rule of (Administrative) Law in International Law' (2005) 68 *Law and Contemporary Problems* 127; Janet McLean, 'Divergent Legal Conceptions of the State: Implications for Global Administrative Law' (2005) 68 *Law and Contemporary Problems* 167; and Eyal Benvenisti, 'The Interplay Between Actors as a Determinant of the Evolution of Administrative Law in International Institutions' (2005) 68 *Law and Contemporary Problems* 319.

[54] Hey, above n. 48, 14–15.

> the calls for access to environmental justice involve at least three distinct issues. First, individuals and public interest groups should be able to hold states accountable in law for the non-observance of international environmental law. Second, individuals and public interest groups should be able to hold non-state actors, such as multinational corporations, accountable in law. Third, individuals, public interest groups and states should be able to hold international organizations accountable in law.

While these rights of non-states remain a yet-to-be-realised ideal, there is a shift that has been observed by international jurist, Simma. He believes that:[55]

> international law has undoubtedly entered a stage at which it does not exhaust itself in correlative rights and obligations running between states, but also incorporates common interests of the international community as a whole, including not only states but all human beings. . . . it is on its way to being a true *public* international law.

This commentary accords with the research findings of the Global Administrative Law Project, which is monitoring the 'use of administrative law-type mechanisms, in particular those related to transparency, participation, accountability and review, within the regulatory institutions of global governance'.[56] It is also incorporated in the thinking of a number of the contributors to this book who assist in contextualising the value of public law beyond jurisdictions. As Craig suggests, an adequate understanding of public law 'requires us to articulate more specifically the type of democratic society in which we live and to have some vision of the political theory which that society espouses'.[57] So the meaning and importance of rights, participation and accountability may well differ depending upon the nature of society, or indeed the type of jurisdiction we place those concepts within. Again, this book seeks to delve into those issues by drawing together public and international lawyers through the environmental lens.

4. Structure of the collection

This collection is divided into five parts, each employing environmental discourses in different ways and drawing upon and making rich

[55] Bruno Simma, 'Universality of International Law from the Perspective of a Practitioner' (2009) 20 *European Journal of International Law* 265, 268.

[56] Institute for International Law and Justice, above n. 27 and references above at n. 53.

[57] Craig, above n. 51, 3.

connections between public and international law. Part I explores environmental discourses founded in philosophy or framed as rights within international law and domestic laws. The principle of intergenerational equity, the notion of environmental justice and concepts of landholder duties and obligations are analysed in ways that critique the limits and opportunities of environmental law to pursue and realise the public law objective of fairness for: future generations, the historically disadvantaged and landholders, balanced with environmental protection. Part II focuses on decision-making, with chapters reviewing administrative functions at the international, regional and domestic level. Discourses are evident, and the authors successfully highlight the dominant paradigms, in both public and international law decisions, about the meaning of sustainable development and precaution, the authorisation of genetically modified foods and the pursuit of a nuclear power industry in Britain.

Part III of the book considers environmental discourses at a higher level, within international institutions: courts, organisations and universal procedural activities. Both reflective and prospective, the chapters here chart the discourses of environmental justice and sustainable development within international courts, reveal drivers behind the present human and environmental security agenda within the Association of South East Asian Nations (ASEAN) and its constituent nations, and reinforce the role of public participation in instilling public law principles within the institution of transboundary environmental impact assessment. Part IV narrows in on the overriding environmental issue of our time: climate change. Each chapter distils environmental discourses shaping or frustrating legal developments to combat human-induced climate change. The chapters analyse discourses of climate limits and apocalypse, market governance, good international citizenship, market liberalism and market failure, and discourses of market and regulation in carbon trading. The chapters in Part V explore the discourses about the common areas of humankind – the seas, the poles and human heritage. The discourses underscore the fragile situation these contentious shared components of the earth are in: perpetually threatened by human exploitation while simultaneously being dedicated for conservation.

4.1 Theories and rights as discourses in environmental law

Part I of the collection, commencing with Lawrence, explores the struggle over the meaning and purpose of the concept of intergenerational equity. He considers that intergenerational equity has been weakly expressed in international environmental law with a tepid infusion into public laws. It is the reluctance of both jurisdictions to give effect to a principle that the global community and national governments claim to adhere to that has meant that laws have been unable to achieve what the principle offers. Lawrence argues that the alternative discourse of ecological modernisation has dominated legal developments instead. However, within the context of climate change, Lawrence offers a modified discourse and understanding of equity and justice across generations, drawing on philosophy and morality[58] to offer an alternative approach to the current public and international law stalemate over the regulation of climate change that is returned to in Part IV of the book.

Jessup connects public and international law through the frame of the discourse of environmental justice. He shows how similar arguments and understandings about justness are evident across legal jurisdictions, and how environmental justice activists have used both public and international laws to advance their causes and how the environmental justice movement has influenced legal developments. In a similar vein to Lawrence, Jessup's chapter is drawn from theory,[59] providing a starting point for other contributors to further explore the contribution of the discourse of environmental justice to the development or understanding of other aspects of environmental laws and law-making.

The chapters by Shepheard and Martin, and Graham offer contrasting insights into sustainable land management through discourses of duty and stewardship on the one hand and the discourse of entitlement on the other. The chapters are based on alternative theories and notions of rights and responsibilities. Shepheard and Martin detail the land management duties of care that exist in legislation. They explain that while there appears on the surface to be consensus about the importance of these duties of care, they demonstrate that different discourses across jurisdictions offer at times inconsistent understandings and expectations of the duty. This inconsistency, when consensus is expected, makes the law troublesome, especially for legal administrators charged with

[58] Lawrence particularly depends on the work of Edith Brown Weiss, *In Fairness to Future Generations: International Law, Common Patrimony, and Intergenerational Equity* (United Nations University, Tokyo, 1989).

[59] Notably the scholarship of David Schlosberg, most recently David Schlosberg, *Defining Environmental Justice: Theories, Movements and Nature* (Oxford University Press, 2007).

implementing and enforcing it. They note that a lesson for public and international law is 'to overcome the problem of multiple hidden meanings that is common in political debate about matters where economics and ethics meet, such as sustainable development'.[60]

Graham challenges the private property law regime to which the duties of care exposed by Shepheard and Martin are attached. Rather than critiquing regulatory efforts to manage land use, Graham focuses her attention on what she sees are systemic failures. She argues that the prevailing Western notions of private property are incompatible with international notions of sustainable development and concerns for environmental protection. Graham extracts discourses of dephysicalisation and entitlement within the property law regime, which she argues leads to an abstract understanding of the land and resources and a misplaced sense of responsibility for their protection.

4.2 Discourses in environmental decisions

The three chapters in Part II of the book tackle discourses from different perspectives and each focuses on a different legal jurisdiction. Ellis draws out the ambitious framework of the precautionary principle in international law and then highlights its limitations as a component of sustainable development when the discourse is dominated by expert opinion. Drawing on principles of public law, Ellis argues for a more collaborative approach to understanding and resolving international environmental issues. Ellis further contributes to the collection through her use of 'boundary objects'. The fact that decisions are made on the boundaries – of science and law, and across legal jurisdictions – indicates the sense in bringing together public lawyers with international lawyers and non-lawyers in this book. It also emphasises the value of this series, which is seeking to overcome, contest and analyse boundaries in different legal and political contexts. According to Ellis, one potential outcome of this endeavour is 'more robust decision-making procedures and better results for the environment'.[61]

While Lange adopts an interpretation of discourse unique within the collection,[62] the arguments she makes tie in with the views developed by

[60] See below Chapter 3 by Mark Shepheard and Paul Martin, 93.

[61] See below Chapter 5 by Jaye Ellis, 141.

[62] For Lange discourses are action in performance, fields of knowledge that generate power. See Michel Foucault, 'What is an Author?' in Colin Gordon (ed.), *Power/*

Ellis. Lange, too, is investigating at the boundary of science and politics, and rationality and emotions. She finds that authorisations approving transgenic agricultural products lack the features of public law governance. European regulation and international trade laws limit the relevant considerations for decision-makers to questions of non-discriminatory market access and scientific assessments of risks, to the exclusion of opposing arguments by large segments of the European community.

Rough addresses an equally contentious matter among environmentalists: nuclear energy. She identifies this issue as being 'trans-scientific',[63] something that can only be understood by looking beyond science. Through her chapter, Rough shows how changing views about a civil nuclear power industry in the United Kingdom are captured in a number of narratives perpetuated within and outside the nuclear industry and politics since the early 1970s. She applies the prism of the environmental discourse to a policy-making struggle, identifying influences from beyond Britain and within the public law tradition. For instance, nuclear fears based on international experiences and responses, and developments to facilitate the nuclear build while 'streamlining' public process are both evident in Rough's nuclear narratives.

4.3 *Environmental discourses in legal institutions*

In the first chapter in Part III, Stephens continues his analysis of the treatment of environmental matters by international courts.[64] Adding to his previous scholarship, Stephens's chapter offers an alternative to the conventional view that international courts do not contribute to the process of forming and transforming environmental discourses. While concluding that this international institution has resisted discourses within the rubric of sustainable development, Stephens demonstrates how international courts will continue to be important fora for the ventilation of competing interpretations and discourses of sustainable development.

Knowledge: Selected Interviews and Other Writings, 1972–1977 (Pantheon Books, New York, 1980) 101.

63 Alvin Weinberg, 'Science and Trans-Science' (1972) 10 *Minerva* 209.

64 See Tim Stephens, *International Courts and Environmental Protection* (Cambridge University Press, 2009); Tim Stephens, 'Sustainability Discourses in International Courts: What Place for Global Justice?' in Duncan French (ed.), *Global Justice and Sustainable Development* (Martinus Nijhoff Publishers, Leiden, 2010) ch. 2.

In contrast, Koh demonstrates the increasing receptiveness of ASEAN to discourses of non-traditional, human and environmental security. Within the context of novel transboundary environmental threats – particularly contagious disease and haze – Koh illustrates the growing discourse of environmental security and analyses the response of ASEAN and its member states in international and domestic laws. Koh argues that owing to the advent of new environmental threats that do not recognise borders, ASEAN must be willing to calibrate the international law doctrine of sovereignty to advance the security of the people of South East Asia from environmental harm.

Finally, Marsden analyses environmental impact assessment, a process that has become institutionalised within the law, from the very agreeable storyline of 'public participation'. Guided by principles of public law, this chapter shows how discourse is now evident in the transboundary setting. It is a process that clarifies and publicises the consequences of states proceeding with development with potential to harm other nations, while not interfering with sovereignty as proposed by Koh. Marsden contributes to the Global Administrative Law Project by arguing that public participation is becoming a principle of international environmental law, largely owing to the symbolic force of the Aarhus Convention on Access to Information, Public Participation in Decision-Making and Access to Justice in Environmental Matters.

4.4 Discourses in climate law

Led by Godden's chapter, Part IV of the collection emphasises the role of market responses in framing the debate about the legal response to climate change. Godden contends that this trend is changing contemporary environmental law at both the public and international level. She argues that law is increasingly becoming deregulated (a shift from 'law' to 'governance'),[65] notwithstanding, and in conflict with, the discourses of limits and survival that are perpetuated across legal jurisdictions. Godden articulates a reflexive environmental law and emphasises the growing need for non-traditional forms of responsibility and accountability, so that law frames more diverse and nuanced forms of regulation. A necessary consequence, according to Godden, will be the rise in

[65] Neil Gunningham, 'Environmental Law, Regulation and Governance: Shifting Architectures' (2009) 21 *Journal of Environmental Law* 179.

concern for accountability, transparency and monitoring within climate law generally, but particularly in negotiated international outcomes.

Cordes-Holland offers a detailed inquiry into the Australian contribution to international climate change negotiations, comparing the language and actions of a nation's government at the domestic level with the international level. Cordes-Holland discerns two discourses: one of good international citizenship and the other of the national interest, and he critically analyses the claims of the Australian government that it continues to be a good international citizen. The chapter shows how an environmental discourse led by politicians can be used strategically to resist change just as it is by segments of society to activate change.

A discourse of market liberalism is the focus of the chapter by McGee and Taplin, who chart the retreat from international cooperation on climate change by the United States and Australia under their previous conservative governments. This retreat culminated in the establishment of the Asia-Pacific Partnership, with its focus on voluntary measures and technology transfer to reduce greenhouse gas emissions within the developed and developing world. In their forensic inquiry into the Asia-Pacific Partnership, McGee and Taplin subtly highlight the absence of public law principles within the institution. They expose the neo-liberal model of international cooperation as circumventing legal norms. For instance, the Partnership has no regard for the principle of common but differentiated responsibilities, and while there has been a noticeable trend within the United Nations Framework Convention on Climate Change to incorporate civil society in the policy-making process, the workings of the Asia-Pacific Partnership remain partly secret.

In her chapter, Bogojević extends her previous work in identifying three models for emissions trading systems.[66] She demonstrates that within the broader emissions trading discourse actors have conceived different legislative models to respond to a shared understanding of the problem of climate change using market mechanisms. Further, her work shows the complex interactions between the mechanisations of international law and public law and reveals the battle between preferences for regulation and deregulation in the design of carbon trading regimes.

[66] Sanja Bogojević, 'Ending the Honeymoon: Deconstructing Emissions Trading Discourses' (2009) 21 *Journal of Environmental Law* 443.

4.5 Environmental discourses in the commons

Part V of the collection returns to the commons, which were the subject of one of the most powerful discourses from the 1960s: the discourse of tragedy.[67] In his chapter, Rothwell discusses the much more contemporary discourses of conservation, sovereignty and governance, which direct international discussions for management of the polar regions. Owing to the trend of states asserting jurisdiction over parts of the poles and their adjacent waters, Rothwell explains how a public law dimension has been introduced into management considerations, but has been problematic to enforce in the Antarctic.

Boer and Gruber introduce numerous understandings and classifications of human heritage, generally protected through international treaty and national protection laws. They then detail the environmental discourses presently recharacterising the importance of heritage and supporting new frameworks for heritage laws. Boer and Gruber argue that heritage is now seen variously as a human right, under threat by development, endangered by climate change, and an entitlement of future generations. As a consequence, particular forms of heritage are prioritised for protection while others are, pragmatically, excluded from the attention of international and public laws.

The final two chapters in the collection, by Akhtarkhavari and Mayo-Ramsay, respectively, consider discourses encouraging and cautioning plans to divert carbon dioxide, a human-generated greenhouse gas, from the atmosphere into or under the oceans. Akhtarkhavari is concerned with the technology of seabed disposal of greenhouse gases. He shows how the laws requiring precautionary action are being interpreted and presented in a discursive fashion, 'as an open-textured norm'[68] inconsistently with their legal meaning. Akhtarkhavari also introduces a novel connection between public and international laws within the collection. Under the 'precautionary' international regime for the regulation of deep seabed disposal of carbon dioxide, states must adopt a set process for permits. The international law has become public law.

The chapter by Mayo-Ramsay illustrates how, for the purpose of ocean fertilisation (making the oceans absorb more carbon dioxide), the oceans are interpreted in a utilitarian or eco-modernist way as a sink for greenhouse gas emissions. Ocean fertilisation still lacks, but

[67] Garrett Hardin, 'The Tragedy of the Commons' (1968) 162 *Science* 1243.

[68] See below Chapter 17 by Afshin Akhtarkhavari, 418.

requires, regulation in the high seas and the territorial waters of states. How the activity is regulated will be intriguing. Will public and international laws characterise the process as a risk to the oceans or as an appropriate solution to climate change? According to Mayo-Ramsay it must do both. She concludes that '[. . .] the governance structure will have to deal with the view of the ocean as an exploitable commons, the principle of precaution and the marketability of any carbon offsets created through this potential opportunity to mitigate climate change'.[69]

5. Conclusion

Through the talking, pondering and strategising about the environment, through the discourses covered in the various contexts in this book: as rights within international law and domestic laws, through decision-making; at the international, regional and domestic level, through international institutions; courts, organisations and universal procedural activities; through climate change and the common areas of humankind, discourse theory illuminates and untangles intersections between public and international law otherwise not extended.

It develops this series' exploration of the complex interactions that occur when legal regimes intersect, merge or collide. In the first volume, *Sanctions, Accountability and Governance in a Globalised World*,[70] public and international lawyers engaged with one another about the legal principles which cross the international law/domestic public law divide. Through concentrating upon sanctions in the domestic and international context it highlighted the tensions and opportunities that emerge from efforts to apply and enforce law across diverse jurisdictions. It opened up understandings of transparency, accountability and fairness, and extended our appreciation of the range of actors involved in the way international and domestic law operates and the important interplay between law and policy.

In *Incentives for Global Public Health: Patent Law and Access to Essential Medicines*,[71] the second volume drew upon international trade law, innovation policy, intellectual property law, health law, human rights and philosophy, to canvass policy solutions encouraging and rewarding worthwhile pharmaceutical innovation while ensuring affordable access to advanced medicines. The collection brought out the interplay of

[69] See below Chapter 18 by Julia Mayo-Ramsay, 435.

[70] Farrall and Rubenstein, above n. 14. [71] Pogge, Rimmer and Rubenstein, above n. 14.

national and international dimensions and, in particular, the great challenges the national health systems of poorer countries confront on account of an international environment they can do very little to influence. The collection highlighted that substantial progress calls for an integrated solution that combines public law and international law elements to form an effective reform package.

If, as Craig suggests, an adequate understanding of public law 'requires us to articulate more specifically the type of democratic society in which we live and to have some vision of the political theory which that society espouses',[72] then our understanding of these concepts becomes fundamental to the way public law plays out in the international context and vice versa, and in the possibility of connections and tensions between the two. Indeed, as he further suggests, the meaning and importance of rights, participation and accountability may well differ depending upon the nature of society, or indeed the type of jurisdiction we place those concepts within. This book has delved into those issues by drawing together public and international lawyers through the environmental discourse lens.

The fact that so much of environmental discourse involves intersections and boundaries – of science and law, and across and within legal jurisdictions – affirms the importance of bringing together public lawyers with international lawyers and non-lawyers in the ways illustrated through this book. It also emphasises the contribution of this series, which seeks to overcome, contest and analyse boundaries in different legal and political contexts. The environment is fundamental to the future of humanity and this volume speaks to the importance of continuing to talk, to ponder and to strategise.

[72] Craig, above n. 51, 3.

PART I

Theories and rights as discourses in environmental law

1

Justice for future generations: environment discourses, international law and climate change

PETER LAWRENCE

1. Introduction

> The climate change problem is at its heart an ethical problem . . . The main impacts are longer-term ones. The most important potential impacts are very long-term ones. And you have to value the welfare of future generations to want to do anything about this problem.[1]

Philosophers, economists and political scientists have written a great deal about intergenerational equity.[2] Curiously, however, with the notable exception of Edith Brown Weiss's *In Fairness to Future Generations*,[3] there has been a paucity of writing by international lawyers on the subject. This chapter proceeds on the basis that fresh insights can be gained from the concept of intergenerational equity by using discourse analysis and drawing upon philosophical literature. This chapter argues that the relatively weak expressions of intergenerational equity in international environmental treaties, that have filtrated into public

[1] Ross Garnaut, keynote address to the Climate Change and Social Justice Conference, University of Melbourne, 3 April 2008.

[2] See Lukas Meyer, 'Intergenerational Justice' (2008) in *Stanford Encyclopedia of Philosophy* at http://plato.stanford.edu/entries/justice-intergenerational/ last accessed 21 August 2009; Nicholas Stern, *The Economics of Climate Change: The Stern Review* (Cambridge University Press, 2007); Ludvig Beckman, 'Do Global Climate Change and the Interests of Future Generations Have Implications for Democracy?' (2008) 17 *Environmental Politics* 610.

[3] Edith Brown Weiss, *In Fairness to Future Generations: International Law, Common Patrimony, and Intergenerational Equity* (United Nations University, Tokyo, 1989). See also Edith Brown Weiss, 'The Planetary Trust: Conservation and Intergenerational Equity' (1984) 11 *Ecology Law Quarterly* 495; Anthony D'Amato, 'Do We Owe a Duty to Future Generations to Preserve the Global Environment?' (1990) 84 *American Journal of International Law* 190; Emanuel Agius and Salvino Busuttil (eds.), *Future Generations and International Law* (Earthscan, London, 1998).

law, reflect the post-1980s dominance of the discourses of 'ecological modernisation' and 'industrialism' and weaker forms of sustainable development. Further, a discourse emphasising intra-generational equity has displaced future generations' interests. This is illustrated by the global climate change negotiations where the interests of entire nations of future generations of island states are at risk, and nationally where future generations' interests are infrequently considered separately from and inferior to the interests of present generations.

An alternate, though not nearly as prevalent, discourse bases intergenerational equity on theories of justice and ethics. The chapter assesses this discourse, particularly in terms of its ability to address the climate change issue. It is argued that the most promising basis for intergenerational equity is a harm avoidance principle, linked to Hart's minimum content of natural law and an interest-based theory of rights. We must shift to an intergenerational equity discourse grounded in justice and ethics for both reasons of principle and pragmatism. International treaties underpinned by common understandings of fairness, as well as science and economics, face better prospects of gaining support and ultimately being implemented through public laws. The urgency of this task is underscored by the chasm between what scientists are calling for in terms of greenhouse gas reductions and the current state of international negotiations and public law stagnation.[4] The United Nations Intergovernmental Panel on Climate Change (IPCC) has called for a global 25–40 per cent reduction in greenhouse gas emissions by 2020 against a 1990 baseline. The Copenhagen Accord of 18 December 2009 involved a pledge and review mechanism with an objective of limiting climate change to 2°C, but emission reduction commitments have fallen well short of what is required,[5] and what is equitable and just.

2. Intergenerational equity and the dominant discourses of industrialism and ecological modernisation

Hajer argues that from the mid-1980s the dominant way of conceptualising environmental policy-making in Europe and then globally can be

[4] See below Chapter 12 by River Cordes-Holland.

[5] Daniel Bodansky, 'The Copenhagen Climate Change Conference – A Post-Mortem' (2010) 104 *American Journal of International Law* 9.

described as 'ecological modernization'.[6] The elements of ecological modernisation include the internalisation of environmental care within economics and incorporation of the polluter pays principle. Eco-modernists see environmental policies as instruments of economic recovery that can create jobs. Thus, the environment and the economy are seen as mutually reinforcing and supportive of technological innovation which can solve environmental problems.[7]

According to Hajer,[8] ecological modernisation was embodied in the 1987 Brundtland Report's definition of sustainable development as 'development that meets the needs of the present without compromising the ability of future generations to meet their own needs'.[9] The Brundtland approach is often described as 'weak sustainability', in that it permits the earth's natural resources to be reduced provided that, overall, each generation passes on to the next generation a combination of natural and human resources that in total is at a level comparable to or better than the generation inherited. This approach is in contrast to strong sustainability, where development is constrained by the requirement to preserve the earth's integrity combined with a notion of ecological justice.[10]

Ecological modernisation is a reaction against the discourse of 'industrialism' and a 'Promethian' discourse which 'denies the existence of ecological resource limits' and assumes that 'human ingenuity' and technology will always find answers to environmental problems.[11] 'Industrialism' and 'Promethian' discourses have strong roots in ways of thinking that reduce environmental problems to issues of economics.[12] While not using the terminology of discourse, Sagoff[13] demonstrates that in the United States from the 1960s through to the 1980s the

[6] Maarten Hajer, *The Politics of Environmental Discourse: Ecological Modernization and the Policy Process* (Clarendon Press, Oxford/New York, 1995) 101.

[7] Ibid. 95–103. [8] Ibid.

[9] World Commission on Environment and Development, *Our Common Future* (Oxford University Press, 1987) 43.

[10] Klaus Bosselmann, 'Ecological Justice and Law', in Benjamin Richardson and Stepan Wood (eds.), *Environmental Law for Sustainability: A Reader* (Hart Publishing, Oxford and Portland, 2006) 129, 150–5.

[11] John Dryzek, 'Paradigms and Discourses' in Daniel Bodansky, Jutta Brunnée and Ellen Hey (eds.), *The Oxford Handbook of International Environmental Law* (Oxford University Press, 2007) 52.

[12] Joseph Des Jardins, *Environmental Ethics* (Wadsworth Publishing Company, Belmont, Calif., 4th edn, 2006) 45–67.

[13] Mark Sagoff, *The Economy of the Earth* (Cambridge University Press, New York, 1st edn, 1988).

only valid justification for environmental regulation was to redress market failures.[14] Sagoff sharply critiques this approach arguing that environmental issues cannot be reduced to economics and 'are problems primarily moral, aesthetic, cultural and political and must be addressed in those terms'.[15]

The dominance of ecological modernisation discourse, including relatively weak versions of sustainable development, explains the weak embodiment of intergenerational equity in current international environmental treaties and public laws. According to the ecological modernisation approach, the interests of future generations are assumed to largely look after themselves: so long as the internalisation of environmental damage occurs through polluter pays mechanisms, economic growth can continue with the help of technology fixes and existing governance.[16] This is reflected in public environmental laws that increasingly embrace biodiversity offsets to justify harmful activities, employ cap and trade systems of regulation in place of more traditional direct control regulation,[17] and impose criminal sentences that attempt to correlate environmental harm and penalties.[18]

The discourse of industrialism has worked hand-in-hand with what Dryzek describes as the Promethean discourse, which involves, first, the notion that human beings can invent new technologies to overcome any environmental problem and, second, the idea that resource scarcity will be addressed by a combination of the market and new inventions.[19] While the phenomenon of climate change poses a serious challenge to this discourse, the Promethean response is to deny there is a problem by emphasising uncertainties in the science[20] or by arguing that climate change will bring a mix of benefits and burdens with, for example, increased agricultural productivity in some areas making up for decline in others.[21]

These views are associated with the views of the Nobel Laureates of the Copenhagen Consensus who in 2004 concluded that:

[14] Ibid. 29. [15] Ibid. 6.

[16] Indeed, ecological modernisation involves foresight and long-term thinking as part of its essential ingredients. See John Dryzek, *The Politics of the Earth: Environmental Discourses* (Oxford University Press, 2nd edn, 2005) 167–8.

[17] See below Chapter 14 by Sanja Bogojević.

[18] For example, under the Environment Protection Act 1970 (Vic), especially ss. 62A and 67AC.

[19] Dryzek, above n. 11, 45–6. [20] Ibid. 58.

[21] See Bjorn Lomberg, *The Skeptical Environmentalist's Guide to Global Warming* (Cyan-Marshall Cavendish, London, 2007).

> future generations that are richer than ours will generally be able to cope with or adapt to climate change … it therefore makes sense – on both efficiency and equity grounds – to invest massively in physical and human capital now, especially in poor countries, and to divert substantial funding for tackling climate change only at a later date.[22]

This squarely raises the issue of how to balance justice concerns between people alive now and between those living and those born in the future.

3. The intra-generational justice storyline

The Brundtland concept of sustainable development contains within it a strong notion of social justice.[23] According to this approach, sustainable development depends on addressing the needs of the poor as well as the needs of future generations. There is no doubt that sustainable development at a political level has been attractive to many countries because of its emphasis on economic development, with the social justice dimension receiving less attention.[24]

Current negotiations for a post-2012 United Nations (UN) climate change treaty illustrate these tensions. Article 3 of the United Nations Framework Convention on Climate Change[25] (UNFCCC) refers to both 'inter' and 'intra' generational equity and the Bali mandate implicitly includes reference to these principles.[26] However, at the Copenhagen conference discussions about a post-2012 climate change framework, North–South 'intra-generational equity' concerns squeezed out inter-generational equity concerns. Pacific Island countries' calls for deep cuts in greenhouse gas emissions to ensure the future survival of their nations were ignored.[27]

Since international climate change negotiations began, developing countries have consistently argued that industrialised countries must

[22] Mike Hulme, *Why We Disagree About Climate Change* (Cambridge University Press, 2009) 133.

[23] World Commission on Environment and Development, above n. 9, 43.

[24] James Meadowcroft, 'Sustainable Development: A New(ish) Idea for a New Century?' (2000) 48 *Political Studies* 379.

[25] Opened for signature 4 June 1992, 1771 UNTS 107 (entered into force 21 March 1994).

[26] *Report of the Conference of the Parties to the UNFCCC on its Thirteenth Session*, Decision 1/CP 13, FCCC/CP/2007/6/Add1 (2007) (Bali Action Plan) 1(a).

[27] International Institute for Sustainable Development, 'Summary of the Copenhagen Climate Conference, 7–19 December 2009' (2009) Earth Negotiations Bulletin Vol. 12 No. 259 at www.iisd.ca/vol12/enb12459.html last accessed 16 May 2010.

act first by making deep cuts in their greenhouse gas emissions, given their historic responsibility in creating the problem and their greater capacity to respond.[28] Thus developing countries have been using a strong intra-generational equity storyline addressing immediate poverty as a top priority and implicitly overlooking the interests of future generations. As Garnaut explains:

> It might make perfect sense for a rich country like Australia to sacrifice some current income for the benefit of future generations. It will not seem quite as simple a matter for a poor country, with most of its people in abject poverty, that needs rather strong economic growth now to get people out of poverty and give people the luxury of thinking about environmental values and the welfare of future generations.[29]

As developing countries will soon overtake industrialised countries as the greatest collective contributors of greenhouse gas emissions, it has become clear that without significant reductions in emissions it will be impossible to reduce greenhouse gas emissions quickly enough to address this problem, thus creating tension between equity and effectiveness.[30] In this respect, the Copenhagen Accord falls well short of what is required in terms of emission reductions. However, it does make progress in terms of 'major developing countries agree[ing] for the first time to reflect their national emissions reduction pledges in an international instrument'.[31]

Are the storylines of intergenerational and intra-generational equity in conflict in relation to climate change? Certainly it would seem that in developing countries, given their generally weaker governance structures, a rapid economic restructuring to reduce greenhouse gas emissions by a shift from coal to renewables and nuclear energy would result in at least a short-term increase in poverty for sections of society.[32] On the other hand, the IPCC has argued that implementing sustainable development in a way that significantly reduces greenhouse gas emissions can be done by developing countries like China in a manner not involving the slowing of economic development.

[28] Bodansky, above n. 5, 3. [29] Garnaut, above n. 1, 2.

[30] Werner Scholtz, 'Equity as the Basis for Future Global Emission Reductions: Between Pragmatic Panacea and Idealistic Impediment. The optimization of the CBDR principle *via* Realism' (2009) 42(2) *The Comparative and International Law Journal of Southern Africa* 167.

[31] See Bodansky, above n. 5, 10.

[32] David Pearce, 'The Social Cost of Carbon and its Policy Implications' (2003) 19(3) *Oxford Review of Economic Policy* 363.

There are certainly overlaps in considering justice for future generations and justice between those alive today. The interests of future generations and even today's younger people are at a considerable disadvantage in the policy-making process, much like the least powerful in our global society. Some have argued that the claim of the unborn being 'voiceless' is exaggerated,[33] given the overlapping interests of generations and parents' concern for their children. Nevertheless, young people and future generations will be more seriously impacted by climate change[34] than those who are now in positions of power, who will have long since died when the worst impacts manifest themselves.[35] Young people today and future unborn generations have little or no possibility of input into the process when negotiating a global climate change regime. Ironically, this is at a time when climate modelling allows policy-makers to simulate with greater accuracy what a climate-changed world would look like.

Government structures, including both democratic and public law mechanisms, appear to be almost exclusively concerned with the interests of the current generation, particularly given politicians' constant interests in the next election.[36] Since the rise of laissez-faire market capitalism, there has been a decline in the long-term planning approach to government policy that characterised many countries in the period immediately after the Second World War, and with it a consideration of future population.

4. Intergenerational equity in public law

Sustainable development, with its intergenerational equity component, has been embodied in various ways in national constitutions and public laws in many countries around the world.[37] However, it is doubtful whether these constitutions and public laws provide meaningful mechanisms for the representation of future generations' interests.

One of the few cases to consider equity issues for future generations is the *Minors Oposa* case.[38] The Supreme Court of the Philippines

[33] Christopher Stone, 'Ethics and International Environmental Law' in Bodansky, Brunnée and Hey (eds.), above n. 11, 291, 304.

[34] See Stern, above n. 2, ch. 3. [35] Garnaut, above n. 1, 1.

[36] Beckman, above n. 2, 611.

[37] Marie-Claire Cordonier Segger, 'Sustainable Development in International Law' in Hans Christian Bugge and Christina Voigt (eds.), *Sustainable Development in International and National Law* (Europa Law Publishing, Groningen, 2008) ch. 2.1.

[38] *Minors Oposa et al.* v. *Secretary of the Environment and Natural Resources Fulgencio Factoran*, GR No. 101083, 30 July 1993, reprinted in (1994) 33 ILM 173.

considered an action brought by living minors represented by their parents and an environmental non-government organisation. The plaintiffs sought to compel the Philippines government to cancel existing timber licence agreements owing to long-term environmental impacts caused by logging. The minors asserted that they represented their generation as well as generations yet to be born. The Supreme Court acknowledged that the parents, on behalf of the plaintiff children, correctly asserted that the children represented their generation as well as generations unborn: 'Their personality to sue on behalf of the succeeding generations can only be based on the concept of intergenerational responsibility in so far as the right to a balanced and healthy ecology is concerned.'[39]

Some commentators viewed this case as affirming intergenerational equity as a legal principle[40] representing a high point in concurrence between public and international law. Intergenerational equity was given primacy only through the agency of present generations. Intragenerational equity was paramount. Lowe has further pointed out that *Oposa* does not involve any direct representation of future generations in that:

> the actual plaintiffs named in the suit were living minors represented by their parents. The minors asserted that they 'represent their generations as well as generations yet unborn'; but that can scarcely be more than a rhetorical device.[41]

5. Sustainability and intergenerational equity

Given that intergenerational equity is usually considered an integral component of sustainable development, can implementation of sustainable development give substance to intergenerational equity in national legal systems? The experience in Australia has been that sustainable development has not been directly implemented as a justiciable principle and at most has been confined to the objectives sections of statutes without guidance to decision-makers on the weight to be given to its

[39] Ibid. 185.

[40] See, e.g., Antonio La Vina, 'The Right to a Sound Environment in the Philippines: The Significance of the *Minors Oposa* case' (1994) 3 *Review of European Community and International Environmental Law* 246, 247.

[41] A. Vaughan Lowe, 'Sustainable Development and Unsustainable Arguments' in Alan Boyle and David Freestone (eds.), *International Law and Sustainable Development: Past Achievements and Future Challenges* (Oxford University Press, 1999) 19, 27.

component principles.[42] However, jurisprudence is emerging where long-term interests of future generations, such as an interest in expanding renewable energy to combat climate change, has been taken into account in land-use planning disputes.[43] Implicitly, the long-term interests of future generations in sustainable fisheries have played a role in Australian Federal Court decisions considering fisheries legislation.[44] This formative jurisprudence offers hopes for a more ethically based understanding of intergenerational equity at the public law level.

Some policy suggests that a shift in discourse is possible. In a number of national jurisdictions, independent statutory bodies have been created to monitor government performance in relation to future generations' interests. Their goal is to be forward looking and less constrained by existing socio-political paradigms. Examples include the Victorian Commissioner for Environmental Sustainability, the Israeli Commissioner for Future Generations and Finnish Parliament's Committee for the Future. This represents a model for giving local effect to intergenerational equity.

5.1 *Intergenerational equity in international environmental law*

Intergenerational equity has been embodied in global environment treaties in various forms. By and large, however, the domination of the discourses of industrialism, ecological modernisation and weak sustainable development have meant that intergenerational equity has been weakly expressed in international environmental law. The 1992 Convention on Biological Diversity[45] contains a vague reference to the sustainable use of biological diversity to meet the needs and aspirations of 'present and future generations' but contains no obligations to guarantee continuation of habitat essential to the survival of endangered species.

The 1992 Rio Declaration on Environment and Development states: 'the right to development must be fulfilled so as to equitably meet

42 Gerry Bates, *Environmental Law in Australia* (LexisNexis Butterworths, Sydney, 7th edn, 2010) 211.

43 See, e.g., *Taralga Landscape Guardians Inc.* v. *Minister for Planning and RES Southern Cross Pty Ltd* (2007) 161 LGERA 1.

44 Jacqueline Peel, *The Precautionary Principle in Practice, Environmental Decision Making and Scientific Uncertainty* (Federation Press, Sydney, 2005) 79.

45 Convention on Biological Diversity, opened for signature 5 June 1992, 1760 UNTS 79 (entered into force 29 December 1993), Art. 2.

development and environmental needs of present and future generations'.[46] Here intergenerational equity is intertwined with intragenerational rights. This mix reappears in the UNFCCC in Article 3:

> The parties should protect the climate system to the benefit of the present and future generations of humankind, on the basis of equity and in accordance with their common but differentiated responsibilities. Accordingly the developed country parties should take the lead in combating climate change . . .

Another expression of the intergenerational equity discourse involves conserving particular elements of nature for the benefit of future generations. This approach is embodied in the 1972 World Heritage Convention,[47] which aims to conserve the cultural and the natural heritage of 'outstanding universal value to the benefit of future generations'.[48]

Finally, it should be noted that there are a series of important international environmental treaties that have not explicitly referred to intergenerational equity but have nevertheless been mindful of the concept. A good example is the 1987 Montreal Protocol on Substances that Deplete the Ozone Layer,[49] which aims to reduce the impact of ozone depleting substances now to ensure a restored ozone layer in the future, and where science discourses in particular overcame political lethargy.[50] Like most treaties, however, the overriding imperative of the Montreal Protocol is to protect the interest of current generations' health and access to food resources,[51] and it is based on a belief in human capacity to redress harm before it is too late.

In summary, there is no consistent treatment in treaties to intergenerational equity. Formulations of intergenerational equity have tended to be vague, involving considerable indeterminacy. This lack of consistency

[46] Rio Declaration on Environment and Development, concluded 14 June 1992, Rio de Janeiro, Brazil, Principle 3.

[47] Convention Concerning the Protection of the World Cultural and Natural Heritage, opened for signature 16 November 1972, 1037 UNTS 151 (entered into force 17 December 1975), Art. 4.

[48] See below Chapter 16 by Ben Boer and Stefan Gruber.

[49] Montreal Protocol for Substances that Deplete the Ozone Layer, opened for signature 16 September 1987, 26 ILM 1550 (entered into force 1 January 1989).

[50] Karen Litfin, *Ozone Discourses: Science and Politics in Global Environmental Cooperation* (Columbia University Press, New York, 1994).

[51] Parliament of Australia Parliamentary Library, *Montreal Protocol on Substances that Deplete the Ozone Layer* (2010) at www.aph.gov.au/library/pubs/ClimateChange/governance/international/montreal.htm last accessed 17 January 2011.

and indeterminacy are an obstacle for intergenerational equity comprising a rule of customary international law.[52] Thus, it is left entirely unclear how one should balance the interests of present generations and future generations in terms of, for example, use of biological resources or climate change policy. In terms of the latter, the UNFCCC envisages further detailed rule-making to flesh out the obligation.

The treatment of sustainable development and intergenerational equity by international tribunals has been dealt with elsewhere.[53] It is sufficient to observe that the concept of intergenerational equity, particularly as part of sustainable development, has begun to play an important role in the reasoning of international tribunals such as the International Court of Justice, often in conjunction with other rules.[54] Hence, there is an opportunity and forum to reshape our understanding of the principle.

Does international human rights law provide for a right to a healthy environment including a stable climate? Neither the Charter of the UN, nor the major UN human rights instruments, including the Universal Declaration of Human Rights (UDHR), contains a right to a healthy environment. Nevertheless, these instruments do contain rights which arguably would *prima facie* be violated by states that fail to take serious action to address environment issues such as climate change. Rights relevant in this context include the right to a standard of living adequate to health and well-being (1948 UDHR,[55] Article 25) and the right to the highest attainable standard of health (1976 International Covenant on Economic, Social and Cultural Rights (ICESCR), Article 12(1) and (2)(b)), the human right to life (1966 International Covenant on Civil and Political Rights (ICCPR), Article 6.1) and the human right to subsistence (ICESCR, Article 11).[56] Caney has argued that these rights would

[52] Cordonier Segger, above n. 37, 121, 135–8.

[53] Cordonier Segger, above n. 37; Tim Stephens, *International Courts and Environmental Protection* (Cambridge University Press, 2009) 183–95.

[54] See, e.g., *Gabcikovo-Nagymaros Project (Hungary/Slovakia)* [1997] ICJ Rep. 7 [140] and separate opinion of Vice President Weeramantry, 88. However, see *Case Concerning Pulp Mills on the Uruguay River (Argentina* v. *Uruguay) (merits)* Judgment of 20 April 2010, where sustainable development played less of a role in the majority judgment. See also Separate Opinion of Judge Cancado Trindale [114]–[131] on intergenerational equity and [132]–[147] on sustainable development, and the Joint Dissenting Opinion of Judges Al-Khasawneh and Simma [26].

[55] GA Res. 217A (III), UN GAOR, 3rd sess., 183 plen. mtg, UN Doc. A/810 (10 December 1948).

[56] International Covenant on Economic, Social and Cultural Rights, opened for signature 19 December 1966, 993 UNTS 3 (entered into force 3 January 1976), Art. 11.

be violated by governments' failure to respond to climate change, given scientists' predictions of increased exposure to malaria and other diseases, deaths from heatwaves and extreme weather events.[57] Indeed, in 2008, the Human Rights Council of the United Nations passed a resolution which concluded that: 'climate change poses an immediate and far-reaching threat to people and communities around the world and has implications for the full enjoyment of human rights'.[58]

International environmental instruments also create rights akin to human rights. A right to a healthy environment is contained in the 1981 African Charter on Human and People's Rights.[59] At the global level, such a right has been asserted in some non-legally binding instruments, including Principle 1 of the Stockholm Declaration, which includes an obligation to improve the environment for present and future generations. Similarly, the 1989 Declaration of The Hague on the Environment recognized the 'duty on the community of nations vis-à-vis present and future generations to do all that can be done to preserve the quality of the environment'.[60]

There is no explicit 'right to sustainable development' in the 1992 Rio Declaration on Environment and Development which contains the rather vague and controversial 'right to development' which embraces social and cultural aspects of human development as well as the environment.[61] The 1993 Vienna Declaration on Human Rights[62] states in paragraph 11 that 'the right to development should be fulfilled so as to meet equitably the developmental and environmental needs of present and future generations'. However, the UN human rights instruments include the right of all peoples to freely dispose of their natural wealth

International Covenant on Civil and Political Rights, opened for signature 19 December 1966, 999 UNTS 171 (entered into force 23 March 1976).

57 Simon Caney, 'Climate Change, Human Rights and Moral Thresholds' in Stephen Humphreys (ed.), *Human Rights and Climate Change* (Cambridge University Press, 2009) 69.

58 Human Rights Council, *Promotion and Protection of All Human Rights, Civil, Political, Economic, Social and Cultural Rights, Including the Right to Developmen*t, 7th sess., Agenda Item 3, UN Doc. A/HRC/7/L.21/Rev.1 (26 March 2008).

59 African Charter on Human and People's Rights, opened for signature 27 June 1981, 1520 UNTS 217 (entered into force 21 October 1986).

60 Hague Declaration on the Environment, concluded 11 March 1989, The Hague, Netherlands, 28 ILM 1308.

61 Alan Boyle, 'Between Process and Substance: Sustainable Development in the Jurisprudence of International Courts and Tribunals' in Bugge and Voigt (eds.), above n. 37, ch. 2.2.

62 Vienna Declaration on Human Rights (Vienna Declaration and Programme of Action), UN Doc. A/CONF.157/23 (12 July 1993).

and resources (1966 ICESR, Article 1(2)) which appears to be directly contrary to an obligation of sustainable development and intergenerational equity.

The European Court of Human Rights has used various rights, including the right to privacy, to allow individuals to protect various aspects of the environment. However, there is no *actio popularis* under the European Convention on Human Rights, and 'if the individual applicant's health, private life, property or civil rights are not sufficiently affected by environmental loss, then he or she has no standing to proceed'.[63] Moreover, in the European Court of Human Rights cases there has been a greater willingness to insist upon due process procedures being followed in relation to the provision of adequate information, public participation and access to judicial review, rather than using human rights to strike down economic policies. This is understandable given that the latter approach would bring the courts into conflict with democratically elected governments, in areas where the courts have no particular expertise.[64]

In relation to climate change and future generations, there clearly would be difficulties in establishing standing (that is: a legal right to bring a claim) where the damage occurs in the future and the impacts were on generations unborn. Such claims would seem to be precluded by the lack of any *actio popularis* in the UN and European human rights instruments. Moreover, courts may be reluctant to intervene where the standards required of governments in terms of mitigating climate change remain highly controversial and arguable issues of government policy which courts should not be deciding.

In short, there is no clear right to a healthy environment, but the rights to life, health and subsistence may be violated by anthropogenic climate change. There are general – albeit vague – obligations on governments to preserve the environment now for both current and future generations. It is difficult to make claims for a breach of human rights in relation to the environment unless one can show a sufficient level of damage. Given there is no *actio popularis* in relation to environmental damage, it is difficult to make claims now on behalf of those who suffer in the future.

6. Justice and ethics approaches to intergenerational equity

We have seen that intergenerational equity has been weakly expressed in current international environmental law rules with a tepid infusion into

[63] Boyle, above n. 61, 207–9. [64] Ibid. 215.

public laws. Discourse theory provides at least one valuable explanation of how this has come about. Opportunities to employ a far-reaching conception of intergenerational equity have been dampened by the dominance of eco-modernist and industrialist discourses in environmental law and policy. However, parallel to the dominant discourses of ecological modernization and industrialism, there has emerged an alternate rationale for intergenerational equity, particularly among philosophers.[65] This rationale, which centres around discourses of justice and ethics, has emerged as a reaction to the mainstream discourses. Mainstream discourses are seen as deficient in not being able to provide a basis for solutions to pressing global environmental problems, and not being able to take into account the non-human ecological system.[66] This alternate discourse has been evident in relation to climate change. The Stern Review argued in 2006 from a conventional welfare economics perspective that the cost of inaction on climate change would far outweigh the costs of mitigation.[67] Interestingly, this report stimulated discussion on the value of future generations arising from Stern's assumption of a low discount rate, which rested on an ethical judgment that future generations were of equal value to persons alive today.[68]

In the following analysis I test various justifications for intergenerational equity in dealing with climate change, drawing on philosophical concepts evident in international and public law and policy.

7. The contribution of Brown Weiss

Brown Weiss's *In Fairness to Future Generations*[69] contains a theory of intergenerational equity that has roots in philosophy. Her theory has had considerable impact on international lawyers, being referred to in a number of the judgments of the International Court of Justice.[70] The essence of Brown Weiss's theory is that:

[65] See Andrew Dobson (ed.), *Fairness and Futurity: Essays on Environmental Sustainability and Social Justice* (Oxford University Press, 1999).

[66] See Bosselmann's interesting survey of attempts to extend liberal theories of social justice to include ecological concerns, above n. 10, 129.

[67] Stern, above n. 2.

[68] Ibid., ch. 2. See Hulme, above n. 22, 120–3 for an overview of this debate.

[69] Brown Weiss (1989), above n. 3.

[70] See, e.g., the Dissenting Opinion of Justice Weeramantry in *Nuclear Weapons Advisory Opinion* [1996] ICJ Rep. 226.

> ... each generation should be required to maintain the quality of the planet so that it is passed on in no worse condition than the present generation received it, and should be entitled to a quality of the planet comparable to the one enjoyed by previous generations.[71]

Brown Weiss's theory has three interrelated elements: first, the idea of a 'trust' with each generation holding the earth 'in trust' for future generations;[72] second, the notion of future generations having rights;[73] and, third, an extension of John Rawls's theory of justice.[74]

Brown Weiss argues that human beings 'as a species, hold the natural and cultural environment of our planet in common, both with other members of the present generation and with other generations, past and future'.[75] She continues that each generation, at any given time, is a 'trustee of the planet for future generations' and derives from this trusteeship an obligation to 'care for the planet' and an obligation towards future generations to pass on the planet in no worse condition.[76]

The concept of a trust, which is a property law construct in domestic legal regimes, has parallels with theories of 'stewardship'. As Shepheard and Martin[77] discuss, ideas of 'stewardship' have relevance in those domestic legal regimes with common law or statutory duties of care. In this respect international and public law scholars have found common ground through notions of trust. They have not yet, though, advanced our understanding of intergenerational equity using a trust or stewardship discourse. This may not be an altogether bad thing. The notion of a trusteeship is a somewhat artificial construct designed to restrain human beings' domain over nature.[78] It can also be seen as grounding intergenerational equity on a religious, particularly Christian basis, where, for example, human beings are under a duty to take care of God's creation.[79] A difficulty with Christian arguments in favour of stewardship is that they can also be interpreted as justifying the exploitation of nature.[80]

Arguably all stewardship or trust-related arguments have a 'quasi theological residue'.[81] The concept of a 'trust' assumes 'ownership' of

[71] Brown Weiss (1989), above n. 3, 38. [72] Ibid. 17. [73] Ibid. 95.

[74] Ibid. 24; John Rawls, *A Theory of Justice* (Oxford University Press, 1972) 289.

[75] Brown Weiss (1989), above n. 3, 17. [76] Ibid. 17 and 25.

[77] See below Chapter 3 by Mark Shepheard and Paul Martin.

[78] Lowe, above n. 41, 19 and 27.

[79] See Alexander Gillespie, *International Environmental Law, Policy and Ethics* (Clarendon Press, Oxford, 1997) 68–71.

[80] Ibid. 71–6. For Islam and other religions, see Brown Weiss (1989), above n. 3, 18

[81] Robert E. Goodin, *Protecting the Vulnerable: A Reanalysis of our Social Responsibilities* (University of Chicago Press, 1985) 175.

the earth's resources in a deity or other entity, and therefore rests on a basis upon which agreement may be very difficult to reach.

Brown Weiss's theory has a strong rights element whereby:

> [t]he present generation has certain obligations to future generations to care for the planet: obligations to conserve options, to conserve quality and to conserve access. Future generations in turn have rights to receive a planet that has been cared for in this manner.[82]

Some have questioned whether future unborn generations can have rights, asking how an entity not yet in existence can have rights.[83] If the *choice theory of rights* is adopted, then there is a problem, as according to this theory a right bearer possesses a right not because of any benefit he or she will derive from another person being constrained, but rather because of being ethically in a position to claim – or waive – the performance of a duty from another by his or her choice.[84]

However, if an *interest theory of rights is adopted*, there is less difficulty. Under this theory 'other things being equal, an aspect of X's well-being (his interest) is a sufficient reason for holding some other person(s) to be under a duty'.[85] Under this theory there seems no reason *per se* why yet-to-be-born persons cannot possess rights. We can assume that 'there will be people who exist in the future, that these people will possess interests that will be vulnerable to harm, and that the actions of existing persons – particularly those affecting the integrity of the natural environment – will have profound effect on these interests'.[86]

[82] Brown Weiss (1989), above n. 3, 96 and 98. These rights are considered by Brown Weiss as group rights in the intra-generational context.

[83] See Ruth Macklin, 'Can Future Generations Correctly Be Said to Have Rights?' in Ernest Partridge (ed.), *Responsibilities to Future Generations* (Prometheus Books, Buffalo, NY, 1981) 151; Ernest Partridge, 'On the Rights of Future Generations' in Donald Scherer, *Upstream/Downstream: Issues in Environmental Ethics* (Temple University Press, Philadelphia, 1990) 11; Edward Page, *Climate Change, Justice and Future Generations* (Edward Elgar, Cheltenham, 2006) 143–4.

[84] Ibid. 143.

[85] Joseph Raz, 'Right-Based Moralities' in Jeremy Waldron (ed.), *Theories of Rights* (Oxford University Press, 1984) 182, 183, quoted in Page, above n. 83, 144.

[86] Ibid. 144–5. The so-called 'non-identity problem' must still be overcome under this theory.

Further, Feinberg[87] and Vanderheiden,[88] in the context of discussing rights, interests and duties of future generations, take the view that future persons, *once they come to exist*, will have interests which give rise to rights, but that until such time it cannot be said that we have any duties with respect to those interests. Under this view, a policy may be wrong not because it violates *now* the rights of unborn persons, but rather because it is likely *in the future* to violate the rights of unborn persons. Thus, adopting a polluting policy today is wrong if, given our current state of knowledge, it will be likely to have harmful effects in the future.[89]

If an interest-based theory of rights is adopted, there does not seem to be any reason in principle why unborn persons cannot possess rights in a contingent sense, overcoming one concern about the lack of knowledge of future generations' interests. This is based on the very reasonable assumption that the interest underlying the right will continue into the future. Moreover, philosophers have pointed out that there is a contingent element to the application of all moral rules in that duties may be linked to rights that will only come into play when certain events occur. Consider the example of a person throwing an old Second World War bomb down a drain in a marketplace. Imagine that six months later the bomb goes off killing a two-month-old child. At the time the bomb was placed in the drain in the marketplace this child was not yet born. Was this child's right to life violated? Here the *duty* not to cause harm certainly extends into the future and is valid regardless of a lack of knowledge about who *in future* will be harmed.[90] Similarly, the right not to be injured or killed through such acts exists now and continues into the future even if the exercise of this right is contingent on certain factors, including the bomb going off and causing harm. The fact that at this moment the right holder is not yet born ought to be irrelevant to whether either the duty or right exists.

Given the foreseeability and indeed high likelihood that a person may in the future be injured by negligence, it is surely irrelevant in terms of the existence of a duty to avoid harm whether, at the moment an old shell is placed in the drain, the potential victim is alive or not. Climate change

87 Joel Feinberg, 'Duties, Rights and Claims' (1996) 3(2) *American Philosophical Quarterly* 139.

88 Steve Vanderheiden, *Atmospheric Justice: A Political Theory of Climate Change* (Oxford University Press, New York, 2008) 132.

89 Ibid.

90 Partridge, above n. 83, 16. Partridge draws on a similar example devised by Galen Pletcher, 'The Rights of Future Generations' in Partridge (ed.), above n. 83, 186.

involves further complications in that we are collectively throwing the old bomb down the drain, raising issues about whether responsibility should be on an individual, corporation, national or sub-national basis.[91]

What about the objection that a right of future generations implies that we (arrogantly) make assumptions about the future values and preferences of persons yet to be born? This objection is flawed, as we can reasonably assume that the basic interests of future persons – including the need for food, water, shelter and clean air – will be similar to ours.[92] Extending this to the climate change context, it seems reasonable to assume that future generations would wish to have as *a minimum* access to a climate that can sustain life at a reasonable standard.

Brown Weiss extends John Rawls's theory of justice.[93] The essence of Brown Weiss's view is that if each generation did not know beforehand when it would be the living generation, it would rationally choose a principle whereby each generation:

> would want to inherit a common patrimony of the planet in as good condition as it has been for any previous generation and to have as good access to it as previous generations. This requires that each generation pass the planet on in no worse condition than it received it and provide equitable access to its resources and benefits.[94]

This concept certainly has appeal in terms of being a compromise between a 'right of exploitation' and deep ecology perspective. Brown Weiss's theory provides flexibility in the management of natural resources: such exploitation is allowed provided that overall the planet is in no worse condition. Thus Brown Weiss's principle involves conservation of the diversity of the natural and cultural resource base, so long as future generations' options are not negated.[95] This is linked to an 'equality' principle, with Brown Weiss stating that 'the theory of intergenerational equity calls for a minimum level of equality among generations'.[96]

Can the concept propounded by Brown Weiss provide a principle of justice which would require the present generation to limit its greenhouse gas emissions even where the benefits of such actions would largely manifest themselves only in the future? Vanderheiden points out that applying Rawls's theory makes no sense in relation to climate change because 'ignorant of the stage of national development in which

[91] See Simon Caney, 'Climate Change and the Duties of the Advantaged' (2010) 13 *Critical Review of International Social and Political Philosophy* 203.

[92] Vanderheiden, above n. 88, 129. [93] Rawls, above n. 74.

[94] Brown Weiss (1989), above n. 3, 24. [95] Ibid. 41–2. [96] Ibid. 24.

they will live, no persons could endorse a standard zero emissions growth, for this would impose a cap on development for those societies in the early stages of industrialisation'.[97] Similarly, it would make no sense to endorse high greenhouse gas emissions caps, as this would in effect endorse climate change. Vanderheiden points out that it would only make sense for countries to endorse strict emission cuts if they could be assured that other nations also endorsed similar cuts, otherwise they would suffer competitive disadvantages in development.[98]

Critics have pointed out that Brown Weiss's concept is limited in its strong anthropocentric bias.[99] It also has built into it a strong concept of progress. Thus, one can legitimately ask why it would not be sufficient for each generation to pass on the earth in sufficient condition to allow future generations to lead a reasonable quality of life.[100] Interestingly, the Stern Review on Climate Change[101] reflects closely Brown Weiss's concept of intergenerational equity. Stern argues that while some resources are substitutable, at the basic level 'the global environmental and ecological system, which provides us with life support functions . . . *cannot be substituted*'.[102]

8. Sustainability and intergenerational equity

Vanderheiden seeks to justify an obligation to future generations in the climate change context on the basis of the concept of sustainability.[103] He posits the question of whether 'there exists a moral obligation to manage the atmosphere in a manner consistent with its sustainable use'.[104] He argues that a duty of resource conservation in the mould advanced by Shepheard and Martin[105] may be found through 'consideration of the nature of environmental harms'. He points out that:

> . . . for conservation to be effective, a steady commitment to its imperatives over time is required. A law that mandated sustainable forestry practices on every day but Sunday would obviously be ineffective in maintaining a sustainable forest.[106]

97 Vanderheiden, above n. 88, 119. 98 Ibid. 120. 99 Gillespie, above n. 79, 124.
100 Wilfred Beckerman, 'Sustainable Development and our Obligations to Future Generations' in Dobson (ed.), above n. 65, 71, 73.
101 Stern, above n. 2, 42. 102 Ibid. Emphasis added.
103 Vanderheiden, above n. 88, 132–8. 104 Ibid. 133.
105 See below Chapter 3 by Mark Shepheard and Paul Martin.
106 Vanderheiden, above n. 88, 133.

He argues that conservation imperatives must allow for causal chains that stretch over time. This argument is circular in that 'conservation', or 'sustainability' includes within its own definition[107] an obligation that extends over time. But it is the basis of this very obligation that is the question, so Vanderheiden's argument seems to assume the very obligation that he is seeking to establish. While it is correct to say that sustainability and conservation policies must stretch out into the future to be 'effective', effectiveness is not what is at question: rather, the justification for taking into account the interests of future generations. A normative rule cannot be deduced from an effectiveness argument. Indeed, an obligation to future generations seems to be the basis of sustainability rather than the other way round.[108]

9. Obligation to avoid harm

A further rationale for intergenerational equity is an obligation to refrain from causing future harm to other human beings. The proposition may be expressed as:

> the current generation, particularly those in positions of power, has an obligation to refrain from action which has a high probability of causing serious harm to the 1) interests of younger people alive today and 2) the interests of future generations (yet to be born). I describe this as a 'harm avoidance principle'.[109]

'Harm avoidance' as a key ethical principle has a long history. John Stuart Mill argued that the prevention of harm to others governed the relationship between the individual and society and was the only basis upon which 'power can be rightfully exercised over any member of a civilised community, against his will'.[110] A similar concept underlies the law of torts and the criminal law. The contrary principle would be: the current generation has a right to take action which has a high probability

[107] Ibid. 132.

[108] Barry takes an opposite view arguing that sustainability is a necessary condition for intergenerational distributive justice: Brian Barry, 'Sustainability and Intergenerational Justice' in Dobson (ed.), above n. 65, 93, 106.

[109] Vanderheiden argues for a similar principle, above n. 88, 137.

[110] John Stuart Mill, *On Liberty* (1859), reprinted in John Stuart Mill, *Utilitarianism, On Liberty, Essay on Bentham* (Fontana, London, 1962) 126, 135. There are parallels here with Thomas Pogge's negative responsibility for world poverty, see Thomas Pogge, 'A Global Resource Dividend' in David Crocker and Toby Linden (eds.), *Ethics of Consumption* (Rowman and Littlefield, Oxford, 1999) 501.

of causing serious harm to those born in the future. This would be problematic, as this would arguably justify actions that could threaten the ongoing survival of significant numbers of human beings. Moreover, the harm avoidance principle is consistent with the instinct and/or responsibility to nurture children and parents' efforts in maximising the likelihood of a successful future for their children.

Action to address climate change can be supported using this principle. Arguably there is a high probability of catastrophic and irreversible impacts on human beings if the current generation does not take mitigation action. Caney has argued for the polluter pays principle as an ethical basis for mitigation of greenhouse gas emissions and adaptation responses to climate change.[111] The essence of the polluter pays principle is that 'if someone has produced a harm . . . then they should rectify that situation. They as the causers are responsible for the ill-effects.'[112] Thus polluter pays is linked to the harm avoidance principle in an environment context. Caney also argues that polluter pays should be qualified so that it cannot require people to pay for emissions needed for their fundamental survival.[113] He argues that the principle needs to be combined with an ability to pay principle to meet these requirements.

Vanderheiden argues that a duty to future generations can be based on the moral duty to avoid causing predictable harm 'conjoined with the equality principle'. He argues that it makes no sense to discount harm 'just because it occurs in the future' and argues that by automatically discounting such harm we are violating the equality principle in the sense that a person's value cannot depend upon when they happen to be born.[114] Vanderheiden concludes that 'if we can foresee that our current actions will, in the future, cause harm to or violate the rights of some future persons, or if they are highly likely to do so, then we should refrain from engaging those actions'.[115]

A potential obstacle to the principle proposed above is that it presumes that a future technological breakthrough which drastically reduces greenhouse gas emissions is impossible. This, however, ignores the fact that the harm principle is based on foresight and knowledge *now*. An ethically justifiable decision cannot retrospectively become unjustifiable because of events which were not foreseeable at the time.[116]

[111] Simon Caney, 'Cosmopolitan Justice, Responsibility, and Global Climate Change' (2005) 18 *Leiden Journal of International Law* 747.

[112] Ibid. 752. [113] Ibid. 763. [114] Vanderheiden, above n. 88, 137. [115] Ibid.

[116] Ibid. 186.

10. Natural law and survival

A shared objective of survival could also provide a foundation for an ethics and justice conception of intergenerational equity. Hart's 'minimum content theory of natural law' has human survival as an underpinning concept.[117] Put simply, Hart argues there are minimum requirements without which there would be no reason to accept other rules. Moreover, the ongoing survival of a society is contingent upon these basic minimum requirements or rules. Hart argues that 'it is the tacit assumption that the proper end of human activity is survival, and this rests on the simple contingent fact that most men most of the time wish to continue in existence'.[118] But he argues that 'survival' has a higher status than merely the sociological fact that in general human beings do desire to live, and he points out that indeed 'whole structures of thought and language' are built upon the assumption of survival being an underpinning value.[119] Hart goes on to specify a minimum content of natural law comprising particular rules of conduct which any society must contain to be viable or, put differently, to survive. He reiterates 'the basic character of such rules may be brought out in a question: if there were not these rules what point could there be for beings such as ourselves in having rules of *any* other kind'.

Some argue that Hart's 'minimum content' is only weakly connected to traditional natural law theory and that he is not making a moral theory. Thus Hart's minimum requirements can be cast as principles of 'prudence' rather than ethical norms: in other words, if society wishes to survive, *as a matter of prudence* the particular principles should be followed.[120]

Hart's argument that there are reasons for restricting violence could be extended to an argument in favour of the harm avoidance principle mentioned above, that is, an obligation not to cause harm to the interests of younger people alive today or future generations. Extending Hart's theory to the climate change context would rest on acceptance of the proposition that a failure to make deep cuts in greenhouse gas emissions will very likely cause actual physical harm to future unborn generations

[117] H. L. A. Hart, *The Concept of Law* (Clarendon Press, Oxford, 1994) 193.

[118] Ibid. 121. [119] Ibid. 192.

[120] Brian Bix, 'Natural Law: The Modern Tradition' in Jules Coleman and Scott Shapiro (eds.), *The Oxford Handbook of Jurisprudence and Philosophy of Law* (Oxford University Press, 2002) 61, 94.

or younger generations alive today. The Stern Review points to the increased worldwide deaths from malnutrition and heat stress projected to flow from anthropogenic climate change, as well as increased risk of malaria, dengue fever and 150–200 million permanent refugees from flooding in East Asia.[121] Given the high likelihood of anthropogenic climate change producing an increased incidence of storm surges with a resultant significant increase in the deaths of large numbers of people, particularly in developing countries, I can see no obstacle to extending Hart's argument in this fashion. Linked to this point is that the harm avoidance principle was framed in terms of harm to *interests* rather than irreparable harm, and is not dependent on a harm being so extensive as to threaten survival of society as a viable entity. Thus, in the climate change context, without acceptance of the harm avoidance principle – and action based on this principle – survival *for significant numbers of human beings* certainly would be at risk. Indeed, there are already signs that the climate change problem is spurring a revival of the 1970s survival discourse.[122]

11. Intergenerational equity, justice and effectiveness

Justification for an ethical principle of intergenerational equity where current generations have an obligation to pass on the planet with a climate that provides for basic life support functions can be grounded in a harm avoidance principle, Hart's minimum content of natural law and a contingent view of rights, given the high probability of current generations' actions impacting on future person's rights. However, owing to the dominance of industrialism and ecological modernisation discourses in international and public law, there has been little discursive space for the alternative ethical-based principle of intergenerational equity.

There is an urgent need for an alternate ethics- and justice-based discourse to become more prominent, for a new coalition to challenge the discourses of industrialism and ecological modernisation. This chapter

[121] Stern, above n. 2, 56 and 77.

[122] An example of this emerging survival discourse is found in United Nations Development Programme, *Human Development Report 2007/2008 Fighting Climate Change: Human Solidarity in a Divided World* (Palgrave Macmillan, New York, 2007) 6, which, in relation to the climate change challenge, states that the future of our children and children's grandchildren 'and maybe their survival – is hanging in the balance'.

offers a philosophical analysis that can be employed to shift the existing paradigm. There is more scope to advance the alternative discourse at the international law level, where there has been the greatest recent reception to environmental law concepts. There is also a greater plurality of environmental ethics and values with opportunity for an alternative discourse to be pursued. To solve global environment challenges it is essential that international environmental treaties be strengthened on the basis of the ethics and justice discourse. This new approach puts a strong onus on those who seek to justify proposed development that destroys irreplaceable aspects of the ecological system. Business as usual in relation to climate change becomes difficult to justify on ethical grounds. While sustainable development in itself cannot provide the basis for an obligation to future generations, if one accepts the basis for intergenerational equity argued for in this chapter, sustainable development in its stronger form[123] becomes a logical framework for its implementation. 'Weak sustainability' allows growth to continue with flexibility as to what type of assets – whether natural or human (for example: education and science, including genetic engineering) is left for future generations. As put by Bosselmann, 'such "capital stock" gift to the future implies the very possibility of destroying the planet's conditions of life'.[124] A less risky approach is strong sustainability which makes '"ecological integrity" of planetary systems . . . a benchmark for any development'.[125]

Intergenerational equity is inevitably an abstract principle, and fleshing out the principle in legal rules at the national and international level is a critical enterprise. Franck has convincingly argued that compliance with international law rules rests upon the perceived moral legitimacy of international rules in terms of their fairness in relation to *substantive outcomes* and fairness in the *process* of negotiation.[126] Brunnée has argued that the process and substance of international law-making is inexorably intertwined and 'internationally shared understandings' of justice must be developed for international law to be effective.[127] While challenges exist, intergenerational justice is an essential element in the tapestry of our public and international laws, which must be woven quickly if we are to address global challenges such as climate change.

123 Bosselmann, above n. 10. 124 Ibid. 151. 125 Ibid. 153.

126 Thomas Franck, *Fairness in International Law and Institutions* (Oxford University Press/Clarendon Press, Oxford/New York, 1995).

127 Jutta Brunnée, 'Climate Change, Global Environmental Justice and International Environmental Law' in Jonas Ebbesson and Phoebe Okawa (eds.), *Environmental Law and Justice in Context* (Cambridge University Press, 2009) 316, 328. See also Hulme, above n. 22, 164 and below Chapter 2 by Brad Jessup.

2

The journey of environmental justice through public and international law

BRAD JESSUP

1. Introduction

The environmental justice discourse has its origins in the 1980s. Then, US academics and activists advocated an alternative environmental concept that promoted the creation of an environmental justice movement. This social movement was characterised by its opposition to potentially harmful industries and activities being permitted in less advantaged neighbourhoods and regions throughout the country. 'Environmental justice' demanded equal access to environmental services and a sharing of potentially environmentally harmful land uses. The social movement argued that governments were discriminating against coloured, ethnic and poor communities by permitting pollution in their environments in greater proportion than in other places. There was a miscarriage of environmental justice even though environmental laws were used and applied to the controversy. In the early 1990s the environmental justice movement successfully agitated for change in US domestic policy and law.[1]

Although the political climate and environmental priorities have changed, the environmental justice argument still resonates and can be understood and observed in other contexts. In the years following the rise of the environmental justice discourse, it has refocused. Environmental justice now also includes rights to participate in environmental decision-making; a trend embraced and promoted heavily by some regional and public laws. The related notion of ecological justice, doing justice for the environment, also now demands rights for the ecosphere. At the same time as the meaning and understanding of environmental justice has broadened, the concept of

[1] David Harvey, 'The Environment of Justice' in Frank Fischer and Maarten Hajer (eds.), *Living with Nature: Environmental Politics as Cultural Discourse* (Oxford University Press, 1999) 153.

environmental justice and its associated movements have internationalised and translocated largely due to the globalisation of environmental concerns and the internationalisation of environmental law. This in turn has led to greater connections between public laws and international laws. Today the concept of environmental justice guides domestic, regional and international law and policy. In particular, the concept is the subject of proposed revived environmental justice laws in the United States[2] seeking to codify earlier guidance for regulators to avoid environmentally unjust outcomes in its assessment and approval of potentially harmful activities. Environmental justice ideals are also now embedded in the European Aarhus Convention on Access to Information, Public Participation and Access to Justice in Environmental Matters.[3] Further, environmental justice concerns are expressed in the context of international trade in hazardous waste[4] and exploited natural resources, and the cause, effect and responsibility to respond to climate change.[5]

This chapter explores how legal advancements, opportunities and failures, legal theories, the establishment and activities of legal institutions and legal disputes have all contributed to the discourse of environmental justice. Further, the chapter looks at how the concept of environmental justice and the principles inherent within it have guided or encouraged legal reforms focusing particularly on public and international legal systems.

The chapter first introduces the origins of the concept of environmental justice and the environmental justice movement. It describes how the notion has changed, broadened and been exposed to the law. Second, the concept of environmental justice is cast as an environmental discourse because conceiving of environmental justice as a discourse helps to explain how and why institutions and communities use the term in different ways. It explains why legal regimes react differently to, and sometimes struggle to make sense of, environmental justice claims. Third, the chapter narrates the rise of the discourse of environmental justice in the context of four socio-legal trends where justice theories and

[2] Health Equity and Accountability Bill, House Bill 3090, 111th Congress of the United States, ss. 421 and 422.

[3] Opened for signature 25 June 1998, 2161 UNTS 447 (entered into force 30 October 2001).

[4] See, e.g., Alastair Iles, 'Mapping Environmental Justice in Technology Flows: Computer Waste Impacts in Asia' (2004) 4(4) *Global Environmental Politics* 76.

[5] See, e.g., Steve Vanderheiden, *Atmospheric Justice: A Political Theory of Climate Change* (Oxford University Press, New York, 2008).

the law have converged. These trends are: the refinement of pollution laws and the initiation of environmental rights; increasing concerns about legal standing in environmental matters; the biodiversity conservation agenda; and the rise of global environmental governance and justice discourses. Finally, the chapter explains both the valuable contributions and occasional indifferent attitude of public and international law to the development of the concept of environmental justice.

2. From origins to contemporary understandings of environmental justice

Most authors writing about environmental justice begin their commentaries by recounting the events of Warren County, North Carolina, in the late 1970s and early 1980s, when a marginalised community was confronted with a poisonous waste dump. This controversy is commonly identified and analysed, along with the Love Canal residential and community development on toxic land in New York State,[6] as the starting point of the environmental justice movement.[7] Indeed, Warren County has become as synonymous with environmental justice as the Brundtland Commission is to sustainable development. However, just as Brundtland's report[8] did not conceive the principle of sustainable development or first expose the philosophy for a reconceptualised development paradigm,[9] the decision and fierce opposition to relocate illegally dumped industrial waste into a poor neighbourhood in North Carolina did not mark the beginning, or restrict the future definition, of the concept of environmental justice. This is despite the controversy being understood as the trigger for the movement that took hold in the United States in the 1980s and 1990s. Many of the ideas, theories, values and beliefs comprising environmental justice, particularly as it has been

[6] Andrew Dobson, *Justice and the Environment: Conceptions of Environmental Sustainability and Theories of Distributive Justice* (Oxford University Press, 1998).

[7] See, e.g., Robert Bullard, *Dumping in Dixie: Race, Class, and Environmental Quality* (Westview, Boulder, 3rd edn, 2000). Julian Agyeman, *Sustainable Communities and the Challenge of Environmental Justice* (New York University Press, 2005) notes that environmental justice concerns date back to the late 1400s.

[8] World Commission on Environment and Development (WCED), *Our Common Future* (Oxford University Press, 1987).

[9] William Adams, *Green Development: Environment and Sustainability in the Third World* (Routledge, London and New York, 2nd edn, 2001).

further theorised and extrapolated, had earlier and plural origins[10] or adopted approaches and strategies of other movements.[11]

Ebbesson argues that 'justice concerns can be traced back in the history of environmental law at least to the 1941 *Trail Smelter Arbitration*'.[12] Warren County was not the first local environmental conflict to capture the attention of a regional or national audience, nor was it the first to be recognised as resulting from an imbalance in power between the state, the community and business enterprise.[13] There are ample historical examples in Australia where potentially harmful industrial facilities or activities have roused organised community opposition[14] or have been involuntarily located on land where the only people most obviously likely to suffer from environmental damage were Aboriginal Australians.[15] What was stark about the Warren County experience as told by participant-academic pair, Burwell and Cole,[16] was the mobilisation of the community, the on-the-street battle, and a shift in power after and resulting from the conflict as the community learned how it could use democratic institutions and the law to achieve socio-political change.

Burwell and Cole[17] provide great insight in explaining how the situating of a contaminated soil disposal site in a mostly African-American and poor community in Warren County provided an impetus for the coalescence of existing groups, concerns and beliefs about the unfair

[10] For example, Christopher Stone, 'Should Trees Have Standing? Toward Legal Rights for Natural Objects' (1972) 45 *Southern California Law Review* 450; Rachel Carson, *Silent Spring* (Houghton-Mifflin, Boston, 1962). Civil rights and social justice movements, as well as humanistic/anthropocentric environmentalism, can be traced from the 1800s.

[11] Clifford Rechtschaffen and Eileen Gauna, *Environmental Justice: Law, Policy and Regulation* (Carolina Academic Press, Durham, 1st edn, 2003).

[12] Jonas Ebbesson, 'Introduction: Dimensions of Justice in Environmental Law' in Jonas Ebbesson and Phoebe Okowa (eds.), *Environmental Law and Justice in Context* (Cambridge University Press, 2009) 1, 5.

[13] Bullard, above n. 7, 3 notes that '[t]he problem of polluted black communities is not a new phenomenon. Historically, toxic dumping and the location of locally unwanted land uses (LULUs) have followed the "path of least resistance".'

[14] See, e.g., Tim Bonyhady, *Colonial Earth* (Melbourne University Press, 2000); Tim Bonyhady, *Places Worth Keeping: Conservationists, Politics and Law* (Allen & Unwin, Sydney, 1993).

[15] For example, nuclear testing at Maralinga, and early uranium mining. See Nicholas Low and Brendan Gleeson, *One Earth: Social and Environmental Justice* (Australian Conservation Foundation, Melbourne, 1999).

[16] See, e.g., Dollie Burwell and Luke Cole, 'Environmental Justice Comes Full Circle: Warren County Before and After' (2007) 1 *Golden Gate University Environmental Law Journal* 9.

[17] Ibid.

distribution of environmentally and socially harmful activities and environmental and social benefits. It is this coalescence, insofar as it was built on the civil rights movement and discourse, and because it had a lasting legacy, that makes the events so important in the anthology of the environmental justice movement.[18] Other events rose to attention and faded, many other grassroots environmental groups dissipated upon defeat, and many communities have not objected at all to the arrival of polluting industries.[19]

The aftermath of Warren County did, however, give rise to the discourse of environmental justice. Irrespective of what went before, it was during the 1980s that academics and communities began speaking about environmental racism, environmental discrimination, and, drawing on notions of social justice and civil rights, began using the term 'environmental justice'.[20] When they did so they implicitly drew on a long legal tradition of justice and rights. Agyeman[21] notes that human understanding of the environment changed as the discursive hegemony of conservation groups was challenged. A new type of environmentalist with interests, history and objectives distinct from the dominant environmental mould championed a more egalitarian environmental ethic[22] and was more prone to engage with the legal system, to fight injustice. Over time the discourse and understanding of environmental justice has broadened. The discourse and legal setting now involves disadvantaged communities and developing nations,[23] environmentalists pursuing ecological conservation[24] and environmental democrats of varying financial standing and class who are affected or concerned by opaque and arbitrary environmental decision-making.[25]

[18] Veronica Eady, 'Warren County and the Birth of a Movement: The Troubled Marriage Between Environmentalism and Civil Rights' (2007) 1 *Golden Gate University Environmental Law Journal* 41.

[19] Harvey, above n. 1.

[20] For instance, Luke Cole and Sheila Foster, *From the Ground Up: Environmental Racism and the Rise of the Environmental Justice Movement* (New York University Press, 2001).

[21] Julian Agyeman, Robert Bullard and Bob Evans, 'Introduction: Joined-Up Thinking: Bringing Together Sustainability, Environmental Justice and Equity' in Julian Agyeman, Robert Bullard and Bob Evans (eds.), *Just Sustainabilities: Development in an Unequal World* (MIT Press, Cambridge, Mass., 2003) 1.

[22] Harvey, above n. 1. [23] Agyeman, Bullard and Evans, above n. 21.

[24] Nicolas Low and Brendan Gleeson, *Justice, Society, and Nature: An Exploration of Political Ecology* (Routledge, London and New York, 1988).

[25] Michael Mason, *Environmental Democracy* (Earthscan, London, 1999).

While some American literature and most US policy and legal documents still define the concept principally in its 1980s form,[26] and some scholars resist a 'retreat from race' as the central tenet of the concept,[27] other theorists, philosophers[28] and practitioners[29] have attempted to define environmental justice to reflect the changed discourse around the concept. Whether or not the broadened conception of environmental justice should retain the terminology so closely aligned with the original understanding of the term is a valid question,[30] but this has not influenced the discourse, which remains fixed on the more emotive and value-laden term 'environmental justice'.[31]

Schlosberg[32] has provided one of the contemporary holistic definitions of environmental justice. Relying on environmental and philosophical theories to explain and justify the change in discourse of environmental justice,[33] he defines environmental justice within four aspects apparent in this chapter: the fair distribution of environmental goods and harm; the recognition of human and non-human interests in decision-making and distribution; the existence of deliberative and democratic participation; and the building of capabilities among individuals, groups and non-human parts of nature.

The law has a primary role in facilitating these components of an environmental justice concept and of overseeing injustice where it remains

26 See, e.g., Robert Bullard (ed.), *Growing Smarter: Achieving Livable Communities, Environmental Justice, and Regional Equity* (MIT Press, Cambridge, Mass., 2007); Agyeman, Bullard and Evans, above n. 21; Health Equity and Accountability Bill, above n. 2, ss. 421 and 422.

27 Clifford Rechtschaffen, 'Strategies for Implementing the Environmental Justice Vision' (2007) 1 *Golden Gate University Environmental Law Journal* 321.

28 Brian Barry, 'Sustainability and Intergenerational Justice' in Andrew Dobson (ed.), *Fairness and Futurity: Essays on Environmental Sustainability and Social Justice* (Oxford University Press, 1999) 93; Low and Gleeson, above n. 24; David Schlosberg, *Environmental Justice and the New Pluralism: The Challenge of Difference for Environmentalism* (Oxford University Press, 1999); David Schlosberg, *Defining Environmental Justice: Theories, Movements and Nature* (Oxford University Press, 2007).

29 For instance, EarthJustice in the United States and the Environment Defenders Office in New South Wales, Australia.

30 See Gabriela Kütting, 'Environmental Justice' (2004) 4(1) *Global Environmental Politics* 115, 120, who suggests a more appropriate term would be 'environmental equity', which 'neatly side-steps the socially constructed nature of the term justice and the need for legal and political theorizing on the nature of justice'.

31 Ibid.

32 Schlosberg (1999), above n. 28; Schlosberg (2007), above n. 28; David Schlosberg, 'Reconceiving Environmental Justice: Global Movements and Political Theories' (2004) 13 *Environmental Politics* 517.

33 Schlosberg (2007), above n. 28.

ignorant of an environmental justice ethic. It was the legal administrators who oversaw the illegal disposal of chemicals in North Carolina in the late 1970s. It was the law that operated to imprison the dumpers of waste, to authorise the waste dump in Warren County and to effect the arrest of hundreds of protestors. It was also the law that disappointed the Warren County community by failing to halt the construction of the waste dump through two unsuccessful legal challenges.[34] Law was called upon and is still seen as an appropriate institution to provide for the fair distribution of environmental harm. However, as this chapter shows, the law still struggles to comprehensively adopt an environmental justice ethic.[35] This is in part due to the complexity of the now multifaceted concept that by and large reflects the dominance of eco-modernist and technocentrist viewpoints on environmental law and policy, and internationally of national self-interest.[36]

3. Environmental justice as a discourse and its legal dimension

Environmental justice is not just a movement or a theory. The adoption of the discourse of environmental justice by a broader coalition of adherents has seen environmental justice ideas expanded, argued and influencing law-makers. The term 'environmental justice' is filled with emotion. It is a rallying point, and has been used as a catch phrase and metaphor[37] to demand legal and political change. It has all the hallmarks of one of Hajer's[38] storylines, used as a common language across social and class structures and giving rise to a powerful social movement. In the 1980s the discourse was filled and understood equally by academics and some of the United States' most disadvantaged communities. Since then the discourse of environmental justice has been shared, and the

[34] Burwell and Cole, above n. 16.

[35] Brad Jessup, 'Investing the Law with an Environmental Ethic: Using an Environmental Justice Theory for Change' in Erika Techera (ed.), *Environmental Law, Ethics and Governance* (ID Press, Oxford, 2010) 21.

[36] See below Chapter 12 by River Cordes-Holland.

[37] Maarten Hajer, 'Coalitions, Practices, and Meaning in Environmental Politics: From Acid Rain to BSE' in David Howarth and Jacob Torfing (eds.), *Discourse Theory in European Politics: Identity, Policy and Governance* (Palgrave Macmillan, Basingstoke and New York, 2005) 297.

[38] Maarten Hajer, 'Discourse Coalitions and the Institutionalization of Practice: The Case of Acid Rain in Britain' in Frank Fischer and John Forester (eds.), *The Argumentative Turn in Policy Analysis and Planning* (Duke University Press, Durham, NC, 1993) 43.

terminology used differently,[39] by a mix of groups and movements often with different, and sometimes competing, agendas and values, but with a common 'way of apprehending the world'[40] and of framing environmental problems.[41] Environmental justice is now concerned with combating environmental colonialism, speaking up on behalf of species and through the law investing citizens with administrative rights and protecting the vulnerable from environmental despoliation. According to these different groups, environmental justice is concerned with fairness, equality and egalitarianism.[42] It fulfils Hajer's simple definition of a discourse as a 'particular way of talking and thinking'.[43]

Dryzek[44] positions the discourse of environmental justice and its actors, principally the members of the environmental justice movement, within a meta-discourse of 'green radicalism'. This is one of four environmental discourses that Dryzek argues is evident within international law.[45] Further, there are innumerably more discourses occurring at national levels in diverse contexts. Environmental justice is a 'radical' discourse as it challenges dominant structures, especially power and legal structures, and promotes political and policy instability. It is nonetheless a discourse in its own right, and as Dryzek acknowledges,[46] has not always been promoted by members of the community who identify as environmentalists. However, it has not been easily co-opted by business and government, like other discourses.[47] Rather, the environmental justice discourse has attracted a diverse range of adherents, including more recently some of the mainstream institutional groups absent from early grassroots pollution struggles that remain a high point of the environmental justice movement.[48]

Analysing environmental justice as an evolving discourse allows for a critique of the law's influence on the movement and how the community

39 Ryan Holyfield, 'Defining Environmental Justice and Environmental Racism' (2001) 22 *Urban Geography* 78.

40 John Dryzek, *The Politics of the Earth: Environmental Discourses* (Oxford University Press, 1st edn, 1997).

41 Hajer, above n. 37. 42 Harvey, above n. 1.

43 Maarten Hajer, *The Politics of Environmental Discourse: Ecological Modernization and the Policy Process* (Clarendon Press, Oxford, 1995) 13.

44 Dryzek, above n. 40.

45 John Dryzek, 'Paradigms and Discourses' in Daniel Bodansky, Jutta Brunnée and Ellen Hey (eds.), *Oxford Handbook of International Environmental Law* (Oxford University Press, 2007) 44. The other discourses are sustainability, survivalism and environmental problem solving.

46 Dryzek, above n. 45. 47 Harvey, above n. 1. 48 Ibid.

has understood the meaning of environmental justice, particularly because the influence of the law is usually marked through abrupt legislative and judicial developments. A discourse analysis avoids trying to define environmental justice in a fixed and, invariably to some groups, objectionable way.[49] It also reveals the changing actors, priorities, theories and content of the concept. Environmental justice can be seen as extending beyond a North American movement concerned with overcoming the maldistribution of environmental harm. An environmental discourse approach also highlights the legal and policy changes that can be attributed to the ideas and theories that comprise the concept of environmental justice and emphasises the (often) slow pace of environmental law reform at the national and supranational levels.

4. The law and environmental justice discourses

4.1 *Movements, rights and pollution laws*

The language used by US activists in the 1970s of 'rights' and 'racism' and the retort to equality, fairness and non-discrimination resembled the claims of civil rights leaders in that country decades earlier. Agyeman[50] explains the environmental justice movement was inspired by the civil rights movement in framing their concerns in this way. Owing to these origins, Eady[51] claims the environmental justice movement was and remains 'inextricably tied to the civil rights movement'. The civil rights movement, of course, was greatly advanced through judicial pronouncement on activities of public dissent, particularly in the United States,[52] and later legislative and treaty instruments. It is this relatively long recent history of public and international civil and human rights legal developments[53] that were foundational ideas for the formation of

[49] Holyfield, above n. 39. [50] Agyeman, Bullard and Evans, above n. 21.

[51] Eady, above n. 18, 43.

[52] Cases like *Brown* v. *Board of Education* 347 US 483 (1954), for example, remain landmarks in the civil rights movement.

[53] In particular the Universal Declaration of Human Rights, GA Res. 217A (III), UN GAOR, 3rd sess., 183 plen. mtg, UN Doc. A/810 (10 December 1948), the International Covenant on Civil and Political Rights, opened for signature 19 December 1966, 999 UNTS 171 (entered into force 23 March 1976), with its non-discrimination and rights focus, and the International Covenant on Economic, Social and Cultural Rights, opened for signature 19 December 1966, 993 UNTS 3 (entered into force 3 January 1976), which seeks to create rights that facilitate equality, and highlight the role and contribution of international law to the broad acceptance of non-discriminatory practices.

the environmental justice movement and still influence values within the discourse of environmental justice today. Groups within the discourse still speak of rights and demand equal access to a healthy environment and to legal processes. As will be discussed later, proponents of environmental justice, especially at the international level, retain their willingness to challenge orthodoxy or authoritarian decrees, and in doing so share the characteristics of civil rights campaigns of years past. This is particularly the case as civil and political rights become more widely legislated in human rights legislation and charters, reaffirmed in regional treaties, inserted into constitutions, interpreted by the judiciary and entrenched in policy and legal directives.[54] Claims are also increasingly becoming more nuanced as they are attached to 'protected' rights under legal regimes in what often appears a battle between legislature, community and judiciary about the scope of human and environmental protections.[55]

There are also parallels at the global or transnational level between the environmental justice movements with labour movements and land rights movements, both of which are supported by international conventions or declarations[56] directed at protecting vulnerable communities from corporate exploitation and discriminatory and paternalistic or custodial governance.

Civil rights, especially as they have been redefined internationally as economic, cultural and social rights, are also the fundamental ideas that are being used to explore human rights to the environment and environmental rights (or rights of the environment).[57] Although these rights are not universally adopted, they are central to the ecological aspects of environmental justice and international advocacy on a right to water.[58] They are also becoming evident at regional and national levels, particularly

[54] Asia Pacific Forum of National Human Rights Institutions (Asia Pacific Forum), *Human Rights and the Environment: Background Paper* (Asia Pacific Forum, Sydney, 2007).

[55] Dinah Shelton, 'Rainforests and Regulation: New Directions in Brazilian Environmental Law and Legal Institutions: Environmental Rights and Brazil's Obligations in the Inter-American Human Rights System' (2009) 40 *George Washington International Law Review* 733; Asia Pacific Forum, above n. 54; Deborah Rook, *Property Law and Human Rights* (Blackstone Press, London, 2001).

[56] For example, the International Labour Organization conventions and the United Nations Declaration on the Rights of Indigenous Peoples, GA Res. 61/295, 62nd sess. (13 September 2007).

[57] See, e.g., Christopher Miller, *Environmental Rights: Critical Perspectives* (Routledge, London and New York, 1998).

[58] World Health Organization (WHO), *Right to Water* (WHO, Geneva, 2003).

in Africa,[59] Europe[60] and the wider Americas.[61] They are also expected to invigorate an international environmental rights legal agenda[62] in a further example of the linkages between public and international law in the development of environmental and human rights laws.

Today, environmental human rights jurisprudence with environmental justice overtones is being led, not necessarily in the US courts, but in diverse institutions across the globe including in Europe, where the European Convention on Human Rights has been interpreted in a way to give Europeans rights not to endure pollution;[63] in India, in domestic public interest litigation;[64] and in the International Court of Justice, which is being confronted with novel environmental justice claims.[65]

The ubiquitous Stockholm and Rio Declarations instilled an environmental equity frame within the rights dialogue that has been significant in the development of environmental discourses generally, and specifically the sustainable development discourse.[66] Since the 1990s the concept of sustainable development has infiltrated public laws in a way that no previous or subsequent environmental theory has before. The reiteration of the discourse domestically has contributed to some commentators suggesting that sustainable development is now an entrenched principle of international law.[67] The concept of sustainable development has also been

59 For example, in the South African Constitution.

60 Through the European Court of Human Rights.

61 Notably in Ecuador's recently changed constitution.

62 Ole Pedersen, 'European Environmental Human Rights and Environmental Rights: A Long Time Coming?' (2008) 21 *Georgetown International Environmental Law Review* 73.

63 Rook, above n. 55.

64 Hans Dembowski, *Taking the State to Court: Public Interest Litigation and the Public Sphere in Metropolitan India* (Asia House, Essen, 2001). Although the nature of the litigation, the class status of applicants and the effect of judgments all raise additional environmental justice concerns. See Lavanya Rajamani, 'Public Interest Environmental Litigation in India: Exploring Issues of Access, Participation, Equity, Effectiveness and Sustainability' (2007) 19 *Journal of Environmental Law* 293.

65 For example, the *Pulp Mills on the River Uruguay (Argentina* v. *Uruguay)* cases, described below in Chapter 8 by Tim Stephens.

66 See, e.g., Principle 1 of the Declaration of Principles for the Preservation and Enhancement of the Human Environment, concluded on 16 June 1972, Stockholm, Sweden, which provides that humans have 'the fundamental right to freedom, equality and adequate conditions of life, in an environment of a quality that permits a life of dignity and well-being' and the 'solemn responsibility to protect and improve the environment for present and future generations'. Further, that 'policies promoting or perpetuating apartheid, racial segregation, discrimination, colonial and other forms of oppression and foreign domination stand condemned and must be eliminated'.

67 See, e.g., Christina Voigt, *Sustainable Development as a Principle of International Law* (Martinus Nijhoff, Leiden, 2009).

reconceived as a development philosophy that can aid in building 'just' and 'sustainable' communities.[68] This approach recasts the discourse of environmental justice to encompass community rights of access to natural resources, decision-making power over their livelihoods and protection from environmental harm from elsewhere – either locally or globally. In doing so it facilitates the fluid movement of ideas and concepts between the public and international sphere seeking to further influence the understanding of an internationally accepted norm.

The environmental justice movement in the United States demanded restorative action and protection from polluting activities relying on Title VI of the Civil Rights Act of 1964,[69] a public law that prevents federally funded agencies like the Environmental Protection Agency from discriminating on the basis of race, ethnicity, or national origin.[70] Under this law they invariably failed.[71] Interestingly, like in Warren County, the discourse of environmental justice did not readily draw from pollution control laws or land use planning laws until more recently. Historically, citizen enforcement action available under those laws was pursued by national environmental groups rather than the grassroots community groups that made up the large proportion of environmental justice discourse actors.[72] Public environmental and land use planning laws, when and where they existed, were often used but failed to halt degrading activities. This continues to be the case, with proposals more likely to be halted through political, media and financing campaigns rather than the application of environmental law and participation in legal processes.[73] This is despite the broadening of rights of objection and challenge under environmental laws, as explained below.

In some of the most highly publicised and devastating environmental incidents in the developing world that gave rise to vocal local and transnational movements, like the Bhopal gas disaster and the Ok Tedi

68 Agyeman, Bullard and Evans, above n. 21.

69 Including in Warren County. See Bradford Mank, 'Title VI and the Warren County Protests' (2007) 1 *Golden Gate University Environmental Law Journal* 73.

70 Olga Pomar, 'Toxic Racism on a New Jersey Waterfront' in Robert Bullard (ed.), *The Quest for Environmental Justice: Human Rights and the Politics of Pollution* (Sierra Club Books, San Francisco, 2005) 125.

71 Mank, above n. 69.

72 Jonathan Adler, 'Stand or Deliver: Citizen Suits, Standing, and Environmental Protection' (2001) 12 *Duke Environmental Law and Policy Forum* 39.

73 See, e.g., Tim Bonyhady and Andrew Macintosh (eds.), *Mills, Mines and Other Controversies: The Environmental Assessment of Major Projects* (Federation Press, Sydney, 2010).

Mine disaster,[74] environmental regulation was shown to be defective at preventing environmental harm or absent altogether, rather than contributing to an environmental justice framework. In those disasters, the law still had a role, post-disaster, when the threat of torts class action claims was effective in procuring financial compensation for victims from industrial, minority world corporate polluters. In both instances the disaster discourse was not one of tortious liability. Rather, mimicking the language of environmental justice, the discourse was of transnational abuse of rights and exploitation of disadvantaged communities. This is a trend in the discourse, unaddressed by international legal developments on the movement of pollution, an idea that will be returned to further when discussing justice in transboundary movement of waste and in climate change action.

It was an acceptance of the deficiency in environmental regulations, notably in how they were administered by the Environmental Protection Agency, that prompted the US Clinton administration to make an executive order on environmental justice.[75] Key actors in the environmental justice movement in the United States who had persisted with an argument that the agency's enforcement policy was discriminatory highlighted this deficiency.[76] The executive order was accompanied by the establishment of the US Office of Environmental Justice and focused on ensuring that adverse environmental effects resulting from administrative action and policy did not fall disproportionately on disadvantaged communities. Both legal institutions remain highly symbolic, even if poorly implemented and incapable of slowing the continued production and disposal of toxic wastes.[77] The order did not prove to be a model for other national jurisdictions and international law, though it remains the preferred approach in the United States where more substantial legislative developments have not occurred nationally. Although environmental justice bills were proposed or enacted in a number of the states of the United States in the fifteen years that followed the introduction of the executive order,[78] the Democrats in the US

[74] See, e.g., Low and Gleeson, above n. 24.

[75] Executive Order 12898 of 11 February 1994: *Federal Actions to Address Environmental Justice in Minority Populations and Low-Income Populations.*

[76] Veronica Eady, 'Environmental Justice in State Policy Decisions' in Agyeman, Bullard and Evans (eds.), above n. 21, 168.

[77] Holyfield, above n. 39.

[78] See Nicholas Targ and Steven Bonorris, 'State Environmental Justice Programs and Related Authorities' in Michael Gerrard and Sheila Foster (eds.), *The Law of Environmental Justice: Theories and Procedures to Address Disproportionate Risks* (American Bar Association, Chicago, 2nd edn, 2008) 157.

Congress, beginning with Al Gore, have failed to give persistent and binding effect to the Clinton policy through environmental justice laws in 1992, 1993, 1999, 2002, 2003, 2005 and 2007.[79] Recent bills have been halted in the committee stages, unable to get broad political support beyond the African-American and Latino constituents of parliament. The current effort to 'codify' the executive order is included in a broader legislative framework, subsumed into the current healthcare discourse with its strong emphasis on equity and combating disadvantage[80] in the United States.[81]

Whereas the law led the development of the discourse of environmental justice through its reception to arguments about civil rights and the enunciation of human rights both internationally and domestically, the law now lags. While 'environmental movements have made significant headway using the discourse of rights'[82] that headway has been most apparent at the theoretical and political levels rather than in law, especially in public laws specifically designed to protect the environment and human health. Despite this, the internationalisation of the concept of environmental justice, and a growing appreciation of the connections between human rights and environmental protection[83] suggests that the next push in the development of environmentally just laws will likely be led by the international legal community at the demand of the developing world.

4.2 *Participation and legal standing*

In the years before and following the first peak of the environmental justice discourse in the 1980s pollution laws were enacted or amended to create procedural rights. This represented a shift in focus from the dominant

[79] Avoice (African American Voices in Congress), *Environmental Justice Timeline* at www.avoiceonline.org/environmental/timeline.html, last accessed 10 August 2009; Govtrack.US at www.govtrack.us, last accessed 10 August 2009; Washingtonwatch.com at www.washingtonwatch.com, last accessed 10 August 2009.

[80] Bruce Siegel and Lea Nolan, 'Leveling the Field: Ensuring Equity through National Health Care Reform' (2009) *The New England Journal of Medicine* Health Care Reform Centre at http://healthcarereform.nejm.org/?p=2461, last accessed 21 January 2010.

[81] Health Equity and Accountability Bill, above n. 2, which was introduced into Congress on 26 June 2009.

[82] Mark Smith and Piya Pangsapa, *Environment and Citizenship: Integrating Justice, Responsibility and Civic Engagement* (Zed Books, London and New York, 2008) 11.

[83] For example, Wolfgang Sachs, *Climate Change and Human Rights: WDEV Special Report 1/2007* (World Economy & Development, Luxembourg, 2007).

distributional justice agenda. These laws are now important constituents of a multifaceted theory of environmental justice.[84] Laws like the 1970 Clean Air Act[85] gave rights to citizens to enforce laws against polluters when the state is an unwilling prosecutor. Administrative laws gave citizens power to challenge decisions of government agencies and ministers. The legal changes were not confined to the United States, although it is there that 'citizen suits' predominate.[86] The US laws also provide the model for elsewhere, including in New South Wales.[87] In both these jurisdictions, however, the promise of citizen suits as community-, or even individual-, initiated court action has not been realised, with agencies and large environment groups more usually the beneficiary of third-party prosecution rights.[88]

The discourse of environmental justice has refocused on participation and procedural justice as a means of empowering communities through the building of capabilities and facilitating distributionally just outcomes. This is documented in the work of scholars, including Schlosberg.[89] However, this refocusing has not been matched by universal agreement within legislatures and courts to broaden standing in environmental or administrative laws where cases cannot be initiated without the need to establish a particular injury or interest. In Australia and the United Kingdom, standing in planning and environmental assessment laws has ceased being contentious, suggesting that ongoing efforts of environmental advocates to broaden access to justice to include groups without direct proprietary interests have succeeded. However, elsewhere, particularly in Europe,[90] the debates about standing persist, notwithstanding the celebrated advent of the Aarhus Convention on Access to Information, Public Participation in Decision-making and Access to Justice in Environmental Matters.[91] This leaves

[84] Schlosberg (2007), above n. 28. [85] 42 USC § 7401 (1970). [86] Adler, above n. 72.

[87] Protection of the Environment Operations Act (NSW) s. 219.

[88] Adler, above n. 72. In NSW, the only recent citizen-suit case under section 219 of the Protection of the Environment Operations Act 1997 (NSW) has been brought by a local council: see *Wyong Shire Council* v. *Thomas Hughes Homes Pty Ltd* (2001) 115 LGERA 56.

[89] Schlosberg's (2007, above n. 28) third aspect of a broad understanding of environmental justice is participation. It is through participation, argues Schlosberg, that participants in environmental controversies are recognised and gain respect.

[90] See, e.g., the European Court of Justice's decision in *Jego-Quere*, analysed in Maria Lee, *EU Environmental Law: Challenges, Change and Decision-Making* (Hart Publishing, Oxford and Portland, 2005).

[91] European Council Regulation (EC) No. 1367/2006 on the application of the provisions of the Aarhus Convention on Access to Information, Public Participation in Decision-Making and Access to Justice in Environmental Matters to Community institutions and bodies, 6 September 2006, Arts. 10 and 11 also give standing to non-government organisations to seek review of decisions made under environmental laws.

community groups in particular, with their often vague or non-existent legal personality and lack of obvious injury, with great difficulty in accessing legal mechanisms to pursue what they see as environmental justice. In common law countries it also leads to stagnation in environmental laws, with courts unable to re-evaluate laws because they are not presented with legal questions for resolution.

Debates and disputes about public participation have been observed in the area of land use planning law and environmental assessment law.[92] These were the laws that gave rights to Warren County community and other like communities to challenge approvals required for the construction and operation of industrial facilities and infrastructure. They are most suited to give effect to Principle 10 of the 1992 Rio Declaration on Environment and Development (Rio Declaration),[93] with its soft-law directive about participation and access to information. In promotion of the Rio principle, the environmental discourse has been about enhancing rights, giving effect to principles of environmental democracy, notably transparency, deliberation and fairness, and counterbalancing the dominance of business, development and government interests in the policy-making process.[94] There is a strong public law undercurrent, as seen in the chapter by Marsden in this collection.[95] Ellis makes the point that the discourse of 'environmental justice sees activism in terms of collective struggles where the marginalised become empowered and thus acclaimed as being redistributive, progressive and just'.[96]

The broadening of understanding and interpretation of human rights, particularly facilitated in the United Kingdom by the passage of the Human Rights Act 1998 and the adoption of the Aarhus Convention, has altered perceptions and treatment of opposition to large-scale development.

[92] Geraint Ellis, 'Discourses of Objection: Towards an Understanding of Third-Party Rights in Planning' (2004) 36 *Environment and Planning A* 1549.

[93] Principle 10 states:

> Environmental issues are best handled with the participation of all concerned citizens, at the relevant level. At the national level, each individual shall have appropriate access to information concerning the environment that is held by public authorities, including information on hazardous materials and activities in their communities, and the opportunity to participate in decision-making processes. States shall facilitate and encourage public awareness and participation by making information widely available. Effective access to judicial and administrative proceedings, including redress and remedy, shall be provided.

[94] Ellis, above n. 92; Mason, above n. 25.

[95] See below Chapter 10 by Simon Marsden.

[96] Ellis, above n. 92, 1553.

Through developments in public law and the UK Parliament giving effect to supranational law, opponents now have 'an enhanced rights regime'[97] supporting participatory decision-making and allowing them to position opposition within a rights and justice discourse and to shift the characterisation of the nature of their objection from self-interest to infringement of human and environmental rights.

A discursive focus on procedural justice in planning and environmental laws and in the Rio Declaration has not resolved power struggles and does not satisfy environmental justice and environmental democracy principles. A narrow view of participation in law, giving community members rights to be heard, to have views considered and to seek judicial review, cannot correct technocentrist policy and equalise access to lawyers and funds to present legal argument. It also fails to engage with consequences of decisions and takes little account of the context within which decisions are made. This is why third-party rights continue to be a focus for reform of planning and development laws, alongside proposals to widen the availability of merits review,[98] strengthen enforcement agencies and invest decision-making functions in specialised bodies and expert courts.[99] Without such changes community groups with a right to initiate proceedings will too often be unsuccessful on technical grounds and burdened with legal costs, with their environmental arguments untested.[100] These calls have been made nationally, but also internationally at the Global Judges Symposium on Sustainable Development and the Role of Law, a quasi-international conference and a prelude to the 2002 Earth Summit. The Johannesburg Principles arising from the symposium called for equipping judges, prosecutors and legislatures with the skills, information and materials to carry out functions in a well-informed way.[101] All are applied measures that respond to elements of Schlosberg's conception of environmental justice. They are directed to further democratising participation by

[97] Ibid.

[98] See the submissions to the Independent Review of the Environment Protection and Biodiversity Conservation Act 1999 (Cth) www.environment.gov.au/epbc/review/index.html, last accessed 21 January 2010.

[99] Lord Woolf, *The Pursuit of Justice* (Oxford University Press, 2008).

[100] See, e.g., *Blue Wedges Inc.* v. *Minister for Environment, Heritage and the Arts* (2008) 167 FCR 463; *Blue Wedges Inc.* v. *Minister for the Environment, Heritage and the Arts (No. 2)* [2008] FCA 1106 (15 July 2008).

[101] Woolf, above n. 99.

increasing its meaningfulness, and the building of capabilities among individuals within the environmental decision-making process.

4.3 *Ecological justice and biodiversity conservation*

Low and Gleeson documented and influenced a shift in the discourse of environmental justice towards a more ecocentric morality[102] in the 1990s. They argued that the scope of morality and society should be extended to include non-human parts of the environment. They claimed that justice should not only be done to humans, which was still the focus of their commentary, but also to the ecosystem. This is a view adopted by Schlosberg in his four-limbed definition of environmental justice. One of the proposals suggested by Low and Gleeson to redress environmental and ecological injustice was the establishment of a World Environment Council and Environment Court with powers to order injunctions and sanctions – including exclusion from world trade – for environmentally unjust activities of a state or its corporations. Although the proposal is unlikely to be progressed any time soon, the significance of the reform proposal is that this academic pair saw international law as the institution to pursue ecological justice.

Low and Gleeson have been joined by other scholars[103] in promoting a more plural and dynamic understanding and breadth of environmental justice, and in doing so enriching the discourse of environmental justice.[104] Commentators on ecological citizenship, drawing on traditional public law doctrines, have also argued that the duties and responsibilities that match the rights of procedural and distributive environmental justice detailed above are obligations of stewardship to the ecosystem and an acceptance of an environmental ethic.[105] Indeed, it is in scholarly work where this branch of the environmental discourse is being pursued. While academic effort has made the discourse of environmental justice less anthropocentric, the discourse change has not corresponded with changes to public and international law. Public laws, for instance, have not given trees standing, a proposition argued in 1972[106] and that

[102] Low and Gleeson, above n. 24.
[103] Particularly led by Schlosberg (1999, 2007), above n. 28.
[104] See Loretta Capeheart and Dragan Milovanovic, *Social Justice: Theories, Issues and Movements* (Rutgers University Press, New Brunswick and London, 2007), especially ch. 7.
[105] See, e.g., Smith and Pangsapa, above n. 82. See below Chapter 3 by Mark Shepheard and Paul Martin, in particular the discussion on stewardship.
[106] Stone, above n. 10.

popularised within public law the idea that non-human components of the environment possess interests that can be legally recognised and protected. Instead, the law has gradually given more scope for interested community and environmental groups to access courts. Those broadened standing rules, though, remain anthropocentric. Further, the law generally still conceives the environment as segmented 'natural resources' available for exploitation, and ecosystems as places where jobs and human interests are balanced with the interests of the ecosystem to maintain integrity and prosperity.

The closest the law has come to addressing ecocentric concerns and reflecting an ecological ethic has been in the development and enforcement of species protection laws. These laws, however, create a hierarchy of protection for aspects of the biosphere – for a combination of ecocentric and anthropocentric reasons. Species are protected because they are rare, valuable or iconic. This prioritisation is also evident within the discourse of conservation and protection, which has encouraged the development and enforcement of species protection laws. By way of recent example, in Australia the environment movement has prioritised whales, old forests and penguins over other marine animals, terrestrial habitats and birds.[107] The ecological justice discourse though, which is mostly employed by philosophers, scholars and 'deep green' environmentalists, avoids this distinction and purports to treat all species (as distinct from individual species)[108] equally.[109] Rarely, though, does the law operate to uniformly and equally preserve the ecosystem. Even the Convention on Biological Diversity,[110] with its concern for maintaining the variety of and within species, and its acknowledgement in its opening text of 'the intrinsic value of biological diversity', creates a regime that does not fully reflect an ecological justice philosophy.

If there is one lesson from Warren County, it is that if an ecocentric conception of environmental justice remains the province of scholars, public and international laws will be slow to respond. This is particularly

[107] See, e.g., *Humane Society International Inc.* v. *Kyodo Senpaku Kaisha* 165 FCR 510; *Brown* v. *Forestry Tasmania (No. 4)* (2006) 157 FCR 1; and the Channel Deepening Project environmental assessment, where concerns about penguins overshadowed other species concerns.

[108] Which has been the focus of recent philosophising in Martha Nussbaum, *Frontiers of Justice: Disability, Nationality, Species Membership* (Belknap Press, Cambridge, Mass., and London, 2006).

[109] See Schlosberg (2007), above n. 28.

[110] Opened for signature 5 June 1992, 1760 UNTS 79 (entered into force 29 December 1993).

so as environmental 'problems', like climate change and land degradation, are rapidly perceived as threats to humans, requiring legal responses to those human threats. Similarly, while conservation is viewed as a threat to economic development, legal protections will be rarely initiated. This suggests that the shared anthropocentric ethic of public and international laws might only be overcome by a new cross-jurisdictional institution altogether, perhaps as envisaged by Low and Gleeson when they foresaw this new course for environmental justice.

4.4 *Global democracy, global toxics and climate justice*

The concern for the unfair distribution of environmental harms observed in the United States in the 1980s is now occurring at the international level.[111] There is a realisation, particularly in light of the climate change experience, that the richest are the polluters while the poorest are expected to endure polluting activities. Oil companies, miners, bio-prospectors, fishers and loggers have all been accused of perpetrating environmental injustices through exploitative practices in the territory, or with the resources, of developing countries. Development theorists[112] began exploring corporate- and government-sponsored exploitation in developing countries as part of the counter-narrative to the individualist, market-structured development discourse. This development discourse was enthusiastically adopted by international financial institutions, conservative governmental institutions[113] and economists,[114] but led to ecological degradation as a corollary to, and sometimes in place of, economic development.[115] The degrading development practices, privatisation agendas, colonialist exploitation and imperialistic prospecting of goods, including greenhouse gas emissions reductions under

[111] Agyeman, Bullard and Evans, above n. 21.

[112] See John Byrne, Cecilia Martinez and Leigh Glover, 'A Brief on Environmental Justice' in John Byrne, Cecilia Martinez and Leigh Glover (eds.), *Environmental Justice: Discourses in International Political Economy* (Transaction Publishers, New Brunswick, 2002) 3.

[113] See, e.g., Thomas Bassett, 'Introduction: The Land Question and Agricultural Transformation in Sub-Saharan Africa' in Thomas Bassett and Donald Crummy (eds.), *Land in African Agrarian Systems* (University of Wisconsin Press, Madison, 1993) 3.

[114] For example, Hernando de Soto, *The Mystery of Capital: Why Capitalism Triumphs in the West and Fails Everywhere Else* (Basic Books, New York, 2000).

[115] James Acheson, 'Institutional Failure in Resource Management' (2006) 35 *Annual Review of Anthropology* 117.

the Kyoto Protocol, have been approved by the law. Sometimes law-makers have promoted such actions enthusiastically as environmentally beneficial without contemplating or articulating the consequences for local communities.[116]

This realisation of a global injustice, due in part to the globalisation of the economy and global dominion over commons areas,[117] has led to calls, with a discourse and movement emerging in developed and developing countries, for a form of international environmental justice to 'fix' distributional inequalities. Agyeman and others[118] note that in this context 'the discourse of environmental justice [is] seen as a unifying process, bringing together diverse situations and sharing understandings and experiences'. Simultaneously, the concept of global democracy with its discourse of human rights, fairness, equality and participation has evolved and been contributed to by administrative laws domestically and internationally, especially through the notion of global administrative law jurisprudence.[119] Arguments about environmental justice have drawn on this discourse.[120]

The issues of relocation of toxic and waste materials and climate change have driven the discourse of environmental justice at the international level.[121] At the negotiation of the Basel Convention on the Control of Transboundary Movements of Hazardous Wastes[122] 'developing countries regularly invoked the concept of environmental justice'.[123] In doing so they foreshadowed the trends that followed. However, the convention did not

116 For example, the proposal to offset greenhouse gas emissions by halting deforestation in the developing world.

117 See Byrne, Martinez and Glover, above n. 112, 8.

118 Agyeman, Bullard and Evans, above n. 21, 9.

119 See below Chapter 10 by Simon Marsden, in particular his discussion on global administrative laws.

120 See David Pellow, *Resisting Global Toxics: Transnational Movements for Environmental Justice* (MIT Press, Cambridge, Mass., and London, 2007); Jutta Brunnée, 'Climate Change, Global Environmental Justice and International Environmental Law' in Ebbesson and Okowa (eds.), above n. 12, 316.

121 André Nollkaemper, 'Sovereignty and Environmental Justice in International Law' in Ebbesson and Okowa (eds.), ibid., 253.

122 Opened for signature 22 March 1989, 1673 UNTS 126 (entered into force 5 May 1992).

123 Chukwumerije Okereke, *Global Justice and Neoliberal Environmental Governance: Ethics, Sustainable Development and International Co-operation* (Routledge, London and New York, 2008) 23.

contemplate the future extent of waste and chemical trade and the difficulties that persist in curtailing it,[124] or the morality and justness of allowing nations to consent to the import of waste on behalf of their citizens.[125] The climate change debate between developed and developing nations has honed in on questions of fairness.[126]

International law provides examples of nations grappling with global environmental justice and contributing to the global discourse. In 1987 the WCED's report[127] emphasised equity and social justice as part of sustainable development. The 2002 Earth Summit, while reaffirming an environmental sustainability agenda, placed a stronger focus on egalitarianism and equity between nations.[128] Earlier, the Rio Declaration[129] adopted the concept of common but differentiated responsibilities between the developed and developing world. Brunnée[130] explains that these changes have created a body of international law that is significantly different from the state of international law after the *Trail Smelter Arbitration*.[131] Contrasted to the 1940s, Nollkaemper[132] highlights that international environmental agreements now oblige states to take protective measures, not simply to avoid doing harm to other nations, even if they disturb state sovereign rights to exploit their natural resources. Meanwhile, international law judicial decisions[133] have identified a requirement on states to protect their environment as a component of sustainable development. The principle of intergenerational equity also looms large,[134] potentially requiring states to avoid harming future non-citizens.[135]

Despite these developments, within the omnipresent and often pessimistic climate change debate, there is an acceptance that the law might not deliver global environmental justice. Brunnée argues, 'it is not enough that the concept is contained in salient legal instruments. The

[124] Pellow, above n. 120; Iles, above n. 4.

[125] See Jonathan Krueger, 'Prior Informed Consent and the Basel Convention: The Hazards of What Isn't Known' (1998) 7 *The Journal of Environment and Development* 115 for a description and analysis of the prior informed consent process in the Basel Convention.

[126] Jeannie Sowers, 'The Many Injustices of Climate Change' (2007) 7(4) *Global Environmental Politics* 140.

[127] WCED, above n. 8. [128] Agyeman, Bullard and Evans, above n. 21.

[129] Principle 7. Also adopted in Article 3(1) of the United Nations Framework Convention on Climate Change, opened for signature 4 June 1992, 1771 UNTS 107 (entered into force 21 March 1994).

[130] Brunnée, above n. 120.

[131] (1938 and 1941) 3 UN Rep. Int. Arb. Awards. [132] Nollkaemper, above n. 121.

[133] See below Chapter 8 by Tim Stephens.

[134] See above Chapter 1 by Peter Lawrence. [135] Nollkaemper, above n. 121.

crucial question is whether it represents a globally shared understanding of distributive justice in the face of climate change.'[136] There is no such shared understanding. Developed countries have framed justice arguments disingenuously and simplistically,[137] solely in terms of the distribution of mitigating action. On the other hand, low-lying island states and non-government organisations argue for drastic emissions reductions so that the burdens of climate change are not unfairly borne by countries least likely to be able to adapt and least responsible for contributing to human-induced climate change.[138] What this emphasises is that the discourse of environmental justice remains fluid and broad, though sufficiently theorised and attentive to fairness and human well-being and environmental protection to detect insincerity and invalidity. However, theoretical purity will be unlikely to motivate consensus from the international community. To attain environmental justice globally the contribution of the international legal community is fundamental. It may not act, however, until the discourse shifts or becomes louder.

5. Conclusion

The final point is important. There is a role for the law to shape understandings of environmental justice; however, the law is traditionally a reactive and cautionary institution. Discourses are far more dynamic and capable of accommodating alternative world views than either public or international laws. What this chapter shows is that environmental discourses do operate at both levels of law, and that public and international laws are responding to claims about environmental justice. Some responses are unique to domestic legal systems and others to global governance. There is, though, much shared between the two legal regimes. Both recognise rights, both converse on Stockholm and Rio objectives, both are moving towards more participatory processes, and both are confronted with dilemmas of an ecological citizenship where rights are balanced with environmental duties. There is also a capacity for international and public law to respond to the refocused concept of environmental justice in ways that each discipline has traditionally, but also by drawing on alternative jurisdictional and disciplinary approaches and agendas. This is seen

[136] Brunnée, above n. 120, 325. [137] Vanderheiden, above n. 5.

[138] See ibid. for a detailed account of justice theories and arguments in the climate change debate.

throughout this chapter with the selective survey of legal and policy environmental law developments. Environmental laws have benefited from civil rights legal advances; international law has used administrative law principles in the promotion of a more environmentally democratic legal system and has the opportunity to learn from the public law response to claims of distributional environmental injustice. Meanwhile, philosophy, political science and development studies theories offer new perspectives on legal responses to environmental issues.

For all the legal reforms inspired by the discourse of environmental justice, the movement has been hampered by a reluctance of environmental laws to shift from their industrial focus to address distributional justice deficits in public environmental law, and to equalise participation and legal power at both law-making levels. It is this focus, too, that has blinded the law to the conception of ecological justice and has caused it to fail to organise a new ecological citizenry. It is the unwillingness of the most powerful to concede economic and political privilege that has led them to cloud conceptions of justice in a way that the law cannot resolve. One lesson from Warren County, though, is that proponents of environmental justice persist, and they rally. The lesson from the years that follow is that the appeal of the theory of environmental justice is broad and as the discourse continues to grow the law, even if reluctantly, will be a part of that journey.

3

The political discourse of land stewardship reframed as a statutory duty

MARK SHEPHEARD AND PAUL MARTIN

1. Introduction

There is a tension between the idea that property rights give rise to minimal legal accountability, and alternatively that property rights holders should exercise care in the enjoyment of their rights. This tension provides a basis for a discourse about stewardship and the practical meaning of a statutory duty of care to protect the environment. The discourse of stewardship and care that ordinarily occurs at the local or national level reflects sustainable development principles advanced in international agreements. The tension created by competing understandings and expectations of property is reflected in administrative rules that seem to make stewardship a legal obligation. These new rules mask the competing meanings embodied in the language used in international environmental dialogue, but in embedding competing meanings of terms in the legal discourse they potentially sow the seeds of future conflicts. This is in part because the pursuit of expanded stewardship responsibility is occurring alongside the creation of ever-broader legally secure property rights to the environment. The tensions are given a public expression in the heated 'farmers' property right' movement, which by 2010 is becoming increasingly strident. Thus there are three parallel forms of discourse about stewardship for natural resources which interact: formalised political discourse about desired norms, spilling over from international to parliamentary contexts; the inchoate legal discourse related particularly to the implementation of instruments; and the informal political discourse of political activism.

All three discourses share characteristics that would be readily identified by a student of Foucault. The symbolic meaning of the language is not shared, and contests about meaning are also contests over power. The form of the discourse is specific to the context and follows 'rules of engagement' specific to that context for discourse. In this chapter we shall consider the interaction between the two formalised discourses that demonstrate competition. The competition we observe is complex. The different contexts and the resulting expectations of the participants in the discourse result in different basic assumptions, including assumptions about the specificity of meaning to be attached to the symbolic words. A contest between world views about humans and the environment, of the type identified by Dryzek,[1] is evident in both discourses. An important distinction between the legal and the policy contexts is that the meaning of symbols that will emerge eventually through formal legal processes will determine which of the categories within Dryzek's taxonomy will emerge as dominant in legal practice. This is a power conflict over the specific meaning to be assigned to a particular set of linguistic symbols.

2. The tension between property rights and social obligation

Sustainable development is a language of political discourse that aspires to marry environmental protection with economic exploitation. Different jurisdictions give substance to this language through economic incentives, administration and legislation.[2] In Australia these expectations are assumed into domestic law in various ways. One is through a statutory environmental duty of care.[3] While the connotations of sustainable development and a duty of care are readily accepted politically, when it comes to denoting particular behaviours with specific, generally economic, consequences, the terminology may prove to be more slippery than one might expect.[4]

A new jurisprudence for the environment is emerging.[5] One core challenge is to reconcile increasing private ownership of rights[6] to the

[1] John Dryzek, *The Politics of the Earth: Environmental Discourses* (Oxford University Press, 1st edn, 1997).

[2] Philippe Sands, *Principles of International Environmental Law* (Cambridge University Press, 2nd edn, 2003) 266. See also World Commission on Environment and Development, *Our Common Future* (Oxford University Press, 1987).

[3] See Table 3.1 below for the list of statutes.

[4] Maria Lee, *EU Environmental Law: Challenges, Change and Decision-Making* (Hart Publishing, Oxford and Portland, 2005) 25.

[5] Paul Martin, 'The Changing Role of Law in the Pursuit of Sustainability' in Michael Jeffrey, Jeremy Firestone and Karen Bubna-Litic (eds.), *Biodiversity Conservation, Law and Livelihoods: Bridging the North–South Divide* (Cambridge University Press, New York, 2008) 49.

[6] See below Chapter 4 by Nicole Graham, who observes a sense of entitlement twinned with property rights.

environment with increasing expectations of public good stewardship. An effective institutional framework is needed to reconcile the minimal accountability expected by property interests and a caring stewardship of resources anticipated by international environmental law. Duties of care represent a step in this direction, but making them effective will require great sophistication of reasoning applied by administrators and industry. It will be necessary to narrow the range of meanings that may be attached to the symbolic phrase, so that the legal system can perform its function of channelling and resolving conflict by reference to specific rules and repeatable processes.

The competing expectations that a statutory duty of care can mandate sustainable management and simultaneously reduce the high transaction costs, complexity and inflexibilities claimed of traditional regulation may not be reconcilable. The view that minimal accountability is all that is legally required within the sanctity of property rights sits uncomfortably alongside the belief that a duty of care legally embeds a higher moral responsibility of care in the relationship between resource users and the environment.

The statutes containing a duty of care produce obligations that are largely implemented through administration rather than civil or criminal action. While making environmental duty an administrative instrument is intended to prevent the courts from being involved in attempting to resolve irreconcilable meanings, this will not prevent political disappointments as the principle is applied. Based on analogous developments in administrative environmental laws, it is expected that the courts will eventually have a fundamental a role in reconciling the tensions between the expectation that private property can only be attenuated by specific rules, and expectations that property is a form of public trust.

This chapter will highlight some practical challenges in society's attempts to translate ideals of stewardship into binding legal principles using a statutory duty of care. Concepts of sustainability and stewardship arise in the political arena, often translated first into international and domestic policy. These are subsequently implemented using mechanisms including funding, taxation and administrative arrangements. Ultimately the ideals of stewardship may be translated into legal principles and applied directly to holders of property rights through policing or civil action or by government agencies exercising administrative oversight of private actions.

The translation from political principle into applied regulation requires the development of precise definitions and legal principles around words that conceal multiple and competing meanings. The term 'duty of care', along with the concepts of 'precautionary principle' and 'sustainable development' have the value of assisting political consensus precisely because of their ambiguity. When their meaning must be defined for the purpose of adjusting individual property rights to exploit resources, the flexibility of meaning becomes a significant problem. This process from international politics to local law may in effect transfer unresolved political tensions into the public law arena, leaving it to the bureaucracy and eventually the courts to determine which world view is reflected in the application of words that can be used to encompass the wide range of perspectives about humans and the environment.

If and when litigation occurs concerning a statutory duty of care, it is likely that a long tradition of judicial application of a duty of care, which reflects minimal obligations of accountability, will inform the ultimate meaning of a farmer's statutory obligation. We suggest this is more likely to involve restating the dominance of the exploitative paradigm of property with some modification to require limited foresight and care, rather than embracing any of the 'greener' world views that have informed the political discourse of care and stewardship.

3. The rhetoric of duty, care and accountability

Property owner responsibilities can be structured around accountability as a minimum required level of behaviour, or around care as a desired standard of ethical stewardship.[7] As discussed below, non-government organization and international agency expectations about sustainable development favour stewardship as a standard. This creates a pressure for concepts of care to expand property owners' responsibilities to the broader community and affected neighbours.[8]

Property owner legal responsibilities for management performance are constituted by accountability to comply with specific statutory obligations, coupled with accountability to neighbours not to infringe their exploitative rights.[9] The paradigm of property embeds a largely unattenuated freedom to exploit, with constraints where parliaments make

[7] Mark Bovins, *The Quest for Responsibility: Accountability and Citizenship in Complex Organisations* (Cambridge University Press, 1998).

[8] Mark Stallworthy, *Sustainability, Land Use and Environment: A Legal Analysis* (Cavendish, London, 2002).

[9] Murray Raff, 'Environmental Obligations and the Western Liberal Property Concept' (1998) 22 *Melbourne University Law Review* 657.

clear this purpose or where exploitation may unjustifiably interfere with the interests of another property owner.[10] Its emphasis is on minimum accountability for environmental harm, with property rights paramount.[11] The common law imposes accountability that is significantly less onerous than the loosely defined public good responsibilities that are implied in stewardship standards of responsibility.[12]

A duty of care within the common law of negligence generates practical meaning to a broadly defined neighbourly duty through consideration of:[13] foreseeability of harm, the circumstances in which harm arises, the objective standard of care relevant to the circumstances determined after the fact, and common practice. A failure to exercise reasonable care in the particular circumstances may result in liability.[14] By a process of court decisions applying this reasoning, society develops well-understood norms of behaviour. The normative nature of these accountabilities means that it is not necessary or expected that they will be fully specified, unlike some 'command and control' regulation.[15]

In the absence of other interpretative support, the long judicial experience with the application of a duty of care is likely to inform the meaning of a farmer's statutory duty of care. This is because the statutory versions provide little clarity about the practical meaning of responsibility in a stewardship context and because of the persistent reluctance of national courts to fully embrace international law principles. Yet people have a right to know what the law is, what it allows and what it does not allow in a way that is pre-stated rather than retrospective.[16] Freedom of action is an overriding interest that is preserved in courts applying a

10 Joseph Sax, 'Environmental Law Forty Years Later: Looking Back and Looking Ahead' in Jeffrey, Firestone and Bubna-Litic (eds.), above n. 5, 9.

11 John Fleming, *The Law of Torts* (Lawbook, Sydney, 9th edn, 1998) 9.

12 Tucker LJ in *Latimer* v. *AEC Ltd* [1953] AC 643.

13 Fleming, above n. 11, 117. The approach is sometimes termed the 'Shirt calculus', since the leading Australian authority is *Wyong Shire Council* v. *Shirt* (1980) 146 CLR 40. For a discussion of breach of duty, see Francis Trindade, Peter Cane and Mark Lunney, *The Law of Torts in Australia* (Oxford University Press, Melbourne, 4th edn, 2007) ch. 8; Jane Stapleton, 'Duty of Care Factors: A Selection from the Judicial Menus' in Peter Cane and Jane Stapleton (eds.), *The Law of Obligations: Essays in Celebration of John Fleming* (Clarendon Press, Oxford, 1998) 59.

14 Mark Lunney and Ken Oliphant, *Tort Law: Text and Materials* (Oxford University Press, 2nd edn, 2003).

15 Tucker LJ in *Latimer* v. *AEC Ltd*, above n. 12.

16 Doreen McBarnet and Christopher Whelan, 'The Elusive Spirit of the Law: Formalism and the Struggle for Legal Control' (1991) 54 *The Modern Law Review* 848, 857.

reasonable care approach.[17] The accountabilities arising from the historical common law approach are more consistent with a property paradigm of freedom to exploit with minimal accountability, than with the more ethically idealised concepts of stewardship based on care. This is because the courts do not conventionally seek to drive the development of community norms. The law is prosaic rather than imaginative in imposing accountabilities.

4. Competing meanings of the stewardship metaphor

'Stewardship' is a component of the political dialogue about resource owner responsibilities. A steward is a person holding a position of responsibility. A steward is the guardian of a place.[18] The metaphorical appeal of the terminology is strong, as it is redolent with a sense of ancestral values, including its use in the bible. Its fiduciary meanings have been picked up to advocate greater farmer responsibility for sustainable natural resource management.[19] Stewardship has been described as an approach that reconnects farming with good environmental practice,[20] recognising constraints on resource depletion as part of an obligation to future generations.[21] This is a response to the belief that modern agricultural production systems demonstrate little of the stewardship role traditionally associated with farming.[22] Instead, industrial agriculture has emerged as a main cause of environmental decay across the landscape.[23]

Stewardship provides a conception of prudent or right behaviour with respect to avoiding environmental harm.[24] Prudence is about ends, how to make important choices using a mix of foresight, morals and

[17] Fleming, above n. 11.

[18] Judy Pearsall and Bill Trumble (eds.), *Oxford English Reference Dictionary* (Oxford University Press, 2nd rev. edn, 2001).

[19] Richard Barnes, *Property Rights and Natural Resources* (Hart Publishing, Oxford and Portland, 2009); Anna Carr, *Grass Roots and Green Tape: Principles and Practices of Environmental Stewardship* (Federation Press, Sydney, 2002) 15.

[20] Policy Commission on the Future of Farming and Food, *Farming & Food: A Sustainable Future* (2002) 9.

[21] United Kingdom, Royal Commission on Environmental Pollution, *Sustainable Use of Soil* (1996) 22. See also above Chapter 1 by Peter Lawrence.

[22] D. Baldock *et al.*, *Growing Greener. Sustainable Agriculture in the UK* (Council for the Protection of Rural England, London, 1996).

[23] Policy Commission on the Future of Farming and Food, above n. 20, 68.

[24] Lee, above n. 4, 207.

self-understanding; in effect, a demonstration of care.[25] For those wishing to see greater emphasis on conservation, the core duties of stewardship are to keep resources for posterity and to save resources from harm.[26] The intention of those using the term is to make property rights subject to norms of environmental responsibility in the same way as the use rights of a steward are constrained by the obligation to hold the resource in trust for others.[27]

The metaphor of the steward is also embraced by farmers, whose world view is often counter to more 'imaginative' perspectives on the relationship between man and the natural world that is present in environmental advocacy. In political discourse, property owners sometimes attach to the metaphor of a good steward their pride in how they have historically managed and used the land. In a Lockean way they impose on the stewardship discourse a sense of moral obligation and justification in exploitative use.[28] This use of stewardship in the debates over their boundaries of responsibility is a bid for continued freedom to exploit. These uses of the word 'stewardship' illustrate how political discourses about sustainability allow for competing meanings to be encompassed in single terms. Whilst useful as language for political discourse, this flexibility of meaning of terms is likely to frustrate legal application of the duty of care. Courts will be forced to find a more technically precise designation, and thereby reduce the scope for uncertainty.

The underlying tension in these discourses is about defining the boundaries between an owner's private rights to exploit and the community's interest in conservation.[29] Secure property rights require the community as a whole to support an owner in defending their interest. This implies a social consensus about responsibility and freedom to exploit.[30] Where the

[25] Bernard Jacob, 'Ancient Rhetoric, Modern Legal Thought, and Politics: A Review Essay on the Translation of Viehweg's "Topics and Law"' (1995) 89 *Northwestern University Law Review* 1622, 1668.

[26] Barnes, above n. 19, 156. [27] Ibid. 161.

[28] For an illustration of these competing views, see Australian Conservation Foundation, *Rights and Responsibilities in Land and Water Management* (2002); Barnes, above n. 19; Andrew Macintosh and Richard Denniss, *Property Rights and the Environment: Should Farmers Have a Right to Compensation?* The Australia Institute, Discussion Paper 74 (2004); Mick Keogh, *Property Rights and Farming in Australia: Defining Duty of Care for Farm Land* (NSW Farmers Federation, Sydney, 2002).

[29] Stallworthy, above n. 8, 78.

[30] Paul Martin and Miriam Verbeek, 'Property Rights and Property Responsibility' in Land and Water Australia (ed.), *Property: Rights and Responsibilities: Current Australian Thinking* (Land and Water Australia, Canberra, 2002) 1.

community is dissatisfied with this bargain it can impose constraints through statutes, or it can apply force or sanctions to ensure that the collective interest is not ignored.[31] While an owner's title is ostensibly clearly defined by law, at a societal level the rules are more variable, and negotiated over time. This duality in the nature of property translates into unresolved tensions about whether the rights of the landowner are only constrained by clearly specified legal accountability, or whether there are broader social responsibilities reflected in the term 'care' that form part of owners' responsibilities that accompany their property rights.

Implicit in this tension, and reflected in the constitutions of many Western democracies, is that property rights are for most purposes paramount. This is translated into a judicial expectation that exploitative interests will be protected except where there is an unambiguous statement by Parliament of its intent to overturn this interest, and where legislation is specific about this intent.

5. The patterns of legal resolution

The failure to resolve the tensions between expectations of freedom to exploit and expectations of caring stewardship is the seed of unproductive and costly disputes. Two examples from New South Wales (NSW) in Australia illustrate this tension with a resolution in the interests of private rights, steering the interpretation of concepts away from an imagining of sustainability towards a prosaic and conservative reflection of world views of property.

With native vegetation legislation the NSW Parliament intended to provide a scientifically rigorous approach to achieve sustainable land management.[32] This administratively rational move was intended to use science to draw the boundary between freedom to exploit and duty to the environment. The Native Vegetation Conservation Act 1997 (NSW) embedded the expectation that scientific data would allow precise categorisation of landscapes, and estimation of the ecological impacts of

[31] Stallworthy, above n. 8, 79. See generally Sean Coyle and Karen Morrow, *The Philosophical Foundations of Environmental Law, Property, Rights and Nature* (Hart Publishing, Oxford and Portland, 2004); Murray Raff, 'Toward an Ecologically Sustainable Property Concept' in Elizabeth Cooke (ed.), *Modern Studies in Property Law*, Vol. III (Hart Publishing, Oxford, 2005) 65.

[32] New South Wales, Legislative Assembly, *Parliamentary Debates*, 19 November 1997, 2075 (Kim Yeadon, Minister for Land and Water Conservation). This is the second reading speech for the Native Vegetation Conservation Bill (NSW).

land use, to enable objective decisions about biodiversity protection.[33] No prosecutions under this legislation were successful in court, principally because of the inability to scientifically prove the breaches and their impacts. In 2002, five years after the legislation was enacted, the Auditor-General found no strategic approach to vegetation conservation had been successfully established and that the regulator lacked comprehensive information about the status of vegetation to efficiently regulate for its conservation.[34] While the data and frameworks were suitable for policy debate, when applied against the background of private rights to exploit they were legally insufficient. The history of environmental law demonstrates that imaginative laws that do not take into account prosaic realities can create cost and complexity even for individuals who are not guilty of doing substantive harm.[35]

The statutory precautionary principle further illustrates the challenges of translating international discourses of environmental responsibility into meaningful local accountabilities.[36] Entering local law to give effect to Principle 15 of the Rio Declaration of 1992, twelve years of judicial interpretation has occurred in the NSW Land and Environment Court[37] about what the principle demands of a decision-making process. It is informative that while the precautionary principle has been implemented only as a principle in administrative decisions, the impact on potential private interests has resulted in an extensive history of administrative litigation. This suggests the ambition to avoid courtroom testing of these principles may be unrealistic, where the principle clashes with the exploitative interests of society.

Judicially the precautionary principle has been characterised as a political aspiration 'with the potential for interminable forensic argument as a legal

[33] Ibid.

[34] Auditor-General of New South Wales, *Performance Audit Department of Land and Water Conservation, Regulating the Clearing of Native Vegetation* (2002).

[35] National Farmers Federation, *Policy on Sustainable Production, Land and Native Vegetation* (2004); Commonwealth of Australia Productivity Commission, *Impacts of Native Vegetation and Biodiversity Regulations* (2004); WWF-Australia, *Native Vegetation Regulation: Financial Impact and Policy Issues* (2005); Auditor-General of New South Wales, *Performance Audit. Regulating the Clearing of Native Vegetation: Follow-Up of 2002 Performance Audit* (2006).

[36] The specific example is the use of the precautionary principle in Protection of the Environment Administration Act 1991 (NSW) s. 6(2)(a).

[37] There are multiple versions of the principle both within Australia and internationally, and this is an example limited to one version in one jurisdiction.

standard'[38] that has gradually been clothed by the courts with a detailed description of what it means to apply the principle.[39] This represents rejection by the legal system of the sort of interpretative pluralism that is useful for political discourse, as counter-productive in the legal and administrative setting. Sustainable development, also a key plank of the Rio Declaration, is recognised as an important management principle for natural resources.[40] To give this term workable meaning the court has had to find ways of specifying what this might mean in particular circumstances. In these examples, in trying to clothe the policy language of sustainability with legal content that is consistent with property and freedom, the courts have moved from a broad 'responsibility' discourse to a narrow 'accountability' mechanism. The imaginative conceptualisation of the relationship between man and the earth is less useful than the prosaic when it comes to the application of the law. This outcome can be argued not as a rejection of the environment, but rather as a reinforcement of human rights to security of legal interests against the excesses of the state.

The jurisprudence of the environment indicated by these examples can be seen as subordinate to the jurisprudence of property. Ownership is intended to convey the freedom to exploit constrained first by specific rules to protect the interest of other owners and neighbours who may be harmed by exploitative acts deemed to be beyond the right of the owner, and by legal sanctions for specific acts where evidence of a suitable standard can be provided to the courts. Overlaid on this are administrative decisions, which do not override ownership interests unless clearly specified to do so and that must be carried out in ways complying with constraints on abuse of administrative power. The overall structure reflects the dominance of exploitative interest constrained only by specified accountabilities. Yet the international discourse seeks to reverse this understanding of the legal relationship between rights to exploit and duties to conserve.

6. The merger of self-interest and social interest

Instead of relying on the moral commitment of resource users to environmental outcomes or to their neighbours, policy-makers increasingly

[38] Talbot J in *Nicholls* v. *Director General National Parks and Wildlife Service* (1994) 84 LGERA 397.

[39] Preston CJ in *Telstra Corporation Ltd* v. *Hornsby Shire Council* (2006) 67 NSWLR 256, [127]–[183].

[40] See *Bentley* v. *BGP Properties Pty Ltd* (2006) 145 LGERA 234, [57].

assume that care is a scarce resource. This is demonstrated by the seemingly inexorable shift from civil law to market instruments. Faith in the ability of citizens to defend their interest was first replaced by faith in regulation reliant on the control capacity of government. The expectation was that self-interest would be constrained by fear of legal sanction. Recently, faith has been transferred to the market with the idea that the self-interest of economic agents will lead them to act in ways that promote the common good. Once again the ghost of Locke is heard in Parliament and the courtroom, even as his conceptualisation of the relationship between humans and the world is considered to be archaic by environmental altruists.

A demonstration of this is water policy. Over the long term the legal model of responsibility has shifted in varying degrees in different jurisdictions from a regime of private riparian rights, to regulation and planning, and then to market mechanisms that reward the pursuit of private good. Under riparian rights a downstream riparian owner has the right to receive water unaltered in flow or quality and the upstream user has an obligation to ensure that is the case.[41] In Australia and the United States of America, reliance on an approximation of moral relationships was diminished by statute, creating reliance on administration to manage resource access and use. This shift from a focus on personal relationship to reliance on administrators was a first step, with administrators arguably representing the collective interest. In Australia the shift to tradable extraction entitlement implies that the extent of moral duty is to be efficient, subject to specific legally defined accountabilities. This shift, from interpersonal relationships with obligations to neighbours, through to reliance on agencies and planning, and then to amoral market transactions, is a recurrent theme in natural resource management.

However, there is a counter-narrative to amorality in relations between people and natural resources. International interest in moral content in natural resource management is reflected in multilateral environmental instruments. For example, reversing natural resource loss is incorporated into one of the United Nations Millennium Development Goals about sustainable development.[42] The Earth Charter also contains commitments to respect and care for the community of life by securing earth's bounty and beauty for present and

[41] William Howarth, *Wisdom's Law of Watercourses* (Shaw, Crayford, 5th edn, 1992).

[42] United Nations Millennium Project, *Investing in Development: A Practical Plan to Achieve the Millennium Development Goals* (Earthscan, London, 2005).

future generations.[43] This includes: respect earth and life in all its diversity, care for the community of life with understanding, compassion and love, build democratic societies that are just, participatory, sustainable and peaceful, and secure the earth's bounty and beauty for present and future generations.[44] This imaginative conceptualisation places a duty or ethic of care as a central guide to practice, encouraging farmers to adopt a sense 'that they are part of a community of responsible neighbours, each guided by a similar vision of sustainable life, each knowing that ownership means duty, that duty means care, and that care, in the end, is our sole source of hope'.[45] Responsible conduct promotes limits on farmers' actions from the inherent social and environmental obligations of ownership, where rights are reconceptualised based on stewardship and where reasonableness is equated to a prudent environmental enquiry.[46] This Earth Charter vision proposes an allocation of responsibility based on care.

Other examples where an ethic of care is placed as central to stewardship include the Stockholm Declaration, Rio Declaration and Agenda 21, World Charter for Nature, World Soil Charter and World soils policy, Convention to Combat Desertification, Convention on Biological Diversity, Ramsar Convention and the United Nations Framework Convention on Climate Change.

Thus, both local and international politics of the environment are now characterised by simultaneous calls for amoral market efficiency alongside calls for caring management. The strangeness of this coupling is largely unnoted in policy debates. However, it does sit comfortably with the observations of discourse theory.

7. How discourses of care translate into action

Mechanisms requiring care in the use of resources span from limited accountability within private property rights (regulation), through informal exercise of community power including the power to constrain or adjust property rights (social licence).[47] In socio-political contexts

[43] Earth Charter International, *The Earth Charter: A Declaration of Fundamental Principles for Building a Just, Sustainable and Peaceful Society in the 21st Century* (2000).

[44] Ibid.

[45] Eric Freyfogle, 'Ethics, Community and Private Land' (1996) 23 *Ecology Law Quarterly* 631, 649.

[46] Raff, above n. 9, 692.

[47] Social licence is a voluntary unwritten consent that a community attaches to resource use. It depends on satisfying social expectations; see Neil Gunningham, Robert Kagan and Dorothy Thornton, *Social License and Environmental Protection: Why Businesses*

expectations are poorly specified and shift, often couched using expressions where what is connoted for different interest groups is more significant than what is denoted. The words used need only be sufficient for the purpose of political debate, and allowing latitude for multiple meanings to co-exist can be advantageous. Examples include 'sustainability', 'sustainable development', 'social justice', 'the precautionary principle', 'stewardship' and 'duty of care'. The linguistic symbols are clothed with different meanings by different people in different contexts.

Sustainable development suggests obligations reflecting needs, limits, equity and systems management.[48] These obligations are intended to avoid harmful behaviour and promote a neighbourly ethos.[49] Such expectations can be translated into concepts of stewardship for the next generation or stewardship for the purpose of production of environmental goods for today's citizens such as biodiversity, clean water and cultural or aesthetic goods. Mechanisms to enforce expectations include: penalty structures applied through regulation or administration, economic incentive structures such as subsidies and fees for production of environmental goods or carrying out of environmental works or for demonstration of good stewardship, and informal exercise of community power to remove or reduce the social licence of the farm sector to carry out their production activities relatively unhindered. These all involve the exercise of power triggered by interpretation.

Regulation is developed within institutions that assume the paramount value of property rights. This results in a need to be specific about accountability. The distribution of government funds and the exercise of discretion in administration are also constrained by rules concerned with the integrity of the use of power. No such constraints exist for communities exercising political power, although respect for law, private property and administrative integrity do channel and constrain the exercise of political power.

As this chapter argues, there is a trend to try to insert elements of a care-focused discourse into the accountability-focused regulatory framework, to close the loop between legal accountability and the desire for

Go Beyond Compliance (Centre for Analysis of Risk and Regulation, London School of Economics and Political Science, London, 2002); Gary Lynch-Wood and David Williamson, 'The Social Licence as a Form of Regulation for Small and Medium Enterprises' (2007) 34 *Journal of Law and Society* 321.

48 Sands, above n. 2.

49 Paul Martin and Miriam Verbeek, *Sustainability Strategy* (Federation Press, Sydney, 2006).

caring stewardship. This is principally through administrative rules intended to translate the language of politics and environmental care into legal requirements. In order to achieve this, words with multiple meanings and connotations need to be refined to create clear accountabilities within the context of private rights.

The European Common Agricultural Policy[50] uses 'good agricultural and environmental practice' as a normative standard for environmentally friendly farming performance.[51] This is the baseline standard of accountability for farmers.[52] Land stewardship incentives encourage good farming practice beyond the good agricultural and environmental condition baseline.[53] Such aspirations are similar to those underpinning Australia's adoption of a statutory duty of care.[54] In England good agricultural and environmental practice (a minimum accountability standard) is implemented using the 'Single Payment System', while good farming practice (the caring performance standard) applies under a tiered 'Stewardship Scheme'. The potential confusion from this plurality of normative guides for farm management performance is illustrated using the example of soil protection.

Both the stewardship aspiration and the minimal accountability approaches make reference to management guidance contained in government guidelines and codes of practice. For example, one document to guide implementation of good agricultural and environmental condition

[50] Council Regulation (EC) No. 73/2009 establishing common rules for direct support schemes for farmers under the common agricultural policy and establishing certain support schemes for farmers.

[51] Christopher Rodgers, 'Agenda 2000, Land Use, and the Environment: Towards a Theory of "Environmental" Property Rights?' in Jane Holder and Carolyn Harrison (eds.), *Law and Geography: Current Legal Issues 2002*, Vol. V (Oxford University Press, 2003) 239; United Kingdom, Rural Payments Agency and Department for Environment, Food and Rural Affairs, *The Guide to Cross Compliance in England* (2009).

[52] United Kingdom, Rural Payments Agency and Department for Environment, Food and Rural Affairs, *Single Payment Scheme Cross Compliance Guidance for Soil Management* (2006) 2.

[53] United Kingdom, Rural Development Service, *Entry Level Stewardship Handbook Terms and Conditions and How to Apply* (2005).

[54] Alex Gardner, 'The Duty of Care for Sustainable Land Management' (1998) 5 *The Australasian Journal of Natural Resources Law and Policy* 29; Commonwealth of Australia, House of Representatives, Standing Committee on Environment and Heritage, *Public Good Conservation: Our Challenge for the 21st Century. Interim Report of the Inquiry into Effects upon Landholders and Farmers of Public Good Conservation Measures Imposed by Australian Governments* (2001); Commonwealth of Australia, Industry Commission, *A Full Repairing Lease. Inquiry into Ecologically Sustainable Land Management* (1998).

and good farming practice is a manual for the assessment and management of soil erosion.[55] This document supports assessment of erosion risk on the farm, but it does not address the risks of cumulative soil and water movement off-farm and potential impacts on the ecological status of receiving waters.[56] Not connecting the farm with the catchment suggests that responsibility is focused upon impacts within the bounds of property (an accountability perspective), not on broader community and environmental effects (a care perspective). Such issues are not restricted to England. The legal uncertainty created by multiple standards of farm performance is a concern across Europe due to its effect on trade.[57]

Competing concepts of stewardship, sustainability and property rights emerge against the background of public rhetoric seeking care of the environment. The dominant paradigm of private property is increasingly expected to be the instrument to protect ecological values. However, to believe that property rights provide a reliable guardian against over-exploitation of the environment requires a leap of faith.[58] The mainstream paradigm of natural resource management emphasises private exploitative rights within a framework of limited and tightly defined environmental accountabilities.

The Australian development of the statutory duty of care intends to establish caring behaviour as the desired norm, guiding land stewards in an economic use that minimises environmental harm. This is unique in the process of moving from political to legal meanings of sustainability because the terminology 'duty of care' comes from the common law, with a rich history of legal interpretation. In this common law setting the words have a particular meaning; in particular, there is a logic of relationships between elements that is accepted by lawyers that dictates the true meaning of the duty. The accepted convention of the process of interpretation is central to the legal meaning of a duty of care, but this

[55] United Kingdom, Department for Environment, Food and Rural Affairs, *Controlling Soil Erosion: A Manual for the Assessment and Management of Agricultural Land at Risk of Water Erosion in Lowland England* (2005).

[56] John Boardman *et al.*, 'Soil Erosion and Risk-Assessment for On- and Off-Farm Impacts: A Test Case Using the Midhurst Area, West Sussex, UK' (2009) 90 *Journal of Environmental Management* 2578.

[57] Rudy Gotzen and Roland Norer, 'Commission III Scientific and Practical Development of Agricultural Law in the EU, in Countries and in the WTO' (Congress conclusions presented at the XXV European Congress and Colloquium of Agricultural Law, Cambridge, 23–26 September 2009).

[58] Sax, above n. 10.

convention is not used outside the legal profession. The layperson's understanding of the symbolic language is quite different to the practitioner's. This legal history focuses on the duty of care to one's legal 'neighbour' and has been applied to the fiduciary duty of trustees and guardians, and in the duty of care for workers. Aspects of this duty have been transformed into statutory duties such as the obligations to provide a safe system of work or for managers and directors to act honestly. How this approach to defining obligations will fit within the framework of sustainability is uncertain.

8. History and legal stewardship

The appeal of the term 'duty of care' lies in the history of its use in the common law, then translated into legislation, with its ability to evolve and adjust to context, and its apparent widespread acceptance in setting norms of behaviour which adjust to changes in the capacity of duty-holders to internalise responsibility to others and the community's acceptance of different forms of harm. The courts clothe a duty of care with content on a case-by-case basis that is evolving, using a sophisticated but deceptively simple-sounding analytic logic rather than a set of rules.[59] This approach is appealing for precisely the reasons that will make it difficult to apply – it requires sophisticated judgments about subjective issues of great complexity. It is a unique concept. Those who do not appreciate the conventions of legal interpretation will find it difficult to understand how the legal profession may apply the term.

The use of a statutory duty of care for land stewardship in Australia is intended to establish a renewed ethical approach to natural resource management.[60] We have argued that the competing expectations that a statutory duty of care will better encourage sustainable management and at the same time reduce the high transaction costs, complexity and inflexibilities claimed of traditional regulation may not be reconcilable in practice.[61] A conservative interpretation is more consistent with the historical traditions of the law than a more imaginative one.

[59] Julius Stone, *Legal System and Lawyers' Reasoning* (Stanford University Press, 1968).

[60] Gardner, above n. 54, 63.

[61] Commonwealth of Australia, House of Representatives, Standing Committee on Environment and Heritage, above n. 54; Commonwealth of Australia, Industry Commission, above n. 54; Gardner, above n. 54; Australian Farm Institute and Land and Water Resources Research and Development Corporation, *Developing a Good Regulatory Practice Model for Environmental Regulations Impacting on Farmers: Overview* (Australia

Table 3.1 *Examples of statutory duties of care for the environment in Australia*

Environmental Protection Act 1994 (Qld)	Section 319 General Environmental Duty
Land Act 1994 (Qld)	Section 199 Duty of Care Condition
Catchment and Land Protection Act 1994 (Vic)	Section 20 General Duties of Land Owners
Environment Protection Act 1993 (SA)	Section 25 General Environmental Duty
Natural Resources Management Act 2004 (SA)	Section 9 General Statutory Duties
River Murray Act 2003 (SA)	Section 133 Specific Duty to a Watercourse
	Section 23 General Duty of Care
Pastoral Land Management and Conservation Act 1989 (SA)	Section 7 General Duty of Pastoral Lessees
Environmental Management and Pollution Control Act 1994 (Tas)	Section 23A General Environmental Duty
Forest Practices Act 1985 (Tas)	Section 31(1) Code of practice to provide reasonable protection to the environment

Source: Mark Shepheard and Paul Martin.

This development, perhaps not accidentally, arises in Australia where market-based instruments have been enthusiastically embraced, in the interest of sustainability and efficiency, that are scarce on requirements for care.

9. The potential for a judicial discourse

Table 3.1 shows where the duty of care has been incorporated into land management statutes in Australian states. These duties have been incorporated into statutes generally in response to parliamentary inquiry recommendations, and they draw significantly on a common law duty

Farm Institute, Sydney, 2007); Corey Watts, *Getting on Track? A Discussion Paper on Australia's Progress Towards Ecologically Sustainable Management of our Rural Landscapes* (Australian Conservation Foundation, Melbourne, 2004); Mike Young, Tian Shi and Jim Crosthwaite, *Duty of Care: An Instrument for Increasing the Effectiveness of Catchment Management* (Department of Sustainability and Environment, Melbourne, 2003); Keogh, above n. 28.

of care,[62] while reflecting efforts of public law institutions to give effect to international law endeavours to promote sustainable development. However, legislatures have avoided promoting taking civil action over a breach of an environmental duty of care, eschewing the traditional private role of a duty of care in relations between citizens. The statutory versions of a duty of care instead focus on boundaries of responsibility between citizens and the state adjudicated through an administrative process. Administrative notices and prosecution for non-compliance are the means to enforce this type of duty.[63]

Generally, the statutory versions require farmers to take 'reasonable and practicable measures' or exercise 'reasonable consideration' or exhibit 'reasonable land management behaviour' to prevent or minimise environmental harm or harm to land. Advocates of this form of duty expect it to offer farmers a self-regulating way to acquit their responsibilities.[64]

The role of the courts in giving practical meaning to the duty of care is downplayed by the administrative enforcement approach. This usually involves issuing an order or notice for which non-compliance is an offence. Action by a third party may be authorised by further administrative action, and costs recovered or court orders issued as a final step in the general process.

The duty of care makes environmental care a rule of accountability by embedding this requirement within administrative frameworks under which government agencies can make orders for private expenditure, and even terminate contractual leases. The bureaucracy, rather than the courts (through criminal action) or the citizen (through civil action), will be charged with determining the moral legitimacy of exploitative acts and giving legal effect to the conscience of the community by taking actions that impose an economic penalty on the environmental wrongdoer. The economic consequences from such orders may be significant, including the termination of private leases over large land areas or costly remediation works at private expense. The incentive to seek judicial

[62] See recommendation 5 of Commonwealth of Australia, House of Representatives, Standing Committee on Environment and Heritage, above n. 54. See recommendations 8.1 and 8.2 of Commonwealth of Australia, Industry Commission, above n. 54.

[63] Gardner, above n. 54, 31 and 61.

[64] Australian Conservation Foundation, above n. 28; Australian Farm Institute, *Statutory Theft* (2001); Wentworth Group of Concerned Scientists, *A New Model for Landscape Conservation in New South Wales* (World Wide Fund for Nature, Sydney, 2003); Watts, above n. 61; Young, Shi and Crosthwaite, above n. 61; Keogh, above n. 28.

review of such administrative decisions seems substantial, particularly as the principles themselves are legally nuanced.

The understandings that are shared between judges and advocates about the relationships that make up a duty of care are unique and specialised. This distinctiveness gives the discourse the character of a specific genre. The duty of care terminology in common law is shorthand for elegant reasoning developed over centuries. This functions as a two-stage process for setting flexible standards of performance. First, contexts and relationships are examined to decide whether one person is under an obligation and has acted reasonably towards another to prevent certain potential harms. The boundary of responsibility for harm depends on whether the harms, harm-causing practices, or people involved ought to be excluded from liability for policy reasons. Second are the behavioural norm aspects of a duty, which arise once the general obligation to take reasonable care is established. These define the practical actions needed to satisfy the duty. The more that common practice of an industry or profession is followed, the more likely that no breach of the duty will be found.

In its new sustainability application, the principal use for a statutory duty of care is in setting boundaries of responsibility between citizens and the state about how the citizen is entitled to treat the environment. There is no clarity about the reasoning process to be applied by the administrators.[65] We expect that in the absence of well-developed precedent the legal interpretation of the new meanings of duty of care is likely to reflect foundational principles from common law history, which is a shared basis for investing meaning in the terms. International law principles may be imported alongside the common law for determining reasonable care. The Australian High Court, for instance, has found that the executive entering into an international agreement raises a legitimate expectation that administrative decisions made by the government will accord with the provisions of the agreement.[66] An international agreement ratified by Australia may influence the court's interpretation of an ambiguous statute, but it is not likely to overturn judicial history.[67]

[65] For example, see Queensland Farmers Federation, *The Environmental Code of Practice for Agriculture* (1998), which is intended to clarify what is required for farmers to meet the general environmental duty of care in Environmental Protection Act 1994 (Qld) s. 319.

[66] *Minister of State for Immigration and Ethnic Affairs* v. *Teoh* (1995) 183 CLR 273.

[67] Ibid. See Mason CJ and Deane J, [26].

Administrative enforcement, rather than private litigation or policing, is intended to remove the spectre of litigation, but as we have noted this may be opening the door for administrative appeals. Administrators do not have a shared interpretative history or a common framework for the discourse about duties. This suggests the potential for a great variety of approaches and outcomes. Administrative enforcement raises significant uncertainties about how a duty of care might be applied, including:

- the reasoning steps that will be applied both in the original decision and for any appeal;
- the type of evidence that may be required as a result;
- whether the enactment will be read to broaden or to narrow the type of obligations on the resource user; and
- the extent to which obligations for sustainable development within international agreements will be relevant.

The potential for complexities in applying the duty of care term to the environment is substantial. The duty of care in its fiduciary and worker safety applications imposes a high standard of obligation on the duty-holder to take a highly precautionary approach to protecting the interests of those to whom they owe the duty. In its application in negligence, however, the duty of care depends on nuanced evaluation by the court of what is foreseeable and reasonably preventable. The level of precaution is only that which is reasonable in the circumstances. The questions that this begs are: 'what is the precautionary onus that must be imposed by an administrator upon the subject of an environmental duty of care?', and then 'what reasoning must be applied by the administrators to demonstrate that they have properly acquitted their obligation to properly apply the test of duty?' before they can act. This judicial discourse is unique and materially different to the discourse of care expressed and understood by farmers and landowners.

Further difficulties arise because, unlike the prior incarnations of duty of care, the environmental duty is protective of non-human interests. This is an imaginative development analogous to the responsibility of those holding market power not to exercise it so as to substantially harm competition in a market. History with Australian trade practices law has demonstrated that moving to consider non-human interests poses particular difficulties for the judicial system. The challenges are illustrated by the early attempts of Australian courts to apply the well-understood concept of 'competition'. In the first case to test this principle,[68] Joske J adopted a definition of competition that was seen as unusually narrow, given the common understanding in economic expert circles of the meaning of this term. The Trade Practices Act 1974 (Cth) was subsequently amended and a more detailed and specific definition of competition was inserted, which directed the courts to specific tests to define the newly created duty not to cause harm to competition. The difficulties arose notwithstanding a range of technical and general guidelines, including overseas cases that were considered by commentators to provide a clear meaning to the policy term. A similar type of process occurred with the precautionary principle, which shares a number of characteristics with a duty of care. In most such cases the approach of the court is to take a prosaic and conservative stance to the extension of legal responsibility, respecting the freedoms to exploit opportunities that are available to the citizen.

10. Competing interpretation in the social genre

The indeterminacy of the accountability coupled with the likelihood of administrative appeal suggests that judicial interpretation will only arise once the duty is applied in ways that adversely affect land users.[69] The indeterminacy also suggests that administrative implementation and judicial interpretation will be complex, and that more specific guidance for land users will be required. This type of dynamic has been evident with interpretation of the statutory, international law-framed, precautionary principle by the courts.

There are a variety of social expectations about what a duty of care is and what it can do for stewardship of natural resources. This is seen in Table 3.2.[70] Few of these expectations reflect the uses of duty in negligence. Many of the interpretations are used in debate without the conflicts between them being highlighted, creating a false sense of coherence between competing interests in the advocacy of a farmer's duty of care.

68 *Top Performance Motors Pty Ltd* v. *Ira Berk (Qld) Pty Ltd* (1975) 24 FLR 286.

69 Stapleton, above n. 13, 76.

70 These twelve versions are distilled from literature and from twenty-eight interviews conducted with individuals from eight stakeholder groupings representing interests in stewardship of natural resources and the use of a duty of care. Groups included: farmers, funding providers, information providers, regional natural resource managers, environmental regulators, farming political lobbyists, conservation political lobbyists and legal practitioners.

Table 3.2 *Diverse and competing expectations of the legal duty of care*

Is it a flexible process for determining responsibility in a range of situations?	OR	Is it specific rules of practice that can be clearly stated?
Is it a method for handling disputes between individuals?	OR	Is it a method for determining compensation claims against the state for 'taking' of private resources?
Is its principal purpose to increase accountability for environmental and public good performance of private enterprise?	OR	Is it a means to safeguard resource use for private enterprise?
Does the term refer to a statutory duty of care, specified by Parliament?	OR	Does it mean a common law duty of care, developed by the judiciary?
Is it principally a tool used to frame political rhetoric?	OR	Is it a legally actionable concept with specific legal content?
Is its purpose to define the collective duty of resource users generally across a generic range of circumstances?	OR	Is it intended to be a tool to evaluate individual performance in particular circumstances?

Source: Mark Shepheard and Paul Martin.

In using the term 'a duty of care', advocates may be expecting quite different outcomes from its application.

These different concepts reflect opposing hopes of interest groups, which include:

- strengthening the property right and compensation claims of farmers;
- strengthening the public interest claim over farmers' management of natural resources;
- creating new civil or government rights to intervene in the management of primary production;
- strengthening 'right to farm' claims;
- shifting of the costs of public good conservation from the private to the public purse; and
- embedding of the costs of conservation as a cost of land tenure.

Not all of these expectations can be met. Further refinement through Parliament or judicial review will take time, and may impose high costs.[71]

11. Conclusion: giving meaning to the legislated discourse

A statutory duty of care for environmental protection and stewardship of natural resources exists in four Australian jurisdictions drawn from common law concepts, international law principles and positions of morality. This development reflects the more imaginative elements of the international discourse of sustainability and environmental responsibility. However, the duty is being applied in a world where the dominant paradigm is the exploitative freedom of property owners constrained only by specific accountability. Although the connotations of care in stewardship and a duty of care are readily accepted politically, in part because of their multiple meanings, when it comes to requiring performance with economic consequences for private interests the application of the terminology may prove slippery.

The potential for complexity when aspirations of moral action interact with the amorality of the market has been illustrated by the experience with implementation of the statutory precautionary principle and native vegetation conservation legislation. Courts, administrators and the legislature will have to overcome the problem of multiple hidden meanings that is common in political debate about matters where economics and ethics meet, such as sustainable development. The economic impact of administrative decisions on property interests suggests the likelihood of court challenges to administrative attempts to bridge these discourses of care.

[71] Bonnie Colby, 'Regulation, Imperfect Markets and Transaction Costs: The Elusive Quest for Efficiency in Water Allocation' in Daniel Bromley (ed.), *The Handbook of Environmental Economics* (Blackwell Publishers, Oxford, 1995) 475; Douglas Heckathorn and Steven Maser, 'Bargaining and the Sources of Transaction Costs: The Case of Government Regulation' (1987) 3 *Journal of Law, Economics and Organization* 69; Robert Baldwin and Martin Cave, *Understanding Regulation: Theory, Strategy, and Practice* (Oxford University Press, 1999); Andrew Dragun, *Environmental Institutional Design: Can Property Rights Theory Help?* (Department of Economics, University of Queensland, Brisbane, 1999); Karen Palmer and Margaret Walls, *Extended Product Responsibility: An Economic Assessment of Alternative Policies* (Resources for the Future, Washington DC, 1999); Kevin Guerin, *Encouraging Quality Regulations Theories and Tools*, New Zealand Treasury Working Paper 03/24 (2003); Barak Richman and Jeffrey Macher, *Transaction Cost Economics: An Assessment of Empirical Research in the Social Sciences*, Duke Law School Legal Studies Research Paper Series, Research Paper No. 115 (2006).

Inevitably, courts must convert words intended to connote care into forms that impose well-specified legal accountability that respect the freedoms of private ownership.

The common law can inform interpretation of the statutory duty of care in the absence of other definitive guidance, but this translation will be doctrinally complex. So, too, can international law as international institutions on the issue of sustainable development provide greater direction.[72] However, practical complexities may emerge from clashes of paradigms, which could significantly impede the effectiveness of the duty of care to extend accountability.

This chapter has attempted to demonstrate that problems arising from a shift of discourse from the political to the legal genres are not idiosyncratic to the Australian land management legislation. Rather, they reflect a clash of philosophies within a discourse that spans legal, social and moral dimensions and that occurs across public and international laws. Unresolved tensions are masked by the use of words that conceal multiple meanings that allow apparent consensus on contentious issues. These in turn reflect world views that mirror those highlighted by Dryzek, but also strongly reflect the continuing political and legal relevance of Lockean views of private property and man's relationship with the world. Eventually these tensions are delegated to bureaucracies to resolve, but in a context in which property interest can be constrained only by unambiguous accountabilities being the legal norm. The form of discourse that is used in the law is unique, and requires levels of semantic precision that are avoidable (and perhaps counter-productive) in the political and social context.

Principles of moral responsibility will need to be far more clearly embedded as counters to the tradition of private exploitation if they are to meet the great expectations that they carry in international political discourse. Achieving this may require improved regulation-making processes, so that the specifics of implementation of sustainability principles are better identified at the time the law is created. This may help to minimise the long periods between promulgation of ecological principles as law, and demonstration of their practical effect. Such processes will also need to ensure that the standards of responsibility expected of property owners are properly specified through Parliament, so that the legal profession can be sure of where along the spectrum of possible positions from conservative (property as paramount) to

[72] See below Chapter 8 by Tim Stephens.

idealistic (strong stewardship ethic) the legislature intends to take society. This is necessary if the dominance of the exploitative paradigm of property is to be shifted by the incorporation of ethical concepts of sustainability.

Regulation-making processes should also improve the capacity of the administration to make the type of decisions that are required of them by such laws. As this chapter has illustrated, what is expected of administrators is a very sophisticated bridging of discourses, for which few are likely to be adequately prepared. Ultimately, administrators and policy-makers will need to accept that legal disputes before the courts over such ambiguities and conflicts are not a demonstration of inefficiency, but a valid process to generate community norms and consensus, in the absence of any other process to do so. The mechanism through which the law works to shape norms is conflict channelled through the legal system. It is false efficiency to bypass this process when the issues are as truly fundamental as those embedded, but hidden, within the simple expression 'a duty of care' for the environment.

4

Dephysicalisation and entitlement: legal and cultural discourses of place as property

NICOLE GRAHAM

1. Introduction

The relationship between environmental degradation and the discourse of property is profound, yet little understood and seldom questioned. Indeed, private property in land and natural resources is sufficiently fundamental to modern society that market-based approaches to environmental regulation are regarded as orthodox components of contemporary environmental law.[1] But there is abundant scope for reform. Property is neither a universal nor static concept. Successful human societies have been those able to adapt their property system to changing environmental contexts. The Anglo-American concept of private property is historically, culturally and geographically specific[2] and has been less than successful at being adaptable to different and changing geographical and climatic contexts. The question of this chapter is not whether the basic legal category of property should or could change to better 'address some of the incentive systems that generate our environmental degradation'.[3] The question is how to do so?

The two constitutive features of the Anglo-American concept of property are precisely what render it unsuitable as a land use and ownership system: dephysicalisation and entitlement. The concept of property works by excluding or abstracting from the property equation the

[1] Jody Freeman and Charles Kolstad, 'Prescriptive Environmental Regulations versus Market-Based Incentives' in Jody Freeman and Charles Kolstad (eds.), *Moving to Markets in Environmental Regulation: Lessons from Twenty Years of Experience* (Oxford University Press, 2007) 3, 4.

[2] Nicole Graham, *Lawscape: Property, Environment, Law* (Routledge, Abingdon, 2011).

[3] Joseph Sax, 'Environmental Law Forty Years Later: Looking Back and Looking Ahead' in Michael Jeffrey, Jeremy Firestone and Karen Bubna-Litic (eds.), *Biodiversity Conservation, Law and Livelihoods* (Cambridge University Press, New York, 2008) 9.

physical specificity of what is owned (dephysicalisation). Consequently, land and natural resources are regarded as no more than the 'thing' of the property relation. Abstraction thus makes possible entitlement to property that, untied from its physicality and the sustainability of its uses over time, furnishes the basis of its ongoing alienability, and the exclusion of all others to its benefits or profits. The conversion, in property law, of particular, unique and non-replaceable 'things' such as land, water and natural resources into abstract rights over non-specific, fungible and replaceable commodities is the intellectual and legal foundation of unsustainable forms of land use. It is the dephysicalisation of and entitlement to 'almost anything'[4] in the world that the legal and cultural discourses of property make possible. Further, 'the rewards' that property 'promotes and encourages'[5] present insurmountable obstacles to the objectives of environmental law.

Current developments in international and public environmental and climate law endeavour to protect both human and non-human biota from a range of tragedies and catastrophes caused by unsustainable levels of natural resource use and consumption. Yet the discourse of property, which facilitates such use and consumption, remains unchallenged. The dephysicalisation of, and entitlement to, the land and natural resources is antithetical and dangerously obstructive to the objectives of environmental law. The extension of the discourse of property into environmental regulation via environmental markets appears perversely inappropriate. Environmental law cannot be effective until lawyers, policy-makers and scholars acknowledge the ubiquity and potency of property as a foundational and facilitative discourse of modern law and society. Property has played and continues to play a constitutive role in current environmental crises. To employ the discourse of property in attempting to solve the problems of its creation is neither rational nor viable.

It is necessary, therefore, to interrogate the concept of property and its associated vocabulary of dephysicalisation and entitlement. Such an inquiry will make possible the introduction or return of the concepts of locally and physically relevant land laws within a discursive structure of responsibilities and place-based knowledge. Property regimes, or land laws, can only be viable, authoritative and enduring where sufficient knowledge and responsiveness to the capacities and limits of the specific places of jurisdiction are developed and exercised. Moreover, it is

[4] Ibid. 12. [5] Ibid.

difficult to imagine how a better relationship between humans and non-human biota is achievable without interrogating the very institution that facilitates the primary dysfunction of that relationship – the person–thing model of property law that separates people and place.[6] According to Sax, 'it is those foundational laws that essentially drive behaviour by creating a deep structure of incentives, and that fundamentally describe the directions the society is going'.[7]

Section 2 of this chapter presents the discourse of property in legal terms as a discourse of dephysicalisation and in cultural terms as a discourse of entitlement. Section 3 argues that the use of the same discourse of property that has contributed to current environmental crises is inappropriate to address those crises. In its place, the chapter suggests that property, as an idea and as a discourse, must reflect what it is in reality: the regulation of physical relations between human communities and particular places in a finite biosphere.

2. Dephysicalisation and entitlement

'Dephysicalisation' describes the gradual socio-legal process whereby the environment, or more accurately the abstract 'thing' (such as land), became excluded from the conventional Anglo-American property relation, known in the literature as the 'person–thing' model.[8] Once the 'thing' of property had become absent and irrelevant, the 'new' or modern property relation was regarded as a relationship only between persons, rather than persons and things. Hence, the literature refers to this as the 'person–person' model.[9] Owning property does not signify the ownership of something physical such as land and natural resources. Owning property signifies the possession of something abstract, a legal right as against the legal rights of others. The expression 'dephysicalisation' is most often used in relation to late nineteenth and twentieth century property scholarship[10] but its origins, which are often overlooked, can be traced back to the marriage of entitlement to property with the improvement of land in the writing of seventeenth century

[6] For an analysis of this model see Graham, above n. 2. [7] Sax, above n. 3, 10–11.

[8] See especially John Locke, *Two Treatises on Government* (ed. Peter Laslett) (Cambridge University Press, 1988, first published 1689); and William Blackstone, *The Commentaries on the Laws of England, Books 1 & 2* (Dawsons, London, 1966) (first published 1765–6).

[9] For an analysis of this model see Graham, above n. 2.

[10] See especially Kenneth Vandervelde, 'The New Property of the Nineteenth Century: The Development of the Modern Concept of Property' (1980) 29 *Buffalo Law Review* 325.

English philosopher John Locke. What is often missed when focusing on the jurisprudence of the nineteenth and twentieth centuries is that the concept of dephysicalised property emerged out of the desire to change land use and ownership in the seventeenth and eighteenth centuries for particular socio-economic reasons.[11] Parliamentary enclosure and the exportation of dephysicalised property, as the dominant paradigm of land ownership and use across the world, were part of a pragmatic political and economic revolution as much as they were part of an intellectual one.[12] The link between the geo-historical origins of dephysicalised property and its relevant practice, industrial-scale food and natural resource production, explains not simply a theory–practice nexus but more significantly, its enduring power in contemporary life. A discourse of property is fundamentally a rationale of a society's land use and resource distribution. It is for this reason that it is important to understand environmental crises confronting public and international law-makers in terms of the discourse of property that describes and prescribes the relevant and dominant land use practices.

Environmental awareness and environmental education have increased during recent decades, yet the legal and cultural discourses of place as property have remained intact and are, indeed, the key mechanisms of environmental policy and regulation. Why? Because 'the same engines are still generating the same developmental incentives that we had before the age of what is called modern environmental law'.[13] The discourse of property as 'rights' or as a 'bundle of sticks' is taught and repeated in law schools and law courts throughout the Anglophone world including the United Kingdom,[14] the United States,[15] Canada[16] and Australia.[17] Legal scholars have described and debated its historical

[11] See Marcel Mazoyer and Lawrence Roudart, *A History of World Agriculture from the Neolithic Age to the Current Crisis* (trans. James Membrez) (Earthscan, London, 2006) 333.

[12] Graham, above n. 2, chs. 2 and 3.

[13] Sax, above n. 3, 11.

[14] Sean Coyle and Karen Morrow, *The Philosophical Foundations of Environmental Law: Property, Rights and Nature* (Hart Publishing, Oxford and Portland, 2004) 59.

[15] Jeanne Schroeder, 'Chix Nix Bundle-o-Stix: A Feminist Critique of the Disaggregation of Property' (1994) 93 *Michigan Law Review* 239.

[16] Crawford Macpherson (ed.), *Property: Mainstream and Critical Positions* (University of Toronto Press, 1978); Jessica Clogg, 'British Columbia at a Crossroads: A Path to Sustainability or the Enclosure of the Commons?' (2004) 14 *Journal of Environmental Law and Practice* 189, 192.

[17] Samantha Hepburn, *Australian Property Law: Cases, Materials and Analysis* (LexisNexis Butterworths, Sydney, 2008).

development and significance for well over a century. The most common theme in the literature pertains to the hollowness of modern property law created by the concept of dephysicalised property. Because property is thought to be merely a series of competing and fragmented rights as between persons, scholars have observed that there is little to distinguish property law from contractual relations at law generally. In doctrinal terms, contemporary property is regarded as being 'devoid of content'.[18] It is neither surprising nor accidental that this is so. Jeremy Bentham insisted that it was only once property was dephysicalised, once the reference to the 'object' of the relation, particularly land, was removed, that society and law would progress. For Bentham and his contemporaries, dephysicalising property was desirable because it afforded the protection of property law to abstract objects and facilitated their marketability. Since Bentham's time, the discourse and law of property has been almost entirely absorbed by the vocabulary and conceptual framework of the market.[19]

As Shepheard and Martin observed in the previous chapter, one of the greatest challenges facing contemporary law and society is to somehow reconcile the increasing private ownership of dephysicalised rights to the environment with 'increasing expectations of public good stewardship'.[20] This is a difficult, if not impossible, challenge precisely because people are imagined to be somehow separate from the environment, rather than part of it. Whether people are regarded as caring for the land or exploiting it, the notion of their mutual separateness remains. The contemporary and dominant discourse of property has its origins in the conceptual separation of people from place. The intellectual and linguistic appellation of almost all non-human biota as the undifferentiated and collective entity 'nature' or 'the environment' highlights this foundational separation. The separation of people and place is also apparent in modern human subjectivity, which defines itself not only by its separateness, even its ontological opposition to its physical 'environment', but also by its superiority to it, as the 'masters and possessors of nature'.[21] Regarding everything other than human as a 'thing', the language of real

[18] David Lametti, 'The Concept of Property: Relations through Objects of Social Wealth' (2003) 53 *University of Toronto Law Journal* 325, 339.

[19] Robin Paul Malloy, *Law in a Market Context* (Cambridge University Press, New York, 2004) 3.

[20] See above Chapter 3 by Mark Shepheard and Paul Martin, 73.

[21] René Descartes, *Discourse on Method and the Meditations* (Penguin, Harmondsworth, 1978).

property law deprives 'things' of meanings and values beyond their utility to the human economy. Nature has become, as Heidegger once complained, 'one vast gasoline station' for human exploitation.[22]

Although anthropocentrism can certainly be said to be a characteristic of the discourse of property, the idea of 'things', such as land and natural resources, being available to human enjoyment does not itself constitute a culture of entitlement. If the availability of those lands, waters and resources were contingent on adaptive and sustainable management, and if ownership were fundamentally connected to those management practices, then entitlement could not be said to characterise that property regime. However, as explained above, the contemporary discourse of property at the basis of contemporary and dominant land use practice is not contingent on a relationship, sustainable or otherwise, to the limits and capacities of the physical world. And because the discourse of property excludes the physical realm, the fact of human agency in the landscape through land use practices is erased. 'Nature' is simply regarded as a resource, and property relations, so far as they have anything to do with 'things', consist only in the entitlement to those things.

The ideas of 'nature' and 'the environment' as being separate and subordinate to human subjectivity are made real by cultural and economic practices including especially land use and natural resource management. The discourse of property as rights and the theory of dephysicalisation are nowhere more apparent than in the landscape itself. The irrelevance of place, its lack of uniqueness, distinctiveness and particularity to human society is tangibly evident on industrial farms and pastures and in the degradation of the atmosphere and hydrosphere. Precisely because the discourse of property is a discourse of abstract rights as between persons, the limits and capacities of the physical world are irrelevant to, and excluded from, the concept of ownership. Ownership is not about responsibilities to and management of place. Ownership is about entitlement to 'things' and 'resources'.[23]

Landholders or proprietors of large tracts of land including farmers, pastoralists and irrigators, sometimes identify themselves as 'battlers' or 'pioneers' and often describe their relationship to land as one of immense

[22] Heidegger, cited in David Harvey, *Justice, Nature & the Geography of Difference* (Wiley-Blackwell, Oxford, 2000) 134.

[23] For a critique of this discourse in practice see, e.g., Paul Lachapelle and Stephen McCool, 'Exploring the Concept of "Ownership" in Natural Resource Planning' (2005) 18 *Society and Natural Resources* 279.

hardship and enduring courage.[24] The land is 'battled' to release its marketable goods. Their ownership of land and water depends on their ability to subdue and appropriate the physical world for its value as a commodity. Perhaps it is in part due to the difficulties experienced by human societies endeavouring to impose foreign and often maladapted land use practices in 'new' lands and on 'frontiers' that when the land does 'yield' its produce those societies perceive the produce as 'things' to which they are entitled. The historical development of property law in former British colonies encouraged and facilitated those land use practices through initiatives such as pastoral leases.[25] As Sax argued: 'the existing property system incentivises the manipulation of land and water to produce those things that promote the displacement of natural services in favour of various kinds of manufactured services'.[26]

Entitlement to 'nature' and 'the environment' is also evident in disputes over land and natural resources that the law categorises and treats as disputes over rights between persons or legal entities. The resolution of the dispute is reached not by assessing and evaluating competing forms of more or less appropriate land use practices, but by comparing legal rights that exist independently of those practices. The culture of entitlement is especially evident in compulsory acquisition and 'takings' case law. In such a setting '[t]here is almost no notion of use entitlements that are withheld because of some interest of the public; nor is there any affirmative obligation to use one's property in a way that is beneficial to the public'.[27] The notion of compensation is therefore central to the idea that persons or entities are entitled by virtue of their property right to a monetary substitute for land, waters and natural resources. In the Australian case of *Newcrest*,[28] for example, the argument that the property rights of a mining corporation would be sterilised not by the compulsory acquisition of its property, but by legislation relating to the recovery of minerals, indicated that the concept of property was utterly dephysicalised. In that case, the Crown granted mining leases over certain land in the Northern Territory of Australia which subsequently became the Kakadu National Park. The National Parks and Wildlife Act 1975 (Cth) prohibited mining. The lessees argued that the government had, if not legally, then effectively acquired the leases, and

[24] See, e.g., Rob Linn, *Battling the Land: 200 Years of Rural Australia* (Allen & Unwin, Sydney, 1999).

[25] For an analysis of this history see Graham, above n. 2. [26] Sax, above n. 3, 12.

[27] Ibid. [28] *Newcrest Mining (WA) Limited* v. *Commonwealth* (1997) 190 CLR 513.

that accordingly compensation was payable under provisions in the Australian Constitution. Their claim was that although the leasehold property rights remained, the purpose of those rights was defeated and thus 'sterilised'. The idea of sterilising property in this case related not to the physical sterilisation of the land by mining the land, but to the abstract sterilisation or destruction of the monetary value of the property right as a commodity. The case demonstrates the prevalence of an understanding of 'nature' as something inherently fungible and therefore capable of monetary substitution, rather than as something inherently irreplaceable and unique. The mining corporation was successful in claiming entitlement to compensation because what was lost, whilst not the property right itself, was its value as a commodity.

Another way in which the culture of entitlement to 'nature' is evident is in the language used when human society encounters events and problems such as atmospheric pollution, drought, floods, salination, soil erosion and loss of biodiversity. These are commonly understood and referred to as 'disasters', 'externalities' and 'environmental issues', an understanding which positions those situations outside both the human economy and human subjectivity. The idea of an 'externality' in economic terms pretends that there is a disconnection between production, consumption and waste which disavows the human agency in the creation of that 'externality'. Malloy asks: 'Why are these effects framed as external or foreign to the activity of the factory? Why aren't the third-party consequences of a manufacturing process considered to be internal effects of the profit-seeking venture within the factory? How might this framing change our thinking?'[29] The language used to describe people–place relations when 'nature' produces benefits to human society is that of ownership. By contrast, the language used to describe people–place relations when 'nature' is damaged or depleted is that of victimhood. This dualism reflects a culture of entitlement in which benefits are regarded as anthropogenic but damage is not. Accordingly, ownership attaches only to benefits. State compensation and support programmes for landowners encountering 'environmental problems', for example, intellectually and politically separate the fact of land ownership from the condition of the land itself.[30] These programmes indicate that, in addition to the entitlement to certain land

[29] Malloy, above n. 19, 183.

[30] See Linda Botterill and Melanie Fisher (eds.), *Beyond Drought: People, Policy and Perspectives* (CSIRO Publishing, Melbourne, 2003).

use practices and to the profits of those practices, landowners are entitled also to the profits of practices that were not physically possible. In other words, entitlement to 'nature' exceeds the real limits of 'nature' or its anthropogenically altered condition.

Environmental regulations that temper property rights are swiftly regarded as 'interference' with necessary structures and institutions of political order and economic prosperity including civil liberties and human rights. The defence of property rights is strongest in the United States,[31] but powerful lobby groups in the United Kingdom,[32] Canada and Australia[33] deploy the same perspectives and strategies to maintain the priority and primacy of the discourse and culture of entitlement. The Policy of the National Farmers Union (US) stated in March 2009 that the union is opposed to the 'acquisition of productive farmland through use of the eminent domain process to extend wildlife habitat'.[34] Any public interest or private obligation to environmentally beneficial land use and ownership is simply antithetical to its purpose. The defence of property rights is powerful and often successful because the defenders tap into existing mainstream understandings and values of people–place relations. In Canada, although there are attempts to introduce new meanings relating to community and environment, property rights remain territorial and individual: 'property ownership and rights are part of a person's framework for comprehending their world'.[35] The discourse of property establishes rules and regulates behaviours that operate at an almost subconscious level of awareness and participation. The default assumption about the ownership of lands and waters is that they are privately owned. As Canadian property scholar David Lametti has observed: '[it] is because private property is so pervasive an institution, especially with respect to traditional, tangible objects of wealth such as land and houses, that X respects the duty not to trespass regardless of

[31] See, e.g., Alfred Olivetti Jr and Jeff Worsham, *This Land Is Your Land, This Land Is My Land: The Property Rights Movement and Regulatory Takings* (LFB Scholarly Publishing LLC, New York, 2003).

[32] Coyle and Morrow, above n. 14, 10.

[33] See Andrew Macintosh and Richard Denniss, *Property Rights and the Environment: Should Farmers Have a Right to Compensation?* The Australia Institute, Discussion Paper 74 (2004).

[34] National Farmers Union, *Policy of the National Farmers Union* (2009) Article VI (P) 'Eminent Domain', Section 10.

[35] Richard Brisbin and Susan Hunter, 'The Transformation of Canadian Property Rights?' (2006) 21*Canadian Journal of Law and Society* 135, 158.

who owns the house'.[36] In the United Kingdom the discourse of property is equally ubiquitous:

> Such is the extent to which rights-talk is embedded in our legal, moral and political culture, it is tempting to assume that the concept of property depends for its existence on that of right. Yet the form of modern property, both legally and in our moral life, is neither historically nor conceptually inevitable.[37]

Environmental law is widely and not incorrectly regarded as a body of public law that has developed in order to restrain and regulate the excesses of private property law.[38] The instrumentalism of property law has long been understood to be at odds with environmental protection. Both English and American scholars observe the tension between the ideals of people–place relations that form the bases of environmental discourse and property discourse. Coyle and Morrow, for instance, note:

> Leopold's observation in his seminal text on conservation, *A Sand County Almanac*, though made in relation to the United States in the mid-twentieth century, is just as apposite in a United Kingdom context: 'Conservation,' he said, 'is getting nowhere because it is incompatible with our Abrahamic concept of land. We abuse land because we regard it as a commodity belonging to us.'[39]

The extent to which environmental law succeeds in delivering effective regulatory solutions is thus the extent to which it is capable of challenging and replacing this 'Abrahamic concept' of the environment at the basis of the discourse of property. Until it succeeds in reshaping property, international and domestic environmental law cannot but 'float at the surface of our legal system' rendering the legal system itself 'handicapped in doing the job it needs to do'.[40]

3. Against dephysicalisation: the need for place

3.1 Sustainability and environmental markets

The discourse of sustainability operates as a corrective to the discourse of property to some extent, in that it identifies the need for land and natural resource use to be modified by a longer-term view of providing the

[36] Lametti, above n. 18, 345. [37] Coyle and Morrow, above n. 14, 10. [38] Ibid. 4.
[39] Ibid. 149. [40] Sax, above n. 3, 10.

benefits of lands and natural resources to human society. The Brundtland Commission's Report, *Our Common Future*,[41] endeavoured to reconcile the twin desires for further economic development and environmental protection. It suggested that both may be possible simultaneously. However, apart from the long-term framework, the instrumentalist view of an undifferentiated 'nature' and 'environment' of the discourse of sustainability is the same as that of the discourse of property. Although there are multiple definitions of sustainability and sustainable development,[42] each of which being 'necessarily contest and contestable',[43] there remains a recurrent theme across the literature notwithstanding the 'weak' and 'strong' emphases.[44] Sustainability is most often defined and debated in terms of time. However, it fails to consider the role of property, in particular the impact of dephysicalisation, on the environment. The concept of property is questioned only to the extent that the benefits of property in land and natural resources are considered too short term and exclude the interests of future generations.[45] It has been argued that a 'sustainable system is one which survives or persists. Biologically, this means avoiding extinction, and living to survive and reproduce.'[46] In more formal terms, sustainable development is defined as 'development that meets the needs of present generations while not compromising the ability of future generations to also meet their needs'.[47] Similarly, Sagoff argues that contemporary environmental discourse must eschew the ideal of conservation and pragmatically embrace the discourse of sustainability. He argues that 'the appropriate principle is no longer reverence but sustainability – the maximisation of human welfare over the very long run'.[48]

[41] World Commission on Environment and Development, *Our Common Future* (Oxford University Press, 1987).

[42] Andrew Dobson, 'Environmental Sustainabilities: An Analysis and a Typology' (1996) 5 *Environmental Politics* 401, 422–3.

[43] Ibid. 402.

[44] For a critical analysis of 'weak' and 'strong' discourses of sustainability, see Dobson, above n. 42, 409–11.

[45] See above Chapter 1 by Peter Lawrence, especially on intergenerational equity.

[46] Robert Costanza and Carl Folke, 'The Structure and Function of Ecological Systems in Relation to Property-Rights Regimes' in Susan Hanna, Carl Folke and Karl-Goran Maler (eds.), *Rights to Nature: Ecological, Economic, Cultural, and Political Principles of Institutions for the Environment* (Island Press, Washington DC, 1996) 19.

[47] Gerry Bates, *Environmental Law in Australia* (LexisNexis Butterworths, Sydney, 5th edn, 2002) 120.

[48] Mark Sagoff, *The Economy of the Earth: Philosophy, Law and the Environment* (Cambridge University Press, 2nd edn, 2008) 159.

The discourse of sustainability is limited, however, in its capacity to address the consequences of the discourse of property and its culture of entitlement because it does not question them. The promise of the discourse of sustainability evident internationally and domestically is that it advocates the need to be mindful of the material limits and capacities of the lands and waters in land use policy.[49] There is also promise in the discourse of sustainability in that it reintroduces the idea of responsibilities[50] in direct contrast to that of rights, which has come to dominate our understanding of ownership. Furthermore, sustainability raises the possibility of collective, rather than individual, interest in land and resource ownership and use,[51] which is an important step in challenging the individualism that supports the discourse of property. However, as promising as these aspects of the discourse of sustainability seem, it is not a counter-discourse to that of property. Indeed, increasingly environmental policies of sustainable development include markets for 'eco-services' that are premised on a vocabulary and conceptual framework that underpin the discourse of dephysicalised and rights-based property. According to Adams and Jeanrenaud:

> Mainstream sustainable development is built on the idea of market-driven approaches and strategies based on technology and intense regulation (termed ecological modernisation). It promises to steer the world towards sustainability in ways that do not demand too many dramatic changes, and that do not upset the comfortable, the rich or the powerful.[52]

The deployment of market instruments in environmental law and policy maintains an outdated and not entirely persuasive critique[53] of direct government regulation of environmental and land use problems whereby regulators are regarded as 'having failed the citizens and squandered common resources'.[54] The market, however, is a creature of the legal and cultural discourses of property in which land and natural resources are dephysicalised and where information about the resource itself is secondary to information about its value to the marketplace. The

[49] See, e.g., Club of Rome, *Limits to Growth* (Universe Books, New York, 1972).

[50] Coyle and Morrow, above n. 14, 162. [51] Ibid. 206.

[52] William Adams and Sally Jeanrenaud, *Transition to Sustainability: Towards a Humane and Diverse World* (IUCN, Gland, 2008) 12.

[53] See below Chapter 11 by Lee Godden.

[54] Sanja Bogojević, 'Ending the Honeymoon: Deconstructing Emissions Trading Discourses' (2009) 21 *Environmental Law Journal* 443, 459.

extent to which environmental markets can deliver the objectives of a suite of environmental laws and policies is prevented by the fact of its preservation and augmentation of the logic of property: the dephysicalisation of, and entitlement to, yet more 'things'.

Unlike the concept of direct environmental regulation, 'the implementation of this broad policy of marketisation has been strong, vigourous, pervasive and has enjoyed bipartisan mainstream political support'.[55] Given the ideological commitment to, and economic dependence on, economic development shared by many contemporary Anglo-American governments,[56] it is unsurprising that market mechanisms are preferred to policies that would 'interfere' with property rights. The use of environmental markets demonstrates the enduring attractiveness, power and ubiquity of the discourse of property. As observed by Shepheard and Martin in the previous chapter, the discourse of sustainability and the frequency with which it accompanies the deployment of environmental markets is arguably political compromise more than legal and economic reform. The marriage of the discourse of sustainability and the mechanism of markets allows the public demand for increased environmental conservation to co-exist with the private owners' demand for a continued 'freedom to exploit'. Shepheard and Martin argue 'both local and international politics of the environment are now characterised by simultaneous calls for amoral market efficiency alongside calls for caring management. The strangeness of this coupling is largely unnoted in policy debate.'[57] The use of markets to address environmental problems also indicates the saturation of legal discourse with law-and-economics scholarship and its vocabulary: 'transaction costs, externalities, efficiency, wealth-maximisation, preference shaping, reasonable investment-backed expectations, and cost-benefit analysis'.[58]

The products and services in environmental markets are both 'things' and processes that human societies use or rely on as resources for life and lifestyle. The possibility of commodifying these things and processes depends on being able to assess their cost or value in precise terms of a monetary equivalence. The use of market-based instruments to solve environmental problems also depends on being able to confidently state or

[55] Stephen Dovers, 'Institutions for Sustainability' (2001) 7 *Tela* 18.

[56] See Samuel Alexander Kirk, *Property Beyond Growth*, unpublished Ph.D. thesis, University of Melbourne (2011).

[57] See above Chapter 3 by Mark Shepheard and Paul Martin, 82.

[58] Malloy, above n. 19, 3.

predict the viable levels of their use, consumption or absorptive capacity.[59] Taken to their logical limits, environmental markets would theoretically be able to price and trade 'the composition of the atmosphere; amelioration of climate, flood controls and drinking water supply; waste assimilation; recycling of nutrients; generation of soils; pollination of crops; provision of food; maintenance of species and a vast genetic library'.[60]

The attractiveness of environmental markets to governments and policy-makers is political and economic rather than scientific. First, environmental markets outsource the task and the cost of restricting the use of and/or reliance on natural resources by individuals and corporations to those individuals and corporations. Second, by creating and regulating these markets, the government simultaneously controls and eschews the responsibility for the restriction of prior (often unarticulated) interests in these products and services. It is thought that '[r]egulatory markets may reduce opposition to regulatory initiatives both by reducing the economic cost of regulation and by reducing tension between interest groups fighting over who will bear the regulatory cost'.[61] The resistance of resource users to the restriction of their use would otherwise be viewed as an interference with their property rights and business interests, whereas the use of environmental markets encourages the users to perceive and experience the restriction as a matter of choice. Fundamentally, this approach to environmental regulation disavows that it is regulation. These 'Regulatory markets represent command-and-control regulation made more consumer-friendly.'[62]

Advocates for environmental markets argue that '[s]ecure property rights provide both powerful incentives for the preservation of natural resources and effective tools to resolve differences over resource use'.[63] In other words, the idea is that people would relate better to place if 'we attached market prices to the products and services it provides'.[64] The idea of the market here presumes 'that there is a relative or close equivalence between the pursuit of self-interest and the promotion of

[59] See, e.g., John Sargent, 'The Economics of Energy and the Environment: The Potential Role of Market-Based Instruments' (2002) 28 *Canada–United States Law Journal* 499, 502.

[60] Costanza and Folke, above n. 46, 17.

[61] Barton Thompson Jr, 'Markets for Nature' (2001) 25 *William and Mary Environmental Law and Policy Review* 261, 262.

[62] Sagoff, above n. 48, 90.

[63] Elizabeth Brubaker, 'Property Rights: The Key to Environmental Protection' (May 2007) *Fraser Forum* 19.

[64] Sagoff, above n. 48, 87.

public interest'.[65] The theory of market behaviour is imported into the discourse of sustainability as manifest in environmental markets. Accordingly, '[p]roperty holders are understood to avoid bad management decisions because their wealth in the property will depend on it'.[66] Theories of market behaviour conventionally suppose that markets are democratic and rational. Specifically, theories of market behaviour attribute to market players rationality that is objective; self-interested rather than in the community interest; grounded in relevant, current, accurate and high-level information; and, that market players enjoy equal purchasing opportunity shared with other market players.[67] Significantly, market behaviour is related only arbitrarily to environmentally sustainable development – it has not been adopted as a policy mechanism on account of the intrinsically environmentally helpful behaviours of market players.

The valuation or pricing methodologies of environmental markets also operate on the basis of a series of assumptions about the possibilities of valuation itself. First, they assume that value can be attributed to anything including processes, such as complex natural water recycling and filtration in the hydrological cycle, and including intangible aspects of 'nature' and 'the environment', such as aesthetic and spiritual values. Contingent valuation methodology approaches environmental products and processes, not from their economic cost, but from their social attractiveness. Contingent valuation endeavours to price 'nature' based on what people would be willing to pay for its products or outcomes.[68] Hedonic valuation methodology assesses the cost of replacing or fixing the loss of a particular product or service by atomising its integrity as a whole product or service into its 'constituent parts'. But both 'hedonic and contingent valuation methods raise normative questions with respect to the ability and desirability of quantifying certain values. They imply a desire to commodify everything when perhaps there are some resources or certain relationships that should not be commodified.'[69]

The expansion of the discourse of property into the discourse of environmental regulation, through the institutionalisation of environmental markets, is inappropriate to address 'environmental problems' for strategic, normative and intellectual reasons. In strategic terms there are substantial problems with market design and implementation such as pricing and predicting market behaviour. As Sanja Bogojević argues in

[65] Malloy, above n. 19, 27. [66] Bogojević, above n. 54, 458.
[67] Malloy, above n. 19, 27. [68] Ibid. 167. [69] Ibid.

her chapter in this volume, despite the scant attention paid by legal scholars to the question of market design, design is not incidental to the effectiveness of a market, but vital to it. Primary issues in design concern the lack of parity of environmental 'products' and 'services' and the absence of discrete geographies that correspond precisely to jurisdictional boundaries and market limits. In this sense:

> It is fairly easy to assign property rights to some resources and ecosystems such as trees or a lake. However, it is much more difficult to assign property rights to resources such as migrating fish populations and in particular to many ecological services such as the role of biological diversity in running nutrient cycles and water cycles in a forest. The reason is that these resources and ecological services are connected to other ecosystems than the forest, and thereby transcend several property-rights regimes. There is a major challenge in designing institutions and property-rights regimes that are in tune with the functions of ecosystems and the goods and services that they generate.[70]

Another problem with markets, regulated or otherwise, is that they do not account for the inadequate and imperfect knowledge and information, relevant to the product or service subject to trade, available to market players. Although we live in a time of sophisticated environmental science, the sufficiency of that knowledge is rarely suitable for decision-making in markets where risks are cumulative and permanent. The precautionary principle of environmental discourse is antithetical to theories of market behaviour because the former accepts the possibility of incomplete or imperfect information whereas the latter does not. A further strategic problem with environmental markets, regulated or otherwise, is that they are arguably too little, too late – the product or service has almost always already been produced or consumed for many years (for example, carbon) prior to the creation of the market, thus frustrating the market's supposed function. Finally, the rationality of market players cannot be objectively determined against a universal standard. Rural communities, for example, whose use of water is central to their economies and cultural identities, do not behave rationally in the eyes of many outside those communities, but their market behaviour may be nonetheless entirely rational and predictable viewed against internal community standards. Malloy notes that '[r]ationality is a behavioural and interpretive concept. As such, it may vary with cultural context.'[71] Finally, the single largest obstacle to the success of

[70] Costanza and Folke, above n. 46, 26. [71] Malloy, above n. 19, 146.

environmental markets as a strategy or mechanism for addressing environmental problems is that their objective is to restrict economic choices that the majority of the developed world regard as rights to which they are entitled. For instance, '[m]any American consumers simply want to pay the lowest possible prices for the products and services that they demand . . . For the consumer it's the best of both worlds, high levels of consumption without responsibility.'[72]

In normative terms, the problem with environmental markets is that they extend rather than question and modify an already deeply anthropocentric view of people–place relations. 'The development of specialised markets transforms the view of nature from a partner to a production input.'[73] As Marx and Heidegger complained, the idea that place is separate to people establishes the possibility of perceiving 'nature' as a resource which is in itself a problem. In Sagoff's view, '[b]y "putting a price on it" we regard nature as a resource to exploit rather than a heritage and endowment to maintain. This is the most self-defeating path environmentalists can take.'[74]

The intellectual problem with the environmental market approach to environmental regulation is that its methodologies focus not on the limits and capacities of those 'products and services', but on the human need and desire for them. In doing so, the economic relationship between people and place is inverted such that the situation of people within place and their dependence on place is erased. For example, pollution markets are founded on the idea that the human need for the absorptive capacity of the atmosphere can and should prevail over (or be consistent with) the actual and finite absorptive capacity of the atmosphere. Differentials such as the particular place and particular time of polluting emissions are considered irrelevant or insignificant because 'if location or timing were to matter, trading would have to be restricted; this would both complicate the system and may reduce the number of participants in any given trading market below the level required for a well-functioning market'.[75] The setting of 'caps' on emissions is similarly not determined by the calculation of the actual limits of the atmosphere, but by the willingness of human societies to incorporate those limits into their economies. Given that until recently pollution has been,

[72] Ibid. 182.

[73] Susan Hanna and Svein Jentoft, 'Human Use of the Natural Environment: An Overview of Social and Economic Dimensions' in Hanna, Folke and Maler (eds.), above n. 46, 35.

[74] Sagoff, above n. 48, 89.

[75] Sargent, above n. 59, 504.

economically speaking, 'cost-free', the debate about pollution markets has most often been concerned with the 'new' costs rather than on the accuracy and viability of the caps themselves.[76]

Scholars and commentators argue that the restriction and regulation of people–place relations using market mechanisms is 'fraught with corruption as each player has insisted on having a supersized initial endowment'.[77] Mark Sagoff argues that the environmental product or service at the basis of the emissions market, the atmosphere itself, is too large to 'divide in pieces or sell in units' so 'we either protect (or "buy") the whole system or forgo it; there is no way to trade in marginal amounts'.[78] This argument challenges the very structure of dephysicalised property which organises property interests into fragmented rights rather than holistic ownership. Legal scholar Brad Sherman has observed a similar problem with dephysicalised property and fragmentation as it pertains to intellectual property in plants and botanical innovation. He argues that patent law 'decontextualises' a botanical innovation or 'invention' from its material conditions to facilitate the tradability and commercial benefit of that invention.[79] The attendant difficulty with this separation of the property right in the invention from the physical thing is that it is not biologically accurate and possible. A more holistic approach is required, he argues, whereby 'plant inventions' are situated within their 'informational and material environments'.[80] The reason for this, he contends, is that 'the environment is not something that is simply external to the object. Instead the environment enters the constitution of the entity: it is folded into and becomes part of the object in question.'[81] The holistic nature of the world, the 'environment', becomes lost in its translation from things with intrinsic values situated in complex natural systems into the non-specific objects of property rights. Holistic ownership, by which I mean a system of ownership situated within the Earth's physical systems of non-fragmented interrelationships (atmospheric and biological, for example) places people not in the centre of a property relation, nor at an imagined periphery, but as one part of a larger economy/ecology.

3.2 *Property-in-place*

Against the 'intuitive appeal of making "things" the mediator of the (property) relationship',[82] the contemporary and dominant discourse

[76] Ibid. 505. [77] Sagoff, above n. 48, 90. [78] Ibid. 88.

[79] Brad Sherman, 'Taxonomic Property' (2008) 67 *Cambridge Law Journal* 560, 565.

[80] Ibid. [81] Ibid. [82] Lametti, above n. 18, 354.

of property in both common law and civil law jurisdictions excludes from their scope the physical realm in which they operate. 'In neither conceptualisation is there mention of the specific features of the resource.'[83] Using a discourse of dephysicalisation to address, and even solve, a problem which has physical causes and physical consequences is neither rational nor viable. In place of a discourse of property characterised by dephysicalisation, entitlement and fragmentation, the law and public policy must develop and elaborate a discourse of property-in-place which is cognisant of and responsive to the real, physical and finite biosphere in which it operates and on which it depends. After all, '[s]ustainability requires that human social systems and property-rights regimes are adequately related to the larger ecosystems in which they are embedded'.[84] If we accept this critical evaluation of the discourse of dephysicalised property, then the question becomes how to develop a re-physicalised discourse or a discourse of property that is situated within place.

First, we must acknowledge the inadequacies of the current preoccupation with the outdated and unhelpful private–public dualism[85] and the associated hybrid of environmental markets. On the one hand, the track record of state intervention through public property or command-and-control approaches to environmental and natural resource ownership and regulation is critiqued for its various and enduring mistakes.[86] Canadian lawyer Elizabeth Brubaker, a staunch defender of private property rights for environmental protection, argues that the public regulation approach is inherently limited by its remoteness from local issues and circumstances as well as by politicisation:

> Governments of all political stripes have given us thousands of reasons not to trust them to protect the environment: they've licensed – and bankrolled – polluters, turned forests into wastelands, emptied oceans of fish, and dammed rivers that were once magnificent.[87]

Counter-arguments contend that the private property approach (such as environmental markets) to environmental regulation is equally and inherently flawed because it is rights-based, individualistic rather than

[83] Ibid. 337. [84] Costanza and Folke, above n. 46, 30.

[85] As discussed by Sanja Bogojević below in Chapter 14.

[86] For an analysis of this critique see Bogojević, above n. 54.

[87] Elizabeth Brubaker, *Property Rights in the Defence of Nature* (Earthscan, London, 1995) 19.

collective in scope, and ultimately self-interested.[88] Almost without exception the scholarship of (or at the very least the argument of) Garrett Hardin's *Tragedy of the Commons* arises in the debate between public (or common)[89] property and private property. But this is ultimately unhelpful because in purely historical terms if nothing else, 'there are a multitude of examples of robust systems and institutions where resources rights are held by a community' and 'where those directly involved have successfully managed complex resource systems over long periods'.[90] The key question is not which socio-political structure best supports a sustainable regime and discourse of property. Rather, the more important question is how any given human economy can adapt and thrive, within the limits of its local and physical conditions – the regime and discourse of property, if sustainable, would merely follow from that.

The second step for developing a re-physicalised discourse of property-in-place would be to acknowledge, draw from and build on existing and often long-standing property systems that take knowledge of local systems as their foundation. By definition, property regimes that have existed for a long period of time are sustainable. The dephysicalised property regime is young as compared with a range of property regimes throughout human history. In fact, '[s]ome of the most sophisticated property rights institutions are found in areas in which these systems have developed over a long period of time, on the order of hundreds of years'.[91] The reason for their sophistication is invariably the opportunity that time presents to develop increasingly in-depth and detailed knowledge of the limits and capacities of local environmental conditions. Furthermore, the observation of biophysical 'things', processes and patterns not only within a short time frame of several years, but over the long term of several generations, builds into a property regime the necessary flexibility to adapt to those processes and patterns. 'The accumulation and transfer of this knowledge between generations has made it possible to be alert to changes and continuously adapt them in an active way. It has been a means of survival.'[92]

Central to these successful and well-established property regimes is their emphasis on the local conditions of particular places. This approach contrasts starkly to the universalising and universalised

[88] William Lucy and Catherine Mitchell, 'Replacing Private Property: The Case for Stewardship' (1996) 55 *Cambridge Law Journal* 566.
[89] The two are often erroneously conflated.
[90] Elinor Ostrom, discussed in Clogg, above n. 16, 191.
[91] Costanza and Folke, above n. 46, 27. [92] Ibid. 28.

approach of dephysicalised property which by definition cannot be responsive to local variance and change in physical conditions. The scholarship of adaptive management is also based on this idea of building natural resource use and management systems on high-level knowledge of specific and changeable local conditions.[93] Longer-established property regimes, like the philosophy of adaptive management, use the specificity of local environments themselves as models of sustainable systems.

Better understanding of ecological systems and how they function and maintain themselves can thus yield insights into designing and managing sustainable economic systems. For example, in mature ecosystems all waste and by-products are recycled and used somewhere in the system or are fully dissipated. This implies that a characteristic of sustainable economic systems should be a similar 'closing the cycle' by finding productive uses for and recycling of currently discarded energy and material, rather than simply storing it, diluting it, or changing its state, and allowing it to disrupt other existing ecosystems and economic systems that cannot effectively use it.[94] Locally derived and longer-established property regimes succeed because the people–place relations are fully integrated into cultural institutions, including semiotic processes, so that a society or community as a whole is cognisant of that relation rather than its being the province of specialists or experts.[95] David Lametti argues that the contemporary discourse of dephysicalised property is not only unsuccessful but unconvincing, because modern property law scholarship 'appear(s) to lack what most people feel intuitively: that property is about things'.[96] To situate people within place and to return place to the legal property relation seems not only intuitive but also necessary for survival.[97]

One of the key critiques of the discourse of dephysicalised property is that it separates rights from responsibilities, building a culture of entitlement. The alignment of property rights with environmental responsibilities into a single, integrated system of property or people–place relations would form a key step in re-physicalising the discourse of property. The notion of the guardian or steward is often discussed in critiques of

[93] See, e.g., Allan Savory with Judy Butterfield, *Holistic Management: A New Framework for Decision Making* (Island Press, Washington DC, 2nd edn, 1999).

[94] Costanza and Folke, above n. 46, 21. [95] Ibid. 27. [96] Lametti, above n. 18, 378.

[97] Costanza and Folke, above n. 46, 21.

private property.[98] Importantly, guardianship or stewardship is formulated in the literature not as a rejection of the notion of right or entitlement but as something attached to the notion of responsibility. Hence:

> The steward is, in essence, a duty-bearer, rather than a right-holder, but this should not be taken to suggest that the steward has no rights. An analogous concept that captures the relationship between duties and rights in something like that of the trust . . . In a similar way, an abstract account of stewardship maintains that the holder, or steward, has some control and rights over the resource, but that control must in the main be exercised for the benefit of specific others.[99]

Stewardship, or this vaguely defined duty of care, is regarded as both an ethic and a logic, capable of correcting existing intellectual, normative and strategic problems with the current discourse of property.[100] 'Stewardship provides a conception of prudent or right behaviour with respect to environmental harm.'[101] But as David Lametti points out, stewardship cannot function without first replacing the 'thing' of property into the discourse. Including the physical realm in the model of people–place relations 'allows us to understand a dimension of private property practice not accounted for in theory: obligations and duties that may attach to a specific resource. These might include an obligation to preserve a valuable resource such as land as a steward, and even to take active steps to conserve it.'[102] Jessica Clogg takes this a step further to argue that stewardship can be adapted for both individualistic and communitarian models of property relations because it includes both place and people in the model. In other words, the responsibilities extend both to people and to place, notwithstanding political structures.[103] Shepheard and Martin argue, however, that while the political breadth of the concept of stewardship provides greater utility at a discursive level, at the level of practice those political structures and the tensions between them persist.[104]

Finally, the reformulation of the discourse of dephysicalised property into a discourse capable of describing and prescribing sustainable people–place

98 See, e.g., above Chapters 1 and 3, respectively, by Peter Lawrence, and Mark Shepheard and Paul Martin.

99 Lucy and Mitchell, above n. 88, 584.

100 See, e.g., Peter Brown, 'Toward an Economics of Stewardship: The Case of Climate' (1998) 26 *Ecological Economics* 11.

101 See above Chapter 3 by Mark Shepheard and Paul Martin, 76.

102 Lametti, above n. 18, 354.

103 Clogg, above n. 16, 192.

104 See above Chapter 3 by Mark Shepheard and Paul Martin.

relations can reconnect the cultural attachment to place that was suppressed by, even lost to, a resource-based view of 'nature'. Economist-sociologist Susan Hanna and sociologist Svein Jentoft suggest that the inclusion of 'respect' into a discourse of property is important. The basis of respect for 'the environment', they argue, is not a lofty sentiment so much as a rational acknowledgement of the dependence of human society on the 'things' of its economy. They say:

> In harsh climates, where a respectful relationship between people and their environment is essential for survival, the oneness between nature and humans is emphasised. This oneness reflects a bond with the environment that is based on dependence. The dependence is illustrated by the detailed knowledge of plants and animals held by the Inuit and other northern peoples, as well as by the ritual acts used to kill animals by the Bushmen of Australia.[105]

Environmental philosopher Mark Sagoff similarly attributes successful property regimes to a human attachment to their physical environment, not in economic terms, but in terms of 'affection'. In his view:

> If you want to understand what makes the economic use of environmental resources sustainable – if you want to know how places survive the vagaries of the global market – then look to the relationships, cultural and political, of the people in them. Look for affection not for efficiency as the trait with which people treat their surroundings.[106]

Sagoff issues an interesting caution to the use of the discourse of property and its situation of 'the environment' as external to human subjectivity and economy. He says that scientific discourse, whilst important, feeds into and from the discourse of property so that when we speak of the absorptive capacity of the atmosphere and other planetary 'support' systems we view the environment 'not as a place or even a collection of places; but rather . . . as a sort of global infrastructure'.[107] The knowledge of 'nature' and 'the environment' is very different to a knowledge of place situated within that specific place. The difference is, of course, that one is fundamentally detached from place, whereas the latter is attached to and founded on place. Such attachment seems at odds with the alienability of property and its centrality to the attractiveness of dephysicalised property as a legal and cultural paradigm. American property scholar Lee Fennell contended that restrictions or adjustments to the alienability of property 'can reduce pressure on

[105] Hanna and Jentoft, above n. 73, 37. [106] Sagoff, above n. 48, 165. [107] Ibid. 163.

common pool resources'.[108] Further, such restrictions can 'complement' and 'substitute' for other, more interventionist measures. The questions raised about the extent to which 'attachment' to and 'affection' for place translate into its inalienability are more numerous than can be considered adequately here. However, it is clear that the alienability and excludability of property at the heart of the Anglo-American discourse of property are fundamental to unsustainable people–place relations. The development of place-specific knowledge, 'respect', 'attachment' and 'affection' for place has long been and remains, for many cultures across the world, the rationale for the inalienability of place that characterises land laws and land use practices that have proven, largely, more sustainable over time.

4. Conclusion

Regardless of whether we call the legal framework and discourse that regulates sustainable land use and ownership 'property law' or 'environmental law' or 'climate law', the fact remains that viable and sustainable (land) laws exist only when and because they adequately describe and prescribe land use practices that are specific to the capacities and limits of particular lands and waters. The reliance of contemporary international and public environmental law on the outdated and maladapted discourse of dephysicalised property and its culture of entitlement is strategically, intellectually and normatively at odds with the imperative of enduring socio-economic viability. To retain and promote the discourse of dephysicalised property risks the obsolescence not only of that particular paradigm of people–place relations, but of the law itself. Law that cannot adequately describe and prescribe viable people–place relations can only ever regulate an imaginary jurisdiction that is not of the earth and its finite systems. The use of the discourse of property in environmental public and international law can change because fundamentally 'change in human societies occurs within, is carried through, and affects institutions'.[109] The discourse of dephysicalised property facilitates and protects institutions and practices that are dangerously detached from the physical conditions of their possibility. The augmentation of dephysicalised legal institutions and land use practices invites their collapse and their continued use is fundamentally unsuited to form the basis of a remedy to the problems of their own creation.

[108] Lee Ann Fennell, 'Adjusting Alienability' (2009) 122 *Harvard Law Review* 1403, 1406–7.
[109] Dovers, above n. 55, 3.

PART II

Discourses in environmental decisions

5

Perspectives on discourse in international environmental law: expert knowledge and challenges to deliberative democracy

JAYE ELLIS

1. Introduction

Many of the greatest difficulties encountered in attempts to craft environmental law and policy spring from the fact that the environment is everywhere. It cannot be confined to a narrow category and delegated to authorities or scientists holding a certain type of expertise. Environmental protection requires coordination and integration among different types of actors, different political authorities and various bodies of knowledge and expertise. Environmental policies must span great distances in time and space, and must be developed and implemented under conditions of uncertainty. Environmental degradation brings to light vast and complex networks of cause and effect, responsibility and obligation. Reining in environmental degradation requires us to mobilise all of our social institutions, and depends on the capacity of these systems to work together. Yet coordination among social systems is an immensely difficult task.

The precautionary approach and the concept of sustainable development are often invoked in attempts to bring together social systems – the economy, law, politics, science – to address environmental problems. They are environmental discourses around which interested actors with diverse interests and expertise rally. A further objective of precaution and sustainable development is to connect these social systems, dominated by expert discourses,[1] with the same discourses also taking place in

[1] By expert discourse, I mean a manner of communicating about problems and approaches to solving them that is defined by a series of assertions about what counts as a good argument, a defensible conclusion, a sound criticism – in brief, assertions about how members of that discipline produce knowledge.

less-expert, public spheres. Precaution is often interpreted as calling for better interaction among scientists, legal and policy experts, public authorities and members of the public.[2] As for the concept of sustainable development, integration among environmental, economic and social spheres is central.[3] We can understand the objective of more effective interaction among social systems in various ways. It could refer to breaking down the boundaries between these spheres and merging them into a unified whole. Alternately, it could involve bringing relevant rules drawn from each body of law together in the context of a legal regime. Or it could involve working out some means for communication and interaction among different spheres. It is this third, more modest approach that will be explored in this chapter. This approach assumes that the boundaries around systems, as arbitrary and inconvenient as they are, can serve important purposes provided they leave some scope for interaction among social systems.

Because precaution and sustainable development are often framed as legal principles, questions are raised regarding the role that law can play in pursuing their objectives. Two such questions will be addressed here: does law have a particular role to play in promoting interaction and collaboration among social systems generally? If so, what role? In addressing these questions, this chapter focuses on the interface between science and law. I consider the notion of a boundary object, that is, a concept, practice or institution – such as risk assessment, patents, or contracts – found in more than one specialised system and that can serve as a point of contact between systems, possibly fostering more or less stable interactions among them. I shall argue that risk is a

[2] Alessandra Arcuri, *The Case for a Procedural Version of the Precautionary Principle Erring on the Side of Environmental Preservation*, Global Law Working Paper No. 09/04 (2004); Tim O'Riordan, 'The Precautionary Principle and Civic Science' in Tim O'Riordan, James Cameron and Andrew Jordan (eds.), *Reinterpreting the Precautionary Principle* (Cameron May, London, 2001) 95; Catherine Larrère, 'Le contexte philosophique du principe de précaution' in Charles Leben and Joe Verhoeven (eds.), *Le principe de précaution: Aspects de droit international et communautaire* (Panthéon-Assas, Paris, 2002) 15.

[3] Daniel Magraw and Lisa Hawke, 'Sustainable Development' in Daniel Bodansky, Jutta Brunnée and Ellen Hey (eds.), *The Oxford Handbook of International Environmental Law* (Oxford University Press, 2007) 613; Philippe Sands, 'International Law in the Field of Sustainable Development' (1994) LXV *British Yearbook of International Law* 303; J. B. Ruhl, 'Sustainable Development: A Five-Dimensional Algorithm for Environmental Law' (1999) 18 *Stanford Environmental Law Journal* 31; Duncan French, *International Law and Policy of Sustainable Development* (Manchester University Press, 2005).

boundary object, operating within both science and law, which can foster interactions between them. I shall further argue that expert and public discourses of precaution and sustainable development can help us understand how this boundary object can be exploited to strengthen that connection.

2. Precaution and sustainable development at the law–science interface

Even once consensus is obtained regarding environmental protection as a moral imperative, the tasks of deciding what constitutes an acceptable environmental risk and how the risks are to be distributed remain very difficult, giving rise to results that are often bitterly contested. Science makes an enormous contribution, permitting us to see complex causal linkages that operate over immense expanses of time and space remaining largely invisible without science's techniques and methods. Science provides public authorities and communities with insights into risk, but cannot itself provide answers to the difficult questions of acceptability and distribution.[4] Discussions of science and its role in literature on environmental studies tend to reflect deep ambivalence. Science is seen as a bulwark against political expediency;[5] as a universal and objective body of knowledge that can help us make decisions in pluralistic societies;[6] as a

[4] See the discussion presented by Elizabeth Rough below in Chapter 7 regarding the contributions of science to the issue of nuclear waste disposal – and regarding the limitations of science in the face of the ethical and political aspects of this issue.

[5] Stewart Elgie, 'Statutory Structure and Species Survival: How Constraints on Cabinet Discretion Affect Endangered Species Listing Outcomes' (2008) 19 *Journal of Environmental Law and Practice* 1. Elgie seeks to explain a strong correlation between constraints on political discretion and decisions to list species as endangered. On page 2 he notes the strong preferences held by environmentalists for giving greater – or exclusive – decision-making authority to scientists and the bitter controversy that this issue caused.

[6] Saskia Young, 'Contemporary Issues of the Convention on International Trade in Endangered Species of Wild Fauna and Flora (CITES) and the Debate over Sustainable Use' (2003) 14(1) *Colorado Journal of International Environmental Law and Policy* 167; Note, 'The CITES Fort Lauderdale Criteria: The Uses and Limits of Science in International Conservation Decisionmaking' (2001) 114 *Harvard Law Review* 1769. The authors recognise that decisions to list species in the appendices to CITES is not a mechanical process, but argue that new listing criteria that place a greater emphasis on scientific evidence of endangerment will, in the words of the author of the Note at 1792, 'improve the deliberations of the parties, not so much by increasing the influence of scientific data as by cooling expressive disputes among the parties, encouraging compromise, and promoting further scientific research'. Both note that many difficulties can

potential threat to democracy;[7] as posing a challenge to non-scientific ways of knowing;[8] and as a driving force behind environmental degradation.[9] Not surprisingly, debates regarding legal institutions for environmental protection reflect this ambivalence: care is taken to protect and promote the role of science so that it can be a force against expediency and capture by powerful interest groups; however, principles such as precaution seem designed to put science in its place.

Precaution and sustainable development, when conceived as legal concepts, seek to guide but not dictate the exercise of public authority in the sphere of environmental protection. Given the essential role played by science in environmental protection, these concepts must provide some assistance to public authorities seeking to integrate scientific knowledge into political decision-making. The role of law in this process is twofold. First, legal instruments are very often the medium through which political decisions about the management of environmental risks are implemented. Second, legal rules, principles and concepts can be called on to aid the evaluation of the appropriateness of exercises of public authority: this is central to the approach taken in literature on the exercise of public authority in local and global contexts.[10] The relevance of these bodies of literature for precaution and sustainable development will be considered below. I shall now turn to a brief discussion of these concepts and their potential contributions to discussions of the science–law interface.

2.1 Precaution

A well-respected definition of precaution is contained in Principle 15 of the Rio Declaration: 'Where there are threats of serious or irreversible damage, lack of full scientific certainty shall not be used as a reason for

be traced back to the unresolved – and probably unresolvable – tension between preservationist and conservationist approaches.

[7] Frank Fischer, 'Democratic Prospects in an Age of Expertise' in Frank Fischer (ed.), *Citizens, Experts and the Environment* (Duke University Press, Durham, NC, 2003) 5.

[8] Karen Warren, 'The Power and Promise of Ecological Feminism' in Michael E. Zimmerman *et al.* (eds.), *Environmental Philosophy: From Animal Rights to Radical Ecology* (Prentice-Hall, Englewood Cliffs, 1998) 325.

[9] Éric Darier presents the deep ambivalence towards science and technology, and towards received wisdom about their contribution to human progress, often held by people concerned about the environment: Éric Darier, 'Foucault and the Environment: An Introduction' in Éric Darier (ed.), *Discourses of the Environment* (Blackwell, Oxford and Maldon, 1999) 1.

[10] Armin von Bogdandy, 'General Principles of International Public Authority: Sketching a Research Field' (2008) 9 *German Law Journal* 1909.

postponing cost-effective measures to prevent environmental degradation.'[11] This definition is certainly not without its flaws,[12] but it does highlight essential features of precaution: the threshold condition of scientific uncertainty and the need for political authorities to act – not prevaricate or delegate – in the face of uncertain risk. Precisely what kind of action must be taken in the face of evidence of a potential risk is left quite open, at least at the level of the general principle, and is rarely filled by discourse adherents. Precautionary action could range from gathering information and deliberating, at one end of the spectrum, to prohibiting substances and activities, at the other end.[13] Central to the concerns reflected in the principle is the division of labour between science and law.[14] While deference to scientists is justified up to a point, political decision-makers cannot abdicate their responsibility in favour of the scientific community; they cannot put off regulatory decisions until the submission of incontrovertible scientific proof.[15]

The precautionary principle has also been interpreted as calling for a thorough re-examination of the relationship between scientists and public authorities.[16] A more expansive interpretation extends this re-examination to the relationship between science and civil society.[17] If scientists are unable to provide us with *the* answer to questions about

[11] Rio Declaration on Environment and Development, concluded 14 June 1992, Rio de Janeiro, Brazil.

[12] Concerns have been raised, for example, about the sliding scale that is implied by the references to the capabilities of states and to cost-effectiveness.

[13] Steve Maguire and Jaye Ellis, 'Redistributing the Burden of Scientific Uncertainty: Implications of the Precautionary Principle for State and Non-State Actors' (2005) 5 *Global Environmental Politics* 505; Olivier Godard, 'Le principe de précaution face au dilemme de la traduction juridique des demandes sociales, leçons de méthode tirées de l'affaire de la vache folle' in Leben and Verhoeven (eds.), above n. 2, 29.

[14] Andy Stirling, 'The Precautionary Principle in Science and Technology' in O'Riordan, Cameron and Jordan (eds.), above n. 2, 61, 62. Stirling argues for a broad regime of risk assessment, which takes into account quantitative and qualitative, direct and indirect effects and accommodates a range of points of view: at 66.

[15] Malcolm McGarvin refers to a criticism made of fisheries biologists, in which the field is described as being 'so accustomed to inaccuracy in its basic models that striking differences between model and observation are scarcely noted ... Nevertheless fisheries biologists fit data to models that are clearly inaccurate and make decisions on that basis': Robert Peters, *A Critique for Ecology* (Cambridge University Press, Cambridge and New York, 1991). McGarvin's comment on this critique hits the mark: 'But perhaps the deeper criticism should be levelled at policies that lead fisheries biologists to attempt the impossible': Malcolm McGarvin, 'Science, Precaution, Facts and Values' in O'Riordan, Cameron and Jordan (eds.), above n. 2, 35, 38.

[16] Larrère, above n. 2; McGarvin, above n. 15; O'Riordan, above n. 2.

[17] Arcuri, above n. 2.

environmental risk, then it stands to reason that other decision-making processes must make a contribution. Given the relevance of scientific knowledge to questions of environmental protection, scientists and non-scientists must be able to work together. This means that they must be able to understand one another to a greater extent, and when mutual understanding is elusive, they must nevertheless function on the basis of mutual respect and accommodation of differences in the production of knowledge and the reaching of judgments.[18] The sophistication and complexity of contemporary scientific debates means we cannot hope for seamless flows of communication between science and other expert discourses, let alone scientists and citizens. But making these diverse communities and bodies of knowledge more intelligible to one another is a realistic objective. In any event, it is essential given the radical and permanent, rather than exceptional and temporary, nature of scientific uncertainty.[19] Precaution can no longer be used as a temporary measure until gaps in knowledge are filled by science.[20]

2.2 Sustainable development

The best-known definition of sustainable development is that found in the Brundtland Report: 'development that meets the needs of the present, without compromising the ability of future generations to meet their own needs'.[21] Two fundamental elements of the concept are integration and equity.[22] In the context of law, sustainable development is described as calling for integration among environmental, economic

[18] See, e.g., O'Riordan, above n. 3, 104 ff; Jean-Jacques Salomon, 'Science, Technology and Democracy' (2000) 38 *Minerva* 33.

[19] Ladeur argues that environmental law has 'reached the limits of complexity'; that it is overtaxed: Karl-Heinz Ladeur, 'Coping with Uncertainty: Ecological Risks in the Proceduralization of Environmental Law' in Gunther Teubner, Lindsay Farmer and Declan Murphy (eds.), *Environmental Law and Ecological Responsibility: The Concept and Practice of Ecological Self-Organization* (Wiley, Chichester, 1994) 299, 303.

[20] Annecoos Wiersema, 'Adversaries or Partners? Science and the Precautionary Principle in International Wildlife Treaty Regimes' (2008) 11 *Journal of International Wildlife Law and Policy* 211, 234–5.

[21] World Commission on Environment and Development, *Our Common Future* (Oxford University Press, 1987).

[22] The most successful definitions of sustainable development are those that seek to identify its core elements. French breaks the concept down into environment, economy, equity and empowerment: above n. 3, 14. Magraw and Hawke identify inter- and intra-generational equity, environmental preservation and integration of social, economic and environmental policies: above n. 3, 618. Sands lists the integration of environment and

and human rights law. As a political or moral principle, integration among environment, society and the economy is one of its central goals.[23] Equity refers to the resolution of justice claims across dimensions of space and time: individuals and groups in different parts of society, whether domestic or international, must be treated equitably, and the needs and interests of future generations must be respected and protected. These two elements, integration and equity, imply a third component, namely living within our means, or treating the environment in a sustainable manner.

To an even greater extent than precaution, sustainable development is an explicitly normative concept, not least because of the key role played by equity.[24] Whereas the call for more fruitful interaction among science, law, policy and civil society is strongly implied by precaution, it is demanded by sustainable development. Respect for democratic principles, notably participation, transparency and accountability, is an integral part of sustainable development. Less obvious are the implications of sustainable development for the interface between law and science, but sustainable development depends heavily on a range of expert discourses, including science as well as policy, law, economics and ethics. One of the messages of sustainable development is that no single expert discourse can dominate; indeed, given the emphasis on equity, the concept suggests that expert discourses generally should not dominate. A plurality of voices must be heard. The question, of course, is how to avoid cacophony.

3. Social systems: systems theory

Precaution and sustainable development point to the conclusion that integration is essential. But how is it to be brought about? Systems theory, or autopoietic theory, as developed by the sociologist Luhmann and legal scholars such as Teubner, sheds light on interactions among highly specialised social systems such as science and law. More

development, equity between states, inter-generational equity and non-exhaustion of environmental resources: above n. 3, 338.

[23] Alhaji Marong, 'From Rio to Johannesburg: Reflections on the Role of International Legal Norms in Sustainable Development' (2003–4) 16 *Georgetown International Environmental Law Review* 21, 31 ff.

[24] On the centrality of questions of justice and equity to sustainable development see below Chapter 8 by Tim Stephens. Brad Jessup, above Chapter 2, discusses the influence of sustainable development, as articulated at the international level in instruments such as the Rio Declaration, on the development of a discourse of environmental justice in the United States and elsewhere.

specifically, this literature helps us to understand why these interactions are so difficult. Luhmann describes modern society as comprising a range of specialised subsystems. This differentiation is necessary as society comes to interact with its environment in increasingly complex ways, but one of the results is that the various subsystems come to function independently of one another, each according to its own logic.[25] These differentiated systems create their own vocabularies and conceptual categories, their own representations of the environment of which they form a part, and their own conceptions of their interactions with, and influences on, that environment. The legal system, when it concludes that a legal obligation has been breached, cannot simply communicate this decision to the parties to the dispute: it must present this conclusion in a form that will have an impact beyond the legal system, such as a financial penalty or the revocation of a licence to do business. In this manner, the consequences of a legal decision are felt in the broader society, but, in the words of Luhmann, the legal system, along with other specialised social systems, is normatively closed: normative meaning is not transmitted across system boundaries.[26]

This conception of society and of the role of law within society has major implications for the integrative projects of precaution and sustainable development. Scholars of autopoietic theory such as Luhmann and Teubner warn that we should not expect a direct, linear relation between the output of a legal system (such as a penalty) and a desired outcome (for example, the party in breach of an obligation fulfils her obligation; other parties, observing this outcome, decide to respect their obligations rather than risk penalties).[27] This is because of the process of transformation that all communications issued by the legal system must undergo as they cross the boundary between system and environment. From the point of view of the economic system, it may be concluded that it is more efficient to pay a penalty than to respect onerous conditions. The legal system can respond to this reaction of the economic system by increasing the penalty, but this may have unpredicted and undesired outcomes, such as driving economic actors away from transactions that

25 Niklas Luhmann, *A Sociological Theory of Law* (Routledge & Kegan Paul, London and Boston, 1985), 104.

26 Ibid. 283.

27 Gunther Teubner, *Law as an Autopoietic System* (Blackwell, Oxford and Cambridge, Mass., 1993) 74.

are beneficial to society and which the legal system had no intention of undermining.

Teubner argues that communication across system boundaries is possible because different systems, though they possess their own vocabularies, structures and images of the world in which they operate, do converge on unique phenomena.[28] For example, while a contract may be understood in many different ways by different systems – law, economics, ethics – and in a different way again by the people who are actually parties to the contract, the transaction viewed from all these different angles is one and the same. In seeking to interpret the transaction, different systems perceive and observe one another, and interpret one another's outputs. The legal system develops its own image of the economic system and reaches its own conclusions about how economics understands contracts. Law then seeks to react to the economic system as it conceives it. However, the economic system to which law seeks to react is not the *actual* economic system as it exists in the world, rather it is law's image of that system.[29] As a result, when systems purport to speak to one another, they actually misspeak, communicating slightly past one another. Although genuinely common ground cannot be found,[30] relatively stable points of contact and dialogue can at least be established.

The phenomenon described by Teubner of an event or transaction that is observed by different social systems is described in literature on science studies as a 'boundary object'. A boundary object can be a social or legal institution, such as a patent, which is understood from the point of view of a range of social systems, including science, law and policy.[31] According to an influential definition and description, boundary objects:

> inhabit several intersecting social worlds; [they are] plastic enough to adapt to local needs . . . yet robust enough to maintain a common identity across sites. They are weakly structured in common use, and become strongly structured in individual-site use. . . . They have different

[28] Ibid. [29] Ibid.

[30] Fischer-Lescano and Teubner propose that specialised legal regimes should (and often do) behave 'as if' they were basing their decisions on reference points common to all legal regimes. The existence of these reference points is, they argue, an 'operative fiction', but one which permits them to look beyond their own areas of competence to rules and approaches developed in other contexts that are of relevance to a given dispute: Andreas Fischer-Lescano and Gunther Teubner, 'Regime-Collisions: The Vain Search for Legal Unity in the Fragmentation of Global Law' (2004) 25 *Michigan Journal of International Law* 999, 1033.

[31] David Guston, 'Boundary Organizations in Environmental Policy and Science: An Introduction' (2001) 26 *Science, Technology and Human Values* 399, 400.

> meanings in different social worlds but their structure is common enough to more than one world to make them recognizable, a means of translation.[32]

In a slightly transposed register, Rehg employs the notion of a 'boundary concept' to describe the possibility of interdisciplinary cooperation. A boundary concept must be capable of playing a 'cross-fertilizing role', which in turn requires that it 'have some purchase in the different disciplines'. It 'must at one level allow a sufficiently flexible or broad interpretation that covers different methods and uses across disciplines, yet at the level of actual exchange and cooperation it must facilitate translation across disciplinary boundaries and generate specific research questions, points of debate, and possibilities for hybrid analysis that combine resources from different disciplines'.[33]

One highly promising candidate for a boundary object that will help us negotiate the science–law interface is risk. Risk is a concept that is proper both to science and to law: both systems bring expertise to bear in attempts to identify, understand and manage risks, but they do so in very different ways. The public legal system depends heavily on scientific input in its own attempts to address risk. It has developed a range of techniques for channelling scientific evidence and expertise into decision-making processes (notably the use of scientific experts in adjudication), and for evaluating the soundness of decisions by public authorities that incorporate scientific evidence, such as the listing of species as endangered or of substances as toxic. In both the adjudicatory and the policy-setting spheres, law seeks to guide decision-making *processes* to promote a range of good governance goals, including transparency, participation and reasoned decision-making. These legal techniques, which occur across the public and international realm, can be seen as attempts to translate scientific conceptions of risk into legal terms.

One way of understanding law's approach to risk is to focus on techniques that are used to reduce questions of risk to a binary structure. These techniques are particularly evident in the context of adjudication, in which parties seek to establish whether the creation of a risk gives rise

[32] Susan Leigh Star and James Griesemer, 'Institutional Ecology, "Translation" and Boundary Objects: Amateurs and Professionals in Berkeley's Museum of Vertebrate Zoology' (1989) 19 *Social Studies of Science* 387, 393.

[33] William Rehg, *Cogent Science in Context: The Science Wars, Argumentation Theory, and Habermas* (MIT Press, Cambridge, Mass., 2009) 6. Footnotes omitted.

to liability: either yes or no. Outside the adjudicatory context, however, it is very difficult to see law's approach to risk as involving a binary categorisation. Instead, actors seeking to avoid legal liability are compelled to work with more open-textured conceptions of risk, in which a range of legal outcomes may be envisaged. This is because the location of the boundary between liability and no liability will very often only be known retrospectively, possibly after the conclusion of a lengthy trial and appeals process. As a result, actors engaged in risk-creating activities will not have the luxury of knowing in advance where the boundary is so they can push up against it without crossing it. Actors will have to engage in a whole range of behaviour in order to satisfy public authorities (and their insurers, shareholders, and constituents) that they are behaving 'reasonably': keeping up to date on the latest scientific and technological developments; conducting environmental impact assessments and monitoring; engaging in research and development; carrying out training of employees and conducting rigorous programmes of implementation and enforcement of environmental standards; and so forth. For actors seeking to avoid liability, risk avoidance appears as a spectrum rather than a binary issue.

Nevertheless, too often, when the legal system turns to science, it seeks what it cannot itself provide, namely a clear, binary distinction: either an activity poses unacceptable risks or it does not; either a species is endangered or it is not; either a substance can be safely ingested or it cannot.[34] Calls for more flexible, adaptable structures and institutions capable of accommodating scientific uncertainties, unexpected outcomes or shifts in scientific consensus are, at one level, calls for a better adaptation of law to the nature of scientific knowledge.[35] I now turn to the questions whether, and how, the discourses of precaution and sustainable development could be deployed to improve the quality of this translation process, bearing the notion of risk as a boundary object in mind.

4. The science–law interface and the exercise of public authority

Decisions about the approval of new pharmaceutical or agricultural products, the inclusion of species on lists of protected species, or the approval of dam construction require a division of labour between

[34] See McGarvin, above n. 15. [35] Arcuri, above n. 2.

scientists and public authorities seeking to assess and manage risks.[36] The shape this division of labour should take is the source of endless controversy, since these tasks are interrelated in complex ways. Many actors favour an expansive role for scientists and strictly limited discretion for political authorities, but others note the dangers of slipping from democratic to technocratic forms of governance and do not wish to give scientists authority to determine whether a risk is politically acceptable. At the international level in particular, where there may be no strong consensus on the underlying goals of a treaty regime[37] or where there may be differing levels of commitment to goals that do attract consensus,[38] the advantages of relying heavily on scientific input and of imposing strong constraints on political discretion may seem great. Insights from autopoietic theory remind us, however, that inputs from one system cannot simply be inserted into another without disruption to both.

Central to these kinds of decision-making procedures are questions about the exercise of public authority. As international legal institutions take on a greater role in matters of public policy that have impacts not only on states but also on sub-sovereign actors, the way in which these policy decisions are made comes to take on great importance. These decision-making processes have been analysed as exercises of administrative authority, but with a distinctly global nature. Scholars of global administrative law argue that we can begin to discern a set of principles operating in an emerging global administrative sphere that seek to promote accountability, transparency, participation, the use of reasons to support decisions, legality and the availability of review of rules and decisions akin to judicial review.[39]

Central to the objectives of global administrative law, argues Kingsbury, is a quality of 'publicness', or 'the claim made for law that it has been wrought by the whole society, by the public, and the connected claim that law addresses matters of concern to the society as

[36] The alignment of risk assessment with science and of risk management with policy is discussed below in Chapter 6 by Bettina Lange.

[37] This is true of CITES, in which disputes between conservationist and preservationist approaches arise in virtually all decision-making processes: see Note, above n. 6.

[38] Examples include regional fisheries management organisations and the climate change regime.

[39] Benedict Kingsbury, Nico Krisch and Richard Stewart, 'The Emergence of Global Administrative Law' (2005) 68 *New York University Journal of Law and Contemporary Problems* 15.

such'.[40] In a similar vein, Bogdandy seeks to articulate 'general principles of international public authority' in order to strengthen 'the publicness of public international law'.[41] Bogdandy is sceptical of certain of the aims of global administrative law,[42] in particular its assertion that the emergence of a common global administrative space requires 'new and distinct principles and mechanisms of accountability through global administrative law' and the 'building of a global administrative law to help govern [global administrative] space'.[43] He sees this approach as being at once too broad – he argues that it tends towards an untenable 'proto-federal conception of global order' englobing international and domestic authorities – and too narrow – focusing only on administrative activity.[44] Bogdandy argues instead for the development of an 'overarching theory and doctrine of public law',[45] focusing not simply on administration but on the exercise of public authority generally, defined as 'any kind of governance activity by international institutions ... [that affects] individuals, private associations, enterprises, states, or other public institutions'.[46] These different but overlapping approaches help us to understand the particular characteristics of political and legal decision-making processes as well as potential contributions of law to negotiating the interface with science.

Both global administrative law and Bogdandy's public law approach have important implications for precaution and sustainable development. As noted above, these concepts embedded in discourses have been employed to call for the promotion of democratic principles and to emphasise the value of different ways of knowing. They cannot tell us what the outcome of a particular adjudication or decision-making process should be, but can help us to understand what is at stake in that process. More particularly, they have the potential to influence the way in which risk assessment and risk management are understood and carried out. As such, they call attention to process – to the manner in which public authority is exercised.

A healthy interaction between science and law could be described in light of the following objectives. Legal structures should create sufficient space for the incorporation not only of scientifically established facts but

40 Ibid. 31. 41 Bogdandy, above n. 10, 1914. 42 Ibid. 1919.
43 Kingsbury *et al.*, above n. 39, 15. 44 Bogdandy, above n. 10, 1919–20.
45 Ibid. 1921.
46 Armin von Bogdandy, Philipp Dann and Matthias Goldmann, 'Developing the Publicness of Public International Law: Towards a Legal Framework for Global Governance Activities' (2008) 9 *German Law Journal* 1375.

also for scientific controversies and uncertainties. Furthermore, they should do so in a way that does not allow political authorities to abdicate their responsibility to make judgments. Criteria may be required to identify cases in which a high degree of deference by an international regime to state authorities is in order, for example to acknowledge different levels of risk aversion in different societies.[47] Protecting the rights and interests of actors affected by measures for which the scientific justification is weak due to uncertainty may require emphasising procedure over substance, as Bogdandy and global administrative law scholars argue.

Precaution and sustainable development are very much concerned with procedure, and when we seek to understand the implications of these concepts for legal systems, procedural questions come sharply into focus. For instance, how to ensure the robustness of decision-making procedures? How to ensure that the range of relevant considerations, and the spectrum of relevant expertise, both lay and expert, are fully aired and given due regard? How to identify the relevant considerations and expertise? What is the proper province for the exercise of judgment by public authorities at the national and international levels? What factors will lead to a conclusion that an exercise of discretion by national authorities is unreasonable, and must be checked by international mechanisms? Embedded in these questions are issues relating to the role of science in the exercise of public authority.

One approach, evident in the World Trade Organization's Sanitary and Phytosanitary Measures Agreement (SPS Agreement), involves treating science with a high degree of deference: unilateral measures must be 'based on' a risk assessment,[48] and standards adopted by scientific bodies within international organisations, such as the Codex Alimentarius Commission, are incorporated by reference.[49] Perez describes this reliance

[47] Caroline Henckels proposes a series of criteria applicable to the application of the SPS Agreement which could be applied to determine instances in which deference to national authorities is in order: 'GMOs in the WTO: A Critique of the Panel's Legal Reasoning in EC–Biotech' (2006) 7 *Melbourne Journal of International Law* 278, 296.

[48] Sanitary and Phytosanitary Measures Agreement, opened for signature 15 April 1994, 1867 UNTS 493 (entered into force 1 January 1995), Art. 5(1).

[49] On the role of international scientific bodies in the setting of standards used to evaluate the legality of SPS measures, see Ravi Afonso Pereira, 'Why Would International Administrative Activity be any Less Legitimate? – A Study of the Codex Alimentarius Commission' (2008) 9 *German Law Journal* 1693; Oren Perez, *Ecological Sensitivity and Global Legal Pluralism: Rethinking the Trade and Environment Conflict* (Hart Publishing, Oxford, 2004) 115.

by the SPS Agreement on science and international standardisation bodies as 'a *functional* appeal for knowledge' but also 'an appeal for *legitimacy*'.[50] The SPS Agreement seems to be attempting to incorporate scientific understandings of risk into a legal framework without going through the process of translation from one expert discourse into another. As Lange argues in this volume, the agreement seeks to shape how arguments to justify health, safety and environmental regulations are to be made.[51] The result is a delegation of significant authority to science and a shirking of responsibility on the part of public authorities. Precaution focuses attention on one potential problem with this approach: in incorporating scientific understandings of risk, the legal system may not be sufficiently attuned to the dynamic nature of those understandings, and of the uncertainties embedded within them. Can the scientific understanding of risk really be taken up by the legal system without undergoing a process of adaptation? Perez argues that this heavy reliance on science is based on two flawed assumptions: first, that science (and by extension the process of standard-setting) can provide an answer to the question whether a state's environmental or health and safety measure is protectionist or not; and second, 'that the criterion of validation which is used by [science] to judge knowledge claims, is the criterion that should be used by the law to resolve risk disputes'.[52] A second set of problems is highlighted by literature on public authority:[53] do the processes through which these scientific conclusions are made meet requirements for the appropriate exercise of public authority? Perez's concern is very similar: can this deference to science *legitimate* the decisions of the SPS regime?[54] Precaution and sustainable development can help us to flesh out the requirements of public authority and therefore develop principles and concepts for evaluating and critiquing exercises of that authority, or rules governing its exercise, such as those found in the SPS Agreement. Precaution reminds us that the acceptability of a risk is a matter for political judgment, not scientific expertise; that the answer provided by scientists is very often provisional and incomplete, in ways that may not be discerned by legal or political authorities; and that science does not

[50] Ibid., 117–18 (emphasis in original). Bettina Lange, below in Chapter 6, also discusses the high degree of deference paid both within the WTO and the EU to science in the process of evaluating SPS measures.

[51] See below Chapter 6 by Bettina Lange.

[52] Perez, above n. 49, 118.

[53] Bogdandy *et al.*, above n. 46; Bogdandy, above n. 10.

[54] Perez, above n. 49, 118.

speak with one monolithic voice. Precaution is thus applicable to 'trans-scientific' issues that science is not capable of resolving. As Rough notes, such issues may exceed the capacity of science because of uncertainty or indeterminacy or because of ethical and moral implications.[55] Precaution insists that policy-makers be informed of potential and poorly understood risks as well as actual and quantifiable risks. This means that political authorities require information not only about risks, but also about the nature of scientific knowledge of risks: in other words, they require some insight into the complexity, plurality and open texture of scientific knowledge.[56] Both precaution and sustainable development suggest that the range of factors to be considered in assessing risk be expanded to include, at a very minimum, damage to the ecosystem itself as well as social and economic impacts, such as impacts on social structures and roles, or impacts on groups that are already disadvantaged or marginalised. Decisions about the acceptability of risks need to be informed by science – indeed, the role of science must be significant. But public authorities cannot delegate such decision-making to standard-setting bodies, nor to other expert procedures such as cost–benefit analysis. The responsibility for determining the acceptability of risk falls on the shoulders of public authorities, as such determinations are based on political and ethical factors. Of course, while public authorities must shoulder the responsibility, decision-making processes will depend for their legitimacy on the extent to which they engage the broader public.

Perez calls for 'a strategy of *active engagement*, which would be based on [a] more open and pluralistic approach to the deliberation of knowledge claims'.[57] This could arouse fears that the contribution of scientific expertise will be weakened, but this need not be the case. In Perez's vision members of the public will not be involved in the production of scientific knowledge. The process involves, as a first step, the reframing of decisions about risk as scientific, political and ethical decisions.[58] Second, public authorities and laypeople must come to understand the indeterminacy of scientific knowledge of environmental risks and, as a corollary, that neither

[55] See below Chapter 7 by Elizabeth Rough.

[56] For an extensive discussion of the implications of precaution for risk assessment see Stirling, above n. 14. Stirling argues that a 'more broadly-based, pluralistic and epistemologically humble precautionary approach is more scientific than traditional narrow risk assessment': at 82. See also the discussion of constructive technology assessment, canvassed in ibid. at 83 ff.

[57] Perez above n. 49, 118. Emphasis in original.

[58] Ibid. at 152–3.

science nor policy can provide perfect control of risks. Processes of risk assessment and risk management must be recognised for what they are: processes of *judgment* rather than of simple *decisions* to which public authorities are driven inexorably by the data. Responsibility for these judgments must be accepted and assumed by public authorities. Third, law can make an important contribution to decision-making processes by setting procedural criteria that will help to ensure the rigour and the fairness of the process as well as the reasonableness of the result. To return briefly to the SPS Agreement, this could involve, as Perez argues, a reflexive approach to regulation whose features would include an acknowledgement of scientific indeterminacy and a resulting emphasis on the quality of the decision-making process, focusing on procedure rather than substance and on criteria such as reasonableness and good faith, which again point in the direction of the decision-making procedure and away from requirements that the final decision meet criteria of *truth* or *correctness*.[59]

On a much more ambitious scale is Latour's recommendation for the establishment of a bicameral legislative assembly including an upper house described as a 'Parliament of Things'. The upper house would comprise representatives of what we tend to think of as the non-human world, although Latour resists this dichotomy. These representatives include, but are not limited to, scientists, who are there because they have some capacity, based on expertise or experience, to provide insights into the impacts on the non-human world of laws and policies proposed in the lower house, which represents humans. In Latour's words, '[n]atures are present, but with their representatives, scientists who speak in their name'.[60]

The issue of representation is both crucial and highly problematic. As Saward argues, claims to represent the interests of non-human entities such as flora, fauna or ecosystems tend to be characterised by what he describes as 'unidirectional approaches, objectivity and authenticity claims', all of which he regards as highly problematic.[61] Rather than a unidirectional process whereby the representative simply transmits information about the represented entity to decision-makers in a

[59] Ibid. 130 ff.; David Winickoff *et al.*, 'Adjudicating the GM Food Wars: Science, Risk, and Democracy in World Trade Law' (2005) 30 *Yale Journal of International Law* 81, 107.

[60] Bruno Latour, *We Have Never Been Modern* (Harvard University Press, Cambridge, Mass., 1993) 144.

[61] Michael Saward, 'Representation' in Andrew Dobson and Robyn Eckersley (eds.), *Political Theory and the Ecological Challenge* (Cambridge University Press, Cambridge and New York, 2006) 183.

completely objective manner, Saward argues that representation is better understood as a 'bi- or multidirectional' process in which the 'representative and represented are in a shifting and mutually constitutive relationship'.[62] He further argues that representatives should not claim to have access to the '*authentic* presence of "nature" or its interests' but must understand that they are interpreting and selecting as they attempt to describe and define the interests of the entity they represent.[63]

How well does Latour rise to the formidable challenge presented by Saward? Latour's approach is very sensitive to the problematic nature of representation.[64] Latour, as a committed social constructivist, does not claim that scientists or anyone else can represent directly, immediately and objectively the nature and interests of ecosystems and their constituent parts. Latour argues that scientists, with all their weaknesses and limitations on their capacity to understand the phenomena they investigate, are nevertheless in a good position to give us insights into the 'natural world'. Elsewhere he describes the construction of scientific knowledge in the following terms: 'Yes, we err often, but not always because, fortunately, (1) *we have time*; (2) *we are equipped*; (3) *we are many*; (4) *we have institutions*.'[65] Importantly, Latour is not advocating a delegation of decision-making authority to scientists. He is instead seeking a way to introduce the insights of scientists – but not only scientists – about the 'natural world' into public deliberation and decision-making.

To return briefly to the exercise of international public authority, two things become clear. First, an obligation imposed on public authorities to refer to scientific evidence in the process of making and justifying their

[62] Ibid. 192. [63] Ibid.

[64] Latour's proposal invites comparison to that of Christopher Stone in the landmark article 'Should Trees Have Standing? Toward Legal Rights for Natural Objects' (1972) 45 *Southern California Law Review* 450. This approach, however, treats the issue of representation as unproblematic: at 466. More than a decade later, Stone returned to his 1972 argument and fleshed out a moral theory which would support his claim. In this article, he had even less to say about issues of representation, though the emphasis here was not so much on the exercise of legal rights as on the moral underpinnings of those rights: Christopher Stone, 'Should Trees Have Standing? Revisited: How Far Will Law and Morals Reach? A Pluralist Perspective' (1985–6) 59 *Southern California Law Review* 1.

[65] Bruno Latour, 'A Textbook Case Revisited – Knowledge as a Mode of Existence' in Edward Hackett *et al.* (eds.), *The Handbook of Science and Technology Studies* (MIT Press, Cambridge, Mass., 3rd edn, 2008) 83, 94–5. Emphasis in original.

decisions can provide some protection against arbitrariness, discrimination, interestedness and caving in to political expediency, among other ills.[66] Second, an obligation to base the exercise of public authority on science alone is untenable: it amounts to a shirking of responsibility on the part of public authorities. The problem is not that science is not democratic.[67] The issue is that scientific knowledge is compounded by particularities; it is produced by a particular group for a particular set of objectives that are particular to the discipline, and these do not encompass the whole of society's ends. Its vital contribution cannot be doubted, and the truths that it helps us to perceive are of great importance, but science cannot give us insights into all the questions that we need to answer in reaching conclusions about what we ought to do in the face of environmental risk.

5. Conclusions

Communication between different discourses, expert and non-expert, is both extremely difficult and absolutely necessary. We cannot hope to attain a seamless relationship among discourses. Interactions among scientists, policy-makers, jurists, economists and members of the public will always be complex and often lead to conflict. Yet the alternatives to pursuing collaboration – leaving decision-making to experts; making decisions without the aid of expert input; or divvying up disputes into their ethical, legal, scientific, economic and political components – are unacceptable.

The notion of a boundary object holds great potential for the project of integration articulated by precaution and sustainable development. It is sufficiently modest, making no promises about the seamless transfer of meaning across system boundaries or the perfect integration between specialised systems. But the notion provides an apt metaphor for the kinds of communication that might successfully pass across system boundaries and may result in more robust decision-making procedures and better results for the environment.

66 On this point, see 'Note', above n. 6; Elgie, above n. 5.

67 On this issue, see Salomon, who notes that while, in one way it is not, because produced by an elite group of people with specialised abilities, in another way it is: 'all who belong and contribute to [the scientific institution] are exposed through their papers to public criticism, to review of their experiments, and open discussion of their results': above n. 18, 33.

Literature on the exercise of public authority raises many crucial points about the role that precaution and sustainable development can play in legal systems as they attempt to interact with science. The approach suggested here is not one of showing science its place and seeking to shore up the authority of law in the face of the growing influence of science. Rather, it is to identify ways in which law can create stable points of interaction between science and law. This involves achieving more sophisticated understandings of the scientific method within legal institutions, finding more effective ways to translate scientific concepts into legal terms, and better understanding the actual and potential roles of law in evaluating, critiquing and, where necessary, disciplining the exercise of public authority.

6

Getting to yes:[1] structuring and disciplining arguments for and against transgenic agricultural products in European Union authorisations

BETTINA LANGE

1. Introduction: conceptual issues and contribution

Within the European Union (EU) regime for the authorisation of transgenic agricultural products, international trade law prioritises a scientific discourse about the risks generated by these products. EU administrative law as well as a 'pure', 'contextualised' and 'meta-scientific' discourse invoked during actual EU authorisations further structure what can be said in what manner about the advantages and disadvantages of transgenic agricultural products during authorisations. Examining this structuring and disciplining of arguments during EU authorisations is important, because how arguments for and against transgenic agricultural products are structured feeds into final authorisation decisions, in practice mostly approvals of authorisation applications despite considerable opposition from citizens and some EU member state governments to transgenic agriculture.[2] Hence this chapter also suggests that attention to the discourses generated during EU authorisations can help to explain why participants in these authorisations focus on and speak to similar themes, notwithstanding their diverging interests, the entrenched conflict between applicants and objectors,[3] as well as different cultural

[1] Roger Fisher, William Ury and Bruce Paton, *Getting to Yes: Negotiating Agreement Without Giving In* (Penguin Books, New York, 1991).

[2] Sylvie Bonny, 'Why Are Most Europeans Opposed to GMOs? Factors Explaining Rejection in France and Europe' (2003) 6(1) *Electronic Journal of Biotechnology* at www.ejbiotechnology.info/content/vol6/issue1/full/4/; Sheila Jasanoff, *Designs on Nature* (Princeton University Press, 2005) 9.

[3] Gilmore, Hankey and Kirke (GHK), Interim Report, *Evaluation of the EU Legislative Framework in the Field of Cultivation of GMOs under Directive 2001/18/EC and Regulation (EC) 1829/2003* (November 2009) 46.

attitudes and political institutional frameworks for understanding the risks of transgenic agriculture among the twenty-seven EU member states.[4]

The chapter suggests that discourses generated during EU authorisations of genetically modified organisms (GMOs) reflect 'boundary work'[5] at the science/politics and the rationality/emotions interface. Distinctions – on a rhetorical level – not just between scientific and political knowledge, between 'facts' and 'interests', but also between emotive public policy debates and rational deliberation in administrative authorisations are central to EU GMO authorisations. But maintaining such boundaries is precarious. 'Boundary work' at the science/politics interface is unstable because scientific knowledge becomes embedded in political governance structures and economic contexts during EU GMO authorisations. Similarly, emotion discourses are not excluded from EU authorisations but are also mobilised through appeals to trust data, science and experts in the light of highly contested scientific claims about the safety of transgenic agricultural products.[6]

In developing these points, this chapter seeks to contribute to two key debates that have implications for how we perceive the relationship between international and public law in the field of risk regulation. The first debate is concerned with the limits and possibilities of a 'rationality project' in risk regulation, which seeks to distinguish between scientific knowledge and politics.[7] Such a distinction becomes a tool for the mediation of conflicts between international and public law arising from different values, such as economic efficiency underpinning free trade provisions in international law, and social protection values embodied in public law. The second debate addresses whether we can and should distinguish between scientific and democratic approaches to risk regulation.[8] It points in particular to the danger of international law

[4] Thomas Bernauer, *Genes, Trade and Regulation* (Princeton University Press, 2003) 168.

[5] See also above Chapter 5 by Jaye Ellis.

[6] Ian Sheldon, 'Regulation of Biotechnology: Will We Ever "Freely" Trade GMOs?' (2002) 29 *European Review of Agricultural Economics* 155, 160.

[7] Karen Litfin, *Ozone Discourses: Science and Politics in Global Environmental Cooperation* (Columbia University Press, New York, 1994) 5, 14; Thorsten Hüller and Matthias Leonhard Maier, 'Fixing the Codex? Global Food-Safety Governance under Review' in Christian Joerges and Ernst-Ulrich Petersmann (eds.), *Constitutionalism, Multilevel Trade Governance and Social Regulation* (Hart Publishing, Oxford, 2006) 267, 286 and 291; Ernst Haas, *When Knowledge Is Power: Three Models of Change in International Organizations* (University of California Press, Berkeley, 1990) 20 and 46.

[8] See, e.g., Joanne Scott, *The WTO Agreement on Sanitary and Phytosanitary Measures: A Commentary* (Oxford University Press, 2009) 4, 77; Hüller and Maier, above n. 7, 267, 294 and 296, who add to the science/democracy dichotomy a tension between national

undermining democratic choices through reliance on science[9] for striking a balance between free trade and social protection aims embedded in regional, such as EU, or national public law. While orientations towards either more scientific or democratic risk regulatory decision-making have been explained with reference to the origins of these styles of decision-making in different, often national traditions of administrative constitutionalism that constitute and legitimate public administration in different ways,[10] this chapter points to a different missing link between science and democracy. It perceives discourses invoked during EU GMO authorisations rather than constitutional traditions as key drivers of social action. By suggesting that both scientific discourses and democratic public policy debates at times involve the invocation of emotion discourses, the chapter directs attention to intersections between different types of knowledge and politics. This is based on the idea that the ability and opportunity to interpret reality is a major source of political power.[11] The chapter thus also contributes to accounts pointing to the limits of a narrowly conceived 'rationality project' in risk regulatory decision-making[12] by highlighting the importance of trust-based emotion discourses in facilitating EU GMO authorisations. This goes beyond traditional critiques of the rationality project which attribute the central role of science in risk regulatory decision-making not to the nature of scientific knowledge itself, but to decision-makers' *beliefs*, for instance, in 'evidence-based regulation'.[13]

Identifying limits to the 'rationality project' has implications for how we think about accountability for risk regulatory decision-making. Since each scientific claim usually generates a new scientific counter-statement,[14] science can only be a provisional basis for decision-making, valid only until new evidence and theories prove existing knowledge as limited or wrong. Knowledge can be mobilised in order to achieve specific policy objectives[15] and thus is not necessarily a source of legitimacy for risk regulation distinct from a political realm. The chapter also suggests that the structuring of arguments further exacerbates the legitimacy deficit of EU

democracy/international economic efficiency; Liz Fisher, 'Beyond the Science/Democracy Dichotomy: The World Trade Organization Sanitary and Phytosanitary Agreement and Administrative Constitutionalism' in Joerges and Petersmann (eds.), above n. 7, 327, 328.

9 Paul Street, 'Constructing Risks, GMOs, Biosafety and Environmental Decision-Making' in Han Somsen (ed.), *The Regulatory Challenge of Biotechnology: Human Genetics, Food and Patents* (Edward Elgar, Cheltenham, 2007) 102, 105.

10 Fisher, above n. 8, 328. 11 Litfin, above n. 7, 8. 12 Ibid. 4. 13 Ibid. 19.

14 Ibid. 36. 15 Ibid. 8.

GMO authorisations because this occurs below the radar of traditional judicial and administrative review. The performative power of discourse, in addition, undermines traditional EU law accountability mechanisms such as a duty of administrators to provide reasons for their decisions because decision-makers are constrained by the discursive frames in which they operate and which cannot be easily dislodged.

The chapter develops its argument in four parts. It first illustrates the significance of the rationality project by providing a brief introduction to the highly contested key arguments for and against GMO agricultural products raised in public policy debates. It also provides an introduction to the main features of a 'rational' bureaucratic system for deciding applications about the authorisation of transgenic agricultural products in the EU and outlines the Foucauldian discourse approach of this chapter. Section 4 of the chapter shows how formal EU law provisions that need to comply with legal obligations arising from World Trade Organization (WTO) Agreements steer arguments within EU GMO authorisations towards scientific discourses that focus upon the potential risks of transgenic agricultural products for human health and the environment.[16] This sidelines socio-economic and ethical considerations, and arguments not relying on natural scientific knowledge. Section 5 discusses different elements of 'scientific discourses', including 'pure', 'contextualised' and 'meta-scientific' knowledge. Section 6 suggests that the structuring of arguments within EU GMO authorisations constitutes a subtle exercise of public powers that is, however, insufficiently controlled through existing administrative EU law accountability mechanisms.

2. Background to debates about transgenic agriculture and its legal regulation in the EU

2.1 The GMO agriculture controversy

Transgenic agriculture has become possible through developments in biotechnology. After the discovery of the chemical structure of DNA, scientists have been able to insert genetic material from one living organism into another – also across species – or to delete genes, thereby

[16] For a further discussion of the dominance of scientific discourses in environmental regulation, see also above Chapter 5 by Jaye Ellis.

altering characteristics of the organism. For instance, genes have been transferred from fish into tomatoes in order to increase their resistance to frost.[17] Hence, transgenic agriculture seeks to optimise agricultural production through novel food and feed products, as well as through increased resistance of crops to pests and weeds.[18] Genetic engineering has also been applied to animals used for food consumption, such as fish whose growth has been accelerated.[19]

Public policy debates about transgenic agriculture are highly contentious. Arguments – sometimes voiced in emotive terms – have focused on its actual and perceived health, environmental and socio-economic impacts.[20] According to proponents of genetically modified (GM) agriculture, it can facilitate a 'second green revolution' and thus contribute to the resolution of the persistent problem of hunger in the developing world.[21] Moreover, GM drought-resistant food crops are seen as vital for adapting to climate change.[22] In the EU, France, Hungary, Bulgaria, Greece, Luxembourg, Germany, Ireland, Austria and Poland,[23] as well as sections of the UK population,[24] people are sceptical about the benefits of GM agriculture, despite its regulation since the early 1990s.[25] Opponents have highlighted potential risks of GM food to health – in

[17] Ed Wallis, 'Fish Genes into Tomatoes: How the World Regulates Genetically Modified Foods' (2004) 80 *North Dakota Law Review* 421.

[18] John Hofer *et al.*, *Yield Potential and Response of Roundup Ready Soybean Varieties to Raptor or Pursuit Herbicides* (1998) Kansas State University, www.biotech-info.net/herb_resist_ksu.pdf, last accessed 21 May 2011.

[19] Shao Jun Du *et al.*, 'Growth Enhancement in Transgenic Atlantic Salmon by the Use of an "All Fish" Chimeric Growth Hormone Gene Construct' (1992) 10 *Bio/Technology* 176

[20] Tom Horlick-Jones *et al.*, *A Deliberative Future? An Independent Evaluation of the GM Nation? Public Debate about the Possible Commercialisation of Transgenic Crops in Britain, 2003*, Understanding Risk Working Paper 04 02 (2004) 126.

[21] Terry Raney and Prahbu Pingali, 'Sowing a Gene Revolution' (2007) 297(3) *Scientific American* 104.

[22] Dick Taverne, *The March of Unreason: Science, Democracy, and the New Fundamentalism* (Oxford University Press, New York, 2005) 98.

[23] France sought to ban Monsanto's MON 810, but EFSA declared the decision to be based on insufficient scientific knowledge. Poland and Austria unsuccessfully sought to ban GM agriculture on their territory.

[24] United Kingdom, Agriculture and Environment Biotechnology Commission, *GM Nation? The Findings of a Public Debate* (Department of Trade and Industry, London, 2003).

[25] European Directive 90/220/EEC on the deliberate release of genetically modified organisms, European Directive 90/219/EEC on the contained use of genetically modified micro-organisms and European Directive 90/679/EEC on the protection of workers from the risks related to exposure to biological agents at work.

particular the digestive system,[26] allergic reactions and antibiotic immunity.[27] There are concerns about contamination of non-GM plants with GM varieties,[28] the displacement of indigenous plants, and the increase of weeds, and of pests tolerant to GM plants which are meant to repel them, giving rise to so-called 'superpests' and 'superweeds'. GM agriculture is also resisted because it is seen as threatening small-scale farming, encouraging a dependence on a narrow and privatised seed base, and because it is 'unnatural' and is meddling with 'nature'.[29] As will become apparent in this chapter, while the concerns about GM agriculture involve a broad range of arguments, EU authorisations are disciplined into a much narrower discussion referring principally to science and EU trade-based arguments.[30]

2.2 An introduction to EU regulation of transgenic agriculture

At the heart of the current EU legal regulatory framework is an authorisation requirement for transgenic agricultural products imported into the EU, cultivated in the EU, or circulated as a domestically produced GM good on the EU internal food and feed market.[31] The legal framework includes two key pieces of EU secondary legislation: the 'Food and Feed Regulation' (Regulation)[32] and the 'Deliberate Release Directive' (Directive).[33] Both pursue similar objectives by seeking to

[26] Stanley Ewen and Arpad Pusztai, 'Effect of Diets Containing Genetically Modified Potatoes Expressing Galanthus Nivalis Lectin on Rat Small Intestine' (1999) 354 *The Lancet* 1353.

[27] Anita Bakshi, 'Potential Adverse Health Effects of Genetically Modified Crops' (2003) 6 *Journal of Toxicology and Environmental Health, Part B Critical Reviews* 211.

[28] Genewatch UK, *Environmental Risks*, at www.genewatch.org/sub-532322, last accessed 17 July 2010.

[29] Vandana Shiva, 'Epilogue: Beyond Reductionism', in Vandana Shiva and Ingunn Moser (eds.), *Biopolitics: A Feminist and Ecological Reader on Biotechnology* (Zed Books, London, 1995) 267, 268.

[30] Similar experiences have been observed with respect to wind farm opposition. See Brad Jessup, 'Plural and Hybrid Environmental Values: A Discourse Analysis of the Wind Energy Conflict in Australia and the United Kingdom' (2010) 19 *Environmental Politics* 21.

[31] Experimental releases of GMOs, for instance for research purposes, are also regulated under Directive 2001/18/EC.

[32] European Council Regulation (EC) No. 1829/2003 on genetically modified food and feed.

[33] European Directive 2001/18/EC on the deliberate release into the environment of genetically modified organisms and repealing Council Directive 90/220/EEC. In fact, no authorisations for cultivation of GM crops have been granted so far under European Directive 2001/18/EC: GHK, above n. 3, 15, 23.

protect human health and the environment, with the Regulation adding protection of animal health, consumer interests and the functioning of the internal market as objectives.

In practice, most applications are processed under the Regulation. In order to limit bureaucratic burdens on biotechnology (or 'biotech') applicant companies, the European Commission has put in place a 'one door – one key' procedure.[34] Where a GMO is covered by both the Regulation and the Directive,[35] the applicant can file the whole application exclusively under the Regulation. The GMO is then assessed for compliance with the criteria of the Directive as well as those of the Regulation. This means that an environmental risk assessment will be required in the case of applications for cultivation – as this is the case for GMOs authorised under the Directive – as well as a safety assessment from the European Food Safety Authority (EFSA). At the end of this procedure a single authorisation will be granted for the GMO and all its uses, including cultivation in the case of plants or seeds, importation, and processing into food/feed or industrial products.

2.3 *A Foucauldian perspective on disciplining argumentation within EU GMO authorisations*

The analysis of the GMO authorisation procedures, in particular how they discipline arguments for and against transgenic agricultural products, is based on a Foucauldian perspective. This approach perceives discourses as disciplines in order to understand the structuring of argumentation in administrative authorisations.[36] It differs from other

[34] European Council Regulation No. 1829/2003/EC covers GMO food and feed, while European Directive 2001/18/EC deals with any type of agricultural GMO, including GM seeds. Some GMO agricultural products and their uses are covered by both the Regulation and the Directive.

[35] Such as in the case of a food product containing GMOs or consisting of GMOs, rather than food or feed produced from a GMO, such as cotton seed oil.

[36] The analysis draws on international and EU administrative law provisions, as well as a preliminary examination of the authorisation dossiers for the 31 GMO products that had been authorised by 6 July 2010 under the new regime that was established by the Food and Feed Regulation and the revised Deliberate Release Directive. The authorisation dossier, different elements of which are published on DG Sanco's, EFSA's and the EU COMPASS website, comprises a summary of the biotech company's application, an assessment report by a national competent authority in the case of applications under the Directive, the Commission Decision on the authorisation application, EFSA's scientific opinion, member states' comments in relation to EFSA's opinion and comments from EU citizens generated during the EU public consultation phase.

contributions to this edited collection that rely on a linguistic conception of discourse. According to the perspective adopted in this chapter discourses perform, rather than just represent, social action. They are defined as historically contingent fields of knowledge expressed, for instance, in talk and text, which generate effects of power.[37] They create the conditions for texts to be meaningful to social actors.[38] Hence, discourses are disciplinary practices located within specific bodies of knowledge and institutions of social control, like public administration.[39] They regulate what can be thought and said about a topic at a particular historical moment in time.

The chapter traces two sources of disciplinary discourses framing EU GMO authorisations. First, formal EU law steers what aspects of transgenic agricultural products can be considered within EU GMO authorisations.[40] This, in turn, is shaped by the EU's international legal obligations arising from the WTO Agreements.[41] Second, disciplinary discourses are also generated during actual communications in EU GMO authorisations. These are relatively independent from the formal legal framework and express the internal relations of power between participants in EU GMO authorisations, including entrenched institutional positions.[42] So, arguments about the pros and cons of transgenic agricultural products do not always emerge out of free and open communication between the various participants in EU GMO authorisations. For instance EFSA is cautious about informal, direct communications between its scientific officers and national experts on its GMO panel, and the national competent authorities and notifiers, in order not to compromise its 'independence' and 'objectivity'.[43] Moreover, EFSA usually provides only very brief written, stock responses in relation to EU

[37] Michel Foucault, 'What Is an Author?' in Colin Gordon (ed.), *Power/Knowledge: Selected Interviews and Other Writings, 1972–1977* (Pantheon Books, New York, 1980) 101, 110.

[38] Alex McHoul and Wendy Grace, *A Foucault Primer: Discourse, Power and the Subject* (New York University Press, 1997) 22.

[39] Ibid. 26.

[40] Joanne Scott, 'European Regulation of GMOs and the WTO' (2003) 9 *Columbia Journal of European Law* 213.

[41] Joanne Scott, *European Regulation of GMOs: Thinking About Judicial Review in the WTO*, Jean Monnet Working Paper 04/04, New York University School of Law (2004) 7. See also Preambles 13 to European Directive 2001/18/EC and 43 to European Council Regulation (EC) No. 1829/2003.

[42] Vivienne Schmidt and Claudio Radaelli, 'Policy Change and Discourse in Europe: Conceptual and Methodological Issues' (2004) 27 *West European Politics* 183.

[43] GHK, above n. 3, 49.

member states' comments on scientific opinions about specific transgenic agricultural products. EFSA frequently states that it has no jurisdiction to engage with member states' comments, particularly if they raise socio-economic arguments.[44] Some member states therefore no longer comment on EFSA's scientific opinions.[45] Others engage in limited communication, repeating the same comments about EFSA's scientific opinions for different applications.[46] This strategy is also occasionally adopted by citizens and environmental non-governmental organisations (NGOs) in relation to EFSA's opinions and applicants' environmental risk assessments.[47] The following section further illustrates the theme of limited communication by showing how discourses generated through the formal legal framework and within EU GMO authorisations turn scientific risk assessments into the main basis for argumentation.

3. Structuring arguments for and against GMO products through the EU legal framework: a limited role for 'other legitimate' and ethical considerations

Risk assessments provide the main grounds for the pros and cons of GMO products to be debated within the EU GMO authorisation procedure. Article 6(3) of the European Council Regulation (EC) No. 178/2002 (Food Law Regulation) enables 'other legitimate factors' to be taken into account in risk management decisions in relation to food safety. Hence, only the Food and Feed Regulation, not the Deliberate Release Directive, provides legal grounds for taking 'other legitimate factors' into account in risk management decisions. According to Article 7(1) of the Food and Feed Regulation, the European Commission takes into account three factors – ranked on an equal level – when preparing its draft decision on the authorisation of a specific GM agricultural product: EFSA's opinion; any relevant provisions of EC law; and 'other legitimate factors relevant to the matter under consideration'. Given the wording of the provision, the Commission may even be *required* to consider other legitimate factors. Citizens and member states sometimes raise socio-economic arguments during authorisations, suggesting there is no market for the GMO product or that it would

[44] Only three out of twenty-two member states who responded to a questionnaire were satisfied with the way in which EFSA deals with their comments: GHK, above n. 3, 5.
[45] Ibid., 36. [46] Ibid. 46. [47] Ibid. 8.

detrimentally affect existing markets in organic food and feed. Some also comment on the potentially negative impact of GM agriculture on the diversity of farming systems in the EU, ranging from small-scale subsistence farming to large farms, as well as the potentially negative impact of GM agriculture on sustainable development.[48]

Nevertheless, there is hardly any consideration of 'other legitimate factors' in EU GMO authorisations.[49] Most applications approved by the Commission are based firmly on EFSA's positive scientific opinion. Hence, science is the dominant discursive frame for arguments advanced in EU GMO authorisations, even more so than the text of the Regulation and the Directive warrant.

Ethical arguments are also limited within EU GMO authorisations.[50] The formal EU legal framework only contemplates consideration of ethical issues of a *general* nature, rather than ethics *in relation to* specific GMO products that are being authorised.[51] This limitation was seized upon by Poland in its defence to an enforcement action brought by the European Commission under the European Community Treaty.[52] The Commission challenged the Polish National Law on Seeds that prevented the marketing of GM seeds in Poland, even though the seed distributors had received authorisation under the Deliberate Release Directive for EU-wide sales.[53] Poland argued that it should be allowed to rely on the 'public morals' ground of Article 30 of the EC Treaty,[54] because the Deliberate Release Directive provided limited consideration

48 For instance, citizens during the EU public consultation phase for maize 1507 suggested that authorisation of this transgenic agricultural product would destroy organic crop markets in the EU, as well as conventional honey production. Similarly, citizens during the EU public consultation phase for maize BT 11 suggested that there is no market for these GM crops in the EU.

49 Author interview with DG Sanco official, DG Sanco, 21 November 2008.

50 See also Mihail Kritikos, 'Traditional Risk Analysis and Release of GMOs into the European Union: Space for Non-Scientific Factors?' (2009) 34 *European Law Review* 405, 414.

51 Article 29(1) Deliberate Release Directive.

52 Now Article 258 of the Treaty of Lisbon amending the Treaty on European Union and the Treaty establishing the European Community on the Functioning of the European Union, opened for signature 13 December 2007 Lisbon (entered into force 1 December 2009)('Treaty on the Functioning of the European Union'). *Commission of the European Communities* v. *Republic of Poland* (Case C-165/08) [2009] ECR I-6843.

53 The European Court of Justice declared as admissible only that part of the Commission's complaint that alleged infringement by Poland of Articles 22 and 23 of European Directive 2001/18/EC.

54 Now Article 36 of the Treaty on the Functioning of the European Union.

of ethical issues in EU GMO authorisations and that therefore no full harmonisation of the authorisation procedure in relation to ethical issues had occurred. Poland's claim was rejected by the European Court of Justice, holding that the real purposes of the Polish law were closely linked to the main objectives of the Deliberate Release Directive; the protection of human health and the environment. Full harmonisation regarding these objectives had occurred through the Deliberate Release Directive and Poland could not rely on any derogation of 'public morals' under Article 30 of the EC Treaty.

Article 33(1) of the Food and Feed Regulation provides a legal power for the Commission to consider ethical issues in EU GMO authorisations. It is, however, phrased in very general terms. The Commission can consult the European Group on Ethics in Science and New Technologies or 'any other appropriate body it might establish'. It can consult either upon its own initiative or upon request of a member state in order to obtain advice on ethical issues. In practice, ethical arguments play even less of a role in authorisations of specific GMO products than socio-economic ones. The European Group on Ethics in Science and New Technologies is not consulted with reference to specific GMO applications,[55] rather, only in relation to wider issues, like the general topic of 'ethics of modern developments in agriculture technologies'.[56] Hence, a scientific discourse is in practice a key frame for arguments in EU GMO authorisations. This focus on scientific knowledge about the potential human health and environmental risks posed by GM agriculture is also a central feature of the international legal framework shaping the EU legal framework. Indeed, the international trade law framework seeks to limit barriers to free trade in transgenic agricultural products, restricting the argumentative space against the authorisation of specific GMO agricultural products.

4. Structuring arguments for and against GMO agricultural products through the international law framework

International trade law steers the EU legal framework by limiting EU powers for restricting trade in transgenic agricultural products and by

[55] Author interview with DG Sanco official, DG Sanco, 21 November 2008.

[56] European Group on Ethics in Science and New Technologies to the European Commission, *Ethics of Modern Developments in Agricultural Technologies*, Opinion No. 24, 17 December 2008.

foregrounding a scientific discourse as the main knowledge base for the pros and cons of transgenic agricultural products to be debated.[57] The powers of the EU to restrict international trade in GMO agricultural products, for instance through non-tariff barriers, are limited by the legal obligations imposed by three WTO Agreements: the General Agreement on Tariffs and Trade (GATT);[58] the Sanitary and Phytosanitary (SPS) Agreement;[59] and the Agreement on Technical Barriers to Trade (TBT Agreement).[60] The SPS Agreement deals with sanitary and phytosanitary measures imposed for the purposes of protecting human, animal and plant life.[61] It applies to restrictions upon the free trade of GMO agricultural products because it captures 'processes and production methods', here the genetic modification of agricultural products.[62] The TBT Agreement covers 'technical regulations', such as product specifications and labelling requirements.

4.1 Limiting arguments against the authorisation of GMO products: the presumption of free trade

These international agreements prioritise free trade, which is presumed to benefit all trading partners.[63] For instance, Articles I and III of the GATT suggest that its main purpose is to ensure free trade between its members. Article I imposes a non-discrimination obligation, whereby imports from WTO members must be treated no less favourably than imports from other states. Article III requires that imported products should not be treated less favourably than domestic products. The WTO Agreements construct social objectives – upon which the authorisation

57 Scott, above n. 8, 2.

58 General Agreement on Tariffs and Trade 1994, opened for signature 15 April 1994, 55 UNTS 194, 1867 UNTS 187 (entered into force 1 January 1995).

59 Sanitary and Phytosanitary Measures Agreement, opened for signature 15 April 1994, 1867 UNTS 493 (entered into force 1 January 1 1995).

60 Agreement on Technical Barriers to Trade, opened for signature 15 April 1994, 1868 UNTS 120 (entered into force 1 January 1995).

61 The SPS Agreement is a specific elaboration of the general exception to free trade under Article XX(b) of the GATT. It is, however, an autonomous agreement, so that no prior breach of the GATT need be established in order for the SPS Agreement to apply. Scott, above n. 8, 10.

62 Ibid., 11.

63 Ernst-Ulrich Petersmann, 'Introduction', in Joerges and Petersmann (eds.), above n. 7, xxxviii.

of transgenic agricultural products can be restricted – as exceptions to free trade.

EU or national restrictions on the trade in GMO agricultural products that are not lawful measures under the SPS or TBT Agreements, discussed below, must instead comply with Article III of the GATT. Article III shapes arguments within EU GMO authorisations by directing attention to the question whether the GM food/feed to be authorised for importation into the EU, and non-GM food/feed already marketed within the EU, can be considered nutritionally alike.[64] A scientific debate about plant and food/feed composition ensues, rather than a debate on the wider risks, benefits and ethics of GMO products.

The public morals exception in Article XX(a) of the GATT is limited. Purely *national* moral perspectives on GMOs not based on a wider, *international* moral consensus may not suffice to justify trade restrictions.[65] It is questionable whether EU member state citizens' moral objections to transgenic agriculture meet this standard. Similarly, criticisms of interference with natural plant reproductive cycles and the potentially negative distributional impacts of transgenic agriculture on conventional and organic farmers are sidelined. Moreover, the WTO Panel's decision in the *EC–Biotech* case further limited arguments against GMO authorisations by declaring the delaying of authorisations in order to respond to EU citizens who are opposed to transgenic agriculture is not possible under the terms of the SPS Agreement.[66]

Restrictions to free trade must be based on the more specific exemptions provided by the SPS and TBT Agreements, rather than general exceptions in Article XX(a) and (b) of the GATT.[67] The SPS Agreement grants states the right to take 'sanitary and phytosanitary measures necessary for the protection of human, animal, or plant life or health'. The TBT Agreement enables measures to be taken for the protection of consumer welfare, such as labelling requirements.

[64] For instance, during the public consultation phase for GM maize 11, EU citizens asserted that GM maize 11 could not be considered as substantially equivalent to non-GM maize, because studies considered during authorisation of GM maize 11 in Canada showed differences in ash, protein and carbohydrate content in the GM and non-GM maize. The Canadian regulator, however, deemed these to be insignificant. The question of substantial equivalence was also discussed during the authorisation procedure for LL Cotton 25.

[65] Maria Lee, *EU Regulation of GMOs* (Edward Elgar, Cheltenham, 2008) 195.

[66] Ibid., 204. See below n. 80. [67] Scott, above n. 8, 29.

The SPS Agreement spells out a specific range of grounds upon which states can adopt trade restricting measures, for example, for protecting animal or plant life or health from certain risks, such as the entry, establishment and spread of pests, diseases or additives, toxins and disease-causing organisms in foods, or diseases carried by animals within the territory of the member. Further, the state adopting an SPS Agreement measure has the right to determine the appropriate level of protection,[68] which may include departing from international standards.[69] However, only *necessary* SPS Agreement measures can be taken,[70] and any unnecessary measures, even if they only have potential, rather than actual trade effects, will infringe the agreement.[71] Measures are necessary when it is not possible to take less trade-restrictive 'reasonably available' measures. Moreover, derogating measures must not be applied 'in a manner which would constitute a means of arbitrary or unjustifiable discrimination between countries where the same conditions prevail, or a disguised restriction on international trade'.[72]

Similar to the test under the SPS Agreement for acceptable trade restrictive measures, Article 2.2 of the TBT Agreement stipulates that a lawful technical regulation will not be more trade restrictive than necessary in order to fulfil an objective of the agreement.

4.2 International law foregrounds scientific knowledge

International trade agreements do not just curtail the grounds upon which free trade in GMO agricultural products can be limited, they also shape how arguments for and against GMO products can be made.

The SPS Agreement requires a science-based discussion of advantages and disadvantages of specific GMO products in order for states to be able to enact necessary restrictive measures.[73] Measures that restrict free trade must be:

> based on an assessment, as appropriate to the circumstances, of the risk to human, animal or plant life or health, *taking into account risk assessment techniques developed by the relevant international organizations.*[74]

[68] SPS Agreement, Art. 5(5). [69] Scott, above n. 8, 6 and 35.
[70] SPS Agreement, Art. 5(5). [71] Scott, above n. 8, 26. [72] GATT, Art. XX.
[73] Naveen Thayyil, 'Deliberative Turning from a Law–Science Cul-de-Sac: Speculations regarding Community Transgenic Regulation' [2008] *Yearbook of European Environmental Law* 153.
[74] Emphasis added. SPS Agreement, Art. 5(1).

There must be an objective and rational relationship between the risk assessment and the SPS Agreement measure.[75] Moreover, an SPS measure must be based on 'scientific principles' and cannot be 'maintained without sufficient scientific evidence'.[76] The *EC–Biotech* WTO Panel's decision further privileged scientific knowledge by stating that the precautionary principle referred to in Article 5.7 of the SPS Agreement could only be invoked in cases where there is insufficient *scientific* evidence. In contrast to this, Lee[77] has argued that application of the precautionary principle should also be triggered if cultural or social information is limited.

In addition, the *EC–Biotech* WTO Panel ruled that members of the SPS Agreement cannot justify national safeguard measures on the basis of objections to the *procedures* adopted for carrying out centralised risk assessments, such as those carried out by EFSA.[78] *Evaluations* of risk assessments are not a risk assessment under Article 5.1 of the SPS Agreement and therefore cannot be relied on as the basis for national safeguard measures. Further, in cases of disputes about the lawfulness of a member's SPS Agreement measures, the WTO Panel and the Appellate Body can rely on advice by scientific experts in order to assess claims that SPS Agreement measures are justified by sufficiently robust scientific risk assessments.[79] Hence, scientific knowledge is also an important element in decisions of the international dispute resolution bodies.

This emphasis on scientific knowledge as the main frame for marshalling arguments both for and against GMO agricultural products within EU GMO authorisations is further strengthened by the Cartagena Protocol on Biosafety. Preamble 13 to the Deliberate Release Directive and Preamble 43 to the Food and Feed Regulation both state that they take into account the legal requirements of the Cartagena Protocol on Biosafety. In the *EC–Biotech* case, the WTO Panel decided that the protocol could shed light on the 'ordinary meaning' of the provisions of the SPS Agreement.[80] The protocol regulates export and import of 'living modified organisms' through a requirement of 'advanced informed

[75] Scott, above n. 8, 105. [76] SPS Agreement, Art. 2(2). [77] Lee, above n. 65, 222.

[78] Scott, above n. 8, 108, especially the discussion on Panel Report: *European Communities – Measures Affecting the Approval and Marketing of Biotech Products* [8.23]–[8.45].

[79] Ibid. 135.

[80] World Trade Organization (WTO), *European Communities – Measures Affecting the Approval and Marketing of Biotech Products*, WTO Document WT/DS 291 R, WT/DS 292 R, WT/DS 293 R (2006), Panel Report [7.92]–[7.95].

agreement'.[81] This advanced informed agreement must be based on a risk assessment carried out 'in a scientifically sound manner . . . [taking] into account recognised risk assessment techniques'.[82]

To summarise, EU and international law, as well as discourses generated within EU GMO authorisations, restrict argumentative space, both in terms of limiting the grounds upon which the advantages of and objections to specific transgenic agricultural products can be debated, as well as the way in which arguments can be marshalled – through a focus on a scientific discourse. The following section discusses in further detail the type of scientific arguments actually deployed in EU GMO authorisations. It shows that argumentation is further narrowed because of an entrenched preference for certain discursive forms of scientific knowledge.

5. Fragmented scientific discourses: from pure, to contextualised to meta-scientific

From a discourse perspective, scientific knowledge constitutes a disciplinary power. This perspective draws attention to rhetorical features of scientific knowledge, moving it closer to forms of everyday communication, such as argumentation and persuasion.[83] This section questions the knowledge/politics, power dichotomy by further developing social constructivist understandings of knowledge. The starting point is a non-positivist understanding of knowledge, where knowledge is not considered as a body of concrete and objective facts but as reflecting specific interests. That scientific knowledge is embedded in relations of power also becomes apparent through its categorisation into 'accepted' and 'rejected' knowledge.[84] This section illustrates within the specific context of EU GMO authorisations the idea that discourses do not consist of homogeneous, uniform thought constructs, but are

[81] Sheldon, above n. 6, 155 and 164.

[82] Cartagena Protocol to the Convention on Biological Diversity, opened for signature 15 May 2000, 2226 UNTS 208 (entered into force 11 September 2003) (Cartagena Protocol), Arts. 10 and 15. But the *grounds of debate* are widened by the Cartagena Protocol, because according to Article 26, countries can consider any socio-economic considerations in their assessments of the impact of living modified organisms on biological diversity, and in particular on the value of biological diversity for indigenous and local communities.

[83] Litfin, above n. 7, 15. [84] Ibid. 25.

characterised by relations of difference and equivalence.[85] One important relation of difference characterising scientific discourses invoked in EU GMO authorisations is a rhetorical distinction between scientific and emotion discourses in public policy debates. According to a recent report by the European Parliament:

> GMOs are often perceived by society in a very emotional way not necessarily based on scientific grounds. Member States should address this issue in a practical and rational [. . .] rather than political way.[86]

From a descriptive perspective, emotion discourses involve the use of emotive terms that constitute a break in register with a more sober, neutral tone for presenting arguments for and against agricultural GMO products. Examples are 'suicide seeds' and 'frankenstein foods' to describe transgenic agricultural products. From a functional perspective, emotion discourses consist of arguments that seek to generate an emotional response. For instance, during the authorisation of maize 1507, one heading of an EU citizen's submission reads: 'Monsanto and Bayer – the matrix of death – using food as a weapon'. The statement continues to assert that 'they [the biotech companies] will even make money out of death' and concludes that biotech companies cannot be 'trusted'.[87] The emotional response encouraged is one of distrust and disgust.

Nevertheless, emotion discourses advancing arguments against GMO products are disciplined because a scientific discourse with its own particular rationality is dominant in EU GMO authorisations. The requirement of international and EU law to justify trade restrictive measures with reference to scientific risk assessments by itself does not exclude the possibility of taking into account emotive arguments against GMO agricultural products based, for instance, on fears relating to that risk.[88] However, emotion discourses, mostly advanced by applicants, invoking trust in science, scientific data, experts and regulatory procedures are at the heart of EU GMO authorisations. Emotion discourses are also evident when biotech applicants and EFSA avoid the terms

[85] Jacob Torfing, *New Theories of Discourse: Laclau, Mouffe and Žižek* (Blackwell, Oxford, 1999), 99.

[86] European Parliament Committee on the Environment, Public Health and Food Safety, *Draft Report on the Implementation of EU Legislation on GMOs, in Particular Directive 2001/18/EC and Regulations (EC) No. 1829/2003 and 1830/2003* (2008) 4.

[87] Comments from members of the public in relation to GM maize 1507.

[88] Scott, above n. 8, 79.

'uncertainty' and 'risk' by EFSA calling its evaluations of applications '*safety*' rather than 'risk' assessments.[89]

Discourses invoked in EU GMO authorisations can, however, also be described as relational not just with reference to the rhetorical binary between 'emotion' and 'scientific' discourses, but also through relationships between various types of scientific knowledge invoked. In particular 'pure', 'contextualised' and 'meta-scientific' science discourses are mobilised in EU authorisations. Tensions exist especially between 'pure' and 'contextualised' scientific discourses since they are founded on different ideas about the certainty and scope of scientific knowledge claims.

5.1 'Pure' scientific knowledge

'Pure' scientific knowledge is generated on the basis of universal laws. It is objective and distinct from cultural, political and economic ways of knowing the social world.[90] It constitutes a value-free 'truth' and can be used in an instrumental manner as a justification for risk regulation decisions. 'Pure' scientific knowledge can be distinguished from 'advocacy science', which employs rhetoric in order to support specific political interest positions.[91]

This conception of 'pure' scientific knowledge seems to be invoked in Article 2.2 of the SPS Agreement and its interpretation through the WTO Panel. In the *Japan Apples* case, non-scientific knowledge was seen as based on a 'non-demonstrated hypothesis' in contrast to scientific knowledge.[92] Moreover, the *EC–Biotech* WTO Panel required actual knowledge, not mere probabilities about risks, in its ruling about the Austrian safeguard measures for GM maize T25.[93]

This conception of 'pure' scientific knowledge is also reflected in the legal provisions of the Deliberate Release Directive and the Food and Feed Regulation, that downplay uncertainty in scientific knowledge. These provisions emphasise the capacity of scientific knowledge to identify and inform solutions to any potential risks arising from GMOs.[94] For instance, the environmental risk assessment to be carried

89 GHK, above n. 3, 37.

90 Scott, above n. 8, 77, 78, 87 and 107.

91 Connie Ozawa, *Recasting Science: Consensual Procedures in Public Policy Making* (Westview Press, Boulder, 1991).

92 *Japan Apples* (Panel) [8.92]–[8.93], discussed in Scott, above n. 8, 86.

93 WTO, above n. 80, [7.30].

94 Les Levidow, 'The Transatlantic Agbiotech Conflict as a Problem and Opportunity for EU Regulatory Policies' in Robert Falkner (ed.), *The International Politics of Genetically Modified Food* (Palgrave Macmillan, Basingstoke, 2007) 134.

out under the Deliberate Release Directive is supposed to capture *any* risks generated by different causal pathways, as well as risks generated over long time periods. Article 2(8) provides:

> Environmental risk assessment means the evaluation of risk to human health and the environment, *whether direct or indirect, immediate or delayed*, which the deliberate release or the placing on the market of GMOs may pose and carried out in accordance with Annex II. (Emphasis added.)

Similarly, Preamble 9 to the Food and Feed Regulation states:

> Thus, genetically modified food and feed should only be authorised for placing on the Community market after *a scientific evaluation of the highest possible standard*, to be undertaken under the responsibility of the European Food Safety Authority, of *any risks* which they present for human and animal health and, as the case may be, for the environment. (Emphasis added.)

A positivist conception of 'pure' scientific knowledge is further buttressed through a distinction between risk assessment and risk management as two separate phases within EU GMO authorisations under the Directive and the Regulation. The main institutional actors in the risk assessment phase – the national competent authorities and EFSA – deliberate the pros and cons of the authorisation of a GMO product on the basis of scientific knowledge. EFSA's opinion and the national assessment reports are then considered in a separate risk management phase by political actors.

5.2 *'Contextualised' scientific knowledge*

The distinction between scientific risk assessment and political risk management is blurred in practice because scientific knowledge becomes embedded in political governance structures. Final political decision-making by the Commission on GMO authorisation applications seems to be closely aligned with, and deferential to, the scientific phase of risk assessment. In most of the GMO authorisations for the thirty-one products so far authorised, the Commission[95] has agreed with EFSA's opinion. This is compounded by the EU member states marginalising themselves in the comitology and Council phase of decision-making. Most of the time they do not form qualified majorities either against or

[95] By 16 August 2010.

for the authorisation of GMOs within the required three-month period. Consequently, they hand over the main institutional decision-making power to EFSA and the Commission. In addition, legally non-binding guidance for EFSA on how to carry out risk assessments further whittles away the distinction between risk assessment and risk management by turning the availability of risk management strategies into an issue relevant for the assessment of risks. That guidance states: 'an evaluation of the overall risk of the GMO should be made taking into account any risk management strategies which are proposed'.[96] However, applicants only ever identify risks to a limited extent, so the risk management measures to date have mainly been limited to general surveillance requirements in relation to GMO releases.[97]

Power relationships between the different participants in EU GMO authorisations are implicated in the generation of scientific knowledge. The EU legal framework determines whose scientific knowledge should count, at what level of governance scientific knowledge should be produced, and how disagreements over scientific knowledge should be handled. For instance, it is the applicant who supplies an environmental risk assessment but also has an interest in the favourable outcome of its application.[98] Moreover, the centralisation of risk assessments at the EU level under the Food and Feed Regulation reflects a preference for harmonised and consensus-based knowledge rather than an open recognition of a plurality of different scientific views of risk in the various EU member states and among their citizens.

Closer examination of the Regulation and the Directive suggests that scientific knowledge is not as 'pure' as supposed, but 'contextualised' also through the economic contexts in which the knowledge is embedded, in particular through the consideration of the costs of producing scientific knowledge.[99] For instance, according to Article 13(2) of the Deliberate Release Directive, applicants can propose that they will not provide certain types of information in their application, such as measures to be taken in the case of the unintended release or misuse of the GMO,

[96] Step 6 referred to in [4.2.6] of European Decision 2002/623/EC establishing guidance notes supplementing Annex II to Directive 2001/18/EC of the European Parliament and of the Council on the deliberate release into the environment of genetically modified organisms and repealing Council Directive 90/220/EEC.

[97] GHK, above n. 3, 41.

[98] Ibid. 33. Environmental NGOs and some member states have described data submitted by applicants as 'biased and of poor quality'.

[99] Hüller and Maier, above n. 7, 279.

instructions or recommendations for storage and handling, further instructions for monitoring, as well as proposed restrictions on the use of the GMO. This provision can be invoked if the applicant thinks that the GMO does not pose risks to human health and the environment on the basis of results from previous experimental releases of the GMO or 'other substantive reasoned scientific grounds'.

The embedding of scientific discourses into economic contexts is significant for the practical operation of EU GMO authorisations. Despite an increase in the number of applications, no additional resources have been allocated to EFSA.[100] Cost, including time considerations, also limits the amount and quality of information that biotech companies provide in their applications. This is a major issue in EU GMO authorisations. Significant delays still occur because it is necessary to 'stop the clock' during authorisations in order to obtain further information from applicants.[101] In addition, a lack of human resources means member states have been reluctant to volunteer to evaluate risk assessments when asked by EFSA.[102] This has generated a distinct pattern of eight member states providing scientific knowledge for risk assessments, with Spain alone having reviewed four applications. This leads to a potentially narrow scientific knowledge base for the risks of GMO products to be evaluated. Member states mainly draw on information about their own specific regional environmental and agro-economic conditions when evaluating risks posed by GMOs, although the application seeks release of the GMO into the territory of the whole of the EU.[103]

5.3 *'Meta-scientific' knowledge*

Meta-scientific knowledge provides a further departure from the idealised conception of 'pure' scientific knowledge and its rhetorical appeal. It is concerned with the interpretation and evaluation of scientific knowledge about potential risks posed by GMOs. This evaluation of especially politically potentially contentious scientific knowledge can occur through 'knowledge brokers'.[104] They can be environmental NGOs, businesses or civil servants.[105] Interpretation of existing scientific studies – a key aspect of the production of 'meta-scientific' knowledge – becomes particularly important in light of significant scientific uncertainty about the long-term effects of GMO agricultural products.[106] By

[100] GHK, above n. 3, 3, 4 and 27. [101] Ibid. 42. [102] Ibid. 3, 29 and 34. [103] Ibid. 34.
[104] Litfin, above n. 7, 5. [105] Ibid. 37. [106] Sheldon, above n. 6, 160.

providing a critical perspective on scientific claims about the impacts of GMOs this meta-discourse opens up debate about the risks of GMOs and allows for more expression of uncertainty within scientific knowledge than the 'pure' science perspective expressed in the formal legal framework and in some submissions during authorisations. For instance, this meta-discourse addresses whether a sufficient number of studies have been carried out in an appropriate range of geographical and climatic regions.[107] This matters because the number of field trials[108] providing scientific knowledge for evaluating the release of GMOs on a commercial scale is declining in the EU. Moreover, field trials are increasingly concentrated in just a few EU member states because of significant opposition to trials by citizens.[109] A scientific meta-discourse also questions the degree to which it is possible to extrapolate from animal GM feeding studies involving earthworms, mice, rabbits and birds[110] to impacts on animal as well as human health and biodiversity more generally.

To conclude, the scientific discourses invoked during EU GMO authorisations in their 'pure', 'contextualised' and 'meta-scientific' dimensions are performative. They structure what can be said about transgenic agricultural products by disciplining discourses that refer to socio-economic impacts of transgenic agriculture and its ethical challenges. This disciplining of the debate within EU GMO authorisations constitutes an exercise of public power, raising questions about its legitimacy and accountability. The following section argues that on their own terms, but in particular from a discourse perspective, traditional EU judicial and administrative review seems to be of limited relevance for ensuring the accountability and legitimacy of the structuring of debate within EU GMO authorisations.

6. Disciplining arguments: challenging traditional EU accountability tools

The structuring and disciplining of arguments further exacerbates an already existing legitimacy deficit of EU GMO authorisations. Current authorisations have limited legitimacy because they rely significantly on

[107] See, for instance, the arguments raised by the Scientific Committee on Food in relation to the authorisation of BT maize 11.

[108] Authorised under Part B of European Directive 2001/18/EC.

[109] GHK, above n. 3, 5. [110] Such as bobwhile quails and laying hens.

scientific expertise, closing off deliberation to those without the qualifications to evaluate or marshal scientific expertise, notably the majority of EU citizens.[111] According to the Court of First Instance,[112] scientific legitimacy is not necessarily 'a sufficient basis for the exercise of public authority'.[113] Most importantly, EU member states' approach to the current decision-making procedures for EU GMO authorisations creates a significant legitimacy deficit. Member states do not build qualified majorities either for or against Commission proposals for authorisation of GMO agricultural products in the regulatory comitology committee and in the Council within the required three-month limit for applications processed under the Food and Feed Regulation.[114] Hence, transgenic agricultural products are currently mainly[115] authorised through a default comitology procedure under which the Commission – an appointed and mainly executive organ of the EU – decides, and most of the time approves its own draft proposals for authorisation submitted by applicants under the Food and Feed Regulation.

6.1 Disciplining arguments below the radar of judicial and administrative review?

This significant legitimacy deficit is exacerbated because traditional EU accountability tools appear to be very limited in controlling discursive narrowing of the grounds of debate. Even after the Treaty on the Functioning of the European Union's modest reforms of standing criteria for EU citizens and environmental groups, access to the European courts is still very limited, and under Article 263 generally requires

[111] Lee, above n. 65, 253; Tamara Hervey, 'Regulation of Genetically Modified Products in a Multi-Level System of Governance: Science or Citizens?' (2001) 10 *Review of European Community and International Environmental Law* 321.

[112] Now called the 'General Court' according to the Treaty on the Functioning of the European Union.

[113] *Pfizer Animal Health SA* v. *Council of the European Union* (Case T-13/99) [2002] ECR II-03305, [201].

[114] In the current debate about the reform of EU GMO authorisations, a broadening of the debate to include socio-economic concerns is seen to allow member states to 'address political issues' and thus to break the deadlock in voting patterns. GHK, above n. 3, 15.

[115] In all of the authorisation procedures for the so-far thirty-one authorised GMO products, the Commission has decided upon its own proposals. It has put forward a proposal for a regulation, COM(2010) 380 final, C(2010) 4822 final, which would enable member states to restrict the cultivation of GMO crops in their territory and thus address the current blockage of EU-wide decisions on cultivation.

non-privileged applicants, such as citizens, to show a 'direct and individual concern'.

More importantly, none of the substantive grounds of review referred to in Article 263 of the Treaty on the Functioning of the European Union, including the duty to provide a careful, diligent and impartial examination of the matter to be decided, the right to be heard, a duty to give reasons and a violation of the precautionary principle, seem to limit the subtle structuring and disciplining of argumentation within EU GMO authorisations.[116] The principle of a careful, diligent and impartial examination requires the Commission to examine the relevant factual and legal aspects of the individual case.[117] Claimants have been able to rely on this principle where they could marshal 'facts' that questioned those facts that had been the basis for the Commission's decision.[118] In the case of EU GMO authorisations, this may require applicants to produce scientific studies that point to new risks of GMO products that have not been considered by the Commission or EFSA. But this option is also limited by the fact that the Court of First Instance is reluctant to allow the Commission to depart from scientific advice, such as EFSA's scientific opinion.[119]

In addition, grounds of internal administrative review provide limited control of the subtle structuring and disciplining of arguments within EU GMO authorisations. Article 36 of the Food and Feed Regulation grants the European Commission a power of administrative review of EFSA's decisions or failure by EFSA to take a decision,[120] but it does not articulate the grounds for this internal review. It also seems unlikely that a subtle structuring of arguments by EFSA, for instance through refusals to accede to member state requests for additional studies that assess the risks of GMOs, will constitute a manifest error, which could potentially be challenged through Article 36.

116 Alexander Fritzsche, 'Discretion, Scope of Judicial Review and Institutional Balance in European Law' (2010) 47 *Common Market Law Review*, 361, 367, 374 and 393.

117 Paul Craig, *EU Administrative Law* (Oxford University Press, 2006) 374.

118 See, e.g., *Nölle* v. *Hauptzollamt Bremen-Freihafen* (Case C-16/90) [1991] ECR I-5163.

119 *France* v. *Commission* (Case T-257/07 R) [2007] ECR II-4153. For a further discussion, see Alberto Alemanno and Stephanie Mahieu, 'The European Food Safety Authority before the European Courts' (2008) 5 *European Food and Feed Law Review* 320.

120 The Commission can act upon its own initiative or upon request from a member state or any person directly and individually concerned.

6.2 *The mediation of public power by discourses raises questions about the relevance of traditional accountability tools*

Finally, from a Foucauldian perspective, it becomes questionable whether traditional EU accountability tools can really restrain the exercise of public power significantly mediated by discourses. Traditional accountability tools are underpinned by the modernist assumption that there are individual administrative 'actors' who can be held accountable for the exercise of specific public powers. Moreover, grounds of judicial and administrative review are based on a representational understanding of social reality. Those who exercise public powers are held accountable by being required to produce narratives that tell 'the truth' about how and why an administrative decision was arrived at, for instance through the requirement to give reasons. These accounts are expected to represent what really happened when an administrative decision was taken. By being subjected to judicial or internal administrative scrutiny they are turned into a tool for controlling future administrative decisions that may be required to conform more closely to standards of good and lawful administrative behaviour.

But from a Foucauldian perspective, discourses in their own right are performative and cannot simply be used strategically by social actors. They cannot necessarily control administrative decision-making through traditional accountability tools, for instance, through the requirement to produce accountability narratives that conform to legal expectations of giving appropriate reasons for decisions or carrying out diligent and careful examination of relevant, including scientific, facts.[121] Speech – one element of the production of discourses – is not the expression of an autonomous subject, but is determined by the way institutions are structured. In the case of EU GMO authorisations, the systems of communication construct the authorisation process and determine what can be said in a particular context.[122] So it is that 'language speaks through the person'.[123] Social 'actors' such as administrators and other participants in EU GMO authorisations cannot

[121] Michel Foucault, 'Chapter 5: 2 Lectures', in Gordon (ed.), above n. 37, 80, 92.

[122] Torfing, above n. 85, 89.

[123] Louise Phillips and Marianne Jørgensen, *Discourse Analysis as Theory and Method* (Sage Publications, London, 2002) 14 and 15. This goes back to Althusser's idea of 'interpellation', according to which language constructs a social location for an individual. Language recruits individuals into particular subject positions. Althusser saw no possibility for individuals to resist these subject positions, while Foucault thought that they always engender resistance.

simply 'step outside' the thought constructs and world views that discourses provide and critically reflect upon these when giving accounts of why they exercised public powers in a particular way.[124] The subjects that discursive power relations generate become part of the operation of this field of power, though they are not merely passive objects of this power.[125] Therefore, traditional accountability mechanisms may only render visible established discursive patterns that underpin administrative decision-making, for instance, when reasons for decisions are given: 'Our cognitions and speech acts only become meaningful within a certain pre-established discourse.'[126] From this perspective, traditional accountability tools do not control how administrative decisions are arrived at in the first instance, but simply add another layer of narrative reflecting entrenched discursive patterning of social action.

7. Conclusion

This chapter has analysed how debate about the advantages and disadvantages of GMO agriculture becomes narrowed in EU GMO authorisations, a field highly regulated by both international and EU public law. EU citizens and some member states are interested in debating critically the role of commercial interests in food production, how to achieve food security and the affirmation of national cultural values through food and particular farming systems, as well as the distribution of power between 'regulatory' bodies, such as the Commission and EFSA, and 'regulated' biotech companies.[127] Nevertheless, GMO authorisations focus overwhelmingly on a scientific examination of the potential risks to human health and the environment posed by transgenic agricultural products. Science here, however, does not include ethics as philosophical inquiry or social science, such as economics. The chapter thus highlights the disciplinary power of scientific discourses that normalise what constitutes acceptable arguments.[128] It further unravels the notion of scientific discourses by distinguishing between 'pure', 'contextualised' and 'metascientific' discourses that open up and close down spaces for voicing

[124] Ibid., 13. [125] McHoul and Grace, above n. 38, 22. [126] Torfing, above n. 85, 84.

[127] A submission from a member of the public in relation to the authorisation of maize 1507 states: 'multinationals are trying to become more powerful than our governments'.

[128] Foucault, above n. 37, 105.

arguments.[129] The chapter argues that discourses not only mediate the exercise of public power through EU GMO authorisations, but also marginalise traditional EU legal and soft law accountability tools. By highlighting these effects of power of discourses the chapter questions the knowledge/politics, power dichotomy and its capacity to mediate conflicts between international trade law and the trade as well as social protection objectives of EU economic and administrative law. It also questions the emphasis on international trade law as undermining social protection objectives enshrined in EU and national administrative law by pointing to the disciplinary force of discourses generated during EU GMO authorisations. They – and not just the formal legal framework – structure in their own right argumentation in EU GMO authorisations. Hence, a deeper understanding of intersections between international and public law may be gained by analysing how heterogeneous discourses mediate these intersections and thus construct the meaning of environmental protection.

[129] Michael Billig, *Arguing and Thinking: A Rhetorical Approach to Social Psychology* (Cambridge University Press, New York, 1996) 14.

7

Nuclear narratives, environmental discourse and UK energy policy and legislation, 1970–2008

ELIZABETH ROUGH

1. Introduction

At the turn of the twenty-first century, the United Kingdom's (UK) civil nuclear industry appeared to be in terminal decline. After reporting a loss of £493 million for 2001, British Energy, the privatised operator of eight of the UK's civil nuclear reactors, faced bankruptcy in the autumn of 2002.[1] Whilst a government-backed loan of £650 million secured the future of the company in the short term, it undermined both the credibility of British Energy and the long-term viability of nuclear power in Britain. Less than a year later the policy repercussions of this 'financial meltdown' were all too apparent. The 2003 Energy White Paper stated that the British government did not support a new nuclear build, asserting that 'current economics make it [nuclear power] an unattractive option for new, carbon-free generating capacity'.[2] The White Paper also drew attention to the ongoing failure to resolve the problem of the disposal of high-level and intermediate-level waste from existing nuclear power stations.

Against this backdrop, the prospects for the nuclear industry in the UK looked bleak; the once-bright promise of the benign atom now appeared to be little more than a mirage. Then, in 2006, a policy turnaround began. Following a positive reappraisal of its role in the UK's energy and climate change strategies,[3] nuclear power was reinstated on

[1] 'British Energy Goes into Meltdown', *ENDS Report* (London), October 2002, 28.

[2] United Kingdom, *Our Energy Future – Creating a Low Carbon Economy*, Cm 5761 (2003) 12.

[3] United Kingdom, *The Energy Challenge. Energy Review: A Report*, Cm 6887 (2006) 8.

the government's agenda and endorsed as a viable energy policy option. The government asserted that:

> Climate Change is quite simply the biggest challenge facing humanity. To meet this challenge we need to take determined long-term action to reduce carbon emissions ... That is why the Government has today concluded that nuclear should have a role to play in the generation of electricity, alongside other low carbon technologies.[4]

By the end of 2008, the government had undertaken several facilitative actions to improve the commercial prospects of nuclear power. Most notably, the Planning Act 2008 seeks to streamline the planning process for large infrastructure projects, like nuclear power stations, in a bid to speed up the approval process.[5]

How can we begin to account for these oscillations between stability and change in domestic UK nuclear energy policy? Shifting economic circumstances, electricity demand projections and anxieties surrounding the security and reliability of the UK's electricity supply have all, at one time or another, impinged upon the position of nuclear power in UK energy policy. Yet the preceding overview suggests that we would miss a great deal if we focused solely on these economic factors and neglected the influence of environmental politics and legislation on the fortunes and image of nuclear power. With these points in mind, this chapter draws on the discourse analysis tradition and unpacks the 'nuclear narratives' – the multiple and often conflicting representations of nuclear power – that have been constructed within the context of environmental politics and law since the 1970s.

After identifying these narratives, the chapter turns to analyse their translation (or otherwise) into policy and public and international law. Whilst primarily focused on domestic UK nuclear energy policy, and its relationship to environmental discourse, it is important to recognise that energy and environmental politics operate at both the national and the international scale. Indeed, it is difficult to account for changes to UK energy policy without situating such change in its European and international context. In this respect, the case offers ample scope to illuminate the relationships between environmental discourses and public and international law.

[4] United Kingdom, *Meeting the Energy Challenge: A White Paper on Nuclear Power*, Cm 7296 (2008) 4.

[5] Planning Act 2008, c. 29.

2. Discourses and narratives

Before employing discourse and narrative in the analysis of nuclear energy policy it is necessary to clarify what is meant by these concepts. Beginning with the former, Jessup and Rubenstein, in the introductory chapter to this collection, offer Dryzek's clear and concise definition of discourse:

> A discourse is a shared way of apprehending the world. Embedded in language, it enables those who subscribe to it to interpret bits of information and put them together into coherent stories or accounts. Each discourse rests on assumptions, judgements and contentions that provide the basic terms for analysis, debates, agreements and disagreements.[6]

When relating this understanding of discourse to the world of policy-making two ideas stand out. The first, put simply, is that language matters. Discourse analysis aims to show how 'language actively shapes the way we perceive and understand [reality]',[7] rendering it comprehensible in such a way that it is amenable to deliberation. As structures or reserves of meaning, discourses can 'channel political thought in certain directions',[8] conditioning our understanding of what is, and what is not, an appropriate response to a particular situation. They do not emanate exclusively from particular individuals or institutions, but rather are the cumulative expression of numerous practices. Thus for Litfin and others, discourses delimit the range of policy options by sanctioning those ideas and voices that resonate with the dominant discourse of the day whilst simultaneously excluding and marginalising those that do not.[9] The concept undoubtedly encapsulates a variety of approaches, yet it is this rejection of language as a 'neutral medium through which ideas and an objective world are represented and discussed'[10] that provides the basic starting point for all discourse analysis.

The second idea that stands out relates to Dryzek's emphasis on 'stories' as organised forms of discourse. A discursive approach to the

6 John Dryzek, *The Politics of the Earth: Environmental Discourses* (Oxford University Press, 1st edn, 1997) 8.

7 Maarten Hajer and Hendrik Wagenaar, *Deliberative Policy Analysis: Understanding Governance in the Network Society* (Cambridge University Press, 2003) 14.

8 William Connolly, *The Terms of Political Discourse* (Robertson, Oxford, 1983) 1.

9 Karen Litfin, *Ozone Discourses: Science and Politics in Global Environmental Cooperation* (Columbia University Press, New York, 1994); Hajer and Wagenaar, above n. 7; Frank Fischer, *Reframing Public Policy* (Oxford University Press, 2003).

10 Keith Jacobs and Tony Manzi, 'Discourse and Policy Change: The Significance of Language for Housing Research' (1996) 11 *Housing Studies* 543, 543.

study of policy-making examines the ways in which we draw on devices like stories (or what I term 'narratives' in this chapter) to bring order and understanding to a situation. Here narratives are understood as a particular type of story, one that renders incoming information meaningful by integrating a variety of seemingly disparate events so as to create a shared understanding.[11] This is not to suggest that everything is an interpretation or that facts do not matter; rather it is that facts, information, knowledge and so on are embedded – explicitly or implicitly – in narrative accounts. By working to simplify a particular set of circumstances, narratives provide stability and orientation as actors grapple with complex issues.

2.1 Narratives and their relationship to policy stability and change

Bridging these two ideas – that both language and 'stories' matter – is one overarching insight: if meaning is not 'ontologically fixed',[12] but is struggled over and contested through numerous interactions and practices, then the nature of a policy problem cannot be assumed as 'given'.[13] A key strength of the discourse analysis tradition is that it begins from this very premise – namely, that shaping both the policy problem and the policy solution through debate, deliberation and argument should be studied as an integral and inherently political part of policy-making.

For Hajer, politics can be conceived of 'as a struggle for discursive hegemony in which actors try to secure support for their definition of reality'.[14] The 'definition of reality'[15] – of what the problem really is and what interventions are needed – is encapsulated in what Hajer terms a 'storyline'.[16] These are 'narratives on social reality through which elements from many different domains are combined and that provide actors with a set of symbolic references that suggest a common understanding'.[17] Achieving a common understanding is possible because the

[11] Multiple interpretations of narratives can be found across the social sciences. For a sociological definition of narrative see Philip Smith, *Cultural Theory: An Introduction* (Blackwell, Oxford, 2001).

[12] Karen Litfin, 'Framing Science: Precautionary Discourse and the Ozone Treaties' (1995) 24 *Millennium: Journal of International Studies* 251, 254.

[13] Ibid.

[14] Maarten Hajer, *The Politics of Environmental Discourse: Ecological Modernization and the Policy Process* (Clarendon Press, Oxford, 1995) 59.

[15] Ibid. [16] Ibid. 62. [17] Ibid.

storyline works to gloss over the complexities and uncertainties of a situation. Not only does this facilitate a heightened degree of flexibility in interpretation, it also enables different, and at times seemingly disparate, actors to come together and unite around a narrative to create a 'discourse coalition'.[18]

Of particular interest to this chapter, given its concern with accounting for stability and change in policy and law, is the way in which new or adapted storylines can precipitate policy and legislative change by reordering meaning. Here conditions that were once seen as inevitable or 'natural' are viewed afresh through new storylines as 'problems' meriting political, and often legal, attention. Similarly, solutions that were previously rejected or were simply unthinkable might be subsequently promoted as potential answers to the problem at hand. The underpinning assumption is that discourses are not set in stone but are always 'incomplete and constantly shifting',[19] thus creating the potential for change.

Despite their instability, toppling existing storylines and usurping them with new ones is not a straightforward process. To judge a coalition's success in their struggle for discursive hegemony, Hajer distinguishes between 'discourse structuration'[20] and 'discourse institutionalisation'.[21] The former occurs when 'policy actors feel obliged to use a certain storyline in order to appear credible'.[22] The latter can be detected when storylines form routine understandings that are translated into concrete policies and are realised through new (or adapted) public laws and institutional arrangements. In some instances, laws may precede policies: instituting new international treaties, or responding to the development of EU law, can require shifts in domestic policy and the institutionalisation of a new storyline.

[18] Ivan Scrase and David Ockwell, 'Energy Issues: Framing and Policy Change' in Ivan Scrase and Gordon MacKerron (eds.), *Energy for the Future. A New Agenda* (Palgrave Macmillan, Basingstoke, 2009) 35.

[19] Maarten Hajer and David Laws, 'Ordering Through Discourse' in Michael Moran, Martin Rein and Robert Goodin (eds.), *The Oxford Handbook of Public Policy* (Oxford University Press, 2006) 251, 253

[20] Hajer, above n. 14, 60. [21] Ibid. 61.

[22] Heather Lovell, Harriet Bulkeley and Susan Owens, 'Converging Agendas? Energy and Climate Change Policies in the UK' (2009) 27 *Environment and Planning C: Government and Policy* 90, 93. At present, for example, it is difficult to find a credible account of nuclear energy that fails to invoke its 'green' credentials.

In the case of civil nuclear power, few studies have considered the development of policy and law from a discourse analysis perspective.[23] This is surprising, given that the advancement of nuclear energy is an excellent example of an 'unstructured problem',[24] one which encapsulates conflicting discourses that leave actors unable to agree on the nature of the problem, let alone the solution. Furthermore, the issues at stake can be described as 'trans-scientific',[25] in the sense that science alone is unable to deliver an answer. As Weinberg acknowledges, trans-scientific questions can be asked of, but cannot be answered by science, because of their intrinsic uncertainty or indeterminacy, or because the questions being asked of science are fundamentally ethical or political in nature.[26] A classic example of a trans-scientific question concerns the disposal of radioactive waste. Whilst a scientific analysis may present a number of feasible, technical solutions, science alone cannot definitively answer the ethical questions that each option may prompt.

Against this backdrop, there appears to be ample scope to consider how storylines or 'nuclear narratives' work to bring order, meaning and stability to a politically charged and value-laden issue like the development of a civil nuclear programme. In the remainder of this chapter, I draw chiefly on Hajer's work to identify and analyse those nuclear narratives that have been constructed within the context of environmental politics in Britain since the 1970s. By studying conflicts between narratives, as well as their relationship to public and international law, I aim to present an alternative approach to understanding oscillations between stability and change in UK nuclear energy policy, one that examines shifts in policy as part of a broader struggle for discursive hegemony in this sector.

3. Identifying nuclear narratives

In order to reflect on the narratives that underpin policy, we must become aware of the elements – the values, facts, beliefs and theories – that combine

[23] For exceptions, see Scrase and Ockwell, above n. 18; John Proops, 'The (Non-) Economics of the Nuclear Fuel Cycle: An Historical and Discourse Analysis' (2001) 39 *Ecological Economics* 13.

[24] Roel In't Veld and A. de Wit, 'Clarifications' in Roel In't Veld (ed.), *Willingly and Knowingly: The Roles of Knowledge about Nature and the Environment in Policy Processes* (Lemma, Utrecht, 2000) 147, 150.

[25] Alvin Weinberg, 'Science and Trans-Science' (1972) 10 *Minerva* 209.

[26] For further detail on the interface between science, policy and law, see above Chapter 5 by Jaye Ellis.

to create them. This is both theoretically and practically difficult: discourses and narratives are influential precisely because so much of what they embody is taken for granted and not amenable to scrutiny. To address some of these problems, a number of methodological approaches were adopted when identifying narratives.

First, numerous sources of evidence were examined in order to attend to the multiple sites at which discursive interactions on nuclear energy policy occurred. These included legislation, official publications and non-official material such as trade journals and newspapers. A number of in-depth, semi-structured interviews were also conducted with senior figures from the nuclear industry and environmental non-governmental organisations (NGOs), all of whom have experience of civil nuclear policy-making. Second, since policy and legislative change is argued to take place over a number of decades, a retrospective approach was adopted. This allowed the researcher to detect any redefinitions of policy problems as well as their translation into policy and law.

Finally, given the practical difficulties associated with identifying narratives, the research built on the approach developed by Chilton and detected narratives through the identification of 'critical discourse moments'[27] in the development of UK energy and environmental policy. These are particular events that stimulate commentary and debate while providing an opportunity for more in-depth coverage of the issue. According to Chilton, it is during these moments that 'meaning is mobilised'[28] and the culture of the issue becomes visible, thus magnifying both the features of narratives as well as possible shifts in their composition.

When identifying critical discourse moments, source triangulation was employed to enhance the analytic reliability of the study. As well as consulting general histories of environmental politics and the UK nuclear power programmes, interviewees were asked to identify any moments or episodes which they thought had influenced nuclear energy policy since the 1970s. Having isolated particular critical discourse moments, narratives were subsequently identified by analysing the underlying definition of the problem at hand, the primary actors or institutions involved, the policy goals and the socio-cultural context in which the critical discourse moment occurred.

[27] Paul Chilton, 'Metaphor, Euphemism and the Militarization of Language' (1987) 10 *Current Research on Peace and Violence* 7, 17.

[28] Ibid.

4. Nuclear energy in the UK

Nuclear energy has been a feature of UK energy policy for over fifty years. The government's first formal commitment to generating electricity from nuclear fission can be found in a 1955 Command Paper entitled 'A Programme of Nuclear Power'.[29] Throughout this early period, civil nuclear power was riding a wave of popular enthusiasm and support. By 'indulging in images which recognized the wider symbolic significance of nuclear power',[30] the government and the nuclear industry worked to downplay the military roots of the civil programme and disassociate 'atomic bombs' from the 'peaceful atoms' of nuclear energy.[31]

Nationally, the technology was presented as a modern, clean and assured way of providing electricity against a backdrop of rising demand, diminishing national coal stocks and security of supply fears. For many it also offered the prospect of economic, industrial and political renewal, ensuring Britain's global significance and boosting national pride at a time when the future of the British Empire was in doubt.[32] Favourable national press coverage, combined with the historically high post-war faith in science, ensured that this positive image of civil nuclear power resonated on a national scale: there was, as one interviewee put it, 'a feeling of almost "the men in white coats will work wonders for us"'.[33] The *promise* of nuclear energy, and the ability to turn 'swords into ploughshares', was *the* narrative underpinning the development of nuclear power in the 1950s and 1960s. Thus it is within this positive, optimistic context that subsequent nuclear narratives should be understood.

In the following sections of this chapter, four critical discourse moments in nuclear energy politics are identified and discussed. Recalling that energy and environmental politics operate at both the national and international scale, it seems appropriate that two of these

[29] United Kingdom, *A Programme of Nuclear Power*, Cmd 9389 (1955).

[30] Ian Welsh, 'The NIMBY Syndrome: Its Significance in the History of the Nuclear Debate in Britain' (1993) 26 *The Journal of the British Society for the History of Science* 15, 20.

[31] The military and civil nuclear programmes were inextricably linked during these early years. For example, the Magnox reactor, on which the UK's first civil programme was based, was designed as an efficient producer of plutonium for nuclear weapons.

[32] Welsh, above n. 30.

[33] Interview with Lorna Arnold, former UK Atomic Energy Authority Official Historian (Oxford, 12 June 2007).

critical discourse moments are international events – the oil crisis in October 1973 and the Chernobyl disaster in April 1986 – whilst the other two moments centre on the publication of seminal domestic reports: the Royal Commission on Environmental Pollution's *Sixth Report: Nuclear Power and the Environment*, in September 1976 and the *Stern Review on the Economics of Climate Change*, in October 2006. As well as discussing these moments, this section of the chapter considers the narratives that they illuminate, as well as their relationship to environmental politics and discourse. Connections between these narratives and public, European and international law are also discussed.[34]

4.1 *Nuclear narrative: the risk of civil nuclear energy*

Until the mid-1970s, a closed, secretive decision-making process, bolstered by the high post-war trust in science and scientists, combined to insulate nuclear energy policy from critical reflection.[35] Accordingly, a range of issues, including safety, cost and risk were kept off the policy agenda. Three critical discourse moments led to a heightened scrutiny of civil nuclear energy policy throughout the 1970s and 1980s. These moments introduced doubts about the safety of civil nuclear energy and encouraged discussion of its risks.[36]

4.1.1 The oil crisis, October 1973

On 16 October 1973, in the midst of the Arab–Israeli War, Organization of Petroleum Exporting Countries (OPEC) members used their leverage over the price-setting mechanism for oil to quadruple its price across the world. High inflation and economic recession ensued, comprehensively challenging one of the underpinning assumptions of nuclear policy – ever-rising energy demand. Throughout this period energy issues became highly newsworthy. Front page headlines heightened the public's awareness of energy and helped to push nuclear energy issues into

[34] For a comprehensive overview of UK civil nuclear policy and law, see Stephen Tromans, *Nuclear Law: The Law Applying to Nuclear Installations and Radioactive Substances in its Historic Context* (Hart Publishing, Oxford, 2010).

[35] Michael Saward, 'The Civil Nuclear Network in Britain' in David Marsh and Rod Rhodes (eds.), *Policy Networks in British Governance* (Clarendon Press, Oxford, 1992) 75, 95.

[36] This section focuses on the *physical* risks of nuclear power. For a detailed analysis of the *financial* risks associated with nuclear power see Simon Taylor, *Privatisation and Financial Collapse in the Nuclear Industry: The Origins and Causes of the British Energy Crisis of 2002* (Routledge, London, 2007).

the limelight. Bitter and often acrimonious quarrels had previously taken place between the UK Atomic Energy Authority[37] and the Central Electricity Generating Board[38] over the scale of nuclear programmes and the reactor design to be adopted.[39] These disputes, however, had occurred behind the scenes and away from public and parliamentary scrutiny. Yet in the wake of the oil crisis they were now in the open and attracting national attention, particularly from a new breed of environmental NGOs.

Documentary analysis of NGO pamphlets and reports reveals how organisations including Friends of the Earth, the Council for the Protection of Rural England and the Town and Country Planning Association gathered momentum throughout the 1970s and 1980s.[40] Encouraged by the publication of the influential yet controversial *Limits to Growth*,[41] their campaigning made explicit the taken-for-granted assumptions, beliefs and values that underpinned nuclear policy which, they argued, had been overlooked by government, industry and the public. The campaigners focused on illuminating the risks introduced by nuclear power to society, the environmental degradation that it caused, and the possibility of dangerous releases of radioactivity from nuclear installations, whether by accident or sabotage. A number of environmental groups went further: their campaigning used the issue of nuclear power to draw attention to a 'bigger' ecological problem; namely, that environmental damage was a direct consequence of many of the most fundamental features of modern industrial economies. For these campaigners, nuclear power was not a 'solution'; it was part of the problem.

In a relatively short period of time, 'the nuclear issue . . . became the metaphor for all that was wrong with society'[42] for a small but growing

37 The Authority, established by the Atomic Energy Authority Act 1954, c. 32, was the government's sole adviser on all aspects of the nuclear programme.

38 Established under the Electricity Act 1957, c. 48, the Board was responsible for generating or acquiring electricity for England and Wales.

39 Saward, above n. 35.

40 Michael Flood and Robin Grove-White, *Nuclear Prospects: A Comment on the Individual, the State and Nuclear Power* (Friends of the Earth, London, 1976); Friends of the Earth, *Nuclear Power? No Thanks!* (Friends of the Earth, London, 1978); Martin Stott, Peter Taylor and the Town and Country Planning Association, *The Nuclear Controversy* (Town and Country Planning Association, London, 1980).

41 Donella Meadows, *The Limits to Growth: A Report for the Club of Rome's Project on the Predicament of Mankind* (Universe Books, New York, 1974).

42 Hajer, above n. 14, 95.

number of people: not only were nuclear power stations 'centralized, technologically complex and hazardous', they also reinforced 'all those trends in society which environmentalists most fear and dislike – the increasing domination of experts, threatening the freedom of the individual, and reinforcing totalitarian tendencies'.[43] Perhaps unsurprisingly, neither the content nor the direction of the UK's civil nuclear energy policy changed in response to environmentalists' challenges. Whilst the oil crisis played an important role in raising the profile of environmental NGOs, as well as the monetary costs and risks of nuclear energy, the government pressed ahead with their nuclear programme and ordered six reactors in 1974. In this instance, concerns surrounding security of supply overshadowed the risks raised by environmentalists.

4.1.2 Publication of the Royal Commission on Environmental Pollution's *Sixth Report: Nuclear Power and the Environment*, September 1976

The Royal Commission on Environmental Pollution's (RCEP) *Sixth Report: Nuclear Power and the Environment*,[44] marked a watershed in environmental politics; published in 1976, it was the first official study of its kind to be produced anywhere in the world. The report authoritatively questioned the UK Atomic Energy Authority and its tacit acceptance of an expanded nuclear programme, the inevitability of the Fast Breeder Reactor within that programme and the implications that the resulting 'plutonium economy'[45] might exert on civil liberties and national security. The prevailing ethos that nuclear energy was a technical matter, devoid of social implications, was shown to be a fallacy. Nuclear power, the Commission argued, raised long-term issues of unusual range and difficulty. These issues were 'political and ethical as well as technical'[46] and there had so far been 'very little official consideration of these matters'.[47] The report also launched an uncompromising critique of the lack of a satisfactory plan for the final disposal of radioactive waste. Sir Brian – later Lord – Flowers, the Chairman of the RCEP during the *Sixth Report*, recalled how he 'became extremely shocked . . . hardly any work had been done, at all, on methods of waste disposal'.[48]

[43] Stephen Cotgrove and Andrew Duff, 'Environmentalism, Middle-Class Radicalism and Politics' (1980) 28 *Sociological Review* 333, 338.

[44] United Kingdom, Royal Commission on Environmental Pollution, *Sixth Report: Nuclear Power and the Environment*, Cmnd 6618 (1976).

[45] Ibid. 73. [46] Ibid. 198. [47] Ibid.

[48] Interview with Lord Flowers (London, 7 June 2007).

Of particular interest to this chapter is the way in which a number of ideas and concepts – some that we now take for granted in environmental discourse – were brought to the fore through the RCEP's report. Perhaps one of the most striking ideas, given the secrecy that the nuclear programme had been shrouded in, was the strong case that the *Sixth Report* made for public deliberation about the risks associated with an emergent technology. A further example of the RCEP's foresight can be found in their considerations on radioactive waste, which explicitly evoked a responsibility to 'our remote descendants'.[49] According to the RCEP:

> it would be irresponsible and morally wrong to commit future generations to the consequences of fission power on a massive scale unless it has been demonstrated beyond reasonable doubt that at least one method exists for the safe isolation of these wastes for the indefinite future.[50]

This duty to 'future generations'[51] – which quickly became known as the 'Flowers' criterion' – was undoubtedly a precursor to today's concern with 'inter-generational equity'; an idea that is now a key principle of international law[52] and is integral to Brundtland's definition of sustainable development.[53] The translation of this 'duty' into UK public law, however, has been a slow affair. Although section 34(1) of the Environmental Protection Act 1990 set out a 'duty of care as respects to waste'[54] it was not until the Environment Act 1995 established the Environment Agency with the principal aim of 'achieving sustainable development'[55] that a duty to future generations was firmly embedded in environmental legislation. This time lag, however, is not necessarily a sign that the 'Flowers' criterion' failed to influence policy and action. Whilst the disposal of radioactive waste from nuclear installations has still to be resolved in the UK,[56] the body now charged with assessing

[49] United Kingdom, Royal Commission on Environmental Pollution, above n. 44, 80.

[50] Ibid. 81. [51] Ibid.

[52] See Edith Brown Weiss, *In Fairness to Future Generations: International Law, Common Patrimony, and Intergenerational Equity* (United Nations University, Tokyo, 1989) and above Chapter 1 by Peter Lawrence.

[53] 'Sustainable development is development that meets the needs of the present without compromising the ability of future generations to meet their own needs.' World Commission on the Environment and Development, *Our Common Future* (Oxford University Press, 1987) 43.

[54] Environmental Protection Act 1990 c. 43, s. 34. It should be noted that the temporal scope of that duty was left somewhat vague in the legislation.

[55] Environment Act 1995 c. 25, s. 4.

[56] International law has had a major impact on preventing the dumping of (radioactive) waste at sea, thus limiting the disposal options available. Treaties include the United Nations Convention on the Law of the Sea, opened for signature 10 December 1982,

options for the long-term management of that waste – the Committee on Radioactive Waste Management[57] – has put considerable emphasis on the importance of ethics and inter-generational equity throughout their most recent assessments and reports.

Here we are reminded that changing mindsets and shifting narratives can take place over a matter of decades rather than months or years. Furthermore, it is important not to underestimate the ways in which an authoritative publication, like the RCEP's report, can perform an important 'enlightenment function',[58] enabling knowledge to 'creep'[59] into the policy process and gradually exert a tangible impact on decision-makers, legislatures and the international community.

4.1.3 The Chernobyl disaster, April 1986

On 26 April 1986 one of four steam-cooled, graphite-moderated (Russian) RBMK[60] reactors at Chernobyl, near Kiev in the Ukraine, suffered a steam explosion, graphite fire and core meltdown.[61] The disaster resulted in fifty deaths among the emergency workers and liquidators from deterministic effects and is expected to result in tens of thousands of cancer deaths.[62] The British government was quick to reassure its citizens that no RBMK reactors had been built outside the Soviet bloc. The damage, however, was already done; Chernobyl was a powerful, visual symbol of the nuclear opposition's fears over nuclear safety and risk. According to one interviewee: 'Chernobyl did more than the whole environmental movement . . . if Chernobyl hadn't happened

1833 UNTS 3 (entered into force 16 November 1994), Arts. 192–4, the Convention on the Prevention of Marine Pollution by Dumping of Wastes and Other Matter, opened for signature 29 December 1972, 1046 UNTS 138 (entered into force 30 August 1975) and the Oslo–Paris (OSPAR) Convention for the Protection of the Marine Environment of the North East Atlantic, opened for signature 22 September 1992 (entered into force 25 March 1998). See below Chapter 17 by Afshin Akhtarkhavari

57 The Committee was established by the Labour government in 2003. See www.corwm.org.uk for further detail.

58 Carol Weiss, 'Research for Policy's Sake: The Enlightenment Function of Social Research' (1977) 3 *Policy Analysis* 351, 351.

59 Claudio Radaelli, 'The Role of Knowledge in the Policy Process' (1995) 2 *Journal of European Public Policy* 159, 164.

60 *Reaktor bolshoy moschnosti kanalniy*: a high-power channel-type reactor.

61 Jonathan Scurlock, 'A Concise History of the Nuclear Industry Worldwide' in David Elliott (ed.), *Nuclear or Not? Does Nuclear Power Have a Place in a Sustainable Energy Future?* (Palgrave Macmillan, Basingstoke, 2007) 24, 32.

62 Ian Fairlie, 'New Information on Radiation Health Hazards' in ibid., 101, 102. The exact figures are still disputed.

we'd be in a very different place than we are now, whatever the campaigning did'.[63]

Taken together, these three critical discourse moments illuminate the establishment of a new 'green ideology',[64] which started to frame issues like pollution and land degradation not as unconnected and localised, but rather as 'symptoms of the same problem', namely 'human society's over exploitation of the natural world'.[65] Nuclear power was undoubtedly the 'emblem' of this emerging 'environmental problematique',[66] yet it was also a symbol of the perils that new technologies posed. Against this backdrop a new nuclear narrative emerged, one that emphasised the 'risks of nuclear energy' rather than its promise. The disaster at Chernobyl was a terrible reminder of the potentially hazardous nature of nuclear power and the potential for uncontrolled releases of radioactivity. In its aftermath, it was all too apparent that such risks do not respect national boundaries; they are pervasive, their effects are long term (in some cases irreversible), and may alter the life conditions for future generations. For Beck, the types of environmental hazards posed by 'new' technologies, like nuclear power, underpin Western societies' movement into a new phase of modernity, one that is characterised by the pervasiveness of risk.[67]

The demonstration of these transboundary risks had an almost immediate impact on international law: less than six months after the Chernobyl disaster, the Convention on Assistance in the Case of a Nuclear Accident or Radiological Emergency and the Convention on Early Notification of a Nuclear Accident[68] were signed by over fifty states at the International Atomic Energy Agency's (IAEA) headquarters in Vienna.[69] A year later, the

[63] Interview conducted with a former campaigner for Friends of the Earth (London, 4 June 2007).

[64] Michael Jacobs (ed.), *Greening the Millennium?: The New Politics of the Environment* (Blackwell, Oxford, 1997) 1, 2.

[65] Ibid. [66] Hajer, above n. 14, 20.

[67] Ulrich Beck, *Risk Society: Towards a New Modernity* (Sage Publications, London, 1992).

[68] Convention on Assistance in the Case of a Nuclear Accident or Radiological Emergency, opened for signature 26 September 1986, 1457 UNTS 134 (entered into force 26 February 1987); Convention on Early Notification of a Nuclear Accident, opened for signature 26 September 1986, 1439 UNTS 276 (entered into force 27 October 1986).

[69] The International Atomic Energy Agency has also taken steps to *reduce* transboundary nuclear risk. For example, the Convention on Nuclear Safety, opened for signature 20 September 1994, INFCIRC/449 (entered into force 24 October 1996), Art. 6 calls on contracting states to upgrade the safety of existing nuclear installations and, if such upgrading cannot be achieved, to shut down the nuclear installation as soon as possible.

European Atomic Energy Community (Euratom) also formalised arrangements amongst member states for the early notification and exchange of information.[70] A number of European countries went further: Italy held three referenda on nuclear power in 1987, whilst the West German and Swedish governments declared their commitment to phase out nuclear facilities.[71] The UK made no such commitment and the construction of a Pressurised Water Reactor at Sizewell, Suffolk went ahead as planned in 1987. In this respect, the narrative's struggle for discursive hegemony had a spatially uneven impact: whilst the 'risk of nuclear power' did achieve both discursive structuration and institutionalisation in a number of European countries, the UK was not among them. However, the narrative did encourage the UK government to become more circumspect as to how such risks should be managed.

Between 1977 and 1985, ministers were compelled to hold two 'big public inquiries'[72] – Windscale in 1977 and Sizewell B between 1983 and 1985 – into the 'implication of the proposed [nuclear developments] for the safety of the public and for other aspects of the national interest'.[73] Both inquiries had broad terms of reference and facilitated wide-ranging discussions on all aspects of Britain's civil nuclear programme. Crucially, they offered advocacy groups a prominent, formal arena in which they could publicly scrutinise nuclear energy *policy* as well as the specific development proposal.[74] This, in turn, enabled the enlargement of the policy agenda to include questions about 'the risks of radiation from nuclear installations and the desirability of the growth ethic underlying arguments for nuclear expansion'.[75]

[70] The European Community Urgent Radiological Information Exchange (ECURIE) system is the technical implementation of the European Council Decision No. 87/600/ Euratom on Community arrangements for the early exchange of information in the event of a radiological emergency, 14 December 1987.

[71] Neil Carter, *The Politics of the Environment: Ideas, Activism, Policy* (Cambridge University Press, 2007) 199.

[72] In the UK, public planning inquiries are an advisory mechanism employed to aid the implementation of a pre-existing policy by informing the minister's mind as to how it may impact upon a locality. 'Big public inquiries' were so-called due to their increasing cost and length throughout this period. For further detail, see Outer Circle Policy Unit, *The Big Public Inquiry* (Outer Circle Policy Unit, London, 1979).

[73] Peter Shore (1977) cited in Patrick McAuslan, 'The Ideologies of Planning Law' (1979) 2 *Urban Law and Policy* 1, 15.

[74] Robin Grove-White, 'Land Use Law and the Environment' in Robin Churchill, John Gibson and Lynda Warren (eds.), *Law, Policy and the Environment* (Blackwell, Oxford, 1991) 32, 37.

[75] Saward above n. 35, 95.

Substantive changes in policy, however, were not forthcoming. Some complained that inquires were simply used as a tool to legitimate decisions that had already been taken.[76] Others focused on the perceived shortcomings of the UK's planning laws. According to McAuslan, the inquiries operated in a system of planning law that had been constructed 'so that the interests of maintaining and preserving the status quo and its institutional bases prevail over the interests of any fundamentally different or alternative point of view'.[77]

Following the enactment of the Planning Act 2008 the planning system has changed considerably and the role of the public inquiry in the UK planning system laws now faces an uncertain future. Changes have also been driven by developments at the EU level. Notably, EU secondary law has played a vital role in ensuring that environmental issues are not marginalised or disregarded when public authorities develop projects, plans, policies and regulations.[78] As a result, it is far more difficult for public authorities and the nuclear industry to neglect negative environmental assessments in the way that they did during the big public inquiries.[79] In this respect, European law not only has the capacity to initiate shifts in domestic policy and regulation, it can also constrain the space within which the UK can pursue its (nuclear) policy agenda.[80]

[76] Ray Kemp, 'Planning, Public Hearings, and the Politics of Discourse' in John Forester (ed.), *Critical Theory and Public Life* (MIT Press, London and Cambridge, Mass., 1985) 177, 179.

[77] McAuslan, above n. 73, 19.

[78] Susan Owens, 'A Balanced Appraisal? Impact Assessment of European Commission Proposals' [2007] 1 *elni Review* 2, 2. See also below Chapter 10 by Simon Marsden.

[79] For example, European Directive 85/337/EEC on the assessment of the effects of certain public and private projects on the environment (as amended by 97/11/EC and 2003/35/EC), which requires a developer to compile an Environmental Statement (ES) describing the likely effects of the development on the environment alongside proposed mitigation measures. More recently, European Directive 2001/42/EC (the Strategic Environmental Assessment Directive) has broadened the focus from specific projects to the plans and programmes from which they derive. For an example of how these directives have (and have not) been applied over arguments about transboundary nuclear risks, see: Simon Marsden, '*MOX Plant* and the Espoo Convention: Can Member State Disputes Concerning Mixed Environmental Agreements Be Resolved Outside EC Law?' (2009) 18 *Review of European Community and International Environmental Law* 312.

[80] I am grateful to Dr Simon Marsden for this insight.

4.2 Nuclear narrative: nuclear energy as a green, low-carbon technology

In December 2006, *The Guardian* ran an article proclaiming 2006 as the year that 'the west awoke . . . to the vast economic, political and social implications of climate change'.[81] This section considers what Lovell *et al.*[82] identify as a key moment in that awakening – the publication of the *Stern Review on the Economics of Climate Change*[83] – and its impact on nuclear energy policy.

4.2.1 The publication of the *Stern Review on the Economics of Climate Change*, October 2006

During the 1990s climate change became the new 'emblem' of environmental discourse: indeed, one could argue that climate change is now so powerful an emblem that it has become almost shorthand for environmental concern. International landmarks and treaties include the formation of the Intergovernmental Panel on Climate Change in 1988, the United Nations Framework Convention on Climate Change, which entered into force in March 1994, and the more recent Kyoto Protocol. At the national level, the Blair Labour government was vocal about its desire to lead the way in climate change diplomacy and to set a positive example to other nations.

The *Stern Review on the Economics of Climate Change*[84] represents an important part of that effort. Written by Sir Nicholas – now Lord – Stern, the former chief economist at the World Bank, the *Review* examines the evidence on the economic impacts of climate change, explores the economics of stabilising greenhouse gases in the atmosphere, and considers the policy challenges involved in managing the transition to a low-carbon economy. Throughout the *Review* climate change is treated as a 'market failure'[85] that must be corrected.[86] To reinforce this message, Stern establishes a powerful discursive construction, one that pitches the

[81] John Vidal, 'The Year the World Woke Up', *Society Guardian*, *The Guardian* (London and Manchester), 20 December 2006, 9.
[82] Lovell *et al.*, above n. 22.
[83] United Kingdom, Her Majesty's Treasury, *The Stern Review on the Economics of Climate Change* (2006), later published as Nicholas Stern, *The Economics of Climate Change: The Stern Review* (Cambridge University Press, 2007).
[84] Ibid. [85] Ibid. viii.
[86] This characterisation has promoted economic responses to climate change as most preferred.

economic benefits of immediate, international action against the risks of doing nothing. He argues that:

> if we don't act, the overall costs and risks of climate change will be equivalent to losing at least 5% of global GDP each year, now and forever. If a wider range of risks and impacts is taken into account, the estimates of damage could rise to 20% of GDP or more. In contrast, the costs of action – reducing greenhouse gas emissions to avoid the worst impacts of climate change – can be limited to around 1% of global GDP each year.[87]

Whilst the *Review* presents a range of options to cut greenhouse gas emissions, a strong emphasis is placed on achieving these cuts through modifications to the energy system. In this respect, the publication of the *Stern Review* reinvigorated the UK government's ambitions to tackle climate change whilst reinforcing its focus on energy policy as the arena through which to realise this goal in practice.

The idea that climate change policy should be delivered through energy policy was first mooted in 2000 with the publication of *Energy: The Changing Climate*, a major report prepared by the RCEP.[88] The report proposed what was then an ambitious target for carbon dioxide emissions – a 60 per cent reduction from 1998 levels by 2050[89] – and outlined four scenarios that detailed how emission reductions could be achieved through changes to the UK electricity system. After the hands-off approach of the 1990s, when 'governments ceased to see it as their responsibility to plan how the demand for energy will be met',[90] the RCEP's report was instrumental in catalysing the government's re-engagement with the energy sector. A plethora of *Energy Reviews*,[91] White Papers[92] and legislation[93] followed in its wake, all of which identified the need to cut carbon dioxide emissions through the energy system. In October 2008, the convergence of these two previously

[87] United Kingdom, Her Majesty's Treasury, above n. 83, vi.

[88] United Kingdom, Royal Commission on Environmental Pollution, *Twenty-Second Report: Energy – The Changing Climate*, Cm 4749 (2000).

[89] Ibid. 199. [90] Ibid. 69.

[91] United Kingdom, Performance and Innovation Unit, *The Energy Review* (2002); United Kingdom, *The Energy Challenge. Energy Review: A Report*, Cm 6887 (2006).

[92] United Kingdom, *Our Energy Future – Creating a Low Carbon Economy*, Cm 5761 (2003); United Kingdom, *Meeting the Energy Challenge: A White Paper on Energy*, Cm 7124 (2007); United Kingdom, *Meeting the Energy Challenge: A White Paper on Nuclear Power*, Cm 7296 (2008).

[93] Sustainable Energy Act 2003 c. 30; Energy Act 2004 c. 20; Climate Change and Sustainable Energy Act 2006 c. 19; Energy Act 2008 c. 32.

discrete policy arenas was institutionalised through the establishment of the Department for Energy and Climate Change.

It is this 'policy convergence'[94] that has helped to reinvigorate the fortunes of nuclear power. By placing a clear emphasis on the need to shift to a low-carbon economy to mitigate the impacts of climate change, the government created a 'business opportunity'[95] for nuclear energy, as a low-carbon technology, to play a prominent role in any future energy policy. The near bankruptcy of British Energy in 2002 undoubtedly prevented the nuclear industry from capitalising on that opportunity in time for the publication of the 2003 Energy White Paper. However, from 2006 onwards, and the publication of the *Energy Review*, nuclear power is continually endorsed by the government as having a role to play in UK energy supply.

The establishment of this new nuclear narrative – nuclear as a 'green, low-carbon technology' – is remarkable on a number of fronts. On the one hand it reinforces the 'promise of nuclear power' whilst also speaking to the 'risk of nuclear power' narrative by implying that the worst possible nuclear disasters are not as bad as the worst possible climate change disasters – what Bickerstaff *et al.* term a 'risk–risk trade-off'.[96] On the other hand, it has been co-produced by a previously unthinkable discourse coalition encompassing figures from industry, the government and business, together with a growing number of environmentalists and citizens.[97] As a result, opponents of nuclear power are increasingly 'portrayed [through this new narrative] as ideologically driven and as undermining their own cause, since nuclear power is low carbon'.[98] Crucially, the narrative also resonates with the prevailing environmental storyline of the day – ecological modernisation – the idea that it is possible to reconcile economic growth and environmental protection through institutional restructuring. Here, then, we have a clear example of a new narrative precipitating policy change by reordering the meaning of nuclear power.

[94] Lovell *et al.*, above n. 22, 91.

[95] Robert Falkner, *Business Power and Conflict in International Environmental Politics* (Palgrave Macmillan, Basingstoke, 2008) 99.

[96] Karen Bickerstaff *et al.*, 'Reframing Nuclear Power in the UK Energy Debate: Nuclear Power, Climate Change Mitigation and Radioactive Waste' (2008) 17 *Public Understanding of Science* 145, 149.

[97] Steve Connor, 'Nuclear Power? Yes Please: Leading Greens Join Forces in a Major U-Turn', *The Independent* (London), 23 February 2009, 1.

[98] Scrase and Ockwell, above n. 18, 50.

Having focused on the uptake of this narrative, it is important to acknowledge that there has been a reaction against one of the ways in which discursive hegemony was achieved by the government. Following the publication of the *Energy Review* in 2006, Greenpeace was successful in a judicial review challenge of the consultation process that, in theory, provided the basis for the *Review*'s findings. Greenpeace argued that the government had effectively endorsed a new nuclear build in the *Energy Review*, but had failed to deliver on the promise made in the 2003 Energy White Paper of holding the 'fullest public consultation'[99] before taking that decision. In February 2007, Sullivan J ruled that the conduct of the consultation had been 'flawed' and that, on the issue of nuclear waste, the government had given information that was both too limited and 'seriously misleading'.[100]

The judicial review process was a valuable mechanism through which to address the procedural legality of the government's decision to support a new nuclear build. However, as a judicial review proceeding does not give the judiciary an opportunity to comment on the merits of the original decision, the eventual policy outcome may not ultimately change, even in cases where procedural illegality is identified. In this instance, the government was forced to hold a further round of consultation, but the outcome – as evidenced by the supportive tone of the 2008 Nuclear White Paper – was essentially the same. Here we see how public law can play an important role in altering policy-making procedures, but that this alone is not always sufficient to impinge upon the content of policy. On 26 November 2008, the Energy Act, Climate Change Act and Planning Act[101] all received Royal Assent. None of these Acts categorically endorses nuclear power. However, they are designed to facilitate and improve the commercial prospects of nuclear power in Britain, and represent a public law culmination of the renewed nuclear discourse.

5. Conclusion

The development of the UK civil nuclear programme is a 'complex tale of many sub-plots'.[102] This chapter focuses on one of those sub-plots,

[99] United Kingdom, *Our Energy Future*, above n. 92, 12.

[100] *Greenpeace Limited* v. *Secretary of State for Trade and Industry* (2007) EWHC 311.

[101] Energy Act 2008, c. 32; Climate Change Act 2008, c. 27; Planning Act 2008, c. 29.

[102] Saward, above n. 35, 75.

namely the role and influence of environmental politics and discourse on nuclear energy policy. Teasing out the influence of 'nuclear narratives' is not straightforward: not only are they 'bound up with regimes, other institutions, material forces, and non-linguistic practices',[103] their impact, as in the case of the RCEP's *Sixth Report*, can be subtle, indirect and long term. Putting these practical difficulties to one side, the approach was helpful in illuminating how the meaning of nuclear power is constituted – and at times reconstituted – through debate, deliberation and argumentative practices. Depending on the narrative and the way in which it frames the technology, particularly in relation to 'the environment', civil nuclear power can be a policy 'problem' or a 'solution'. From the preceding discussion it is clear that these differing (and sometimes conflicting) nuclear narratives have competed for the attention of policy-makers with varying results.

Until the twenty-first century, environmental discourse had a marginal impact on the content of UK civil nuclear policy. Whilst environmentalists attempted to turn nuclear power into a policy problem, concerns about the health, environmental and safety risks of nuclear power failed to destabilise the government's commitment to expanding the civil nuclear programme. The alluring 'promise of nuclear energy' that had captivated policy-makers since the 1950s continued to have a profound influence over the shape of UK energy policy and provided stability in the face of repeated challenges from anti-nuclear groups.

Conversely, environmental discourse, and particularly the risk narrative, did play an important part in gradually overhauling the governance of nuclear technology. Responding to pressure from below, and to developments in EU and international law, the UK government started to adjust national environmental policies and procedures from the late 1970s onwards. These adjustments had two significant results. First, they facilitated greater public participation in the nuclear decision-making process, particularly through the 'big public inquiries'. Second, the transposition of the European environmental assessment directives into UK law has ensured that environmental considerations must now be taken into account when formulating civil nuclear policy and siting nuclear installations. In this respect, environmental discourse has helped to

[103] John Dryzek, 'Paradigms and Discourses' in Daniel Bodansky, Jutta Brunnée and Ellen Hey (eds.), *The Oxford Handbook of International Environmental Law* (Oxford University Press, 2007) 44, 62.

destabilise and open up the decision-making process to different voices and knowledge.[104]

More recently, a remarkable turn of events has seen the emergence of a new nuclear narrative that draws on climate change, as the new emblem of environmental discourse, to frame nuclear power as an energy solution once more. As policies to mitigate the impacts of climate change have increasingly centred on reducing carbon dioxide emissions, particularly through the energy system, so the meaning of nuclear power has been reordered to focus on its low-carbon status. The result is a pervasive narrative underpinned by a previously unthinkable discourse coalition and the endorsement of nuclear power by the government. Only time will tell if this new narrative, and the Energy Act and Climate Change Act that have flowed from it, will deliver the much-anticipated new nuclear build in the UK.

[104] The outcome of the 'big public inquiries', however, suggests that we should remain circumspect about the potential for adapted policy-making procedures to fundamentally alter the content of policy.

PART III

Environmental discourses in legal institutions

8

International courts and sustainable development: using old tools to shape a new discourse

TIM STEPHENS[1]

1. Introduction

'Sustainable development' has been the hegemonic global environmental policy for nearly three decades,[2] not only because it offers the tantalising prospect that economic development can be reconciled with environmental protection, but also because it is a highly pliable concept, and can embrace quite different views about how this reconciliation is to be achieved.[3] The plasticity of sustainability has hamstrung efforts to embed the concept in international law, either in treaty form or as a customary rule, while at the same time ensuring that it remains the main discourse through which environmental and developmental challenges are debated.[4] The discursive character of sustainable development also makes it susceptible to multiple, contested and changing interpretations over time through the influence of a variety of domestic and international actors.

[1] A version of the paper upon which this chapter is based was also presented at the Global Justice and Sustainable Development Conference held at the University of Sheffield School of Law, 26–27 August 2009. Ms Meredith Simons provided valuable research assistance, for which I am most grateful.

[2] John Dryzek, 'Paradigms and Discourses' in Daniel Bodansky, Jutta Brunnée and Ellen Hey (eds.), *The Oxford Handbook of International Environmental Law* (Oxford University Press, 2007) 44, 56–8.

[3] William Adams, *Green Development: Environment and Sustainability in the Third World* (Routledge, London and New York, 2nd edn, 2001) 4. See also Thomas J. Willbanks, '"Sustainable Development" in Geographic Perspective' (1994) 84 *Annals of the Association of American Geographers* 541, 543 ('different people can accept [sustainable development] sincerely while they mean different things by it').

[4] John Dryzek, *Deliberative Global Politics: Discourse and Democracy in a Divided World* (Polity Press, Cambridge, 2006) 56 ('sustainable development is a discourse, not a concept, and still less a scientific concept').

Among the voices contributing to this dialogue are the growing number of international judicial bodies and arbitral tribunals that are increasingly being called upon to address disputes raising environmental and developmental issues. In this regard, this chapter is concerned not with the formal, legal status of sustainable development, but rather with broader questions about how judicial decisions may shape the meaning of sustainability as an environmental and developmental discourse, an enquiry that is attracting growing legitimacy.[5] The chapter first examines the value that discourse theory can bring to understanding the judicial development of international law relating to sustainable development. It then turns to consider this process in the context of select cases relating to transboundary environmental disputes. The discussion hones in upon specific legal sub-discourses or narratives that have been influential in the resolution of disputes over natural resources, namely the notion that justice requires an equitable distribution of environmental goods, and that fair processes should accompany the making of environmental decisions. It is seen that these orthodox legal conceptions of equity and justice may be invoked for more than mere rhetorical reasons, and provide a language through which contemporary understandings of sustainable development may be accommodated within a formal legal framework. The due-process storyline is particularly important, demonstrating the growing international influence of domestic public law principles relating to transparency, accountability and participation in environmental decision-making.

2. International courts and sustainability discourses

International environmental law in the late twentieth and early twenty-first centuries has been characterised by the rapid growth of a range of regulatory regimes on a host of issues, from wildlife protection to the abatement of pollution. Nonetheless, it remains the case that much of international environmental law is animated by general principles that

[5] As the International Law Association's (ILA) Committee on the International Law on Sustainable Development has acknowledged, whether 'sustainable development' is a binding rule of international law is to a large extent a 'sterile' question, and our attention should be focused on the substantive content and 'effective impact' of the concept, and the role of institutions such as international courts, in developing and implementing sustainability: ILA Committee on the International Law on Sustainable Development, *Third Report* (2008) 9.

continue to be subject to ongoing discussion and debate.[6] Sustainable development is pre-eminent among these, but it is at the centre of a constellation of other principles including permanent resource sovereignty, prevention of transboundary harm, the polluter-pays principle, and the precautionary principle/approach.[7] Understanding how environmental principles evolve, and influence state behaviour, is therefore critical to a full appreciation of the function of public international law in environmental governance.

In this regard discourse theory has considerable value. Writing in the mid-1990s, Daniel Bodansky argued that 'sustainable development' is fundamentally 'discursive' in nature. In his view, sustainable development is concerned with 'how states speak to one another', rather than their domestic or cross-jurisdictional actions.[8] Hence, environmental principles can be understood as constituting 'regularities in discourse rather than regularities in state behaviour'.[9] Bodansky nonetheless accepted that these discursive international environmental norms can have a practical impact on international governance in setting policy objectives, because they also specify the terms of debate and therefore the apparent limits to agreement on environmental goals.

Bodansky further argued that over time environmental principles may congeal and be expressed in binding form in environmental treaties and other texts. However, he cautioned against rushing to judgment on the customary status of environmental principles. Indeed, finding evidence of sustainable development's customary status remains a Sisyphean task, given the many competing visions as to its meaning. Similarly, while other principles such as precaution have been given more concrete effect, as seen in the extent to which they are implemented through specific provisions in particular environmental treaties,[10] it is impossible to

[6] Duncan French, *International Law and Policy of Sustainable Development* (Manchester University Press, 2005) 59–62.

[7] Philippe Sands, *Principles of International Environmental Law* (Cambridge University Press, 2nd edn, 2003) 231.

[8] Daniel Bodansky, 'Customary (and Not So Customary) International Environmental Law' (1995–6) 3 *Indiana Journal of Global Legal Studies* 105, 115.

[9] Ibid. 116.

[10] See, e.g., the use of the precautionary principle in the Agreement for the Implementation of the Provisions of the United Nations Convention on the Law of the Sea of 10 December 1982 relating to the Conservation and Management of Straddling Fish Stocks and Highly Migratory Fish Stocks, opened for signature 4 December 1995, 34 2167 UNTS 3 (entered into force 11 December 2001). See the discussion in Donald R. Rothwell and Tim Stephens, *The International Law of the Sea* (Hart Publishing, Oxford, 2010) ch. 13.

speak in general terms of precaution applicable in all circumstances of environmental risk. The operationalisation of environmental principles is therefore highly context-specific.

In his analysis Bodansky adverted to, but did not expressly adopt, the discourse theory approach, deployed by John Dryzek and others, as a way of explaining how governments and other actors deal with challenges of environmental governance in a context where there are relatively weak formal institutions.[11] By contrast to other areas of international law, collective security and trade being obvious examples, in international environmental law authority is highly disaggregated through an array of institutions, including a multiplicity of multilateral environmental treaty bodies. In this context, environmental discourses have particular relevance because they provide a conceptual framework through which policy priorities are identified and debated and can be given consistency across a variegated institutional architecture.

As has been emphasised throughout this book, the insight of the discourse theory approach is that the language and terminology used in the process of articulating international environmental policy priorities constructs and conditions the ways in which environmental issues are perceived, and the legitimacy of possible regulatory responses.[12]

Discourse theory has been wholeheartedly embraced by many writers on international relations and by New Stream, or critical, legal scholars, who take a functionalist approach in explaining patterns of normativity. It has been particularly important in understanding how governments address environmental and developmental issues nationally, regionally and internationally.[13] The emergence and consolidation of environmental jurisprudence in many municipal jurisdictions shows the complex ways in which the language of sustainability has been deployed, debated and accepted or resisted. While new ideas of sustainability have been shunned in some instances, in others sustainable development has been

[11] John Dryzek, *The Politics of the Earth: Environmental Discourses* (Oxford University Press, 2nd edn, 2005). See also Dryzek, above n. 2, 12.

[12] Dryzek (2005), above n. 11.

[13] See, e.g., for an analysis of one aspect of development policy in the Pacific from a discursive perspective: Tim Stephens, 'Fishing-Led Development in the South Pacific: Charting a Pacific Way to a Sustainable Future' (2008) 39 *Ocean Development and International Law* 256.

used creatively to develop the law.[14] Nevertheless, mainstream jurists have been very reticent in considering the utility of the discursive perspective, even though it is fully compatible with many conventional accounts of the international law-making process, concerned as it is with the power of words, most particularly in the context of customary international law.[15]

Dryzek has argued that discourse theory need not be regarded as providing a complete or grand theory for understanding environmental governance, nationally or internationally. Discourses are instead one influence among many. In the context of international regimes, discourses can provide a language or 'software' which allows international institutions to function, while more formal organisations and rules provide the basal structure or 'hardware'.[16] Dryzek does not specifically refer to international courts among such institutions, but it is clear that in an era where environmental disputation is becoming increasingly 'judicialised', that is subject to the strictures of third party settlement according to law, the 'software' provided by environmental discourses is important, and increasingly so.

Another lesson of discourse theory is that the discursive products from the institutional 'hardware' can have a much more dynamic impact on the content and development of environmental policies than their positioning within formal structures or hierarchies of international legal authority might otherwise suggest. Viewing environmental principles through discourse theory levels the field for participation by a wider range of actors in the discourse and avoids complex questions about the legal status of the principles. For example, Charlotte Epstein makes the point that the emergence of an anti-whaling discourse within key nations has had international resonance, and effectively transformed the formal rules of the international whaling regime.[17] In her view, a major

[14] See, e.g., a string of recent decisions in the New South Wales Land and Environment Court, including *Telstra Corporation Limited* v. *Hornsby Shire Council* (2006) 67 NSWLR 256, in which Preston CJ engaged in a wide-ranging analysis of the precautionary principle by reference to several jurisdictions in North America and Europe. For comment, see: Jacqueline Peel, 'When (Scientific) Rationality Rules: (Mis)Application of the Precautionary Principle in Australian Mobile Phone Tower Cases' (2007) 19 *Journal of Environmental Law* 103.

[15] See generally Michael Byers, *Custom, Power and the Power of Rules* (Cambridge University Press, 1999).

[16] Dryzek, above n. 11, 60.

[17] International Convention for the Regulation of Whaling, opened for signature 2 December 1946, 161 UNTS 72 (entered into force 10 November 1948).

advantage of discourse theory is that '[i]ndividuals, NGOs, states, are all potentially the subjects (the I/we) of a discourse' and there is therefore 'a degree of *equivalence between subjects* pertaining to otherwise different levels of analysis'.[18]

There is clearly no formal legal equality among such subjects. States remain the dominant actors in international law, a privileged position exemplified by Article 34(1) of the Statute of the International Court of Justice (ICJ), which provides that only states may be parties in cases before the Court. However, states may in important respects act as proxies or agents of discourse coalitions, which can include not only other states, but also civil society groups also potentially aggrieved by public legal systems. Witness, for instance, the role of popular environmental concerns in prompting the Hungarian government to withdraw from a joint dams project undertaken with Slovakia, a decision that led to the litigation in the ICJ in the *Gabčíkovo-Nagymaros Project* case.[19] The protest of vocal environmental and community groups was also a factor in Argentina bringing proceedings in the ICJ in the *Pulp Mills* case[20] against Uruguay in relation to the authorisation and construction of pulp mills on the River Uruguay.

3. Sustainability, justice and international courts

There is a tendency in international relations literature to dismiss the contribution of international courts to the deliberative process through which environmental discourses are formed and transformed. The view of Hans Morgenthau, that international courts are an ineffectual and idealistic gesture to liberal multilateralism,[21] remains prevalent even among scholars who are otherwise hostile to the realist vision of international affairs.[22] This perspective overlooks the reality that states are

[18] Charlotte Epstein, *The Power of Words in International Relations: Birth of an Anti-Whaling Discourse* (MIT Press, Cambridge, Mass., 2008) 16 (emphasis in original).

[19] *Gabčíkovo-Nagymaros Project (Hungary* v. *Slovakia)* [1997] ICJ Rep. 7.

[20] *Pulp Mills on the River Uruguay (Argentina* v. *Uruguay) (request for provisional measures by Argentina)* (2006) 45 ILM 1025; *(request for provisional measures by Uruguay)* (2007) 46 ILM 311; *Case Concerning Pulp Mills on the Uruguay River (Argentina* v. *Uruguay) (merits)* Judgment of 20 April 2010.

[21] Hans Morgenthau, *Politics Among Nations: The Struggle for Power and Peace* (Knopf, New York, 1948) 211.

[22] See, e.g., Dryzek, above n. 4, 145–6, who categorically dismisses the ICJ as 'an irrelevance because it cannot find a supportive discourse, and cannot assert itself against strong conceptions of national sovereignty'.

increasingly turning to international courts in relation to critical issues requiring inter-state coordination, including in disputes over environmental protection and natural resources,[23] and that international courts have become important actors in their own right in international politics, especially in some regional settings such as Europe.[24] In this regard, the International Law Association has recognised the central role of adjudication in underlining that when it comes to the evolution and implementation of sustainable development 'not all legal process is dependent on the will of States', and that 'the role of the judiciary – both domestically and internationally – should not be underestimated'.[25]

The nature of the international adjudicative process, as one involving independent judges, reaching conclusions on the basis of reasoned arguments, according to fair process and international law, means that it is uniquely positioned by comparison with political institutions for giving independent and authoritative recognition to environmental and developmental values of concern to the international community at large. As Thomas Franck pointed out, in the absence of truly democratic political institutions, decisions of an international court such as the ICJ according to a fair and 'principled process' carry particular global influence.[26] Franck's analysis was an important precursor to the contribution made by scholars of global administrative law in highlighting the importance of principles of administrative law to structures of intergovernmental regulation, particularly procedural fairness, participation, transparency and legality.[27] Indeed, according to Franck, international courts by extolling these values have a privileged role compared to political institutions in engaging with discourses addressing public interest concerns such as environmental protection and sustainable development.

Franck's analysis was not restricted only to matters of fair process. Instead, he sought to establish a general theory of 'compliance pull' to

[23] Tim Stephens, *International Courts and Environmental Protection* (Cambridge University Press, 2009) 12.

[24] See Lawrence Helfer and Anne-Marie Slaughter, 'Toward a Theory of Effective Supranational Adjudication' (1997) 107 *Yale Law Journal* 273 and Alex Mills and Tim Stephens, 'Challenging the Role of Judges in Slaughter's Liberal Theory of International Law' (2005) 18 *Leiden Journal of International Law* 1.

[25] ILA, above n. 5, 31.

[26] Thomas Franck, *Fairness in International Law and Institutions* (Oxford University Press/Clarendon Press, Oxford/New York, 1995), 347.

[27] See, e.g., Sabino Cassese *et al.* (eds.), *Global Administrative Law: Cases, Materials, Issues* (Institute for International Law and Justice, New York, 2nd edn, 2008).

explain why states follow some rules and precepts of international law and not others. According to Franck, the likelihood of compliance is to a large degree a function of whether the decision-making process by the relevant law-making institution or process is fair. However, Franck argued that compliance also depends 'upon perceptions of the distributional justice' in terms of the 'costs and benefits' associated with a decision or rule.[28] As a consequence, it is not only appropriate but necessary for international courts and other fora to engage with '[f]airness discourse' when it comes to the allocation of natural resources.[29] Franck did not refer to sustainable development; however, it is clearly a concept that is based on substantive notions of fairness and justice.[30] Justice is at the forefront of the mainstream definition of sustainability as 'development that meets the needs of the present without compromising the ability of future generations to meet their own needs'.[31] This formulation highlights intergenerational environmental justice, although also implicit in the reference to the 'needs of the present' is intra-generational environmental justice.[32]

The implication of Franck's analysis is that sustainable development will have greater discursive influence if actors, including courts, engage with its justice dimensions in a manner that is perceived as promoting an equitable distribution among peoples of the public goods that the environment provides. International courts and individual judges have seldom sought to address the justice dimensions of sustainability in such sweeping terms. However, they have made a contribution by dealing with specific sub-discourses of fairness by addressing particular ideas of equity and justice. The following discussion assesses the ways these concepts have been relevant to the international judicial examination of sustainability questions, and where opportunities for future development may lie.

3.1 Legal conceptions of equity and sustainable development

For most of the history of international law, the primary way in which considerations of justice and fairness have informed international

[28] Franck, above n. 26, 353. [29] Ibid. 19. [30] French, above n. 6, 28.

[31] World Commission on Environment and Development, *Our Common Future* (Oxford University Press, 1987) 43.

[32] Daniel Magraw and Lisa Hawke, 'Sustainable Development' in Bodansky, Brunnée and Hey (eds.), above n. 2, 613, 619.

adjudication on environmental matters is through the use of concepts and principles of equity. These have a far longer history than sustainable development, which has emerged relatively recently in international law. However, the significance for this analysis is that ideas of equity are consonant with sustainable development, and can be used in order to advance a just international legal framework for achieving sustainability.[33]

When reference is made to 'equity' in international law, it is to three different ideas. The first is the use of general principles of law as referred to in Article 38(1)(c) of the Statute of the ICJ to address lacunae in international law, or to soften what would be an otherwise harsh and clearly inequitable application of a rule of international law. Included in this category are equitable doctrines such as acquiescence, estoppel and 'clean hands', familiar to domestic lawyers, and which can have a bearing on international disputes,[34] although usually only in a procedural sense. A second notion of equity is a more substantive one, involving situations where conceptions of fairness themselves constitute the relevant legal rule, as can be seen in certain situations requiring cross-border cooperation such as shared natural resources (including watercourses) and pollution. Both of these procedural and substantive conceptions of equity are quite different from a third notion of equity as a complete supererogation for legal rules, as for instance, would be the case were the ICJ to be asked to resolve a dispute *ex aequo et bono* under Article 38(2) of the Statute of the ICJ. None refer to sustainability; however, they are clearly relevant to sustainability, and provide a means by which international courts can contribute to the development of sustainability within accepted categories of legal reasoning.

3.1.1 International watercourses

There are several hundred transboundary rivers, lakes and aquifers globally and international law has had to develop in order to regulate competition for, and conflict over shared freshwater resources that are becoming increasingly scarce. Decisions of international arbitral

[33] Dinah Shelton, 'Describing the Elephant: International Justice and Environmental Law' in Jonas Ebbesson and Phoebe Okowa (eds.), *Environmental Law and Justice in Context* (Cambridge University Press, 2009) 55, 58. See also Dinah Shelton, 'Equity' in Bodansky, Brunnée and Hey (eds.), above n. 2, 639; Owen McIntyre, *Environmental Protection of International Watercourses under International Law* (Ashgate, Aldershot, 2007) 121.

[34] *Diversion of Water from the River Meuse (Netherlands* v. *Belgium)* [1937] PCIJ (Ser. A/B) No. 70, 76–7.

tribunals and international courts have been particularly influential in effecting a shift in this area of international law away from absolutist positions favouring specific states (such as upstream users over downstream users, or vice versa).

The overarching principle is now recognised to be that of 'equitable utilisation', which requires a reasonable sharing of available freshwater resources.[35] This principle is an example of equitable considerations providing guidelines for achieving a reasonable sharing of a natural resource.[36] As expressed in the 1997 United Nations Convention on the Law of the Non-Navigational Uses of International Watercourses,[37] which codifies custom on this point, equitable utilisation essentially involves a process of balancing the interests of states, rather than defining an outcome in advance.[38] This seemingly narrow, and partly process-oriented equitable principle, can influence and be influenced by broader conceptions of fairness in resource allocation. As Goldie put it, the principle supplies a means through which 'society's contemporary sense of justice and fairness' can be brought to bear in natural resource disputes.[39]

The case most often cited in this context is the *Lake Lanoux* case,[40] which examined a French scheme to generate electricity by diverting waters from Lake Lanoux, an alpine lake in the French Pyrenées, to the Ariège river. The project would have reduced the volume of water in the lake's natural drain, the Carol river, which flowed into Spain. Following Spanish protests, France agreed to return to the Carol river, from another source, the exact quantity of water that was diverted from its headwaters. As a result, the arbitral tribunal was not asked to achieve an equitable apportionment of water resources, and instead the tribunal was more concerned with the defects in France's behaviour towards Spain when designing and implementing the works. In this regard the arbitral award strongly emphasised equity in a procedural public law sense, in finding that in proposing changes to a shared watercourse an upper

[35] Convention on the Law of Non-Navigational Uses of International Watercourses, opened for signature 21 May 1997, 36 ILM 700 (not yet in force), Art. 5(1) ('Watercourse states shall . . . utilize an international watercourse in an equitable and reasonable manner . . .'). See generally McIntyre, above n. 33, 53–86.

[36] Franck, above n. 26, 65. [37] Above n. 35, Art. 5(1). [38] McIntyre, above n. 33, 133.

[39] L. F. E. Goldie, 'Equity and the International Management of Transboundary Resources' in Albert E. Utton and Ludwik A. Teclaff (eds.), *Transboundary Resources Law* (Westview Press, Boulder, 1987) 103, 107.

[40] *Lake Lanoux (France* v. *Spain)* (1957) 12 UN Rep. Int. Arb. Awards.

riparian should negotiate in good faith with states downstream, during which 'account must be taken of all interests, of whatsoever nature, which are liable to be affected by the works undertaken, even if they do not correspond to a right'.[41] This is a significant statement of the importance of procedural fairness in environmental decision-making, especially where there are transboundary impacts.

3.1.2 Transboundary pollution

Equity has been raised in similar terms in litigation concerning transboundary atmospheric pollution. In the landmark *Trail Smelter* case,[42] an arbitral tribunal was asked to resolve a dispute over air pollution damaging to the United States that originated from a lead and zinc smelter in Canada, and in so doing to 'reach a solution just to all parties concerned'.[43] This reference to justice in the arbitral agreement left the way open for the tribunal to incorporate equitable considerations in the orders made. This occurred both in the interim award requiring Canada to compensate the United States (an instance of retrospective or corrective justice), and in the final award requiring Canada to take costly steps to reduce transboundary pollution into the future (an instance of prospective and distributive justice). In the final award the Tribunal articulated the well-known dictum that states must not permit their territory to be used in ways causing significant damage to the territory of other states by atmospheric pollution. It has been argued that this obligation, and its application on the facts, 'reflect[ed] an equitable allocation of the capacity of the airshed to accommodate pollution from the smelter'.[44]

While it is doubtful whether equity would have been given such a prominent role but for the requirement within the arbitral agreement

[41] Ibid. 314–15. For a discussion of this aspect of the case, see Ellen Hey, 'Distributive Justice and Procedural Fairness in Global Water Law' in Ebbesson and Okowa (eds.), above n. 33, 351, 353.

[42] *Trail Smelter (Canada* v. *United States)* (1938 and 1941) 3 UN Rep. Int. Arb. Awards.

[43] Convention for the Settlement of Difficulties Arising from the Operation of the Smelter at Trail between Great Britain and the United States, opened for signature 15 April 1935, 162 LNTS 73 (entered into force 14 January 1936), Art. IV.

[44] Stephen McCaffrey, *The Law of International Watercourses: Non-Navigational Uses* (Oxford University Press, 2nd edn, 2007) 231. See also Jonas Ebbesson, 'Introduction: Dimensions of Justice in Environmental Law' in Ebbesson and Okowa (eds.), above n. 33, 1, 6 (arguing that the mandate of the arbitral tribunal to reach a 'just' solution evidences an important precedent for incorporating justice considerations in international judicial settlement of environmental disputes).

that the tribunal reach a 'just' outcome,[45] the language of equitable balancing was later endorsed by the International Law Commission in the Draft Articles on Prevention of Transboundary Harm from Hazardous Activities.[46] Article 9(1) of the Draft Articles provides that originating and potentially affected states should enter into consultations in order to reach agreement on measures to prevent or minimise significant transboundary harm, and Article 9(2) states that these consultations should be directed at achieving a solution 'based on an equitable balance of interests'. The significance of this formulation is that it is open-ended, and as with the principle of equitable utilisation in the context of watercourses, allows international courts to draw upon contemporary conceptions of sustainability devised by international and public law scholars in arriving at an appropriate equilibrium of interests. These adjustments can influence the trajectory taken by sustainability discourse.

3.2 Broader conceptions of justice

The preceding discussion illustrates how justice as equity can be used as a process and as a conceptual framework for environmental decision-making in circumstances where there is a need for fairness and flexibility. Conceived in this way, the primary interest served by justice is promoting the peaceful and durable resolution of a particular dispute. However, excluded from this is any systematic effort to address inequalities between the disputants, or any concern for other equities, such as the effect of the decision on the international community at large, on the interests of future generations, or on the natural environment.[47]

An example of the limitations of using 'old tools' to influence the new discourse of sustainability is the categorical rejection of substantive conceptions of equity when addressing disputes over territorial and maritime boundaries. The United Nations Convention on the Law of

[45] See Stephens, above n. 23, 151–60.

[46] *Report of the International Law Commission*, 53rd sess., 366, UN Doc. A/56/10 (2001).

[47] On the failure of environmental justice to recognise the importance of ecological integrity, see Klaus Bosselmann, 'Ecological Justice and Law' in Benjamin Richardson and Stepan Wood (eds.), *Environmental Law for Sustainability* (Hart Publishing, Oxford and Portland, 2006) 129.

the Sea specifically requires the delimitation process to be directed towards an 'equitable solution';[48] however, as the ICJ noted in the *North Sea Continental Shelf* cases, 'it is not a question of applying equity simply as a matter of abstract justice, but of applying a rule of law which itself requires the application of equitable principles'.[49] As seen in the recent *Case Concerning Maritime Delimitation in the Black Sea*,[50] such equitable principles have only the most limited of corrective functions.[51] The ICJ has previously held that its task in maritime boundary delimitation is not to compensate for inequalities of nature, and that it cannot consider the marine ecology, the natural resources of the delimitation area, relative levels of development, the extent of land territory, or population size in setting a delimitation line for overlapping continental shelves or exclusive economic zones.[52]

However, there are some indications in several other cases that it is possible to envisage situations in which international courts and tribunals could potentially make a more substantive contribution to the discourse of sustainability.

3.2.1 Preservation of wildlife

One of the most significant cases in this respect is also one of the earliest: the *Bering Sea Fur Seals* case.[53] The dispute giving rise to the case arose in 1886 following the arrest of Canadian sealing schooners that were catching Alaskan fur seals. Britain contended that the Canadian vessels

[48] Opened for signature 10 December 1982, 1833 UNTS 397 (entered into force 16 November 1994), Art. 83(1) ('The delimitation of the continental shelf between States with opposite or adjacent coasts shall be effected by agreement on the basis of international law . . . in order to achieve an equitable solution'). See also Art. 74(1) in relation to the delimitation of the exclusive economic zone.

[49] *North Sea Continental Shelf Cases (Germany* v. *Denmark; Germany* v. *Netherlands)* [1969] ICJ Rep. 3 [85].

[50] *Case Concerning Maritime Delimitation in the Black Sea (Romania* v. *Ukraine)* Judgment of 3 February 2009.

[51] Ibid. 122 and 214.

[52] *Case Concerning the Continental Shelf (Libya* v. *Malta)* [1985] ICJ Rep. [46]. See Robin R. Churchill and A. Vaughan Lowe, *The Law of the Sea* (Manchester University Press, 1999) 190. But see the separate opinion of Judge Weeramantry, in which he argued that equity should be viewed in 'global terms', and that among the relevant equitable considerations in the process of delimitation was 'the sacrosanct nature of earth's resources, harmony of human activity with the environment, respect for the rights of future generations, and the custody of earth's resources with the standard of due diligence expected of a trustee'.

[53] *Bering Sea Fur Seals Arbitration (Great Britain* v. *United States)* (1893) 1 Moore International Arbitrations 755 ('*Bering Sea Fur Seals* case').

enjoyed complete freedom on the high seas, while the United States advanced inventive arguments that made express reference to equity in a substantive and intergenerational sense. Specifically, the United States argued that it was the trustee for 'preserving and cherishing this valuable interest', and that this obligation to protect marine wildlife derived from the 'natural trust' held for the benefit of future generations. In this respect, counsel for the United States described the earth and its natural resources as a 'gift in common' to mankind, that may only be the subject of usufructuary possession and not absolute beneficial ownership, and which must be protected for the interests of 'succeeding tenants'.[54]

There was no discussion of these ideas in the British submissions, and neither were they considered in the brief award of the tribunal, which found in favour of Britain's assertion of the high seas freedom to fish. The main practical legacy of the decision is the detailed regulations set down, at the request of the parties, to protect and preserve the fur seal population. Nonetheless, a question remaining to this day is what legal and discursive impact the decision would have had if it had found that the United States possessed the trusteeship rights it asserted, rights that are potentially able to be given expression through established legal concepts. In this regard, one of the arbitrators appointed by the United States, Justice John Marshall Harlan, in his carefully reasoned dissenting opinion, held that in the absence of precedent it was appropriate to turn to 'the law of nature; that is . . . the principles of justice, sound reason, morality, and equity, as recognized and approved by civilized peoples'.[55]

The *Bering Sea Fur Seals* case occupies an important position in the canon of international environmental jurisprudence, as seen most obviously in the significant attention it attracts in the leading texts, notwithstanding the limited compass of the decision itself.[56] This confirms that when assessing the discursive impact of international litigation it is necessary to look beyond the formal documentary products of the dispute settlement process, the decisions and orders of the relevant court or tribunal concerned, and to examine the oral and written submissions of the parties, and the broader social and political context in which litigation was made possible, and the way in which the litigation is interpreted over time by international actors and commentators.

[54] Written argument by Mr Carter, Counsel for the United States, reproduced in ibid., 833–4.
[55] Ibid., 914. [56] See, e.g., Sands, above n. 7, 561–5.

3.2.2 Nuclear weapons and intergenerational equity

Much more recently, the concept of intergenerational equity was expressly invoked by the ICJ in the *Legality of the Threat or Use of Nuclear Weapons (Nuclear Weapons Advisory Opinion)*[57] in 1996.[58] The proceedings were the third occasion in which the environmental effects flowing from the military use of nuclear technology had been brought before the Court, the previous instances being the 1974 *Nuclear Tests* cases[59] and 1995 *Nuclear Tests* case,[60] both concerning French nuclear testing in the South Pacific. Neither the 1974 nor 1995 decision engaged with substantive issues of environmental law that could have a bearing on sustainable development in the pre- or post-Rio Conference stages of its emergence.[61] Nonetheless, in the 1995 *Nuclear Tests* case, Judge Weeramantry issued a strong dissenting judgment in which he considered the concept of 'intergenerational rights'.[62] New Zealand had not made an argument along these lines, however Judge Weeramantry considered it implicit in the long-lasting environmental effects occasioned by nuclear testing that the Court was being asked to consider in the matter. Judge Weeramantry argued that the ICJ is a 'trustee' of the rights of generations yet unborn.[63]

By contrast, in the *Nuclear Weapons Advisory Opinion*, the ICJ did recognise both the notion of intra-generational and intergenerational equity as matters 'imperative' for correctly applying the United Nations Charter and international humanitarian law.[64] Evidently neither idea constrained the Court from reaching its controversial finding that it 'cannot conclude definitively whether the threat or use of nuclear weapons would be lawful or unlawful in an extreme circumstance of self-defence, in which the very survival of a State would be at stake'.[65] However, it is significant that the Court did expressly recognise that 'the environment is not an abstraction but represents the living space,

57 *Nuclear Weapons Advisory Opinion* [1996] ICJ Rep. 226.

58 UNGA Res. 49/75 K.

59 *Nuclear Tests (Australia* v. *France) (merits)* [1974] ICJ Rep. 253; *Nuclear Tests (New Zealand* v. *France) (merits)* [1974] ICJ Rep. 457.

60 *Nuclear Tests, Request for an Examination of the Situation in Accordance with Paragraph 63 of the Court's Judgment of 20 December 1974 in the Nuclear Tests (New Zealand* v. *France)* [1995] ICJ Rep. 288.

61 Stephens, above n. 23, 137–50.

62 *Nuclear Tests*, above n. 60, 341.

63 Ibid. 341–2.

64 Edith Brown Weiss, 'Opening the Door to the Environment and to Future Generations' in Laurence Boisson de Chazournes and Philippe Sands (eds.), *International Law, the International Court of Justice and Nuclear Weapons* (Cambridge University Press, 1999) 338, 349.

65 *Nuclear Weapons Advisory Opinion*, above n. 57, 105.

the quality of life and the very health of human beings, including generations unborn'.[66] It also noted '[t]he destructive power of nuclear weapons cannot be contained in either space or time' and that they 'could be a serious danger to future generations' as they may 'damage the future environment, food and marine ecosystem, and ... cause genetic defects and illness in future generations'.[67] In his dissenting judgment, Judge Weeramantry advanced this analysis further, explaining the way this dimension of sustainable development could be incorporated within established legal rights. He referred expressly to 'the principle of intergenerational equity' and held that the Court can and should recognise and respect the rights of future generations, as these rights 'have woven themselves into international law through major treaties, through juristic opinion and through general principles of law recognized by civilised nations'.[68]

3.2.3 'Community of interest' in international watercourses

Shortly after the *Nuclear Weapons Advisory Opinion*, the ICJ decided the *Gabčíkovo-Nagymaros Project* case,[69] rendering a decision in which the Court made express reference to sustainable development for the first time.[70]

The case turned on a joint project between Hungary and Slovakia executed under a 1977 treaty[71] between Hungary and Czechoslovakia, to which Slovakia succeeded in 1993. Ultimately the Court concluded that the environmental concerns raised by Hungary in relation to the project could appropriately and effectively be addressed within the framework of the 1977 treaty, and that therefore Hungary could not withdraw from the regime. The decision was highly procedural in its focus. However, the Court affirmed the statement it made in the *Nuclear Weapons Advisory Opinion*, that 'the environment is not an abstraction but represents the living space, the quality of life and the very health of human beings, including generations unborn'.[72] In addressing the future conduct of the

[66] Ibid. 29. [67] Ibid. 35. [68] Ibid. (Dissenting Opinion of Judge Weeramantry) 17.

[69] *Gabčíkovo-Nagymaros Project (Hungary* v. *Slovakia)* [1997] ICJ Rep. 7.

[70] Although in the *Nuclear Weapons Advisory Opinion*, above n. 57, 30, the Court did refer to Art. 24 of the Rio Declaration, which provides that '[w]arfare is inherently destructive of sustainable development'.

[71] Treaty Concerning the Construction and Operation of the Gabčíkovo-Nagymaros System of Locks, opened for signature 16 September 1977, 32 ILM 1247 (entered into force 30 June 1978).

[72] *Nuclear Weapons Advisory Opinion*, above n. 57, 112.

parties under the joint regime, the Court noted the importance of 'vigilance and prevention' in the field of environmental protection 'on account of the often irreversible character of damage to the environment'.[73] It referred to new norms having been established in recognition of the risks posed 'for mankind – for present and future generations' by constant interference with nature.[74] And it placed these concerns specifically within the concept of sustainability in stating that the 'need to reconcile economic development with protection of the environment is aptly expressed in the concept of sustainable development'.[75]

There has been extensive analysis of the extent to which this analysis has influenced international environmental law and the discourse of sustainability in general. It cannot be argued that it has led to the recognition of sustainable development and the subsidiary notion of intergenerational equity as binding legal norms. The most realistic assessment is that provided by Vaughan Lowe, who argues the decision shows that while sustainable development cannot be applied as a binding rule, it may be used as a 'meta principle' that exercises an 'interstitial normativity' in reconciling conflicting developmental and environmental norms.[76] This recognises the discursive impact of sustainability in providing a conceptual language in resolving disputes on environmental issues that run up against traditional norms of international law that otherwise seem hostile, or at least non-responsive, to contemporary environmental concerns. The Court found that new developments in international environmental law could have a legitimate impact on the interpretation and application of a treaty concluded many years beforehand in 1977, a conclusion described as being of potentially radical importance.[77] The Court's affirmation of the 'community of interest' concept significantly advanced the sub-discourse of justice within sustainability. Slovakia had contended that in the face of Hungary's intransigence it could proceed unilaterally to divert up to 90 per cent of flows of the Danube to a bypass canal on its territory, where the water would be used to generate electricity. The Court rejected this as an unlawful countermeasure, finding that Hungary had not 'forfeited its basic right to an equitable and reasonable sharing of the resources of an

[73] Ibid. 140. [74] Ibid. [75] Ibid.

[76] A. Vaughan Lowe, 'Sustainable Development and Unsustainable Arguments' in Alan Boyle and David Freestone (eds.), *International Law and Sustainable Development: Past Achievements and Future Challenges* (Oxford University Press, 1999) 19, 31.

[77] Philippe Sands, 'International Environmental Litigation and its Future' (1999) 32 *University of Richmond Law Review* 1619, 1632.

international watercourse'.[78] In support of this principle the Court cited the dictum of the Permanent Court of International Justice in the *Territorial Jurisdiction of the International Commission of the River Oder* case, that the 'community of interest in a navigable river becomes the basis of a common legal right'.[79]

The Court did not elaborate on what the community of interest approach requires, but there is in the notion the seeds not only of *inter partes* equitable adjustment as seen in the *Lake Lanoux* case, but also a wider concern with the global equitable dimensions of sustainable development. The issue of equitable sharing of transboundary water resources is treated in depth in various instruments, including the 1997 Watercourses Convention, referred to with approval by the Court. However, in relation to the broader question as to access to freshwater resources by disadvantaged states, there has been limited treaty-law development, underlying the need for greater conceptual development. In this regard, McCaffrey argues the community of interest theory could potentially be developed in line with the concept of common heritage of humankind which underpins the regime of the United Nations Convention on the Law of the Sea in relation to the mineral resources of the deep seabed.[80] He observes that when it comes to oceanic resources the international community has devised a system for resource sharing, with particular regard for landlocked and geographically disadvantaged states, and that it is 'equally important that [there be an] elaboration of a system for the sharing of the world's freshwater resources equitably among all states, especially those that are *hydrologically* disadvantaged'.[81] For McCaffrey, the principles of equitable allocation underlying the deep seabed regime have even more pressing relevance in the context of freshwater resources which are essential for human life.[82] Ellen Hey has similarly observed that the main impediment to addressing the global water crisis, in which over one billion people lack access to safe and affordable water, is the absence of fair and equitable distribution.[83]

[78] *Gabčíkovo-Nagymaros Project*, above n. 69, 78.

[79] *Territorial Jurisdiction of the International Commission of the River Oder* [1929] PCIJ (ser. A) No. 23, 27.

[80] Opened for signature 10 December 1982, 1833 UNTS 3 (entered into force 16 November 1994), Part XI.

[81] McCaffrey, above n. 44, 169 (emphasis in original).

[82] Ibid.

[83] Hey, above n. 41, 351.

4. International courts and discursive transformation

The community of interest theory has not received attention in the proceedings recently brought by Argentina in relation to the authorisation and construction by Uruguay of pulp mills on the River Uruguay,[84] although the decision on the merits carries important implications for several procedural dimensions of sustainable development.

Unlike the *Gabčíkovo-Nagymaros Project* case, which related primarily to diversion of water from an international river, the *Pulp Mills* case was concerned with potential pollution impacts on the River Uruguay from two pulp mills, and there was therefore of limited relevance for the community of interest notion. There are, however, other significant aspects of the litigation, both in the interlocutory phase and on the merits, for the discourse of sustainability. One particularly notable feature was the reference made by the Court in its first provisional measures order to sustainability in a radically different way to its formulation in the *Gabčíkovo-Nagymaros Project* case. In rejecting Argentina's application for provisional measures, the Court noted that 'the present case highlights the importance of the need to ensure environmental protection of shared natural resources while allowing for *sustainable economic development*'.[85] As the concept of sustainable development already seeks to balance ecological protection with economic growth, something the Court made express reference to in the *Gabčíkovo-Nagymaros Project* case, this novel accenting of the economic dimension of sustainable development suggested that the Court was on the cusp of a major reframing of the discourse of sustainability.

However, this new formulation, which had been suggested to the Court by counsel for Uruguay, Alan Boyle, in order to bring into focus the economic interests of Uruguay,[86] was not subsequently repeated in the judgment on the merits, a decision that added no new substantive content to the concept of sustainable development as set out by the Court

[84] *Pulp Mills on the River Uruguay (Argentina* v. *Uruguay) (request for provisional measures by Argentina)*, above n. 20; *Pulp Mills on the River Uruguay (Argentina* v. *Uruguay) (request for provisional measures by Uruguay)*, above n. 20.

[85] *Pulp Mills on the River Uruguay (Argentina* v. *Uruguay) (request for provisional measures by Argentina)*, above n. 20, 80. Emphasis added.

[86] Verbatim Record, Thursday 8 June 2006, [44]. See further Alan Boyle, 'Between Process and Substance: Sustainable Development in the Jurisprudence of International Courts and Tribunals' in Hans Christian Bugge and Christina Voigt (eds.), *Sustainable Development in International and National Law* (Europa Law Publishing, Groningen, 2008) 203.

in the *Gabčíkovo-Nagymaros Project* case. Rather than stepping again into this contested territory, or considering the range of multilateral environmental agreements cited by Argentina, the Court largely confined itself to an examination of the obligations imposed upon the parties by the applicable river treaty: the 1975 Statute of the River Uruguay.[87]

Argentina claimed that Uruguay had breached several procedural and substantive obligations under the river regime, including by discharging pollutants into the river having damaging effects on riverine biodiversity. In presenting its case, Argentina sought to link its claims under the 1975 statute with the international law of sustainable development in its broadest sense, by referring to a number of multilateral environmental conventions and environmental principles, including sustainable development.[88] Exemplifying the strict jurisdictional confines within which international adjudication normally operates, the Court found that the 1975 statute did not incorporate these standards, and that it did not have jurisdiction to look beyond the 1975 statute to measure Uruguay's compliance against the 1973 Convention on the International Trade in Endangered Species of Wild Flora or Fauna, the 1971 Ramsar Convention on Wetlands of International Importance, the 1992 United Nations Convention on Biological Diversity or the 2001 Stockholm Convention on Persistent Organic Pollutants.[89] While the Court did acknowledge that this body of law and principle could be taken into account in interpreting the 1975 statute, consistent with customary rules of treaty interpretation as codified in the 1969 Vienna Convention on the Law of Treaties,[90] there is no indication that this material had any real impact on the reasoning of the Court.

Ultimately the ICJ, while making several references to sustainable development,[91] did not explore the meaning of the term in reaching its conclusion that Uruguay had breached certain procedural obligations to notify the river commission of planned works before their authorisation, but had not violated substantive obligations, including the obligation under Article 41 of the 1975 statute to prevent pollution and preserve the river environment. In relation to the latter obligation, the Court held that proper performance required the carrying out of an environmental

[87] Opened for signature 16 February 1975, 1295 UNTS 340 (entered into force 18 September 1976).

[88] *Pulp Mills on the River Uruguay (Argentina* v. *Uruguay) (merits)* Judgment of 20 April 2010, 53.

[89] Ibid. 63. [90] Ibid. 65. [91] Ibid., especially 75, 177.

impact assessment (EIA);[92] a position both parties accepted although they disagreed on the content that the EIA should have. Significantly, the Court held that EIA had 'gained so much acceptance among States that it may be considered a requirement under general international law' to undertake such an assessment 'where there is a risk that the proposed industrial activity may have a significant adverse impact in a transboundary context'.[93] However, it found that neither the 1975 statute nor general international law specified the reach or the detailed content of an EIA. The Court found that Uruguay was in breach of a procedural obligation under the 1975 statute by failing to notify Argentina of the EIA,[94] something akin to a procedural defect giving rise to administrative law jurisdiction, but not on the substantive question as to whether the EIA was satisfactory. Argentina argued that the EIA had failed to consider possible alternative sites for one of the mills, and had not involved sufficient consultations with affected populations on the river. The Court concluded that the assessment had considered alternatives,[95] and that affected communities had indeed been consulted.[96]

The Court was therefore unwilling to engage in a substantive sense with the discourse of sustainability, and confined its assessment to procedural issues. Nonetheless, it is significant that the procedural issues were placed within the conceptual framework of sustainable development, with the Court referring to the concept more frequently in its judgment than in any previous case, and in a context in which it could potentially have ignored it altogether in its interpretation of the 1975 statute. The persistent appearance of the language of sustainability in the reasons, if not concrete notions of sustainable development, is in this respect reflective of the way in which the case was argued by the parties, with both sides making repeated reference to the concept in their submissions.

5. Conclusion

This chapter has offered an analysis of only a small cross-section of international jurisprudence of relevance to the discourse of sustainable development. The discursive influence of this case law, and the broader body of arbitral awards and judicial decisions of which it is representative, should not be overestimated, as its impact is relatively weak in comparison with the other forces that have shaped legal and policy

[92] Ibid. 203. [93] Ibid. 204. [94] Ibid. 119–20. [95] Ibid. 210. [96] Ibid. 219.

debates around sustainability. Beyond statements by one former judge of the ICJ, Christopher Weeramantry (who once famously described sustainable development as among 'the most ancient of ideas in the human heritage'[97]), there is little willingness among international courts and their judges to engage in any comprehensive and overt way with the concept of sustainable development.

In this respect, the position which international courts occupy in the international legal system needs to be appreciated. The 'hardware' of international adjudication – its consensual basis – limits the capacity of international courts to consider and apply sustainable development and other environmental principles and thereby contribute to the 'software' provided by discourses to environmental governance. This restricted position is most obvious in the context of ad hoc arbitration, which is less independent of party control than judicial settlement.[98] However, even in permanent international courts, which enjoy greater isolation from political pressure, there is a tendency to take the narrowest and most uncontroversial path in the reasoning, and to facilitate an amicable settlement to environmental disputes where this is possible.[99] Nonetheless, the reality is that the judicialisation of environmental governance continues apace, as litigants increasingly seek a resolution to disputes within international courts. Despite their jurisdictional limitations, international courts remain unique as institutions for addressing such controversies, as their separation (even though only a partial one) from the cut and thrust of international polities imbues courts with the capacity to render decisions, and develop the law incrementally, in a rational and reasoned way which will tend to command authority and legitimacy above and beyond the cacophony of voices in debates over sustainability.

The crucial environmental and developmental challenges of our time will therefore continue to be raised in international environmental litigation in the absence of their clear resolution in treaty and customary law. Hence, we shall continue to see cases such as the *Pulp Mills* case where pressure is brought to bear upon international courts to adjust the notion of sustainable development towards one of the oppositional developmental and environmental priorities that the discourse purports

[97] *Gabčíkovo-Nagymaros Project (Hungary* v. *Slovakia)*, above n. 69, 110.

[98] Robert Keohane, Andrew Moravcsik and Anne-Marie Slaughter, 'Legalized Dispute Resolution: Interstate and Transnational' (2000) 54 *International Organization* 457.

[99] Stephens, above n. 23, 97–102 and 109–12.

to syncretise. The challenge for international courts will be to continue to walk the 'tightrope' between the party consent and international legitimacy when addressing such disputes. It has been suggested in this chapter that international courts may seek to make a contribution to the discourse of sustainable development, while at the same time retaining their legitimacy by using what are labelled 'old tools'; traditional legal concepts and categories of equity and justice. A more recent discursive strategy utilised by international courts to stay aloft is to avoid the substantive dimensions of sustainability altogether. This strategising is seen most obviously in the approach adopted by the ICJ in the *Gabčíkovo-Nagymaros* case and the *Pulp Mills* case in focusing on the means of achieving, rather than ends to be achieved by, sustainable development. Both of these decisions considered in detail procedural environmental obligations, and these were expressly assessed within the rubric of sustainable development. This is, it might be thought, an unremarkable achievement, and one which confirms the 'proceduralisation' and public law infiltration of international environmental law in which major controversies are not resolved, or only partially addressed, with the parties left to themselves to come to an acceptable accommodation.[100] Nonetheless, these decisions can and should be regarded as important expressions of a broader movement in international environmental law to improve the quality of environmental decision-making, and part of a longer tradition of judicial engagement with specific narratives or themes within the larger discourse of sustainable development.

[100] Martti Koskenniemi, 'Peaceful Settlement of Environmental Disputes' (1991) 60 *Nordic Journal of International Law* 73.

9

The discourse of environmental security in the ASEAN context

KHENG-LIAN KOH*

> Freedom from want, freedom from fear, and *the freedom of future generations to inherit a healthy natural environment* – these are the interrelated building blocks of human – and therefore – national security.[1]

1. Introduction

The Association of South East Asian Nations (ASEAN) was established in 1967 as a grouping of five countries – Indonesia, Malaysia, Philippines, Singapore and Thailand. The subsequent inclusion of Brunei, Vietnam, Laos and Myanmar, and Cambodia, between 1984 and 1999, enlarged ASEAN. Its institutional mandate has also widened, from the maintenance and strengthening of peace, security and stability in the region, to the active promotion of an ASEAN Community by 2020,[2] but has since been targeted at 2015. The conceptualisation of its security mandate has similarly expanded. ASEAN is no longer only concerned with traditional security. It is now called on to address non-traditional security issues, including transboundary environmental issues. At the same time, 'human security', which is embedded in non-traditional security and focuses on the individual rather than the state, is gradually entering ASEAN's policy agenda.

The promotion of an ASEAN community and a broadening of understanding of security offer greater scope for environmental law and policy

* The author thanks and acknowledges the assistance of Lovleen Bhullar in preparing this chapter.

1 Kofi Annan, 'Secretary-General Salutes International Workshop on Human Security in Mongolia' (Ulan Bator, press release, 8–10 May 2000). Emphasis added.

2 Declaration of ASEAN Concord II (Bali Concord II), concluded 7 October 2003, Bali, Indonesia.

development within ASEAN that builds on its long-standing environmental governance agenda. It also offers opportunities to strengthen the position of ASEAN as a conduit between public and international legal systems.

ASEAN's earliest environmental initiative was the ASEAN Subregional Environment Program, which went through three phases from 1978 to 1992, setting the framework for regional cooperation on environmental protection. The 1981 Manila Declaration on the ASEAN Environment was intended to ensure the conservation and protection of ASEAN's natural resources. Likewise, the ASEAN Agreement on the Conservation of Nature and Natural Resources of 1985 recognised the link between conservation and socio-economic development, and in 1992, ASEAN Member States further pledged to protect the environment by cooperating to promote and integrate sustainable development into all aspects of development.[3] Since then, ASEAN has developed many policies, plans, programmes, strategies and regional agreements, drawing on public law initiatives and international law advancements to address environmental issues in the region.[4]

Today, transboundary environmental issues have opened up space for novel discourses in ASEAN. This is particularly the case in a time of new environmental threats to the ASEAN region and a rejuvenated environmental governance structure within ASEAN that better facilitates the transmission of ideas, laws and policies between public and international laws through a cooperative regional institution with legal personality under the ASEAN Charter.[5]

This chapter focuses on the role of ASEAN in the broader context of shaping the emerging discourse of securitisation of transboundary environmental issues. Section 2 identifies and discusses the different security approaches, focusing on 'human security'. It then examines the ASEAN approach towards securitisation, including environmental security. The next section illustrates the important features of ASEAN's

[3] ASEAN Agreement on the Conservation of Nature and Natural Resources, opened for signature 9 July 1985, 15 EPL 2 (not yet in force); Singapore Declaration of 1992, concluded 28 January 1992, Singapore.

[4] Kheng-Lian Koh (ed.), *ASEAN Environmental Law, Policy and Governance: Vol. I* (World Scientific, New Jersey, 2009).

[5] ASEAN Charter, opened for signature 18 November 2007 (entered into force 15 December 2008) ('ASEAN Charter'). ASEAN was granted observer status at the United Nations in December 2006. See *Observer Status for the Association of Southeast Asian Nations in the General Assembly*, GA Res. 61/44, 61st sess., 64th mtg, Agenda Item 153, UN Doc. A/RES/61/44 (4 December 2006).

environmental governance structure, particularly under the ASEAN Charter. These features show how ASEAN is now better equipped to engage with discourses concerning human and environmental security. The penultimate section considers the interface of environmental law with some rethinking of the principles of international law and international relations, such as the classical notion of 'security', the principle of sovereignty and non-interference with domestic affairs, and 'human security'. Three case studies relating to non-traditional security issues in ASEAN are examined for this purpose. The conclusion considers some lessons for the future.

2. Human/national security and the environment

The framing of an issue as a 'security' issue has important implications. It heightens political awareness of the issue and encourages a government response. It can then be included in the decision-making agenda, and receive public attention.[6] This is partly because of the way the word 'security' has been employed. Traditionally, 'security' is defined in geopolitical terms and confined to relationships among nation states.[7] The realist and neo-realist state-centric view, which sees the defence of the state's territory from external attack as the overarching goal of security, shaped this understanding. The end of the Cold War in 1989 provided the opportunity for a reconceptualisation of security and, particularly through the framing of 'security' issues, increasing attention is now paid to individuals as the victims of security threats.[8]

The term 'non-traditional security' was first used in the mid-1990s by several European and North American writers to widen the scope of security studies and alert governments and the public to new and emerging threats to states and people.[9] It was, though, the growing recognition of the state's responsibility to provide a safe and secure environment for its citizens to pursue their normal life beyond the military security of the state alone that led to the broad and flexible

[6] Yizhou Wang, 'Defining Non-Traditional Security and its Implications for China' (2004) 12(5) *China & World Economy* 59.

[7] Ibid.

[8] Kofi Annan, *'We the Peoples': The Role of the United Nations in the 20th Century: Report of the Secretary-General*, 54th sess., Agenda Item 49(b), UN Doc. A/54/2000 (27 March 2000)32.

[9] See Wang, above n. 6.

concept of 'human security'.[10] Like most environmental discourses, there is no single universally accepted definition or understanding of human security. However, some common elements do exist.[11] The advocates of human security call for a reorientation of the security referent, moving it away from the exclusive focus on the state to the security of individuals, societies and groups, and for expanding the scope of security to reflect the chronic and complex insecurities commonly faced by individuals and societies.[12] This conception of human security provides a deliberative space to identify the sources of emerging threats, examine their linkages, study their evolution, and to adopt more holistic policy responses.[13]

The United Nations Development Programme first used the term 'human security' in its *Human Development Report* in 1994.[14] It identified two main aspects of 'human security': first, safety from chronic threats such as hunger, disease and repression, and second, protection from sudden and hurtful disruptions in the patterns of daily life. According to the report, human security is a summation of seven distinct elements of security, namely: economic security, food security, health security, environmental security, personal security, political security, and community security.[15]

The 2003 report of the United Nations Commission for Human Security provided a holistic definition of human security 'to protect the vital core of all human lives in ways that enhance human freedoms and human fulfilment. Human security means protecting fundamental freedoms – freedoms that are the essence of life.'[16] The United Nations' (UN) concept of human security, focusing on putting 'humans first', was

[10] Ralf Emmers, Mely Caballero-Anthony and Amitav Acharya (eds.), *Studying Non-Traditional Security in Asia: Trends and Issues* (Marshall Cavendish Academic, London, 2006) v.

[11] Andrew Mack, *Human Security Report 2005: War and Peace in the 21st Century* (Oxford University Press, New York, 2005).

[12] Mely Caballero-Anthony, 'Non-Traditional Security and Infectious Diseases in ASEAN: Going Beyond the Rhetoric of Securitisation to Deeper Institutionalization' (2008) 21 *The Pacific Review* 507, 509–10; Andrew T. H. Tan and J. D. Kenneth Boutlin (eds.), *Non-Traditional Security Issues in Southeast Asia* (Select Publishing for Institute of Defence and Strategic Studies, Singapore, 2001).

[13] Ibid. 510.

[14] United Nations Development Programme, *Human Development Report* (Oxford University Press, New York, 1994) 23.

[15] Ibid. 24–5.

[16] United Nations Commission on Human Security, *Human Security Now* (United Nations, New York, 2003) 4.

subsequently adopted by several developed countries, including Canada, Norway, the Netherlands and Japan. The report of the International Commission on Intervention and State Sovereignty (ICISS) perceives the concept of human security as wider than human rights, much like the United Nations focuses on human fulfilment, not just freedoms. According to the report, this broad notion of human security has also become an increasingly important element in international law and international relations by offering a conceptual framework for international action to advance the livelihoods of the international citizenry.[17]

However, some scholars are wary of categorising all human risks as issues of human security. According to Walt, the discourse around human security runs the risk of expanding security studies excessively and destroying its intellectual coherence, which would 'make it more difficult to devise solutions to any of these problems'.[18] The conceptual ambiguity surrounding human security is the result of the uncertainty about its meaning, and because 'individuals and human race levels are difficult to construct as referent objects for security'.[19]

Among those nations to have adopted the concept of human security, there are two different views about its benefactors.[20] Canada supports protective human security, which extends traditional security to the individual level and stresses the responsibility to protect the individual from physical threats.[21] Japan supports development human security, which stresses chronic threats at the community level and avoids grappling with civil and political rights. This view encourages a long-term

[17] International Commission on Intervention and State Sovereignty (ICISS), *The Responsibility to Protect* (International Development Resource Centre, Ottawa, 2001).

[18] Stephen Walt, 'The Renaissance of Security Studies' (1991) 35 *International Studies Quarterly* 211, 213. See also Daniel Deudney, 'The Case Against Linking Environmental Degradation and National Security' (1990) 19 *Millennium* 461.

[19] Barry Buzan, 'Human Security in International Perspective' in Mely Caballero-Anthony and Mohamed Jawhar Hassan (eds.), *The Asia Pacific in the New Millennium: Political and Security Challenges* (ISIS Malaysia, Kuala Lumpur, 2001).

[20] S. Neil MacFarlane and Yuen Foong Khong, *Human Security and the UN: A Critical History* (Indiana University Press, Bloomington, 1st edn, 2006). See also Otto von Feigenblatt, *ASEAN and Human Security: Challenges and Opportunities*, RACPS Working Paper No. 09–5 (2009).

[21] The controversial international 'responsibility to protect' refers to the right and duty of the international community to intervene, with force if necessary, in order to protect individuals in other countries from genocide or other physical threats beyond the capability of their home governments, with or without their approval. See Edward A. Kolodziej, *Security and International Relations* (Cambridge University Press, 2005).

viewpoint to threats and prevention rather than offering short-term protection to citizens.

Some ASEAN Member States have expressed reservations about these elements of human security, such as a responsibility to protect and to respond to issues as they arise, because they are perceived to contravene the principles of sovereignty and non-interference in domestic affairs embodied in the ASEAN Charter.[22] Although the issue is far from uncontroversial, the concept of 'human security' has nevertheless entered the discourse and has promoted a shift in international thinking about humans and the ecosystems in which they live.

Within the broad ambit of human security, this chapter is concerned with 'environmental security' against environmental risks, which includes prevention of ecosystem degradation (resulting, for example, from transboundary pollution), zoonotic and infectious diseases, impacts of climate change and ocean acidificiation,[23] and other transboundary environmental issues (acid rain, nuclear wastes, ozone depletion, soil degradation, and sea-level rise). Transboundary environmental issues[24] have reminded us of a world without borders – what affects one country or a region can have a ripple effect globally. The resulting damage can be potentially severe, in terms of loss of lives and environmental damage, and no one country can tackle these problems. The ICISS Report pointed out that 'the end of the Cold War has held out the prospect of effective joint international action to address issues of . . . human rights and sustainable development on a global scale'.[25] According to former UN Secretary-General Kofi Annan:[26]

> The demands we face also reflect a growing consensus that collective security can no longer be narrowly defined as the absence of armed conflict, be it between or within States . . . environmental disasters present a direct threat to human security.

Relevant to environmental security being a subset of human security, there is some recognition of the inextricable link between the protection

[22] Before the ASEAN Charter, these principles were recognised in the Declaration of ASEAN Concord 1976, concluded 24 February 1976, Bali, Indonesia.

[23] See below Chapter 18 by Julia Mayo-Ramsay; Ross Allen and Anthony Bergin, 'Ocean Acidification: An Emerging Australian Environmental Security Challenge' (2009) 1(2) *Australian Journal of Maritime and Ocean Affairs* 49.

[24] See below Chapter 10 by Simon Marsden. [25] ICISS, above n. 17, 3.

[26] Kofi Annan, *Report of the Secretary-General on the Work of the Organization*, UN GAOR, 55th sess., Supp No. 1, UN Doc. A/55/1 (30 August 2000) 4. See also Kofi Annan, 'Two Concepts of Sovereignty', *The Economist* (London), 18 September 1999.

of human rights and the ecosystem. For instance, on 17 April 2007, for the first time in its history, the United Nations Security Council debated the security implications of climate change, including their impacts on conflict issues such as energy, water, food and other scarce resources, and displacement of populations.[27]

3. Conceptualisation of security in ASEAN: towards the new 'human security' discourse

The principle of state sovereignty forms an integral element of the foreign policies of Southeast Asian countries. The history of colonial rule explains the adoption of the traditional security approach by several of these countries despite most of their security threats having internal origins. Initially, ASEAN provided a forum for regional leaders to meet and discuss issues affecting the entire region. Improved communication led to increased flows of information, which helped build trust and assuage the security concerns of Member States.[28]

Over the years, however, the scope of conventional security has broadened in Asia. This trend was initiated during the 1970s, when Japan coined the concept of 'comprehensive security' to take into account external and internal, military and non-military threats. In 1987, even before the end of the Cold War, ASEAN Member States, including Indonesia, Malaysia and Singapore, had also developed their own versions of comprehensive security.[29]

Non-government institutions,[30] such as the ASEAN Institutes of Strategic and International Studies (ASEAN-ISIS) and the Council for Security and Cooperation in the Asia Pacific (CSCAP), have been instrumental in enlarging ASEAN's mainstream traditional security discourse to include comprehensive security. ASEAN-ISIS recommended the creation of a multilateral forum for political and security cooperation in the

[27] UN SCOR, 62nd sess., 5663rd mtg, UN Doc. S/PV.5663 (17 April 2007). See also Chris Abbott, Paul Rogers and John Sloboda, *Global Responses to Global Threats: Sustainable Security for the 21st Century* (Oxford Research Group, Oxford, 2006).

[28] Rodolfo Severino, 'ASEAN Beyond Forty: Towards Political and Economic Integration' (2007) 23 *Contemporary Southeast Asia* 406.

[29] Mely Caballero-Anthony, 'Revisioning Human Security in Southeast Asia' (2004) 28(3) *Asian Perspective* 155, 160–1.

[30] Often referred to as 'track two' institutions, which refers to a network of academics, experts, members of civil society and government officials who act in their private capacities. See Pauline Kerr, 'The Security Dialogue in the Asia-Pacific' (1994) 7 *The Pacific Review* 397.

Asia Pacific, which led to ASEAN's proposal for the ASEAN Regional Forum. CSCAP, which comprises several research institutes in the Asia Pacific region, contributed to the development of the notion of human security through its definition of 'comprehensive security' as 'the pursuit of sustainable security in all fields (personal, political, economic, social, cultural, military, environmental), covering both the domestic and external spheres, essentially through cooperative means'.[31]

Arising from this shift in discourse, ASEAN now considers 'comprehensive security' as the 're-organised security concept' where security 'goes beyond (but does not exclude) the military to embrace the political, economic and socio-cultural dimensions'.[32] However, ASEAN has not gone so far as to fully embrace 'human security'. It retains the Member States (rather than individuals) as the security referent in an effort to emphasise regime stability and economic development.[33]

The comprehensive security approach came under intense criticism, particularly in the aftermath of the Asian financial crises of 1997–8, the resulting socio-economic, political and security challenges and their devastating consequences. This highlighted the inadequacy of the state as the main security referent.[34] During this period, the concept of 'human security' entered the regional security lexicon, leading to the deepening of comprehensive security. Thailand became the first and only country in the ASEAN region to officially adopt the human security approach in its foreign and domestic policy. It was also responsible for proposing the concept of human security to ASEAN and calling for the adoption of a more people-centric approach to development. ASEAN responded positively and created a Caucus on Human Security at the ASEAN Post-Ministerial Conference in Manila.[35]

[31] Council for Security Cooperation in Asia Pacific, *CSCAP Memorandum No. 3: The Concepts of Comprehensive and Cooperative Security* (1995) 1.

[32] Muthiah Alagappa, *Asian Security Practices: Material and Ideational Influences* (Stanford University Press, 1998) 624. See also Muthiah Alagappa, 'Comprehensive Security: Interpretations in ASEAN Countries' in Robert Scalapino *et al.* (eds.), *Asian Security Issues: Regional and Global* (Institute of East Asian Studies, University of California, Berkeley, 1988) 50.

[33] Caballero-Anthony, above n. 29, 161–2. See also Zarina Othman, 'Human Security Concepts, Approaches and Debates in Southeast Asia' in Hans Günter Brauch *et al.* (eds.), *Facing Global Environmental Change – Environmental, Human, Energy, Food, Health and Water Security Concepts* (Springer, Berlin, 2009) 79.

[34] Caballero-Anthony, above n. 12, 509.

[35] David Capie and Paul Evans, *The Asia-Pacific Security Lexicon* (Institute of Southeast Asian Studies, Singapore, 2nd edn, 2007) 144.

Non-traditional security issues challenge the survival and well-being of peoples and states arising primarily out of non-military sources, such as climate change, resource scarcity, infectious diseases, irregular migration, famine, people smuggling, drug trafficking and transnational crime.[36] Their common characteristics are:[37]

- They have non-military sources and they are transnational in scope.
- They arise at very short notice, but are rapidly transmitted.
- It is difficult to prevent them, but coping mechanisms can be developed.
- Unilateral national solutions are often inadequate and they require regional and multilateral cooperation.
- The state is no longer the only security referent; the people – at the individual and community levels – are also included.

The fact that the term 'non-traditional security' designates what something is not rather than what it is, has posed analytical problems.[38] However, within ASEAN, the labelling of certain issues as non-traditional security issues has been effective in drawing attention to them, conveying urgency and commanding governmental resources to address them.[39] ASEAN policy-makers are reconsidering their security agendas to find new and innovative ways to address these new and complex non-traditional security challenges. This, in turn, has profound implications on the nature of regional security cooperation among Member States.[40]

ASEAN envisions the establishment of an ASEAN Community consisting of three intertwined and mutually reinforcing pillars – the ASEAN Political-Security Community (APSC), the ASEAN Economic Community and the ASEAN Socio-Cultural Community (ASCC) – to ensure durable peace, stability and shared prosperity in the region. The Annex for the ASEAN Security Community Plan of Action includes a section on promoting cooperation on non-traditional security (environmental) issues including haze, pollution and floods.[41]

36 Caballero-Anthony, above n. 12, 510. 37 Ibid. 508.

38 Caballero-Anthony, above n. 29, 173.

39 Mely Caballero-Anthony, 'Non-Traditional Security and Infectious Diseases in Asia: The Need for a Global Approach for Health and Human Security' (Paper presented at the conference 'East Asia in Transition – Comprehensive Security in the Pacific Rim', Institute of East Asian Studies, University of California, Berkeley, 29 September 2006).

40 Caballero-Anthony, above n. 12, 508.

41 ASEAN, *Annex for the ASEAN Security Community Plan of Action*, official website of the Association of Southeast Asian Nations (2009) www.aseansec.org/16829.htm, last accessed 21 April 2010.

Under the ASEAN Vientiane Action Programme (2004–10), ASEAN began to consider transboundary environmental issues, such as zoonotic and infectious diseases (notably SARS, avian flu and H1N1), and climate change, not merely as environmental issues falling within the ambit of the ASCC, but also the APSC, which deals with 'transboundary problems' requiring enhanced regional cooperation. By categorising these environmental problems under the APSC, ASEAN has 'securitised' them.

The Roadmap for an ASEAN Community 2009–2015 (Roadmap), which consists of the APSC Blueprint, the ASEAN Economic Community Blueprint, the ASCC Blueprint and the Initiative for ASEAN Integration Work Plan 2, replaced the Vientiane Action Programme. The APSC Blueprint states that: 'ASEAN subscribes to the principle of comprehensive security which goes beyond the requirements of traditional security but also takes into account non-traditional aspects vital to regional and national resilience, such as the economic, socio-cultural, and environmental dimensions of development.'[42]

The APSC Blueprint also includes a separate section on non-traditional security issues, which states that a 'key purpose of ASEAN is to respond effectively and in a timely manner, in accordance with the principles of comprehensive security, to all forms of threats, transnational crimes and transboundary challenges'.[43] The APSC can, for example, activate the ASEAN disaster management arrangements (including for environmental disasters) in accordance with the ASEAN Agreement on Disaster Management and Emergency Response 2005. ASEAN has also entered into a Memorandum of Understanding with the UN and the World Bank to strengthen disaster risk reduction and disaster management.

The APSC Blueprint envisages transboundary challenges, such as pandemics (like avian flu, SARS and H1N1, which ASEAN has tackled in recent years), and climate change being elevated to the same status as transnational crimes under it. ASEAN also recognises the proactive role of its defence mechanisms as part of an integrated approach and collective efforts to address non-traditional security issues.[44]

[42] *ASEAN Political-Security Community Blueprint* (2009) 8. [43] Ibid. 12.
[44] See *Joint Declaration of ASEAN Defence Ministers on Strengthening ASEAN Defence Establishments to Meet the Challenges of Non-Traditional Security Threats* (26 February 2009).

4. ASEAN's restructured environmental governance: coping with transboundary environmental issues

The implementation of transboundary environmental issues as security issues requires a stronger governance structure, which is now reflected in the ASEAN Charter. The form of governance structure influences how ASEAN will reorientate its internal and external relations to mobilise national and international support to tackle non-traditional security issues. ASEAN is also changing the way it engages with the region, which is demonstrated through ASEAN Plus 3, East Asia Summit and the ASEAN Regional Forum.[45]

The previous mandate was inadequate to meet the challenges of transboundary environmental problems, while ASEAN's governance structure was piecemeal, limiting its capacity to effectively respond to complex environmental concerns. The ASEAN Charter, which was formally adopted on 20 November 2007 and came into force on 15 December 2008, has vastly improved ASEAN's governance mechanisms.[46] In particular, ASEAN has established new mechanisms for cross-sectoral coordination for the implementation of the Roadmap. This section highlights some of the refinements and structural changes and overall strengthening of the governance architecture of ASEAN and its external relations under the ASEAN Charter that have made ASEAN more receptive to the discourse of environmental security and better equipped to act as an intermediary between public and international environmental laws. One of the significant changes is the upgrading of the secretariat to provide enhanced administrative, research and technical support. The Secretary-General is empowered to work towards integration and to address those new and emerging transboundary environmental challenges that require interaction between the Member States and the global community.

The newly established ASEAN Coordinating Council coordinates ASEAN's performance against the three mutually reinforcing pillars. The ASEAN Socio-Cultural Community Council also coordinates the

[45] For instance, ASEAN and China have signed the Joint Declaration of ASEAN and China on Cooperation in the Field of Non-Traditional Security Issues (4 November 2002).

[46] See also Mely Caballero-Anthony, 'The ASEAN Charter: An Opportunity Missed or One that Cannot Be Missed?' [2008] *Southeast Asian Affairs* 71; Paul Davidson, 'The Role of International Law in the Governance of International Economic Relations in ASEAN' (2008) 12 *Singapore Year Book of International Law* 213.

work of the different sectors under its purview, and on issues that cut across other community councils, while the ASEAN Sectoral Ministerial Bodies implement agreements and decisions of the ASEAN Summit.[47]

ASEAN has also established working groups on the environment.[48] Specific ASEAN centres and other governance mechanisms promote the coordination and implementation of ASEAN's work, for example, on biodiversity, haze pollution, food security, energy and humanitarian assistance.[49] In coping with transboundary environmental problems, ASEAN has to coordinate with international organisations: it has already developed external relations with the UN, World Health Organization, Food and Agricultural Organization and International Organization of Epizootics. Now the Charter institutionalises a system of 'external relations',[50] promoting the position and role of international law within the region.

On environmental issues, ASEAN interacts with its dialogue partners and trading partners, including the European Union, India, China, Australia, New Zealand, Canada, Republic of Korea, United States and Japan, as well as with other sub-regional, regional and international organisations and institutions. ASEAN has also strengthened its local networks and interactions with civil societies and public law systems.

Despite these changes, the ASEAN Charter has not redressed some of the limits to environmental decision-making. In particular, the Charter codified the long-standing ASEAN practice of decision-making by consensus, meaning that decisions reflect the lowest common denominator, and has not deviated from ASEAN's strict adherence to the principle of non-interference. Nevertheless, it is important to remember that the Charter is a living document;[51] it will keep evolving. For instance, on 8 April 2010, ASEAN Member States signed the Protocol to the ASEAN Charter on Dispute Settlement Mechanisms, overcoming a previous criticism of a lack of a dispute settlement process.

[47] See Arts. 8–10 of the ASEAN Charter.

[48] These include working groups on nature conservation and biodiversity; marine and coastal environment; multilateral environmental agreements; environmentally sustainable cities; water resources management, and the Haze Technical Task Force.

[49] These include the ASEAN Centre for Biodiversity, the ASEAN Coordinating Centre for Transboundary Haze Pollution Control, the ASEAN Centre for Energy and the ASEAN Coordinating Centre for Humanitarian Assistance.

[50] See Arts. 41–6 of the ASEAN Charter.

[51] Tommy Koh *et al.*, 'The ASEAN Charter' (2007) 331 *PacNet Newsletter* (7 September 2007).

5. Environmental security in ASEAN and the interface with international law and relations: the Indonesian haze[52]

As transboundary environmental issues lack borders, territorial boundaries act as constraints to international cooperation to address environmental problems, because consent of the affected state is required before administering external assistance. The traditional principle of sovereignty and non-interference in internal affairs of a state, which have been the lynchpin of international relations since the Treaty of Westphalia in 1648, serves as a powerful political tool for non-cooperative states.

These principles are now embedded in the ASEAN Charter,[53] raising several significant questions for 'environmental security'. Does the traditional principle of sovereignty and non-interference in domestic affairs constrain the effective implementation of securitisation of transboundary environmental issues? Should the principle be calibrated? This section attempts to answer these questions by focusing on the Indonesian haze problem.

The problem of Indonesian haze illustrates the challenges posed by the application of the principles of sovereignty and non-interference in the internal affairs of a state for the resolution of non-traditional security issues. The raging fires in Indonesia, commonly referred to as the 'haze', have been an ASEAN concern since the early 1980s. These fires have wrought ecological disaster in terms of pollution, deforestation and the destruction of watersheds, biodiversity and ecological buffer zones. Thus, they represent a threat to the human and environmental security of the region. There were a number of ASEAN instruments dealing with the problem, culminating in the 2002 ASEAN Agreement on Transboundary Haze Pollution, which entered into force on 25 November 2003 with ratification by seven of the ten Member States. Indonesia still has not ratified the Agreement.

During the recurrence of the haze in 2006, the Prime Minister of Singapore, Lee Hsien Loong, raised the issue at the meeting of the United Nations General Assembly on 26 October 2006 to seek assistance

[52] This section is based on the author's previous article, Kheng-Lian Koh, 'A Breakthrough in Solving the Indonesian Haze' in Sharelle Hart (ed.), *Shared Resources – Issues of Governance*, IUCN Environmental Policy and Law Paper No. 72 (2008) 225, which has been updated.

[53] See Art. 2.

from the UN to deal with the problem.[54] He approached the Indonesian representatives to issue an ASEAN statement on the haze. However, Indonesia's representative, Adiyatwidi Adiwoso Asmady, stated that the haze was a domestic problem and that Indonesia did not want any interference in its domestic affairs. She characterised Singapore's call for international assistance as 'badgering', claiming that 'it is tantamount to interference in the domestic affairs of Indonesians'. Ms Asmady even suggested that there might be 'some malice' on the part of Singapore in bringing the matter to the attention of the General Assembly.[55]

The Indonesian response was 'startling' and exaggerated. All that had been done was to '[suggest] that the haze is a staggering problem, that Indonesia and ASEAN cannot cope with it themselves, and that international assistance is urgently needed?'[56] The prime minister of Singapore's call for assistance from the UN was reasonable, as the objective of the Agreement is to prevent and monitor 'tranboundary haze pollution' through 'concerted national efforts and intensified regional and international co-operation'. It is an agreement that appreciates the collective contribution of public and international laws to address a locally produced problem that is experienced across borders. Singapore was of the view that ASEAN Member States had to identify and address this serious, long-term environmental problem as an issue that has now been included in the discourse of human and environmental security. It saw the benefits in linking legal and political systems at local, regional and international levels. On the other hand, Indonesia argued that ASEAN members should limit legal options to the Agreement (to which Indonesia is not a party).[57]

This example highlights the importance of the concomitant re-examination of the interrelationship of transboundary environmental law on the one hand, and international law and relations on the other,

[54] Jeff Ooi, 'Haze: Balls on UN Table, Indonesia Upset', *Asian Correspondent.com*, 6 November 2006 at http://asiancorrespondent.com/jeff-ooi-blog/2006/11/haze_balls_on_un_table_and_ind.php, last accessed 22 July 2009.

[55] Janadas Devan, 'Haze: Why Jakarta Should Accept International Help', *Straits Times* (Singapore), 4 November 2006. See also 'ASEAN Needs Help to Tackle Haze: PM: International Expertise Needed to Help Nip Problem in the Bud', *Straits Times* (Singapore), 6 November 2006.

[56] Devan, above n. 55. See also 'Jakarta Using Sand Ban to Put Pressure on Spore', *Straits Times* (Singapore), 17 February 2007; Derrick Paulo, 'Between the Sand and a Flooded Place', *Today* (Singapore), 13 February 2007.

[57] 'Haze on Line', *FIRE Information Bulletin*, 9 November 2006, 3.

with the development of the concept of non-traditional security in ASEAN and other fora. In this regard, the United Nations High-Level Panel on Threats, Challenges and Change explains the concept of 'responsibility to protect' as follows:

> In signing the Charter of the United Nations, States not only benefit from the privileges of sovereignty but also accept its responsibilities. Whatever perceptions may have prevailed when the Westphalian system first gave rise to the notion of State sovereignty, today it clearly carries with it the obligation of a State to protect the welfare of its own peoples and meet its obligations to the wider international community.[58]

The Indonesian haze problem calls for a calibration of the principles of sovereignty and non-intervention, potentially triggered by the new perspectives on human and environmental security. As Koh and Robinson point out: 'it can be argued that the inability to avert an environmental disaster is a greater loss of sovereign authority than cooperation in agreed programs to control the harm'.[59]

However, at least when dealing with the haze, ASEAN has remained deferential to domestic affairs and public laws, rather than upholding the obligations of states not to harm others. It is surprising that while the APSC Blueprint includes some transnational environmental issues, such as climate change, which therefore have the status of a non-traditional security issue, the Indonesian haze problem is not included. It is instead contained in the ASCC Blueprint. The politically sensitive nature of 'transboundary haze pollution' may explain its non-inclusion under the APSC Blueprint. The practical significance of classifying a transboundary environmental issue as a 'security' issue under the APSC Blueprint is that ASEAN will respond effectively and in a timely manner in accordance with the principle of comprehensive security. Nevertheless, the two pillars are not mutually exclusive and if required, a transnational problem under the ASCC Blueprint may invoke the comprehensive security approach. However, this has not happened with the haze problem.

[58] United Nations Secretary-General's High-Level Panel on Threats, Challenges and Change, *A More Secure World: Our Shared Responsibility* (United Nations, New York 2004) [29].

[59] Kheng-Lian Koh and Nicholas Robinson, 'Strengthening Sustainable Development in Regional Inter-Governmental Governance: Lessons from the "ASEAN Way"' (2002) *Singapore Journal of International and Comparative Law* 640, 676.

6. Towards mainstreaming human security in ASEAN's environmental security agenda

Non-traditional security issues are gradually, if slowly, redefining ASEAN's security architecture.[60] The need for regional cooperation to address what are non-traditional security issues dominates the agenda of ASEAN summits and ministerial meetings. As discussed, even though there is reluctance on the part of Member States to rely on legal avenues and to combat all environmental issues, ASEAN is playing an important role in supporting regional capacity-building efforts as Member States recognise their growing vulnerability to some non-traditional security issues and their limited capacity to address them. This has led to a gradual shift from ASEAN's traditional reactive approach, towards meaningful action and future institutionalisation of security cooperation in ASEAN. This section discusses two non-traditional security issues – zoonotic and infectious diseases and climate change – where there has been an ASEAN environmental discourse around security.

In the past decade, three zoonotic diseases[61] – Severe Acute Respiratory Syndrome (SARS), Highly Pathogenic Avian Influenza (HPAI or avian flu) and H1N1 (swine flu) – have affected countries including ASEAN Member States. Between 2003 and 2005, avian flu recurred in some of the ASEAN countries and the region, and spread to other parts of the world. There was also an outbreak of SARS. The concept of human security (and in the ASEAN context, non-traditional security) has led to the inclusion of health-related issues in the security discourse. The SARS and HPAI crises were watershed events, as they led to the securitisation of infectious diseases in the region.[62]

In December 2004, ASEAN established the HPAI Task Force to address the spread of avian flu. In October 2005, it established a regional fund for avian flu and a three-year action plan. The 2005 Regional Framework for Control and Eradication of HPAI subsumed this regional fund.[63] In the framework, ASEAN also envisages cooperation to strengthen the capacity of relevant regional networks to meet the needs of ASEAN and Member States in communicable disease surveillance and response. This includes strengthening national and regional capacity in

[60] Caballero-Anthony, above n. 12, 516–17.

[61] Any disease or infection that is naturally transmissible from vertebrate animals to humans and vice versa is classified as a zoonosis.

[62] Caballero-Anthony, above n. 12, 514. [63] Ibid. 515.

epidemiological surveillance; early warning and response to avian influenza and other emerging and resurging infections; and to strengthen the capacity of the member countries to prepare for a global influenza pandemic.[64]

These diseases were not confined to the ASEAN region, but spread to other parts of the world, and there was a threat of future recurrences. This promoted the formation of measures across public and international regimes by ASEAN and other organisations. These included:

- The ASEAN Plus Three Emerging Infectious Diseases Programme, which linked multiple sectors and countries to collaborate on responses that complemented regional and national priorities.
- The East Asia Summit Declaration on Avian Influenza Prevention, Control and Response 2005, which emphasises and supports national and regional efforts towards pandemic preparedness and response planning. It calls for national legislation and technical expertise to minimise the impact of a pandemic, and the strengthening of institutional capacities.
- ASEAN collaboration with the World Health Organization to implement the Asian Pacific Strategy for Emerging Diseases, including avian flu.

Because of the experience gained in tackling SARS and avian flu in the region, ASEAN was well placed to manage the outbreak of influenza (H1N1), which originated from Mexico in April 2009.

ASEAN's robust response to avian flu, SARS and H1N1 illustrates its non-traditional security approach under the APSC Blueprint of the ASEAN Charter. However, in tackling zoonotic and infectious diseases, ASEAN has only focused on human health, and not biodiversity aspects. 'Non-traditional security' must include an ecosystem approach. The culling of animals (such as poultry, wild migratory birds and waterfowl) believed to be the source of these diseases, has implications for conservation and sustainability under the 1992 Convention on Biological Diversity, the 1971 Ramsar Convention and the 1979 Convention on Migratory Species of Wild Animals.[65]

[64] Draft Directions for ASEAN Regional Cooperation on Highly Pathogenic Avian Influenza Control and Prevention, 18 October 2005.

[65] Kheng-Lian Koh, 'Animal Health, Biodiversity Conservation and Sustainable Development: A Case Study of Avian Influenza' (2005/6) *Environmental Law Programme Newsletter* 12.

The resulting ecological effects may also threaten food and health security. ASEAN ought to work with the secretariats of international nature conservation agreements to address the issue of culling or over-culling, which does not solve the problem of disease spread and has adverse effects on the ecosystems.

The impacts of climate change are all-encompassing – they affect biodiversity, human and ecosystem health, food production, water scarcity, migration of populations and much more. Climate change has also been identified as a cause of environmental disasters, requiring disaster management and humanitarian relief. Consequently, ASEAN has identified climate change as a security threat. The climate change challenge calls for new approaches, innovative governance and an interface of regional organisations and the international community.

ASEAN has securitised climate change issues within the ambit of non-traditional security. Ministers have noted that 'climate change constitutes a major threat to sustainable development and requires urgent concerted and coordinated actions at national, regional and international levels',[66] while ASEAN has created a series of programmes and policies. ASEAN Member States have also agreed to work closely together for a comprehensive multilateral arrangement to address climate change beyond 2012,[67] building upon the non-binding Copenhagen Accord in the international climate change negotiations process.[68]

On the public law front, ASEAN has encouraged the development of adaptation strategies and the conservation and sustainable management of coastal and marine ecosystems. Further, it has promoted policies and laws relating to integrated water resource management, a 'low carbon

[66] See ASEAN Foreign Ministers, *Acting Together to Cope with Global Challenges*, Joint Communiqué of the 42nd ASEAN Foreign Ministers Meeting, 20 July 2009, Phuket, Thailand, [33]. See also ASEAN Declaration on Environmental Sustainability, concluded 20 November 2007, Singapore.

[67] ASEAN Declaration on the 13th Session of the Conference of the Parties (COP) to the United Nations Framework Convention on Climate Change (UNFCCC) and the 3rd Session of the Conference of the Parties Serving as the Meeting of the Parties (CMP) to the Kyoto Protocol, concluded 20 November 2007, Singapore. See also ASEAN Joint Statement on Climate Change to the 15th Session of the Conference of the Parties to the United Nations Framework Convention on Climate Change and the 5th Session of the Conference Parties serving as the Meeting of Parties to the Kyoto Protocol, concluded 24 October 2009, Cha-am-Hua Hin, Thailand.

[68] ASEAN Leaders' Statement on Joint Response to Climate Change, concluded 9 April 2010, Ha Noi, Vietnam.

society', 'compact cities', 'eco-cities'[69] and 'environmentally sustainable transport'.[70] Following the failure of the international climate meeting at Copenhagen to deliver an international agreement, several countries, including ASEAN Member States, are shifting their focus to a 'Plan B', that is, adaptation to climate change, which is more local or regional in focus. The move towards a 'networked dialogue' mechanism seems to be the preferred ASEAN way in building resilience to climate change. There already exist within ASEAN and the region a few such initiatives, like the Asian Cities Networked Resilience and the Nairobi Network. To provide adaptation solutions, they must be invigorated.

In order to address non-traditional security threats, ASEAN's regional security approach focuses on norm-building, building trust and confidence and developing cooperative approaches with states.[71] However, in order to realise the goals of the Roadmap, the engagement of Member States and the implementation of ASEAN's environmental instruments through public laws must be enhanced, even where this may interfere with the internal affairs of Member States.

As more transboundary environmental issues affect human security, the discourse shifts to focus on whether they should be seen as human rights issues. This is a shift that is intended to capture further issue attention. There is, however, a basis for it within ASEAN. The Terms of Reference under Article 14 of the ASEAN Charter envisage the promotion of human rights to include energy security, prevention of pandemics and sustainable development. Further, ASEAN has established a consultative body, the ASEAN Intergovernmental Commission on Human Rights, which aims to promote 'human rights, including sustainable development, and disaster management and pandemic preparedness'.[72] If this is indeed the current focus, it marks a significant step towards the emerging trend to invoke human rights to advance environmental protection and refashion human and environmental security.

According to the ASEAN Secretary-General, Dr Surin Pitsuwan: 'human security needs a new mindset, requires a new look at the issue

[69] Singapore is now involved in developing China's ecocities in Tianjin and Nanjing. See 'After Tianjin, S'pore-Nanjing "Mini Eco-City" Mooted', *Straits Times* (Singapore), 24 April 2008.

[70] Singapore Declaration on Climate Change, Energy and the Environment, concluded 21 November 2007, Singapore.

[71] Caballero-Anthony, above n. 29, 162.

[72] 'ASEAN Agrees on Role of Human Rights Commission', *Straits Times* (Singapore), 21 July 2009. See also ASEAN Foreign Ministers, above n. 66.

of security. To shift from national security to human security requires a major shift of mindset of policymakers.'[73] Non-traditional security issues could be pivotal in encouraging ASEAN to recalibrate its existing institutional arrangements and to move towards credible and effective policies. This is contingent on the way ASEAN reconceptualises security – from comprehensive security to a more holistic, human security approach, perhaps directed by a human rights framework.[74]

7. The way forward: a new categorisation

The foregoing case studies raise the question of securitisation of transboundary environmental issues and the question of environmental and human rights – all under the new classification of non-traditional security. This approach has implications for traditional international law and public law, and for international relations. The Indonesian haze case study illustrates how the principle of sovereignty and non-interference with internal affairs can stifle effective public and international law and policy responses to a regional environmental problem. While making recommendations for the Charter, members of the ASEAN Eminent Persons' Group debated this issue; however, ultimately the principles of sovereignty and non-interference were entrenched in the Charter. However, this chapter has highlighted a basis for the inveterate Westphalian doctrine of sovereignty being calibrated in the context of environmental law.

As we share one stratosphere, climate change and its linkages to biodiversity and with it questions of the vulnerabilities to human security, such as health security, food security, and water security are all interconnected to the web of life not only in ASEAN, but the world at large. These linkages impact on sustainable development and ASEAN has taken a step forward in shaping the securitisation of transboundary environmental issues in a proactive and innovative manner.

[73] Surin Pitsuwan (keynote address at the 'Launch of the RSIS Centre for Non-Traditional Security Studies', Singapore, 6 May 2008).

[74] Caballero-Anthony, above n. 12, 517.

10

Public participation in transboundary environmental impact assessment: closing the gap between international and public law?

SIMON MARSDEN

1. Introduction

Public participation is an acknowledged part of environmental decision-making and is included in most domestic and international law. The notion of 'public participation' varies, with the term having subtle differences of meaning to different groups. It is, however, part of a discourse of sustainable development and its adherents share an understanding about it involving the public at all stages of decision-making. This results in better outcomes for the environment and more acceptance by the public.[1] In examining the relationship between international and public law concerning environmental protection, the role of the public stands out. Under municipal public law, opportunities to participate in decision-making and challenge regulatory failings in judicial review proceedings are commonly made by individuals and non-governmental organisations (NGOs).[2] In public international law, Principle 10 of the Rio Declaration[3] recognises the role of individuals and NGOs, with the Aarhus Convention providing more opportunities to challenge state governments for similar failings when applicable.[4] International law is no longer confined to the relationship between states and international

[1] See Klaus Bosselmann, *The Principle of Sustainability: Transforming Law and Governance* (Ashgate, Aldershot, 2008) 116.

[2] See Paul Craig, *Administrative Law* (Sweet & Maxwell, London, 6th edn, 2008) 372, who sets out the rationale for procedural rights.

[3] Rio Declaration on Environment and Development, concluded 14 June 1992, Rio de Janeiro, Brazil, Principle 10.

[4] Convention on Access to Information, Public Participation in Decision-Making and Access to Justice in Environmental Matters, opened for signature 25 June 1998, 2161 UNTS 447 (entered into force 30 October 2001) ('Aarhus Convention').

organisations, and in an environmental context it is as appropriate to emphasise the relationship between individuals and states as in international human rights and humanitarian law.[5] In international environmental law, therefore, individuals and NGOs now have an important role in environmental regulation.[6]

This chapter focuses on the discourse, principle and practice of public participation, contributing in particular to the growing debate concerning the globalisation of administrative law.[7] As discussed in the first section of the chapter, the globalisation of administrative law is seen in many ways,[8] including in the regulatory cooperation established through international treaties providing for public participation in transboundary environmental impact assessment (transboundary EIA), the UN Economic Commission for Europe Espoo[9] and Aarhus Conventions. The decision-making body for each treaty, the Meeting of the Parties,[10] has been active in adopting decisions and developing guidance, including for public participation. The non-compliance procedures of each treaty, in particular the Compliance Committee of the Aarhus Convention, informs the argument in this chapter that administrative law mechanisms are permeating public international law so that the traditional gap between municipal and international law in the public domain is closing.

[5] Sam Blay, 'The Nature of International Law' in Sam Blay, Ryszard Piotrowicz and Martin Tsamenyi (eds.), *Public International Law: An Australian Perspective* (Oxford University Press, Melbourne, 2nd edn, 2005) 1, 1.

[6] Peter Spiro, 'Non-Governmental Organisations and Civil Society' in Daniel Bodansky, Jutta Brunnée and Ellen Hey (eds.), *The Oxford Handbook of International Environmental Law* (Oxford University Press, 2007) 770.

[7] See, e.g., Simon Chesterman, 'Globalisation and Public Law: A Global Administrative Law?' in Jeremy Farrall and Kim Rubenstein (eds.), *Sanctions, Accountability and Governance in a Globalised World* (Cambridge University Press, 2009) 1.

[8] See, e.g., Benedict Kingsbury, Nico Krisch and Richard Stewart, 'The Emergence of Global Administrative Law' (2005) 68 *Law and Contemporary Problems* 15, 16; Daniel Esty, 'Good Governance at the Supranational Scale: Globalizing Administrative Law' (2006) 115 *Yale Law Journal* 1490; Francesca Spagnuolo, 'Beyond Participation: Administrative-Law Type Mechanisms in Global Environmental Governance. Toward a New Basis of Legitimacy?' (2009) 15 *European Public Law* 49, 50 and 59, which considers the role of the Aarhus Convention.

[9] Convention on Environmental Impact Assessment in a Transboundary Context, opened for signature 25 February 1991, 1989 UNTS 309 (entered into force 10 September 1997) ('Espoo Convention').

[10] See generally Robin Churchill and Geir Ulfstein, 'Autonomous Institutional Arrangements in Multilateral Environmental Agreements: A Little Noticed Phenomenon in International Law' (2000) 94 *American Journal of International Law* 623; Jutta Brunnée, 'COPing with Consent: Law-Making under Multilateral Environmental Agreements' (2002) 15 *Leiden Journal of International Law* 1.

Public participation is viewed through the lens of EIA[11] because although it is domestically derived and implemented (public law), it is also applied in a transboundary context (international law).[12] This is partly due to the implementation of treaties with EIA provisions, and partly as a result of jurisprudence in international courts and tribunals.[13] Some have suggested that transboundary EIA is not as effective as domestic EIA, because the success of the latter is the administrative law context for its enforcement;[14] in the international law sphere, it is argued, the absence of this context means enforcement is problematic for individuals and NGOs.[15] This chapter challenges this argument by suggesting that the non-compliance procedures in the Espoo and Aarhus Conventions, particularly the Aarhus Compliance Committee,[16] while not directed at individual remedies, provide opportunities to challenge procedural failings regarding public participation in transboundary EIA and are an excellent example of administrative law-type mechanisms operating in the international law context.

In fact, there are at least four potential ways in which procedural failings with transboundary EIA by state parties to these treaties can be remedied by individuals. This is through public participation obligations and other processes like access to information. First, a member of the public can ask its government to remedy its own breaches or challenge a non-compliant state through the Implementation Committee of the Espoo Convention. Second, individuals and NGOs can challenge procedural failings directly

[11] Pierre Andre *et al.*, *Public Participation – International Best Practice Principles*, Special Publication Series No. 4 (International Association for Impact Assessment, Fargo, 2006); Ciaran O'Faircheallaigh, 'Public Participation and Environmental Impact Assessment: Purposes, Implications and Lessons for Public Policy Making' (2010) 30 *Environmental Impact Assessment Review* 19.

[12] Neil Craik, *The International Law of Environmental Impact Assessment* (Cambridge University Press, 2008); Kees Bastmeijer and Timo Koivurova (eds.), *Theory and Practice of Transboundary Environmental Impact Assessment* (Martinus Nijhoff, Leiden and Boston, 2008).

[13] See above Chapter 8 by Tim Stephens, together with Tim Stephens, *International Courts and Environmental Protection* (Cambridge University Press, 2009).

[14] Charles Kersten, 'Rethinking Transboundary Environmental Impact Assessment' (2009) 34 *Yale Journal of International Law* 173, 175.

[15] Stephens (2009), above n. 13, 247, 253–6 discusses opportunities for public interest proceedings in relation to international courts and tribunals.

[16] Veit Koester, 'The Compliance Committee of the Aarhus Convention: An Overview of Procedures and Jurisprudence' (2005) 37 *Environmental Policy and Law* 83; Malgosia Fitzmaurice, 'Environmental Justice through International Complaint Procedures? Comparing the Aarhus Convention and the North American Agreement on Environmental Cooperation', in Jonas Ebbesson and Phoebe Okowa (eds.), *Environmental Law and Justice in Context* (Cambridge University Press, 2009) 211, 213.

through the unique Compliance Committee of the Aarhus Convention. Third, the Aarhus Convention's access to justice obligations provide opportunities for the public to take proceedings, so a member of the public must be allowed to access the courts of its own state or of another party when it has breached its obligations. Fourth, for parties that are also EU Member States, the obligations of these international treaties have been largely implemented by EU secondary law, and the EIA Directive has vertical direct effect. This means that justiciable individual rights against Member State governments are created.[17] Although each of these has relevance to the relationship between international and public law, the focus of this chapter is on the first and second of these mechanisms.

The chapter first explains the relevance of public participation as developed in municipal law to the establishment of a global administrative law, and second, analyses the position of public participation as a principle of international environmental law. The procedural role of the public in relation to the various stages of the EIA process leading up to its contribution to decision-making is explored in the third section, with reference to the provisions of the Espoo and Aarhus Conventions, and in the fourth section in relation to their non-compliance procedures. In conclusion, the chapter argues that in establishing procedures for enforcement of individual rights regarding transboundary EIA, in particular in relation to the Aarhus Compliance Committee, there is evidence that 'global administrative law' is permeating international environmental law.

2. Public participation and 'global administrative law'

The emergence of a growing body of global administrative law has recently been identified in the literature as a response to global

[17] See Simon Marsden, 'Transboundary Environmental Impact Assessment in European Law', in Simon Marsden and Timo Koivurova (eds.), *Transboundary Environmental Impact Assessment in the European Union: The Espoo Convention and its Kiev Protocol on Strategic Environmental Assessment* (Earthscan, London, 2011); Simon Marsden, 'Enforcing Non-Discrimination in Transboundary Environmental Impact Assessment: Advantages for EU Citizens from the Transposition of the Espoo and Aarhus Conventions?' (2009) 6 *Journal for European Environmental and Planning Law* 437; Aine Ryall, *Effective Judicial Protection and the Environmental Impact Assessment Directive in Ireland* (Hart Publishing, Oxford, 2009) For explanation in an administrative law context, see Craig above n. 2, 303, 308, 957, 1006. Note that since the Lisbon Treaty came into force on 1 December 2009, there is no longer any distinction between EC and EU law; the EC has now ceased to exist and the three-pillar structure has been consolidated.

interdependence, including in environmental protection. The inability to address the consequences of this interdependence through isolated national systems has influenced the need to establish transnational systems, frequently through international treaties. Administrative functions not subject to direct control by municipal legal systems have in many cases resulted, having implications for private parties. The Global Administrative Law Project at the New York University School of Law has been responsible for much of this work, which has been examined in the environmental protection context by others.[18] Global administrative law has been defined as:

> comprising the mechanisms, principles, practices, and supporting social understandings that promote or otherwise affect the accountability of global administrative bodies, in particular by ensuring they meet adequate standards of transparency, participation, reasoned decision, and legality, and by providing effective review of the rules and decisions they make.[19]

The accountability of global administrative bodies like institutions established by treaties is a key component of this definition, and adequate standards of participation are seen as essential to this, backed up by the potential for effective review by those affected by decision-making. Global administrative bodies are distinguished as comprising certain models, one of which is the formal intergovernmental regulatory body, established under an international treaty.[20] The definition suggests that global governance can be understood and analysed as administrative action, such as 'rulemaking, administrative adjudication between competing interests, and other forms of regulatory and administrative decision and management'.[21] 'Standards and rules of general applicability adopted by subsidiary bodies' and 'informal decisions taken in overseeing and implementing international regulatory regimes' are identified as examples,[22] many of which derive from the Meeting of the Parties and the implementation of non-compliance procedures.

Two of the subjects of global administration are individuals and NGOs.[23] This is significant when international bodies make decisions having direct legal consequences, including changes in private conduct.

[18] See references in n. 8 above. [19] Kingsbury *et al.*, above n. 8, 17.

[20] Ibid. 21, which identifies the non-compliance procedure of the Montreal Protocol as an example.

[21] Ibid. 17. [22] Ibid. [23] Ibid. 23.

In other instances, while states may be the primary subject of regulation, the intention may be to protect or benefit certain groups.[24] Another perspective on individuals and NGOs is the internal mechanisms adopted by global institutions for participation and accountability, raising the issue of legitimacy in international law. As Spagnuolo emphasises, traditionally legitimacy issues in international (environmental) law have relied on state consent and legality; the rise of global governance, in particular 'the increased delegation of decision-making authority to global institutions and the growing distance between those exercising authority and the public', has created the need for alternative standards of legitimacy, such as public participation.[25] In environmental governance in particular, the case of participatory rights is highlighted as having different functions and justifications in a global context. Three are identified:

> First of all, by forcing global regulators to be more transparent and openly justify rules, public participation increases social consensus and leads to greater legitimacy. Secondly, it ensures exchange of information and provides a forum for debate and discussion. Thirdly, and more similarly to domestic legal orders, participation is a means to provide due process to other States and nationals and to grant the right of national authorities or private individuals to have their views considered before a decision is taken.[26]

The Aarhus Convention is a prominent example, although the role of the Compliance Committee is only indicated by way of a footnote, despite calls for greater procedural guarantees.[27] It is the Aarhus Convention in particular where concerns are identified. In Kersten's 'Rethinking Transboundary Environmental Impact Assessment', he argues that information alone will not produce an effective EIA regime which also 'requires the support of other institutions to achieve maximum effect'.[28] He points to those institutions established under the US Administrative Procedure Act, which empower courts to overturn an agency action when not in accordance with the law. The US domestic law on EIA, the National Environmental Policy Act, has largely been successful because of this administrative law context.[29]

[24] Ibid. 24–5. [25] Spagnuolo, above n. 8, 53–4. [26] Ibid. 58.
[27] Ibid. 59–60 (footnotes 53 and 59). [28] Kersten, above n. 14, 182.
[29] Ibid. 191. National Environmental Policy Act, 42 USC (1969) ss. 4321–7; Administrative Procedures Act, 5 USC (1946) s. 706.

In contrast to this US domestic law, Kersten points to the vague language and weak enforcement mechanisms in the international context for transboundary EIA.[30] Yet while he identifies the Aarhus Convention generally as a means for individuals to challenge procedural failings in national courts, he fails to highlight the role of the Compliance Committee, which can be used as a forum to complain about breaches of participatory rights in transboundary EIA when it is not possible to meet national requirements for standing, or overcome other technical restrictions. Although the Compliance Committee procedure is not directed specifically to the enforcement of individual rights, and is in no way comparable to the binding enforcement mechanisms in domestic law such as the US Administrative Procedures Act which supports the National Environmental Policy Act, the relationship between it and the public participation provisions in the Espoo Convention at least allows for individual complaints to be raised and followed up with the non-compliant state through the Meeting of the Parties. As such, it is an excellent example of global administrative law in action in the environmental sphere.

The guidance produced on the compliance mechanism gives substance to this claim.[31] This is replete with provisions concerning 'rulemaking, administrative adjudication between competing interests, and other forms of regulatory and administrative decision and management'. They are 'administrative action' in the context of global governance.[32] The introduction to the guide details the composition of the Compliance Committee, its nomination for election, functions, powers and triggers for compliance review. Concerning its modus operandi, general principles of the Committee's operation, procedures for handling submissions and referrals, and for processing communications and gathering information are detailed. The final two sections concern the relationship between NGOs and the Committee and public communications, followed by two annexes further specifying information requirements. In relation to public communications, formal criteria to be satisfied are set out, including taking into account the availability of any domestic remedy.[33] All of these provisions are administrative in character.

[30] Kersten, above n. 14, 193.

[31] *Guidance Document on Aarhus Convention Compliance Mechanism, Volume 11* (2008) www.unece.org/env/pp/compliance/manualv8.doc, last accessed 21 May 2011.

[32] Kingsbury *et al.*, above n. 8. [33] Ibid. 32.

3. Public participation as a principle of international environmental law

Public participation is part of the discourse of sustainable development, which has come to require not only sustainable outcomes but also environmentally democratic processes. While those advocating public participation sometimes have different perspectives on the nature, coverage and form of both 'public' and 'participation', all use the terms to argue for a common change – to empower those often ignored in decision-making processes. Of particular relevance to transboundary EIA, notably principles of consultation, participation and non-discrimination have been advanced in the jurisprudence of international courts and tribunals, treaties and soft law instruments.[34] In particular, many of them have been raised in the context of international watercourses.[35] Although there has been argument over whether transboundary EIA may have attained customary status,[36] the general obligations flowing from state responsibility have accepted customary status following earlier decisions reached in the *Trail Smelter*,[37] *Lake Lanoux*[38] and *Nuclear Test* cases.[39] Yet prevention of harm to the environment was a limited part of the reasoning to most of these cases,[40] and it has been

[34] Kees Bastmeijer and Timo Koivurova, 'Introduction' in Bastmeijer and Koivurova (eds.), above n. 12, 3.

[35] Lilian del Castillo-Laborde, 'Case Law on International Watercourses' in Joseph Dellapenna and Joyeeta Gupta (eds.), *The Evolution of the Law and Politics of Water* (Springer, Dordrecht, 2009) 319.

[36] Jack Jacobs, 'A New Look at Environmental Impact Assessments: Using Customary Law to Prevent Domestic and Transboundary Environmental Damage' in Michael Faure and Song Ying (eds.), *China and International Environmental Liability* (Edward Elgar, Cheltenham, 2008) 22; Alexander Gillespie, 'Environmental Impact Assessments in International Law' (2008) 17 *Review of European Community and International Environmental Law* 221; Bastmeijer and Koivurova, above n. 12, 355–7; Craik, above n. 12, 120–6; John Knox, 'The Myth and Reality of Transboundary Environmental Impact Assessment' (2002) 96 *American Journal of International Law* 291.

[37] *Trail Smelter Arbitration (United States* v. *Canada)* (1938 and 1941) 3 UN Rep. Int. Arb. Awards.

[38] *Lake Lanoux Arbitration (France* v. *Spain)* (1957) 12 UN Rep. Int. Arb. Awards. It is notable that the duty to cooperate has also featured heavily in international water law; see Maria Manuela Farrajota, 'International Cooperation on Water Resources' in Dellapenna and Gupta (eds.), above n. 35, 337.

[39] *Nuclear Tests (New Zealand* v. *France) (merits)* [1974] ICJ Rep. 457; *Request for an Examination of the Situation in Accordance with Paragraph 63 of the Court's Judgment of 20 December 1974 in the Nuclear Tests (New Zealand* v. *France)* [1995] ICJ Rep. 288.

[40] Stephens (2009), above n. 13, 134–7.

left to dissenting jurists[41] and academics[42] to argue that sustainable development, precaution and potentially EIA with public participation central to it has acquired customary status.

The *Lake Lanoux Arbitration*[43] sets out the duty to cooperate in transboundary situations, such as the use of a shared natural resource, including the principle of 'state' participation, potentially in the procedures of another.[44] Proper observance of the duty requires states to undertake EIA, give prior notice and consult and negotiate with any state whose interests may be affected. However, there remain limitations, as under the doctrine of state sovereignty states only have to negotiate in good faith. States are not required to obtain the prior consent of states potentially affected by intended activities in their own jurisdiction. In relation to emergency situations and accidents, the duty to notify is enhanced by a need to take timely action if they might cause harm to others, as shown in the *Corfu Channel* case.[45] Connected with the duty to notify is the duty to assist others, which, while a feature of some treaty regimes, is unlikely to exist as a customary norm.

The duty to cooperate is also seen in a number of international agreements, for example the Convention on the Law of Non-Navigable Uses of International Watercourses 1997.[46] The earliest, with specific reference to transboundary EIA, is found in the 1974 Nordic Environmental Protection Convention,[47] requiring an assessment of the effects in the territory of one party of activities carried out in the territory of another. Emergency situations have received particular emphasis in treaties, for example the Convention on Early Notification

41 Weeramantry J in the 1995 *Nuclear Tests* case and later *Gabčíkovo-Nagymaros Project (Hungary* v. *Slovakia)* [1997] ICJ Rep. 7.

42 For a recent evaluation with respect to sustainability as distinct from sustainable development, see Bosselmann, above n. 1.

43 Above n. 38.

44 This needs to be distinguished from any principle of public participation, which clearly has different results. Public participation has been developed in the specific context of water governance; see Jona Razzaque, 'Public Participation in Water Governance' in Dellapenna and Gupta (eds.), above n. 35, 353.

45 *Corfu Channel (United Kingdom* v. *Albania) (merits)* [1949] ICJ Rep. 4.

46 Convention on the Law of the Non-Navigational Uses of International Watercourses, opened for signature 21 May 1997, 36 ILM 700 (not yet in force).

47 Nordic Convention on the Protection of the Environment, opened for signature 19 February 1974, 13 ILM 511 (entered into force 5 October 1976). See Timo Koivurova, 'Transboundary Environmental Impact Assessment in International Law' in Marsden and Koivurova (eds.), above n. 17, 16.

of a Nuclear Accident 1986,[48] prepared in response to the failure of the then USSR to notify the international community in a timely or adequate manner about the Chernobyl incident the same year.

Principle 10 of the Rio Declaration is a classic exposition of the participatory principle in soft law, applied in a public context.[49] This calls for environmental information to be made public and distributed as widely as possible, so that the public can participate in environmental decision-making, and for access to justice to be granted to the public.[50] Pallemaerts[51] cites the 1985 ASEAN Agreement on the Conservation of Nature and Natural Resources,[52] as the first regional agreement to give effect to the principle, and more recently the African Union's 2003 African Convention on the Conservation of Nature and Natural Resources.[53] He defines the principle:

> The participatory principle essentially calls for environmental information to be made public and disseminated as widely as possible, for public participation to be guaranteed in decision-making on projects, plans and programmes with significant environmental implications, and for access to justice to be granted to the public in environmental matters.

State practice and judicial opinion have therefore ensured the participatory principle is widely accepted by the international community, largely as a result of national law preceding developments at the international level, as several countries have had such provisions in their national law for some time, as set out by Kiss and Shelton when they discuss the full range of environmental rights, including participation, access to information and access to justice. They also consider human rights, environmental justice and equity, and discuss national case law where challenges to EIA procedures have been upheld on the basis of failure to

[48] Convention on Early Notification of a Nuclear Accident, opened for signature 26 September 1986, 1439 UNTS 276 (entered into force 27 October 1986).

[49] Above n. 3.

[50] Other soft law pronouncements on the participatory principle include the World Charter for Nature, GA Res. 37/7, 48th plenary mtg, UN Doc. A/RES/37/7 (28 October 1982).

[51] Marc Pallemaerts, 'An Introduction to the Sources, Principles and Regimes of International Environmental Law' in Marko Berglund (ed.), *International Environmental Law Making and Diplomacy* (University of Joensuu, Department of Law, 2004) 69.

[52] ASEAN Agreement on the Conservation of Nature and Natural Resources, opened for signature 9 July 1985, 15 EPL 2 (not yet in force).

[53] African Convention on the Conservation of Nature and Natural Resources (Revised Version), opened for signature 11 July 2003 (not yet in force).

comply with various aspects of the duty to cooperate, which sometimes includes transboundary elements.[54]

The participatory principle developed from the duty to cooperate as a result of the expansion of procedural environmental rights. This is most clearly outlined in the Espoo and Aarhus Conventions,[55] which also grant these rights to non-citizens, in accordance with the principle of non-discrimination. Together they give legal recognition to Principles 10 and 17 of the Rio Declaration[56] (the latter setting out the EIA requirement), with widespread implementation particularly into European and domestic law since. Article 9 of the 1992 Helsinki Watercourses and Lakes Convention[57] deals with bilateral and multilateral cooperation, and requires states to enter into agreements to prevent, control and reduce transboundary impact. These agreements must establish joint bodies to serve as a forum for information exchange and in order to participate in the implementation of EIA. Article 12 of the 1997 International Watercourses Convention[58] requires notification of planned measures with possible adverse effects before implementation, including the results of any EIA carried out.

Many other treaties contain provisions for EIA and participation that incorporate obligations to cooperate. These include Article 7 of the Convention on Long Range Transboundary Air Pollution,[59] the Convention on the Law of the Sea,[60] Articles 4 and 10 of the Convention on the Transboundary Movement of Hazardous Waste,[61] the EIA Annex to the Madrid Protocol,[62] Articles 3 and 9 of the Helsinki Watercourses and

[54] Alexandre Kiss and Dinah Shelton, *Guide to International Environmental Law* (Martinus Nijhoff, Leiden and Boston, 2007), 113.

[55] Above nn. 9 and 4, respectively. [56] Above n. 3.

[57] Convention on the Protection and Use of Transboundary Watercourses and International Lakes, opened for signature 17 March 1992, 1936 UNTS 269 (entered into force 6 October 1996).

[58] Above n. 46.

[59] Convention on Long Range Transboundary Air Pollution, opened for signature 13 November 1979, 335 UNTS 211 (entered into force 16 March 1983).

[60] United Nations Convention on the Law of the Sea, opened for signature 10 December 1982, 1833 UNTS 3 (entered into force 16 November 1994).

[61] Basel Convention on the Control of Transboundary Movements of Hazardous Wastes and Their Disposal, opened for signature 23 March 1989, 1673 UNTS 57 (entered into force 5 May 1992).

[62] Protocol on Environmental Protection to the Antarctic Treaty, opened for signature 4 October 1991, [1998] ATS No. 6 (entered into force 15 January 1998) ('Madrid Protocol').

Lakes Convention,[63] Article 4 of the Climate Change Convention,[64] Articles 7 and 14 of the Convention on Biological Diversity,[65] and Article 12 of the International Watercourses Convention.[66]

In the *Gabčíkovo-Nagymaros* case, separate judicial opinion supported the view that EIA had assumed the status of a principle of customary international law. Judge Weeramantry referred to the need for 'continuing EIA', acknowledging the significance of ongoing assessment and monitoring of a project while in operation.[67] He also stated that a duty of EIA is to be read into treaties whose subject can reasonably be considered to have a significant impact on the environment. The earlier comments of Judges Palmer[68] and Weeramantry[69] (in the minority) in the *Nuclear Tests* case tend to suggest that while the status of the precautionary principle in customary international law may be uncertain, the status of EIA is a little clearer. However, that is not to say that the latter has yet attained the status of a customary norm, with Judge Palmer's comment only establishing that 'EIA is a means of establishing a process to comply' rather than the legal duty itself. More recently, in the *MOX Plant*[70] proceedings and especially the *Pulp Mills*[71] case, EIA again featured, and although no further elaboration has been forthcoming about its customary nature, in relation to the ICJ 'the Court clearly perceives that EIA and other procedural duties form part and parcel of the principles of no-harm and due diligence'.[72] Despite this, state practice may support its customary status through growing compliance with the Espoo Convention in particular.

[63] Above n. 57.

[64] United Nations Framework Convention on Climate Change, opened for signature 4 June 1992, 1771 UNTS 107 (entered into force 21 March 1994).

[65] Convention on Biological Diversity, opened for signature 5 June 1992, 1760 UNTS 79 (entered into force 29 December 1993).

[66] Above n. 46.

[67] *Gabčíkovo-Nagymaros Project*, Separate Opinion, above n. 41, 108–10.

[68] *Nuclear Weapons Advisory Opinion* [1996] ICJ Rep. 226, Dissenting Opinion Judge Palmer.

[69] Ibid., Dissenting Opinion Judge Weeramantry.

[70] *MOX Plant (Ireland* v. *United Kingdom) (provisional measures)* [1997] ICJ Rep.; *MOX Plant (Ireland* v. *United Kingdom) (suspension of proceedings on jurisdiction and merits and request for further provisional measures)* (order 3, of 24 June 2003) (2003) 42 ILM 1187 (order 4, of 14 November 2003) (order 5, of 22 January 2007).

[71] *Pulp Mills on the River Uruguay (Argentina* v. *Uruguay) (request for provisional measures by Argentina)* (2006) 45 ILM 1025.

[72] See Koivurova, above n. 47, 23–5. See also Jan de Mulder, 'Case Note' (2010) 19 *Review of European Community and International Environmental Law* 263.

4. Public participation in the transboundary EIA procedures of the Espoo and Aarhus Conventions

Transboundary EIA is a process applied by one or more states to evaluate the significant environmental effects from proposals within their own territory (e.g. a nuclear power plant, like the Sellafield 'MOX Plant' in the UK) or which physically cross borders (e.g. a gas pipeline, like the Baltic Sea 'Nordstream' between Russia and Germany[73]), and which may affect the territory of another state or states. The process is designed to provide better information for decision-makers, as well as to involve public and government stakeholders in the process. The terminology 'party of origin' and 'affected party' is used under the Espoo Convention to differentiate the obligations and rights of each. As discussed, transboundary EIA is based on domestic EIA as applied within a state, sometimes conducted by national or state authorities, or by a mixture of both.[74] There may be more than one party of origin and affected party, and where proposals physically cross boundaries, each state will be both a party of origin and an affected party.

Proposals with a strategic dimension, commonly known as policies, plans and programmes, may also be subject to transboundary EIA. Whether limited to the territory of a particular state or crossing the boundaries of states, their assessment may expedite or avoid the need for assessment of specific projects at a later time. Because of the improved benefits of what is called strategic environmental assessment (SEA) over project-level EIA, (such as determining priorities while all options are open and avoidance of cumulative effects) it is an area of growing interest to many states.[75] While practice with project-level transboundary EIA is significant, there has been limited practice at the strategic level so far.[76] This may change

[73] Timo Koivurova and Ismo Pölönen, 'Transboundary Environmental Impact Assessment in the Case of the Baltic Gas Pipeline' (2010) 25 *The International Journal of Marine and Coastal Law* 151.

[74] See generally Bastmeijer and Koivurova, above n. 12; Kersten, above n. 14.

[75] See Thomas Fischer, *The Theory and Practice of Strategic Environmental Assessment: Towards a More Systematic Approach* (Earthscan, London, 2007); Simon Marsden, *Strategic Environmental Assessment in International and European Law* (Earthscan, London, 2008); Bastmeijer and Koivurova, above n. 12; Regional Environmental Center for Central and Eastern Europe and United Nations Development Programme, *Benefits of an SEA* (2003).

[76] See Simon Marsden, 'Assessment of Transboundary Environmental Effects in the Pearl River Delta Region: Is There a Role for Strategic Environmental Assessment?' (2011) 31

following the coming into force of the SEA Protocol to the Espoo Convention in 2010.[77]

The procedure that applies in all instances for transboundary EIA is very similar to that for domestic EIA, although there are differences based on the underlying agreement between the parties. Schrage and Bonvoisin identify several procedural matters relevant to most systems of transboundary EIA. These include: notification by the party of origin to the affected party of the planned activity and likely significant effects (or the opportunity of the affected party to request such a procedure[78]), response by the affected party as to whether it wishes to be involved in the EIA procedure, sharing of information, preparation of documentation and distribution in the affected party, consultation between authorities and participation of the public in both states, decision-making taking into account documentation and comments, sharing of information as to the decision and monitoring and post-project analysis.[79]

Determinations of harm significance are first made in order to trigger the procedure (known as *screening*), which may be in accordance with a list approach of major activities (as in the Espoo Convention), through a

Environmental Impact Assessment Review 593; Nick Bonvoisin, 'Transboundary Issues in Strategic Environmental Assessment' in Barry Sadler *et al.* (eds.), *Handbook of Strategic Environmental Assessment* (Earthscan, London, 2011) 396; Eike Albrecht, 'Transboundary Consultations in Strategic Environmental Assessment' (2008) 26 *Impact Assessment and Project Appraisal* 289; Jan de Mulder, 'The Institutional Context for Transboundary Environmental Impact Assessment in Belgium: Multi Level Setting – A Matter of Smooth Governance?' (2008) 26 *Impact Assessment and Project Appraisal* 282.

77 Protocol on Strategic Environmental Assessment to the Convention on Environmental Impact Assessment in a Transboundary Context. Opened for signature 21 May 2003, [2010] ECE/MP.EIA/2003/2 (entered into force 11 July 2010). See United Nations Economic and Social Council, *Report of the Working Group on EIA on its 12th meeting*, Geneva, 11–13 May 2009, 4.

78 The Inquiry Procedure has been established under the Espoo Convention in order that effect significance can be determined by an independent panel when a potentially affected party disputes the determination made by the party of origin. This procedure was used for the first time in the *Danube Delta* case involving Ukraine and Romania. See Mari Koyano, 'The Significance of the Convention on Environmental Impact Assessment in a Transboundary Context (Espoo Convention) in International Environmental Law: Examining the Implications of the Danube Delta Case' (2008) 26 *Impact Assessment and Project Appraisal* 299; Kersten, above n. 14, 198–9; and Simon Marsden, '*MOX Plant* and the Espoo Convention: Can Member State Disputes Concerning Mixed Environmental Agreements Be Resolved outside EC Law?' (2009) 18 *Review of European Community and International Environmental Law* 312.

79 Wiek Schrage and Nick Bonvoisin, 'Transboundary Impact Assessment: Frameworks, Experiences and Challenges' (2008) 26 *Impact Assessment and Project Appraisal* 234.

general determination based on criteria such as location or scale (also in the Espoo Convention, which may be combined with the list approach), or, rarely, requiring assessment for all activities undertaken (as in the Madrid Protocol to the Antarctic Treaty[80]). Once the procedure has been triggered, then terms of reference for the assessment are decided upon (known as *scoping*), sometimes taking into account a broader range of stakeholders, including the public and NGOs. Requirements for consultation and participation may also be included in the stages that lead up to the production of a report, usually known as an environmental impact statement. Sometimes opportunities are given in aspects of the decision-making process itself, which is intended to be informed as a result of the information found in the environmental impact statement and the views of the stakeholders. Reasons for a decision should also be provided.

The Aarhus Convention has had an even greater influence on the development of information provision, public participation and access to justice,[81] and has also contributed to the development of democratic and constitutional principles in the Eastern European members of the United Nations Economic Commission for Europe,[82] and indeed, beyond the nation state.[83] Where democracy may not be attainable at the international level, the Aarhus Convention may also provide significant assistance to 'enhanced transparency, participation, more balanced voting procedures and effectiveness of decisions as possible ways of

[80] See EIA Annex to the Madrid Protocol, above n. 62. On the potential for this legal instrument to address SEA, note Simon Marsden, 'Introducing Strategic Environmental Assessment to the Antarctic Protocol: Lessons from International Experience' (2011) 1 *The Polar Journal* 36.

[81] Peter Davies, 'Public Participation, the Aarhus Convention, and the European Community' in Donald Zillman, Alistair Lucas and George Pring (eds.), *Human Rights in Natural Resource Development: Public Participation in the Sustainable Development of Mining and Energy Resources* (Oxford University Press, 2002) 155; Maria Lee and Carolyn Abbot, 'The Usual Suspects? Public Participation under the Aarhus Convention' (2003) 66 *Modern Law Review* 80.

[82] Jerzy Jendroska and Stephen Stec, 'The Aarhus Convention: Towards a New Era in Environmental Democracy' (2001) 9 *Environmental Liability* 140; Michael Zschiesche, 'The Aarhus Convention – More Citizens' Participation by Setting Out Environmental Standards?' (2002) 1 *Environmental Law Network International* 21; Jeremy Wates, 'The Aarhus Convention: A Driving Force for Environmental Democracy' (2005) 2 *Journal for European Environmental and Planning Law* 2.

[83] Elena Petkova and Peter Veit, *Environmental Accountability Beyond the Nation State: The Implications of the Aarhus Convention* (World Resources Institute, Washington DC, 2000).

making decisions more legitimate'.[84] It has also served to link the environment and human rights in international law.[85] The convention is open to accession by any United Nations member with the approval of the parties,[86] and even where not directly applicable, has influenced state behaviour globally, especially in conditions attached to loans provided to developing states by international institutions.[87] Article 1 indicates the objective of the convention is to guarantee procedural rights in order to contribute to protection of the right of current and future generations to live in an environment adequate for health and well-being. The convention deals with access to and collection of environmental information in Articles 4–5 (pillar 1), public participation in decision-making in Articles 6–8 (pillar 2) and access to justice in Article 9 (pillar 3). The provisions in pillar 1 require that environmental information progressively becomes available in electronic databases, easily accessible to the public through public telecommunications networks. Information in this form should include text of legislation on or about the environment, and, 'as appropriate', policies, plans or programmes on the environment and environmental agreements. There are also measures for the dissemination of legislation and policy documents, and progress reports on their implementation, prepared at various levels of government.

The convention distinguishes between three areas of environmental decision-making for which public participation is required in pillar 2: specific activities, plans, programmes and policies, and environmental legislation. Plans and programmes on one hand and policies on the other are distinguished; the more specific the decision, the greater the procedural guarantees available. The access to justice provisions in pillar 3 deal with three situations: where the right of access to environmental information is impaired, where the right to public participation is impaired,

[84] Steinar Andresen and Ellen Hey, 'The Effectiveness and Legitimacy of International Environmental Institutions' (2005) 5 *International Environmental Agreements* 211.

[85] Elisa Morgera, 'An Update on the Aarhus Convention and its Continued Global Relevance' (2005) 14 *Review of European Community and International Environmental Law* 138; Sean McAllister, 'Human Rights and the Environment: The Convention on Access to Information, Public Participation in Decision Making, and Access to Justice in Environmental Matters' (1998) 9 *Colorado Journal of International Environmental Law Yearbook* 187.

[86] Article 19(3).

[87] Jona Razzaque, 'Participatory Rights in Natural Resource Management: The Role of Communities in South Asia' in Ebbesson and Okowa (eds.), above n. 16, 117.

and access to justice where acts and omissions of public authorities or private persons are in breach of the law.

5. Public participation practice via the Espoo Convention Implementation Committee and Aarhus Convention Compliance Committee

As discussed earlier, non-compliance procedures are now a common feature of modern environmental treaties, including the Implementation Committee of the Espoo Convention and the Compliance Committee of the Aarhus Convention.[88] Together with the role played by the Meeting of the Parties in decision-making, they illustrate the globalisation of administrative law in an environmental context. The relationship between these procedures and domestic law operates both upstream and downstream. While the focus of this chapter is on the former, decisions reached by the committees are ultimately subject to implementation in the latter context.[89] While examples of this to date have not involved public participation in transboundary EIA, they have involved public participation in domestic processes, where Albania and Armenia have been found in breach and measures put in place to encourage compliance.[90] A recent report from Albania to the Implementation Committee and the Compliance Committee discusses progress made in implementing the required action plan and further measures to address compliance.[91] This section considers the role of these procedures through the recent 'jurisprudence' of the Compliance Committee.

The objective of the Implementation Committee is to review compliance by the parties with their obligations under the Espoo Convention,

[88] See Tullio Treves *et al.* (eds.), *Non Compliance Procedures and Mechanisms and the Effectiveness of International Environmental Agreements* (TMC Asser Press, The Hague, 2009).

[89] See Implementation Committee of the Convention on Environmental Impact Assessment in a Transboundary Context, *Opinions of the Implementation Committee 2001–2010*, 20th sess., Agenda Item 9, ECE/MP.EIA/IC/2001/INF.1 (13 January 2011).

[90] See Compliance Committee of the Aarhus Convention, *Implementation of Decisions of the Meeting of the Parties on Compliance by Individual Parties*, United Nations Economic Commission for Europe at www.unece.org/env/pp/CCimplementation.htm, last accessed 24 October 2010.

[91] See Republic of Albania, Ministry of Environment, *Forests and Water Administration, Progress Report for Implementation of Action Plan in Response to the Recommendations of the Compliance Committee of the Aarhus Convention*, 31 December 2009.

in order to assist them fully to meet their commitments.[92] Public involvement is a matter discussed by the Implementation Committee, and takes into account the guidance on public participation that was adopted at the Third Meeting of the Parties by Decision III/8. Case studies on public participation in transboundary EIA were submitted by thirteen parties and are included in the guidance, which indicates that 'equivalent' opportunities for public participation have been provided for those in affected states.[93] In one instance the proponent of the project advised the public in both the party of origin and affected party; the obligation overall, however, is on both parties to ensure this is carried out. Time limits are also considered, with one of the case studies highlighting how the competent authorities in the party of origin provided more time for comment from the public in the affected party than for its own public.[94] Specific matters are raised with parties when a response to an implementation questionnaire indicates non-compliance. In a few instances, these matters have included failings to comply with provisions related to public participation, such as in Finland, where NGOs were notified, but not the public generally. This was explained by time restrictions and isolation of the area where effects may occur.[95]

The Implementation Committee has been especially busy evaluating Ukraine's compliance with the convention, after it was raised by Romania in relation to the Bystroe Canal Project[96] proposed for the Danube Delta.[97] Designated a Wetland of International Importance

[92] Decision III/2 of the Third Meeting of Parties to the Convention on Environmental Impact Assessment in a Transboundary Context, Doc. ECE/MP.EIA/6, annex II, 1–4 June 2004, Cavtat, Croatia (replacing Decision II of the Second Meeting of the Parties), which provides the structure and functions of the Implementation Committee and procedures for review of compliance. Para. 14 of Decision III/2 states that the Implementation Committee is 'a non-adversarial and assistance-oriented procedure'.

[93] Decision III/8, *Guidance on Public Participation in Environmental Impact Assessment in a Transboundary Context*, of the Third Meeting of Parties to the Convention on Environmental Impact Assessment in a Transboundary Context, Doc. ECE/MP.EIA/6, annex VIII, 1–4 June 2004, Cavtat, Croatia.

[94] Ibid. [17]. [95] In this instance Finland was found not to be in breach.

[96] United Nations Economic Commission for Europe, Working Group on Environmental Impact Assessment, *Inquiry Procedure – Review of the First Inquiry Procedure, Note by the Secretariat*, Tenth Meeting of the Parties to the Convention on Environmental Impact Assessment in a Transboundary Context, Geneva, 21–23 May 2007.

[97] Koyano, above n. 78, credits its success with the fact that the parties were cooperative, NGOs and external experts were involved, the conclusion was unanimous and its work also covered mediation through the recommendations. See also Wiek Schrage, 'The Convention on Environmental Impact Assessment in a Transboundary Context' in Bastmeijer and Koivurova (eds.), above n. 12, 29, 46–7.

under the Ramsar Convention,[98] it was inscribed on the list of the World Heritage Convention,[99] and is listed as a Biosphere Reserve under UNESCO's Man and Biosphere Programme.[100] Romania requested an inquiry under Appendix IV of the Espoo Convention, believing there were likely to be significant adverse effects, and after the scientific evaluation the Inquiry Commission (a different body to the Implementation Committee) agreed, and the provisions of the Espoo Convention were held to apply. Ukraine was obliged to send a notification about the canal to Romania to commence the transboundary EIA procedure, including communication between the parties and public participation. During the Fourth Meeting of the Parties in Bucharest in May 2008, the Ukrainian delegation committed to fulfil its obligations under the Espoo Convention, and this is now being done, with the Implementation Committee monitoring the situation closely.

The Aarhus Compliance Committee is a significant innovation in ensuring access to justice for individuals and NGOs. Both have the right to submit complaints about a state's compliance with the convention, the latter regardless of demonstrating a specific interest or needing to prove they are affected by the decision. Proceedings of the Compliance Committee are also largely in public, and members of the Compliance Committee are independent, serve in their personal capacity, and may also be nominated by environmental NGOs. As with the Implementation Committee of the Espoo Convention, the Aarhus Compliance Committee in part depends on the reporting function of the parties in response to circulated questionnaires. Another novel feature of the Aarhus Convention is the requirement of the party to consult with the public when national reports are being prepared. All consultations with the public concerning national reports, public submission of complaints and the openness of proceedings before the Compliance Committee make practical sense, given that substantive provisions of the convention relate to the public, rather than to other states.

A total of sixty cases under the Compliance Committee have been initiated by communications from the public, and some have been

[98] Convention on Wetlands of International Importance Especially as Waterfowl Habitat, opened for signature 2 February 1971, 996 UNTS 246 (entered into force 21 December 1975).

[99] Convention Concerning the Protection of the World Cultural and Natural Heritage, opened for signature 16 November 1972, 1037 UNTS 151 (entered into force 17 December 1975).

[100] At the Sixteenth Session of General Conference of UNESCO, Programme on Man and the Biosphere, 1970.

discussed in the literature;[101] a few of these involving national or European courts.[102] Many of the public communications have concerned a failure to fully implement Articles 6–8 (public participation), or Article 9 (access to justice). Although several of the parties in breach are non-EU Member States, a few EU Member States have recently been challenged for failing to comply with the third pillar rights of the convention. Since the EU is a party to the convention, it is perhaps not surprising that it has also been challenged, in one case following the failure of one of its financial institutions to allow public participation in relation to a recent investment decision, although in this instance it was not held in breach. In another case of some significance, the EU was challenged for failing to provide access to justice in relation to its own institutions.[103]

Although many of the cases relate to failings to ensure access to information or public participation in relation to domestic EIA, only one case relates to transboundary EIA; the Danube Delta dispute discussed above in relation to the Espoo Implementation Committee.[104] At the same time as the Inquiry Commission procedure was initiated in 2004, both Romania and a Ukrainian NGO, Ecopravo-Lviv, made a 'submission' (by a party) and a 'communication' (by the public) in relation to Ukraine's decision to construct the navigation canal. Ecopravo-Lviv, as a member of the 'public' and 'public concerned', contended that Ukraine had breached Article 6 by failing to consult; Romania, as the affected party, raised similar issues in relation to its own public. The Compliance Committee agreed with both sets of contentions and recommended the matter be determined by the Meeting of the Parties to ensure Ukraine fully complied with its obligations.

[101] Fitzmaurice, and Koester, both above n. 16.

[102] Ludwig Krämer, 'Environmental Justice in the European Court of Justice' in Ebbesson and Okowa (eds.), above n. 16, 195; Stephen Stec, 'Environmental Justice Through Courts in Countries in Transition' in ibid., 158.

[103] See Findings and Recommendations of the Compliance Committee with regard to Communication ACCC/C/2008/38 concerning compliance by the European Union, adopted on 14 April 2011.

[104] United Nations Economic Commission for Europe, *Communication concerning non-compliance by Belarus with the UN ECE Convention on Access to Information, Public Participation in Decision-Making and Access to Justice in Environmental Matters* (Communication ACCC/C/2009/37), 14 March 2009, may also relate to transboundary EIA because it makes reference to a hydro-power plant on the Neman River which passes Belarus, Lithuania and Russia. Findings and recommendations were adopted on 24 September 2010.

Despite the issuance of a caution, Ukraine appears still to have some work to do to fully comply.

6. Conclusions

Public participation in environmental governance is a beneficiary of the expansion of procedural rights in international law and an example of the globalisation of public and administrative law. The analysis of these rights in the context of transboundary EIA emphasises the role of the non-compliance procedures in the Espoo and Aarhus Conventions, and the underlying procedure and practice of both treaties that are closely related. Although these treaty provisions are currently limited to parties in the UN Economic Commission for Europe region, they have been effective in promoting limited behavioural change and improving decision-making influence of the public; the common goal of the discourse coalition advocating public participation. This is illustrated by the few examples discussed regarding public participation. Examples of compliance with the other pillars of the Aarhus Convention (access to information and access to justice) can also seen regarding Belgium, which changed its jurisprudence concerning access to justice following the recommendation of the Committee.[105]

In the case of the Aarhus Compliance Committee a direct opportunity for individuals and NGOs to pursue grievances is therefore available, although this has mostly been used by well-organised environmental NGOs so far. This is clearly an administrative law process suggesting that the gap between international and public law may be closing. Beyond the UN Economic Commission for Europe region currently comprising the parties to these two treaties, the situation is rather different. While there may be opportunities for non-UN Economic Commission for Europe states in the future to become parties to the Espoo[106] and Aarhus[107]

[105] See generally Jan Wouters, André Nollkaemper and Erika de Wet (eds.), *The Europeanisation of International Law: The Status of International Law in the EU and its Member States* (TMC Asser Press, The Hague, 2008).

[106] The second amendment (not yet in force) reads: 'Any other State, not referred to in paragraph 2 of this Article, that is a Member of the United Nations may accede to the Convention upon approval by the Meeting of the Parties. The Meeting of the Parties shall not consider or approve any request for accession by such a State until this paragraph has entered into force for all the States and organisations that were Parties to the Convention on 27 February 2001.'

[107] Article 19 reads: 'Any other State, not referred to in paragraph 2 above, that is a Member of the United Nations may accede to the Convention upon approval by the Meeting of the Parties.'

Conventions, and for NGOs and individuals in other states to challenge actions by their own government or that of another party, it is probably unlikely that the Espoo Convention will ever become a fully global treaty.[108] After all, there are regional arrangements elsewhere in the world, as well as different priorities and a focus on bilateral arrangements that operate against multilateralism. Notwithstanding this, the growing 'jurisprudence' of the Aarhus Compliance Committee may result in demands for similar procedures to be established in other treaty regimes in the future.

[108] Kevin Gray, 'International Environmental Impact Assessment: Potential for a Multilateral Environmental Agreement' (2000) 11 *Colorado Journal of International Environmental Law and Policy* 83; Knox, above n. 36; Bastmeijer and Koivurova, above n. 12.

PART IV

Discourses in climate law

11

Climate change: limits discourses at the interface of international law and environmental law

LEE GODDEN*

1. Introduction

Climate change effects are linked by scientific evidence to anthropogenic causes that typically are associated with industrialisation and global economic development.[1] Ironically these patterns of growth and development were integral to the historical trajectories designed to overcome earlier 'limits' scenarios. Apocalyptic discourses of global warming echo many of the earlier warnings about the limits of civilisation, where the 'civilised world' was regarded as veering toward an ecological disaster with accompanying human catastrophe. Catastrophe was averted as the European nation states from the early sixteenth century colonised the environment and peoples of the newly 'discovered' world. Central to the processes of colonisation were the constructs of trade, treaty and contractual ordering, working in conjunction with the emerging principles and practices of international law.[2]

* The author acknowledges the support provided by Australian Research Council Discovery Project grant, 'Responding to Climate Change: Australia's Environmental Law and Regulatory Framework', including the valuable research assistance provided by Anne Kallies and Naomi Wynn.

[1] Ross Garnaut, *The Garnaut Climate Change Review: Final Report* (Cambridge University Press, Melbourne, 2008) 4. See the section entitled: 'A decision-making framework'.

[2] There are a number of commentators examining the role of international law in the colonial period: see, e.g., Martti Koskenniemi, 'Miserable Comforters: International Relations as the New Natural Law' (2009) 15 *European Journal of International Relations* 395. For an examination of the historical development of international law, see Anthony Anghie, *Imperialism, Sovereignty and the Making of International Law* (Cambridge University Press, 2004). From an indigenous perspective, see S. James Anaya, *Indigenous Peoples in International Law* (Oxford University Press, New York, 2nd edn, 2004).

In a more recent era of globalisation, with the recognition of climate change, the constructs of limits, trade and contractual ordering once again are pervasive modes in international policy and legal discourses.[3] In the twenty-first century, there is an uneasy tandem between international law and the rising dominance of forms of environmental governance based in markets, exchange and offsets. Indeed, the rise of governance in tension with the formal, traditional account of law as moral obligation[4] is central to the argument advanced in this chapter. In part this tension arises as public international law increasingly has assumed a regulatory presence as a definer of normative rights and obligations within, as well as between, nations.[5] There are inherent tensions within the international law climate change framework. The framework encompasses both public international environmental law principles guiding nation state obligations to set limits on emissions, as well as the implementing 'flexibility measures' effecting a contractual form of governance that extends regulation beyond the typical scope of formal public law.

In this context, this chapter considers the nature of the dynamic but uneasy relationship between international environmental law and public law for climate change regulation in an era marked by a resurgence of contractual law and ordering within the corporatist state, exchange-related, economic instruments, and the rise of reflexive environmental law. Briefly, 'reflexive', or as it is sometimes known, 'responsive' environmental law refers to the trend to use a range of regulatory tools in addition to, or substitution for, legal rules in order to induce changes in behaviour toward the environment.[6] It is characteristic of so-called deregulatory regimes where governments (and indeed, other actors) use many modes based in law, markets and even media communication for initiating self-regulatory or 'responsive' change in environmental behaviours in pursuit of policy goals.[7] The chapter also situates the

[3] Peter Newell, 'The Political Economy of Global Environmental Governance' (2008) 34 *Review of International Studies* 507, 510.

[4] This is not to suggest that international law is not law, as was proposed by positivist accounts such as that put forward by John Austin, see Wayne Morrison, *Jurisprudence from the Greeks to Post-Modernism* (Cavendish Publishing, London, 1997) 218.

[5] Peter Danchin, 'Whose Public? Which Law? Mapping the Internal/External Distinction in International Law' in Jeremy Farrell and Kim Rubenstein (eds.), *Sanctions, Accountability and Governance in a Globalised World* (Cambridge University Press, 2009) 27, 28.

[6] Neil Gunningham, 'Environmental Law, Regulation and Governance: Shifting Architectures' (2009) 21 *Journal of Environmental Law* 179, 181.

[7] Daniel Fiorino, *The New Environmental Regulation* (MIT Press, Cambridge, Mass., 2006) 11.

relationship between international law, public law and environmental law within a wider discourse of climate change mitigation, reflexive governance and a growing role for law in the 'facilitation of life'. In this way the more specific modes of 'disciplining' people's behaviour via mitigation and adaptation strategies in order to respond to the limits imposed by climate change are a manifestation of the changes that have culminated in the move from 'law' to 'governance'.

2. Deconstructing the discourse of climate change law

In unpacking the complex legal relationships in the climate change regulatory sphere, the chapter adopts a methodology exploring law's relationship to the governance of life as a genealogical discourse analysis or deconstruction that informs the examination of those relationships. This approach is associated with 'biopower' analyses.[8] Biopower typically encompasses the idea that the state and other sources of 'power' are fundamentally concerned with the promotion of the biological across many spheres of bodily 'intervention'. Pursuant to these discursive narratives, humanity is understood as a species whose existence must be managed and controlled and its behaviour disciplined in order to continue to reproduce, grow and flourish.[9] This idea of the role of law and power challenges the traditional conception of the individual as the holder of rights and obligations, that is: the subject of law. Instead it institutes the concept that law and other forms of power constitute biological life through a pervasive governmentality.

To apply these views, the governance of 'life' is realised simultaneously through the international public law frameworks, such as the United Nations Framework Convention on Climate Change (UNFCCC),[10] Kyoto Protocol,[11] as well as in the public law that provides the

[8] Leading theorists of this view are Michel Foucault, *The Foucault Effect: Studies in Governmentality* (eds. Graham Burchell, Colin Gordon, and Peter Miller) (University of Chicago Press, 1991); however, the term has gained more general currency, see Angela Oels, 'Rendering Climate Change Governable: From Biopower to Advanced Liberal Government?' (2005) 7 *Journal of Environmental Policy and Planning* 185.

[9] See generally, Michel Foucault, *The History of Sexuality* (trans. Robert Hurley) (Vintage Books, New York, 1978).

[10] United Nations Framework Convention on Climate Change, opened for signature 4 June 1992, 1771 UNTS 107 (entered into force 21 March 1994) ('UNFCCC').

[11] Kyoto Protocol to the United Nations Framework Convention on Climate Change, opened for signature 16 March 1998, 2303 UNTS 148 (entered into force 16 February 2005) ('Kyoto Protocol').

architecture for environmental regulation and climate change laws, like those within Australia.[12] In concert, the interface between international law and public law is progressively reshaped as part of that wider transition. The exact boundaries and parameters, however, are still evolving as the respective priorities shift between pursuing solutions within the UNFCCC and in seeking to achieve emissions reductions through global financial measures and economic 'governance'. The rise of governance via technical and economic rules and incentives is regarded by many as a concomitant of increasing globalisation.[13] While globalisation may have contributed to shifting attention from sovereign nation states to specialist functionalist regimes and international organisation, as yet, according to some, 'it has hardly transformed the dynamics of such engagement'.[14] Nonetheless, as Krisch and Kingsbury write, 'we are witnessing the emergence of a "global administrative space": a space in which the strict dichotomy between domestic and international has largely broken down, in which administrative functions are performed in often complex interplays between officials and institutions on different levels, and in which regulation may be highly effective despite its predominantly non-binding forms'.[15]

Further, while a dynamic interface has always existed between international environmental law and public environmental law within nations,[16] the importance of the articulation between international law and public law will grow in future efforts to implement legal frameworks for responding to climate change. The growing difficulty in achieving broad multilateral agreements between nations regarding their respective obligations around greenhouse gas emissions will enhance the importance of the international law and public law interface as the forms of agreement making splinter among power blocs in the international community.

In light of these transitions occurring in the international climate change sphere as part of the rise of biopower and governmentality,

[12] Exposure Draft Clean Energy Bill 2011 (Cth).

[13] See generally, Arthur Mol (ed.), *Globalization and Environmental Reform: The Ecological Modernization of the Global Economy* (MIT Press, Cambridge, Mass., 2001).

[14] Koskenniemi, above n. 2, 4.

[15] Nico Krisch and Benedict Kingsbury, 'Introduction: Global Governance and Global Administrative Law in the International Legal Order' (2006) 17 *European Journal of International Law* 1.

[16] See, e.g., Ben Boer, 'The Globalisation of Environmental Law: The Role of the United Nations' (1995–6) 20 *Melbourne University Law Review* 109.

several themes are explored in the following sections of the chapter. First is an exploration of the de-centring of the traditional hierarchical model of the nation state and law. This trend is accompanied by a concurrent move to adopt forms of reflexive law and economic ordering to discharge some 'public' environmental governance functions within nations.[17] Second, a growing interpenetration of international law and national environmental law has occurred in pursuit of the diffuse governance of life. In this regard a legal process for transcending the limits imposed by climate change is considered critical. Both of these earlier themes are consistent with the broad movements in the shift from law to governance.[18] This shift marks a corresponding change from a situation where power as law was exercised by the sovereign as a control using the threat of death to modern societies where power, and particularly governmental power, is used to facilitate and promote life and growth.[19] Thus the modern age is marked by a pervasive governance that manifests in part as an overwhelming concern with the promotion of life, growth and development. Perversely, in a climate change context the promotion of life must be achieved by setting limits to development and growth. Given the all-pervading modes of governance that this change represents, a third element in these transformations can be discerned whereby 'the increasing exercise of public power in these structures has given rise to serious concerns about legitimacy and accountability, prompting patterns of responses to those concerns in many areas of global governance'.[20]

3. The governance of climate change

Against the backdrop of major transformations in the nature and function of law, the international community has endeavoured to use the institutions of public international law for the global governance of anthropogenic atmospheric warming by setting limits for greenhouse gas emissions. The principle of 'common but differentiated responsibility' emerged in early climate change negotiations under the UNFCCC as

17 See Thomas Cottier, Olga Nartova and Sadeq Z. Bigdeli (eds.), *International Trade Regulation and the Mitigation of Climate Change* (Cambridge University Press, 2009).

18 See Gunningham, above n. 6, 180.

19 Benjamin Richardson, 'Environmental Law in Postcolonial Societies: Straddling the Local–Global Institutional Spectrum' (2000) 11 *Colorado Journal of International Environmental Law & Policy* 1.

20 Krisch and Kingsbury above n. 15, 2.

a compromise to quell debates about the respective responsibilities of developed and developing nations for greenhouse gas emissions. Under that construct, redress for former industrialisation and economic development that 'caused' global warming is to be effected by imposing current 'limits' on the most developed countries identified in Annex 1 to the UNFCCC. The mechanisms to implement the limits are a mixture of reduction targets and market measures and the associated monitoring and compliance. Market measures take the form of three types of flexibility measures under the UNFCCC – emissions trading, Joint Implementation Initiatives and the Clean Development Mechanism. The failure to achieve a firm multilateral agreement for the post-2012 period at the Copenhagen Conference of the Parties,[21] however, has cast some doubt on the efficacy of strategies such as emissions trading to achieve substantial greenhouse gas emissions reductions. Nonetheless, it remains clear that international public law processes will continue to play a major role in climate mitigation and adaptation efforts. At the same time, normative rules around voluntary exchange, trade and associated financial and funding arrangements[22] will assume even more prominence in the absence of overarching multilateral agreements.[23] Concurrently, renewed attention is being directed to national and bilateral approaches to climate change mitigation, and in this context the interpenetration of international and public environmental law will increase.

Public administrative law concepts, as they are progressively rearticulated to meet new demands of accountability and transparency in the international and transnational sphere, will provide an important impetus for the expansion of international climate change law. This expansion is likely to occur in areas previously seen as more strictly within the preserve of private normative ordering. Historically, in its classical nation state dimensions, public administrative law is associated with principles that seek to act as a constraint on executive power where the state is regarded as the central rule-making and sanctioning

[21] UNFCCC, Copenhagen Accord, Decision 2/CP. 15, FCCC/CP/2009/11/Add.1, 18 December 2009, Copenhagen, Denmark.

[22] UNFCCC Ad Hoc Working Group on Long-Term Cooperative Action under the Convention, *Text to Facilitate Negotiations Among Parties, Tenth Session Bonn, 1–11 June 2010*, FCCC/AWGLCA/2010/6.

[23] Daniel Bodansky, 'The Copenhagen Climate Change Conference: A Post-Mortem' (2010) 104 *American Journal of International Law* 230, 231.

institution, albeit that citizens may consent to such governance.[24] However, if the state is no longer the unitary mode of rule-making, and normative regimes are more diffuse, then in turn the role of public law is progressively transformed. In the climate change context the diffusion of normative sources is clearly apparent in the enhanced reliance on economic regulation, contract and trading and specialist regimes, such as that exemplified by the Kyoto Protocol.

More widely, these diffuse regimes underline the exponential growth of global administrative structures that has given rise to a corresponding concern to ensure effective constraints to power within these expanded institutional and organisational structures.[25] At one level, the emphasis on accountability, transparency, monitoring and compliance as a normative ordering replicating the primary diffusion of power over life by the state will grow as reliance upon binding international instruments that seek to apportion responsibility and obligation for climate change mitigation become more uncertain.[26] On the other hand, the principles and mechanisms of monitoring, compliance and accountability articulate with, and merge into, the mechanisms of surveillance, self-report and disciplining that resonate with the advent of governmentality,[27] or at the very least, a deregulatory state.[28]

Yet the transition from law to governance remains incomplete in the climate change sphere as all modes of power find a point of conjunction in an ambivalent relationship with 'life' and an ultimate limit of 'death'. Therefore, in a large measure climate change itself might be thought of as a cumulative outcome of law's shift in focus from sovereign control by means of the power to impose 'death' to a modern preoccupation with life and the regulation of the conditions of life and sustainability. Law

[24] See, e.g., Daniel Bodansky, 'The Legitimacy of International Governance: A Coming Challenge for International Environmental Law' (1999) 93 *American Journal of International Law* 604 and Charles Sampford, 'The Potential for a Post-Westphalian Convergence of "Public Law" and "Public International Law"' in Farrell and Rubenstein (eds.), above n. 5, 56.

[25] Simon Chesterman, 'Globalisation and Public Law: A Global Administrative Law?' in Farrell and Rubenstein (eds.), above n. 5, 75, 78.

[26] Bodansky above n. 23. See also, Richard Mulgan, 'AWB and Oil for Food: Some Issues of Accountability' in Farrell and Rubenstein (eds.), above n. 5, 334, who suggests that a key element of global administrative law is accountability, which in part is to be achieved through the allocation of responsibility.

[27] Timothy Luke, 'Environmentality as Green Governmentality' in Eric Darier (ed.), *Discourses of the Environment* (Blackwell, Oxford, 1999) 121, 121–8.

[28] Gunningham, above n. 6, 181.

under the climate change imperative enables life but disciplines the manner of living by setting limits. This conundrum is addressed at two levels. First, it outlines the current modes promoting life through economic growth that have been imperfectly limited by law. Second, it sheds insights on a wider problematic for law that some have phrased as the 'controlling paradox of the liberal project'.[29] The paradox might be expressed as the situation where law to preserve freedom (or life) must create order to restrict it.[30] This paradox resonates in climate change laws where the underlying assumption of growth and development, which is fostered by law in constructs of state sovereignty, is now challenged by limits to that sovereignty. Paradoxically, however, those limits, ushered in by ideas of impending climate crisis, are to be implemented by reflexive legal modes based in freedom of contract (like markets and trade) that have their genesis in the very legal forms used for facilitating growth and life.

3.1 Climate change as the apocalypse

> If civilisation is to survive, this century will have to be a time of dramatic transformation, not just in technological capacity but also in our approach to the natural world – and each other. The road we are travelling now can only end in disaster.[31]

This pronouncement by environmentalist and scientist Ian Lowe of a looming environmental apocalypse that threatens the consensual realm of the natural order of society and state is analogous to similar dire predictions with respect to climate change. Similarly, the leading scientific body, the Intergovernmental Panel on Climate Change, while relatively conservative in its predictions due to the need for collective communiqués, clearly recognised the need for strong 'intervention' in current policy and legal trajectories in order to avoid 'dangerous climate change'.[32] Scientific predictions of a climate crisis have parallels in

[29] Danchin, above n. 5, 28 and 31.

[30] Ibid., in reference to Immanuel Kant, *Critique of Pure Reason* (trans. Norman Smith) (Macmillan, London, 1933) 601–2.

[31] Ian Lowe, *A Big Fix: Radical Solutions for Australia's Environmental Crisis* (Black Ink Press, Sydney, 2005) 20.

[32] See Intergovernmental Panel on Climate Change ('IPCC'), *Climate Change 2007. Synthesis Report: Summary for Policy-Makers* (IPCC, Geneva, 2007) and Intergovernmental Panel on Climate Change Working Group II, *Climate Change 2007. Impacts, Adaptation and Vulnerability* (Cambridge University Press, 2007).

arguments by McKibben in *The End of Nature*.[33] McKibben argued that nature could no longer exist outside the social realm once humans were able to fundamentally alter the climate system. By contrast, Lovelock's Gaia thesis[34] has received increased attention as tipping points and exponential feedback loops are predicted for the climate system as global warming takes effect.[35] In this discourse, a resurgence of nature against 'human life' will occur once the tipping point in the ecosystem has been reached.

Climate change limits discourses potentially displace a traditional hierarchical model of law. The construct of natural limits threatens not only human life and society but the very institution of law as traditionally understood – that is, law must be founded beyond the state of nature and the realm of the natural body and unregulated conditions for thriving. In situating the debates around climate change very firmly 'in nature', and by raising the spectre of death and bodily destruction, the limits discourses question whether it remains possible to continue to regard law as continuing to exist only in a social realm that implicitly is predicated upon the maintenance of growth and development under the prevailing 'social contract'.

In this regard, the main thrust of scientific research already confirms that some degree of climate change is inescapable;[36] some limit to human society is already in place; the apocalypse is assured. As a reaction against such deterministic outcomes, climate scepticism has resurfaced to counter scientific evidence of the anthropogenic causes of global warming. The resulting confusion of 'truth claims'[37] has paralysed many policymakers. In a neat conflation of 'nature endorsing' claims about the environment with 'nature sceptical' claims,[38] there is growing acknowledgement that 'humanity' may be a major contributor to global warming, but intense conflict over the attribution of responsibility, the

[33] Bill McKibben, *The End of Nature* (Anchor Books, New York, rev. edn, 1999).

[34] James Lovelock, *Gaia: A New Look at Life on Earth* (Oxford University Press, rev. impression, 1987). See also Tim Flannery, 'Now or Never, A Sustainable Future for Australia?' (2008) 31 *Quarterly Essay*.

[35] Ian Allison *et al.*, *The Copenhagen Diagnosis: Updating the World on the Latest Climate Science* (The University of New South Wales Climate Change Research Centre, Sydney, 2009) 40–2.

[36] IPCC, above n. 32, 19–20.

[37] Diana Liverman, 'Conventions of Climate Change: Constructions of Danger and the Dispossession of the Atmosphere' (2009) 35 *Journal of Historical Geography* 279, 280.

[38] Eric Darier, 'Foucault and the Environment: An Introduction' in Darier (ed.), above n. 27, 1.

'fundamental' causes of the problem and the guiding parameters to be adopted for collective legal responses beyond 2012. This confusion provides an open texture for the development of reflexive, self-responsive forms of climate change governance ranging from voluntary offsets[39] to government and non-government-initiated adaptation programmes.[40]

4. Ecological limits to life

Death is raised again as a pressing problem that human society thought it had virtually conquered, or at least banished to the realm of the outer limits of the probability statistics that construct the governing parameters of modern risk society.[41] Admittedly, while not explicitly couched in terms of epidemics, plagues and chaos, climate change threatens a maelstrom of social, ecological and economic malaise that questions the core paradigm of continued growth and development. In the more prosaic terms of models, quantitative analyses and careful predictions of degrees of warming, it presents the twenty-first century equivalent to Milton's vision of purgatory in *Paradise Lost* – which, of course, used 'warming' as a much more dramatic metaphor of human suffering and death.

This is not to denigrate the severity of the current problems, but to reveal the historical genealogies to current limits discourses and the changing meta-narratives of how societies, in particular Western societies, have configured notions of life, law and death against an environmental and, more latterly, ecological backdrop. Indeed, environmental conservation discourses have been significant undercurrents to the dominant progress narratives since the Enlightenment.[42] These alternative narratives hinge upon future scenarios largely predicated upon the

[39] See, e.g., Lisa Moore, 'Voluntary Carbon Offsets: A Legal Perspective' in Wayne Gumley and Trevor Daya-Winterbottom (eds.), *Climate Change Law: Comparative, Contractual & Regulatory Considerations* (Lawbook Co., Sydney, 2008) 159; Jolene Lin and Charlotte Streck, 'Mobilising Finance for Climate Change Mitigation: Private Sector Involvement in International Carbon Finance Mechanism' (2009) 10 *Melbourne Journal of International Law* 10.

[40] Philippa England, 'Doing the Groundwork: State, Local and Judicial Contributions to Climate Change Law in Australia' (2008) 25 *Environmental and Planning Law Journal* 360.

[41] Bronislaw Szerszynski, 'On Knowing What to Do: Environmentalism and the Modern Problematic' in Scott Lash *et al.* (eds.), *Risk, Environment and Modernity: Towards a New Ecology* (Sage Publications, London, 1996) 104.

[42] Richard Grove, *Ecology, Climate and Empire: Colonialism and Global Environmental History, 1400–1940* (White Horse Press, Isle of Harris, 1997).

authority of science,[43] which produce competing responses to the perceived problems of 'limits' to growth and progress.[44]

The most well-known historical 'limits prediction' was posed by Thomas Malthus in the late eighteenth century. Malthus argued that excessive population growth would outstrip the carrying capacity of land and resources in Europe, with widespread death from famine and disease as population numbers increased.[45] His name is now synonymous with the need for population control. Malthusian constructs exemplify many ideas now recognised as ecological limits, especially when aligned with population control.[46] In the mid-twentieth century, 'limits' constructs reappeared in a new ecological form that challenged the dominant economic growth paradigm. Seminal analyses from population biology and ecology, such as Garret Hardin's *Tragedy of the Commons*,[47] forecast ecological crises and environmental degradation. A similar critique, predicated on the emerging disciplines of systems theory and computer modelling, was advanced in 1972 by the Club of Rome in *Limits to Growth*.[48] Other notable research includes 'Spaceship Earth'[49] and 'Small Is Beautiful'.[50] Scenario-based computer modelling around climate change is much more sophisticated than earlier efforts to define limits.[51] Nonetheless, many underlying assumptions on which such modelling is based still remain highly contested.[52] At the same time

43 For a comparable discourse surrounding forestry policy and international soft law, see David Humphreys, 'Discourse as Ideology: Neoliberalism and the Limits of International Forest Policy' (2009) 11 *Forest Policy and Economics* 319.

44 John Dryzek, *The Politics of the Earth: Environmental Discourses* (Oxford University Press, 1997) 46–51.

45 Paul Neurath, *From Malthus to the Club of Rome and Back: Problems of Limits to Growth, Population Control, and Migrations* (M. E. Sharpe, Armonk, 1994).

46 Ibid.

47 Garrett Hardin, 'The Tragedy of the Commons' (1968) 162 *Science* 1243. Hardin's article has generated literature challenging its central premise. See, e.g., Elinor Ostrom, *Governing the Commons: The Evolution of Institutions for Collective Action* (Cambridge University Press, New York, 1990).

48 Donella Meadows *et al.*, *The Limits to Growth: The 30 Year Update* (Earthscan, London, 2005).

49 For a representative publication, see Kenneth Boulding *et al.*, *Economics of Pollution* (New York University Press, 1971).

50 Eric Schumacher, *Small Is Beautiful: A Study of Economics as if People Mattered* (Blond and Briggs, London, 1973).

51 Garnaut, above n. 1, 75–96.

52 This can be categorised as a 'Promethean response' that effectively suggests 'Nature' does not exist except as a source of raw materials for human flourishing. See Dryzek, above n. 44, 46–60.

there has been a perceptible shift in societal attitudes, as captured by Beck-Gernsheim:

> The more our life world is determined by technology, by our own interventions and appropriations, and the more the consequences are perceived as potentially problematic, even threatening, the more too a new guiding principle is coming to the fore: 'nature' . . . employed very effectively to mobilise public criticism and resistance.[53]

The alternating 'growth' and 'limits' cycles of discourse have tipped into the 'limits' spectrum with recent climate change analyses. Indeed, the re-emergence of an understanding of 'nature' as a fundamental limit is central to governance frameworks that seek to impose norms on human behaviour to avoid dangerous climate change. Underpinning such discursive limits are the embedded power and knowledge relationships integral to the governmentality of climate change laws.[54] Law acts as a key locus for the generation and affirmation of discursive knowledge about the environment.[55] In turn, though, this knowledge frames the assessment of the efficacy of various types of legal responses. Most recently, the discursive consensus has favoured reflexive, market measures, notwithstanding the key environmental discursive agenda around targets and limits.

5. Transitioning from law to governance

A discursive conception of law challenges more deterministic views of the relationship between environment, law and nature. Older models of environmental law and governance conveyed the idea that the science of ecology, systems theory and climatology was the foundation for legal responses to climate change based on a hierarchical model of the nation state governing its territory and resources and adjusting legal goals in response to objective scientific predictions. By contrast, Foucault's work on archaeological constructs of knowledge illuminates a changing episteme[56] around central narratives of life and law. Operating in tandem is

[53] Elizabeth Beck-Gernsheim, 'Life as a Planning Project' in Lash *et al.* (eds.), above n. 41, 139, 148.

[54] Oels, above n. 8, 194. [55] Liverman, above n. 37.

[56] Michel Foucault, *The Archaeology of Knowledge* (trans. A. M. Sheridan Smith) (Pantheon Books, London, 1972). Briefly, the idea of an episteme is that a prevailing paradigm of knowledge gains currency at particular historical periods and displaces earlier 'world views'.

'the entry of life into history'[57] as part of the rise of a normative paradigm of biopower. For Foucault, the question of life and its relationship to the state changed to one whereby the individual as the central subject was then to be characterised in the following terms as:

> [i]f the question of man [*sic*] was raised – insofar as he was a specific being, and specifically related to other beings – the reason for this is to be sought in the new mode of relation between history and life: in the dual position of life that placed it at the same time outside history, in its biological environment, and inside human historicity.[58]

A specific consequence of this change in the climate change law context is that life became susceptible to expert, specialist techniques of governance. Thus 'life', now regarded as species or populations, was then open to being disciplined in behaviour through reflexive and responsive technical modes, including those adopted in regulatory regimes. Life was 'outside' history or previous visions of law and society, located in a purely biological or material realm. In such a position the human is placed beyond the sovereign sphere. At the same time, the governance of life through the body became central to the manner in which the modern state sought to achieve the ends, goals or outcomes of human historicity. A critical goal of the modern state under the UNFCCC framework, for example, is to achieve global targets for greenhouse gas emissions and thus achieve the biological imperatives of sustaining life through a particular 'technique' of governance. Such governance is the legal 'method' or apparatus that facilitates life and which manifests as an expert managerialism by the state working in concert with a plethora of other actors in the environmental field: all concerned to ensure the maintenance of life's sustaining conditions.[59]

More widely, the advent of a regulation of bodies and populations under biopower marks a change from the earlier sovereign model of the state premised upon the inherent power of the sovereign to take the life of a subject or to let the subject live. In Western history this sovereign power over time was progressively replaced by a diffuse power to foster life.[60] This key shift in the construction of sovereign power and law reflects a change from law to governance. If these epistemic, discursive shifts are translated into the doctrinal language of modern

[57] Darier, above n. 38, 12. [58] Foucault, above n. 10, 143. [59] Ibid. 92–102.

[60] For a discussion of the sovereign-juridico model of law and power, see generally, Michel Foucault, *Discipline and Punish* (trans. Alan Sheridan) (Vintage Books, New York, 1979) 85.

environmental law and more specifically into a climate law regime, we can see a move from prescriptive obligations backed by explicit sanctions to a regime that matches legal institutions with an ever-expanding administrative bureaucracy, prioritising a responsive, self-regulation approach assisted by the market.[61]

This shift exists in tandem with a rising concern over the health and moral well-being of populations.[62] Promotion of life manifests as a control over 'body' as the crucial target of 'a power organised around the management of life rather than the menace of death'.[63] The power resonates not just in direct 'medical' control over humans, but in the conditions for the flourishing of populations that law can institute. These conditions, when facilitated by the nation state, might now begin to employ a terminology of sustainability borrowed from ecology as the objectives of legislation. The ends of human civilisation and of law might now be couched in terms of achieving a sustainable balance in the face of dwindling resource bases and cataclysmic threats to species survival. The construction of life through these paradigms of biopower has become normalised, even in law,[64] while the focus of control has extended from purely human populations to a concern with populations inhabiting ecosystems, and to biodiversity protection.[65]

Now all species, all life, is threatened by global warming. Whether the 'cause' of climate change is to be seen as overpopulation and burgeoning economic growth in developing countries or the continued affluence of developed countries, if we deconstruct these causes, each may have an underlying locus in the 'entry of life into history' that has outstripped the limits of law to control that growth. Most acutely for legal analyses, it places in profile questions about the appropriate legal model of constraint or limit that might be employed in international law and at a national level to deal effectively with climate change.[66]

[61] Some commentators adopt the terminology of neo-liberalism to explain these trends. See also Gunningham, above n. 6, 181, 190.

[62] For a discussion, see generally, Alan Hunt and Gary Wickham, *Foucault and the Law: Towards a Sociology of Law as Governance* (Pluto Press, London, 1994) 25–7.

[63] Foucault, above n. 9, 147.

[64] Note the extent to which ecologically sustainable development is set as the objective for international environmental law instruments and national legislation.

[65] Wendy Larner, 'Neoliberalism: Policy, Ideology and Governmentality' (2000) 63 *Studies in Political Economy* 3.

[66] Martin Parry, 'Climate Change Is a Development Issue, and Only Sustainable Development Can Confront the Challenge' (2009) 1 *Climate and Development* 5, 5.

6. The response of international law to climate change

Resolution of this question at international law around setting targets and responsibilities for reductions was mediated by calls for flexibility.[67] Subsequently, in the aftermath of the fifteenth Conference of the Parties in Copenhagen, even reaching international consensus on targets for greenhouse emissions reductions (whether or not assisted by flexibility measures and trade) seems increasingly problematic. This highlights the central dilemma facing legal models employing neo-liberal and private ordering modes of governance – is it possible to constrain the growth and consumption that result in anthropogenic global warming if the overarching governance mode is one which remains embedded in the facilitation of life? Therefore, climate change law, as an interface between public international law, environmental law and global administrative law, must evolve beyond a traditional account of law as a limit on sovereign nation state power. It must change its assumptions and modes of implementation based on deterministic 'limits' models if it is to effectively resonate with the pervasive diffusion of the governance of life that characterises current modes of global governance. In this mode, contractual and economic ordering occupies an increasingly dominant normative position. Any such engagement is not without its own inherent risks, as the disparities inherent to the diffusion of public law, private law and 'voluntary' normative ordering underpinning world trade can illustrate.[68] Moreover, as noted previously, global administrative law may have a growing role to play here, if its assumptions and forms can co-evolve to provide a regulatory safety-net to the ever-expanding international bureaucracies and private law realms.[69] For example, the World Bank's role has increased to include 'indirect' governance of climate change through carbon financing, and in schemes such as the United Nations Collaborative Programme on Reducing Emissions from Deforestation and Degradation.

[67] Farhana Yamin, 'The Kyoto Protocol: Origins, Assessment and Future Challenges' (1998) 7 *Review of European Community and International Environmental Law* 113.

[68] Andreas Fischer-Lescano and Gunther Teubner, 'Regime-Collisions: The Vain Search for Legal Unity in the Fragmentation of Global Law' (2004) 25 *Michigan Journal of International Law* 999.

[69] In this context, note International Law Commission, *Fragmentation of International Law: Difficulties Arising from the Diversification and Expansion of International Law: Conclusions* (A/CN.4/L.702) (2006).

Market measures retain their dominance as the preferred instruments to institute 'limits', but issues of the accountability and transparency of these measures themselves are being raised. Critiques have arisen most directly in the operation of the Clean Development Mechanism,[70] but are by no means limited to it. More acutely, the problems inherent to the use of reflexive forms are raised by the extent to which these measures might continue to allow 'business as usual' scenarios in both developed and developing economies. It is therefore imperative to question who wins and who loses from flexibility measures. The use of polluter 'pays' principles in this context may take on a new meaning – although one familiar in domestic pollution regulation, where the 'costs' of continuing to 'do business' are simply factored into industry 'bottom lines' or passed onto third parties including consumers, without generating fundamental change in practices. The weak targets set by nation states for mitigation within their public laws, as well as the ineffective design of those emissions trading schemes that have been implemented like the European Union scheme,[71] exemplify these difficulties. The availability of the 'offset' option, whether instituted through public international law or the private law ordering of contract under voluntary schemes of carbon 'neutrality', remains a central problematic in assessing whether a reflexive law approach can be truly effective in addressing climate change.[72]

There is a widening dichotomy between the objectives of climate change instruments at international law and the mechanisms deployed to implement them. Once discursively anchored around the principles of sustainable development,[73] the methods and procedures of the UNFCCC are increasingly associated with private law ordering and reflexive

[70] Some critiques call for greater monitoring and reporting controls, see, e.g., Lin and Streck, above n. 39, while other commentators point to the lack of substantive sustainability achievements of the mechanisms, see, e.g., Paul Desancker, 'The Kyoto Protocol and the CDM in Africa: A Good Idea But [. . .]' (2005) 56 *Unasylva* 24.

[71] For a comprehensive discussion of phase 1 of the EU scheme, see Michael Fauré and Marjan Peeters, *Climate Change and European Emissions Trading: Lessons for Theory and Practice* (Edward Elgar, Cheltenham, 2008). See also below Chapter 14 by Sanja Bogojević.

[72] For a discussion, see David Driesen, 'Sustainable Development and Market Liberalism's Shotgun Wedding: Emissions Trading under the Kyoto Protocol' (2008) 83 *Indiana Law Journal* 21

[73] Laura Horn, 'Intra-generational Equity' (Paper presented at the Australian Law Teachers Association Conference, *Law and Public Policy: Taming the Unruly Horse?*, The University of Western Australia, Perth, Australia, 23–26 September 2007).

governance.[74] In this vein, the adoption of the legal 'instruments' of trade and the technicalities of flexibility mechanisms reveal a governmentality of climate change regimes with origins in economic growth that must now control the heat-producing pollution of modern consumer life. The UNFCCC must hold together life and law and governance in a framework constituting the means for the nation state to sustain life by reducing emissions, while at the same time supporting the rights of individuals as consumers to the conditions supporting life. Climate law must constitute a reworked 'mechanics of power'[75] directed to securing life against limits. These modes of governance produce a tension between the public and private forms of law and ordering that operate in the interstices of multilateral conventions,[76] and at the national level. The climate change regime now functions more as a body of norms, practices and expectations associated with technical idioms of global penetrating power, rather than having a firm anchor in equity, justice and responsibility.[77] These liberal principles were fashioned around a model of a strong sovereign state having duties and responsibilities, which is a model where law can establish the conditions necessary for community and social order by setting limits.[78]

7. Limiting the freedom of consumers in the nation state

Ironically, this mode of limiting the 'freedom' of the subject through law remains at the core of environmental law and regulation at a domestic level within most industrialised nations. Most recently this model has been castigated as 'command and control',[79] and identified by some commentators as highly inefficient.[80] Nonetheless, the concept of a strong interventionist state promulgating laws for environmental

[74] Anne-Marie Klijn, Joyeeta Gupta and Anita Nijboer, 'Privatizing Environmental Resources: The Need for Supervision of Clean Development Mechanism Contracts?' (2009) 18 *Review of European Community and International Environmental Law* 172.

[75] See Foucault, above n. 9, 85.

[76] Jed Ela, 'Law and Norms in Collective Action: Maximizing Social Influence to Minimize Carbon Emissions' (2009) 27 *UCLA Journal of Environmental Law and Policy* 93.

[77] Brad Jessup, 'Investing the Law with an Environmental Ethic: Using an Environmental Justice Theory for Change' in Erika Techera (ed.), *Environmental Law, Ethics and Governance* (ID Press, Oxford, 2010) 21. See also above Chapters 1 and 2, by Peter Lawrence and Brad Jessup, respectively.

[78] Danchin, above n. 5, 27. [79] Gunningham above n. 6, 182–3.

[80] See, e.g., Cass Sunstein, 'The Paradoxes of Regulation' (1990) 67 *University of Chicago Law Review* 408.

protection, including various forms of pollution control, was highly influential in the early development of international environmental law. At a national level it was effective in instituting the initial legal frameworks for pollution control, biological conservation, environmental impact assessment and in the reorientation (at least partially) of natural resource management.[81] The move to detailed prescriptive legislation as a key component of environmental law is indicative of a more general trend to 'substantive law' in the latter part of the twentieth century. This trend was 'characterised by detailed, particularised policies, programmes and rules through which governments seek to mould social behaviour in pursuit of specific social goals'.[82] Substantive law largely displaced 'formal or juridical law', which was exemplified by the use of common law actions, such as nuisance, for achieving relatively constrained levels of environmental protection through the courts. This laid down broad generic forms of liability for economic and environmental harm, but left large discretion in terms of overall compliance. This outcome largely depends on the initiation of litigation by affected parties. The re-emergence of legal action through the courts in climate change contexts where there has been a failure by the respective nation state to engage with international climate law or to implement national greenhouse emissions mitigation laws is an interesting development.[83] This trend, where the primary form of normative ordering occurs within the private law sphere, correlates with similar trends in the international arena.

By contrast, as an example of the public institution of substantive law, environment protection agencies are now prominent across most nations, including all Australian jurisdictions.[84] They administer an increasingly complex, detailed and prescriptive range of statutes, delegated legislation and policies seeking to implement standards and procedures for environmental protection. In some instances these agencies also embrace a wider range of regulatory or 'reflexive' approaches

[81] Gunningham above n. 6, 182.

[82] Carolyn Abbott, 'Environmental Command Regulation' in Ben Richardson and Stepan Wood (eds.), *Environmental Law for Sustainability* (Hart Publishing, Oxford, 2006) 64.

[83] The United States exemplifies one such jurisdiction where civil action in tort or judicial review of administrative decision-making have sought to fill the void in the absence of direct state laws governing climate change. See, e.g., *State of Connecticut* v. *American Electric Power Co. Inc.* 582 F 3d 309 (2d Cir 2009); *Re Xstrata Coal Queensland Pty Ltd* [2007] QLRT 33; *Queensland Conservation Council Inc.* v. *Xstrata Coal Queensland Pty Ltd* (2007) 155 LGERA 322.

[84] Gunningham above n. 6, 182.

incorporating business and community actors in the regulatory compass.[85] It would be possible to treat greenhouse gas emissions as yet another suite of atmospheric pollutants to be addressed in statute law by the introduction of prescriptive air quality standards.[86] In concert, theoretically, it would be possible to engage science, industry and community groups in standard setting for emissions reductions that could then be reflected in existing pollution control laws. These legal and regulatory options were not extensively canvassed in most Australian jurisdictions. Detailed standard setting for emissions controls was only adopted in a very small number of jurisdictions in respect of narrow sectors, particularly transport. Typically models seeking to directly 'limit' growth and consumption face strong resistance. These situations highlight the extent that climate change policy discourses favouring highly prescriptive law have been supplanted by reflexive, regulatory regimes. There has been a 'de-centring of the state, its resources and powers as a result of privatisation and regulatory growth',[87] which has brought about accountability problems, 'that traditional control mechanisms – judicial control and political accountability – may not address'.[88]

Emerging patterns in public environmental law more generally reveal that the highly prescriptive nature of much environmental law has led to calls by industry to 'cut red tape' and for greater flexibility in environmental standard setting for industry, commercial organisations and community activities.[89] In part, the response has been to differentiate the application of industrial regulation by identifying 'leaders and laggards' and in adapting the scale and expectations of the relevant regulation.[90] A new focus looks to achieve the diffuse social goals of integrated environmental protection as a component of sustainability,

[85] Gunningham uses the Victorian EPA as an example of an agency that has employed a wide diversity of regulatory and governance approaches, ibid. 191–2.

[86] In this regard, see *Massachusetts* v. *EPA* 549 US 497 (2007).

[87] Hitoshi Nasu, 'Who Guards the Guardian? Towards Regulation of the UN Security Council's Chapter VII Powers through Dialogue' in Farrell and Rubenstein (eds.), above n. 5, 128.

[88] Ibid.

[89] Robyn Eckersley, 'Markets, the State and the Environment: An Overview' in Robyn Eckersley (ed.), *Markets, the State, and the Environment: Towards Integration* (Macmillan Education Australia, Melbourne, 1995).

[90] See, e.g., Neil Gunningham and Darren Sinclair, 'New Generation Environmental Policy: Environmental Management Systems and Regulatory Reform' (1998) 22 *Melbourne University Law Review* 592.

rather than a defined standard-setting approach. Flexible performance standards, based around agreement models, are more indeterminate than traditional 'command and control' standards, for they allow increasing levels of discretion for delegated authorities in governing regulatory frameworks. The growing discretion of authorities in the implementation of pollution standards has been accompanied by the emergence of reflexive law in many areas of environmental pollution regulation.[91] These administrative discretions are often not caught by traditional models of transparency and accountability, which administrative law frameworks are historically designed to address.

The trends are illustrative of the shifts to a 'facilitation of life' as opposed to a state-based model built upon hierarchical sovereign control and sanction. For example, within Australia, conflicting interests largely immobilised the former Howard federal government until events finally drew the concession that climate change had to be addressed by other than 'voluntary' or self-regulatory measures for business and industry.[92] By contrast, the first act of the incoming Rudd federal government was to ratify the Kyoto Protocol, committing Australia as a nation state to an internationally binding emissions reduction target. An intensive process of policy development followed, with the release of government Green and White Papers on climate change mitigation.[93] The national process culminated in the issue of the first draft legislation for the establishment of an Australian emissions trading scheme.[94] A decision to shelve the scheme until 2013 was taken, but a new legislative scheme was later introduced for meeting any international emissions reduction targets and limits. The proposed carbon price mechanism if enacted does represent a hybrid form of an emissions trading, regulatory tool.

[91] Elim Papadakis and Richard Grant, 'The Politics of "Light-Handed Regulation": "New" Environmental Policy Instruments in Australia' (2003) 12 *Environmental Politics* 27.

[92] Jacqueline Peel, 'The Role of Climate Change Litigation in Australia's Response to Global Warming' (2007) 24 *Environmental and Planning Law Journal* 90, 91.

[93] For a discussion of these trends, see Jacqueline Peel, 'Climate Change Law: The Emergence of a New Legal Discipline' (2008) 32 *Melbourne University Law Review* 922, 946–55.

[94] This legislative package consisted of six different pieces of legislation, including the Carbon Pollution Reduction Scheme Bill 2009 (Cth). The subsequent draft package of legislation included the Clean Energy Bill 2011 (Cth).

The national difficulties in adopting firm measures mirror international law developments. The process by which limits discourses might have been translated from 'anxiety' to robust and enforceable domestic public law measures to address climate change remains in suspension. Some initiatives, such as the mandatory renewable energy target schemes, do remain.[95] In summary, to date, a general acknowledgement of the looming apocalypse has not been matched by comprehensive Australian legal and regulatory measures capable of providing an effective response to the broad, cumulative environmental impacts predicted as a result of climate change.[96] Instead, there has been a reversion to non-statutory responses, such as enhanced research funding, a renewed belief in technological innovation, such as carbon capture and storage, and perhaps most surprising of all, a return to exploring land-use change as a form of climate change adaptation.[97]

8. Reflexive and responsive environmental law and climate change regulation

A complex aggregation of deregulation, flexible, collaborative and agreement-oriented (or dialogue-based) trends in environmental governance that can be subsumed under the rubric of reflexive law has been brought to bear in the climate change sphere. These reflexive models operate within an overarching legal framework that is predominantly procedural rather than substantive, where the key modes are report and monitoring. The National Greenhouse Energy Reporting Act 2007 (Cth) implemented by the Australian federal government as a baseline emissions reporting platform for the potential adoption of an emissions trading scheme is illustrative of the process. It is a powerful exemplar of the intersection of public law and reflexive law modes of disciplining industry behaviour as it relies on self-report of emissions, but with relatively punitive sanctions imposed by the state for 'mis-report': that is, for a failure to abide by the norms of self-discipline. Similarly, many law and economic analyses argue for stronger normative ordering

95 For a general discussion of the laws, see Chris McGrath, 'Australia's Draft Climate Laws' (2009) 26 *Environmental and Planning Law Journal* 26.

96 Peel, above n. 93.

97 See Commonwealth of Australia, Department of Climate Change, *Adapting to Climate Change in Australia: An Australian Government Position Paper* (Department of Climate Change, Canberra, 2010)

through the adoption of property rights,[98] as one way in which law might address the need for limits to avoid the tragedy of atmospheric commons. Social cost theory has been highly influential in the trends to institute responsive, flexible, self-correcting approaches to environmental protection.[99]

The dominance of discourses based around a reflexive model of climate change regulation can be most clearly demonstrated by the progressive legal redefinition of greenhouse gas emissions. Emissions have been progressively recoded in line with the shifts from law to governance as: first, an atmospheric pollution, a 'waste' and a threat to life; then, as a 'tradable permission'; and ultimately a 'commodity' in terms of emissions trading schemes that can be used in futures markets.[100] The redefinition of greenhouse gas emissions from pollutant to a commodity within climate change legal frameworks is symptomatic of the deeply entrenched ambivalence and tensions that inhere in simultaneously holding together public law and private law normative orderings in international and national environmental law for mitigation of climate change. It also identifies a 'deeper' contradiction that would use the techniques of the governance of life and growth to impose ecological limits at law in order to sustain life.

9. Conclusion

This chapter has explored how reflexive environmental governance operating at the intersection of public international law, environmental law, and indeed global administrative law, might address the complex problems of impending ecological limits around climate change. Competing, yet at times congruent, discourses of growth and limits to growth are most clearly articulated at the level of international law. On the one hand, there are arguments advocating the need for a 'strong state', or at least a coalition of nations to impose international legal frameworks for national mitigation efforts. On the other hand, the

[98] Richard Posner, *Economic Analysis of Law* (Little, Brown, Boston, 1972).

[99] Clearly emissions trading regimes exemplify these trends. For a discussion of property rights models in environmental sustainability laws, see Lee Godden, 'Governing Common Resources: Environmental Markets and Property in Water' in Aileen McHarg *et al.* (eds.), *Property and the Law in Energy and Natural Resources* (Oxford University Press, 2010) 413.

[100] Karan Capoor and Philippe Ambrosi, *State and Trends of the Carbon Market 2009* (World Bank, Washington DC, 2009).

failure to achieve a binding agreement post-2012 within the formal structures of public international law points to the resilience of the facilitation of life through economic growth that remains embedded in many international regimes, including trade and contractual forms of governance. However, the UNFCCC still emphasises, as do other public environmental law conventions, the role of law as a means of defining responsibility and in ensuring some degree of accountability among nations.[101] Increasingly, though, it seems anachronistic as a platform to implement the targets and trajectories that will control the behaviours of nations and their populations sufficiently to avoid the descent into 'dangerous climate change'.[102]

So, what is the practical outcome? This chapter has identified the need for a fundamental rethinking of how law as governance operates in the climate change regime in public international law and in Australian public environmental law. It has sought to deconstruct some of the more fundamental discourses which underpin the various policy and legal mechanisms for climate change that are advocated and implemented. This is particularly pertinent within Australia, given the current stasis in its choice of regulatory measures to address climate change, given the postponement of an emissions trading scheme. Accordingly, it is an appropriate point to critically evaluate the respective advantages and disadvantages of a spectrum of legal instruments and regulatory tools. It is clear that Australia and the international community must take the hard decisions and impose limits on carbon emissions by a range of measures if it is effectively to institute a sustainable governance of life that is cognisant of the limits posed by the anticipated ecological crisis. While the limits may be discursively constructed in specific ways, their ramifications will be material. In understanding the articulation between public international law under the UNFCCC, reflexive environmental law and the growing need for non-traditional forms of responsibility and accountability, law may begin to frame more diverse and nuanced forms of regulation that are iterative with the pervasive modes of the governance of life, so as to avoid once again the spectre of death as the ultimate limit.

[101] Jurgen Habermas, *Between Facts and Norms: Contributions to a Discourse Theory of Law* (Polity Press, Cambridge, 1996).

[102] Driesen, above n. 72.

12

The national interest or good international citizenship? Australia and its approach to international and public climate law

RIVER CORDES-HOLLAND*

1. Introduction

This chapter examines the influence of two discourses on Australian government approaches to international and public climate law since the late 1980s, namely, 'national interest' and 'good international citizenship'. Neither discourse is peculiar to the environmental field; both are relevant to the broad range of global issues to which governments must respond. However, both national interest and good international citizenship discourses are important to understanding how Australian governments have defined and implemented their environmental responsibilities, including on global climate change.

The labelling of national interest discourse requires some clarification. The notion of the 'national interest' is, of course, heavily contested, including by good international citizenship discourse. In using this label, this chapter refers to a particular conception of the national interest that promotes the advancement of narrow security and economic interests. It will be seen that in relation to climate change, national interest discourse – as most fervently espoused by the conservative Howard government – has encouraged the pursuit of Australia's short-term economic prosperity over the adoption of potentially costly measures to reduce greenhouse gas emissions.

Good international citizenship discourse – as chiefly promulgated by centrist Labor governments – has promoted a more ethical view of Australia's global responsibilities. Popularised in the late 1980s by

* The author wishes to thank the referees and editors for their helpful comments.

Labor Foreign Minister, Gareth Evans, good international citizenship accepts that states have legitimate security and economic needs. However, it calls for these to be pursued in a more enlightened fashion that also advances the common good. On climate change, Labor's good international citizenship discourse has acknowledged the need for governmental restraint in promoting the immediate economic interests of its constituents (whether individuals, business, or other interest groups) in order to safeguard the longer-term needs of future generations, the international community and the environment.

This chapter examines the influence of national interest and good international citizenship discourses on the Hawke, Keating, Howard and Rudd governments, a period spanning close to three decades.[1] Section 2 first outlines how Australian governments have articulated each discourse at a general level. Sections 3 to 5 then consider how these discourses have been expressed in relation to climate change and their impact on Australian government approaches to international and public climate law, through a select examination of each government's political rhetoric and practice. The chapter argues that domestic national interest ultimately trumps international citizenship and that a particular nationalised discourse directs global behaviour, thus connecting the public and international legal and political spheres.

2. Introducing national interest and good international citizenship discourse

There is a commonly held view that '[s]ecurity and prosperity will always be the *primary* foreign policy motivations of any government elected to protect and advance the interests of its society'.[2] This statement reflects the type of national interest discourse to which this chapter refers. Gyngell and Wesley further recognise, however, that Australian governments have typically also acknowledged the importance of promoting less self-interested values in foreign policy 'that are more concerned with a nation's sense of self and responsibilities to people and institutions beyond its borders'.[3] In the late 1980s, during Evans's foreign ministership, Australian governments began articulating this more ethical aspect

[1] Hawke 1983–1991, Keating 1991–6, Howard 1996–2007, Rudd 2007–10.

[2] Allan Gyngell and Michael Wesley, *Making Australian Foreign Policy* (Cambridge University Press, New York, 2nd edn, 2007) 273. Emphasis added.

[3] Ibid.

of foreign policy explicitly in terms of good international citizenship.[4] Since popularised by Evans, all Australian governments have made a commitment to being a good international citizen – albeit with varying levels of sincerity – including in relation to climate change.

Good international citizenship does not depart radically from traditional national interest discourse; Evans also regarded the advancement of security and economic interests to be of critical importance for government.[5] In addition, however, Evans argued that Australia had a national interest 'in being, and being seen to be, a good international citizen'.[6] Good international citizenship was partly characterised by Evans as the pursuit of 'purposes beyond ourselves'.[7] In other words, good international citizenship was about helping to realise an idealistic vision of a 'peaceful and prosperous Australia and a peaceful and prosperous world'.[8] But good international citizenship was not just 'the foreign policy equivalent of Boy Scout good deeds'.[9] Rather, Evans saw good international citizenship as a logical response to an increasingly globalised and interdependent world in which the promotion of Australian interests necessarily involved pursuing global solutions to global problems.[10] For Evans, good international citizenship was an exercise in 'enlightened self-interest'[11] which sought to mutually advance both national and global interests.

Evans' good international citizenship discourse was characterised by several other features. In particular, it encouraged internationalism (actively seeking to address global issues, whether human rights abuses, AIDS, environmental problems, or other); the demonstration of leadership; and a commitment to multilateralism, international institutions

[4] Note that while Evans's explicit adoption of good international citizenship discourse was new, it is often regarded as taking its cue from a broader international and Australian tradition of liberal internationalism, see, e.g., Richard Leaver and Dave Cox, 'Introduction: The World According to Gar' in Richard Leaver and Dave Cox (eds.), *Middling, Meddling, Muddling: Issues in Australian Foreign Policy* (Allen & Unwin, Sydney, 1997) 1, 6. On Evans and good international citizenship generally, see, e.g., David Goldsworthy, 'Australia and Good International Citizenship' in Stephanie Lawson (ed.), *The New Agenda for Global Security: Cooperating for Peace and Beyond* (Allen & Unwin, Sydney, 1995) 171.

[5] Gareth Evans, *Making Australian Foreign Policy* (Australian Fabian Society and Pluto Press, Sydney, 1989) 9–11.

[6] Ibid. 9. There are, of course, other discussions about international citizenship beyond international relations; however, this chapter concentrates upon this specific international relations discourse.

[7] Ibid. 11. [8] Ibid. 46. [9] Ibid. 42. [10] Ibid. [11] Ibid. 43.

and international law.[12] Evans was a strong advocate of international law, believing that it was essential to promoting international cooperation and 'setting new and higher standards of both international and national behaviour'.[13] As such, he thought it necessary for Australia to be active in the development of international law, as well as always to comply with its international obligations.[14]

Good international citizenship was encouraged by Evans to counteract a more traditional national interest discourse that he later likened to a 'disease'.[15] In the period of review, this narrower type of national interest discourse was most openly advocated by the conservative Liberal/National Howard government, elected in 1996. The Liberal Party's election manifesto, *A Confident Australia*, made clear that – unlike Labor – it did 'not subscribe to unrealistic notions of global idealism'.[16] The government's 1997 foreign policy White Paper, *In the National Interest*, instead promised an emphasis on 'the hard-headed pursuit of the interests which lie at the core of foreign and trade policy: the security of the nation and the jobs and standard of living of the Australian people'.[17] This 'basic test of national interest' would guide all future foreign and trade policy.[18] The coalition's foreign policy rhetoric also lacked Labor's enthusiasm for multilateralism, international institutions and international law, committing instead to a renewed focus on bilateral diplomacy.[19]

A sense of higher purpose was largely absent from the Howard government's national interest discourse, but it did make some concessions to good international citizenship. While the term was dropped from the coalition's White Paper, it did acknowledge the importance of promoting less self-interested 'national values' in its foreign policy (such as respect for human rights), and the benefits of enjoying an 'international reputation as a responsible member of the international

[12] See Gareth Evans, 'Foreign Policy and Good International Citizenship' (speech, Canberra, 6 March 1990).

[13] Gareth Evans and Bruce Grant, *Australia's Foreign Relations: In the World of the 1990s* (Melbourne University Press, 2nd edn, 1995) 153.

[14] Gareth Evans, 'International Law and Australia's Interests' [1989] *Australian International Law News* 185, 187.

[15] Moises Naim and Dave Case, 'True Believer' (2001) (Mar/April) *Foreign Policy* 26, 29.

[16] Commonwealth of Australia, Department of Foreign Affairs and Trade, 'New Australian Government: Foreign Policy' (1996) 5 *Insight* 3, 6.

[17] Commonwealth of Australia, *In the National Interest: Australia's Foreign and Trade Policy White Paper* (1997) iii.

[18] Ibid. [19] Ibid. iii, 47.

community'.[20] Elsewhere, the government, including Prime Minister Howard, also expressed that it was Australia's desire to be a 'good international citizen' on a range of global issues, including climate change,[21] although with much less frequency than its Labor predecessors.

In opposition, Labor heavily criticised the Howard government's alleged acts of 'bad international citizenship', including its refusal to ratify the Kyoto Protocol to the United Nations Framework Convention on Climate Change (UNFCCC).[22] Labor leader, Kevin Rudd, committed to return Australia to its role as a 'good global citizen' if elected.[23] After regaining office in 2007, the Rudd Labor government made good international citizenship a more prominent feature of the national government's vocabulary, reminiscent of the Evans era. Foreign Minister Stephen Smith, for example, declared that '[t]he new Australian government came to office intent on making a difference as a good international citizen'.[24] Led by Prime Minister Rudd, the government's foreign policy rhetoric took its cue from Evans, but provided a new expression of good international citizenship discourse. In Rudd's first address to the United Nations (UN) General Assembly, for example, he called upon the international community to recognise that 'national interests are invariably best served by the simultaneous prosecution of the international interest' and 'to act for the common purposes of the planet we all share'.[25] Labor also reiterated the importance of international leadership, multilateralism, international institutions and international law to the government's foreign policy agenda.[26]

[20] Ibid. 11, 13.

[21] See, e.g., Malcolm Farr, 'Clean Coal Powers Howard', *Herald Sun* (Melbourne), 14 November 2006.

[22] Robert McClelland, 'Time to Repair our Reputation: The Rise and Fall of Australia as a Good International Citizen' (speech delivered at the Lowy Institute for International Policy, Sydney, 14 March 2007); Kyoto Protocol to the United Nations Framework Convention on Climate Change, opened for signature 16 March 1998, 2303 UNTS 148 (entered into force 16 February 2005) ('Kyoto Protocol').

[23] Kevin Rudd, 'An Action Agenda for Climate Change' (speech delivered at the Annual Fraser Lecture, Canberra, 30 May 2007).

[24] Stephen Smith, 'A New Era of Engagement with the World' (speech delivered at the Sydney Institute, Sydney, 19 August 2008).

[25] Kevin Rudd, 'Address by Prime Minister Kevin Rudd to the United Nations General Assembly' (speech delivered at the UN General Assembly, New York, 25 September 2008).

[26] Smith, above n. 24.

3. The Hawke and Keating Labor governments (1983–96)

3.1 The Hawke Labor government

The Hawke government was quick to recognize global warming, and atmospheric protection generally, as 'the biggest ecological problem, the biggest challenge, faced in this or any other age' and consequently the need for a new international legal regime to reduce greenhouse gas emissions.[27] Indicative of his good international citizenship approach, Evans stated that the negotiation of a new treaty would 'require careful balancing between national interests *and* international responsibilities'.[28] Evans recognised that Australia had plenty of self-interested reasons to act, for example: climate change could potentially create 'massive' long-term 'economic, social and security costs'; 'large costs' may be involved in meeting 'new environmental responsibilities'; and new regulations could have 'potential implications for [Australia's] ... energy exports, especially coal'.[29] More altruistically, Evans suggested that the possibility of rising sea levels to displace South Pacific peoples – and its associated 'human misery' – was ample reason for concern,[30] and also highlighted the international community's 'responsibility to protect the environment for future generations'.[31]

In its practice, the Hawke government took several early steps to address climate change through the emerging field of international climate law. In March 1989, Evans represented the government at the Hague Environment Summit. The Summit's Declaration acknowledged that industrialised nations had the primary historical responsibility for greenhouse gas emissions, the greatest resources to deal with the problem, as well as 'special obligations' to assist developing countries respond.[32] In October 1990, Labor adopted an Interim Planning Target to stabilise emissions at 1988 levels by 2000, and then cut emissions by 20 per cent by 2005, which it announced internationally at the Second World Climate Conference in Geneva.[33] Tellingly, however, the government's commitment came with the caveat that Australia would

[27] Gareth Evans, 'Foreign Policy and the Environment' (1990) 61 *Australian Foreign Affairs and Trade: The Monthly Record* 112, 116–17.

[28] Evans, above n. 14, 191. Emphasis added. [29] Evans, above n. 27, 113. [30] Ibid.

[31] Evans, above n. 14, 190.

[32] Hague Declaration on the Environment, concluded 11 March 1989, The Hague, Netherlands, 28 ILM 1308.

[33] Ros Taplin, 'International Co-operation on Climate Change and Australia's Role' (1995) 26 *Australian Geographer* 16, 17.

not adopt measures that would cause 'net adverse economic impacts nationally or on Australia's trade competitiveness in the absence of similar action by major greenhouse gas producing countries'.[34] This was an early example of the tension in Australian governments' desire to be a good international citizen and concern not to harm Australia's economic interests.

3.2 The Keating Labor government

Bob Hawke was deposed as prime minister by Treasurer Paul Keating, in December 1991. As such, the strength of the Hawke government's commitment to good international citizenship discourse was never properly tested. The responsibility for formulating Australia's international and public law response to climate change instead fell to the Keating government. The pressing task for the Keating government was to help finalise negotiations on the UNFCCC,[35] which would be adopted at the 1992 UN Conference on Environment and Development in Rio. The Keating government adopted an activist diplomatic approach, sought to be recognised as a leader in the negotiations,[36] and following Rio, quickly ratified the treaty and encouraged other nations to do likewise.[37]

The UNFCCC represented a landmark in the development of international climate law, being the first treaty to regulate greenhouse gas emissions. But it was also a highly flawed agreement, especially because it failed to establish legally binding emission reduction obligations for developed countries, primarily due to opposition by the United States (US).[38] Instead, Annex I countries (developed countries and former Soviet countries in transition to a market economy) agreed only to a non-binding goal to stabilise their emissions at 1990 levels by 2000.[39] Environment Minister Ros Kelly indicated that Australia had 'negotiated for stronger outcomes'[40] and that the UNFCCC had not gone as far as

[34] Clive Hamilton, *Running from the Storm: The Development of Climate Change Policy in Australia* (University of New South Wales Press, Sydney, 2001) 33.

[35] United Nations Framework Convention on Climate Change, opened for signature 4 June 1992, 1771 UNTS 107 (entered into force 21 March 1994) ('Climate Change Convention').

[36] Dave Cox, 'The Road from Rio: Multilateral Cooperation Gives Way to National Interest' in Leaver and Cox (eds.), above n. 4, 215, 219–20.

[37] Ratified 30 December 1992. Taplin, above n. 33, 17.

[38] Ibid. 19.

[39] Climate Change Convention, Art. 4(2)(a) and (b).

[40] Cox, above n. 36, 219.

the government would have liked.[41] While the government's behaviour at Rio has been described as that of a good international citizen, 'committed to significant reductions in greenhouse gas emissions and more generally multilateralism in environmental policy',[42] others have been more circumspect. Cox, for instance, suggests that 'it was relatively easy to appear [to be] one of the leading states when the major CO_2 producing state [the US] refused to negotiate stringent policy'.[43] He further points out that while the Keating government wanted to be regarded as a leader, it also acknowledged that 'there ha[d] always been a caveat in our negotiations that . . . [the UNFCCC wouldn't] be at an economic cost to Australia'.[44]

The strength of the government's concern not to jeopardise Australia's economic interests became clearer in its weak attempts to implement its UNFCCC obligations. In 1992, the government introduced the National Greenhouse Response Strategy.[45] This Strategy primarily included voluntary measures to encourage the greening of Australia's energy supply and the improvement of national energy efficiency.[46] Typical of voluntary emissions reduction approaches, the scheme failed to reduce Australia's growing emissions. By October 1994, Australia's emissions were tracking to rise 7 per cent above 1990 levels by 2000.[47] In response, the government downplayed expectations regarding its UNFCCC commitment. In February 1995, for example, Treasurer Ralph Willis stated that while the government would do 'everything in its power' to meet its goal of stabilising emissions by 2000, the UNFCCC contained 'let-out clauses' and the government might decide that a less ambitious target was appropriate.[48] While Labor did introduce a new policy to curb emissions – Greenhouse 21C – this again emphasised voluntary measures and failed to curb emissions growth.[49] Potentially effective laws such as a carbon tax or an emissions trading scheme (ETS) were mooted within government,[50] but it lacked the resolve to introduce such measures which, by

[41] Matt McDonald, 'Fair Weather Friend? Ethics and Australia's Approach to Global Climate Change' (2005) 51 *Australian Journal of Politics and History* 216, 223.

[42] Simon Lightfoot, 'A Good International Citizen? Australia at the World Summit on Sustainable Development' (2006) 60 *Australian Journal of International Affairs* 457, 459.

[43] Cox, above n. 36, 220. [44] Ibid. 223.

[45] Commonwealth of Australia, *National Greenhouse Response Strategy* (1992).

[46] See, e.g., Hamilton, above n. 34, 34–9. [47] Cox, above n. 36, 222, 224.

[48] Ibid. 225. [49] See, e.g., Hamilton, above n. 34, 40–50. [50] See Cox, above n. 36, 224.

deliberately putting a price on carbon pollution, would necessarily entail economic cost.

In March/April 1995, parties to the UNFCCC held their first Conference of the Parties (COP 1). A key purpose of COP 1, held in Berlin, was to discuss stronger emission reduction targets.[51] New measures could not be agreed on at Berlin, but the COP adopted the Berlin Mandate, establishing a formal process to guide further negotiations.[52] Before considering the Keating government's behaviour at Berlin, it should be noted that the UNFCCC established several principles to 'guide' parties' future efforts to achieve the objective of the UNFCCC (to 'prevent dangerous anthropogenic interference with the climate system').[53] According to Article 3: parties should act 'on the basis of equity and in accordance with their common but differentiated responsibilities and respective capabilities'; developed countries should 'take the lead'; the atmosphere should be protected for both 'present and future generations'; and parties should take 'precautionary measures' to prevent climate change notwithstanding 'lack of full scientific certainty' (the precautionary principle).[54] Developed countries were expected to show leadership because, as noted in the Preamble, 'the largest share of historical and current global emissions … originated in developed countries', per capita emissions in developing countries remained relatively low, and developing countries had 'priority needs' of 'sustained economic growth and the eradication of poverty'. The extent to which a party respects the UNFCCC's principles has since provided a good indicator of whether good international citizenship or narrow self-interest is motivating its behaviour.

At Berlin, the Association of Small Island States (AOSIS) (low-lying island nations that are particularly vulnerable to climate change) urged parties to adopt a protocol requiring developed countries to reduce carbon dioxide (CO_2) emissions by 20 per cent below 1990 levels by 2005,[55] the same target once committed to by the Hawke government. Yet Australia refused to support the AOSIS proposal, in part because of

[51] See International Institute for Sustainable Development, *COP-1 Report* (1995) Earth Negotiations Bulletin Vol. 12 No. 21 at www.iisd.ca/vol12/1221000e.html, last accessed 31 May 2011.

[52] *Report of the Conference of the Parties to the UNFCCC on its First Session*, Decision 1/CP 1, FCCC/CP/1995/7/Add1 (1995).

[53] Climate Change Convention, Art. 2.

[54] Climate Change Convention, Art. 3(1) and (3).

[55] International Institute for Sustainable Development, above n. 51, 3.

this target.[56] The Keating government and several other developed countries also sought to have larger developing country emitters agree to undertake emission cuts (a strategy designed to minimise its own future emissions reduction burden).[57] This was despite the fact that Australia – which would not meet its existing UNFCCC commitment – had yet to demonstrate the leadership called for by the UNFCCC. Labor's position was ultimately rejected at Berlin, with the Mandate deciding that only developed countries would be required to strengthen their targets.[58] But the Keating government's negotiations at Berlin demonstrated that its good international citizenship goals had diminished in the face of traditional national interest considerations.

4. The Howard Coalition government (1996–2007)

The Hawke and Keating governments' enthusiasm for good international citizenship discourse perhaps helped to mask, at least early on, the true strength of its concern to protect the Australian economy. The Howard government, however, stated upfront that narrow economic interests would guide its approach to international climate law. With the upcoming COP 3 in mind, where the Kyoto Protocol would be adopted, the government's 1997 White Paper declared that it would be prepared to 'stand aside from an international agreement' that did 'not adequately protect Australia's national interests' and if others could not be convinced that Australia's proposals were 'superior in terms of both the environment and the global economy'.[59]

At Kyoto, the government's negotiating strategy reflected its desire to protect the national interest, narrowly defined. As noted, the Berlin Mandate had stipulated that only developed countries would be required to strengthen their emission reduction commitments at Kyoto. Notwithstanding this, the coalition sought to have new obligations imposed on developing countries.[60] This was unsuccessful, but the government did win two significant concessions intended to minimise economic costs. First, Australia gained a very generous target under Kyoto. Annex I countries

[56] Ibid. 11. [57] Cox, above n. 36, 226.

[58] *Report of the Conference of the Parties*, above n. 52, 2(a)(b).

[59] Commonwealth of Australia, above n. 17, 49.

[60] Lorraine Elliott, 'Australia in World Environmental Affairs' in James Cotton and John Ravenhill (eds.), *The National Interest in a Global Era: Australia in World Affairs 1996–2000* (Oxford University Press and the Australian Institute of International Affairs, Melbourne, 2001) 235, 249, 251.

agreed in the Kyoto Protocol to collectively reduce emissions by at least 5 per cent by 2008–12 on 1990 levels. Intense negotiations took place concerning the individual target each developed country would adopt.[61] The European Union (EU) showed some leadership in adopting an emissions reduction target of 8 per cent[62] (and had been prepared to go as high as 15 per cent).[63] In contrast, the Howard government won Australia the right to *increase* emissions by 8 per cent.[64] The government argued that Australia's special circumstances warranted this target, including the importance of fossil fuels to its export and domestic energy sectors, both of which were crucial to jobs.[65] Although the Berlin Mandate had indicated that parties' 'individual circumstances' would be relevant to the allocation of targets,[66] it appears that Australia won its unreasonably weak target only by threatening to otherwise withdraw from negotiations, not because other parties regarded it as fair.[67]

Second, the Howard government gained the inclusion of the so-called 'Australia clause'. This provided that emissions of CO_2 caused by land clearing could be included in Kyoto's 1990 baseline emission figures.[68] This increased Australia's baseline emission figure by 30 per cent, yet land clearing rates had already dropped – by 33 per cent between 1990 and 1995 – and the government had already committed to phasing it out.[69] The coalition could have used this as an opportunity to adopt a far more ambitious target, but instead chose to pursue its generous emissions allowance.[70]

Following Kyoto, Federal Minister for Primary Industries and Energy, John Anderson, boasted that Australia's Kyoto deal would 'preserve the interests of [Australia's] farmers, miners, manufacturing industry and

[61] See International Institute for Sustainable Development, *Report of the Third Conference of the Parties to the United Nations Framework Convention on Climate Change: 1–11 December 1997* (1997) Earth Negotiations Bulletin Vol. 12 No. 76 at www.iisd.ca/vol12/enb1276e.html, last accessed 31 May 2011, 7–8.

[62] Kyoto Protocol, Annex B.

[63] International Institute for Sustainable Development, above n. 61, 3.

[64] Kyoto Protocol, Annex B. [65] Elliott, above n. 60, 250.

[66] *Report of the Conference of the Parties*, above n. 52, (2)(a).

[67] See The Australia Institute, *A Poisoned Chalice: Australia and the Kyoto Protocol*, Background Paper No. 13 (1998) 11.

[68] International Institute for Sustainable Development, above n. 61, 7–8; Kyoto Protocol, Art. 3(7).

[69] The Australia Institute, above n. 67, 5, 12–13. [70] Ibid.

the economy in general'.[71] Despite this, the Howard government later refused to ratify the agreement. According to its 2003 foreign policy White Paper, *Advancing the National Interest*, the government would 'continue to strive for an effective global response' that did 'not unfairly compromise the competitiveness of Australian industry'.[72] The coalition argued that Australia would lose competitive advantages in emission-intensive and trade-exposed industries like oil, gas, coal and aluminium, unless a global agreement included the US (the only other developed nation not to ratify) and major developing countries like China.[73] Further, it claimed that because Australian emissions represented only 1.5 per cent of global emissions, ratifying Kyoto would in any case have negligible impacts on global warming.[74] This argument ignored the fact that Australia was one of the top emitters on a per capita basis, in the top 15 polluters outright,[75] and as a developed country was expected to show leadership in reducing emissions.

In 2002, Federal Environment Minister David Kemp disingenuously boasted that 'increasingly the international community recognises that although we have taken the view that it is not in Australia's national interest to ratify the Kyoto Protocol, we are actually at the forefront of nations that are taking the responsible attitude', adding, 'we have to be a good international citizen'.[76] Yet the government's repudiation of Kyoto indicated that its concession to good international citizenship discourse was only superficial. In addition to withdrawing from the agreement, the Howard government called for Kyoto to be abandoned in international forums.[77] In preference, it espoused the virtues of the six-nation Asia-Pacific Partnership

[71] Anthony Albanese, *Fact Sheet: What the Howard Government Has Said About Kyoto* (2009) at www.anthonyalbanese.com.au/file.php?file=/news/ZFYZABAMQVQJUKZLYOBILLHQ/index.html, last accessed 2 December 2009.

[72] Commonwealth of Australia, *Advancing the National Interest: Australia's Foreign and Trade Policy White Paper* (2003) x.

[73] Ibid. 67.

[74] Commonwealth of Australia, *Australia's Climate Change Policy: Our Economy, Our Environment, Our Future* (2007) v.

[75] Ross Garnaut, *The Garnaut Climate Change Review: Final Report* (Cambridge University Press, Melbourne, 2008) 54.

[76] Australian Broadcasting Corporation, 'Minister Defends Position on Greenhouse Gas Emissions', *Insiders*, 18 August 2002 www.abc.net.au/insiders/content/2002/s651631.htm, last accessed 2 December 2009.

[77] See Friends of the Earth Australia, *Australia Isolates Itself at Climate Change Negotiations* (2006), www.foe.org.au/media-releases/2006-media-releases/mr_14_11_06.htm, last accessed 2 December 2009.

on Clean Development and Climate, a non-binding technology agreement which lacked emission reduction targets.[78]

Somewhat paradoxically, the Howard government stated that it remained committed to achieving Australia's Kyoto target,[79] even though it was not legally obliged to do so. This likely reflected a political need for the government to allay both domestic and international concerns about its withdrawal from Kyoto. But its public law and policy response largely continued the weak approach of the Keating government. Other than a Mandatory Renewable Energy Target of 10 per cent, the government placed its faith in voluntary programmes.[80] These policies did put Australia on track to meet its Kyoto goal – made easy by the 108 per cent target and the Australia clause – but longer-term emissions were predicted to rise to 127 per cent of 1990 levels by 2020.[81] Under considerable public pressure, the government announced prior to the 2007 federal election that it would finally introduce an ETS, as well as a 15 per cent Clean Energy Target.[82] With its election loss, however, the Howard government left behind a poor legacy of international and public climate law practice, clearly shaped by its narrow national interest discourse.

5. The Rudd Labor government (2007–10)

A commitment to adopt strong action on climate change was a 'totemic part' of the Rudd Labor government's winning 2007 election campaign.[83] Highly critical of the Howard government's international and domestic response, Rudd promised 'real action', to 'restore Australia's international leadership' and return Australia 'to its role as a good global citizen' on climate change.[84] Shortly after the election, Rudd personally

[78] Asia-Pacific Partnership on Clean Development and Climate, *About the Asia-Pacific Partnership on Clean Development & Climate* (2009), www.asiapacificpartnership.org/english/about.aspx, last accessed 2 December 2009. See also below Chapter 13 by Jeffrey McGee and Ros Taplin.

[79] Commonwealth of Australia, above n. 74, 6.

[80] See Commonwealth of Australia, Prime Ministerial Task Group on Emissions Trading, *Report of the Task Group on Emissions Trading* (2007) 37–43.

[81] Australian Greenhouse Office, *Tracking to the Kyoto Target 2006* (2006) 1.

[82] Commonwealth of Australia, above n. 74, 7; Australian Government, 'National Clean Energy Target' (press release, 23 September 2007).

[83] Australian Broadcasting Corporation, 'ETS Postponed by Rudd Government', *The 7.30 Report*, 27 April 2010.

[84] Rudd, above n. 23.

attended COP 13 in Bali, December 2007, to present Australia's instrument of ratification to Kyoto.[85] Rudd's speech to the COP marked the return of political rhetoric on climate change consistent with good international citizenship. Rudd cautioned delegates that climate change represented 'one of the greatest moral, economic and environmental challenges of our age' and that their choices would 'impact all future generations'.[86] The community of nations were 'custodians of the planet' and 'its future', and Australia, for its part, was willing to put its 'shoulder to the wheel'. In his September 2009 address to the UN General Assembly, Rudd further called upon nations to 'reach beyond their self interests and instead fashion a "Grand Bargain" between the developed and developing countries of the world'.[87]

Regarding the international domain, the Rudd government's ratification of Kyoto was certainly a positive step. But because Howard-era policies had already put Australia on track to meet its Kyoto target, it also involved a healthy dose of symbolism. The much bigger test of the Rudd government's commitment to good international citizenship discourse concerned its negotiations on a post-2012 legal framework (when the first commitment period of the Kyoto Protocol expires). At COP 13, parties to the UNFCCC adopted the Bali Roadmap, establishing a two-track process to guide negotiations under both the UNFCCC (called the Bali Action Plan (BAP)) and Kyoto. Parties intended to conclude a new agreement, with stronger commitments on mitigation, adaptation, finance and technology, at COP 15 in Copenhagen, 2009.[88] A legally binding agreement, however, could not be reached. To salvage the conference, many parties, including Australia, signed the non-binding Copenhagen Accord.[89] While significant – for example, signatories agreed to limit global temperature rise to no more than 2°C and to assist developing countries with US$100 billion of finance annually by 2020 – the Accord represented only a small political step. At the time of writing,

[85] Ratified 3 December 2007.

[86] Kevin Rudd, 'Address to the High Level Segment of the 13th Conference of the Parties' (speech delivered at the High Level Segment of the 13th Conference of the Parties, UNFCCC, Bali, 12 December 2007).

[87] Kevin Rudd, 'Address to the 64th Session of the United Nations General Assembly' (speech delivered at the United Nations General Assembly, New York, 23 September 2009).

[88] See UNFCCC, *The United Nations Climate Change Conference in Bali* (2010) at unfccc.int/meetings/cop_13/items/4049.php, last accessed 15 January 2010.

[89] *Report of the Conference of the Parties to the UNFCCC on its Fifteenth Session*, Decision 2/CP 15, FCCC/CP/2009/11/Add1 (2009).

negotiations for a new legally binding protocol to complement or replace Kyoto remained ongoing.

International negotiations on a post-2012 agreement have been the most complex of any climate negotiations to date. Due to space considerations, this chapter will only comment on one aspect of the Rudd government's negotiations, namely its mitigation target. Developed countries' lack of ambition on this issue has been a major contributory factor to the slow progress of international negotiations.[90] In 2007, the Intergovernmental Panel on Climate Change (IPCC) *Fourth Assessment Report* indicated that Annex I parties would need to collectively reduce their emissions by at least 25 to 40 per cent by 2020 in order to stabilise atmospheric emissions at a level to avoid 'dangerous' climate change.[91] For its part, the Rudd government committed to reduce Australia's greenhouse emissions by 5 to 25 per cent by 2020.[92] This target came with many caveats.[93] The upper figure was conditional on an 'ambitious global agreement' which, inter alia: could stabilise atmospheric emissions at 450 ppm CO_2-e and obliged developed countries to collectively reduce emissions by at least 25 per cent by 2020, and 'major developing economies' by at least 20 per cent on business-as-usual levels. The medium target of 15 per cent was conditional on developed countries adopting 'comparable' commitments to Australia, and major developing economies committing to 'substantially restrain' emissions. If neither scenario was realised, the Rudd government had an unconditional target of just 5 per cent.

Scrutiny of this target suggests that the Rudd government's approach to mitigation was strongly influenced by traditional national interest considerations. This was evident from both its conditional nature and level of ambition. Regarding the former, Australia was not unique in adopting a conditional approach which tied the level of its national ambition to that of other countries.[94] But such an approach was arguably inconsistent with Labor's emphasis on leadership in its good international citizenship

[90] Note that the author attended COP 15 in Copenhagen as an observer.

[91] On 1990 levels. See International Alliance of Research Universities, *Synthesis Report from Climate Change: Global Risk, Challenges and Decisions* (2009) 18.

[92] On 2000 levels (4–24 per cent on 1990 levels). UNFCCC, *Ideas and Proposals on the Elements Contained in Paragraph 1 of the Bali Action Plan*, FCCC/AWGLCA/2009/MISC4/Add3 (2009) [3].

[93] Ibid.

[94] See UNFCCC, *Appendix I – Quantified Economy-Wide Emissions Targets for 2020* (2010) at unfccc.int/home/items/5264.php, last accessed 15 March 2010.

discourse. Indeed, the Rudd government justified the conditionality of its target by stating that Australia would 'do no less and no more than the rest of the world'.[95] This approach was clearly motivated by the same desire held by earlier Australian governments not to jeopardise Australia's economic and trade competitiveness. In setting a conditional target tied to the ambition of the international community (or lack thereof), rather than to the demands of science, Labor demonstrated that it actually had little real desire to be an international leader.

Regarding the ambition of its individual target, Labor claimed that it intended to make a 'fair' contribution to an 'effective' global agreement.[96] The Rudd's government's 5 and 15 per cent targets were clearly inconsistent with the science as outlined by the IPCC. The 25 per cent target, however, appeared to be more in accordance with its common but differentiated responsibility and respective capabilities. By comparison to other national targets submitted to the Copenhagen Accord, the goal was much higher than the US and Canada (3 per cent) and matched that of Japan.[97] However, it was lower than many others, for example: Iceland (30 per cent); Norway (30 to 40 per cent); the EU-27 (20 to 30 per cent – if its upper goal were adopted); and individual EU nations like Germany (40 per cent).[98] It must be noted that the BAP envisaged that parties' targets need not be uniform in ambition. Rather, they should reflect 'comparability of effort' and differences in 'national circumstances'.[99] The Rudd government justified its less ambitious target by pointing to Australia's higher economic costs in reducing emissions, chiefly caused by its high share of emission- and energy-intensive industries and the dominance of low-cost coal in electricity generation.[100] While this claim reflected the narrow national interest arguments previously

[95] Kevin Rudd and Penny Wong, 'Joint Press Conference with the Minister for Climate Change' (press conference, Copenhagen, 19 December 2009).

[96] Penny Wong, 'Australia's Contribution to a Global Agreement on Climate Change' (speech delivered at the Lowy Institute for International Policy, Sydney, 20 April 2009).

[97] The US and Canada target is converted to a 1990 base year from the stated targets of 17 per cent on 2005 levels. Joeri Rogelj *et al.*, 'Copenhagen Accord Pledges Are Paltry' (2010) 464 *Nature* 1126, 1126–8.

[98] Ibid.; Reuters, 'Germany Sticking to Ambitious CO_2 Target: Adviser' *Reuters*, 11 January 2010 at www.reuters.com/article/idUSTRE60A4D020100111, last accessed 15 February 2010.

[99] *Report of the Conference of the Parties to the UNFCCC on its Thirteenth Session*, Decision 1/CP 13, FCCC/CP/2007/6/Add1 (2007) 1(b)(i).

[100] UNFCCC, *Ideas and Proposals on the Elements Contained in Paragraph 1 of the Bali Action Plan*, FCCC/AWGLCA/2009/MISC1/Add3 (2009) [22].

employed by the Howard government, the 25 per cent target was within the IPCC's proposed target range, and was considered a proportionate contribution by the government's independent climate change adviser, Ross Garnaut.[101]

Most developing countries, however, did not accept the IPCC's recommended 25 to 40 per cent target range for developed countries, instead calling for much higher minimum aggregate reductions, for example, 40 per cent (the African Group and China); and 45 per cent (AOSIS).[102] Under these more ambitious scenarios, Australia's upper target would necessarily need to be higher.[103] Developing countries insisted on higher emission reductions from developed countries for a variety of reasons.

First, the IPCC's proposed target range did not account for the historical responsibility of developed countries for current greenhouse gas emission levels.[104] Second, many developing countries were concerned that developed countries based their targets on a 450 ppm CO_2-e emissions scenario, with the goal of limiting global warming to no more than 2°C. A major concern is that the 450 target only provides a 50 per cent chance of actually keeping warming below 2°C.[105] As such, AOSIS, and the Least Developed Countries, called for a stabilisation target that genuinely respected the precautionary principle.[106] In preference, these highly vulnerable countries insisted on a 350 ppm CO_2-e target,[107] which offered a more favourable 92 per cent chance of keeping warming below 2°C.[108] This would also have the benefit of providing a better chance of keeping warming below 1.5°C. AOSIS insisted that warming be limited to this lower level, arguing that the 2°C goal (favoured by Australia and other developed countries) would result in 'devastating consequences' for their nations and jeopardise their 'rights to survival' because of likely climate impacts such as sea-level rise and more extreme weather events.[109] This view was backed by the science, with a major scientific

[101] Garnaut, above n. 75, 277.
[102] UNFCCC, *Documentation to Facilitate Negotiations by Parties*, FCCC/KP/AWG/2009/10/Add4/Rev2 (2009) 12–13.
[103] See, e.g., the Philippines and South Africa's proposals: ibid. 2, 4.
[104] See, e.g., UNFCCC, *Ideas and Proposals on the Elements Contained in Paragraph 1 of the Bali Action Plan*, FCCC/AWGLCA/2008/MISC5/Add2 (Part II) (2008) [48].
[105] See International Alliance of Research Universities, above n. 92, 18.
[106] See, e.g., UNFCCC, above n. 104, (Part I) [42]. [107] Ibid.
[108] Bill Hare and Malte Meinshausen, 'How Much Warming Are We Committed To and How Much Can Be Avoided?' (2006) 75 *Climatic Change* 111, 131.
[109] See, e.g., UNFCCC, above n. 104, (Part I) [46–7] (Small Island States).

congress prior to Copenhagen declaring that a 2°C target carried 'significant risks of deleterious impacts for society and the environment'.[110] Given these factors, it must be questioned whether Australia's 25 per cent target really did seek to make a fair contribution to a genuinely effective global agreement. While the Rudd government judged that a 450 ppm CO_2-e/2°C stabilisation target was in Australia's national interest, it had poor prospects of safeguarding the environment for future generations and of meeting the needs of the most vulnerable countries.

As with its approach to international law, the Rudd government's public law approach looked positive early, but later fell victim to short-term economic considerations. An important election commitment by Labor was to introduce an ETS to put a price on carbon pollution for the first time in Australia.[111] The government claimed that its ETS, the Carbon Pollution Reduction Scheme (CPRS), would 'transform ... [Australia's] economy, putting it on a low-emissions path'.[112] Detailed analysis of the proposed scheme is not possible in this chapter. However, there were several factors suggesting that the CPRS was more concerned with protecting jobs in fossil fuel-based industries than actually transforming the Australian economy. A Grattan Institute report, for example, found that the over $20 billion in free emission permits that would be awarded to Australia's emission-intensive and trade-exposed industries was far more generous than was legitimately necessary to prevent carbon leakage (polluting industries relocating to countries without comparable regulations) and would mute incentives for these industries to actually reduce emissions (the key purpose of an ETS).[113] A second example is that the CPRS was not designed to encourage the electricity industry to switch from coal-fired power stations – Australia's largest source of emissions – to renewable and clean forms of power such as wind or solar.[114] Highly respected climate scientists, like NASA's James Hansen, argue that coal must be phased out worldwide if dangerous

[110] See International Alliance of Research Universities, above n. 92, 16.

[111] Rudd, above n. 23.

[112] Commonwealth of Australia, *Carbon Pollution Reduction Scheme: Australia's Low Pollution Future* (2008), 1–7.

[113] John Daley and Tristan Edis, *Restructuring the Australian Economy to Emit Less Carbon*, Grattan Institute Report (2010) 12.

[114] See Richard Dennis, *Harder to Do Than to Say? The Failure of the CPRS to Reduce Emissions from Coal-Fired Power Stations*, The Australia Institute Policy Brief No. 5 (2009) 1, 2–3.

climate change is to be avoided.[115] Instead of encouraging this, the CPRS gambled that new coal-fired power stations would be fitted with carbon capture and storage technology, and that existing stations could be retrofitted.[116] Yet carbon capture and storage technology is yet to be commercially demonstrated, and there is no guarantee that retrofitting technology will become available.[117] Nor can it be certain that CO_2 captured and buried underground will not leak into the atmosphere in future.[118] Rather than encouraging a transition to proven renewable energy technologies, which can guarantee emission reductions, the CPRS adopted a pro-coal approach in order to maintain the competitive advantages provided to Australia by its abundance of this fossil fuel.

In the final months of the Rudd government, evidence emerged that its early resolve to introduce an ETS, even a pro-jobs one, had dissipated. Initially, the government promised to introduce the CPRS by 2010.[119] This was then deferred until 2011, ostensibly due to the economic impacts of the global financial crisis.[120] In 2009, the CPRS Bill[121] was twice rejected by the Australian Senate, as the government did not have the support of non-Labor senators. Liberal Opposition leader, Tony Abbott, insisted that passing the CPRS prior to the adoption of a new international agreement would 'damage the Australian economy' and put Australia at a 'competitive disadvantage vis-à-vis the rest of the world'[122] (reiterating a traditional national interest argument). Citing the Senate's hostility, and the slow progress of international negotiations, in April 2010 the government announced that it would further delay the CPRS until 2013.[123]

The Rudd government cannot take the full blame for failing to pass the CPRS, nor for the slow pace of international negotiations, which involve over 190 states. But neither of its justifications for delay was entirely credible. First, where a government's bill has been twice rejected by the Senate, the Australian Constitution allows it to request that the Governor-General

[115] Nicky Phillips, 'We're Dealing to Coal Addicts: Hansen', *Sydney Morning Herald* (Sydney), 4 March 2010.

[116] Dennis, above n. 114, 2–3. [117] Ibid.

[118] Jeff Angel, *Green is Good* (ABC Books, Sydney, 2008) 130.

[119] Commonwealth of Australia, above n. 112, xxv.

[120] Kevin Rudd, 'Carbon Pollution Reduction Scheme: Support in Managing the Impact of the Global Recession' (press release, 4 May 2009).

[121] Carbon Pollution Reduction Scheme Bill 2009 (Cth).

[122] Tony Abbott and Julie Bishop, 'Transcript of Joint Doorstop Interview' (Canberra, 2 December 2009).

[123] Kevin Rudd, 'Transcript of Doorstop Interview' (Penrith, 27 April 2010).

dissolve both houses of Parliament, and if re-elected, hold a joint sitting of Parliament.[124] Moreover, a regular federal election was already due in 2010.[125] The government, however, decided to delay the CPRS even before testing support for the scheme, or similar legislation, in a new Parliament.

Second, prior to Copenhagen, the Rudd government argued that the passage of its CPRS Bill was essential, in part because it would help to build 'momentum' in international negotiations by demonstrating to other nations 'that it is possible to integrate a carbon price into the economy and reduce emissions with only modest economic impacts'.[126] Rudd suggested that political opponents who had called for delay had demonstrated 'absolute political cowardice' and an 'absolute failure of leadership'.[127] He further argued that if 'every nation ... [made] the decision not to act until others have done so, then no nation will ever act' leading to a 'permanent stand-off' in international negotiations'. In delaying the CPRS, the Rudd government, by its own admission, demonstrated a clear failure of international leadership, and signalled that its early enthusiasm for good international citizenship discourse had gone walkabout in the face of short-term economic and political concerns. Ultimately, Labor's backflip on the CPRS gave the impression 'of a PM without convictions',[128] and resulted in great personal cost to Rudd. Having lost the confidence of his party and much of the Australian electorate,[129] Rudd was ousted by Julia Gillard as Labor leader and prime minister in June 2010.

6. Conclusion

This chapter examined the influence of good international citizenship and national interest discourse on Australia's approach to international and public climate law during the term of four governments. These discourses have transcended the public international law divide, occurring concurrently in the law-making spheres of national politics and international negotiations. Good international citizenship – as chiefly espoused by Labor – was characterised as a discourse that counters a

[124] Australian Constitution s. 57. [125] Australian Constitution ss. 7, 13, 28.

[126] Commonwealth of Australia, above n. 112, 4–15.

[127] Kevin Rudd, 'Address to the Lowy Institute' (speech delivered at the Lowy Institute, Sydney, 6 November 2009).

[128] Paul Kelly, 'Internal Polling Tipped Gillard Over Line', *The Australian* (Sydney), 30 June 2010.

[129] Ibid.

traditional and narrow approach to the national interest that emphasises short-term security and economic interests. In contrast, good international citizenship recognized the importance of these needs, but encouraged the state to also fulfil their ethical responsibility to promote the common good. In the context of climate change, Labor governments have typically identified their broader obligations as extending to future generations, the international community and the environment.

From an environmental perspective, good international citizenship is undoubtedly the more attractive discourse. Indeed, traditional national interest discourse – as most forcefully adopted by the Howard government – can only be described as environmentally reckless, because its encouragement of short-term national prosperity comes at the expense of longer-term planetary needs. By contrast, good international citizenship discourse has some potential to help address global environmental problems like climate change, because it acknowledges that the material interests of present generations cannot be responsibly pursued in such a short-sighted fashion.

Yet while good international citizenship discourse appears to have environmentally beneficial possibilities, this chapter has found that Australian governments' rhetorical commitment to good international citizenship discourse has had little lasting impact on their approaches to both international and public climate law. This is not surprising in relation to the Howard government, whose employment of good international citizenship discourse was entirely superficial. However, the consistency of Labor's rhetorical commitment to good international citizenship suggests that its philosophical attraction to the discourse does have some depth. It is particularly troubling, then, that Labor government approaches to international and public climate law have also consistently fallen short, given that it has been unique among the two major political parties in showing any real promise of taking strong action to reduce greenhouse emissions.

Traditional national interest discourse clearly remains very powerful within, and outside, government in Australia. Despite often invoking good international citizenship discourse, domestic political pressures to advance economic prosperity have seen Australian governments develop an aversion to taking effective international and public law measures. Australian governments, both Labor and conservative, have continually judged that adopting measures that involve economic costs for their constituents (whether individuals, business or other interest groups) would be politically toxic. This is deeply problematic, given that

Australian governments' good international citizenship discourse has at most implied that short-term economic interests must be moderated. Yet an effective global response to climate change is likely to require that wealthy nations like Australia make some genuine economic *sacrifice* if the needs of future generations, the most vulnerable countries and the environment are to be met.

13

The Asia-Pacific Partnership: a deepened market liberal model for the international climate regime?

JEFFREY McGEE AND ROS TAPLIN

1. Introduction

In December 2007 the nations of the world commenced a two-year period of negotiations under the 1992 United Nations Framework Convention on Climate Change (UNFCCC) to arrive at a new global climate agreement to succeed the 1997 Kyoto Protocol to the UNFCCC (Kyoto Protocol).[1] However, the international dialogue on climate change over the last decade has extended well beyond the negotiation process under the UN climate regime. After withdrawing from the Kyoto Protocol in 2001, the United States (US) George W. Bush administration was active in forming and participating in a range of international climate-related agreements outside the UN climate change process. The US has joined bilateral climate change partnerships,[2] multilateral technology partnerships,[3] the Asia-Pacific Partnership on Clean Development and Climate (Asia-Pacific Partnership),[4] the G8 Climate process,[5] the APEC Sydney Declaration 2007[6] and also facilitated the US

[1] UNFCCC, *United Nations Climate Change Conference in Bali* (2007) at http://unfccc.int/meetings/cop_13/items/4049.php, last accessed 7 February 2009.

[2] United States of America Department of State, *Bilateral and Regional Climate Partnerships* (2009) at http://2001–2009.state.gov/g/oes/climate/c22820.htm, last accessed 7 February 2009.

[3] Methane to Markets Partnership, *Partners* (2009) at www.methanetomarkets.org/partners/country/index.htm, last accessed 7 February 2009.

[4] Asia-Pacific Partnership, *Asia-Pacific Partnership on Clean Development and Climate* (2009) at www.asiapacificpartnership.org/, last accessed 7 February 2009.

[5] Pew Center on Global Climate Change, *Summary of G8 Summit 2005 in Gleneagles Scotland* at www.pewclimate.org/policy_center/international_policy/summary_of_g8.cfm, last accessed 7 February 2009.

[6] *Sydney Leaders Declaration on Climate Change, Energy Security and Clean Development*, concluded 9 September 2007, APEC meeting, Sydney, Australia.

Major Economies Process.[7] The Australian government of Prime Minister John Howard adopted a similar approach of favouring a proliferation of avenues for international dialogue on climate change.[8] At the very least, these non-UN climate initiatives represent a significant fragmentation of the international dialogue on any post-2012 global climate agreement.[9] At the domestic level this agnosticism to climate change commitments was reflected in a stagnation or outright opposition to the development or strengthening of public laws to address climate change.

The US and Australia, at the time both opposed to the Kyoto Protocol, were key actors in engineering this fragmentation of the international dialogue on climate change.[10] It is therefore important to critically examine the claims that these non-UN climate initiatives established by the Bush administration and Howard government were designed to act in consort with the UN climate treaties.[11] Notwithstanding the change of government in the US and Australia, these claims persist, emphasising the continuing relevance of an inquiry as to whether these fora external to the UN climate regime are supportive or undermining of it. This question is brought into particularly sharp relief following the problems of international climate negotiations under the UN umbrella at Copenhagen in December 2009.

[7] United States of America, Department of State, *Major Economies Process on Energy Security and Climate Change* at http://2001–2009.state.gov/g/oes/climate/mem/index.htm, last accessed 7 February 2009.

[8] Peter Lawrence, 'Australian Climate Change Policy and the Asia Pacific Partnership on Clean Development and Climate. From Howard to Rudd: Continuity or Change?' (2009) 9 *International Environmental Agreements: Politics, Law, Economics* 281, 283–7.

[9] On fragmentation in international law, see: Frank Biermann *et al.*, 'The Fragmentation of Global Environmental Governance Architectures: A Framework for Analysis' (2009) 9(4) *Global Environmental Politics* 14; International Law Commission, *Fragmentation of International Law: Difficulties Arising from the Diversification and Expansion of International Law: Conclusions* (A/CN.4/L.702) (2006) and Tim Stephens, *International Courts and Environmental Protection* (Cambridge University Press, 2009) 304–7.

[10] Lawrence, above n. 8.

[11] For analysis of claims of 'complementarity' between the Asia-Pacific Partnership and Kyoto Protocol, see: Jeffrey McGee and Ros Taplin, 'The Asia-Pacific Partnership on Clean Development and Climate: A Complement or Competitor to the Kyoto Protocol?' (2006) 18 *Global Change Peace and Security* 173. For similar analysis of the claims of 'consistency' between the Asia-Pacific Partnership and UNFCCC, see: Jeffrey McGee and Ros Taplin, 'The Asia-Pacific Partnership on Clean Development and Climate: A Retreat from the Principle of Common but Differentiated Responsibilities?' (2009) 5 *McGill Journal of Sustainable Development Law and Policy* 11.

This chapter focuses on the Asia-Pacific Partnership as one controversial example of fragmentation. Given that the Asia-Pacific Partnership emerged in the wake of US and Australian contestation of the Kyoto Protocol, it is important to focus on the political as well as legal doctrinal significance of the partnership.[12] This chapter uses interpretative international relations theory to further understanding of the political significance of the Asia-Pacific Partnership. Interpretative theory analyses the ideas and inter-subjective meanings that underlie interaction between actors in international affairs, including in the formation of international agreements and institutions.[13]

Dryzek's discourse analysis,[14] a form of interpretative theory, is used to explore the ideas, assumptions and inter-subjective meanings that lie behind the Asia-Pacific Partnership. The partnership is thereby situated within the wider political landscape of ideas regarding the architecture for post-Kyoto international climate change policy that will be influential on public law developments. Dryzek's interpretative international relations theory is used to complement the more traditional analysis of legal policy principles.

In this chapter we first outline Dryzek's discourse theory and the theoretical concepts of 'market liberalism' and 'market failure' deployed in our analysis later in this chapter. Second, we provide a descriptive overview of the formation, structure and activities of the Asia-Pacific Partnership. Third, we provide an analysis and comparison of the key design principles of both the Asia-Pacific Partnership and UN climate treaties. Finally, we use Dryzek's discourse theory to analyse and compare the normative structures of the Asia-Pacific Partnership and UN climate treaties and consider whether the Asia-Pacific Partnership represents a deepened market liberal discourse for the international climate regime.

2. Dryzek's discourse analysis

Discourse theory is an interpretive approach to research, concerned with the varying ways actors talk about, understand and give meaning to the

[12] Shirley Scott, *The Political Interpretation of Multilateral Treaties* (Martinus Nijhoff Publishers, Leiden, 2004) 4.

[13] Mark Neufeld, 'Interpretation and the "Science" of International Relations' (1993) 19 *Review of International Studies* 39.

[14] John Dryzek, *The Politics of the Earth: Environmental Discourses* (Oxford University Press, 2nd edn, 2005) and John Dryzek, 'Paradigms and Discourses' in Daniel Bodansky, Jutta Brunnée and Ellen Hey (eds.), *Oxford Handbook of International Environmental Law* (Oxford University Press, 2007) 44.

world.[15] Dryzek's concept of discourse helps to provide a theoretical bridge between the text of an international agreement and the wider political understandings and inter-subjective meanings in which it was created. Discourse theory is used to contextualise the ideas, concepts and categories contained in an international agreement within the political circumstances in which it formed.[16] This adds a critical layer to the debates, assumptions and informal understandings guiding the generation and application of international legal principles.

3. The discourse of market liberalism

Market liberalism[17] is a political-economic discourse based on principles of deregulation, marketisation and privatisation where individual choice through market exchange is viewed as a preferred means of governance.[18] The market is viewed as a self-regulating mechanism of governance where state planning, state provision and state intervention in markets is minimised.[19] The role of the state in market liberalism is essentially limited to building institutions to facilitate the establishment and operation of market activity.[20] Market liberal policy emphasises the need to remove impediments to international trade or capital mobility, and the withdrawal of all regulation that does not have a direct market-facilitating function.[21] International economic policy is therefore most usefully seen to be directed towards creating market-friendly institutions to curtail organised labour, privatise state enterprises and open domestic

[15] Marianne Jorgensen and Louise Phillips, *Discourse Analysis as Theory and Method* (Sage Publications, London, 2002) 1. See also above Introduction by Brad Jessup and Kim Rubenstein.

[16] Shirley Scott's 'Cognitive Structures of Cooperation' theory provides a similar theoretical bridge between the text of a treaty and its wider political context. See Scott, above n. 12, 97–117.

[17] See Dryzek, above n. 14, 121 where he explains that the terms 'market liberalism', 'neoliberalism', 'classical liberalism' and 'economic rationalism' are used interchangeably to refer to a discourse of management of environmental problems by employment of market mechanisms.

[18] David Harvey, *A Brief History of Neoliberalism* (Oxford University Press, New York, 2005).

[19] John Gray, *False Dawn: The Delusions of Global Capitalism* (Granta Publications, London, 2nd edn, 2002) 1–7.

[20] Simon Lee and Stephen McBride (eds.), *Market Liberalism, State Power and Global Governance* (Springer, Dordrecht, 2007) 6.

[21] Dryzek, above n. 14, 2.

markets as much as possible to foreign capital and trade.[22] The US in particular has been a strong advocate of market liberal economic policy at an international level over recent decades.[23] While there has been some retreat from market liberalism in international development policy over the last decade, the imprint of market liberalism on shaping the international economic order remains significant.[24]

Market liberals view environmental problems as caused primarily by 'lack of economic growth, poverty and distortions and failures of the market'.[25] Poverty is viewed by market liberalism as a key driver of environmental degradation that should be attacked by liberalising international trade.[26] Distortions in trade and investment markets and lack of secure property rights are viewed as hampering the ability of the market to foster growth and reduce poverty.[27] Further trade and investment liberalisation to open and integrate global markets is viewed as the best path to environmental protection.[28] Market liberalism also places faith in the ability of science, technology and human ingenuity to avoid the worst aspects of environmental problems.[29] In the event of environmental problems being the result of a failure in market activity, market liberalism prescribes a least interventionist approach by the state.[30] This might involve the provision of better information to market participants to assist in market decision-making,[31] voluntary undertakings to reduce environmentally damaging activity or market-based regulation such as the use of tradable pollution or resource extraction permits.[32] Strongly interventionist regulation such as mandatory and non-tradable restrictions on environmentally damaging activity is to be avoided. Market liberalism prefers least interventionist regulatory options, such as individual recourse to tort litigation, or voluntary industry codes of conduct.

[22] Anwar Shaikh, 'The Economic Mythology of Neoliberalism' in Alfredo Saad-Filho (ed.), *Neo-liberalism; A Critical Reader* (Pluto Press, London, 2004) 42.

[23] Gray, above n. 19, 3; Harvey, above n. 18, 23–9.

[24] John Gray, 'The Rudd Essay and the Global Financial Crisis', *The Monthly* 45, May 2009; Kevin Rudd, 'The Global Financial Crisis', *The Monthly* 42, February 2009; Harvey, above n. 18, 4–38.

[25] Jennifer Clapp and Peter Dauvergne, *Paths to a Green World; The Political Economy of the Global Environment* (MIT Press, Cambridge, Mass., 2005) 5.

[26] The environmental Kuznets curve suggests that as per capita income initially increases, the rate of environmental decline will also rise. However, as incomes reach a certain threshold, environmental damage will level off, and then rapidly decline. See ibid. 91–2.

[27] Ibid. 5. [28] Ibid. 6. [29] Ibid. [30] Ibid. 6–7.

[31] Ross Garnaut, *The Garnaut Climate Change Review: Final Report* (Cambridge University Press, Melbourne, 2008) 406–10.

[32] Clapp and Dauvergne, above n. 25, 7.

If more interventionist regulation is required, then the creation of tradable pollution rights is preferred in order to give flexibility to market participants in how they meet any required level of environmental performance imposed.

Okereke[33] observes that the Kyoto Protocol flexibility mechanisms of international emissions trading, Clean Development Mechanism (CDM) and Joint Implementation (JI), are the foundation of an international carbon trading market that places market mechanisms at the centrepiece of international climate policy.[34] Okereke argues that these flexibility mechanisms of the Kyoto Protocol contain a market liberal conception of justice that marginalises developing world equity concerns regarding the unequal distribution of wealth/emissions in the global community and developed world contribution to global environmental problems.[35]

4. The discourse of market failure and climate change

The concept of 'market failure' from economics literature is important in determining the circumstances in which market liberal discourse will support regulatory intervention at a national or international level. The UK Treasury's *Stern Review of the Economics of Climate Change* (Stern Review) describes climate change as the 'greatest and widest-ranging market failure ever seen'.[36] The Australian government's *Garnaut Climate Change Review* (Garnaut Review) adopts a similar premise in stating that the correction of 'market failure is the central task of climate change policy in Australia and the world'.[37] According to this conventional economics literature, climate change is the result of two distinct market failures.[38] First, markets for the production of goods and services 'fail' by not taking into account the full costs of production decisions. This occurs when a part of the cost of production is 'externalised' and hence borne by society, rather than by those involved in the

[33] Chukwumerije Okereke, *Global Justice and Neoliberal Environmental Governance; Ethics, Sustainable Development and International Co-operation* (Routledge, London and New York, 2008) 3.

[34] Ibid. 117–21. [35] Ibid. 176–82.

[36] United Kingdom, Her Majesty's Treasury, *The Stern Review on the Economics of Climate Change* (2006) Executive Summary.

[37] Garnaut, above n. 31, 299.

[38] Adam Jaffee, Richard Newell and Robert Stavins, 'A Tale of Two Market Failures; Technology and Environmental Policy' (2005) 54 *Ecological Economics* 164.

transaction.[39] The externality leads to an over-supply of the polluting product, and an increase in the societal level of pollution above that which would be optimal.[40] Environmental policy should thus be directed at raising the incentive for the producer to internalise the cost of greenhouse gas emissions. This might be achieved by an environmental tax or emission trading scheme, or by imposing limits on the level of the polluting activity.[41] Market liberals would prefer a market facilitating rather than limiting approach, such as an emissions trading scheme.

5. Overview of the Asia-Pacific Partnership

The Asia-Pacific Partnership is a US- and Australian-inspired arrangement that was launched in mid-2005. Initially termed the 'AP6', the partnership was limited to six member nations: China, India, Japan, South Korea, Australia and the US. However, in October 2007 Canada was admitted as the seventh member. The Asia-Pacific Partnership brings together an influential group of nations responsible for approximately half of the world's population, economy and energy use.[42]

The Asia-Pacific Partnership is a non-binding or 'soft law' agreement[43] directed at international cooperation on development, energy, environment and climate change issues.[44] Its charter indicates the partnership is directed at 'international cooperation to facilitate the development, diffusion, deployment, and transfer of existing, emerging and longer term cost-effective, cleaner, more efficient technologies and practices'.[45] It claims to operate as a 'unique public–private partnership model to bring together industry stakeholders and government officials to achieve Partnership goals'.[46] The Asia-Pacific Partnership is headed by a Policy and Implementation Committee, comprised of three government

[39] Ibid. 165. [40] Garnaut, above n. 31, 299.

[41] Jaffee, Newell and Stavins, above n. 38, 165.

[42] Asia-Pacific Partnership, *About the Asia Pacific Partnership on Clean Development and Climate* (2009) at www.asiapacificpartnership.org/english/about.aspx, last accessed 2 December 2009, www.app.gov/app/about/, last accessed 7 February 2009. For a discussion of ASEAN, another Asia-Pacific forum that has taken on some environmental governance roles, see above Chapter 9 by Kheng-Lian Koh.

[43] Alan Boyle and Christine Chinkin, *The Making of International Law* (Oxford University Press, New York, 2007) 212–13.

[44] Asia-Pacific Partnership, *Charter of the Asia Pacific Partnership on Clean Development and Climate*, concluded 13 January 2006, Sydney, Australia, Preamble, 1.

[45] Ibid., clause 2.1.1. [46] Asia-Pacific Partnership, above n. 4.

officials from each of the seven partner countries.[47] The Policy and Implementation Committee sets the overall direction of partnership activities and has the role of approving action on specific technology-related projects. There have been seven Policy and Implementation Committee meetings and two ministerial-level meetings since its formation.[48]

The formulation of proposals for projects and their implementation occurs through eight sectoral task forces covering the following industries: aluminium, building and appliances, cement, fossil fuel, coal mining, power generation/transmission, renewable energy and steel.[49] These task forces are led by representatives from the governments of the seven countries.[50] Developed countries occupy the chair positions of the eight task forces, while the developing countries, China and India, each have two co-chair roles.[51] The task forces are also open to participation from public research bodies and private business interests but not environmental non-governmental organisations. The Asia-Pacific Partnership task forces are designed to meet independently to formulate projects for endorsement by the Policy and Implementation Committee and monitor progress of existing projects.

In 2006 the eight task forces formulated initial Action Plans containing a total of over 100 projects that were endorsed for implementation by the Policy and Implementation Committee.[52] Eight of these projects have been completed, most relating to information gathering and exchange through workshops, conferences and visits.[53] By mid-2009 there were 140 Asia-Pacific Partnership projects in the implementation phase.[54] The US is the only Asia-Pacific Partnership member that has publicly released information on the identity of its representatives on the eight Asia-Pacific Partnership task forces. The US has two government

47 Asia-Pacific Partnership, above n. 44, clause 4.4.

48 Asia-Pacific Partnership, *Asia-Pacific Partnership Meetings and Events*, (2009) at www.asiapacificpartnership.org/english/meeting_events.aspx, last accessed 26 July 2009.

49 Ibid.

50 Asia-Pacific Partnership, *Asia-Pacific Partnership Public–Private Sector Task Forces* at asiapacificpartnership.org/task_forces.aspx, last accessed 8 February 2009.

51 Asia-Pacific Partnership, *Asia-Pacific Partnership – Organisation* at www.asiapacificpartnership.org/english/organization.aspx, last accessed 26 July 2009.

52 Asia-Pacific Partnership, *Asia-Pacific Partnership on Clean Development and Climate: Executive Summary of Task Force Action Plans* (2006).

53 Asia-Pacific Partnership, *Asia-Pacific Partnership Project Roster* (2009) at www.asiapacificpartnership.org/english/project_roster.aspx, last accessed 29 July 2009.

54 Ibid.

and two private sector representatives sitting on each task force.[55] Despite the fact that the private sector is expected to play a key role in implementing Asia-Pacific Partnership projects, there is no publicly available information on the exact level of private sector participation in Asia-Pacific Partnership task force projects.

In October 2006, the Asia-Pacific Partnership provided information on the nature of the initial projects approved by the Policy and Implementation Committee.[56] Across all task forces only 5 per cent of the initial projects were devoted to deployment of technology, demonstration projects or technology-based research.[57] The initial batch of task force projects were primarily for gathering information about current practices within industry sectors, dispersing information about 'best-practice' and building expertise and knowledge within target markets to encourage trade in cleaner technologies and practices. The Asia-Pacific Partnership acknowledges that the initial task force projects were directed at 'soft' activities. However, it claims this reflects:

> both the opportunity to make significant improvements in the use of existing energy and industrial technologies, as well as the need to undertake further analysis and scoping of more ambitious technology projects and opportunities in order to overcome specific market barriers.[58]

A further seventy projects have been approved since 2006 and show a similar pattern of preference for projects based on information exchange, standard setting and capacity building.[59] The bulk of current task force projects have therefore been directed at easing informational failures in markets for cleaner technologies and management practices. The level of government funding committed to the Asia-Pacific Partnership to date has been very modest, with the US providing $US65 million out of a total of $US200 million committed by the seven Asia-Pacific Partnership countries.[60]

[55] Government of the United States of America, *Asia Pacific Partnership on Clean Development and Climate Website; Program Office and Task Force Contacts* at http://2008–2009.app.gov/about/taskforce/index.htm#alum, last accessed 5 February 2009.

[56] Asia-Pacific Partnership, above n. 52, 2.

[57] From analysis of Asia-Pacific Partnership Task Force Action Plans, see Asia-Pacific Partnership, above n. 52.

[58] Asia-Pacific Partnership, *Asia Pacific Partnership on Clean Development and Climate Brochure* (2008) 9.

[59] Ibid.

[60] Government of the United States of America, *US Involvement in the Asia-Pacific Partnership on Clean Development and Climate* at www.app.gov/library/111306.htm, last accessed 8 February 2009.

6. Key principles of the UN climate treaties

The ultimate objective of the UNFCCC is to stabilise 'greenhouse gas concentrations in the atmosphere at a level that would prevent dangerous anthropogenic interference with the climate system'.[61] This is a non-economic, politically determined objective regarding the level of climate risk that humanity will accept. However, this non-economic objective is qualified in that the timing of stabilisation of greenhouse gas concentration in the atmosphere must enable 'economic development to proceed in a sustainable manner'.[62] The UNFCCC contains the important equity principle of common but differentiated responsibilities designed to guide burden sharing between developing and developed countries in responding to climate change.[63] The common but differentiated responsibilities principle in Article 3(1) of the UNFCCC creates different obligations for developed and developing nations based on non-economic criteria like responsibility for emissions and greater capacities to respond.[64] The developed countries have a higher initial level of emission reduction obligation under the Kyoto Protocol so as to 'lead the way' in emission reduction and protecting sinks in accordance with Article 4(2)(a) of the UNFCCC. This higher level of developed country obligation is also present in Article 4(3) of the UNFCCC requiring developed countries to provide new and additional finance for developing countries to implement commitments under the treaty, including calculating[65] and reporting their emissions.[66] Article 4(3) of the UNFCCC also requires developed countries to provide new and additional technology transfer to allow developing countries to develop and diffuse lower emission technology.[67] The UNFCCC therefore establishes important non-economic principles intended to guide the evolution of the climate regime.

However, there is also significant evidence of protection of economic growth, trade liberalisation and economic efficiency embodied in the

[61] United Nations Framework Convention on Climate Change, opened for signature 4 June 1992, 1771 UNTS 107 (entered into force 21 March 1994) ('UNFCCC') Art. 2.

[62] Ibid.

[63] Lavanya Rajamani, 'The Principle of Common but Differentiated Responsibility and the Balance of Commitments under the Climate Regime' (2000) 9 *Review of European Community and International Environmental Law* 120. See also above Chapter 1 by Peter Lawrence, which discusses Art. 3 of the UNFCCC in terms of intergenerational equity.

[64] Ibid. [65] UNFCCC Art. 4(1). [66] UNFCCC Arts. 4(1)(b) and 12.

[67] UNFCCC Art. 4(1)(c).

UNFCCC. The preamble to the UNFCCC clearly states that the human response to climate change is to be framed to avoid adverse impacts on economic development and sustained economic growth in developing countries.[68] The overriding goal of the UNFCCC of avoiding dangerous climate change is therefore subject to sustainable economic growth.[69] The developed countries' commitment to adopt national policies and measures to take the lead in reducing emissions is also subject to 'the need to maintain strong and sustainable economic growth'.[70]

The UNFCCC states that economic efficiency is one of its key principles so that 'policies and measures to deal with climate change ... be cost-effective so as to ensure global benefits at the lowest possible cost'.[71] The requirement for countries to take precautionary measures to reduce emissions is qualified by the pursuit of economic efficiency in reducing emissions. The UNFCCC also states that the parties will support an open international economic system leading to sustainable economic growth in all countries, but particularly developing countries, to enable the problems of climate change to be addressed.[72] Economic development through trade-induced growth is therefore viewed as a key path to 'adaptation' to climate change. The UNFCCC also disavows use of protectionist or trade-distorting policies in responding to climate change.[73] The UNFCCC is couched in language making action on reducing emissions contingent on protecting sustained economic growth, economic efficiency and trade liberalisation.

At first glance, the Kyoto Protocol appears to adopt an interventionist approach of setting politically negotiated binding emission reduction targets for developed countries to meet in the period 2008–12.[74] The protocol is the strongest implementation of the equity-based burden sharing principle of common but differentiated responsibilities agreed in the UNFCCC. However, the Kyoto Protocol also displays significant evidence of pursuing principles of economic efficiency and marketisation. As mentioned previously, the Kyoto Protocol flexibility mechanisms of JI,[75] international emissions trading[76] and the CDM[77] are primarily designed

[68] UNFCCC Preamble [21].

[69] World Commission on Environment and Development, *Our Common Future* (Oxford University Press, 1987) 93–6.

[70] UNFCCC Art. 4(2)(a). [71] UNFCCC Art. 3(3). [72] UNFCCC Art. 3(5).

[73] UNFCCC Art. 3(6).

[74] Kyoto Protocol to the United Nations Framework Convention on Climate Change, opened for signature 16 March 1998, 2303 UNTS 148 (entered into force 16 February 2005) ('Kyoto Protocol') Annex B.

[75] Kyoto Protocol Art. 4.1. [76] Kyoto Protocol Art. 17. [77] Kyoto Protocol Art. 12.

to promote economic efficiency in meeting national targets by allowing developed countries to be credited with emission reductions in other countries that have a lower marginal cost of emissions abatement.[78] The Kyoto Protocol and associated Marrakesh Accords[79] are the foundations for the international carbon market allowing developed countries to be credited with emission reductions occurring outside their borders. However, to do this, the developed countries must purchase emission reduction credits on the international emissions trading market. The price developed countries pay for these emission reduction credits should make carbon-intensive forms of production less attractive for future investment.[80] The Kyoto Protocol carbon market is therefore a significant marketisation of international climate policy directed at developed countries' preference for pursuit of economic efficiency in meeting their binding emission reduction targets for the first commitment period. The market liberalism of the Kyoto Protocol was a contentious issue in the negotiations leading up to the formation of this agreement in 1997. It was pushed hard by the US and resisted, initially, by Europe and developing countries.[81]

7. Key principles of the Asia-Pacific Partnership

The Kyoto Protocol has market-liberal elements, but these are placed within the setting of the UNFCCC's overarching principles, which emphasise additional, non-economic values and priorities going to issues of inter- and intra-generational justice. By contrast, the Asia-Pacific Partnership adheres to market liberalism in a much purer and more unalloyed way. The Asia-Pacific Partnership approach to international climate policy is to facilitate trade in cleaner technologies and management practices that have the potential to reduce the partner countries' greenhouse gas intensities.[82] The task force projects are primarily directed at remedying informational failures (lack of information, lack of capacity to use information, information asymmetries) in international markets for cleaner technologies and management practices.

78 Larry Lohmann, 'Marketing and Making Carbon Dumps: Commodification, Calculation and Counterfactuals in Climate Change Mitigation' (2006) 14 *Science as Culture* 203, 205–8.

79 *Report of the Conference of the Parties to the UNFCCC on its Seventh Session*, FCCC/CP/2001/13 (2002).

80 Lohmann, above n. 78.

81 Okereke, above n. 33, 138–9.

82 McGee and Taplin (2006), above n. 11, 182.

This is evidenced by the task force activities focusing mostly on information collection about industry conditions, identification of best industry practice, information exchange and capacity building for adoption of cleaner technologies.

As Asia-Pacific Partnership activities are primarily directed at informational failures in technology markets, they fail to follow the UN climate treaties in intervening to establish national emission reduction targets and institutional structures of the carbon market. The Asia-Pacific Partnership abandons any notion that a regulatory system at international level, or across public laws based in part on market constraint, may be necessary to pursue a collective goal of stabilisation of emissions at a level to avoid dangerous climate change. Instead, multinational regulation of climate change arises from facilitation of the dispersed market decisions of individual private sector actors involved in trade in cleaner technologies and management practices. The prime 'intervention' in market activity is to facilitate better informational flows in technology markets.

The Asia-Pacific Partnership fails to follow the UN climate treaties' desire to seek global political agreement on the level of climate change risk to be tolerated and on allocating binding emission reduction targets to achieve this end. The willingness of the Asia-Pacific Partnership to abandon a politically negotiated compromise on the level of climate change risk is evident in the Australian government's economic modelling supporting the initial Asia-Pacific Partnership Ministerial Meeting in 2006.[83] The modelling analysed best-case scenarios for the operation of an Asia-Pacific Partnership-style climate change policy at a global level. The model would allow global greenhouse gas emissions to rise by at least 100 per cent above 2005 levels by 2050.[84] Instead of a global political settlement to define the level of dangerous climate change in Article 2 of the UNFCCC, the Asia-Pacific Partnership model at a global level offers a global emission increase which is determined by private decision-making within markets for cleaner technologies and practices. The law, at the public or international level, is sidelined. The Asia-Pacific Partnership favours a private interest regulatory approach to international climate policy in which regulation emerges 'from the actions of

[83] Brian Fisher *et al.*, *Technological Development and Economic Growth*, ABARE Research Report 06.1 – Inaugural Ministerial Meeting of the Asia Pacific Partnership on Clean Development and Climate (2006).

[84] Ibid. 34.

individuals or groups motivated to maximise their self-interest'.[85] The private interest regulatory approach of the Asia-Pacific Partnership allows individual, self-interested decision-making of the Asia-Pacific Partnership task force participants to determine the outcome of international climate change policy without any collective global goal for limiting climate change risk and locally without any avenues of administrative review. The Asia-Pacific Partnership model seeks to shift international climate change policy from a regulatory system based on the pursuit of a global public interest of stabilisation of greenhouse gas emissions at a safe level, informed by climate science, towards a private interest regulatory system in which outcomes of the global climate regime are determined by individualised market decision-making. Any difference in the level of obligation between developed and developing countries (or their corporations) in reducing emissions will simply arise from ad hoc commercial bargaining in the implementation of task force projects. The Asia-Pacific Partnership provides a private interest approach to regulation are largely determined by individualised decision-making in a market setting.

7.1 The Asia-Pacific Partnership: a deepening of market liberal discourse?

The preceding two sections identify the key legal policy principles of the UN climate treaties and the Asia-Pacific Partnership and note some significant inconsistencies. This section takes this analysis further by using discourse analysis to explore the inter-subjective meanings and assumptions lying beneath the legal policy principles of the UN climate treaties and Asia-Pacific Partnership. This discourse analysis allows for a deeper and more nuanced understanding of the normative structures of the UN climate treaties and the Asia-Pacific Partnership. This approach situates the Asia-Pacific Partnership within the wider context of political ideas from which it emerged. It also allows for consideration of how discourses are used by actors to contest and shape inter-subjective meaning and the possibilities for international and national legal policy design in an issue area like climate change. This section analyses the UN

[85] Bronwen Morgan and Karen Yeung, *An Introduction to Law and Regulation: Texts and Materials* (Cambridge University Press, 2007) 43.

climate treaties and Asia-Pacific Partnership using the five elements of Dryzek's discourse theory.[86] These elements are: *Ontology* (the key entities whose existence is recognised or denied); *Agents* (the human or non-human actors, individual or collective, who are recognised as either having the ability to act or be acted upon); *Motives* (the assumptions made about the motivation for actors doing things); *Natural Relationships* (the relationships that are assumed to be natural between different actors or entities); and *Metaphors and other Rhetorical Devices* (the concepts or ideas designed to convince or persuade by likening one situation with another).

7.2 Ontology

The UNFCCC and Kyoto Protocol make a key ontological distinction between developed countries (listed in Annex 1 of the UNFCCC) and developing countries. This is used to allocate obligations and responsibilities. The Asia-Pacific Partnership does not make any formal distinction between developed and developing countries in terms of obligations or ability to participate in partnership activities. Another key ontological difference is that the UN climate change process formally recognises and provides legitimacy to the participation of non-governmental organisations as observers of Conference of the Parties (COP) meetings.[87] However, non-governmental organisations have not received recognition as legitimate participants in the Asia-Pacific Partnership Policy and Implementation Committee or task force meetings. The Asia-Pacific Partnership has only recognised elite business, public research, international finance bodies and government actors as participants at Policy and Implementation Committee and task force meetings.

7.3 Agents

The UNFCCC/Kyoto Protocol provides state parties with the key role of acting to enter global agreements to pursue global collective goals for limiting climate change risk. Civil society has a more limited role of lobbying state parties and observing the process of the UN climate change negotiation process. The private sector also has the ability

[86] Dryzek, above n. 14, 16–19.

[87] UNFCCC, *Parties and Observers* (2009) at http://unfccc.int/parties_and_observers/items/2704.php, last accessed 7 February 2009.

under the UNFCCC/Kyoto Protocol to lobby states parties, but has an important further role of implementing the carbon market through profit-making activities.[88] The Asia-Pacific Partnership provides agency to states to enter into a regional agreement to facilitate trade in markets for technology and cleaner development. However, the Asia-Pacific Partnership also gives the private sector an equally important role in the proposal and implementation of task force projects through public–private partnerships.

7.4 Motives

The UNFCCC/Kyoto Protocol frames states as motivated to cooperate to reach a global political settlement on the level of acceptable climate change risk and arrangements to share the burdens of adjustment in accordance with the equity principle of common but differentiated responsibilities. The private sector has an important but secondary role in implementation of this political settlement through the anticipated least-cost emission abatement of the carbon market. In contrast, the Asia-Pacific Partnership views states as primarily interested in regional cooperation to facilitate a lessening of informational failures in technology markets and thereby indirectly reducing greenhouse gas emissions and local pollution problems. The Asia-Pacific Partnership fails to view states as pursuing any global political settlement of the level of climate risk or broad issues of distributing the costs of mitigation or adaptation. The level of climate risk that states are prepared to tolerate is simply determined by the success of technology markets in producing lower emitting technologies. The Asia-Pacific Partnership and UN climate treaties both view private sector participation as being driven by profit-making concerns.

7.5 Natural relationships

The UNFCCC/Kyoto Protocol and Asia-Pacific Partnership both assume a natural relationship between economic growth, trade liberalisation and mitigation of greenhouse gas emissions. The UN climate

[88] One example being the verification role of the private sector under the CDM mechanism: see Eva Lovbrand, Teresia Rindefjall and Joakim Nordqvist, 'Closing the Legitimacy Gap in Global Environmental Governance? Lessons from the Emerging CDM Market' (2009) 9(2) *Global Environmental Politics* 74, 79–80.

treaties assume that states are global citizens prepared to act to pursue a global common good of avoiding dangerous climate change. In contrast, the Asia-Pacific Partnership assumes that the natural relationship between states is that of facilitators of individualistic competitive trade relationships in markets for cleaner technologies, with any reduction in greenhouse gas emissions a fortunate by-product of increased trade in such technologies.

7.6 Key metaphors and rhetorical devices

The UN climate treaties frame climate change as a global problem requiring a global solution in the form of near universal state participation in the UN treaty process. The UN climate treaties also emphasise the shared inheritance or commonality of all states' reliance on the atmosphere and hence the necessity for a global response. The metaphor of the countries of Annex 1 of the UNFCCC 'taking the lead' in mitigating emissions and providing funding for developing country adaptation and treaty compliance is also prominent.[89] In contrast, the rhetoric supporting the Asia-Pacific Partnership has characterised the partnership as a practical, result-oriented, bottom-up climate policy at a regional level that taps into public–private partnerships and the power of the market.[90]

8. Deepening market liberal discourse through the Asia-Pacific Partnership

The Bush administration and the Howard government were openly hostile to the binding targets and timetables approach of the Kyoto Protocol, but key advocates for the Asia-Pacific Partnership. Members of the Howard government in particular were not shy in calling for a more 'free-market' response to climate change. In a key speech on climate policy in 2007, Prime Minister Howard was forthright in criticising international regulation of greenhouse gas emissions and advocating

[89] UNFCCC Arts. 3(1) and 4(2)(a).

[90] For example, see Government of the United States of America, above n. 60; United States of America, Department of State, *Asia-Pacific Partnership on Clean Development and Climate: Concluding Press Conference* (2006) http://2001–2009.state.gov/g/oes/rls/or/2006/59213.htm, last accessed 2 August 2009; John Howard, Prime Minister of Australia (address to the Melbourne Press Club, Hyatt Hotel, Melbourne, 17 July 2007) at http://pandora.nla.gov.au/pan/10052/20070823–1732/www.pm.gov.au/media/Speech/2007/Speech24445.html, last accessed 5 February 2009.

for more intensive reliance upon markets as the central human response to climate change:

> The good news is that mankind [*sic*] has powerful tools for the task ahead, none more so than the spirit of discovery inspired and channeled by rational science and free markets ... The false prophets are those preaching Malthusian pessimism or anti-capitalism. They are the real climate change deniers because they deny rational, realistic and sustainable policy solutions. The moralising tone of utopian internationalism is also not helpful. Institutions will only work and endure if they harness national interests. The world needs less Woodrow Wilson and more Adam Smith to effectively tackle climate change.[91]

Senior Australian climate change diplomat, Ms Adams, reinforced this free-market message at the 2007 Asia-Pacific Partnership meeting in New Delhi, claiming the partnership:

> is a model which embraces the power of the market, and the innovation of our businesses, researchers and entrepreneurs. After all, we do not need to rethink capitalism to solve climate change, we need to harness it.[92]

From an Australian perspective, the Howard government's use of this market liberal discourse to support the Asia-Pacific Partnership was not surprising. Guy Pearse, a past employee of a former Howard government environment minister, describes a strong market liberal influence upon the Howard government's approach to public environmental law and policy:

> a neoliberal approach has come to dominate party thinking about environmental issues too. Calls for government intervention to protect the environment are reflexively viewed with suspicion: government intervention should be kept to the bare minimum. Scepticism and denial of the scientific justification for such intervention is almost automatic. From protecting endangered species to controlling greenhouse emissions, anything that might be detrimental to the cost of doing business is viewed as an illegitimate affront to economic freedom.[93]

In Pearse's view, the Howard government's general approach to environmental issues was driven by a strong market liberal, anti-interventionist

[91] Ibid.

[92] Australian Statement to the Second Ministerial Meeting of the Asia-Pacific Partnership on Clean Development and Climate, 15 October 2007.

[93] Guy Pearse, *High and Dry: John Howard, Climate Change and the Selling of Australia's Future* (Penguin, Melbourne, 2007) 133.

sentiment that favoured the Asia-Pacific Partnership over the binding international targets of the UN climate treaties.[94] The US position in international climate policy under George W. Bush followed a similar path.[95]

The above comments reflect significant attempts by key Australian climate policy actors to shape the policy landscape on climate change through the formation and advocacy of the Asia-Pacific Partnership. This is confirmed by discourse analysis that indicates the Asia-Pacific Partnership instantiates a significant shift in inter-subjective meaning on the human response to climate change. First, the Asia-Pacific Partnership significantly depoliticises international climate change policy by shifting decision-making on an acceptable level of climate change risk from a global political settlement, to simply the establishment of markets for cleaner technologies and practices. Under the Asia-Pacific Partnership, the level of acceptable climate risk is determined by the operation of technology markets rather than science and global political compromise. The role of states is reframed from that of global citizens pursuing a political compromise of a matter of common concern, to facilitators of competitive trade relationships in cleaner technologies. Second, the Asia-Pacific Partnership retreats from the extensive carbon market regulatory structure of the UN climate treaties in favour of voluntary information-sharing measures carried out through public–private task forces. The Asia-Pacific Partnership avoids engagement with opportunities for states to develop their national laws. This makes the Asia-Pacific Partnership significantly deregulatory compared to the binding targets for emissions reduction and carbon market of the UN climate treaties, both of which depend on public laws for their structure and implementation. Third, the Asia-Pacific Partnership's reframing of climate change from a global public concern requiring regulatory constraint to an issue for resolution by private interest in technology markets, marginalises the existing equity principle of common but differentiated responsibilities that form the foundation of the UN climate treaties and displaces all forms of public administrative law review of decisions. Fourth, the Asia-Pacific Partnership's focus upon market facilitation appears to have caused a retreat from the UNFCCC/Kyoto

[94] Ibid. 112–16, 130–4.

[95] Jeffrey McGee and Ros Taplin, 'The Asia-Pacific Partnership and the United States' International Climate Change Policy' (2008) 19(2) *Colorado Journal of International Environmental Law and Policy* 213–15.

Protocol engagement with civil society in the process of policy-making. The Asia-Pacific Partnership has failed to recognise civil society groups, like environmental non-governmental organisations, as legitimate participants or observers or lobbyists at Policy and Implementation Committee and task force meetings. Similarly, key information regarding operations of the Asia-Pacific Partnership, including the identity of members of the sectoral task forces, has not been made public. The Asia-Pacific Partnership favours a shift to market-facilitating governance by elite state and business actors at odds with recent trends towards greater transparency, participation and public review of decision-making in international institutions.[96] The Asia-Pacific Partnership therefore instantiates a technology-focused market liberal discourse that elevates technology markets to a central role in international climate change policy.

The UN climate treaties adopted market mechanisms as a means of pursuing least-cost emission reduction. However, the strong market liberal discourse within the UN climate regime was constrained by overarching political decisions on stabilising climate change at a safe level and equity-based burden sharing between developed and developing countries. The Asia-Pacific Partnership instantiates an inter-subjective understanding of the human response to climate change in which the institution of the market is liberated from these overarching political constraints and, in the guise of technology markets, elevated as the central element of international climate change policy. Discourse analysis is useful in looking beneath the legal policy principles of the Asia-Pacific Partnership and UN climate treaties to trace this contest over the inter-subjective understanding of the possibilities of the human response to climate change.

From the election of the Australian government under Prime Minister Rudd in late 2007 and the Obama administration in late 2008, there were some outward signs from Australia and the US of the possibility of a return to engagement with the Kyoto model of binding emission reduction targets for developed countries and the principle of common but differentiated responsibilities.[97] However, during this period Japan openly advocated key elements of the Asia-Pacific Partnership

[96] For a description of this trend towards a 'global administrative law' of greater transparency, participation and public review, see: Nico Krisch and Benedict Kingsbury, 'Introduction: Global Governance and Global Adminstrative Law in the International Legal Order' (2006) 17 *European Journal of International Law* 2.

[97] See, for example, United States of America, Department of State, *Intervention of the United States: Plenary Session of Ad Hoc Working Group on Long Term Cooperative*

technology-focused market liberal discourse (greenhouse gas intensity targets and sectoral approaches) in the post-2012 climate negotiations as an alternative to further targets and timetables for reducing greenhouse emissions.[98] Ultimately, the agreement coming out of COP 15, the Copenhagen Accord,[99] contains some significant similarities to the Asia-Pacific Partnership in abandoning binding emission reduction targets in favour of voluntary pledges for emission reduction and a weakening in the application of common but differentiated responsibilities. It appears that the Asia-Pacific Partnership represents an early and significant institutional step in a general strengthening of market liberal discourse within international climate change negotiations. This strengthened market liberal discourse will, in contestation with other emerging discourses, continue to shape inter-subjective understanding of the possibilities of the human response to climate change and hence the range of policy options considered to be available.[100]

9. Conclusion

The UNFCCC contains an uneasy tension between market liberal principles of protecting economic growth, trade liberalisation and economic efficiency and the equity-based, non-market burden sharing principle of common but differentiated responsibilities. The Kyoto Protocol effects an extensive marketisation of international climate change policy in search of an economically efficient human response to climate change. However, in establishing the international carbon market, the Kyoto Protocol must put into place an extensive, interventionist, international regulatory structure of binding emission reduction targets for developed countries and flexibility mechanisms for which national public laws have

Action under the Convention (2009) at www.state.gov/g/oes/rls/remarks/2009/120974.htm, last accessed 10 August 2010.

98 At the UNFCCC COP 13 meeting in Bali in December 2007, Japan advocated greenhouse gas intensity targets for both developed and developing countries and sectoral approaches as key elements of any post-2012 global climate agreement: see Antto Vihma, 'Friendly Neighbour or Trojan Horse? Assessing the Interaction of Soft Law Initiatives and the UN Climate Regime' (2009) 9 *International Environmental Agreements: Politics, Law, Economics* 239–62.

99 UNFCCC, *Copenhagen Accord*, Decision 2/CP.15, FCCC/CP/2009/11/Add.1, 18 December 2009, Copenhagen, Denmark.

100 Dryzek identifies two emerging discourses; first an 'energy security' and second a 'climate justice' discourse, in John Dryzek, *Green Democracy*, Occasional Paper 2/2010, The Academy of Social Sciences of Australia (2010) 4–5.

a key role in giving local effect and administrative oversight. In responding to the market failure of greenhouse gas emissions the UN climate treaties attempt to walk a mid-path between market liberal and politically based regulatory structures. The goal of the UN climate treaty process of avoiding 'dangerous climate change' is defined and determined by a global political compromise on the amount and distribution of climate change risk. The Kyoto carbon market is indeed a marketisation of environmental policy, but only as a process to implement the politically determined goal of avoiding a certain level of climate risk. Under the UN climate treaties the market has a secondary and procedural role in pursuing the previously established goals for emission reduction and avoidance of climate risk.

In contrast to the UNFCCC/Kyoto Protocol, the Asia-Pacific Partnership promotes voluntary greenhouse intensity targets and sectoral-technology cooperation in place of the binding emission reduction targets and the flexibility mechanisms of the carbon market. The Asia-Pacific Partnership is directed primarily at the correction of market failures with regard to technology product information and coordination of actors in markets for cleaner technologies and management practices. Member State activity is largely confined to overcoming informational and coordination failures through organising venues for cooperation between actors in technology markets. Legal structures at the international and national level are sidelined. The Asia-Pacific Partnership is far more deregulatory compared to the UN climate treaties. The binding emission reduction targets and regulatory structures to establish and support the international carbon market are not required under the Asia-Pacific Partnership approach. The Asia-Pacific Partnership model provides that the goals for international climate change policy, in terms of emissions reduction and exposure to the risks of climate change, should be determined by the performance of markets for cleaner technologies and management practices. The Asia-Pacific Partnership elevates the market to the key determinant of the level of emission reduction and climate risk that will be tolerated.

The discourse analysis supporting the arguments in this chapter found the Asia-Pacific Partnership embodied a strong technology-focused market liberal discourse chiefly advocated by the two developed countries who stood outside the Kyoto Protocol, the US and Australia. This is to be distinguished from the provisional approach taken by the international community in the UNFCCC and Kyoto Protocol. However, as evidenced by recent developments in international climate policy, most recently the outcome of the COP 15 meeting in Copenhagen, the

Asia-Pacific Partnership technology-focused market liberal discourse appears to be strengthening and conventional regulatory models employed at the international and public law level are becoming less favoured. The Asia-Pacific Partnership may trigger an unlikely connection between the two spheres of law: a shared abandonment of avoiding dangerous climate change.

14

Global gazing: viewing markets through the lens of emissions trading discourses

SANJA BOGOJEVIĆ

1. Introduction

A key legal response to the global problem of climate change is emissions trading schemes. This regulatory strategy is set out in international law as part of the Kyoto Protocol (Protocol), which identifies emissions trading as a pollution control system to help parties to the Protocol to meet their quantified emission limitation and reduction commitments.[1] Although the Protocol does not prescribe how emissions trading schemes ought to be constructed and implemented in domestic jurisdictions, emissions trading schemes tend to be understood as being based on common 'design features'.[2] This understanding sparks and encourages generalisations about the legal effects and characteristics of emissions trading, and so when these trading schemes are analysed they tend to be examined through a so-called 'global gaze',[3] without taking the

[1] Kyoto Protocol to the United Nations Framework Convention on Climate Change, opened for signature 16 March 1998, 2303 UNTS 148 (entered into force 16 February 2005) Art. 17.

[2] See, for instance, Tom Tietenberg, *Emissions Trading: Principles and Practice* (Resources for the Future, Washington DC, 2nd edn, 2006) 17; Carol Rose, 'Common Property, Regulatory Property, and Environmental Protection: Comparing Community-Based Management to Tradable Environmental Allowances' in Elinor Ostrom *et al.* (eds.), *The Drama of the Commons* (National Resource Council, Washington DC, 2003) 233, 235–7; Dimitrios Mavrakis and Popi Konidari, 'Classification of Emissions Trading Scheme Design Characteristics' (2003) 13 *European Environment* 48, 52.

[3] This term is borrowed from Fogel. She argues that in global discourses, such as surround the Protocol, common tendencies are to simplify environmental problems and overlook local particularities in favour of 'existing elites'. The reason why this is done, Fogel explains, is to be able to 'rule from afar': Cathleen Fogel, 'The Local, the Global, and the Kyoto Protocol' in Sheila Jasanoff and Marybeth Long Martello (eds.), *Earthly Politics: Local and Global in Environmental Governance* (MIT Press, Cambridge, Mass., 2004) 103, 104.

legal context in which they operate into consideration. As a result, emissions trading schemes are often understood to be merely instrumental from a legal viewpoint;[4] they are seen as a simple tool that can be integrated or imposed in public law from jurisdiction to jurisdiction to quickly fix political problems, such as complying with international obligations to tackle climate change.

The aim of this chapter is to demonstrate that although emissions trading schemes are part of a global governance system responding to a global problem, they are more than a simple tool with applicability across all public law regimes. Rather, these schemes are complex regulatory strategies that are shaped according to different legislative models and dependent on the legal setting in which they operate. By exploring various ways in which the market – a central component of emissions trading – is understood in emissions trading discourses, this chapter highlights the breadth of legal responses to an international agreement that lists emissions trading as a possible method of compliance. In doing so, I set out three models: *Economic Efficiency, Private Property Rights* and *Command-and-Control.*[5] These models see emissions trading as having differing objectives – from employing markets for economic benefit, to embracing liberalism, to offering a neo-regulatory mechanism. The relationship with public law under each model also differs.

As this chapter explains, these models shed light on two important points. First, they show that in emissions trading discourses markets bear fundamentally different meanings. The way in which the market is viewed is, however, directly linked to the way in which other institutions (the public institution being a prime example) are understood. More precisely, the market is rarely defined on its own terms, but rather, in a residual manner with regard to what the role of the state is understood to be.[6]

[4] Fisher notes that assuming that environmental law is simply about functional matters (that is, law being a type of 'toolbox' and thus focusing on mere 'instrumentality' as the law) is a common oversimplification present in legal scholarship: Elizabeth Fisher, 'Unpacking the Toolbox: Or Why the Public/Private Divide Is Important in EC Environmental Law' in Mark Freedland and Jean-Bernard Auby (eds.), *The Public Law/Private Law Divide: Une Entente Assez Cordiale? La Distinction du Droit Public et du Droit Privé: Regards Français et Britanniques* (Hart Publishing, Oxford, 2006) 215, 217.

[5] I first used the models in Sanja Bogojević, 'Ending the Honeymoon: Deconstructing Emissions Trading Discourses' (2009) 21 *Journal of Environmental Law* 443. Here I build on this previous publication.

[6] Market and state, or public and private interrelationships are common in legal scholarship; see, for instance, Charles Sampford, 'Law, Institutions and the Public/Private Divide' (1991) 20 *Federal Law Review* 185.

This private/public relationship shows that despite the fact that emissions trading schemes are applied under a global agreement, these cannot exist without the state and absent from a particular public law regime.

Second, the models demonstrate that when markets are discussed in emissions trading discourses, the focus is almost exclusively on their function. The construction of emissions markets, on the other hand, tends to be oversimplified by presenting it as a mere legal technicality that stands independent from legal particularities.[7] By using the European Union Emissions Trading Scheme (EU ETS) as a reference point, I intend to shed light on difficult legal dilemmas arising in constructing an emissions market in an EU context. In this way, it shows that emissions trading schemes cannot be understood to be simple instrumental responses to a global climate change framework; rather, the full complexity of the legal environment in which these schemes operate must be taken into account.

This chapter is structured as follows. In section 2, emissions trading discourses are briefly identified and the 'global gaze' in the literature explained. Subsequently, in section 3, the discourses are deconstructed by setting out three models: the *Economic Efficiency, Private Property Rights* and *Command-and-Control* models. In section 4, the models and their implications are explained and evaluated, which is followed, in section 5, by an overview of legal complexities in constructing an emissions market, in which the EU ETS is employed as a case study. In section 6, the findings in the chapter are summarised and further discussed.

2. Emissions trading discourses

The study of discourses is a topic in itself,[8] and the word 'discourse' has come to mean many different things in many different places.[9] Jessup and Rubenstein explicate the different kinds of environmental discourses this collection of essays is based upon,[10] also referring to general understandings

[7] As suggested by describing emissions trading schemes as being based on common 'design features', above n. 2.

[8] Alan Bryman, *Social Research Methods* (Oxford University Press, 3rd edn, 2008) 501.

[9] Maarten Hajer, *The Politics of Environmental Discourse: Ecological Modernization and the Policy Process* (Clarendon Press, Oxford, 1995) 43.

[10] See the above Introduction by Brad Jessup and Kim Rubenstein.

of a discourse as 'stories . . . shared ways of apprehending the world',[11] 'an ensemble of ideas, concepts, and categories' to which disparate views, values and interests may be attached,[12] providing the basic terms for analysis, debates, agreements and disagreements.[13] On these accounts, the role of a discourse is to paint a picture and encompass a particular attitude, position or world view.

In literature on emissions trading, this pollution control system tends to be described and debated from the viewpoint of a so-called 'global gaze'. This particular phrase is employed to explain that emissions trading schemes are portrayed with a public law starting point, but with the *presumption* that these trading schemes can be replicated and applied across borders, without considering the legal context in which they operate. In other words, emissions trading is depicted and understood as a simple tool that can be integrated or imposed in public law from jurisdiction to jurisdiction in a legal attempt to tackle climate change, but regardless of legal specificities. As a result of this framing,[14] the way in which emissions trading schemes are regarded from a legal perspective adheres to this particular global view.[15] I have previously listed and described the literature that forms this outlook.[16] In this chapter I do not revisit these scholarly contributions but instead explain, with reference to the EU ETS, why emissions trading literature is fixated on viewing emissions trading through a global, rather than local lens.

[11] John Dryzek, *The Politics of the Earth: Environmental Discourses* (Oxford University Press, 2nd edn, 2005) 9.

[12] Maarten Hajer, 'Coalitions, Practices, and Meaning in Environmental Politics: From Acid Rain to BSE' in David Howarth and Jacob Torfing (eds.), *Discourse Theory in European Politics: Identity, Policy and Governance* (Palgrave Macmillan, Basingstoke, 2005) 297, 300.

[13] Dryzek, above n. 11.

[14] For a discussion on 'framing', see Sheila Jasanoff, 'Heaven and Earth: The Politics of Environmental Images' in Jasanoff and Long Martello (eds.), above n. 3, 31, 49.

[15] For an explanation as to how descriptions prescribe a certain way of viewing what is described, see Jerry Mashaw, *Greed, Chaos, and Governance: Using Public Choice to Improve Public Law* (Yale University Press, New Haven, 1997) 1.

[16] Emissions trading literature, which is the basis of my current research on the legal complexities of emissions trading schemes, is categorised as theory-based, promotional, pragmatic, cross-jurisdictional and pervasively interdisciplinary. In short, my argument is that these scholarly contributions overlook and oversimplify legal aspects of emissions trading, and in this fashion help create and secure a so-called 'honeymoon period' in environmental law scholarship: Bogojević, above n. 5.

2.1 The 'global gaze'

The EU ETS is the European Union's (EU) regulatory response to the Protocol; it is understood to help the EU and its Member States comply with this international treaty, and thereby also fight a global problem, which is climate change.[17] I identify four key reasons why this regulatory option is furthered through a global outlook.

First, the fact that the EU ETS is initiated as a response to the Protocol and linked to a global emissions trading scheme helps to project the EU ETS as a component of a global legal framework rather than an isolated legal scheme. In short, the EU ETS would not exist if it were not for the Protocol.[18] Despite this top-down impact, it is important to note that the Protocol does not prescribe how emissions trading schemes must be implemented at national or regional level. Considering that various legal systems are involved in the Protocol – each having a different concept of trading – means that the Protocol allows for multiple emissions trading schemes to take form.[19] The global vision of the EU ETS arises, however, due to the possibility of linking among national, regional and the global carbon markets that form part of the global legal framework that the Protocol constitutes. In short, and in the context of the EU ETS, linking means that each emissions allowance under this trading scheme may be identified, or linked to, an assigned amount under the Protocol, thereby enabling cross-market trade to take place. Subsequently, each Member State may allow operators of covered installations to acquire emissions reduction units in accordance with Kyoto rules and use them for compliance purposes under the EU ETS.[20] Linking is described to be 'the de jure or de facto post-2012 international architecture' for climate mitigation,[21] and a phenomenon that is understood to maintain a global

[17] See Preamble to European Directive 2003/87/EC establishing a scheme for greenhouse gas emission allowance trading within the Community and amending Directive 96/61/EC ('EU ETS Directive').

[18] Denny Ellerman and Paul Joskow, *The European Union's Emissions Trading System in Perspective* (Pew Center on Global Climate Change, Arlington, 2008) 1.

[19] Rutger de Witt Wijnen, 'Emissions Trading under Article 17 of the Kyoto Protocol' in David Freestone and Charlotte Streck (eds.), *Legal Aspects of Implementing the Kyoto Protocol Mechanisms: Making Kyoto Work* (Oxford University Press, 2005) 403, 415.

[20] For an overview of this mechanism, see Jürgen Lefevere, 'The EU ETS Linking Directive Explained' in Jos Delbeke (ed.), *EU Energy Law: The EU Greenhouse Gas Emissions Trading Scheme* (Claeys & Casteels, Leuven, 2006) 117.

[21] Robert Stavins, 'Linking Tradable Permit Systems: Opportunities, Challenges, and Implications' (7th Annual Workshop on Greenhouse Gas Emissions Trading, 9 October 2007, Paris, France).

market in carbon emissions, even in the case of diplomatic collapse of attempts to create such a system under international agreements.[22] This offsets a view of emissions trading schemes, not only as a mere component of a bigger international climate change jigsaw, but also as a global scheme in which the importance of national public law regimes is underplayed.

Second, while initiating, deciding, and implementing the EU ETS, officials relied on 'foreign' advice, which helps portray the EU ETS as a global rather than inherently European, or local, regulatory alternative. The EU relied primarily on US expertise from officials in the Environmental Protection Agency, who had pioneered successful markets for air pollutants from the period of the US sulphur dioxide programme.[23] The support and input from the United States is described to have been 'an inspiration'[24] to the EU officials working on an emissions trading scheme, in the context of the EU, which helps strengthen the belief that the EU ETS is an 'alien' legal option.[25] From this perspective, framing the EU ETS through a global gaze may seem a justifiable way of viewing this regulatory strategy.

Third, European officials continuously promote a global rather than culture-specific profile of the EU ETS. This regulatory strategy is understood to be the future 'nucleus of a single global carbon market'[26] and the 'global standard-setter'[27] with regard to carbon trading. The prediction is that rules established by the EU ETS can be adopted around the world, thereby presenting the legal framework of the EU ETS as a possible 'blueprint' for a global system in emissions trading. Such a legal transplant, it is

[22] Christian Flachsland *et al.*, *Developing the International Carbon Market: Linking Options for the EU ETS* (Report to the Policy Planning Staff in the Federal Foreign Office, Potsdam Institute for Climate Impact Research, May 2008) 8.

[23] See Jon Skjærseth and Joergen Wettestad, *EU Emissions Trading: Initiation, Decision-Making and Implementation* (Ashgate Publishing, Burlington, Vt, 2008) 154.

[24] Jos Delbeke, Deputy Director General, DG Environment, 'Putting the Emerging Global Carbon Market on a Solid Footing' (speech for the opening of ICAP Global Carbon Market Forum, 19–20 May 2008, Brussels).

[25] Harro van Asselt, 'Emissions Trading: The Enthusiastic Adoption of an "Alien" Instrument?' in Andrew Jordan *et al.* (eds.), *Climate Change Policy in the European Union* (Cambridge University Press, 2010) 125.

[26] Stavros Dimas, 'The EU and the Fight Against Climate Change' (Speech to the European Commission Responsible for Environment during a seminar on climate change organised by the Finnish Institute for International Affairs, Helsinki, 4 May 2006).

[27] European Commission, *A Single Market for 21st Century Europe* (Communication) COM(2007) 724 final, 20 November 2007.

suggested, will make the EU into a 'strong global player'[28] and offer the EU countless benefits of becoming a leading economy.[29] From this perspective, the EU ETS is encouraged to set out and follow a global rationale that establishes the world's prototype for international emissions trading.[30] From this viewpoint, legal particularities of emissions trading are deliberately overlooked.

Fourth, the reason why the EU ETS tends to be framed in a global perspective may be explained with a more broad reference to the 'contemporary obsession with globalisation'.[31] To start with, the concept of 'globalisation', or even 'global' in environmental discourses, is contested and broad.[32] Although difficult to define, globalisation impacts legal scholarship, including emissions trading discourses, in two important ways. First, whether of an economic or cosmopolitan humanist kind, globalisation has, on the one hand, sharpened the awareness of varieties of laws (for example, information regarding laws in different jurisdictions is quickly transmitted across the globe) and, on the other hand, helped portray a picture of a homogeneous world in which law is unified rather than diversified.[33] From this viewpoint, debates regarding the singularity of regulatory options or the application of *a* particular kind of regulation across different jurisdictions is a legitimate methodology – despite the fact that it undermines the autonomy and particularities of national public law regimes. Second, and similarly, rhetoric that applies to debates regarding globalisation – including concepts regarding the 'new world',[34] 'new global order'[35] and the powerless state,[36] as opposed

[28] Stavros Dimas, 'Climate Change, International and EU Actions' (speech, Prague, 31 October 2008).

[29] Ibid.

[30] Anita Engels, 'Market Creation and Transnational Rule-Making: The Case of CO_2 Emissions Trading' in Marie Laure Djelic and Kerstin Sahlin-Andersson (eds.), *Transnational Governance: Institutional Dynamics of Regulation* (Cambridge University Press, 2006) 329, 343.

[31] For an analysis of the impact of the idea of globalisation on law, see Sionaidh Douglas-Scott, *Law After Modernity* (Edward Elgar, Cheltenham, forthcoming).

[32] Jasanoff, above n. 14, 33.

[33] Douglas-Scott, above n. 31. Note that in this context Douglas-Scott refers to the impact of globalisation on laws more generally rather than discussing the effect it has on environmental discourses *per se*.

[34] Anne-Marie Slaughter, *A New World Order* (Princeton University Press, 2004).

[35] David Levi-Faur and Jacint Jordana, 'The Making of a New Regulatory Order' (2005) 6 *Annals of the American Academy of Political and Social Science* 598.

[36] See Linda Weiss, *The Myth of the Powerless State: Governing the Economy in a Global Era* (Polity Press, Cambridge, 1998).

to the 'global state',[37] help portray international treaties as existing against the backdrop of a diminishing power of the state,[38] or even without the direct agency of the state.[39] De Saadeler notes in a similar fashion that the pressure of a globalised world has meant that 'the State has lost its monopolist role as a producer of norms of multilateral and supranational institutions'.[40] The impact of the idea of globalisation on emissions trading discourses is the inducement to commit to global framing on this topic, which, in this regard, means to both overlook legal particularities of emissions trading schemes, and to question the role of the state therein.

These four reasons as to why the EU ETS is furthered and envisioned as a global trading scheme are not employed so as to claim that the EU ETS, deriving from international law and drawing from the regulatory experience of the United States, constitutes a problem *per se*. The legal difficulty lies in the fact that emissions trading schemes, inspired by the successful story of US trading with sulphur dioxide, are replicated across jurisdictions and environmental problems with the *presumption* that they will work equally well.[41] As a consequence, legal complexities particular to a certain trading scheme are overlooked. By viewing regulation of this kind in an exclusively global rather than culture-specific context, law is mistakenly framed as an easily applicable tool that will seek to achieve the sought-for regulatory results at all times and in all public law settings.

3. Viewing markets through models

Beneath the 'global gaze' of emissions trading schemes in emissions trading discourses, distinct portrayals of the market, and its function in emissions trading, exist. By deconstructing emissions trading discourses and inquiring into the set of shared ideas and values that are imposed on

[37] Martin Shaw, *Theory of the Global State: Globality as an Unfinished Revolution* (Cambridge University Press, 2000).

[38] Bern Hansjürgen (ed.), *Emissions Trading for Climate Policy: US and European Perspectives* (Cambridge University Press, 2005).

[39] Alfred Aman Jr, 'Administrative Law for a New Century' in Michael Taggart (ed.), *The Province of Administrative Law* (Hart Publishing, Oxford, 1997) 90, 91.

[40] Nicolas de Saadeler, *Environmental Principles: From Political Slogans to Legal Rules* (Oxford University Press, 2002) 223.

[41] Lisa Heinzerling, 'The Environment' in Peter Cane and Mark Tushnet (eds.), *The Oxford Handbook of Legal Studies* (Oxford University Press, 2003) 701, 712 and Michael Hanemann, 'Cap-and-Trade: A Sufficient or Necessary Condition for Emission Reduction?' (2010) 26 *Oxford Review of Economic Policy* 225.

emissions markets and influence the way in which emissions markets are portrayed in emissions trading debates, more diverse pictures emerge and the 'global gaze' becomes coloured and bounded. These show that different understandings of emissions markets exist and that these correspond to different legislative models upon which trading schemes are based. This also confirms that emissions trading schemes cannot be generalised. As mentioned above, in order to highlight the diverse storylines through which the market is viewed, I use models – the *Economic Efficiency, Private Property Rights* and *Command-and-Control* models. Each model imagines a different framework within which emissions markets may be created and operate.

Differences in understanding the market in emissions trading literature are manifested in the various rhetorics, catch phrases, vocabularies of motive, metaphors and analogies employed in discussing this pollution control system.[42] It is important to understand *how* different discourses have been distinguished and mapped out in other models before I use my models in this chapter.

In the *Economic Efficiency Model*, the focus is on the cost-effectiveness of the market. Advocates of these discussions stem from the economics field and the language deployed includes economics terms such as 'internalising externalities', creating 'incentives', 'bargaining systems' and 'profit-centre' that produce 'cost-efficient' results. This model reflects views underpinning international climate negotiations and global trade agreements.[43] In the *Private Property Rights Model*, on the other hand, the focal point is to illustrate the market as a 'free' forum in which citizens of a community, rather than the state, are able to make decisions over and control common resources. Key phrases embedded in these discourses include 'liberty', 'bureaucratic coercion', 'privatisation' and 'private property rights'. As a distinguishing feature from the other two models, opinions encompassed in this model, and in particular with regard to the government, are shared with certain public choice theorists.[44] This may help explain why in the *Private Property Rights Model* any common or top-down approaches of public and international law

[42] Method as applied in René Kemp, 'Why Not In My Backyard? A Radical Interpretation of Public Opposition to the Deep Disposal of Radioactive Waste in the United Kingdom' (1990) 22 *Environment and Planning* 1239. See also above Introduction by Brad Jessup and Kim Rubenstein.

[43] I thank Brad Jessup for this comment.

[44] Public choice literature is vast. For classic public choice examples, see Anthony Downs, *An Economic Theory of Democracy* (Harper, New York, 1957); James Buchanan and

are rejected. In the *Command-and-Control Model*, the discussion shifts to regulatory reform and the manner in which markets can help to comply with regulatory obligations. Key words in this model are subsequently 're-regulation', 'regulatory flexibility', 'permits' and 'authorisation', rather than private property rights. This model, by contrast to the two previous models, has a strong public law tradition in which implementing flexible regulation is the focal point of discussion. Overall, understanding the emphasis in rhetoric in these models is essential, because it frames the way in which markets are presented and understood in emissions trading discourses. To a certain extent, the models may seem to overlap. However, their disconnection is clear in the language used in defining and explaining markets.

It is important to point out that my intention is not to try to convince the reader that the categorisation of the emissions trading literature presented in this chapter is the only possible or correct one. In other words, the models in this chapter are not intended to be exhaustive and so they do not create a strict pattern of how markets must be understood, nor do they necessarily reflect the way in which existing markets operate.[45] My argument is rather that although we may disagree about the exact distinctions as to how markets are thought of in emissions trading literature, and set out in the models, it is nonetheless obvious that different concepts about the market and its functions exist in these debates and often dominate them. The role of the models, therefore, is to help to illustrate the multifarious ways of understanding the operation of markets as described in emissions trading discourses and thereby help defy generalising remarks regarding markets and emissions trading schemes. If we are to better understand emissions trading models, there is a better hope of creating systems mindful of local culture and public law traditions.

Gordon Tullock, *The Calculus of Consent: Logical Foundations of Constitutional Democracy* (University of Michigan Press, Ann Arbor, 1965); Kenneth Arrow, *Social Choice and Individual Values* (Yale University Press, New Haven, 1963). For a recent overview, see Jerry Mashaw, 'Public Law and Public Choice: Critique and Rapprochement' in Daniel Farber and Ann O'Connell (eds.), *Research Handbook on Public Choice and Public Law* (Edward Elgar, Cheltenham, 2010) 19.

45 The models encompass only certain scholarly debates on this topic: for example, environmental ethics literature is omitted from this chapter. For a brief overview of this type of debate, see Mark Sagoff, 'Controlling Global Climate: The Debate over Pollution Trading' in Verna Gehring and William Galston (eds.), *Philosophical Dimensions of Public Policy* (Transaction Publishers, New Brunswick, 2002) 311.

3.1 *The Economic Efficiency Model*

In the *Economic Efficiency Model*, the market plays a central role in emissions trading because it is understood to provide the most cost-effective allocation of externalities. As a consequence, questions such as what 'interest should prevail' or what payment is made for the right to externalities should not be defined by the regulator, but are decided instead according to market mechanisms.[46] In effect, price and allocation of externalities in this model are seen to depend on the shrewdness of the various bargainers in the market.[47] This theory is, however, based on the premise that there are no transaction costs.[48] In real life, transaction costs exist, and when these are high, the *Economic Efficiency Model* explains that government intervention in the market may be required. To be more specific, if the government provides solutions for internalising externalities at less cost than the market, the role of the government should be to limit the costs of trading by regulatory intervention.[49] Therefore, when a regulatory strategy is applied to common resources, it should be constructed to provide the most cost-effective solutions instead of assuming that either the government or the market works without cost.[50] From this viewpoint, markets are seen as forming part of a pragmatic economic process of allocation of externalities rather than complying with a strict doctrinal laissez-faire theory.[51] In sum, this overview of the *Economic Efficiency Model* shows that markets are seen as providing a forum in which externalities can be internalised at the lowest cost. It is therefore the cost-effective function of a market which is in focus in this model; it also being the reason why emissions markets are understood to be best suited for controlling pollution.

[46] For example, Pigou argued that the government should internalise externalities by taxation: Arthur Pigou, *Wealth and Welfare* (Macmillan, London, 1912). Coase's study contrasts with Pigou's theory in the sense that it is not the government but the market, due to its allocative efficiency, which should internalise externalities: Ronald Coase, 'The Problem of Social Cost' (1960) 3 *Journal of Law and Economics* 1.

[47] Ibid. 5. [48] Ibid. 18.

[49] Depending on where the high costs lie, the government could, for instance, set allocation mechanisms: Harold Demsetz, 'The Cost of Transacting' (1968) 82 *The Quarterly Journal of Economics* 33, 33–4; Garrett Hardin, 'The Tragedy of the Commons' (1968) 162 *Science* 1243, 1245–6.

[50] Richard Posner, 'Nobel Laureate: Ronald Coase and Methodology' (1993) 7 *Journal of Economic Perspectives* 195.

[51] Ibid. 202.

3.2 Private Property Rights Model

In the *Private Property Rights Model*, markets are understood to be vital components not only of emissions trading schemes, but society at large. Markets in this model are portrayed not simply as cost-effective, but as the cornerstones of 'free' society.[52] Only the market, it is argued, can provide individual liberty, 'and without that human freedom, environmental quality will be of little consequence'.[53] Freedom in this context consists of the breadth of possibilities that the market offers every citizen for finding exchanges of private property rights on the best terms possible for that particular person.[54] The element of freedom that is understood to exist in markets is contrasted with coercive bureaucratic control. Regulators are described as having failed the citizens and squandered common resources.[55] From this perspective, the market is seen as 'the only non-arbitrary solution',[56] and also as a substitute for non-functioning government control of common resources.

Clearly there are overlaps between this and the previous model. Both models put forward arguments in favour of managing common resources according to market behaviour and without government meddling. They see limited obvious scope for a public law contribution. The difference is, however, that in the *Economic Efficiency Model* markets are understood to be the most *cost-effective* way of internalising externalities, while in the *Private Property Rights Model* it is the empowerment of markets, their ability in offering citizens the possibility to manage common resources on their own terms, that is in focus. Due to this distinction, in the latter model, markets are seen as 'free', meaning free from state intervention, whilst in the previous model, state intervention is envisaged if costs of transactions become too high. In sum, in this model, markets are portrayed in a libertarian light and shown to have the function of securing liberty in society at large.

[52] See above Chapter 4 by Nicole Graham, particularly her focus on the notion of entitlement.

[53] See Terry Anderson and Donald Leal, 'Free Market Versus Political Environmentalism' (1992) 15 *Harvard Journal of Law and Public Policy* 297, 310.

[54] Armen Alchian, *Pricing Society* (The Institute of Economic Affairs, Leicester, 1967) 8.

[55] Elizabeth Brubaker, *Property Rights in the Defence of Nature* (Earthscan, London, 1995) 162.

[56] Walter Block, 'Environmental Problems, Private Property Rights Solutions' in Walter Block (ed.), *Economics and the Environment: A Reconciliation* (The Frasier Institute, Vancouver, 1990) 281, 302.

3.3 *Command-and-Control Model*

In comparison to the *Economic Efficiency* and *Private Property Rights* models, the *Command-and-Control Model* is far more critical of the role of the market in emissions trading. In the two previous models, the market is depicted as 'free', meaning that no room is envisaged for governmental intervention in relation to emissions trading[57] – unless it is cost-effective, in the case of the *Economic Efficiency Model.* In the *Command-and-Control Model*, markets are not understood to exist in this kind of legal vacuum, but in the constant presence of the regulator. The task of the regulator is defined as ensuring fair competition via government intervention in the emissions market – a view contrary to the *Private Property Rights Model.* Unregulated markets are described to give rise to dominant market players who have the possibility of raising costs for rivals or blocking the entry of new competitors by means of predation, pre-emption, exclusion and collusion, unless the regulator intervenes.[58] Emissions trading is viewed as a regulatory strategy in which the government through a range of measures in the public law tradition should artificially shape competition so as to prevent this.[59] Moreover, the regulator should set the limits and targets – and not the market – for the quantity of emission allowances so as to create scarcity and ensure that the market functions.[60] Therefore, the market is not understood as 'free' in the *Command-and-Control Model*, but at best as 'partial or incomplete',[61] and a mere device through which the regulation in question can be carried out.[62]

[57] Ibid. 312.

[58] Walter Misiolek and Harold Elder, 'Exclusionary Manipulation of Markets for Pollution Rights' (1989) 16 *Journal of Environmental Economics and Management* 156.

[59] Eckard Rehbinder, 'Market Based Incentives for Environmental Protection' in Richard Revesz, Philippe Sands and Richard Stewart (eds.), *Environmental Law, the Economy and Sustainable Development* (Cambridge University Press, 2000) 245, 245.

[60] The European Commission and the Member States are referred to as the 'regulator' in the EU in this particular literature: Skjærseth and Wettestad, above n. 23; Jürgen Lefevere, 'Greenhouse Gas Emission Allowance Trading in the EU: A Background' [2004] *Yearbook of European Environmental Law* 149, 151.

[61] Bronwen Morgan and Karen Yeung, *An Introduction to Law and Regulation: Texts and Materials* (Cambridge University Press, 2007) 316.

[62] Ibid.

4. Evaluating the models

Table 14.1 summarises and illustrates the different roles and connotations that that market has in emissions trading discourses. In the *Economic Efficiency Model* the market is understood to provide the most cost-effective forum for internalising externalities and thus the significance of markets is cost-effectiveness. The tone is different in the *Private Property Rights Model*, according to which the market is portrayed as a cornerstone of 'free' society that enables citizens to manage common resources on their own terms, and thus independently of governmental bureaucracy. This stands as a contrast to the *Command-and-Control Model*, in which the market is seen as a regulatory device through which a regulatory obligation, such as reducing emissions of certain gases, is complied with. The models show that in discussing the market, emissions trading discourses do not adhere to *one* prevailing definition of what constitutes a market, nor what role it plays or ought to play in emissions trading schemes: rather, *diverse* views of the market exist.

The models help highlight two further points. First, they show that in emissions trading discourses the market is not defined on its own terms,

Table 14.1 *The models compared*

	Economic Efficiency Model	Private Property Rights Model	Command-and-Control Model
Role of the market	Ensure cost-effectiveness	Safeguard personal liberty (i.e., ensure that transfer of private property rights occurs on the terms of property holders)	Regulatory device
Role of the state	Regulatory intervention if cost-effective	Legislator has a role of defining rights and judiciary in enforcing them	Creating and managing the emissions market

Source: S. Bogojević, modified from S. Bogojević, 'Ending the Honeymoon: Deconstructing Emissions Trading Discourses' (2009) 21 *Journal of Environmental Law* 443.

but by direct reference to the role of the state in emissions trading schemes. This shows that a strong correlation between the public and the private exists in these debates. For instance, in the *Economic Efficiency Model*, the way in which the market is viewed depends on the cost-effectiveness of state intervention in the market. According to the *Private Property Rights Model*, on the other hand, the market is viewed as 'free' and as a direct contrast to 'government coercion'. In the *Command-and-Control Model*, the market is simply a device with which government bodies can control pollution. The models, therefore, help explain that emissions markets cannot be discussed or viewed in legal isolation, but within the framework of the state and its legal and cultural setting – even if applied under an international agreement.

Moreover, the models demonstrate that in discussing the market in emissions trading discourses, the outlook point is on the function of these: cost-effectiveness in the *Economic Efficiency Model*, substitution of government control and thus safeguarding personal liberty in the *Private Property Rights Model*, and acting as a regulatory device in the *Command-and-Control Model*. Each model is underpinned by a different belief as to what the role of the market is or ought to be. The construction of markets, on the other hand, tends to be oversimplified. Ackerman and Stewart, for example, identify four bureaucratic tasks in the setting up and managing of trading schemes before concluding 'that's that'.[63] Constructing a market, from this perspective, is seen to be a mere technicality of setting the framework and thereafter letting the market 'do its work'.[64] In order to draw attention to legal complexities and important implications in constructing an emissions market, I shall explain the various stages in determining an emissions market by using the EU ETS as a reference point.

5. Emissions market in a European legal context

The EU ETS is the world's largest emissions market. It was implemented in the EU legal order in 2003 in order to promote reductions of greenhouse gas emissions and to help the then European Community and its Member States comply with obligations under the United Nations

[63] Bruce Ackerman and Richard Stewart, 'Reforming Environmental Law' (1985) 37 *Stanford Law Review* 1333, 1347.

[64] Popular phrase used, for instance, by Paul Krugman, 'Building a Green Economy', *New York Times*, 5 April 2010.

Framework Convention on Climate Change and the Kyoto Protocol. The fact that the EU emissions market is established as a legal response to an international convention, however, bears no particular importance in the construction of this emissions market, as the Protocol simply establishes 'the barest skeleton of a market'.[65] The EU emissions market is therefore an EU – rather than global – legal creation.

5.1 Constructing the EU ETS

The EU emissions market is based on a so-called 'cap-and-trade' principle. The term 'cap-and-trade' suggests that establishing and managing an emissions market of this kind is a straightforward task that involves the setting of the cap from which emission allowances are allocated and thereby a carbon market is created.[66] Constructing the EU emissions market is, therefore, perceived to be an 'intuitively simple'[67] process, which also helps explain why the application of emissions trading schemes, across different public law regimes, is regarded to be unproblematic.

Upon closer scrutiny of the EU ETS, and in particular the method of determining the cap, it is clear that constructing this emissions market is far more complex and administratively burdensome than the notion 'cap-and-trade' reveals. First, there is not a single, but twenty-seven different national caps under the current EU ETS. According to the EU ETS Directive, each Member State has to develop its national cap, or the so-called 'National Allocation Plan' (NAP), which states the total quantity of allowances and their intended allocation.[68]

When the national authorities grant emissions permits, they in fact determine their total national cap. The cap is crucial to 'get right', as it reflects the desired environmental effects,[69] which also means emissions permits are allocated according to the overall environmental ambitions of their government. Each Member State has, in addition to granting emissions permits, monitoring, reporting and verification responsibilities. This process of determining NAPs is, however, not an entirely

[65] Donald MacKenzie, *Material Markets: How Economic Agents Are Constructed* (Oxford University Press, 2009) 153.

[66] Sanja Bogojević, 'Litigating the NAP: Legal Challenges for the Emissions Trading Scheme of the European Union' (2010) 3 *Carbon and Climate Law Review* 217.

[67] Skjærseth and Wettestad, above n. 23.

[68] European Directive 2003/87/EC, Art. 9(1).

[69] Tom James and Peter Fusaro, *Energy and Emissions Markets* (John Wiley and Sons, Chichester, 2006) xi.

decentralised activity. According to Article 9(1) of the EU ETS Directive, each NAP shall be based on 'objective and transparent criteria', including a wide range of principles such as non-discrimination and consistency with other EU-based legislation and policy instruments. The interpretation of these criteria is set out in the European Commission's (Commission) Guidelines[70] to help Member States in determining NAPs in accordance with the EU ETS Directive. The criteria and guidelines insert a public law dimension into the trading system. There is, however, no clear guidance as to how, who, and to what extent Member States' discretion in determining their NAP ought to be controlled. Further, under Article 9(3) of the EU ETS Directive, a second phase exists in which the national caps have to be approved by the Commission.

The scope of the Commission's discretion to approve or reject NAPs is fiercely contested. Indeed, Article 9 of the EU ETS Directive is the Article most often subject to administrative review.[71] In fact, Article 9 has proven to establish ineffective control measures in determining caps; in the first period of emissions trading, Member States repeatedly over-allocated their emissions levels and the Commission showed it is unsuccessful in controlling the over-allocation ad hoc and via litigation.[72] In 2009 it was concluded that the EU ETS Directive had to be amended in this regard. In the next period of emissions trading (2012 onwards), rules regarding cap setting are stipulated by a revised EU ETS Directive,[73] which states that instead of the Member States, the Commission will determine the cap for the entire EU.

5.2 *Implications and evaluation*

Determining the cap under the EU ETS raises difficult legal questions about multilevel governance, which, in the case of the EU, is particularly problematic. The cap-setting system under the current EU ETS Directive

[70] European Commission, *Guidance to Assist Member States in the Implementation of the Criteria Listed in Annex III to Council Directive (EC) 2003/87* (Communication) COM (2003) 830 final, 7 January 2004.

[71] See, for example, *United Kingdom* v. *Commission* (Case T-178/05) [2005] ECR II-4807; *EnBW* v. *Commission and Germany* (Case T-387/04) [2007] ECR II-1195; *Germany* v. *Commission* (Case T-374/04) [2007] ECR II-4431.

[72] European Commission, *Building a Global Carbon Market: Report Pursuant to Article 30 of Directive 2003/87/EC* (Communication) COM(2006) 676 final, 13 November 2006.

[73] European Directive 2009/29/EC amending Directive 2003/87/EC so as to improve and extend the greenhouse gas emission allowance trading system of the Community.

is based on a system that offers a certain degree of autonomy to both the Member States and the Commission: the Member States are allowed to determine NAPs and the Commission has the authority to review these. By altering this system to allow the Commission alone to set a centralised cap shows that regulatory power in this context is tipped in favour of the Commission. Under the revised cap-setting procedures, the Commission will therefore have additional discretion and obligations in terms of information collection and policy integration. This move of authority under the EU ETS raises numerous questions regarding power balance in the EU and accountability of decision-making power under the EU ETS. By centralising power in this manner, it might be suggested that the Commission has committed a 'Commission coup',[74] leaving Member States without an effective input in the construction of emissions markets.[75] The point to be made in this chapter is that determining caps, and thereby constructing emissions markets, may appear to be a simple legal technicality, or a so-called mere 'design issue'. Upon closer scrutiny, however, it is clear that this procedure evolves around difficult legal dilemmas concerning power allocation. Discussions regarding the construction of emissions markets thus highlight not only the legal complexities of emissions trading schemes, but also the importance of legal cultures in understanding how emissions markets are constructed and their legal consequence.

Examining the construction procedure of the EU emissions market also helps demonstrate that this market is heavily regulated. From this perspective, the EU emissions market overlaps with the understanding of markets as described in the *Command-and-Control Model* that builds on new administrative laws. The fact that discourses encompassed in the *Private Property Rights* and *Economic Efficiency* models portray markets in a fundamentally different light, highlights the importance of initiating a debate on the differences of markets, as understood to operate and be constructed in emissions trading discourses, and thus rejecting the current generalisation and omission of trading particularities on this topic.

[74] Jorgen Wettestad, 'Revising EU Emissions Trading: A "Requested Revolution"?' (lecture given as part of the European Union and the Fight against Global Climate Change Lecture Series, 29 October 2008).

[75] For a broader analysis of legal changes under the revised EU ETS Directive, see Sanja Bogojević, 'The EU ETS Directive Revised: Yet Another Stepping Stone' (2009) 11 *Environmental Law Review* 279.

In addition, the construction procedure of emissions markets at EU level demonstrates that the way in which the EU emissions market is constructed and perceived is not deterministic or static. Rather, EU ETS directives may be revised and rules regarding the construction of markets changed, showing there is no *one* single method of constructing markets or *one* prevailing lens through which these are viewed. In fact, the EU ETS is an 'experiment'[76] *in vivo*, or more precisely, an experiment of 'action and reflection'[77] developed in different phases, each phase evolving based on the experiences gained in the previous trading episode.[78] Still, the way in which an emissions market is constructed matters not only for the economic outcomes of emissions trading[79] but also for legal implications, as this chapter has intended to show.

In sum, exploring the construction process of the EU emissions market shows that concepts developed at the international level and framed by market discourses cannot be adopted and applied uniformly and effortlessly across different public law regimes. There is a willingness of the public realm to intervene under the EU ETS scheme, a kind of intervention that is extremely difficult, and perhaps impossible, at a global level. Viewing emissions trading schemes through a so-called 'global gaze' is therefore a flawed and oversimplified picture of this particular pollution control system.

6. Conclusion

This chapter shows that emissions trading schemes are complex legal constructions that cannot simply be viewed in the abstract through a global, generalising gaze. By deconstructing emissions trading discourses, and thereby applying models, I have shown that different lenses exist through which emissions markets – a cornerstone of emissions trading schemes – may be viewed and conceived. The models – *Economic Efficiency, Private Property Rights* and *Command-and-Control* – demonstrate that when emissions trading schemes are discussed, different

[76] MacKenzie, above n. 65, 154.

[77] See Fabian Muniesa, Yuval Millo and Michel Callon, 'An Introduction to Market Devices' (2007) 55 *The Sociological Review* 1.

[78] MacKenzie, above n. 65, 166 and 171.

[79] Axel Ockenfels, 'Empfehlungen für das Auktionsdesign für Emissionsberechtigungen' (2009) 2 *Zeitschrift für Energiewirtschaft* 105, 106.

types of legislative models are referred to, in which each emissions market is understood to play fundamentally different roles. According to the *Economic Efficiency Model*, markets are understood to provide the most cost-effective fora for internalising externalities, with only moderate government influence; in the *Private Property Rights Model*, markets are portrayed as cornerstones of 'free' society that enable citizens to manage common resources on their own terms, and thus independently of governmental bureaucracy, whilst in the *Command-and-Control Model*, markets are seen as a device through which a regulatory obligation, such as reducing emissions of certain gases, is complied with.

These models highlight that when markets are debated in emissions trading schemes, not only are different type of markets referred to, but these are also defined in direct correlation to the prescribed role of the state. This means that in responding to an obligation under international law and implementing an emissions trading scheme, the role of the market, as well as the role of the state under such a scheme, may vary from jurisdiction to jurisdiction. Legal and cultural traditions may favour or exclude certain trading options. Clearly, this shows that viewing emissions trading schemes in a generalising fashion overlooks important legal divergences across different public law regimes.

Additionally, the models demonstrate that the emissions trading literature focuses on the function, as opposed to the construction, of emissions trading schemes. The reason for this is that constructing emissions markets tends to be viewed as a simple technicality. Closer scrutiny of cap setting under the EU ETS, however, shows that constructing an emissions market raises difficult legal dilemmas and implications regarding power allocation that more often will be unique rather than global in character. This legal theme has only been touched upon in this chapter, but hopefully in this way I have helped to initiate a debate that ought to be developed further.

On a concluding note, allow me to summarise the key points in this chapter by drawing what may seem unlikely parallels between emissions trading schemes and the Wizard of Oz. The wizard and this particular pollution option are similar in the sense that they both enjoy a special status in their respective domain: the wizard is understood to possess the most forceful and potent witchcraft of all witches in Oz, whilst emissions trading schemes, using the EU ETS as an example, are labelled as the 'flagship measure',[80] 'pillar',[81] 'cornerstone',[82] and 'jewel in the crown'[83] of the EU's climate change policy. Both are therefore regarded as significant and powerful amongst their peers. The wizard, however, when confronted by Dorothy and her friends, confesses that he is not a great wizard, but instead 'just a common man'.[84] In a similar fashion I have aimed to show that emissions trading is not the type of regulatory strategy it is often assumed to be: simple and seen through a global gaze. Rather, emissions trading schemes are complex legal options that exist both at global and national levels and are influenced by the legal environment in which they operate.

This, however, is not synonymous with disapproving of the use of emissions trading schemes. In the case of the wizard, it is clear that he may not be what Dorothy and her friends expected him to be: the greatest wizard of all. Yet, the wizard succeeds in leading Dorothy and her company to what they demanded from him in the first place; the Cowardly Lion found courage, the Scarecrow brains, the Tin Man a heart and Dorothy her home in Kansas, simply because they were forced to look inside and challenge themselves. In this chapter my intention has been to show that environmental law scholars ought to follow Dorothy's example and challenge existing perceptions of emissions trading schemes as global pollution control. This may not provide us with definite solutions as to whether we should regulate pollution via emissions trading or not, but it will lead us to a yellow brick road on which we shall be able to critically assess emissions trading schemes as a global regulatory strategy and thus better understand national responses to the global initiative to tackle climate change.

80 European Commission, *Cheap Carbon Only Temporary in the EU ETS* (20 August 2009) Environment for Europeans ec.europa.eu/environment/news/efe/climate/20090820_carbon ets_en.htm, last accessed 21 May 2011.

81 Jos Delbeke, 'Environmental Policy in the Times of Economic Crisis – the Example of the EU ETS' (acceptance speech at the Smith Prize Award, Rotes Rathaus, Berlin, 20 May 2009).

82 Margaret Wallström, 'Emissions Trading' (speech, Berlin, 8 November 2002); Opinion delivered by AG Maduro (21 May 2008); *Arcelor Aquitaine et Lorraine and Others* v. *Commission* (Case C-127/07) [2008] OJ C44/8.

83 Dimas, above n. 28.

84 Lyman Frank Baum, *The Wonderful Wizard of Oz* (Bibliolis, London, 2010 edn) 94.

PART V

Discourses in the commons

15

Polar opposites: environmental discourses and management in Antarctica and the Arctic

DONALD R. ROTHWELL

1. Introduction

In 2009 the 1959 Antarctic Treaty[1] celebrated its fiftieth anniversary. Its resilience in managing the Antarctic continent and parts of the adjacent Southern Ocean is generally seen as one of the great 'success stories' of contemporary international law. This is especially the case when it is considered that the treaty was negotiated during the height of the Cold War at a time when the then USSR and United States had significant interests in Antarctica, and that the treaty never sought to resolve simmering sovereignty tensions over parts of the continent, especially those between Argentina, Chile and the United Kingdom over their competing claims to parts of the Antarctic Peninsula. Now, in the early part of the twenty-first century, and notwithstanding the lack of recognition which has been granted to the seven territorial claims to the Antarctic continent, the Antarctic Treaty includes not only the original twelve states parties, but an additional thirty-six states parties from varied parts of the globe, and retains its capacity to effectively manage Antarctic affairs.

At the other pole, the Arctic attracts attention as a region in need of an effective regime.[2] Whilst the Arctic is not plagued by unresolved territorial disputes, there is the spectre of rising tension over yet to be asserted maritime claims over the vast Arctic Ocean, and consequential issues arising as to the legitimacy of those claims and how maritime boundaries between the Arctic states may be delimited. When this issue is added to the growing alarm over the impact of climate change upon the Arctic,

[1] The Antarctic Treaty, opened for signature 1 December 1959, [1961] ATS No. 12 (entered into force 23 June 1961) ('Antarctic Treaty').

[2] See generally, Donald R. Rothwell, 'The Arctic in International Affairs: Time for a New Regime?' (2008) 15 *Brown Journal of World Affairs* 241.

bringing with it not only associated significant environmental change but also increased access, it becomes clear that a once marginalised region for much of the twentieth century has the potential to take centre stage as state interests are awoken and global concerns advance.[3]

These events for both the Arctic and Antarctic heightened increased attention being given to their legal regimes when there is ever-increasing attention to their intrinsic scientific value, and their role as sentinels to climate change. The legal issues include not only the adequacy of the international legal frameworks governing the polar regions,[4] but also the national legal regimes adopted by states to regulate and manage their polar possessions. Moreover, questions about national legal regimes include both the capacity of these national laws to give effect to international obligations, and their capacity to reflect the sovereign rights and interests of the claimant states. Given that many of the national laws have strong environmental dimensions, the merger of national environmental laws (seeking to regulate activities that may cause environmental harm in some of the most environmentally sensitive parts of the planet, but also increasingly becoming more accessible as a result of the effects of climate change), poses challenges for international and national legal frameworks that so far have rarely been encountered in the polar regions. Whether these regimes are sufficiently robust to deal with the challenges ahead is emerging as a key issue.[5]

Against this backdrop, this chapter reviews 'environmental discourse' in the polar regions, focusing on how international and national environmental laws have interacted in Antarctica and the Arctic, and the issues arising as a result of that interaction. An environmental discourses approach, particularly when a discourse is understood as a 'shared set of concepts, categories and ideas that provides its adherents with a

[3] Some of these issues are reflected in Michael Byers, *Who Owns the Arctic?* (Douglas & McIntyre, Vancouver, 2009); Ken Coates *et al.* (eds.), *Arctic Front: Defending Canada in the Far North* (Thomas Allen, Toronto, 2008).

[4] See the discussion in Christopher Joyner, *Governing the Frozen Commons: The Antarctic Regime and Environmental Protection* (University of South Carolina Press, Columbia, 1998); Donald R. Rothwell, *The Polar Regions and the Development of International Law* (Cambridge University Press, 1996); Monica Tennberg, *Arctic Environmental Cooperation: A Study in Governmentality* (Ashgate, Aldershot, 2001); Jessica Shadian, and Monica Tennberg (eds.), *Legacies and Change in Polar Sciences: Historical, Legal and Political Reflections on the International Polar Year* (Ashgate, Aldershot, 2009).

[5] See Rosemary Rayfuse, 'Melting Moments: The Future of Polar Oceans Governance in a Warming World' (2007) 16 *Review of European Community and International Environmental Law* 196.

framework for making sense of situations',[6] raises for consideration the environmental discourses taking place in the polar regions, and the constraints, limitations, opportunities and capabilities provided in addressing some of the current environmental issues confronting the poles. In undertaking this analysis, consideration is given to the Antarctic and the Arctic environmental discourse, with particular attention to how a particular environmental issue has been addressed within each region.

2. Antarctic governance

The 1957–8 International Geophysical Year provided the mechanism for the various states with an interest in Antarctic affairs to come together in the name of scientific research and work collaboratively on the continent. This proved to be the catalyst to move forward ongoing debates over the future of Antarctica and was the spur to the eventual November 1959 gathering of interested states in Washington, where the Antarctic Treaty was negotiated.

2.1 The Antarctic Treaty and the treaty system

The treaty became the foundation for the development of the so-called 'Antarctic Treaty System', including a framework of additional conventions and instruments in addition to the decisions and recommendations adopted at Antarctic Treaty Consultative Meetings. Over five decades the Antarctic Treaty System has proven itself capable of promoting the freedom of scientific research and continuing the spirit of the International Geophysical Year. It has also gradually acquired a much stronger environmental focus, reflected in two additional Antarctic Treaty System instruments: the 1980 Convention for the Conservation of Antarctic Marine Living Resources;[7] and the 1991 Madrid Protocol on Environmental Protection.[8]

[6] John Dryzek, 'Transnational Democracy in an Insecure World' (2006) 27 *International Political Science Review* 101, 104.

[7] Convention on the Conservation of Antarctic Marine Living Resources, opened for signature 20 May 1980, 1329 UNTS 47 (entered into force 7 April 1982).

[8] Protocol on Environmental Protection to the Antarctic Treaty, opened for signature 4 October 1991, [1998] ATS No. 6 (entered into force 15 January 1998) ('Madrid Protocol').

2.2 Article IV and Antarctic sovereignty

Much of the success of the Antarctic Treaty is founded upon Article IV and its provisions dealing with sovereignty, adopted against a backdrop of contested Antarctic sovereignty during the height of the Cold War.[9] Article IV(1) provides that nothing in the treaty shall be a basis for an interpretation supporting a renunciation or diminution of previously asserted, or existing, or even potential claims to Antarctica, and in particular as not prejudicing the position of those states who had a possible basis of claim which had not yet been asserted. This provision sought to deal with the position concerning the existing territorial claims, and potential claims that could be made in Antarctica, dealing with the interests of a variety of states. These include the seven territorial claimants,[10] those territorial claimants who may be in dispute with other claimants over the validity of their claims,[11] and others such as the United States or Russian Federation (as the successor to the USSR) that may wish to assert a claim in the future. The formula provided that all of the principal parties in Antarctic affairs could come together in 1959 under the control of a single regime without compromising their position on the status of sovereignty claims, or potential sovereignty claims.[12]

Furthering the scope of Article IV(1), Article IV(2) provides that 'no acts or activities taking place while the present Treaty is in force' shall be a basis for 'asserting, supporting or denying a claim' to sovereignty in Antarctica. At one level, Article IV(2) places limitations on the enhancement of pre-existing territorial claims, with the effect that nothing occurring during the lifetime of the Treaty would further embellish the status of the existing claims. The second aspect creates an outright prohibition on the assertion of new claims or the enlargement of existing claims while the treaty is in force. The effect of this was that all claims, bases of claims, or potential claims were in effect suspended as of the entry into force of the treaty in 1961 and nothing occurring while the treaty is in force affects the pre-existing position of all of the interested

[9] See generally, Donald R. Rothwell, 'Sovereignty and the Antarctic Treaty' (2010) 46 *Polar Record* 17.

[10] Argentina, Australia, Chile, France, New Zealand, Norway and the UK.

[11] The claims made by Argentina, Chile and the UK to parts of the Antarctic Peninsula overlap.

[12] Arthur Watts, *International Law and the Antarctic Treaty System* (Grotius, Cambridge, 1992) 127–9.

parties – both the claimants and the non-claimants.[13] As a complement to Article IV, Article VIII of the treaty addresses the related issue of jurisdiction over certain activities in Antarctica, making clear that nationality jurisdiction is to apply with respect to designated treaty activities such as scientific research. One result is that Antarctic Treaty parties have traditionally been very reluctant to apply jurisdiction in Antarctica against non-nationals. The result of these key provisions is that Antarctica was made 'sovereignty neutral' for the lifetime of the treaty.

2.3 Antarctic maritime claims and the treaty

In recent years controversies have erupted over the assertion of new maritime claims offshore Antarctica. As a result of the extensive developments occurring in the law of the sea, some of the claimant states have sought to take advantage of those developments by asserting maritime claims consistent with the 1982 United Nations Convention on the Law of the Sea.[14] In particular, expanded territorial sea and continental shelf claims have been asserted, as have claims to an exclusive economic zone (EEZ), which was a maritime zone not recognised by international law in 1959.[15] The most contentious maritime claims have been to an outer continental shelf going beyond the nominal 200-nautical-mile limits set by the Law of the Sea Convention.[16] By 1 January 2010, Southern Ocean continental shelf submissions had been made to the Commission on the Limits of the Continental Shelf by Australia, Norway and Argentina, while New Zealand, France, the United Kingdom and Chile all sought to reserve their position on future claims.[17] While the maritime claims of

[13] Rothwell, above n. 4, 75–80; F. M. Auburn, *Antarctic Law and Politics* (C. Hurst, London, 1982) 104–10; Gillian Triggs, *International Law and Australian Sovereignty in Antarctica* (Legal Books, Sydney, 1986) 137–50.

[14] United Nations Convention on the Law of the Sea, opened for signature 10 December 1982, 1833 UNTS 3 (entered into force 16 November 1994) ('Law of the Sea Convention').

[15] See Patrizia Vigni, 'Antarctic Maritime Claims: Frozen Sovereignty and the Law of the Sea' in Alex Oude Elferink and Donald R. Rothwell (eds.), *The Law of the Sea and Polar Maritime Delimitation and Jurisdiction* (Martinus Nijhoff, The Hague, 2001) 85.

[16] See Stuart Kaye, 'The Outer Continental Shelf in the Antarctic' in ibid., 125; Alan Hemmings and Tim Stephens, 'Extended Continental Shelves from Sub-Antarctic Islands: What Implications for Antarctic Governance?' (2010) 46 *Polar Record* 312.

[17] Andrew Serdy, 'Some Views Are More Equal than Others: Submissions to the Commission on the Limits of the Continental Shelf and the Strange Loss of Confidence in Article IV of the Antarctic Treaty' (2009) 28 *Australian Year Book of International Law* 181.

the Antarctic claimant states may be characterised principally as efforts to consolidate territorial claims predating the Antarctic Treaty and position themselves for a time when the treaty may no longer be operative, they also raise issues for municipal law, as in nearly all instances the formal assertions are made in reliance upon national legal frameworks.[18] Once these zones have been proclaimed, however, they also become subject to other management and regulatory mechanisms, especially relevant environmental law.[19]

2.4 *Southern Ocean whaling and Antarctic Treaty constraints*

In the case of the regulation of whaling in the Southern Ocean, the Antarctic Treaty has acted as something of a brake on national environmental laws. The current global whaling regime is based on the 1946 International Convention for the Regulation of Whaling (Whaling Convention),[20] which predates the Antarctic Treaty and originally had as its focus the orderly regulation of the commercial whaling industry. Over time the Whaling Convention evolved into a regime with a strong focus on the conservation of whales reflected in the Whaling Convention Schedule, which introduced a moratorium on commercial whaling from 1986.[21] The Whaling Convention has also recognised a 'Southern Ocean Sanctuary' where no commercial whaling activity is to occur;[22] however, the Convention does not prohibit the killing or taking of all whales. Article VIII of the Convention permits state parties to issue special permits authorising the taking and killing of whales for scientific purposes, which is commonly referred to as 'special permit' whaling.

Notwithstanding the moratorium on commercial whaling, since 1987 there has been growing controversy over Japanese 'special permit' whaling in the Southern Ocean. At the heart of this controversy is whether Japan is conducting legitimate whaling for research only purposes, or

[18] In Australia, for example, all claims to maritime zones are made via the Seas and Submerged Lands Act 1973 (Cth) under which proclamations identify the limits of Australia's various maritime zones, including those offshore of the Australian Antarctic Territory (AAT).

[19] See, e.g., Antarctic Mining Prohibition Act 1991 (Cth); Antarctic Treaty (Environment Protection) Act 1980 (Cth) s. 19A and B, which created offences directed against mining activities in Antarctica.

[20] International Convention for the Regulation of Whaling, opened for signature 2 December 1946, 161 UNTS 72 (entered into force 10 November 1948).

[21] International Convention for the Regulation of Whaling, Schedule, para. [6].

[22] International Convention for the Regulation of Whaling, Schedule, para. [7](b).

whether in reality Japan is undertaking commercial whaling contrary to the Whaling Convention.[23] In the 1987/8 whaling season, Japan introduced the Japanese Whale Research Program under Special Permit in the Antarctic (JARPA), which was continued until 2004/5. JARPA had a principal focus upon research into minke whales in the Southern Ocean, with initially a sample size of 300 (+ or −10 per cent) being taken each season. In 2005, Japan announced the Second Phase of JARPA (JARPA II) with projected annual sample sizes being 850 minke whales, 50 humpback whales and 50 fin whales (+ or −10 per cent). Notwithstanding sustained criticism of JARPA and JARPA II from within the International Whaling Commission (IWC),[24] Japan has continued its 'special permit' whaling in the Southern Ocean in apparent defiance of the moratorium on commercial whaling and the 'Southern Ocean Sanctuary'. In response to Japan's ongoing conduct of JARPA II, on 31 May 2010 Australia commenced proceedings against Japan in the International Court of Justice, challenging the legitimacy in international law of JARPA II.[25]

In addition to the international regulation of whaling by the Whaling Convention, some states have extensive national laws regulating whaling by their nationals and within their territorial sea and EEZ. Australia has an extensive array of these laws extending not only to the waters adjacent to the Australian continent, but also to Australia's external territories including the Australian Antarctic Territory. Under the Environment Protection and Biodiversity Conservation Act 1999 (Cth) (EPBC Act), all whaling activity is prohibited within the declared Australian Whale Sanctuary, which is conterminous with the Australian EEZ and applies within the waters of the Southern Ocean 200 nautical miles offshore of the Australian Antarctic Territory,[26] thereby encompassing parts of the Southern Ocean where Japan regularly conducts its whaling activities. Notwithstanding these provisions, Japan has ignored Australian law and

[23] Reuben Ackerman, 'Japanese Whaling in the Pacific Ocean: Defiance of International Whaling Norms in the Name of "Scientific Research", Culture and Tradition' (2002) 25 *Boston College International and Comparative Law Review* 323; Tanya Wansbrough, 'On the Issue of Scientific Whaling: Does the Majority Rule?' (2004) 13 *Review of European and International Environmental Law* 333.

[24] See, e.g., International Whaling Commission, Resolution 2007–1, 59th Annual Meeting, Anchorage, Alaska, 2007.

[25] International Court of Justice Application Instituting Proceedings, *Dispute Concerning Japan's JARPA II Program of 'Scientific Whaling' (Australia* v. *Japan)* (31 May 2010).

[26] See Environment Protection and Biodiversity Conservation Act 1999 (Cth) (EPBC Act) s. 225.

been regularly conducting whaling activities within the Australian Whale Sanctuary; however, the Australian government has been reluctant to enforce Australian law against the Japanese whalers.

In 2004 a non-governmental organisation, Humane Society International, commenced proceedings before the Federal Court of Australia asserting that the activities of the Japanese whalers were contrary to the EPBC Act.[27] In a series of proceedings before the Federal Court from 2004 to 2008,[28] declaratory and injunctive relief was sought concerning whaling alleged to have been carried out by Kyodo Senpaku Kaisha, a corporation holding a licence from the Japanese government to conduct 'special permit' whaling in the Australian Whale Sanctuary offshore of the Australian Antarctic Territory. In the initial 2004 hearing, Allsop J exhaustively reviewed the applicable international legal regime dealing with Antarctica and whaling, and also the relevant provisions of the EPBC Act. Allsop J was concerned about a potential conflict between the Act and the Whaling Convention, which:

> may be seen to conform with a conclusion that whatever the rights in public international law that Japan enjoys under Article VIII of the Whaling Convention, the content of the relevant municipal law can be seen to be such as to prohibit the killing of whales for any purpose within Australian territory, including the Antarctic EEZ.[29]

In light of the international dimensions of the matter, the judge ensured that the Commonwealth Attorney-General be served with the relevant documents and given an opportunity to consider the matter.[30]

Subsequently, in 2005, submissions to the Federal Court were filed by the Commonwealth Attorney-General,[31] where the following points were made:

- only four other states recognised Australia's claim to Antarctica, those being Norway, France, New Zealand and the United Kingdom;
- Japan did not recognise Australia's claim to the Australian Antarctic Territory or the assertion of its adjacent EEZ;

[27] Humane Society International was considered to have standing to bring proceedings seeking an injunction under the EPBC Act, s. 475(7): *Humane Society International Inc.* v. *Kyodo Senpaku Kaisha Ltd* (2008) 165 FCR 510, [4].

[28] Commencing with *Humane Society International Inc.* v. *Kyodo Senpaku Kaisha Ltd* (2004) 212 ALR 551.

[29] Ibid. [62]. [30] Ibid. [75]–[76].

[31] *Humane Society International Inc.* v. *Kyodo Senpaku Kaisha Ltd* (2004) 212 ALR 551 [NSD 1519 of 2004] Federal Court of Australia, 'Outline of Submissions of the Attorney-General of the Commonwealth as Amicus Curiae'.

- Japan would consider any attempt to enforce Australian law against Japanese vessels to be in breach of international law;
- enforcement of Australian law against Japanese vessels could 'reasonably be expected to prompt a significant adverse reaction from other Antarctic Treaty parties'; and
- Japan had indicated that enforcement of Australian law against Japanese vessels would be likely to give rise to an international disagreement with Japan.

The Attorney-General asked that the court take these matters into account when making its decision in the matter.

In due course when Allsop J reconvened the court, the judge was of the opinion that the views of the Executive Government in this matter were relevant,[32] and that in exercising a discretion as to whether leave should be granted to issue service out of the jurisdiction it was appropriate to take into account the matters raised by the Commonwealth Attorney-General.[33] Allsop J concluded that:

> Japan will view service or any attempt at service in Japan of process of this Court seeking orders under the EPBC Act as the attempted enforcement of rights that it does not recognise and as an interference with rights, under international law, of its nationals to ply the high seas and conduct themselves conformably with Japan's rights under international law, in particular by acting conformably with the Whaling Convention. ... I can also conclude that Japan would take the view that an attempt to invoke the exercise of federal jurisdiction under the EPBC Act was itself contrary to international law and that the claim by this Court to the exercise of jurisdiction was based on an impermissible claim by Australia under international law to the Antarctic Territory.[34]

Principally upon these grounds, Allsop J did not grant leave to serve the originating process on the respondent in Japan. However, when the matter went to appeal in 2006, the Full Court of the Federal Court took a different view and dismissed the 'political considerations' in determining whether leave should have been granted.[35] Accordingly,

[32] *Humane Society International Inc.* v. *Kyodo Senpaku Kaisha Ltd* [2005] FCA 664 (27 May 2005), [24].

[33] Ibid. [27]. [34] Ibid.

[35] *Humane Society International Inc.* v. *Kyodo Senpaku Kaisha Ltd* (2006) 154 FCR 425 (Black CJ and Finkelstein J).

Humane Society International was granted leave by the Full Court to serve the originating process upon the respondent in Japan.[36]

In January 2008, Allsop J delivered a further judgment, following orders issued for service upon the respondent in Japan in 2007. Judgment was reserved in late 2007 in order once again to give the Commonwealth Attorney-General an opportunity to express a view on the matter. The Attorney-General's response was that service by the applicant was defective and that 'Japan would view neither the proceedings nor any judgment arising from them as legitimate'.[37] Nevertheless, given the Full Court's judgment in the matter, Allsop J felt bound to accept that service in Japan was permissible. Satisfied that a 'significant number of whales were taken inside the Australian Whale Sanctuary' by the respondent,[38] Allsop J concluded that Kyodo had contravened a number of relevant provisions of the EPBC Act in relation to both minke whales and fin whales and issued orders that they be restrained from engaging in any further such acts.[39] Humane Society International arranged for the Federal Court's judgment to be served upon Kyodo in Japan in late January 2008.[40] This did not deter the Japanese whalers, however, from continuing their activities within the Australian Whale Sanctuary, and they completed their 2007/8 season and returned again in 2009/10.[41]

These events highlight an environmental discourse over the protection of the marine environment, and in particular whales that, despite the moratorium on commercial whaling and Australia's efforts to conserve and protect whales within the Australian Whale Sanctuary, has been very difficult to translate into a legally enforceable regime. Therefore, and notwithstanding the Australian Federal Court's 2008 judgment against Kyodo of having engaged in activity contrary to the EPBC Act, actual enforcement of the judgment remains problematic because of a mixture of private international law arising from the fact

[36] For comment on the decision of the Full Court of the Federal Court, see Tim Stephens and Donald R. Rothwell, 'Japanese Whaling in Antarctica: *Humane Society International Inc.* v. *Kyodo Senpaku Kaisha Ltd*' (2007) 16 *Review of European Community and International Environmental Law* 243.

[37] *Humane Society International Inc.* v. *Kyodo Senpaku Kaisha Ltd*, above n. 27, [26].

[38] Ibid. [39]. [39] Ibid. [55].

[40] Peter Alford, 'Aussie Judgment Served on Whalers', *The Australian* (Sydney), 24 January 2008, 7.

[41] In the 2008/9 whaling season the Japanese whalers principally conducted their whaling operations in the Southern Ocean within the Ross Sea area adjacent to the New Zealand claimed 'Ross Dependency' sector of Antarctica.

that Kyodo has no presence within the jurisdiction of the court which can be directly made the subject of a court order,[42] but also due to the interaction of public international law and national environmental law. This is particularly so because of the limitations created for a country like Australia in the actual enforcement of its environmental law in the Southern Ocean by the Antarctic Treaty in an area where Australian sovereignty and maritime jurisdiction is not widely recognised by the international community. While there may be common goals and objectives between the international and the national legal regimes, in this instance the international legal regime placed constraints on the national legal regime, ultimately compromising the effectiveness of that regime, thereby frustrating the common discourse of environmental protection.

3. Arctic governance

The management of Arctic affairs has traditionally fallen under the purview of littoral states whose territories are washed by the Arctic Ocean or whose lands extend north of the Arctic Circle.[43] In distinction to Antarctica, with the exception of some minor disputes,[44] territory in the Arctic is not contested between the eight claimant states. Therefore the Arctic has traditionally been seen as within the sovereign domain of each of the territorial states, meaning that also unlike the Antarctic, there has been less incentive for the Arctic states to work together at a bilateral or regional level to address common issues. With the exception of a ground-breaking 1973 agreement concerning conservation of polar bears,[45] there has not been any long-standing history of cooperation amongst Arctic states on environmental matters.[46] However, during the past twenty years, the Arctic states have gradually been engaged in levels of regional environmental cooperation, first through the 1991 Arctic

[42] *Humane Society International Inc.* v. *Kyodo Senpaku Kaisha Ltd*, above n. 27, [46].

[43] These states: Canada, Denmark, Finland, Iceland, Norway, Russia, Sweden and the United States and in the past two decades they have often been referred to as the 'Arctic Eight'.

[44] Canada and Denmark have an ongoing dispute over Hans Island, located in Davis Strait: Christopher Stevenson, 'Hans Off! The Struggle for Hans Island and the Potential Ramifications for International Border Dispute Resolution' (2007) 30 *Boston College International and Comparative Law Review* 263.

[45] Agreement on the Conservation of Polar Bears, opened for signature 15 November 1973 (1974) 13 ILM 13 (entered into force 26 May 1976).

[46] See Donald R. Rothwell, 'International Law and the Protection of the Arctic Environment' (1995) 44 *International and Comparative Law Quarterly* 280.

Environmental Protection Strategy,[47] and since 1996 through the Arctic Council.[48] Nevertheless, these initiatives at regional environmental governance in the Arctic remain tentative and the dominant environmental discourse occurring in the region remains at the national level where it is often characterised by the need for governments in the 'south' to adopt appropriate laws for the 'north'.[49]

3.1 Arctic legal regime

As the Arctic states had their sovereign rights over Arctic lands progressively confirmed throughout the early part of the twentieth century,[50] the way was cleared for development to take place across parts of the Arctic. Post the Second World War, and despite the fact that the United States and the then USSR effectively 'faced off' against each other in the Bering Strait, mineral and industrial development occurred across parts of the Arctic, especially in Alaska and Siberia. The development of these parts of the Arctic was subject entirely to the laws of the relevant states. When some offshore development activities commenced in the 1960s resulting in significant oil and gas exploration in areas such as the Beaufort Sea in the 1970s, they were once again subject to national environmental law.

During this period developments in the law of the sea did not have immediate Arctic implications, due to the impossibility of surface navigation in the central Arctic Ocean,[51] though there was an awareness of the potential for sea routes to be developed along the Canadian coastline via the Northwest Passage and along the Soviet/Russian coastline via the Northeast Passage.[52] Nevertheless, the Law of the Sea Convention was

[47] Arctic Environmental Protection Strategy, concluded 14 June 1991, 30 ILM 1624.

[48] Timo Koivurova, 'Limits and Possibilities of the Arctic Council in a Rapidly Changing Scene of Arctic Governance' (2010) 46 *Polar Record* 146.

[49] This is especially the case for the three largest Arctic States: Canada, Russia and the United States.

[50] Through decisions such as that by the Permanent Court of International Justice in *Legal Status of Eastern Greenland (Denmark* v. *Norway)*, Judgment, PCIJ Reports, Series A/B, No. 53.

[51] This is to be distinguished from submarine navigation of the Arctic, which was actively undertaken by the UK, United States and then USSR during the Cold War: see W. Harriet Critchley, 'Polar Deployment of Soviet Submarines' (1984) 39 *International Journal* 828.

[52] Also referred to as the 'Northern Sea Route', which more accurately reflects a shipping route substantially within USSR/Russian Federation waters: Leonid Tymchenko, 'The Northern Sea Route: Russian Management and Jurisdiction over Navigation in Arctic Seas' in Oude Elferink and Rothwell (eds.), above n. 15, 269.

not a catalyst for enhanced Arctic cooperation and it was not until the Arctic Environmental Protection Strategy in 1991 that the Arctic states began to genuinely engage in a discourse about the state of the Arctic environment and the merits of regional cooperation to tackle common problems.[53] A major institutional breakthrough in the Arctic regime came with the creation of the Arctic Council in 1996, which over the past decade has evolved to have much greater oversight for the ongoing monitoring and implementation of the Arctic Environmental Protection Strategy.[54]

There has been a strong institutional resistance to giving the Arctic Council a legal foundation, and accordingly it has remained what can best be described as a 'soft law regime'.[55] The future of the Arctic Council and its ability to represent with one voice the views of Arctic states was cast into doubt by the May 2008 independent gathering of only five of the eight Council members to discuss Arctic Ocean issues.[56] The resulting Ilulissat Declaration stressed the 'sovereignty, sovereign rights and jurisdiction in large areas of the Arctic Ocean' of the five participating Arctic states.[57] To an extent this summed up the Arctic legal regime as based on the sovereign rights of the littoral states founded upon the legitimacy of their territorial claims and the law of the sea providing a capacity to assert claims to the adjacent maritime areas, including the continental shelf.

3.2 Contemporary Arctic issues

A number of contemporary Arctic environmental issues have significant legal implications influencing Arctic environmental discourses centring around environmental regulatory control and responsibility. The first is the rising tension associated with outer continental shelf claims. Whilst such claims are a legitimate part of the contemporary oceans governance regime, the challenge they create for the Arctic is that they will inevitably

[53] Donald R. Rothwell, 'The Arctic Environmental Protection Strategy and International Environmental Cooperation in the Far North' (1995) 6 *Yearbook of International Environmental Law* 65.

[54] See Timo Koivurova and David VanderZwaag, 'The Arctic Council at 10 Years: Retrospect and Prospects' (2007) 40 *University of British Columbia Law Review* 121.

[55] Erika Lennon, 'A Tale of Two Poles: A Comparative Look at the Legal Regimes in the Arctic and the Antarctic' (2008) 8(3) *Sustainable Development Law & Policy* 32, 33.

[56] Iceland, Finland and Sweden were presumably not invited on the basis that they do not have a significant interest in the Arctic Ocean.

[57] Ilulissat Declaration, Arctic Ocean Conference, 27–29 May 2008, Ilulissat, Greenland.

converge in the central Arctic Ocean, resulting in the need for resolution of additional maritime boundaries to settle overlapping claims. This will result in the need to delimit maritime boundaries across the Arctic Ocean, and given the resource potential of the region, this may prove contentious. The second factor at play is the melting of the Arctic sea ice. In recent years the effect of the melt has been dramatic, with significant tracts of open water appearing in parts of the Arctic Ocean and a shifting ice pattern becoming discernible.[58] The impact of retreating ice will have considerable environmental implications for Arctic fauna and flora, especially for iconic species such as the polar bear, which in May 2008 was listed as threatened by the US Department of the Interior.[59] A third and related factor is climate change, which is becoming evident not only in the retreating ice, but also in the thawing of permafrost. This will radically change the landscape for Arctic flora and fauna. In turn, there is the potential for impact on the lifestyles and culture of the indigenous peoples of the north.[60] A final factor is that melting of the ice also has resource access implications. Previously inaccessible areas of the Arctic Ocean will potentially become accessible for various forms of resource exploitation ranging from the non-living resources of the seabed, to fish stocks and other living resources of the water column. A July 2008 report of the US Geological Survey estimated that 90 billion barrels of undiscovered but technically recoverable oil existed to the north of the Arctic Circle.[61] Reports such as this further concentrate attention on the resource capacity of the region. With increased resource exploitation, there is clearly the potential for enhanced risk of environmental impact,[62] and associated demands for greater foreign access by states which may not previously have expressed an interest in the Arctic. This

[58] William Snape III, 'Overview: Radical Environmental Change in the Polar Regions Is the Globe's Wake-Up Call' (2008) 8(3) *Sustainable Development Law & Policy* 2, 2.

[59] Voice of America, 'Polar Bear Added to List of Threatened Species in US', *VOANews.com*, 16 May 2008, at www.voanews.com/english/news/science-technology/a-13–2008–05–16-voa27.html, last accessed 17 January 2011.

[60] See, e.g., Australian Broadcasting Corporation, 'Record Heat Forces Closure of Canada Arctic Park', *ABC News* at www.abc.net.au/news/stories/2008/08/02/2322340.htm, last accessed 2 August 2008, discussing the closure of the Auyuittuq National Park, on Baffin Island in Canada's north, due to melting permafrost.

[61] Q. Wong, 'Study Estimates Vast Supplies of Arctic Oil and Gas', *Anchorage Daily News*, 24 July 2008, A6.

[62] 'Climate Change Raises Spill Risks in Oil-Rich Arctic', *Calgary Herald*, 26 July 2008, E5.

may especially be the case with respect to Arctic fisheries.[63] Enhanced accessibility to the Arctic Ocean will also raise issues of increased navigational interest by members of the international community eager to gain access to new shipping routes between the North Pacific and North Atlantic via an ice-free Arctic Ocean.

3.3 *Northwest Passage dispute*

To date, the response of the Arctic legal regime to existing environmental issues and those increasingly looming on the horizon has been founded upon national environmental law. This is highlighted by Canada's efforts at Arctic marine environmental protection within its so-called 'Arctic waters'. The Northwest Passage is a series of interconnected straits falling between continental North America and the Canadian islands comprising the 'Arctic Archipelago'. The Passage provides access between the Beaufort Sea in the west to Davis Strait in the east, where vessels can gain access to the North Atlantic. Notwithstanding the waters of the Northwest Passage fall on either side of Canadian territory, the status of navigation through the Passage has been the subject of ongoing dispute between Canada and the United States ever since the 1969 voyage of the SS *Manhattan*. This voyage provoked considerable controversy in Canada; seen as an attempt by the United States to challenge Canadian sovereignty in the Arctic, notwithstanding that there was never any suggestion that the United States was seeking to assert any form of claim to Canadian Arctic territory.

In response to the *Manhattan* voyage, the Government of Canada adopted the Arctic Waters Pollution Prevention Act,[64] placing significant environmental controls upon shipping passing through waters within 100 nautical miles of the Canadian Arctic. The effect of this was that all navigation through the Northwest Passage became subject to the Act, whether the waters of the Passage were internal waters of Canada, Canadian territorial sea, or parts of the adjacent high seas. The intent of the legislation was to recognise the environmental vulnerability and significance of Canadian Arctic waters and to reassert Canadian jurisdiction over the waters of the Canadian Arctic. In addition, and realising the potential weakness of its position in the international law of the sea

[63] Michael Distefano, 'Managing Arctic Fish Stocks' (2008) 8(3) *Sustainable Development Law & Policy* 13.
[64] Arctic Waters Pollution Prevention Act, SC (1970), c. 47.

(which at that time did not recognise the capacity of states to exercise any comprehensive environmental jurisdiction in waters beyond the limits of the territorial sea) Canada also varied its position with respect to the jurisdiction of the International Court of Justice so that the United States could not commence proceedings before the court on this issue.

Canada's national environmental law initiative proved to be a success, and ongoing commercial navigation through the Northwest Passage by oil-carrying supertankers was halted. In addition, Canada was able to successfully argue during the Third United Nations Conference on the Law of the Sea that there was a need for a more proactive position to be taken on the environmental protection of ice-covered waters. With the support of the then USSR, Canada was able to promote the adoption of Article 234 in the Law of the Sea Convention recognising the rights of coastal states to adopt and enforce non-discriminatory laws for the prevention, reduction and control of marine pollution within the limits of an EEZ where there are 'particularly severe climatic conditions and the presence of ice covering such areas for much of the year'. Recognition in international law of the need to enhance environmental protection for ice-covered areas effectively endorsed the Canadian position which it had adopted via the Arctic Waters Pollution Prevention Act, providing a foundation in international law for the Canadian national law response.

In 1985 Canada was confronted with another apparent challenge by the United States to its Arctic sovereignty when the US Coast Guard vessel *Polar Star* sought to navigate the Northwest Passage without prior permission. Canada responded by declaring a series of straight baselines around the outer limits of the islands comprising the Canadian Arctic Archipelago so that any future navigation of the waters would be within Canada's internal waters as recognised by international law and accordingly fall exclusively within Canadian jurisdiction.[65] On this occasion, Canada principally responded by using international legal principles to reaffirm its national jurisdiction over the Northwest Passage. However, its actions in 1985 can be characterised as seeking to confirm Canadian sovereignty rather than an assertion of new environmental jurisdiction. Nevertheless, once Canadian sovereignty had been firmly asserted over

[65] The significance of Canada's initiatives has been to convert waters that may at one time have been a part of the territorial sea or EEZ, within which certain navigational rights existed for foreign ships, into waters over which Canada has complete sovereignty and the capacity to regulate all shipping – including the right to deny entry to foreign vessels: see Donat Pharad, *Canada's Arctic Waters in International Law* (Cambridge University Press, 1988).

the Northwest Passage, this provided the basis for clearer assertion of Canadian environmental jurisdiction over all maritime activities within the Passage, impacting upon navigation by both Canadian-flagged and foreign-flagged vessels.[66] The effect of these Canadian initiatives is that there is now no doubt in international law that the waters of the Northwest Passage are Canadian, in the sense of being a part of either Canadian internal waters, the territorial sea, or the EEZ. Canada's sovereign rights and jurisdiction over these waters is very clearly articulated by the operation of Canadian environmental law and the Arctic Waters Pollution Prevention Act, subject only to possible rights of innocent passage that may rest with foreign flagged vessels, but which must still be undertaken in conformity with Canadian law.

4. Polar environmental discourses

A review of polar environmental discourses reveals both an existing vertical discourse and emerging horizontal discourse. The vertical discourse is the more familiar one in the polar regions that has been taking place since the 1950s with the initial adoption of the Antarctic Treaty. That discourse was initially dominated by science and the value of Antarctica to international scientific discovery and was reflected in how the treaty perpetuated the freedom of scientific research that was founded in the International Geophysical Year. However, over time the Antarctic discourse has also become an environmental one, and this is reflected in the developments taking place within the Antarctic Treaty System, where the regime has been shaped by global, regional and national environmental discourses about the need for enhanced environmental protection and management of especially fragile ecosystems. The 1991 Madrid Protocol with its prohibition on mining in Antarctica is a clear illustration of the changing discourse.

The Antarctic environmental discourse has, however, also been influenced by sovereignty where the treaty sought to address the issue in 1959, with implications over fifty years later. Sovereignty sensitivity remains in Antarctica, highlighted by some of the responses to the

[66] Between 1985 and 2009 there have been a total of five transits of the Northwest Passage by US Coast Guard icebreakers, but these have not been contentious, as they have been conducted consistently with the 1988 Agreement on Arctic Cooperation between Canada and the US, concluded 11 January 1988 [1988] Canadian Treaty Series 29; see discussion in Ted McDorman, *Salt Water Neighbours* (Oxford University Press, New York, 2009) 248–51.

assertion of outer continental shelf claims. Australia's submission of data to the Commission on the Limits of the Continental Shelf regarding its outer continental shelf offshore of the Australian Antarctic Territory provoked a sharp response in 2005 from some of the treaty parties.[67] Likewise, Britain's 2009 claims before the Commission on the Limits of the Continental Shelf provoked a similar controversy with Chile and Argentina.[68] Sovereignty, and how it may be exercised, therefore remains a traditional area of Antarctic controversy, highlighting a tension between regional governance under an international law framework, and sovereign states still seeking to retain their public law rights. The Australian Whale Sanctuary offshore of the Australian Antarctic Territory highlights some of the tensions occurring within some environmental discourses. Notwithstanding the Australian objective of seeking to adopt measures for the protection and conservation of whales, aligned with the global initiatives being pursued within the IWC, Australia has been reluctant to actively enforce its national environmental laws against the Japanese whalers because of the constraints created by the Antarctic Treaty and the need not to compromise Australia's claim to Antarctic sovereignty.

In the case of the Arctic, the environmental discourse has a different dynamic, because sovereignty has a much firmer foundation and the regional legal regime is much weaker. This has allowed 'space' for national law to play a more dominant role in the environmental discourse about regulatory control and responsibility. It has also provided opportunities for individual states to take bold environmental initiatives not likely possible if they were working within a regional legal framework. Canada's actions to regulate and control navigation through its Arctic waters, and especially the Northwest Passage, highlight the capacity of national environmental law when it is not subject to certain international legal constraints. The Arctic Waters Pollution Prevention Act was an innovative legal response at a time when marine environmental

[67] Six states – Germany, India, Japan, Netherlands, Russian Federation and the United States – all parties to the Antarctic Treaty, made it clear that in their view Article IV of the treaty placed constraints on the capacity of treaty parties to assert rights or claims over the seabed offshore of Antarctica. See, e.g., Germany, Permanent Mission of Germany communication to the United Nations, Note No. 88/2005 (5 April 2005) at www.un.org/Depts/los/clcs_new/submissions_files/aus04/clcs_03_2004_los_deu.pdf, last accessed 4 January 2007.

[68] 'Chile and Argentina Unite Against UK Claim', *The Independent* (London), 8 March 2009, 36.

measures were principally focused on ship-sourced pollution and little attention was given to regulating the environment in areas beyond the limits of the territorial sea. This initiative allowed Canada to more actively assert its Arctic sovereignty, and ultimately Canada's position was strengthened by the reliance upon national environmental law, but it also subsequently had an effect on the Law of the Sea Convention and provided a further legal basis for initiatives which both Russia and the United States could undertake in their Arctic waters.

A further aspect of the polar environmental discourse is the horizontal discourse between the polar legal regimes. In 2009, during fiftieth anniversary celebrations of the Antarctic Treaty in Washington, US Secretary of State Hillary Clinton addressed the first joint meeting of Antarctic Treaty parties and the Arctic Council.[69] While only ceremonial in nature, this may signal the commencement of an ongoing polar environmental discourse of polar cooperation. After all, notwithstanding some significant differences between the two polar legal regimes, they face a number of very common challenges in coming decades, especially as they confront issues of sovereignty, environmental protection and climate change.

5. Concluding remarks

The polar regions have been considered distinctive in modern international law because of the unique legal issues arising within areas dominated by ice. To that end there has been much debate as to whether the poles appropriately are a part of the common heritage and can be equated with outer space, the deep seabed and the high seas.[70] Global governance of the polar regions has attracted considerable attention, and the 1959 Antarctic Treaty is a clear outcome of that project. However, Kirsch and Kingsbury argue that 'much of global governance can be understood as regulation and administration, and that we are witnessing the emergence of "global administrative space"'.[71] This represents not

[69] 'Secretary of State Clinton Speaks on Joint Session of the Antarctic Treaty Consultative Meeting, The Arctic Council, 50th Anniversary of the Antarctic Treaty', *US Fed. News*, 11 April 2009.

[70] See Jonathan Charney, *The New Nationalism and the Use of Common Spaces* (Allenheld, Osmun, Totawa, 1982); Philip C. Jessup and Howard Taubenfeld, *Controls for Outer Space and the Antarctic Analogy* (Columbia University Press, New York, 1959).

[71] Nico Krisch and Benedict Kingsbury, 'Introduction: Global Governance and Global Administrative Law in the International Legal Order' (2006) 17 *European Journal of International Law* 1, 1.

only a critique of the international legal system, but also a warning about accountability of the system which is increasingly seen as having a 'democratic deficit'.[72] What these brief studies of the polar regions demonstrate is that there will always remain a need for a discourse to occur between and sometimes within legal systems. Notwithstanding the attractions of global governance in areas like the polar regions, there remains a clear role for national law. As Dryzek has observed, '[h]uman action takes place within the context that discourses provide: discourses themselves both enable and constrain actions'.[73] This is reflected in the constraints and opportunities arising in the relationship between international and national law in the polar regions. Neither, however, is supreme, and accordingly environmental discourses, especially around science, environmental protection, regulatory control, responsibility and cooperation need to be ongoing and capable of discursive changes in uncertain times if appropriate environmental protection and management outcomes are to be achieved for Antarctica and the Arctic.

[72] Stephan observes: 'But in important if sometimes subtle ways, international bodies have supplanted national law with international rules and standards': Paul Stephan, 'The New International Law – Legitimacy, Accountability, Authority, and Freedom in the New Global Order' (1999) 70 *University of Colorado Law Review* 1555, 1557.

[73] Dryzek, above n. 6, 105–6.

16

Heritage discourses

BEN BOER AND STEFAN GRUBER

1. Introduction

Heritage encompasses a wide variety of ideas and concepts. While many people feel very strongly about heritage, their views about the meaning of the term vary widely. The concept is fluid, as it is continuously shaped by social, political and ideological developments at international and national levels, as well as differing interests and varying beliefs.[1] On the other hand, the way societies and individuals express, evaluate and celebrate heritage heavily influences the way they construct their own identity.[2] Therefore, heritage is not only a fluid concept, but also a very active one, which makes it an engaging subject for discourse analysis. Different concepts of 'heritage' reflect shared ways of apprehending the world.[3] These conceptions are based on assumptions and judgments that provide the basis for any discussion, analysis, agreement and disagreement.[4]

This chapter explores a variety of discourses in heritage protection. It starts by explaining and exploring the multiple ways of characterising and classifying heritage. Within public and international law, selected forms of heritage are protected in mostly consistent, though at times culturally distinct, ways. The chapter emphasises the influence of international law as providing a universal protection regime for widely accepted forms of heritage that has generally been incorporated into public laws of nations or has acted as an overarching influence which has been gradually

[1] Ben Boer and Graeme Wiffen, *Heritage Law in Australia* (Oxford University Press, Melbourne, 2006) 7, 8.

[2] Denis Byrne, Helen Brayshaw and Tracy Ireland, *Social Significance: A Discussion Paper* (NSW National Parks and Wildlife Service, Sydney, 2nd edn, 2003) 58.

[3] John Dryzek, *The Politics of the Earth: Environmental Discourses* (Oxford University Press, 2nd edn, 2005) 9.

[4] Ibid.

adopted by initially reluctant nations. It also highlights how other forms or interpretations of 'heritage' at a national level are perceived and protected, often mimicking the international regime, while not necessarily being protected under it.

Presenting the different categories and understandings of 'heritage' underscores the term's dynamism. Heritage does not mean just one thing, and it is not used consistently in language and argument. Heritage concepts change over time and this evolution is reflected in policies and legal instruments at an international and domestic level. The chapter shows how 'heritage' is used as a discourse in a variety of contexts relying on environmental theories to promote conservation of places, communities and cultures. While this continuing flux of heritage discourses can be confusing, it is often a richly rewarding interplay between what is regarded as of value and worth legally protecting, and what can be left to one side in the continuous march of seemingly inevitable 'development'.

2. Cultural and natural heritage

Generally, heritage is divided between cultural and natural heritage. Both cultural and natural heritage can be further divided into tangible or intangible. Tangible cultural heritage encompasses ancient buildings, monuments, archaeological sites and movable items. However, in many cases, cultural and natural heritage are closely linked. Many heritage sites are shaped by their surroundings and reflect the capacity, as well as the fundamental need of humans, to adapt to the environment. Other sites or items were inspired by, or incorporate materials derived from, the local natural environment.[5] In international law, the connection between cultural and natural heritage is reflected in the framework of the Convention Concerning the Protection of the World Cultural and Natural Heritage[6] of 1972 ('World Heritage Convention').[7] The convention defines both cultural and natural heritage and the World Heritage Committee generally treats them equally. However, an increasing number of sites are recognised as mixed cultural and natural heritage sites.

[5] Roger-Alexandre Lefèvre, *The Materials of Cultural Heritage in their Environment* (Edipuglia, Bari, 2006).

[6] Convention Concerning the Protection of the World Cultural and Natural Heritage, opened for signature 16 November 1972, 1037 UNTS 151 (entered into force 17 December 1975) ('World Heritage Convention').

[7] See further, Francesco Francioni and Federico Lenzerini, *The 1972 World Heritage Convention: A Commentary* (Oxford University Press, 2008).

The basis for this is the last leg of the definition of cultural heritage in Article 1 of the convention, which refers to the 'combined works of nature and man':

> sites: works of man or the combined works of nature and man, and areas including archaeological sites which are of outstanding universal value from the historical, aesthetic, ethnological or anthropological point of view.

Since 1992, the *Operational Guidelines for the Implementation of the World Heritage Convention*[8] ('Operational Guidelines') have specifically recognised the possibility of inscribing 'cultural landscapes' which are 'illustrative of the evolution of human society and settlement over time, under the influence of the physical constraints or opportunities presented by their natural environment and of successive social, economic and cultural forces, both external and internal'. The *Operational Guidelines* recognise landscapes designed and created intentionally by people, organically evolved landscapes, and associative cultural landscapes for inscription on the World Heritage List. Associative cultural landscapes are 'justifiable by virtue of the powerful religious, artistic or cultural associations of the natural element rather than material cultural evidence, which may be insignificant or even absent'.[9] This example shows that it is often difficult, if not impossible, to distinguish cultural and natural heritage sites. Further, these items are now recognised as having intangible elements as well, and social values and cultural components are seen to play an important role in the protection of natural heritage.[10]

Inhabited sites are particularly vulnerable to the blurring of these distinctions, as some will have clearly identifiable material evidence of human interactions, whereas others may manifest quite minimal evidence of such interactions, as recognised in the various categories of

[8] World Heritage Committee, *Operational Guidelines for the Implementation of the World Heritage Convention*, UNESCO Doc. WHC. 08/01 (January 2008) ('*Operational Guidelines*').

[9] Definitions of the individual categories of cultural landscapes can be found in *Operational Guidelines*, Annex 3, [10].

[10] See Thomas Schaaf and Mechtild Rössler, 'Sacred Natural Sites, Cultural Landscapes and UNESCO's Action' in Bas Verschuuren *et al.* (eds.), *Sacred Natural Sites Conserving Nature and Culture* (Earthscan, London, 2010) 161; Erika J. Techera, 'Synergies and Challenges for Legal Protection of Sacred Natural Sites in the South Pacific' in ibid. 170; Susan McIntyre-Tamwoy, 'Social Value, the Cultural Component in Natural Resource Management' (2004) 11 *Australasian Journal of Environmental Management* 289.

cultural landscapes.[11] These developments are particularly important within discourses on heritage, as they manifest a marked expansion of what is considered valuable, which in turn reflects a shift in the discourse over how people conceive of their relationship to the natural and cultural environment in general and what components of human surroundings ought be conserved. Our identity and memory is often connected to locations, which makes the landscapes we live in – both rural and urban[12] – so important to our heritage.[13] The shift to recognising cultural landscapes particularly illustrates the changing attitudes towards the heritage of indigenous people and local communities whose economies and identities are geographically and ecologically specific.

Placing a value on cultural landscapes, whether within the realm of the World Heritage Convention or beyond it, can add strength to the claims of indigenous and local communities to a continued right to occupy their traditional lands, notwithstanding pressures from governments and development interests to move them away and to exploit those lands for mining and extraction purposes. Once properties are inscribed on international heritage lists for their value to local communities, national attempts, including through the passage of public laws, to decrease or even destroy such sites, can attract a much stronger international response and political pressure, which might contribute to discouraging unjustifiable interference from development interests.

One example of the development of the concept of cultural landscapes is found in Uluṟu-Kata Tjuṯa National Park in Australia. The area was originally inscribed on the World Heritage List in 1987 as a natural site, but was renominated as a mixed site in 1994, recognising its cultural landscape value,[14] and the occupation by the Aṉangu, the traditional owners of the land. The area is of great importance in the belief system of the Aṉangu, who have lived in the area for tens of thousands of

[11] *Operational Guidelines*, Annex 3, [10].

[12] See Dolores Hayden, *The Power of Place: Urban Landscapes as Public History* (MIT Press, Cambridge, Mass., 1995).

[13] See, e.g., several case studies from Ireland, England, Scotland and the United States in Niamh Moore and Yvonne Whelan (eds.), *Heritage, Memory and the Politics of Identity* (Ashgate, Aldershot, 2007).

[14] For relevant decisions by the World Heritage Committee and the evaluations of the site by IUCN in 1987 and ICOMOS in 1994 respectively, see World Heritage Centre, *Uluṟu-Kata Tjuṯa National Park* http://whc.unesco.org/en/list/447/documents/, last accessed 18 April 2011.

years.[15] While they did not transform the landscape in any major way (except by fire regimes), rock art and other significant elements remain in evidence.[16] The area was identified under the World Heritage Convention as an associative cultural landscape as one of the most sacred sites to Australia's Aborigines.[17]

Links between cultural and natural heritage are not limited to cultural landscapes. For example, Maffi and Woodley argue that the conservation of cultural diversity and biodiversity are two sides of the same coin.[18] Conserving the knowledge, thinking and practices for survival and adaptation to their environment that local communities have accumulated throughout the ages adds to our civilisation's resilience to new environmental challenges.[19]

3. Tangible and intangible heritage

The division of heritage into tangible and intangible heritage is, from a legal point of view, relatively recent. According to Blake, it was initiated by 'a growing awareness of the need to employ a broader and more "anthropological" notion of cultural heritage that encompasses intangibles associated with material culture'. In the 1990s this idea was accompanied by a greater understanding of the relationship between culture and development at the international level.[20] Tangible cultural heritage consists of heritage sites and movable heritage, the latter often referred to as heritage objects or cultural objects.[21] While tangible heritage is more obviously identified as representative of a nation's

[15] See further, Commonwealth of Australia, Department of Environment, Water, Heritage and the Arts, *Uluru-Kata Tjuta National Park* www.environment.gov.au/parks/uluru/, last accessed 18 April 2011.

[16] See, e.g., Josephine Flood, *Archaeology of the Dreamtime: The Story of Prehistoric Australia and its People* (Collins, Sydney, 1989); Sarah Colley, *Uncovering Australia: Archaeology, Indigenous People and the Public* (Allen & Unwin, Sydney, 2002).

[17] See generally Robert Layton and Sarah Titchen, 'Uluru: An Outstanding Australian Aboriginal Cultural Landscape' in Bernd von Droste, Harald Plachter and Mechtild Rössler (eds.), *Cultural Landscapes of Universal Value: Components of a Global Strategy* (Gustav Fischer Verlag, Jena, 1995) 174.

[18] Luisa Maffi and Ellen Woodley, *Biocultural Diversity Conservation: A Global Sourcebook* (Earthscan, London, 2010).

[19] Ibid.

[20] Janet Blake, *Commentary on the 2003 UNESCO Convention on the Safeguarding of the Intangible Cultural Heritage* (Institute of Art and Law, Leicester, 2006) 8.

[21] See Ana Filipa Vrdoljak, *International Law: Museums and the Return of Cultural Objects* (Cambridge University Press, 2006).

heritage and cultural identity, intangible heritage is at least equally important. By its nature, it is impossible for intangible heritage, *by itself*, to be included in a list of properties, to be displayed in museums, or to be offered for sale on the art market, although generally it is closely associated with the tangible heritage. Intangible heritage for these reasons may be wrongly perceived as less valuable than tangible heritage, except in association with items of the tangible heritage. However, its importance to the cultural identity of societies and any culturally distinct groups, and the way they are recognised by others, should not be underestimated. Intangible heritage can in fact be seen as crucial to a nation's or other community's cultural identity. Only by maintaining an active cultural interaction is it generally possible to sustain the distinct cultural features of groups, communities and societies.

The international legal framework reinforces these ideas. The 2003 Convention for the Safeguarding of the Intangible Cultural Heritage[22] ('Intangible Cultural Heritage Convention') defines intangible heritage as:

> practices, representations, expressions, knowledge, skills – as well as the instruments, objects, artefacts and cultural spaces associated therewith – that communities, groups and, in some cases, individuals recognize as part of their cultural heritage. This intangible cultural heritage, transmitted from generation to generation, is constantly recreated by communities and groups in response to their environment, their interaction with nature and their history, and provides them with a sense of identity and continuity, thus promoting respect for cultural diversity and human creativity.[23]

The Intangible Cultural Heritage Convention also stresses the connection between people and their environment, and in particular their interaction with nature. Humans, potentially through discourses about heritage, can delineate intangible cultural heritage. The convention recognises that the environment has a significant influence on human culture and that humans must be seen as part of the environment. Many cultural differences between societies reflect the ecological influences of different natural environments. Further, the intangible natural heritage is coming to be perceived as a significant concept capable of legal protection.[24]

[22] Convention on the Safeguarding of the Intangible Heritage, opened for signature 3 November 2003, 2368 UNTS 1 (entered into force 20 April 2006) ('Intangible Cultural Heritage Convention').

[23] Intangible Cultural Heritage Convention, Art. 2(1).

[24] See Techera, above n. 10.

In a similar way to cultural and natural heritage, the distinctions between tangible and intangible heritage should not be drawn too strictly. The Intangible Cultural Heritage Convention recognises the 'deep-seated interdependence between the intangible cultural heritage and the tangible cultural and natural heritage'.[25] Some World Heritage sites, such as the Nazi concentration and death camp Auschwitz-Birkenau in Poland and the Hiroshima Peace Memorial, have been inscribed on the World Heritage List solely for their intangible heritage values, reminding humankind of some of the worst atrocities in human history.[26] Tangible heritage cannot be simply reduced to its material, financial or exchange value. Its true value flows from its meaning to people. Bouchenaki argues that 'symbols, technologies and objects are tangible evidence of underlying norms and values. Thus they establish a symbiotic relationship between the tangible and the intangible. The intangible heritage should be regarded as the larger framework within which tangible heritage takes on shape and significance.'[27] They are equally important to the collective memory of societies and the survival of traditions and cultural identities. Further, both tangible and intangible heritage contribute to the development and conservation of each other.

While questions of ownership of tangible heritage might be easy to answer in many cases, this issue is much more complex with respect to intangible heritage. In particular, the relationship between intangible cultural heritage and intellectual property needs also to be considered.[28] To what extent can groups and communities claim ownership of the value in the intellectual property associated with their intangible heritage? At this stage, the international instruments on intellectual property and associated documents do not give much guidance. That is a significant gap in international law needing attention in order to provide appropriate protection to such intangible heritage.

25 Intangible Cultural Heritage Convention, Preamble.

26 See Olwen Beazley and Harriet Deacon, 'Safeguarding Intangible Heritage under the World Heritage Convention: Auschwitz, Hiroshima and Robben Island' in Janet Blake (ed.), *Safeguarding Intangible Cultural Heritage: Challenges and Approaches* (Institute of Art and Law, Builth Wells, 2007) 93.

27 Mounir Bouchenaki, 'The Interdependency of the Tangible and Intangible Cultural Heritage' (keynote address delivered at the ICOMOS 14th General Assembly and Scientific Symposium, Victoria Falls, 2003).

28 An overview of many related issues can be found at Toshiyuki Kono (ed.), *Intangible Cultural Heritage and Intellectual Property: Communities, Cultural Diversity and Sustainable Development* (Intersentia, Antwerp, 2009).

4. Cultural heritage and identity

Culture is one of the binding forces within societies. It is one of the elements that most clearly distinguish communities from each other at international, national and local levels.[29] Without their cultural identity recognised, kept intact, and mutually respected, culturally or ethnically distinct groups generally cannot easily survive as constituent parts of diverse human communities. It can even be argued that the survival of some nations is dependent on the conservation of their culture.[30] Cultural heritage can be seen as a synchronised relationship involving society, norms and values.[31] In many cases, the denial of cultural differences, or even suppression of the cultural identities of communities, has led to political instability, open hostilities and armed conflict.[32] While it might be possible for the state and groups to suppress specific cultural expressions of people for periods of time, the underlying repressed culture will eventually re-emerge and, in some cases regenerate in a stronger form than before the suppression.[33] Distinct cultural communities are often also the most vocal among discourse coalitions arguing for heritage conservation.[34]

[29] Laurajane Smith (ed.), *Cultural Heritage: Critical Concepts in Media and Cultural Studies* (Routledge, London, 2007) Vol. II, Part 4.

[30] See, e.g., Thubten Tsering, 'The Status of Tibetan Language' in Karubaki Datta (ed.), *Essays on Tibetan Cultural Heritage* (Serials Publications, New Delhi, 2008) 80.

[31] Bouchenaki, above n. 27.

[32] For example, the unrest in Tibet in 2008 was triggered by the detention of protesting monks who were calling for an end of religious restrictions and the release of imprisoned monks. What started as peaceful protests soon turned into violent events, with harsh countermeasures by the Chinese authorities. See 'Monks on the March', *The Economist* (London), 15 March 2008; Human Rights Watch, 'China, India, Nepal: Free Tibetan Protesters' (News Release, 14 March 2008) http://china.hrw.org/press/news_release/china_india_nepal_free_tibetan_protesters, last accessed 18 April 2011.

[33] For instance, while in the former Soviet Union any form of religious life was suppressed, the traditions survived underground. Nowadays, religion – especially Islam in many former Soviet countries – emerged in a significant way, partly as a form of political protest. See Vitaly Naumkin, 'Islam in the States of the Former USSR' (1992) 524 *Annals of the American Academy of Political and Social Science* 131.

[34] For example, the Inuit Peoples of the North American Arctic in their pursuit of the United States of America over climate change impacts on the melting of the Arctic. In 2005, a petition was filed with the Inter-American Commission on Human Rights on behalf of all Inuit of the Arctic Regions of the United States and Canada, entitled *Petition to the Inter-American Commission on Human Rights Seeking Relief from Violations Resulting from Global Warming Caused by Acts and Omissions of the United States* at www.ciel.org/Publications/ICC_Petition_7Dec05.pdf, last accessed 18 April 2011.

Cultural identity, no matter how current and contemporary it might appear, inevitably flows from the past, sometimes from the distant past. The natural and cultural inheritance is at once the basis and the key to that identity. It influences to a great extent who we are and how our future development as a society is determined. Our cultural heritage is a direct link to our forebears, as well as to the current members of the communities of which we are part.[35] It influences the way we see the world and often has a bearing on how we make our decisions. Cultural heritage is recognised by the international human rights regime, even though its protection largely depends on nationally based public laws ensuring the continuation of cultural practices (for instance, through land rights regimes), the protection of the human right to culture and the prohibition of discrimination of those people who belong to a distinct cultural group.

5. Differing perceptions of heritage

While there may be a general understanding about the meaning of heritage, there is often a level of disagreement regarding its form in specific cases. One of the main challenges is thus to explore the meanings of heritage. Defining a place, a practice or an object as part of the heritage can play a significant role in determining what we decide to conserve. It is obvious that this can be a highly political task, as individuals and communities can be quite divided on what is worthy of conservation and what is less important. It is in large part this division of views that promotes and sustains discourses about heritage. Coalitions will vary, depending on differing cultural and political backgrounds, religious beliefs, age, gender, nationality, ethnicity and family history, among other characteristics. There are many examples of destruction of heritage in order to rewrite history, downplay events, humiliate others, or create political advantage. Deciding what is heritage and what is not is often in itself the exercise of political power. It includes the power to influence how our past and present will be evaluated in the future. Having said that, opinions on heritage might change over the course of time. Some

[35] For example, in Nepal multicultural groups are identified by their tangible and intangible heritage. Apart from being identified as the inhabitants of different regions, those groups also identify themselves by their caste, ethnic groups and religions. See Tulasi Diwasa, Chura Mani Bandhu and Bhim Nepal, *The Intangible Cultural Heritage of Nepal: Future Directions* (UNESCO, Kathmandu, 2007) 7.

things that we do not consider heritage today might be seen as culturally valuable and thus heritage items in the future.

For example, in Australia, indigenous culture and language had long been regarded in some quarters as primitive and as a hindrance to the possibility of Aboriginal and Torres Strait Islander children leading a meaningful life. That policy environment led to the infamous era of the Stolen Generations,[36] when Aboriginal children around Australia and children from the Torres Strait Islands were taken from their families by force and given to non-Aboriginal foster families and 'welfare' institutions to raise.[37] The thinking of non-Aboriginal people regarding Aborigines and their culture has shifted dramatically since those days. Today, Aboriginal culture is generally regarded as inseparably bound up with the broader Australian heritage and is unashamedly used to market the country as a tourist destination. Meanwhile, in 2008 the Australian government acknowledged the mistakes of its forerunners and extended a formal apology to the Aboriginal communities and families affected.[38]

Another example is the Great Proletarian Cultural Revolution in China,[39] a country where the political system and ways of thinking have always been very much influenced by traditions and customs. However, in an attempt to eliminate political rivals and to keep total control of the Communist Party of China, Chairman Mao Zedong initiated a movement over the whole country to remove suspected bourgeois elements. That resulted not only in the deaths of hundreds of thousands of people,[40] but also in the nearly complete cessation of traditional cultural practices and ways of living. Universities and schools were closed, academics and teachers were sent to the fields, countless artefacts and reminders of China's cultural past were destroyed, with over 6,000 monasteries demolished in Tibet alone, and many traditional Chinese customs suffered significantly.[41] That dark era was one of the world's greatest human disasters both in general and for cultural heritage in particular; the damage done is almost inestimable.

[36] Approximately 1869–1969.

[37] See further Commonwealth of Australia, Human Rights and Equal Opportunity Commission, *Bringing Them Home: Report of the National Inquiry into the Separation of Aboriginal and Torres Strait Islander Children from their Families* (1997).

[38] Kevin Rudd, 'Formal Apology to the Stolen Generations' (speech delivered to the Parliament of Australia, Parliament House, Canberra, 12 February 2008).

[39] The Cultural Revolution lasted from 1966 to 1976.

[40] Roderick MacFarquhar and Michael Schoenhals, *Mao's Last Revolution* (Harvard University Press, Cambridge, Mass., 2006) 262.

[41] Ibid. 258.

In 1981, the Central Committee of the Communist Party of China condemned the Cultural Revolution as a grave mistake that brought serious harm to the Chinese people and the Communist Party.[42] The attitude towards China's cultural heritage has changed dramatically since then[43] and the importance of its protection has been underlined in all recent Five Year Plans.[44]

Decisions about what to conserve and legally protect as heritage are often bound up with issues of cultural identity, which are inherently political and the subject of continuously changing discourses about what is of value at a particular time, and what can be ignored or discarded. In that sense, national developments are also influenced significantly by international concepts of heritage which espouse a different approach.

Heritage law discourses can thus operate in two-way mode: international heritage law can influence domestic law and policy, while legal principles and mechanisms developed at the domestic level can influence international heritage law. Heritage conventions – as with all international treaties – are negotiated by individual states, and there is always a significant transfer from domestic concepts of heritage and culture.[45] Several factors may operate here, including the religious background of a country, its political and legal system, whether it has a significant indigenous population or whether it is a source country or a major destination in the case of illegally acquired artefacts.

The domestic approach to cultural heritage also influences whether countries become parties to heritage conventions. For example, the 2001 Convention on the Protection of the Underwater Cultural Heritage has been ratified by very few countries (thirty-seven, as of early 2011),[46] but nevertheless has met its minimum number of signatories to enter into force in 2009. Among the several reasons for this are conflicting interests and the

[42] The 11th Central Committee of the Communist Party of China, *Resolution on Certain Questions in the History of our Party Since the Founding of the People's Republic of China* (6th Plenary Session, 27 June 1981).

[43] See further Stefan Gruber, 'Protecting China's Cultural Heritage Sites in Times of Rapid Change: Current Developments, Practice and Law' (2007) 10 *Asia Pacific Journal of Environmental Law* 253.

[44] See, e.g., the 16th Central Committee of the Communist Party of China, *The Outline of the Eleventh Five-Year Plan for National Economic and Social Development of the People's Republic of China* (5th Plenary Session, 11 October 2005), Chapter 12.

[45] See, e.g., the drafting process of the Intangible Cultural Heritage Convention as described in Blake, above n. 20.

[46] Convention on the Protection of the Underwater Cultural Heritage, opened for signature 2 November 2001, 41 ILM 40 (entered into force 2 January 2009).

financial resources available to countries. While some countries do not wish to give up their rights to salvage shipwrecks, other states do not have the resources or technical skills to protect the underwater cultural heritage in their waters. From a heritage point of view, post-colonial countries do not always regard the protection of shipwrecks of the former colonial powers as a priority.[47]

6. Positive and negative heritage

Most endeavours to conserve heritage have focused almost entirely on accentuating the positive aspects, conserving the beautiful and masterful creations that reflect centuries of human genius, and the beauty of natural and cultural landscapes.[48] Increasingly, however, places that represent a painful period in global history are being considered as heritage items, often characterised as 'negative' heritage. In discussing negative heritage, heritage discourses become even more complex. It is not just a matter of whether this type of heritage is conserved, but also how to deal with it in terms of the politics of presentation. The rationale behind remembering, conserving or even consciously forgetting painful or shameful heritage is very different from dealing with 'positive' heritage.

For example, during the Communist rule in Poland, Auschwitz was used mainly as a nationalist memorial, symbolising the aggression from the fascist West and Polish martyrdom during the Second World War. Initially it was a concentration camp for Polish political prisoners, but became a camp for the extermination of Jewish people in 1942. However, the suffering of the Jewish people was hardly mentioned in the onsite exhibitions and educational material in the 1970s and 1980s.[49] While the international Jewish community was rightfully upset, things changed significantly after the end of Communist rule. Nowadays, Auschwitz is regarded by the general public as a symbol for the sufferings of the Jewish people, at least internationally.[50] Gilbert reports of a non-Jewish Polish

[47] See, e.g., Lyndel Prott (ed.), *Finishing the Interrupted Voyage: Papers of the UNESCO Asia-Pacific Workshop on the Protection of the Underwater Cultural Heritage* (Institute of Art and Law, Builth Wells, 2006).

[48] See William Logan and Keir Reeves (eds.), *Places of Pain and Shame: Dealing with 'Difficult Heritage'* (Routledge, London, 2009).

[49] Katie Young, 'Auschwitz-Birkenau: The Challenges of Heritage Management Following the Cold War' in ibid., 50.

[50] Martin Gilbert, *Holocaust Journey: Travelling in Search of the Past* (Columbia University Press, New York, 1998) 140.

Auschwitz survivor who reflected '25 years ago they were the centre of attention, but today . . . only an addendum'.[51] It is difficult to find the right approach (if there is one) when dealing with such places of horror and sadness.

Things are even more complicated when dealing with heritage feared to be used to reinterpret the past. For example, controlling history as a victorious nation after a war is a powerful political tool, which societies will not give up easily. Atrocities committed by the defeated party will always be emphasised, while the victorious side does its best to make its actions appear as justified as possible. How this affects dealing with heritage on an international scale became evident during the nomination and inscription of the Hiroshima Peace Memorial on the World Heritage List in 1996.[52] The site commemorates the first use of an atomic bomb as a weapon and consists of the only building left standing near the hypocentre of the explosion. Some 140,000 people died as a direct consequence of that tragic event, and countless others were maimed for life. What was meant as a reminder of the destructive power of the most deadly weapon humankind has ever invented and as a symbol for the hope for peace and ultimate elimination of nuclear weapons, triggered strong responses from the United States and China. China justified its reservations to the World Heritage inscription by stressing that 'during the Second World War, it was the other Asian countries and peoples who suffered the greatest loss in life and property. But today there are still [a] few people trying to deny this fact of history. As such, if Hiroshima's nomination is approved to be included on the World Heritage List, even though on an exceptional basis, it may be utilized for harmful purpose[s] by these few people.'[53] The United States, insisting that killing civilians in this manner was a legitimate action to hasten the capitulation of Japan, was openly concerned that the World Heritage inscription would question their interpretation of history: "The United States is concerned about the lack of historical perspective in the nomination of Genbaku Dome. The events antecedent to the United States' use of atomic weapons to end the Second World War are key to understanding the tragedy of Hiroshima. Any examination of the period

[51] Ibid.

[52] Yushi Utaka, 'The Hiroshima "Peace Memorial"' in Logan and Reeves (eds.), above n. 48, 34.

[53] World Heritage Committee, *Report, World Heritage Committee, Twentieth Session, Merida, Yucatan, Mexico – 2–7 December 1996*, UNESCO Doc. WHC-96/CONF.201/21 (10 March 1997), Annex V.

leading up to 1945 should be placed in the appropriate historical context.'[54] As with every example of negative heritage, the main problems arise from the way heritage is commemorated and conserved. Unlike the case of positive heritage, debate and discursive frames over negative heritage mainly revolve around perspectives and historical and political contexts.

7. Heritage as a human right

As the heritage forms part of the identity of every human being, all people have the right to the conservation of their cultural identity and their heritage in its many manifestations. Taking away or abusing the heritage violates the right to human dignity and freedom. This is recognised by Article 22 of the 1948 Universal Declaration of Human Rights,[55] which states that:

> Everyone, as a member of society, has the right to social security and is entitled to realization, through national effort and international cooperation and in accordance with the organization and resources of each State, of the economic, social and cultural rights indispensable for his dignity and the free development of his personality.

Also of importance in that regard, especially to intangible cultural heritage, is the Convention on the Protection and Promotion of the Diversity of Cultural Expressions of 2005.[56] Its preamble stresses the right of people to their own heritage and its protection:

> . . . Celebrating the importance of cultural diversity for the full realization of human rights and fundamental freedoms proclaimed in the Universal Declaration of Human Rights and other universally recognized instruments . . .

Similarly, Article 15 of the International Covenant on Economic, Social and Cultural Rights of 1966[57] explicitly mentions the duty of states to recognise the right to take part in cultural life, while Article 27 of the

[54] Ibid.

[55] Universal Declaration of Human Rights, GA Res. 217A (III), UN GAOR, 3rd sess., 183 plen. mtg, UN Doc. A/810 (10 December 1948).

[56] Convention on the Protection and Promotion of the Diversity of Cultural Expressions, opened for signature 20 October 2005, 2440 UNTS 311 (entered into force 18 March 2007).

[57] International Covenant on Economic, Social and Cultural Rights, opened for signature 19 December 1966, 993 UNTS 3 (entered into force 3 January 1976).

International Covenant on Civil and Political Rights of 1966[58] underlines the right of ethnic, religious or linguistic minorities 'to enjoy their own culture, to profess and practise their own religion, or to use their own language' in community with the other members of their group. Those rules oblige states to provide adequate protection for cultural groups to protect all property and intangible heritage that they require for their existence as culturally distinct communities.[59]

This human rights regime has been employed to advocate for heritage conservation on the basis of upholding human rights. This was evident in the aftermath of the destruction of the Buddha statues of Bamiyan in Afghanistan by the Taliban in 2001, in an attempt to erase any evidence of pre-Islamic culture in the country. In a resolution, the Thirteenth General Assembly of States Parties to the World Heritage Convention condemned the destruction as a 'crime against the common heritage of humanity'.[60] The notion of heritage destruction amounting to human rights infringements was adopted by the United Nations Educational, Social and Cultural Organization (UNESCO) in its *Declaration concerning the Intentional Destruction of Cultural Heritage* of 2003[61] in response to the Taliban actions. The Preamble to that declaration especially underlined the connection between cultural identity and human rights and linked them to human dignity, stating that:

> Mindful that cultural heritage is an important component of the cultural identity of communities, groups and individuals, and of social cohesion,

[58] International Covenant on Civil and Political Rights, opened for signature 19 December 1966, 999 UNTS 171 (entered into force 23 March 1976).

[59] Francesco Francioni, 'Culture, Heritage and Human Rights: An Introduction' in Francesco Francioni and Martin Scheinin (eds.), *Cultural Human Rights* (Martinus Nijhoff Publishers, Leiden and Boston, 2008) 1, 9.

[60] UNESCO, *Summary Record of the Thirteenth General Assembly of States Parties to the Convention Concerning the Protection of the World Cultural and Natural Heritage (UNESCO Headquarters, Paris, 30–31 October 2001)*, UNESCO Doc. WHC-2001/CONF.206/8 Rev. (29 July 2003), Annex 3 ('*Resolution on the Protection of the Cultural Heritage of Afghanistan, adopted by the General Assembly of States Parties to the World Heritage Convention at its Thirteenth Session (Paris, 30–31 October 2001*'). See further, UNESCO, *Records of the General Conference, 31st Session, Paris, 15 October to 3 November 2001, Vol 1: Resolutions*, UNESCO Doc. 31C/Resolutions (2002, adopted 2 November 2001) Resolution 26 ('*Acts Constituting a Crime against the Common Heritage of Humanity*').

[61] UNESCO, *Records of the General Conference, 32nd Session, Paris, 29 September to 17 October 2003, Vol 1: Resolutions*, UNESCO Doc. 32C/Resolutions (2004, adopted 17 October 2003), Resolution 33 ('*Declaration Concerning the Intentional Destruction of Cultural Heritage*').

> so that its intentional destruction may have adverse consequences on human dignity and human rights.

Intentional destruction of cultural heritage must be judged as an offence against all humankind, as it violates the dignity of those whose heritage it is, as well as those *identifying* with it for cultural or religious reasons. As heritage forms part of the cultural identity of people, its intentional destruction is clearly contrary to the basic foundations of human rights law and is a further important aspect of the way international legal principles impact on culture and heritage.

The right of people to interact with and conserve their heritage in accordance with their traditions, and the concept of heritage being a good for all humankind, may sometimes lead to dispute. For example, it has been a tradition of many of Australia's Aboriginal people to repaint fading rock paintings under the supervision of Aboriginal elders in order to preserve them as a part of their ancient responsibilities and thus maintain their community's cultural life.[62] However, such activities sometimes meet significant opposition from non-Aboriginal people. The repainting of a presumed 3,000-year-old site in the Kimberley region in 1987 attracted a good deal of protest, as some people regarded it as the destruction of a significant archaeological site.[63] In fact, only the youngest layer of that ancient rock painting was still visible when it was repainted. That dispute raises several central questions on cultural heritage conservation. Who really 'owns' such Aboriginal cultural 'property'? Must the sites be conserved in their original state for the public good or is it preferable to maintain them in a recognisable state for the benefit of the cultural (right holding) groups? Should cultural groups have a right to protect and manage their heritage? How do we weigh up the importance of conserving archaeological sites with the active continuation of that living culture?[64]

8. Heritage threatened by development

Heritage is threatened in a wide variety of ways in contemporary times. Threats include pressure of modern residential and industrial development obliterating heritage sites, the process of gentrification and

[62] See Josephine Flood, *Rock Art of the Dreamtime* (Angus & Robertson, Sydney, 1997) 298–300.

[63] See Sandra Bowdler, 'Repainting Australian Rock Art' (1988) 62 *Antiquity* 517.

[64] Ibid.

the disappearance of the centres of ancient cities, urbanisation causing the loss of rural cultural landscapes and cohesion of rural communities, the pillaging of heritage sites, illicit art trafficking and both anthropogenic and natural influences, such as sea-level rise and desertification. Inhabited heritage sites are often especially threatened, as they are susceptible to the impacts of poverty, social transformations, conflicts between various interested parties and development proposals that may destroy or significantly alter the values of a site.[65] The World Heritage Convention recognises those kinds of threats by 'noting that the cultural heritage and the natural heritage are increasingly threatened with destruction not only by the traditional causes of decay, but also by changing social and economic conditions which aggravate the situation with even more formidable phenomena of damage or destruction'.[66]

Protection of heritage is often employed to halt development or change socio-cultural patterns. Moreover, arguments are made not just with respect to tangible heritage, but also intangible heritage that is perceived as threatened, especially by changing social norms and laws. For instance, the displacement of local populations due to economic pressure or other social impacts often not only leads to the loss of inhabited heritage sites, but also to a loss of local traditions and both cultural and ecological knowledge. For example, the self-image and cultural influence of nations is closely linked to the importance and uniqueness of the nation's language and writing system.[67] If the use of a language in both its written and spoken form is made illegal, or discouraged either directly by displacement of communities through emigration, infrastructure development or colonisation, the cultural heritage expressed by that language is, over time, lost to those communities and, except for archival storage, to the world. This is as true

[65] See, e.g., the Dresden Elbe Valley, which was delisted as a World Heritage Site in 2009 after the construction of a four-lane bridge across the river valley destroyed the outstanding universal value of the site (World Heritage Committee, *Final Decisions of the 33rd Session of the World Heritage Committee (Seville, 2009)*, UNESCO Doc. WHC-09/33.COM/20 (Seville, 20 July 2009), Decision 33COM 7A.26). See also the World Heritage Site of Kathmandu Valley, where several monuments were threatened by new construction in their immediate vicinity. When the Nepalese authorities did not manage to respond to that threat effectively, the site was inscribed on the List of World Heritage in Danger in 2003 (World Heritage Committee, *Decisions Adopted by the 27th Session of the World Heritage Committee in 2003*, UNESCO Doc. WHC-03/27.COM/24 (Paris, 10 December 2003), Decision 27COM 7B.52).

[66] World Heritage Convention, Preamble; see also Art. 11(4).

[67] Tsering, above n. 30.

for Australian indigenous communities[68] as it is for any other community or ethnic group around the world that is subjected to such forces.

Thus, the loss of tangible heritage also fuels the loss of intangible heritage; this link is recognised in the Preamble to the Intangible Cultural Heritage Convention:[69]

> . . . the processes of globalization and social transformation, alongside the conditions they create for renewed dialogue among communities, also give rise, as does the phenomenon of intolerance, to grave threats of deterioration, disappearance and destruction of the intangible cultural heritage, in particular owing to a lack of resources for safeguarding such heritage.

Examples of the impact of social transformations include the World Heritage cultural landscape of the Rice Terraces of the Philippine Cordilleras which date back between 2,000 to 6,000 years. As many local farmers can no longer see a future on the land for themselves, many are leaving the area to find other employment. The lack of maintenance of the rice terraces has caused severe deterioration, resulting in the site being inscribed on the List of World Heritage in Danger in 2001.[70] Similar developments can be witnessed at many other cultural landscapes around the world.[71] Other examples include the ongoing destruction of the hutongs in Beijing.[72] These narrow, heavily populated laneways with ancient houses and courtyards, of which there were several thousand fifty years ago, are seen as important buffer zones for the nearby World Heritage sites, including the Forbidden City.[73] In

[68] In the context of demographic processes and language in Aboriginal Australia, see Peter Sutton, 'The Pulsating Heart: Large Scale Cultural and Demographic Processes in Aboriginal Australia' in Betty Meehan and Neville White (eds.), *Hunter-Gatherer Demography: Past and Present* (University of Sydney Press, 1990) 71.

[69] Intangible Cultural Heritage Convention, Preamble.

[70] See further World Heritage Committee, *Report of the 25th Session of the World Heritage Committee (Helsinki, Finland, 11–16 December 2001)*, UNESCO Doc. WHC-01/CONF.208/24 (Paris, 8 February 2002) VIII.111–120, Decision 25COM X.3; Save the Ifugao Terraces Movement, *IMPACT: The Effects of Tourism on Culture and the Environment in Asia and the Pacific: Sustainable Tourism and the Preservation of the World Heritage Site of the Ifugao Rice Terraces, Philippines* (UNESCO Bangkok, 2008).

[71] See UNESCO World Heritage Centre, *Cultural Landscapes: The Challenges of Conservation* (UNESCO World Heritage Centre, Paris, 2003).

[72] See further, Gruber, above n. 43, 279–81.

[73] World Heritage Committee, *Decisions Adopted by the 27th Session of the World Heritage Committee in 2003*, above n. 65, Decision 27COM 7B.43; World Heritage Committee, *State of Conservation of Properties Inscribed on the World Heritage List*, UNESCO Doc. WHC-04/28.COM/15B (Paris, 15 June 2004), Report 54; World Heritage Committee, *Decisions Adopted at*

recent years, many of the original inhabitants have been evicted by force and the housing in the hutongs is either being torn down to make room for development projects or upgraded for wealthier people. Over the centuries, a unique social life developed in the hutongs, which are regarded as the 'heart of Beijing'. With the eviction of the original inhabitants, whose families have sometimes lived in the same location for hundreds of years, the whole area is losing its soul, people are losing their social networks and a unique way of living is disappearing.

However, pressure from development affects not only urban areas, but also rural and forest communities. Indigenous communities are often the most vulnerable to those threats. For example, the Penan people of Sarawak in Malaysia have inhabited rainforest areas and led a fully sustainable way of life in co-existence with their natural environment for generations. These rainforest areas have clearly become part of the Penan culture, which the outside world now also recognises. However, their homelands are increasingly threatened by commercial logging and dam projects, forcing many of them to leave. Although the land has not been substantially altered by them, it is a cultural landscape because of the way it has been used by indigenous people in a unique and irreplaceable way of life. Thus, destroying their home areas also obliterates the very existence of the Penan as an indigenous community, as they are being forced to live in towns and villages, which are essentially alien environments for them.[74]

9. Heritage under threat from climate change

A dramatic example of international issues impacting on the domestic heritage is climate change, which poses significant threats to all kinds of heritage. The expected and already-observed impacts of climate change will result in increases of extreme weather events, changes in precipitation in many regions, increasing ground instability in permafrost regions, rock avalanches in mountainous regions, changes in ecosystems and enlargement and increased numbers of glacial lakes.[75] Those meteorological changes will not only severely affect Earth's biodiversity

the 28th Session of the World Heritage Committee (Suzhou, 2004), UNESCO Doc. WHC-04/28 COM/26 (Paris, 29 October 2004), Decisions 28COM 14B.30, 28COM 15B.54.

74 See Sahabat Alam Malaysia (ed.), *The Battle for Sarawak's Forests* (World Rainforest Movement/Sahabat Alam Malaysia, Penang, 2nd edn, 1990).

75 Intergovernmental Panel on Climate Change, *Climate Change 2007. Synthesis Report, Summary for Policy-Makers* (IPCC, Geneva, 2007) 30 ff.

and landscapes, they will also have an enormous impact on many aspects of cultural heritage.[76]

Some of the worst climate threats to heritage are increasing desertification and other types of land degradation in many regions, the rise of water levels and extreme weather events. These environmental influences can affect built structures, for example either by sandstorms or floods, or by the faster decay of still-buried relics. People whose forebears have lived there for centuries have abandoned some settlements because of the effects of climate change.

Responding to arguments about heritage being threatened by climate change effects, the World Heritage Committee recently expressed its awareness of those threats[77] and commissioned comprehensive and representative case studies on the dangers that climate change poses not only to natural, but also to cultural World Heritage sites. Examples include the increased effects of the El Niño weather phenomenon on the Chan Chan Archaeological Zone in Peru, which is one of the largest and most important pre-Hispanic earthen-architecture cities in the Americas. At the Chavin Archaeological Site, also in Peru, catastrophic avalanches caused by melting glacier headwalls have wreaked havoc on both the structures and the people. In Canada, we see the effects of catastrophic landslides, the deterioration of permafrost and drastic reduction of sea ice on Ivvavik/Vuntut/Herschel Island on the Canadian World Heritage Tentative List. In the United Kingdom, the potential flooding of London's World Heritage sites caused by sea-level rise and increasing storm surges is evident. In Italy, the increasing frequency of floods in Venice is wreaking even more destruction on the fragile fabric of the city's historic buildings. In the West African nation of Mali, damage to World Heritage sites in Timbuktu has been caused by desertification and heavy rainfall.[78]

[76] See further Stefan Gruber, 'The Impact of Climate Change on Cultural Heritage Sites: Environmental Law and Adaptation' (2011) 2 *Carbon & Climate Law Review* 209.

[77] World Heritage Committee, *Decisions of the 29th Session of the World Heritage Committee (Durban, 2005)*, UNESCO Doc. WHC-05/29.COM/22 (Paris, 9 September 2005), Decision 29COM 7B.a. Specifically on the World Heritage Convention and climate change, see Erica Thompson, 'The World Heritage Convention and Climate Change: The Case for a Climate-Change Mitigation Strategy Beyond the Kyoto Protocol' in William Burns and Hari Osofsky (eds.), *Adjudicating Climate Change* (Cambridge University Press, 2009) 255.

[78] UNESCO World Heritage Centre, *Case Studies on Climate Change and World Heritage* (UNESCO World Heritage Centre, Paris, 2007).

Not only tangible, but also intangible heritage is threatened by climate change, when people are forced to leave their home regions and to adapt their ways of living. One of the most dramatic cases (which is likely to become more common) is that of the Carteret Islanders, who have become the world's first widely identified climate refugees.[79] The Carteret Islands are part of Papua New Guinea and located 120 kilometres northeast of Bougainville. A culturally unique Halia-speaking community of some 2,500 people have inhabited them. The very existence of the Carteret Islanders as a community is now threatened by climate change. Because of a maximum elevation of only 1.2 metres of the islands, the rising sea level and an increased number of tidal waves and storm surges are washing away gardens and homes and polluting fresh water supplies, making the islands uninhabitable. Despite fighting storm surges and rising seas for over twenty years by building sea walls and planting mangroves, the islands will soon be lost forever to human habitation. Since 2007, the Carteret Islanders have been evacuated steadily to Bougainville. The resettlement and land allocation is being carried out with the assistance of the Catholic Church, a local government organisation and through family connections on Bougainville. The migration will have a devastating impact on the lives of the Carteret Islanders, as they will have to adapt to a different livelihood and living conditions. The islanders themselves identify the maintenance of their cultural identity as their top priority, and some insist in any case that they will continue to fish their traditional reefs, even though all other aspects of their way of living as islanders will soon no longer exist.[80]

Heritage is not only threatened by rising sea levels, but also by rising temperatures. The Inuit of northern Canada, who traditionally live by hunting polar bears, seals, caribou and whales, are a case in point. As the sea ice appears later in the year and starts melting earlier, the habitat areas of several Arctic species are shrinking dramatically. Because of that shortened cycle, the Inuit can no longer go hunting as often as in earlier times. Sea ice that used to be strong enough to carry people in the winter now more frequently breaks and hunters sometimes fall through

[79] See further, Stefan Gruber, 'Human Displacement and Climate Change in the Asia Pacific Region' (2011) 12(1) *Harvard Asia Pacific Review* (forthcoming); Eric Kwa, 'Climate Change and Indigenous People in the South Pacific: The Need for Regional and Local Strategies' in Ben Richardson *et al.* (eds.), *Climate Law and Developing Countries: Legal and Policy Challenges for the World Economy* (Edward Elgar, Cheltenham, 2009) 102.

[80] Taloi Havini, 'An Uncertain Future' (2008) (September to November) *Explore* 14.

the ice with their dog sleds and drown. Whole villages could collapse into the ocean. To make up for the shortened hunting season, the Inuit are in need of infrastructure such as freezers to keep the meat of their prey fresh until they can go hunting again. Their traditional means of living is highly threatened and parts of Inuit culture are consequently similarly threatened.[81]

10. Heritage as intergenerational justice

Intergenerational justice is a central tenet of heritage discourse. This concept is used in the international law framework to recognise the rights of future peoples to the values and collective memories expressed in objects, ruins, rituals and musical performances, and is another way of expressing the principle of intergenerational equity, as part of a package of concepts which coalesce under the broad principle of sustainable development.[82] In the context of heritage, it obliges the present generation not to exploit their cultural and natural heritage in a way that compromises the ability of future generations to benefit from, treasure and enjoy it.[83] As today's decisions inevitably affect what will be left for future generations, we must recognise the implications of our decisions regarding heritage, as their negative effects will often be permanent, while the benefits of retention of the heritage remain in the collective psyche of groups, communities and nations for generations.

In whatever way we decide each case of heritage protection, the rights of future generations must always be considered, in so far as it is possible to imagine their preferences. They might have very different ideas from the present generation as to what is important. The responsibility that comes with those decisions thus cannot be underestimated. Prott and O'Keefe argue, 'heritage creates a perception of something handed down; something to be cared for and cherished. These cultural manifestations have come down to us from the past; they are our legacy from our

[81] Australian Broadcasting Corporation, 'Inuits Need Cash for Freezers in Warming Arctic', *ABC News* (online), 13 December 2009 www.abc.net.au/news/stories/2009/12/13/2770156.htm, last accessed 18 April 2011.

[82] See World Commission on Environment and Development, *Our Common Future* (Oxford University Press, 1987).

[83] See Philippe Sands, *Principles of International Environmental Law* (Cambridge University Press, 2nd edn, 2003) 256; Alexandre Kiss and Dinah Shelton, *International Environmental Law* (Transnational Publishers, Ardsley, 3rd edn, 2004) 16; Stephen Turner, *A Substantive Environmental Right* (Wolters Kluwer Law & Business, Austin, 2009).

ancestors. There is today a broad acceptance of a duty to pass them on to our successors, augmented by the creations of the present.'[84] All decisions relating to cultural heritage conservation should be made in the spirit of that argument in order for the present generation to meet its obligations to the generations to come.

An important factor is the recognition of values and traditions shared by local people, which are deeply rooted in their native context.[85] Kawaguchi argues, 'whether the public wishes to pass on their cultural heritage to future generations is highly dependent on whether that cultural heritage adequately expresses the current values and memories of the society. Too often, attempts to create cultural heritage reveal themselves as mere political constructions posing as memory and history.'[86] When such values and traditions do not represent the current views and values of the public and authorities, the way they are being conserved (if at all) might paint a very 'sanitised' picture, or they receive a different meaning once they are 'wrapped in cellophane when they are removed from their local context'.[87] In the light of intergenerational justice, not only the fact that cultural heritage is passed on is important, but the way it is done also matters, as selective transmission of the heritage can alter or even obliterate its meaning.

11. Conclusion

This chapter has demonstrated that heritage is not a fixed concept; rather, it is a cultural *process*.[88] Its meaning can vary depending on what people regard as worth being conserved. Cultural and natural heritage are related in many aspects. Both are non-renewable resources; they cannot be brought back once they are gone, and this is one of the reasons why in many aspects the approaches and legal mechanisms for their protection are very similar. Not every site or object might appear as being worthy of protection to outsiders. However, both tangible and intangible heritage can be of enormous importance to local communities, whether as their traditional homes or by playing central roles

[84] Lyndel Prott and Patrick O'Keefe, "'Cultural Heritage" or "Cultural Property"?' (1992) 1 *International Journal of Cultural Property* 307, 311.

[85] Yukiya Kawaguchi, 'Covering Heritages, Erasing Locals: Passing on History to the Next Generation' in Kenji Yoshida and John Mack (eds.), *Preserving the Cultural Heritage of Africa: Crisis or Renaissance?* (James Curry/Unisa Press, Muckleneuk, 2008) 129, 137–8.

[86] Ibid. [87] Ibid.

[88] Laurajane Smith, *Uses of Heritage* (Routledge, London, 2006) 44–84.

in their belief systems and social structures. Whether, what or how heritage is protected will depend on which international and national governance bodies are persuaded by the range of heritage discursive frames that each prioritise places, things, people or cultures as most threatened and warranting protection. As this chapter has illustrated, the discourse rationale for protection varies from human rights, justice, or combating climate change. Because of this variation, heritage discourses need to be conducted in a way that allows broad participation, in recognition of the fact that heritage in many contexts is a common good and should be treated accordingly.[89]

Heritage discourses are also an important tool in the context of the concept of environmental, economic and political/cultural sustainability. It is impossible to conserve and protect absolutely everything. From time to time heritage sites will need to be destroyed to create open space for development, in the process creating 'new' pasts, and recognising that the removal of some heritage resources might not only be unavoidable, but on occasion even desirable.[90] It is for the present generation to choose what to protect and hand down to coming generations. The success of discourses to rise to dominance and influence laws at the international and public level will indeed influence what tangible and intangible heritage the current generation chooses to pass on, and what it does not.

[89] See further Federico Mayor, *Memory of the Future* (UNESCO, Paris, 1995).

[90] Cornelius Holtorf, 'Is the Past a Non-Renewable Resource?' in Robert Layton, Peter Stone and Julian Thomas (eds.), *Destruction and Conservation of Cultural Property* (Routledge, London, 2001) 286, 295.

17

Environmental principles and social change in the ocean dumping regime: a case study of the disposal of carbon dioxide into the seabed

AFSHIN AKHTARKHAVARI

1. Introduction

In international environmental law it is common to use the term 'principle' to describe a type of legal doctrine that functions differently to a 'rule'. Environmental principles, like the precautionary approach, often with origins in public law and policy settings, can appear in international instruments as an abbreviated and abstract configuration of a complex set of ideas and culture which has been developing for a period of time across jurisdictions and within institutions. Alternatively, environmental principles can be conceptualised as norms which, instead of being captured in an abbreviated form, are stated in a longer and more open-textured configuration. An example is found in Principle 25 of the 1992 United Nations Declaration on Environment and Development ('Rio Declaration'), which states that '[w]arfare is inherently destructive of sustainable development. States shall therefore respect international law providing protection for the environment in times of armed conflict and cooperate in its further development, as necessary.'[1] This principle is open to various interpretations because of the open-textured solutions that are provided to a somewhat generic case or situation. What 'respecting

[1] Rio Declaration on Environment and Development, concluded 14 June 1992, Rio de Janeiro, Brazil ('Rio Declaration'). For commentary on the Rio Declaration see, for example, David Wirth, 'The Rio Declaration on Environment and Development: Two Steps Forward and One Back, or Vice Versa' (1995) 29 *Georgia Law Review* 599; Ileana Porras, 'The Rio Declaration: A New Basis for International Cooperation' in Philippe Sands (ed.), *Greening International Law* (Earthscan, London, 1993) 20.

international law' means is open to differing interpretations; so, too, is the meaning of environmental protection and of facilitating the development of international law and sustainable development. However, despite their abstract or open-textured nature, individuals or groups of actors can draw on environmental principles to understand each other, or to contest and influence a particular approach to social change.

In the Introduction to this book, Jessup and Rubenstein use the term 'discourse', as defined by Dryzek, to refer to:

> a shared way of apprehending the world. Embedded in language, it enables those who subscribe to it to interpret bits of information and put them together into coherent stories or accounts.[2]

Defined in this way, the difference between a discourse and an environmental principle, as described above, is not particularly pronounced or obvious. A discourse and an environmental principle both focus on the reasons why, despite the individual preferences of actors, there is the potential for groups to develop a common knowledge or an understanding about a particular issue or practice. The concepts of discourse and principle both prioritise the role of participation and interaction amongst actors in understanding the discourse or principle and their relationships to the external world. As this book demonstrates, discourses and principles also aid the transfer and understandings of legal knowledge between public and international legal systems.

This chapter asserts that an environmental principle, such as the precautionary approach,[3] can steer social and legal change within a treaty regime by functioning as a discourse, in a similar way to how Jessup and Rubenstein have conceptualised it in the Introduction of this book.[4] This chapter explores how the precautionary principle has operated within the ocean dumping regime comprising the 1972 London Convention[5] and the 1996 Protocol to the London Convention ('London

[2] John Dryzek, *The Politics of the Earth: Environmental Discourses* (Oxford University Press, 1st edn, 1997), 8.

[3] For the difference between the precautionary approach and the principle, see Jacqueline Peel, 'Precaution – A Matter of Principle, Approach or Process?' (2004) 5 *Melbourne Journal of International Law* 483.

[4] See above Introduction by Brad Jessup and Kim Rubenstein.

[5] Convention on the Prevention of Marine Pollution by Dumping of Wastes and Other Matter, opened for signature 29 December 1972, 1046 UNTS 138 (entered into force 30 August 1975) ('London Convention'). The agreement is more commonly known as the 1972 London Convention.

Protocol').[6] The precautionary approach is an important principle because of its common usage and ubiquity in both public and international law and politics. However, there are a variety of views on what the precautionary principle or approach means – in policy-making and within public law systems.[7] It is argued in this chapter that as the precautionary approach gradually embedded itself within the ocean dumping regime, the nature of how states participated and interacted with each other within the regime changed. The precautionary principle changed how states were presenting 'legal opportunities' to each other and coming up with 'legal responses' to issues.[8]

Although this study is based on the ocean dumping regime, it examines more specifically how state parties to the London Convention and the London Protocol responded to requests for legalising the disposal of CO_2 into sub-seabed repositories and how public laws became the institution to approve such disposal. This case study is important because the request to legalise the disposal of CO_2 came after both the London Convention and the London Protocol had been in operation for a number of years. More importantly, largely reflecting the state of environmental policy thinking at the time of their development, the earlier London Convention, unlike the London Protocol, did not contain a reference to the precautionary approach. The large number of states that negotiated the request to legalise the placement of CO_2 into sub-seabed repositories were members of the London Convention, but not of the later London Protocol. It is therefore significant that the views of these various state actors (despite the fact that some of them were not parties to the London Protocol) in permitting the placement of CO_2 in sub-seabed repositories were being creatively shaped or socially restrained during negotiations by the discourse of precaution.

[6] Protocol to the Convention on the Prevention of Marine Pollution by Dumping of Wastes and Other Matter, opened for signature 7 November 1996, 36 ILM 1 (entered into force 24 March 2006) ('London Protocol'). The term 'ocean dumping regime' will be used to refer to the collective impact of the London Convention, London Protocol and the resolutions of the Consultative Committee to both agreements. The London Protocol, as of 31 March 2008, has thirty-four contracting parties compared to the eighty-two that have signed and ratified the London Convention.

[7] See Peel, above n. 3; Arie Trouwborst, 'The Precautionary Principle in General International Law: Combating the Babylonian Confusion' (2007) 16 *Review of European Community and International Environmental Law* 185; Arie Trouwborst, *Precautionary Rights and Duties of States* (Martinus Nijhoff, Leiden and Boston, 2006); Joakim Zander, *The Application of the Precautionary Principle in Practice: Comparative Dimensions* (Cambridge University Press, 2010).

[8] See above Introduction by Brad Jessup and Kim Rubenstein.

This chapter initially describes the ocean dumping regime and the role of the precautionary approach within it. It then assesses the way in which the regime, dependent on public law permitting processes, has dealt with the storage and disposal of CO_2 in sub-seabed repositories. The chapter concludes with an analysis of the effect the precautionary approach had on the negotiations leading to states seeking to permit the storage of CO_2 in sub-seabed repositories in accordance with national laws.

2. The ocean dumping regime

Over recent decades states and international institutions have articulated a concern within public and international laws about the effect of increased CO_2 output from inland activities on the global climate system. More recently, these concerns have extended to include the impacts of burning fossil fuels and other CO_2 activities on our oceans. Scientists have predicted that the oceans, the world's largest common resource, are threatened not only by climate change impacts (for instance by a changed climate altering currents, sea temperatures and sea levels), but also by acidification, as the oceans sequester ever greater quantities of carbon dioxide. Whereas in the past the oceans were seen instrumentally as being capable of absorbing CO_2, now they and their inhabitants are seen as threatened by climate change like the land masses and their inhabitants. The dire marine and other global consequences of high levels of CO_2 have, however, generated much interest in the possibility of storing it, not within the water body of the oceans, but in the geological formations in the sub-seabed, including in disused oil and gas reservoirs, deep saline aquifers and un-mineable coal seams. However, the sequestration of CO_2 and its storage in sub-seabed geological formations is not without risk to the integrity of the marine environment, given the possibilities of leakage which would be particularly harmful if the stored CO_2 was contaminated.

Since 2006, the storage or disposal of CO_2 in the ocean has been regulated internationally through the regime established by the London Convention and the London Protocol. The London Convention in particular has widespread support internationally, with eighty-four contracting parties who contribute about 68 per cent of the world's CO_2 tonnage.[9] It established what Birnie and Boyle have called the most successful

[9] See the official website of the International Maritime Organization, www.imo.org, last accessed 15 May 2011. World tonnage is significant because it represents the number of countries and the percentage of vessels that can potentially engage in disposing of waste at sea.

regulatory treaty of the 1970s.[10] Now that the ocean dumping regime includes the London Protocol it is 'generally regarded as one of the more successful international legal instruments, having led to an apparently significant reduction in the volume and type of waste being dumped at sea'.[11] The disposal of waste at sea, generally known as dumping, has long been an attractive option for states, particularly because the oceans are typically beyond the oversight of national public laws.[12] It is estimated that approximately 10 per cent of the pollutants entering the marine environment are the result of deliberate dumping activities undertaken by coastal states.[13] Ocean dumping is conceptually different from direct land-based and vessel-sourced marine pollution. Unlike these other forms of marine pollution, ocean dumping is an intentional or deliberate act. Because of this, ocean dumping is particularly amenable to regulation. By the late 1990s, the London Convention had helped states to value the idea of waste minimisation and not to see the oceans as having an unlimited capacity to assimilate it. Under the convention, state parties were prohibited from dumping listed wastes and were required to implement programmes to assess the need and effects of dumping wastes at sea. General permit procedures were devised to permit dumping. The London Protocol, which came into force in 2006 but has not been ratified by all the convention parties, takes a more stringent approach. It prohibits the disposal of all waste at sea with only some exceptions. In order to dispose of wastes at sea, parties to the Protocol must seek to list the specified waste materials in what is known as Annex I of the London Protocol. Only then are permits issued under their national public laws for their disposal.

In the 1990s the precautionary approach was embedded in the ocean dumping regime. States were directed first through a resolution under the London Convention, and then in the London Protocol, to take preventative measures rather than to support activities with potentially

[10] Patricia Birnie and Alan Boyle, *International Law and the Environment* (Clarendon Press, Oxford, 1st edn, 1992) 320, 330.

[11] Submission by the Netherlands, 'Future Work Programme Implementation and Review of the Long-Term Programme', to the Twenty-Fourth Consultative Meeting of Contracting Parties to the Convention on the Prevention of Marine Pollution by Dumping of Wastes and Other Matter, LC 24/14, 9 August 2002.

[12] Office for the London Dumping Convention at the International Maritime Organization, *The London Convention: The First Decade and Beyond* (International Maritime Organization, London, 1991) 44.

[13] Ibid. See also John Kindt, *Marine Pollution and the Law of the Sea* (W. S. Hein, Buffalo, 1986) 1087.

disruptive impacts on the ocean and its sub-seabed. The idea of capturing and storing CO_2 in sub-seabed repositories therefore came as a serious challenge to long-held assumptions within the ocean dumping regime. The advantages of storing CO_2 are significant, but the possibility of its leaking into the marine environment and atmosphere, and the consequent adverse marine and climate change impacts, is high.[14] Despite this, in 2006 the consultative meeting of the London Protocol and the London Convention considered a proposal by Australia (co-sponsored by France, Norway and the United Kingdom) to amend the Protocol, allowing the disposal of CO_2 into sub-seabed repositories. The proposal, which later formed the basis of the changes to the regime, was simple and general. The state parties amended Annex 1 of the London Protocol to allow the disposal into sub-seabed geological formations of streams consisting overwhelmingly of CO_2.[15]

3. The precautionary approach and the ocean disposal regime

Environmental principles did not play a direct role within the ocean dumping regime until 1991, when the consultative meeting to the London Convention adopted a resolution to apply a version of the precautionary 'approach' to the framework established by the convention.[16] The resolution required contracting parties when implementing the London Convention to be 'guided' by a 'precautionary approach to environmental protection'.[17] The use of the word 'guide' does not adequately convey the difficulties experienced by the contracting states in formally adopting the principle.

[14] See OSPAR Commission for the Protection of the Marine Environment of the North-East Atlantic, *Placement of Carbon Dioxide in Sub-Sea Geological Structures in Note by the Secretariat, Continuation of a Review of the Benefits of Carbon Dioxide Sequestration in Sub-Seabed Geological Structures and of New Information Relevant to the Protection of the Marine Environment*, Meeting of the SG Intercessional Technical Working Group on Carbon Dioxide Sequestration, 3–6 April 2006, LC/SG-Carbon Dioxide.1/INF.2, Annex, 6.

[15] Submission by Australia (co-sponsored by France, Norway and the United Kingdom), 'Carbon Dioxide Sequestration in Sub-Seabed Formations: Consideration of Proposals to Amend Annex 1 to the London Protocol', to the First Meeting of Contracting Parties to the 1996 Protocol to the Convention on the Prevention of Marine Pollution by Dumping of Wastes and Other Matter 1972, LP 1/6, 28 April 2006.

[16] *The Application of a Precautionary Approach in Environmental Protection within the Framework of the London Convention*, Res. LDC.44(14) of the Fourteenth Consultative Meeting of Contracting Parties to the Convention on the Prevention of Marine Pollution by Dumping of Wastes and Other Matter, LC 14/16, 30 December 1991, Annex 2.

[17] Ibid.

This is seen, for instance, in the text of the resolution, which makes reference to the contracting parties becoming aware 'that the quantity, diversity and complexity of chemical compounds entering the environment' make it difficult to 'determine the overall threat to the environment'.[18] The resolution also raised concerns about the need to 'limit contamination of the marine environment by wastes and other matter'.[19]

Building upon this resolution, Article 3(1) of the London Protocol was drafted to require states to apply a 'precautionary approach to environmental protection'. The Article requires states to take 'preventative measures ... when there is reason to believe that wastes or other matter introduced into the marine environment are likely to cause harm even when there is no conclusive evidence to prove a causal relation between inputs and their effects'. The drafting history of the various instruments in which the precautionary approach has been discussed confirms that this formulation was intended to be open-textured and abstract. Its open-textured nature goes beyond questions about whether the contracting parties should 'apply' or only be 'guided' by the precautionary approach. In the discussions during the consultative meeting that approved Resolution LDC.44(14) (1991), it was noted that the precautionary approach was 'a new policy based on the recognition of the failure of past approaches to environmental protection [and this failure] ... required new measures to be adopted'.[20] This statement recognises the need to move away from past practices but expresses uncertainty about what the future direction of precautionary policy measures should be.

Article 3(1) of the London Protocol, as well as Resolution LDC.44(14), specify that precaution must be taken when 'there is reason to believe' that dumping of wastes and other matter into the sea is 'likely to cause harm even when there is no conclusive evidence to prove a causal relation between inputs and their effects'.[21] Contracting parties rejected Sweden's proposals during negotiations to replace the words 'likely to cause harm' with 'may cause harm'. Sweden argued for this alternative because, in its view, the words 'may cause harm' better balance the differences between prevention and precaution.[22] The final text, however, narrows the range of measures that states can take as a precaution

[18] Ibid. [19] Ibid. [20] Ibid. [4.4]. [21] Ibid. [1]; London Protocol, Art. 3(1).

[22] Proposal by Sweden in 'List of Documents Issued in Connection with the First Meeting of the London Convention 1972 Amendment Group', London Convention 1972 Amendment Group (First Meeting), LC/AM 1/INF.2, 19–23 July 1993, 15.

to protect future generations. Measures can only be taken when a situation already presents a risk of harm. By contrast, the form of the precautionary principle adopted in Principle 15 of the Rio Declaration is less directive. Principle 15 requires that cost-effective measures to prevent environmental degradation not be postponed where there is a lack of full scientific uncertainty about environmental damage. This difference, however, does not appear to have influenced the direction taken by the contracting parties, and in fact the inter-subjective meaning of the precautionary principle developed out of practice appears to value the risk to environmental damage in a very uncertain way.

4. Injecting carbon dioxide into the sub-seabed as waste disposal

The application of the London Convention and the London Protocol to the problem of reducing the significant amounts of CO_2 emitted into the atmosphere and dissolved into the ocean is complex. This is because the regime was designed to eliminate pollution by dumping, rather than to accommodate the potential climate change 'solution' of storing captured CO_2. It was only in the context of finding a disposal site for excess waste gas mostly generated offshore that contracting parties had previously considered storing waste in offshore wells.[23] The use of the seabed for disposal or storage of waste had also been brought up in discussions relating to the disposal of high-level radioactive wastes that might not have found a safe disposal site on land.[24]

In 1992 the contracting parties to the London Convention were first made aware of the possibility of disposing of CO_2 in the deep ocean waters by injecting it into the water column itself.[25] At that stage, on advice from the Scientific Group of the London Convention, the contracting parties bypassed the issue because of 'numerous uncertainties and limitations of the scientific understanding' of the process of

[23] *Report of the Seventeenth Consultative Meeting of Contracting Parties to the Convention on the Prevention of Marine Pollution by Dumping of Wastes and Other Matter*, LC 17/14, 3–7 October 1994, [3.25].

[24] See also below Chapter 18 by Julia Mayo-Ramsay, which explores another ocean 'solution' to climate change – that of ocean fertilisation.

[25] *Report of the Fifteenth Consultative Meeting of Contracting Parties to the Convention on the Prevention of Marine Pollution by Dumping of Wastes and Other Matter*, LC 15/16, 9–13 November 1992, [6.22].

disposing of CO_2 in deep ocean waters.[26] The idea of injecting CO_2 into 'oceanic deepwater' was later considered and dismissed as an option for the ocean dumping regime.[27] It is an option that would contribute to ocean acidification.

In 2006 the London Protocol was amended to allow CO_2 to be injected into sub-seabed geological formations in certain circumstances.[28] This amendment only regulates certain kinds of CO_2 capture and storage because of the jurisdictional reach of the London Convention and the London Protocol. For instance, the disposal of waste generated offshore during normal operations on platforms or other artificial structures is not dumping according to the London Protocol, so the disposal of CO_2 in such circumstances is permitted.[29] Also, injecting CO_2 into sub-seabed geological formations using pipelines originating from land is allowed. This is because the definition of 'sea' in the London Protocol does not include the sub-seabed which is accessed only from land.[30] The broad definition leaves states to define for themselves whether they will regulate the use of pipelines from land to directly inject CO_2 into geological formations. It is also generally accepted that the London Convention does not regulate this kind of activity.

The 2006 amendment to the London Protocol lists the injection of CO_2 into geological formations in the sub-seabed in Annex I, making it a permissible disposal in accordance with national permit laws. Of course, as discussed previously, under the older London Convention the disposal of any waste not listed within the convention (in Annex I and II) can occur in accordance with a general permit granted under national laws, and often subject to minimal regulation.[31]

While disposal of CO_2 is now permitted under both arms of the ocean dumping regime, there is a noticeable difference in approach. Under the

[26] Ibid.

[27] *Consideration of the Report of the Scientific Group: Ocean Storage of Carbon Dioxide*, at the Twenty-First Consultative Meeting of Contracting Parties to the Convention on the Prevention of Marine Pollution by Dumping of Wastes and Other Matter, LC 21/INF.2, 25 June 1999.

[28] Res. LP.1(1) of the Twenty-Eighth Consultative Meeting of Contracting Parties to the 1972 Convention on the Prevention of Marine Pollution by Dumping of Wastes and other Matter LC 28/15, October 2006 and 1st Meeting of Contracting Parties to the 1996 Protocol to the Convention on the Prevention of Marine Pollution by Dumping of Wastes and Other Matter 1972, LP 1/1, October–November 2006 ('Resolution LP.1(1) (2006)').

[29] London Protocol, Art. 1.4.2.1.

[30] London Protocol, Art. 1.7.

[31] London Convention, Art. 4(1)(c).

London Convention a general permit can be issued for CO_2 disposal without risk management strategies being carried out. However, under the London Protocol, as a waste listed in Annex I, a state can issue a permit for disposal of gas streams that consist overwhelmingly of CO_2. However, within its public law regime it must also have processes in place to support the assessment of applications using the Waste Assessment Framework found in Annex 2 of the London Protocol.[32] This framework imposes detailed and prescriptive international law obligations within the public law sphere. It operates as a boundary between science and law and between international law and public law.[33] It is indeed an example of public law regulation-making by international convention. The framework requires states to assess the suitability of waste disposal at sea depending on the type and characteristics of the materials. National regulatory agencies must, among other things: aim to reduce waste production; give consideration to managing waste; develop an 'action list' for screening wastes in terms of their impact on human health and the marine environment; consider dumpsite selection; and undertake monitoring and regular reviews of permits. National laws are required to support this regime. In Australia this is achieved by the Environment Protection (Sea Dumping) Act 1981 (Cth), an Act that allows permits to be subject to administrative challenge.[34]

At present, the Scientific Group of the London Protocol is developing specific guidance on the application of the Waste Assessment Framework to the capture and storage of CO_2 in sub-seabed geological formations.[35] These guidelines will reflect the general framework established in Annex 2, but with specific applicability to sequestered CO_2.

Aside from the 'reverse listing' differences to be found between the London Protocol and the London Convention, the amendment to the London Protocol allowing CO_2 to be injected into the sub-seabed classifies the act of injecting it as 'disposal' rather than 'storage'.[36] There are different conceptual possibilities for dealing with the sequestration of CO_2, but the

[32] The drafting history reveals that the inclusion of the 'precautionary approach' in Art. 3.1 of the London Protocol is directly related to the introduction of 'reverse listing' and the 'waste assessment framework'.

[33] See above Chapter 5 by Jaye Ellis, in particular her discussion on boundaries in environmental law.

[34] Environment Protection (Sea Dumping) Act 1981 (Cth) s. 24.

[35] International Maritime Organization, *Notification of Amendments to Annex 1 to the London Protocol 1996*, LC-LP.1/Circ.5, 27 November 2006.

[36] Resolution LP.1(1) (2006), above n. 28.

amendment adopts only the language of referring to the process as 'disposal'. This is consistent with the London Protocol more generally, which in Article 4 classes the storage of waste in the seabed and its subsoil as disposal and therefore prohibited.[37] The drafting history of the London Protocol confirms this, by showing that the party states were trying to address excess gas production in offshore wells, and in particular 'the need to avoid an inadvertent prohibition of this practice'.[38] In classifying the injection of CO_2 in this way, the amendment to the London Protocol avoids giving legitimacy to the activities of those states that are members of only the London Convention, and that might have interpreted the classification of CO_2 into geological formations as 'storage' as an implicit permission to carry out the activity entirely outside the ocean dumping regime.

Finally, there is one further difference of note and relevance to the forthcoming discussion on the precautionary approach in the ocean dumping regime. The London Protocol defines the term 'sea' in a broader way than the London Convention, by including the seabed and subsoil in addition to the marine waters above it.[39] Article 1.7 of the London Protocol merely confirms and validates earlier decisions of the consultative meetings to include disposal at sea of wastes under the sea-bed as part of the remit of the London Convention. It also confirms the decision of the twelfth consultative meeting in 1989 that disposal into repositories accessed from land would not constitute dumping:[40] at that meeting, it was specifically stated that the sea does not include sub-seabed repositories accessed only from land.

5. Role and function of environmental principles

The capture and injection of CO_2 into sub-seabed geological formations appears to be of relatively low risk compared to the potential harm from ocean acidification resulting from the absorption of CO_2 by the ocean. It appears safer than the direct release of CO_2 into the 'ocean water column or onto the deep seafloor'.[41] Despite the relative low risk, there is a degree

[37] London Protocol, Art. 1.4.1.3.

[38] *Report of the Seventeenth Consultative Meeting of Contracting Parties to the Convention on the Prevention of Marine Pollution by Dumping of Wastes and Other Matter*, LC 17/14, 3–7 October 1994, [3.25].

[39] London Protocol, Art. 1.7.

[40] Ad Hoc Group of Legal Experts on Dumping, *Report of the Fourth Meeting of the Ad Hoc Group of Legal Experts on Dumping*, LDC/LG 4/WP.2/Rev.1, 22–26 October 1990, [3.1.3].

[41] Bert Metz *et al.*, *Carbon Dioxide Capture and Storage* (Cambridge University Press for the Intergovernmental Panel on Climate Change, 2005) 3.

of uncertainty about whether CO_2 injected into the sub-seabed will leak into the marine environment.[42] The OSPAR Commission for the Protection of the Marine Environment of the North-East Atlantic recently noted that 'in appropriately selected and managed geological reservoirs, the fraction' of CO_2 which is 'retained is very likely to exceed 99 per cent over 100 years and is likely to exceed 99 per cent over 1000 years'.[43] However, what is uncertain is the impact that impurities will have on the CO_2 injected into deep-seabed geological formations. Lastly, as highlighted by this OSPAR comment, states have to regulate a number of matters to ensure the safe storage or disposal of captured CO_2. As noted, however, there is minimal safety guidance and requirements imposed under the London Convention.

How states have politically and legally managed the risk associated with this kind of activity can only be understood in the context of the discourses within the ocean dumping regime. As illustrated earlier, there are significant differences between the London Convention and the London Protocol. The focus of the latter is on eliminating or managing permitted disposal activities so that either they do not happen again or that their effects on the marine environment are minimal, whereas the key focus of the London Convention is on prohibiting the disposal of listed harmful wastes. The strength of this difference resonates with the contracting parties to the London Protocol having adopted the precautionary approach in Resolution LDC.43(14) and more formally in Article III(1) of the Protocol itself (and implicitly in other Articles of the agreement).[44]

Given that the London Protocol was drafted much later than the London Convention, the approach of the contracting parties to managing CO_2 capture and disposal highlights the impact that the precautionary principle has had on states. In managing the interests of future generations, particularly in relation to risks associated with disposing of sequestered CO_2, the precautionary principle gave creative impetus to arguments during negotiations, but also had the effect of constraining other arguments and points of view during the discussion process. The

42 OSPAR Commission for the Protection of the Marine Environment of the North-East Atlantic, above n. 14.

43 Ibid. 6.

44 It should be pointed that this does not mean that it is only the precautionary approach which is solely responsible for this difference. The discourses within the regime are richer and stronger than having their foundations built solely on the precautionary approach.

discourse of precaution worked in different ways in relation to the London Convention and London Protocol to stimulate change.

6. Giving arguments a fresh impetus

During the negotiations leading to the London Protocol, contracting parties rejected the idea that states should take a precautionary approach to situations that 'might' cause harm.[45] Article 3(1) instead reflected arguments that states should only be required to manage risks that were 'likely' to eventuate. This meant that states adopted a precondition to the application of the precautionary principle that would be less likely to be satisfied. Nevertheless, states do not have to judge how severe the pollution is likely to be from disposal into the sea.[46] Disposal activities do not have to give rise to serious or significant grounds for concern before relying on the precautionary principle.[47] States can use the principle once satisfied that a disposal activity is 'likely' to cause harm should it be permitted to go ahead. This is reflected in the London Protocol's 'reverse listing' of materials for disposal at sea, which presumes that everything dumped at sea may be or is 'likely' to cause harm, irrespective of how serious it might be for the marine environment. What this does is to place an extraordinary onus on states when considering whether to introduce resolutions for amending the 'reverse list' in Annex 1 and hence adding additional permissible waste disposals. In fact, since the London Protocol was drafted, the only amendment has been in relation to the disposal of CO_2 in sub-seabed geological formations.

This less permissive approach to precaution[48] appears to have given states a creative impetus to favour arguments protecting the environment

[45] Proposal by Sweden, above n. 22.

[46] The precautionary approach or principle can be expressed in many ways; see, for instance, Andre Nollkaemper, '"What You Risk Reveals What You Value", and Other Dilemmas Encountered in the Legal Assaults on Risks' in David Freestone and Ellen Hey (eds.), *The Precautionary Principle and International Law: The Challenge of Implementation* (Kluwer Law International, The Hague and Boston, 1996) 73; Nicolas de Sadeleer, 'The Effect of Uncertainty on the Threshold Levels to which the Precautionary Principle Appears to be Subject' in Maurice Sheridan and Luc Lavrysen (eds.), *Environmental Law Principles in Practice* (Bruylant, Bruxelles, 2002) 32.

[47] See, for instance, the United Nations Framework Convention on Climate Change, opened for signature 4 June 1992, 1771 UNTS 107, Principle 3.3 (entered into force 21 March 1994), which requires that states act in situations where there are 'threats of serious or irreversible damage'.

[48] The term is developed by Nicolas de Sadeleer, *Environmental Principles: From Political Slogans to Legal Rules* (Oxford University Press, 2005 reprint) 160.

more generally rather than those that simply argue for reducing pollution caused by dumping of wastes at sea. That is, unlike the London Convention which concerns itself with weighing the risks of one kind of ocean disposal of waste against another, the London Protocol is focused more on managing waste and its impact on the natural environment more generally, and not just the marine environment. In considering how states should approach the issue of capturing and disposing of CO_2 the contracting parties were, in addition to weighing the risks and potential effects of this activity, also taking into account the wider problems posed by 'elevated atmospheric levels of carbon dioxide'.[49]

Contracting parties to the London Protocol could have rightfully rejected the disposal of CO_2 into the sub-seabed because of the likelihood of the risk of leakage from repositories. They could have done so, citing the precautionary principle, on the basis that such dumping would be particularly problematic if the CO_2 contained significant amounts and types of impurities. However, the precautionary approach in fact led states to view this risk as less than the harm to the marine environment if states did not reduce ocean acidification from the natural absorption of CO_2 by sea. That is, the focus of the contracting parties was shifted from preventing marine pollution through dumping alone to broader considerations of the likelihood of damage to the capacity of the ocean if states were not allowed to safely store CO_2 in sub-seabed repositories. The states interpreted the precautionary principle creatively by not limiting their perspective to the potential harm of actions, but by also imaging the likely harm of their failure to act. Further, the resolution amending Annex 1 of the London Protocol also helps develop the expertise that will favour environmentally safer methods of disposing CO_2 in the ocean instead of, for instance, its injection into the ocean floor or the marine columns above it.[50]

Importantly, the resolution amending Annex 1 only permits disposal of streams that 'consist overwhelmingly of carbon dioxide'.[51] This was a clear adoption of the precautionary principle made in light of scientific knowledge about the security of storage being dependent on the purity of the injected gases. It was known that captured CO_2 can contain a host of other substances (some of which may be intentionally introduced) which

[49] OSPAR Commission for the Protection of the Marine Environment of the North-East Atlantic, above n. 14, 1.

[50] On this, see Metz *et al.*, above n. 41.

[51] Resolution LP.1(1) (2006), above n. 28.

might affect both its 'transport and storage'.[52] Given the potential 'health, safety and environmental impacts' of impure captured CO_2 streams, this requirement confirms the discourse established since the adoption of Resolution LDC.43(14) encouraging a precautionary approach.[53] That is, the risk associated with the activity is dealt with by requiring states to manage the purity of the captured CO_2 streams which are to be injected into sub-seabed geological formations. Further, as discussed above, states must act in accordance with Annex 2 of the London Protocol and subject all disposal activities to its framework on risk and waste management assessment when giving effect to its public law permitting system. States also resolved to develop a specific framework for the assessment of captured CO_2 in line with Annex 2 of the London Protocol. This means that not only must the permit that is granted for the injection of CO_2 deal with purity, but also a host of other factors which will avert the risks associated with disposal. The creativity of response extended to the acceptance by states of imposing stringent and prescriptive requirements within public laws through international conventions.

The above discussion shows that regulating what is done in the sub-seabed, as part of efforts to protect the marine environment itself, involves a creative approach that is persuasively integrated into the ocean dumping regime. Both the London Protocol and London Convention are not particularly decisive in terms of whether they extend to geological formations that are thousands of kilometres below sea level.[54] However, the resolution listing the disposal of CO_2 into geological formations in the sub-seabed decisively extends the regime to protect the marine waters from potentially polluting activities on the seabed.[55]

[52] See draft of the 'Risk Assessment and Management Framework for Carbon Dioxide Sequestration in Sub-Seabed Geological Structures (CS-SSGS)', which will complement Annex 2 of the 1996 Protocol in *Report of the Meeting of the SG Intersessional Technical Working Group on Carbon Dioxide Sequestration*, LC/SG-Carbon Dioxide 1/7, 3–7 April 2006, annex 3, 11.

[53] Ibid.

[54] See in particular *Report of the Twenty-Seventh Consultative Meeting of Contracting Parties to the Convention on the prevention of Marine Pollution by Dumping of Wastes and Other Matter 1972*, LC 27/6 Annex, 24–28 October 2005, 18 points 102–5.

[55] Submission by the Netherlands, 'Explanatory note accompanying the proposal for restructuring and amending the London Convention', in Note by the Secretariat, 'Inventory of Amendment Proposals' in Amendment Group – First Meeting, LC/AM 1/3, 10 June 1993, 42.

7. The constraining influence of the precautionary principle

The discourse of precaution constrained how actors 'characterised' certain initiatives and activities in terms of whether they were to be exempt from the prohibition on dumping wastes at sea.[56] In other words, the discourse of precaution had constrained how actors argued and characterised certain activities as more or less harmful as others and therefore whether they should be prohibited or allowed under the regime. It did not necessarily 'determine the particular substantive choices of the parties', but gave meaning to how they interpreted the arguments that were being presented to them and therefore affected the ultimate choices and decisions that they made.[57]

This is evident, for instance, in the range of alternative options to the injection of CO_2 into the sub-seabed that were canvassed in reports and studies before the contracting parties amended the London Protocol. The secretariat of the consultative meeting to the London Convention first supported a study in 1999, which it presented to contracting parties, from the Greenhouse Gas Programme of the International Energy Agency of the Organisation for Economic Co-operation and Development relating to the idea of injecting CO_2 into 'oceanic deep-waters'.[58] In another study prepared by the Intergovernmental Panel on Climate Change, which was presented to the contracting parties in 2005, the possibility of disposing of CO_2 in the water column or on the sea floor was highlighted with a note of caution that the ecological impact of such

[56] This particular way of interpreting the constraining nature of norms is taken from Friedrich Kratochwil's characterisation of them as constitutive of what actors do. See Friedrich Kratochwil, 'How Do Norms Matter?' in Michael Byers (ed.), *The Role of Law in International Politics: Essays in International Relations and International Law* (Oxford University Press, 2000) 34, 47. For instance, he writes, that:

> In so far as they are 'constraints' at all, it is only in the sense identified above, in that they allow us to characterize an action as falling within a certain class, such as the making of a contract. However, these rules will not determine the particular substantive choices of the parties.

On the difference between constitutive and regulatory norms, see also Nina Tannenwald, 'The Nuclear Taboo: The United States and the Normative Basis of Nuclear Non-Use' (1999) 53 *International Organization* 433.

[57] Kratochwil, above n. 56, 47.

[58] *Consideration of the Report of the Scientific Group: Ocean Storage of Carbon Dioxide*, at the Twenty-First Consultative Meeting of Contracting Parties to the Convention on the Prevention of Marine Pollution by Dumping of Wastes and Other Matter, LC 21/INF.2, 25 June 1999, agenda item 5.

a venture was still being researched.[59] At the early stages of the debate the idea of simply injecting CO_2 into the water column was seen as something that would eventually happen anyway, because of the atmosphere–ocean exchange process that naturally absorbed CO_2 into the ocean.[60]

It is clear that the resolution of only permitting the injection of CO_2 into sub-seabed geological formations implicitly rejected any alternative approaches to disposing of sequestered CO_2. The constraining potential of the discourse is seen in the way that the regime made an issue out of the potential for leakage while CO_2 is being transported to the storage site or in the long term after it has been stored. This suggests that contracting parties gradually narrowed their choices in terms of what they should be allowed to do with sequestered CO_2 and how much they would tolerate risk to the marine environment. As a result, arguments pressing for alternatives to injecting CO_2 into the sub-seabed were constrained by what contracting parties had come to learn and appreciate as the level of risk they were willing to cope with in terms of pollution from the intentional disposal of CO_2 into the marine waters.[61] Contracting parties did not state that their decision to permit the injection of CO_2

[59] Metz *et al.*, above n. 41, 7. On this possibility see also support from the OSPAR Commission for the Protection of the Marine Environment of the North-East Atlantic, above n. 14.

[60] *Consideration of the Report of the Scientific Group: Ocean Storage of Carbon Dioxide*, at the Twenty-First Consultative Meeting of Contracting Parties to the Convention on the Prevention of Marine Pollution by Dumping of Wastes and Other Matter, LC 21/INF.2, 25 June 1999.

[61] Their concern with risk was also confirmed in a statement that the contracting parties to the London Convention and the London Protocol issued in 2007, and confirmed again in 2008, identifying their concerns about the idea of states engaging in large-scale 'fertilization of ocean waters using micro-nutrients such as iron to stimulate phytoplankton growth in order to sequester carbon dioxide': London Convention and London Protocol Circular, *Statement of Concern Regarding Iron Fertilization of the Oceans to Sequester Carbon Dioxide*, LC-LP.1/Circ.14, 13 July 2007. In particular, their statement of concerns drew from the work of Metz *et al.*, above n. 41, which had noted that 'ocean iron fertilization remains largely speculative, and many of the environmental side effects have yet to be assessed'. Although not rejecting the option as yet, the contracting parties to the London Convention and London Protocol have requested states to carefully consider whether to engage in such an activity and whether it would be contrary to the aims of the London Convention and the London Protocol. In January 2008 the London Convention and London Protocol Circular asked contracting parties to 'use the utmost caution when considering proposals for large-scale ocean fertilization operations at this stage': London Convention and London Protocol Circular, *Preparation for the Scientific and Legal Discussions in 2008 of Ocean Fertilization with a View to its Regulation under the London Convention and Protocol*, LC-LP.1 Circ.20, 29 January 2008, [12.1].

into the sub-seabed, in contrast to other alternatives, was driven by precaution. However, this seems to have been the way that they did proceed, given that the contracting parties listed sub-seabed injection of CO_2 as a permissible disposal activity under Annex 1 of the London Protocol.

Another example of the constraining effect of the precautionary principle is evident from the way that contracting parties approached the issue of whether the injection of CO_2 into the sub-seabed was to be classed as 'placement', because it is being stored, or 'dumped', as it will be disposed of. The precautionary approach worked to narrow the meaning that contracting parties gave to the term 'placement' in Article 2(2) of the London Protocol. To have interpreted the term 'placement' in broad terms would have meant that contracting parties had encouraged the potential of leakage of CO_2 from sub-seabed repositories by not regulating the activity in any way.[62] That is, if the injection of CO_2 in the sub-seabed is interpreted as storage, then it is likely to be classified as 'placement,' in which case the London Protocol regime would not regulate the activity.

The idea that the injection of CO_2 into sub-seabed repositories could be interpreted as 'placing' it in them was difficult to sustain because of the requirement that the activity should be consistent with the objectives of the London Protocol. Arguments developed during negotiations suggesting that injecting CO_2 into sub-seabed geological formations would protect the oceans from acidification were not seen as consistent with the need to protect the marine environment from 'all sources of pollution'.[63] That is, the injection of CO_2 was seen as presenting risks for the marine environment, and an interpretation of the London Protocol that ignored these risks was not acceptable to the contracting parties. According to the scientific reports distributed through circulars to the contracting parties, there was a fair amount of uncertainty as to what would make an effective site for storage and whether there would be any leakage from it or not.[64] Given the level of uncertainty around whether leakage can occur or not, the contracting parties preferred to avoid classifying the injection of CO_2 into sub-seabed geological formations as 'placement'. This meant that it could be regulated through the London Protocol.

[62] On this, see in particular Submission by the United Kingdom, 'Sequestration of Carbon Dioxide in Sub-Seabed Geological Structures', LP 1/6, 28 April 2006, annex, 11 [65].

[63] *Report of the Meeting of the CM Intercessional Legal and Related Issues Working Group on Sequestration*, LC/CM-Carbon Dioxide 1/5, 10–12 April 2006, point 3.6.

[64] For example, Metz *et al.*, above n. 41.

The constraining potential of the discourse of the precautionary principle on what the parties accepted as good arguments seemed also to extend to an alternative, though ultimately rejected, suggestion. Some states had argued that they should be allowed to 'place' CO_2 in sub-seabed repositories if they could provide a statement that illustrated how their practices were consistent with the objectives of the London Protocol, which include preventing, reducing and where practicable, eliminating pollution at sea.[65] This proposal was also rejected in part because the uncertainty of the harm associated with CO_2 leaking from storage meant that contracting parties wanted to regulate through a public international law legal system the choice of sites for disposal and the mechanism for transporting the CO_2 to the storage sites.

Storing CO_2 in sub-seabed repositories is an option which is less risky for the oceans than the alternatives, such as injecting it into the water column above the deep seabed or leaving it in the airspace to be naturally absorbed by the sea. Clearly, states could have avoided the disposal of sequestered CO_2 in geological formations in the sub-seabed. They considered several options, but favoured the one that prohibited the activity unless it was regulated through public laws according to the provisions of the London Protocol. In this instance, contracting parties were cautious and sought to regulate not only states that might harm the environment, because the techniques they use for transporting or injecting and storing CO_2 into the sub-seabed might cause leakage, but also those that could seal sites with little or no chance of CO_2 escaping into the water column within 1,000 years.

In the first example discussed in this sub-section, contracting parties had been constrained to adopt alternate ways of injecting sequestered CO_2 into the ocean. In the second example they appear to have gone further, by taking precautionary measures whereby actors might inadvertently dispose of sequestered CO_2 into the deep seabed by classifying it as storage or placement. In both instances contracting parties adopted a counterintuitive approach to what had been the ocean dumping regime

[65] *Report of the Meeting of the CM Intercessional Legal and Related Issues Working Group on Sequestration*, LC/CM-Carbon Dioxide 1/5, 10–12 April 2006. The argument that this should be the case was first put by the United States as one of three ways to deal with sequestration of carbon dioxide. See Submission by the United States, 'Facilitation and/ or Regulation of Carbon Dioxide Sequestration in Sub-Seabed Geological Structures: Options and Implications' at the Meeting of the CM Intersessional Legal and Related Issues Working Group on Carbon Dioxide Sequestration, 10–12 April 2006, LC/CM – Carbon Dioxide 1/3/1, point 4.

until then. They permitted the storage – or disposal – of CO_2 in the sub-seabed because the risks of its being absorbed by the oceans were larger than those associated with its leaking into the ocean after it had been stored.

8. Conclusion

This chapter highlights the significance of the precautionary approach or principle as a type of discourse within the ocean dumping regime. The principle does not appear to have been used by appealing to its exact provisions or wording in Article 3(1) of the London Protocol. For instance, in drafting the London Protocol itself the idea of reverse listing appeared to have been an appeal to the idea of taking precautionary measures rather than whether the alternative approach in the London Convention was 'likely' to cause harm to the marine environment. Instead the precautionary principle appears to be functioning more as an open-textured norm or as an abstraction that points states to a discourse which takes them beyond just wanting to prevent harm, and has encouraged a transformation of international laws into public law systems. The London Protocol did not just prevent states from disposing of their waste in the water column. Rather, it regulated how only a very select group of materials could be dumped and as long as this was done as part of a waste management programme adopted by the state in their public legal system. The discussion around the 2006 amendment to the London Protocol has also shown that the contracting parties were not simply consenting to states disposing of CO_2 into sub-seabed repositories, but that they were demanding the management of waste in a way that seeks to protect the ocean waters that would naturally absorb CO_2 if it were left in the atmosphere.

The contracting parties to the London Convention and the London Protocol developed their arguments during negotiations by appealing to precautionary measures required to prevent pollution. For instance, the requirement that CO_2 injected into sub-seabed repositories should contain very few impurities is part of the precautionary measures taken to ensure that leakage has little adverse impact on the ocean itself. This suggests that the discourse developed through varying appeals to the notion of taking precautionary measures. States learned that sub-seabed repositories were important as part of the overall waste management strategy that the London Protocol had been pursuing. Not only did the precautionary approach encourage consideration of this, but also constrained how they regulated activities that permitted its use for the disposal of CO_2. That is, sub-seabed repositories could not be used if the CO_2 that was being injected into geological formations had impurities which could impact the marine waters in the long term.

There are variable though significant ways that an environmental principle like the precautionary principle can influence legal opportunities or responses to particular issues within a particular regime. At the international level, states appear to have been constrained within the consultative meeting as to what they could do with sequestered CO_2, as well as encouraged to consider its disposal into the sub-seabed as part of an overall strategy to further protect the marine environment. In this way, the discourse of precaution did not direct or cause change, but established the necessary background for a more subtle, indirect – but nevertheless extremely important – way for states to learn and change their public law responses to waste management in the oceans.

18

Environmental discourses in the ocean commons: the case of ocean fertilisation

JULIA MAYO-RAMSAY

1. Introduction

As human populations expand and their activities on the coast and on the seas increase, pollution of the marine environment is worsening. Meanwhile, ocean resources are being diminished through overfishing and destructive fishing practices damaging species' habitats, endangering biodiversity and jeopardising the future viability of the oceans as a food source. With so little known about them, our oceans appear in a precarious state. Under international law the responsibility for stewardship of the oceans and activities, including conservation and sustainable use of marine resources, falls to the nation managing an exclusive economic zone (EEZ), or whose flag vessels fly. However, enforcement of these laws on the high seas is notoriously difficult. Public laws apply to coastal activities, within the territorial sea of a coastal state. Here, laws are more likely to be enforced, though law-makers are still reluctant to regulate land-based pollution sources and near shore fisheries in ways that might aggravate rural constituencies.

Now climate change further threatens the quality of the oceans and presents greater regulatory and enforcement problems at international and public law levels. The oceans, which cover the vast majority of the earth's surface, are critical to maintaining equilibrium in the global carbon cycle. They are responsible for the uptake of about half of all anthropogenic carbon dioxide.[1] The threat, which is the subject of this chapter, is the acidification of the ocean through the natural uptake of the increased levels of atmospheric carbon dioxide (CO_2) by way of the

[1] Ben McNeil *et al.*, 'Anthropogenic CO_2 Uptake by the Ocean Based on the Global Chlorofluorocarbon Data Set' (2003) 299 *Science* 235.

biological and solubility pump, and further, through plans to 'fertilise' the oceans with additional carbon dioxide, beyond their natural uptake. The rationale for ocean fertilisation is that it will mitigate climate change by removing additional carbon dioxide from the atmosphere.

Ocean fertilisation is a dilemma, because it is at the same time an environmental 'solution' and an environmental 'problem'. It is complex, interconnected and multidimensional. The law has not yet found a way to deal with it. Even the Law of the Sea Convention,[2] with its multiple objectives of peaceful use of the oceans, the equitable and efficient utilisation of their resources and the preservation and conservation and protection of marine living resources and environment, does not appropriately deal with ocean fertilisation. Public laws, though particularly relevant for coastal ocean fertilisation projects, are mute on the issue. Ocean fertilisation is connecting these two legal regimes as they both grapple with legal responses to proposals that are simultaneously lauded and feared. Within this complex setting, ocean fertilisation in theory and in proposals has been advanced and opposed by a mix of scientists, government officials, business and environment groups. Among them there are a variety of perspectives and they have, both explicitly and implicitly, employed a number of environmental discursive frames to advance their arguments about the opportunities and threats of ocean fertilisation and the manner of its regulation at the international and national levels.

This chapter introduces the science and rationale for ocean fertilisation and explains the risks of ocean acidification arising from this new technology. It then identifies and analyses a number of environmental discourses discernible from the promotion of the technology and the caution articulated by those who presently oppose it or who advance the cause of greater management of the oceans. Overlaying this discussion will be the question: how can our governments and the international community devise a legal and governance structure for such an opportunistic but largely untested technology in a largely unknown environment?

[2] United Nations Convention on the Law of the Sea, opened for signature 10 December 1982, 1833 UNTS 3 (entered into force 16 November 1994) ('Law of the Sea Convention').

1.1 The freedom and responsibility of the ocean commons

The dominant theme in the international law of the sea, dating from the seventeenth century,[3] has been that the high seas are common property,[4] making the oceans the greatest commons, free to all, on earth. This freedom of the high seas is open to all nations and is defined in Part VII of the Law of the Sea Convention.

The Law of the Sea Convention allows freedom of the high seas, subject to rights to cooperation under Article 64,[5] including fishing[6] and other uses,[7] which have far-reaching effects on both the biodiversity of the oceans and its ecosystems. The critical situation that the global oceans commons are currently in is exemplified by widespread over-fishing,[8] particularly in waters beyond national jurisdiction. In many locations technological developments have allowed fishers to easily locate fish, and take catches far in excess of what is sustainable.[9] For these people, the oceans are an unregulated bounty ripe for exploitation. Now geoengineering options are being tested or proposed as methods to further enhance the ocean as a carbon sink. Proposals to store anthropogenic carbon dioxide in the deep ocean have gained momentum over the past decade as a potential way of mitigating the increasing atmospheric levels of CO_2 from industrial and other anthropogenic sources. There are, however, concerns about the stability of the deep sea as a storage repository and the ability of species to adapt to a rapid change in their environment.[10] Nevertheless, it is the freedom of the seas that helps make these methods imaginable, as the oceans are vast and often seen as providing limitless, and poorly governed, opportunities.

The freedom of the seas, however, is subject to constraints and is in part subject to national regulations. The use of the seas has always been

[3] Hugo Grotius, *On the Laws of War and Peace* (1st edn, 1625) available at gallica.bnf.fr/ark:/12148/bpt6k580227.capture, last accessed 1 October 2009.

[4] Brian Fitzgerald, 'Port State Jurisdiction and Marine Pollution under UNCLOS III' (1995) 11 *Maritime Law Association of Australia and New Zealand Journal* Part 1, 33.

[5] Law of the Sea Convention, Art. 64.

[6] Law of the Sea Convention, Art. 87(1)(e).

[7] Law of the Sea Convention, Art. 87(1)(a), (c), (d) and (f).

[8] General situation of world fish stocks, United Nations Food and Agriculture Organization (FAO) at www.fao.org/newsroom/common/ecg/1000505/en/stocks.pdf, last accessed 1 November 2009.

[9] R. Quentin Grafton, *Too Few Fish and Too Many Boats*, Policy Briefs – Fishing Futures, Crawford School of Economics and Government, ANU (2006).

[10] Brad Seibel and Patrick Walsh, 'Biological Impacts of Deep-Sea Carbon Dioxide Injection Inferred from Indices of Physiological Performance' (2003) 206 *The Journal of Experimental Biology* 642.

limited by the customary law that allows exclusive national jurisdiction over the marine zone adjacent to the land.[11] After the Second World War, led by the United States (US),[12] nations also began declaring control over continental shelves, and investing themselves with the natural resources upon and within the continental shelf.[13] Nevertheless, the oceans, particularly the high seas, remain no country's property and, especially given the fluidity and expanse of the oceans, for environmental management purposes they are better considered common property, shared by all and the responsibility of all. Despite this, in recent years there has been a notable lack of stewardship of the oceans, particularly on the high seas.

While the oceans have been pillaged and polluted, human-induced climate change has further damaged them through warming of the sea surface temperature and ocean acidification from the increase in atmospheric CO_2.[14] That the biogeochemical composition of the oceans has changed because of human fossil fuel use demonstrates that the oceans are not limitless and bountiful, rather, a finite resource. It is a 'resource', as well as a habitat for many life forms susceptible to what humans may perceive as very small changes in the oceans. For example, a change of only one degree celsius in the sea surface temperature may prevent some species from breeding.[15] Even small changes in the pH of seawater will prevent some animals from forming a shell.[16] Within this conflicted setting of freedoms and responsibilities, of common property and nationalised territories, and of ongoing deterioration of the oceans and new proposals to further exploit their resources, there are three technologies that are publicly being considered or trialled as ways of enhancing the oceans as a carbon sink.

[11] David Hunter, James Salzman and Durwood Zaelke, *International Environmental Law and Policy* (Foundation Press, New York, 2nd edn, 2002) 658.

[12] President Truman, 'Policy of the United States with Respect to the Natural Resources of the Subsoil and Sea Bed of the Continental Shelf' (White House News Release, 28 September 1945).

[13] Hunter *et al.*, above n. 11, 658.

[14] Thomas Trull *et al.*, *Ocean Fertilisation: Science and Policy Issues*, Position Analysis 3 (Antarctic Climate & Ecosystems Cooperative Research Centre, Hobart, 2008).

[15] Taro Takahashi *et al.*, 'Global Sea-Air CO_2 Flux Based on Climatological Surface Ocean pCO_2, and Seasonal Biological and Temperature Effects' (2002) 49 *Deep-Sea Research Pt II* 1601.

[16] James Orr *et al.*, 'Anthropogenic Ocean Acidification Over the Twenty-First Century and its Impact on Calcifying Organisms' (2005) 437 *Nature* 681.

First is geosequestration, involving the storage of CO_2 in geological formations (like coal, oil and gas wells) including in the seabed.[17] This technology is under consideration by the Australian government.[18] Second is deep-ocean storage of carbon dioxide in the ocean water column, involving injecting CO_2 into the water column to form lakes on the sea bottom or solid CO_2 hydrates at 3,000 metres below sea level or deeper.[19] Deep-ocean injection of CO_2 can be seen as a way to expedite the natural oceanic uptake of CO_2, which would normally occur over many hundreds of years. It is suspected, however, that due to local super-saturation and the pattern of ocean currents, a large portion of injected CO_2 might be returned to the atmosphere after only a few hundred years.[20] Third is ocean fertilisation, which uses artificially stimulated primary production to increase the natural absorption of CO_2 by the ocean.

1.2 Ocean fertilisation

Stimulating the growth of phytoplankton in the ocean by using a limited nutrient such as iron was first identified by Haakon Gran in 1931.[21] However, it was not until more than fifty years later that American oceanographer John Martin[22] further developed Gran's theory as a method of drawing excess CO_2 from the atmosphere into the ocean, with his 'iron hypothesis'.[23] Martin recognised that the primary source of iron to the surface waters of the oceans is from land, in the form of dust and run-off. Through a series of experiments in the late 1980s, Martin[24] confirmed that phytoplankton productivity in the Southern Ocean is

17 See above Chapter 17 by Afshin Akhtarkhavari.

18 Offshore Petroleum and Greenhouse Gas Storage Act 2006 (Cth).

19 Bert Metz, 'Ocean Storage' in Bert Metz *et al.*, *Carbon Dioxide Capture and Storage* (Cambridge University Press for the Intergovernmental Panel on Climate Change, 2005) 289.

20 Kurt Zenz House, 'Permanent Carbon Dioxide Storage in Deep-Sea Sediments' (2006) 103(33) *Proceedings of the National Academy of Sciences of the United States of America* 12291.

21 H. Gran, 'On the Conditions for the Production of Plankton in the Sea' (1931) 75 *Rapports et Procès-Verbaux des Reunions Conseil International pour l'Exploration de la Mer* 37.

22 John H. Martin, Steve E. Fitzwater and R. Michael Gordon, 'Iron Deficiency Limits Phytoplankton Growth in Antarctic Waters' (1990) 4(1) *Global Biogeochemical Cycles* 5.

23 John H. Martin, 'Glacial-Interglacial CO_2 Change: The Iron Hypothesis' (1990) 5 *Paleoceanography* 1.

24 Ibid.

limited by iron deficiency. Hence, the phytoplankton in the Southern Ocean cannot take advantage of other available nutrients in the sea water to grow in greater number. At a conference at Woods Hole Oceanographic Institution in 1993, Martin was purported to have announced: 'Give me half a super tanker of iron and I'll give you another ice age.'[25]

Around 30 per cent of anthropogenic carbon dioxide[26] is drawn down into the oceans naturally, through the biological and solubility pumps. However, ocean scientists, such as Martin, believe that if phytoplankton growth could be stimulated with iron or other nutrients, the growth would 'take in so much carbon from the atmosphere that they could reverse the greenhouse effect and cool the Earth'.[27]

Ocean fertilisation works by introducing a limiting nutrient into the sea to stimulate phytoplankton growth. The main limiting nutrients in the open ocean are micro-nutrients, such as iron, and macro-nutrients such as nitrogen and phosphorus. Whereas ocean iron fertilisation uses iron to stimulate the growth of phytoplankton in high-nutrient low-chlorophyll areas of the ocean, the macro-nutrient model uses urea, a common farm fertiliser and nutrient, as the main catalyst for the stimulation and growth of phytoplankton in low-nutrient areas of the ocean.

There are a number of environmental concerns associated with ocean fertilisation. One known side effect of increasing nutrients in coastal waters is eutrophication, which can trigger anoxic events resulting in hypoxia or dead zones, where marine life is destroyed. These dead zones have been particularly prevalent in the Gulf of Mexico and other areas where there is considerable farm run-off into the sea.[28] In ocean fertilisation using macro-nutrients, liquid urea or other nutrients are mixed to produce a nutrient solution or pellet which is delivered, via a marine pipeline, ship or barge, into nutrient-depleted areas of the ocean. It is claimed[29] that this nutrient solution stimulates the growth of

25 Kenneth Coale, 'Preface' (1998) 45 *Deep Sea Research II* 915.

26 Intergovernmental Panel on Climate Change (IPCC) Working Group I, *Climate Change 2007. The Physical Science Basis. Summary for Policy-Makers* (Cambridge University Press, 2007)

27 John Weier, *John Martin 1935–1993* (2001) NASA earthobservatory.nasa.gov/Library/Giants/Martin/, last accessed 6 June 2009.

28 Jocelyn Kaiser, 'Gulf's Dead Zone Worse in Recent Decades' (2005) 308 *Science* 195. See also Patricia Glibert *et al.*, 'Ocean Urea Fertilization for Carbon Credits Poses High Ecological Risks' (2008) 56 *Marine Pollution Bulletin* 1049.

29 Gavin Sequeira and Ian S. F. Jones, *Financial & Economic Modelling of the Sulu Sea Ocean Nourishment Project*, OTG Report No. 5/99, University of Sydney (1999).

phytoplankton, which then increases the draw-down of CO_2 into the ocean through the biological pump. At the same time, the solution invigorates the base of the food chain, resulting in increased marine productivity. The phytoplankton life cycle is short (approximately five days), after which time the plants decompose and either sink directly to the ocean floor or re-mineralise and initiate further phytoplankton growth. Although ocean fertilisation has a short life cycle, for any benefit to be gained there would need to be constant stimulation of the phytoplankton, possibly resulting in a disruption to the ecosystem. Models predict that sustained ocean fertilisation in the Southern Ocean would change patterns of primary production globally by reducing the availability of nitrogen and phosphorous in the Pacific. There could also be a shift of the microbial community towards organisms that produce methane, another greenhouse gas.[30]

Despite the uncertainty surrounding the science of ocean fertilisation, private organisations plan to conduct large-scale ocean fertilisation releases to generate carbon offsets.[31] They will do so by building on the evidence from the thirteen large-scale *in situ* ocean iron fertilisation field experiments undertaken since 1993. Each trial has released small amounts of iron, and while this research has greatly increased the understanding of carbon dynamics and the role iron plays in the ocean ecosystem, the experiments were not specifically designed to test ocean iron fertilisation as a carbon mitigation strategy.[32]

The tests have proceeded, and will continue to proceed, before any international agreement dealing with ocean fertilisation in the high seas is negotiated and with scant public laws dealing with the process in national waters. Nevertheless, a considerable amount of work has been undertaken by scientists worldwide in the drafting of guidelines for ocean fertilisation research. For instance, Annex 2 of the Report of the Thirty-Second Meeting of the Scientific Group of the London Convention and the Third Meeting of the Scientific Group of the London Protocol sets out the draft assessment framework for scientific research involving ocean fertilisation. Additionally, at the Thirtieth Meeting of the Contracting Parties to the London Convention and the

[30] Jagat Adhiya and Sallie Chisholm, *Is Ocean Fertilization a Good Carbon Sequestration Option?* White Paper, Massachusetts Institute of Technology (2001) 309.

[31] Ibid.

[32] Ken Buesseler *et al.*, 'Ocean Iron Fertilization – Moving Forward in a Sea of Uncertainty' (2009) 319 *Science* 162.

Third Meeting of the Contracting Parties to the London Protocol,[33] a resolution on the regulation of ocean fertilisation was adopted.[34] The resolution did not, however, approve the commercial employment of ocean fertilisation. Rather, it noted that there was insufficient knowledge on the effectiveness and potential environmental impacts of ocean fertilisation to justify activities other than *legitimate scientific research*.[35] It was also agreed that research proposals should be assessed on a case-by-case basis, using an assessment framework to be developed by the Scientific Groups under the London Convention and Protocol, and that the resolution should be reviewed at appropriate intervals, when new and relevant scientific information and knowledge becomes available.

The draft assessment framework aims to ensure competent bodies use the framework in an interactive manner, to make sure all elements of risk are considered before any decision is made to carry out ocean fertilisation research. It is a policy document that connects public and international laws, as it is expected that the same framework will be used irrespective of ocean boundaries.[36] It is a further example, like the Kyoto Protocol with respect to greenhouse gas emissions and the Rotterdam Convention dealing with persistent organic pollutants, where an international grouping of esteemed scientists outlines a cautious response to a global problem that depends on international cooperation together with national efforts. In the meantime, there is still an unenforceable moratorium on ocean fertilisation operations pursuant to the decision of the parties to the Convention on Biological Diversity in Bonn on 30 May 2008, when 191 nations agreed to prohibit large-scale commercial ocean fertilisation schemes to mitigate climate change.[37]

[33] Convention on the Prevention of Marine Pollution by Dumping of Wastes and Other Matter, 29 December 1972, 1046 UNTS 138 (entered into force 30 August 1975) ('London Convention') and Protocol to the Convention on the Prevention of Marine Pollution by Dumping of Wastes and Other Matter, opened for signature 7 November 1996, 36 ILM 1 (entered into force 24 March 2006) (London Protocol).

[34] *Regulation of Ocean Fertilization*, Res. LC-LP. 1 (2008) of the Thirtieth Meeting of the Contracting Parties to the London Convention and the Third Meeting of the Contracting Parties to the London Protocol, LC 30/16, 31 October 2008.

[35] Emphasis added.

[36] *Report of the Thirty-Second Consultative Meeting of Contracting Parties to the Convention on the Prevention of Marine Pollution by Dumping of Wastes and Other Matter*, LC/SG 32/15, 11–15 October 2010, Annex 2, 2–3.

[37] Jeff Tollefson, 'UN Decision Puts Brakes on Ocean Fertilization' (2008) 453 *Nature News* at www.nature.com/news/2008/080604/full/453704b.html, last accessed 18 December 2009.

Potentially exploiting the regulatory gap between public and international laws, a commercial entity, Ocean Nourishment Corporation, is currently trialling ocean fertilisation using macro-nutrients (urea) in near shore environments. The activities are occurring within the realm of public laws. Ocean Nourishment Corporation is investing in ocean fertilisation for both carbon sequestration and to produce fish in low-nutrient areas of the ocean. The corporation plans to sell area-based licences,[38] allowing organisations to generate carbon credits using the Ocean Nourishment™ process.[39] The concerns for ocean urea fertilisation differ from those for ocean iron fertilisation, as they relate not only to the management of the biodiversity in the open ocean, but also to the social implications of the coastal fishing industry and the livelihood of those people who live in the areas adjacent to fertilisation projects. Whereas ocean iron fertilisation, due to its very nature, is most likely to be carried out in the open ocean in waters beyond national jurisdiction, ocean fertilisation using urea or other nutrients is almost certain to be carried out within national jurisdictions.[40]

1.3 *The ocean fertilisation environmental discourses*

The complex and multifaceted features of ocean fertilisation have meant that a number of environmental discourses are evident from the discussions, positioning and views about it. As this section of the chapter will show, depending on how the environment of the oceans is perceived, the risk of climate change is understood, and preferences about markets, ocean fertilisation is characterised, advocated and opposed using different discursive frames. Further, the need for and the form of the public and international legal response to the process are affected by these perceptions, understandings and preferences.

Arguments and representations about ocean fertilisation, and concerns expressed for the oceans can be seen as reflecting at least four discourses. They are: responding to climate change; human dominion over ocean commons; markets for environmental protection; and precaution.

[38] Sequeira and Jones, above n. 29. [39] Ibid.

[40] D. Harrison, *Ocean Nourishment in the Philippines – Proof of Concept Report for Sulu Sea* (Earth, Ocean & Space Pty Ltd, Sydney, 2007) 4.

1.4 *A techno-fix for climate change*

The Intergovernmental Panel on Climate Change was established in 1988 after the World Meteorological Organization and the United Nations Environment Programme recognised that human activities were starting to interfere with the natural global climate systems. Although there has been considerable dialogue and a greater public awareness in relation to climate change since then, there has been no reduction in global emissions. Instead, global emissions have escalated in the last two decades, particularly in developing countries. According to Myhre and others, '[i]n China and India, fossil fuel CO_2 emissions have more than doubled, with the largest increase in China (emissions higher by almost a factor of three). The percentage contribution to the CO_2 emissions was 11% of the total for China in 1990 and has doubled to 22% in 2008.'[41] For the same period the increase in emissions in the US was 17 per cent and in Japan 12 per cent.[42]

Because of this trend of increased emissions in the face of scientific knowledge about climate change risks, geoengineering principles such as CO_2 removal from the atmosphere are presented as a way to keep CO_2 levels within a safe level.[43] This is evident in the way Ocean Nourishment Corporation presents itself and its activities. On its Internet home page, for instance, the corporation claims it 'is an ethical organisation established with the ... [goal] of managing planet wide greenhouse gas concentrations' and that '[i]ncreasing the storage of carbon in the oceans represents a transitional solution to mitigate the potentially catastrophic effects caused by carbon dioxide emissions, pending the full development of a low carbon global community'.[44]

Ocean fertilisation supporters vest faith in technology to overcome an environmental problem, while also presenting the process as a necessary short-term solution to a larger problem. Another ocean fertilisation start-up, Climos, claims that:

[41] G. Myhre, K. Alterskjær and D. Lowe, 'A Fast Method for Updating Global Fossil Fuel Carbon Dioxide Emissions' (2009) 4 *Environmental Research Letters* 034012.

[42] Ibid.

[43] The IPCC's 2007 Report (above n. 26) found stabilisation at around 450 parts per million (ppm) may avoid a two-degree rise in global temperature. Above this point, dangerous climate change is predicted.

[44] Ocean Nourishment Corporation Pty Ltd, *Ocean Nourishment Corporation*, www.ocean nourishment.com, last accessed 21 October 2010.

> While aggressive emission reductions are essential to addressing our currently elevated levels of atmospheric CO_2, various climate intervention techniques may be necessary to bridge us in the interim. Ocean fertilization may be one such technique.[45]

These organisations are, adopting the classification of environmentalists by Dryzek,[46] Prometheans, with a view that ingenuity can overcome environmental limits to development. They are also eco-modernists, believing that environmental governance at the public and international level should be technocratic and opportunistic,[47] and they see their contribution as altruistic. They are problem solvers rather than disbelievers. Ocean fertilisation is presented as a techno-fix within a scientific discourse, even though there is much scientific concern over the environmental consequences of large-scale ocean fertilisation and whether any carbon sequestered will have an effect on the climate at all.[48]

2. Human dominion over commons

The promoters of ocean fertilisation, despite their apparent good will, self-proclaimed ethical conduct and sincere motivations to address climate change, are perpetuating the long-recognised discourse of human dominion over common property. Since the birth of civilisation, humans have exploited the resources of the oceans and used the sea as a dumping ground for pollutants, mostly from land-based sources. As long ago as 1791 Raymond Bastoulh, the *procureur-général-syndic* of the department of the Aude, intoned to his departmental administration:

> People are complaining on all sides about the misguided greed of peasants who are spending every day clearing the woods and the uncultivated land on mountainsides, without realizing that this soil will only be productive for a year or two . . .[49]

[45] Climos, *About Us*, www.climos.com/aboutus.php, last accessed 20 October 2010.

[46] John Dryzek, 'Paradigms and Discourses' in Daniel Bodansky, Jutta Brunnée and Ellen Hey (eds.), *Oxford Handbook of International Environmental Law* (Oxford University Press, 2007) 44.

[47] Karin Bäckstrand, 'Scientisation vs. Civic Expertise in Environmental Governance: Eco-Feminist, Eco-Modern and Post-Modern Responses' (2004) 13 *Environmental Politics* 695.

[48] Adhiya and Chisholm, above n. 30.

[49] Peter McPhee, 'The Misguided Greed of Peasants? Popular Attitudes to the Environment in the Revolution of 1789' (2001) 24 *French Historical Studies* 247.

This attitude is still reflected today, only on a far greater scale. Governments are more likely to be charged with the responsibility of looking after the environment, with public law control now asserted and exercised over the continental shelf and EEZ of the seas. However, for the corporation, the legal entity most likely to pursue ocean fertilisation, what happens to the ocean environment, especially ten, twenty, or fifty or more years from now, may be of little concern or have little impact on its present day profitability. With no government charging levies or requiring leases in the high seas, it is therefore not surprising that the oceans continue to be seen opportunistically as a free commons, exploitable at will. In this sense, ocean fertilisation can be seen as a potential modern day tragedy of the ocean commons.

In 1968, Garrett Hardin's influential essay, 'The Tragedy of the Commons',[50] sparked much controversy.[51] Hardin's logic of the commons was simple. If each grazier is allowed to graze as many cows as possible without considering the long-term needs of the community, the pastures will inevitably become overgrazed, thereby ruining the commons for all others.[52] This type of action can be directly conveyed to what is happening at the present time in the world's oceans. With regard to fishing on the high seas, each fisher wants to obtain the biggest catch possible, within any legal restraints. Often fishers have huge overheads in running their vessels and concern for the sustainability of the target fish, by-catch or damage to other marine life in the process of fishing, usually takes second place to profit margins. Oosterveer claims the level of by-catch[53] alone is around 29 million tons worldwide, and is a large contributor to the loss of ocean biodiversity.[54] This is further exacerbated by many countries offering government grants for the building of commercial fishing vessels.

[50] Garrett Hardin, 'The Tragedy of the Commons' (1968) 162 *Science* 1243.

[51] Beryl Crowe, 'The Tragedy of the Commons Revisited' (1969) 166 *Science* 1104. See also Thomas Dietz, Elinor Ostrom and Paul Stern, 'The Struggle to Govern the Commons' (2003) 302 *Science* 1907.

[52] Hardin, above n. 50.

[53] By-catch are non-targeted or other fish or wildlife caught in the nets alongside targeted species. By-catch can include sharks, dolphins, turtles, sea birds and undersized or other fish.

[54] Peter Oosterveer, 'Governing Global Fish Provisioning: Ownership and Management of Marine Resources' (2008) 51 *Ocean & Coastal Management* 797.

Pollution of the world's waterways follows a similar route.[55] With the cost of disposing of pollutants escalating,[56] each polluter endeavours to discard the maximum amount of pollutant possible for the least cost, often with little consideration as to any environmental damage sustained in the process. It is not surprising, then, that what is perceived as a relatively benign pollutant, CO_2, should be proposed for disposal in the vast seas.[57] In the case of ocean fertilisation, it is a pollutant that can be made more readily absorbed into the ocean commons. If ocean resources were infinite, then people could populate, consume, pollute and fish at will.[58] However, we know the oceans are not infinite, and there is evidence that fertilisation of oceans for the purpose of carbon sequestration may lead to ocean acidification. Hence, by maintaining their technological faith in ocean fertilisation, proponents are ignoring known and suspected limits and treating the oceans as an inexhaustible commons where international and public law has a minimal role.

2.1 Markets for environmental protection

Although the science has yet to be proven and the environmental consequences of large-scale ocean fertilisation are still unknown, ocean fertilisation is being presented as a means through which marketable carbon mitigation permits can be created. It is the opportunity of this market measure that is a powerful incentive for companies to exploit the oceans. Adopting the language of 'offsets', Ocean Nourishment Corporation asserts that:

> One Ocean Nourishment™ site will remove approximately 5–8 million tonnes of CO_2 from the atmosphere for each year of operation, equivalent to offsetting annual emissions from a typical 1000MW coal-fired power station or the short-term sequestration from one million hectares of new growth forest.[59]

[55] Michelle Allsopp *et al.*, *Plastic Debris in the World's Oceans*, Greenpeace Online Report at oceans.greenpeace.org/en/documents-reports/plastic_ocean_report, last accessed 10 December 2009.

[56] State of Queensland Environment Protection Authority, *State of the Environment Queensland 2007* (2008).

[57] See above Chapter 17 by Afshin Akhtarkhavari.

[58] John Dryzek, *The Politics of the Earth: Environmental Discourses* (Oxford University Press, 1st edn, 1997) 25.

[59] Ocean Nourishment, *Technology* at www.oceannourishment.com/technology.asp, last accessed 20 October 2010.

Meanwhile, Climos claims that it:

> intends to use emerging environmental markets to help fund the research into OIF. The ultimate purpose of these environmental markets is to protect or restore the environment by creating a financial incentive that will stimulate action and innovation within the private sector.[60]

Although all commercial applications of ocean fertilisation have been temporarily put on hold due to the moratorium,[61] if the science can be proved to be viable and safe, then commercial ocean fertilisation may well be a part of the future carbon market, a structure that dominates the dialogue about climate change regulation at international and national levels.[62]

2.2 *Precaution in the ocean commons*

Much opposition to ocean fertilisation is framed either explicitly or implicitly within the precautionary principle, a legal standard defined in Principle 15 of the 1992 Rio Declaration on Environment and Development. For instance, the Hands Off Mother Earth network opposes ocean fertilisation on the basis of rejecting the oceans being used as a 'laboratory';[63] a place where untested experiments are conducted. More explicitly, the Global Forum on Oceans, Coasts, and Islands claims that 'concerns for the inherent risks and costs to the environment [associated with ocean fertilisation] suggest the precautionary approach is appropriate'.[64]

An essential element of the precautionary principle is that it is applied to those situations where the potential outcome is irreversible. This is especially relevant to ocean fertilisation, where there is little knowledge or control over the impacts on the biodiversity of the ecosystems through fears of eutrophication and acidification having permanent effects on the oceans.

The degree to which people consider a risk acceptable will vary, depending on the magnitude of damage likely to occur, as well as the dimensions of the risk.[65] For some, ocean fertilisation presents too great

[60] Climos, *What Is Climos' Funding/Business Model*? at www.climos.com/faq.php#9, last accessed 20 October 2010.

[61] Tollefson, above n. 37. [62] See above Chapter 11 by Lee Godden.

[63] Hands Off Mother Earth, *Ocean Fertilization* at www.handsoffmotherearth.org/learn-more/what-is-geoengineering/ocean-fertilization/, last accessed 20 October 2010.

[64] Biliana Cicin-Sain (ed.), *Oceans and Climate Change: Issues and Recommendations for Policymakers and for the Climate Negotiations, Global Forum on Oceans, Coasts, and Islands*, Draft Policy Briefs prepared for the World Ocean Conference, 11–15 May 2009, Manado, Indonesia, 143.

[65] Jeroen Van der Sluijs and Wim Turenburg, 'Climate Change and the Precautionary Principle' in Elizabeth Fisher, Judith Jones and René Von Scomberg (eds.), *Implementing*

a risk in the form of ocean acidification and other uncertainties. This framing of opposition to ocean fertilisation appears to be having some influence on the decision of governance bodies. It has led to Climos mounting an argument that the precautionary principle ought not to apply, largely on the basis of lack of clear meaning of the principle, and its characterisation as a 'philosophy' rather than a legal standard. Climos instead prefers 'adaptive management' and monitoring as a form of self-regulation within the public and international law realms.[66]

3. Governance of ocean fertilisation

The unique characteristics of the oceans contribute to the problem of devising governance regimes to protect the resource and control behaviour. The sheer size and difficulty of measuring the resources and biodiversity contained within only makes the task more complex. On the high seas there have been instances of ships evading the rules.[67] Technology such as satellites may assist in monitoring phytoplankton blooms stimulated by ocean fertilisation, but this shows only the extent, not the depth,[68] of the blooms and does not monitor the health of the ecosystems. The international legal community must confront the difficulties presented by ocean fertilisation governance.

Technological developments, such as ocean fertilisation, while having the potential to improve one set of socio-ecological conditions, may increase the potential for damage to the ecosystems.[69] One such example was the ocean urea fertilisation trials carried out off the Tawi-Tawi islands of the Philippines in 2007. This proposal, a collaboration between the University of Philippines Visayas and the Ocean Technology Group from the University of Sydney, involved no consultation with the Tawi-Tawi people. Following the trials, the seaweed was observed to be whitening, which the locals call 'ice-ice'.[70] With the people of

the Precautionary Principle: Perspectives and Prospects (Edward Elgar, Cheltenham, 2006) 254.

66 Climos, *How Does the Precautionary Principle Apply?* www.climos.com/faq.php#50, last accessed 20 October 2010.

67 Matthew Gianni and Walt Simpson, *The Changing Nature of High Seas Fishing. How Flags of Convenience Provide Cover for Illegal, Unreported and Unregulated Fishing* (Australian Department of Agriculture,Fisheries and Forestry, International Transport Workers' Federation, and WWF International, Canberra, London and Gland, 2005).

68 Glibert *et al.*, above n. 28.

69 Trull *et al.*, above n. 14.

70 Philippines, *Parliamentary Debates*, 27 November 2007, Question of Privilege of Rep. Jaafar, Government Journal No. 40.

Tawi-Tawi relying on the sea for their income and living, mostly from fishing and the growing of seaweed, any damage to the ecosystem could be catastrophic to their livelihoods.[71] The experience made stark the need for a public law regime to preserve their interests even in the interim, before any commercialisation of ocean fertilisation.

4. Conclusion

As with any human intervention concerning the environment, ocean fertilisation carries with it many potential risks as well as possible benefits. Whether society is willing to accept any form of large-scale ocean fertilisation that is likely to result in the alteration of the ocean ecosystems, especially while many consequences are still unforeseen, is yet to be determined. However, the view of the community to the concerns associated with ocean fertilisation and its collective view about responding aggressively to climate change will impact on future decisions in this area.[72] So, too, will the various discourses evident within the debates about the merits and risks of ocean fertilisation. It is within this setting that public and international laws, connected by an environmental issue occurring across jurisdictions, will be devised. The regime will most likely reflect other ocean conventions, where the high seas and national waters are subject to almost identical laws. The governance structure will have to deal with the view of the ocean as an exploitable commons, the principle of precaution and the marketability of any carbon offsets created through this potential opportunity to mitigate climate change. This will be the dominant consideration. After all, the problem of climate change is global and concerns every man, woman and child on this planet, and the 'solutions' to this problem have not been readily agreed upon. So while '[t]here is hardly a place on earth where human activity does not influence the environment's current condition or its prospects for the future',[73] the largely unregulated and unmanaged ocean commons might be facing further exploitation.

[71] Ibid.

[72] Julia Mayo-Ramsay, 'Taking a Precautionary Approach to Climate Mitigation Measures in the Southern Ocean' (2008) 12 *Antarctic & Southern Ocean Law & Policy Occasional Papers* 33.

[73] As cited in Timothy W. Luke, *Generating Green Governmentality: A Cultural Critique of Environmental Studies as a Power/Knowledge Formation*. Department of Political Science, Virginia Polytechnic Institute and State University Blacksburg (June 1996) at www.cddc.vt.edu/tim/tims/Tim514a.pdf, last accessed 8 May 2011, 11.

Concluding remarks

Discourse versus strategy

THOMAS POGGE

Lawyers love law. It is not hard to see why. Law facilitates the peaceful settlement of conflicting claims – not entirely cost-free, but vastly cheaper than most other ways of battling it out. Law forestalls many conflicts by setting out in advance, in a mutually consistent way, what various agents are required, entitled, permitted, or forbidden to do. By disposing society to punish those who overstep their bounds, law deters conduct likely to entail conflict. Moreover, insofar as it is not merely known but also internalised, law civilises social intercourse by placing illegal conduct outside the realm of options that agents typically consider. By clarifying and policing the limits of each agent's freedom, law ensures that agents can act with security and confidence within these limits.

All these virtues of law are compatible with gross injustice – compatible with systems of laws that recognise, for instance, property in persons (slavery) or an entitlement to rape one's wife. Gross injustice in the law may balance law's virtues through the special hideousness of officially sanctioned wrongs. Rape is rendered even more intolerable if it is socially approved as lawful or even comes right after the victim has been turned over, by dutiful enforcers of the law, to her rightful owner or husband.

Those who love law recognise that it can be gravely unjust. Typically, though, they believe that law has an inherent tendency to progress morally. This happens, according to them, through the cleansing power of legal discourse which is inherently related with broader cultural and intellectual discourses about justice, fairness, equity and the common good. Much legal scholarship on the evolution and likely future of law, including the majority of chapters in this volume, is informed by this optimistic background assumption that law is trending, slowly but with some steadiness, toward convergence with morality.

Such optimism about the self-cleansing tendency of law is less common outside the law. It is denied or downplayed by realists and Marxists, for example, who view the content of law as tending to reflect and to track the distribution of power. They recognise that law can over time become more just or more protective of the vulnerable, but they add that law may as easily become less just or more oppressive. As they see it, the explanation of changes in the law, in either direction, is to be found in extra-legal developments. It may become possible for women to achieve equality of legal status when changing economic conditions enhance their economic value and hence their bargaining power, and possible for slaves to achieve their freedom when powerful industrialists need cheap and mobile labour for their proliferating factories. Equally it may happen that powerful agents find it in their interest to work for legal changes that make law less just – for instance, the introduction of slavery or the suppression of the trade in generic medicines. On this less optimistic analysis, law is likely always to remain unjust to some considerable extent. The strong and more powerful have greater opportunities to affect the content of law and they tend to give greater weight than justice allows to the advancement of their own interests and less weight to protecting the needs and interests of the weak and vulnerable. Law can then be expected to disfavour those who are naturally disadvantaged and to perpetuate social disadvantages that those who suffer them are too weak to overcome on their own.

This realist analysis of law cannot be dismissed. It is undeniable that the evolution of law does not take place in a vacuum: through intelligent discourses among disinterested jurists and intellectual citizens about how law should be shaped so as best to fulfil the concerns of justice and equity. The content of the law substantially affects the economic and political power of agents and groups of agents as well as the evolution of this distribution over time. Understanding this well, agents and groups seek to influence the content of the law in their own favour; and there is no reason to believe that the net effect of such competitive lobbying is either naught or else consistent with basic requirements of justice. In fact, there is good reason to expect the opposite: that competitive self-interested lobbying tends to shift the law in favour of more privileged agents and groups, as these have better opportunities and stronger incentives to lobby, in part because they can – far more easily than poor and marginalised groups – form sufficiently strong coalitions and acquire the expertise necessary to lobby effectively.

Still, it would not be warranted to conclude from the realist analysis that law simply manifests a dynamic bargaining equilibrium among competing interests and thus is impervious to any public discourses about justice and the common good. Law plays an important role in maintaining the legitimacy of the social order and, to fulfil this role, must be presented as just. This need is reflected, for instance, in expressions like 'Department of Justice', 'Ministry of Justice', and 'criminal justice system' for the law enforcement segment of governmental administration and also in the title 'Justice' for certain officers of the law. And this need would not be met if the law, or sections of it, were too closely tailored to the advantage of specific persons or organisations. To fulfil its legitimating role, the law must, then, be formulated in general terms. It must, for example, eschew proper names and then tax competing corporations on the basis of the same tax rate schedule. Even where the law draws impactful distinctions in general terms, these distinctions require a comprehensible rationale: were law to impose without good reason different tax schedules on lawyers and dentists, it would suffer in its legitimating role.[1] And this fact exerts some discipline that tends to move the law toward justice.

So how much can we expect from this gravitational pull toward justice? Realists will contend that this pull is much diminished by three important phenomena. First, legitimacy of law can be preserved not merely by sound rationales for legal discriminations, but also by specious rationalisations. Agents capable of influencing those who make law are often also in a position to hire or otherwise reward economists or other experts.[2] Given the complexity of law in many areas – including environmental law[3] – and the complexity of the arguments brought to bear in shaping it, and given the immense proliferation of legal rules in the modern world, it is not hard to avoid public notice of the fact that some formulations of the law were corruptly designed to serve special interests.

[1] In the United States, we actually have such a case. The managers of hedge funds owe federal income tax at a maximal rate of 15 per cent, while the members of any other profession face top marginal income tax rates of 35 per cent. The discrepancy persists thanks to continuous lobbying – and helps undermine the legitimacy of Congress and the law in the eyes of the public.

[2] In Chapter 5 above, Jaye Ellis argues further that experts are dominating the discourses of sustainability and precaution at international law, while Bettina Lange in Chapter 6 above analyses the entrenched and dominant position of experts in deciding on the authorisation of genetically modified organisms in Europe.

[3] See the Introduction by Brad Jessup and Kim Rubenstein.

Second, people judge what is just and reasonable in light of the conceptions of justice prevalent in their time and jurisdiction.[4] Such dominant conceptions themselves may well reflect the prevailing distribution of power. There is, then, an inherent tendency of law to gravitate only toward 'justice' – that is, toward justice as conceived by those who might be able to influence the making or revising of law. Such 'justice' might well be consistent with existing unjust practices – such as slavery and the subjection of women or, in our age, environmental degradation and resource purchases from corrupt and oppressive rulers. As Karl Marx memorably put the general point in his 'German Ideology':

> The ideas of the ruling class are in every epoch the ruling ideas, ie the class which is the ruling material force of society, is at the same time its ruling intellectual force. The class which has the means of material production at its disposal, has control at the same time over the means of mental production, so that thereby, generally speaking, the ideas of those who lack the means of mental production are subject to it. The ruling ideas are nothing more than the ideal expression of the dominant material relationships, the dominant material relationships grasped as ideas.[5]

A third phenomenon that should temper the optimism of those who delight in the law's drift toward justice is defection by agents who find the law too demanding on themselves.[6] To be fully effective, law must meet two requirements that may not be compatible and may then pull it in opposite directions: law must be perceived as basically just by the general public and it must also keep the most powerful agents sufficiently content so that they do not have excessively large temptations to defect. Defection can take three forms. There is undesirable conduct designed to defeat the law's purpose without violation of the law (as in tax avoidance, where those subject to a tax seek to identify and exploit loopholes that allow them legally to reduce their tax on given earnings). There is straightforward violation of the law (as in tax evasion, where those subject to a tax seek to conceal their wealth or earnings in order illegally to escape the taxes they owe). Further, there is choice of jurisdiction (as

[4] See above Chapter 8 by Tim Stephens, which provides an example of how the International Court of Justice has conceived environmental justice.

[5] Karl Marx, 'The German Ideology: Part 1' in Robert C. Tucker (ed.), *The Marx–Engels Reader* (W.W. Norton & Co., New York, 1978) 146, 172–3.

[6] The members of the Asia Pacific Partnership can be considered defectors from the international climate law regime. See above Chapter 13 by Jeffrey McGee and Ros Taplin.

when a resourceful agent locates or relocates away from a jurisdiction in order to avoid being bound by its laws).

All three corrosive phenomena tend to be more serious when power inequalities among the law's subjects are larger. And the third phenomenon of defection becomes more serious when there is poorer enforcement of the law. Poor enforcement affects not merely the conduct of those who have no moral allegiance to the law by reducing their reluctance to be law breakers; it also affects the conduct of those who have such an allegiance. It does so by feeding the belief that others are probably breaking the law and that it is therefore less wrong (more excusable) to defect oneself, that is, to avoid doing what one would otherwise recognise as one's fair share. When one firm believes that many of its competitors are violating the law to get ahead, then it will feel that its own defection (in any of the three ways) is excused by the need to avoid competing at an unfair disadvantage.

Massive inequality and poor enforcement have been hallmarks of international law, and indeed we find that international law faces more serious hurdles on its path to justice than does the domestic law of democratic national jurisdictions.[7] All three corrosive phenomena are prominent in the international arena. Substantial resources are expended on cosmetic efforts toward showing that existing legal arrangements are morally good or at least well intentioned,[8] as paradigmatically exemplified by myriad efforts to justify as 'pro-poor' legal arrangements that really benefit powerful states and their corporations. The international justice discourse is very heavily dominated by the more powerful states' media companies whose profitability depends on beautifying and defending the status quo. Strong states routinely defect when they find legal constraints inconvenient, as is best illustrated in recent decades by the conduct of the United States which, to cite just three well-known instances, ignored the 1984 judgment of the International Court of Justice (finding that the mining of Nicaragua's harbours and the building and arming of the Contras was in violation of international law), ignored the UN Security Council's decision not to authorise the 2003 invasion of Iraq, and also repeatedly ignored WTO rulings against its protectionist violations (for example cotton subsidies) of the WTO Treaty.

[7] Compare, for instance, Chapters 8 and 2 above by Tim Stephens and Brad Jessup, respectively.

[8] See, e.g., the discussion of the 'good international citizen' in Chapter 12 above by River Cordes-Holland. This is a term the Australian government has applied to itself to justify its approach to international engagement on matters including climate change.

The chapters in this volume explore how and to what extent reasoned discourse centrally involving contested conceptions of justice and equity is influential in creating and shaping authoritative and effective law in an area where such an influence must appear especially improbable. This area is environmental protection, the preservation of conditions on our planet that enable human beings and other species to live here in good health and comfort for centuries and millennia to come. This possibility is currently under threat: most immediately from climate change driven by various greenhouse gases, principally CO_2. Somewhat less immediate threats are posed by the rapid depletion of non-renewable natural resources such as crude oil (also used in the production of fertiliser), natural gas, coal, uranium, lithium, copper, phosphorus and fossile water (which collects in aquifers far more slowly than it is currently extracted).

These threats to the long-term survival and health of humanity and many other species appear especially difficult to tackle on a realist analysis of law. This is so because of three main misalignments. First, there is, in the temporal dimension, a dramatic mismatch between power and vulnerability. Climate change and resource depletion may well devastate the lives of billions of people in the future, but these people are yet unborn or at best children, and thus can do nothing to affect the rules that might now be put in place to protect them.[9] On the other hand, those who can exert real influence on the content of these rules are mature adults whose remaining life expectancy saves them from having to bear the brunt of the problem if and when it materialises.

In response to this observation it is often said that members of each generation care at least about their children and the children of close relatives and friends. But here the second misalignment comes into play: the dramatic mismatch between power and vulnerability across income groups. Those who contribute most to environmental degradation and could do the most, individually or politically, to slow it down, are affluent people in affluent countries. So long as they can bequeath their economic advantages to their descendants, the latter are well positioned to protect themselves from environmental harms. Should energy, water or food become scarce and therefore expensive, they will still be able to buy enough for themselves and their families. Should climate change bring on uncomfortable temperatures, they can afford to air-condition their homes. Should rising sea levels or extreme weather events make specific locations or entire regions inhospitable, they can afford to move and will

[9] See above Chapter 1 by Peter Lawrence.

be welcomed even as immigrants in other countries. Conversely, those who have most reason to worry about the fate of their descendants are poor people in poor countries: people in many island states and low-lying coastal regions (including much of Bangladesh), which are threatened by rising sea levels, and people in Africa, which is facing water scarcity and desertification. These future people will not be able to keep up with competitive bidding for shrinking supplies of food, water and energy. They will not be able to do much to insulate themselves from temperature extremes. And they are also unlikely to be able to move to a more hospitable location. Unfortunately for them, their currently living ancestors are almost entirely powerless to protect their interests.

This second misalignment among contemporaries brings an ancillary problem in its wake. Clearly, any just or equitable distribution of the relative burdens of slowing environmental degradation would impose the largest burdens on populations that are now doing the most damage and are benefiting the most from past pollution and past depletion of non-renewable resources: the United States, Australia, Canada, Europe and Japan. But these populations have little to lose from non-agreement – less, certainly, over the next century than they would lose by bearing their fair share of solving the problem. Of course, any of these countries might be convinced by moral reasons to commit itself to a just international legal framework under which it forgoes unfair gains for its own population for the sake of protecting much poorer present and future populations from much larger harms. But convincing such a country to do this is much harder when other, similar countries fail to join. The prospects of convincing Canada or Australia to join such a regime will be greatly diminished, for instance, if the United States refuses to join. Canada and Australia can then more easily likewise refuse to join, pointing out that their own 'sacrifice' would mean little without a matching effort by the United States and also that they should not be asked to place their own constituents at an unfair competitive disadvantage vis-à-vis their US competitors. In the real world, of course, things would be less clear-cut. The countries interested in avoiding a fair agreement will make various plausible but incompatible proposals and will then with deep regret announce that, due to the intransigence of others, they could not reach a compromise. This way they can get the best of both worlds: each continues to cause a grossly disproportionate share of pollution and depletion of non-renewable resources while blaming the resulting harm on some other country's supposedly unreasonable negotiating posture. Negotiations in which key parties gain from non-agreement are likely to result in non-agreement so long as each of these key parties can plausibly deny that the failure was chiefly its responsibility.

The third misalignment, finally, is the divergence between the incentives of members of the global elite and the interests of those on whose behalf they are supposedly acting. This misalignment is driven by two factors. Because the position of most leaders is precarious – politicians face re-election, CEOs need to keep their board and shareholders satisfied – such leaders tend to focus excessively on the near term; those who accept some short-term underperformance for the sake of future gains rarely survive in office long enough to reap the benefits of their wisdom. The other, related factor is that leaders tend to partake in their successes far more fully than in their failures and are thereby incentivised to take excessive risks. For example, it makes a huge difference to a CEO whether his company is performing in the second decile or the ninth.[10] With a second-decile performance, the CEO will fetch large contingency rewards in the form of profit-sensitive bonuses and stock options; with a ninth-decile performance he will likely receive no discretionary rewards and lose his job fairly fast. By contrast, it makes little difference to a CEO whether his company is performing in the ninth decile or the tenth. The CEO has no self-interested reason, then, to sacrifice corporate profits in order to avert the risk of catastrophe.

Let me illustrate the point with a simplified version of a recent event. Suppose it would cost BP $600 million annually to eliminate the 2 per cent annual risk of a major offshore oil spill that would cost the company $40 billion. This is clearly a good deal for the company: the probability-weighted annual gain is $800 million (2 per cent of $40 billion) and the cost is only $600 million. But it may not be a good deal for BP's CEO when the extra $600 million expense would make him an underperformer liable to lose his job. The CEO is then vastly better off taking the gamble, because his prospective winnings are both *much more probable* and *much larger* than his prospective losses. Regarding probability, if the CEO is five years from retirement, the chance of the catastrophe happening on his watch is 10 per cent, if he is eleven years from retirement, the chance is 20 per cent, and even if he is twenty years from retirement, the chance is still only one-third. Regarding pay-offs, if the CEO is lucky and

[10] Deciles are one-tenth segments of a rank distribution. Thus a CEO performing in the second decile means that the company is, under his leadership, doing better than at least 80 per cent and worse than at least 10 per cent of its competitors.

the spill does not occur, he will keep his job and partake in the greater profits of his firm through performance bonuses and stock options. If he is unlucky, he will be losing his job somewhat more ignominiously on account of the oil spill rather than on account of plain underperformance.[11] With so much upside and so little downside, the CEO's self-interested reasons overwhelmingly favour his taking the gamble – against the best interests of the company's owners and workers. Moreover, given that the gamble is so lucrative for the CEO, he is then also incentivised to use corporate funds to lobby against stricter regulations that would force him to spend the money necessary to eliminate the risk of a major spill. This lobbying is likely to be successful, because the relevant politicians, too, face an attractive gamble when they decide to accept support from the CEO in exchange for laxer regulation[12] – a gamble whose prospective winnings are both much more probable and larger than its prospective losses.

Considered through the lens of strategic rationality, the environmental problem at the centre of this book is something like a perfect storm.[13] Though humanity clearly has the capacity to organise itself to master the challenge, this mobilisation will not happen because of the three dramatic misalignments. These misalignments will persist. The first arises from a necessary fact: that the present generation is in a position unilaterally to benefit itself at the expense of future generations. The third misalignment might be corrected by introducing draconian punishments for leaders who make decisions that go against the interests they were entrusted to protect. China imposes occasional such punishments for clear-cut cases of corruption – witness, for instance, the execution of Zheng Xiaoyu, the former head of China's Food and Drug Administration. But most Chinese officials enrich themselves with impunity and resist any systematic efforts to curb the massive corruption in their country.[14] And Western political and corporate officials are similarly unlikely to permit the

[11] He may also lose some money on any company shares he may own.

[12] Lee Godden, in Chapter 11 above, explores the movement towards more reflexive, 'flexible' and 'responsive' environmental regulation, which she suggests is in large part driven by industry demands.

[13] Stephen M. Gardener, 'A Perfect Moral Storm: Climate Change, Intergenerational Equity, and the Problem of Moral Corruption' (2006) 15 *Environmental Values* 397.

[14] One main indicator of corruption is illicit financial outflow which can be measured through indirect methods. The non-profit organisation, Global Financial Integrity, estimates that, in the 2000–08 period, China accounted for one-third of all illicit financial outflows from less developed countries, or a staggering \$2.18 trillion (= \$746 million *per day*). See Dev Kar and Karly Curcio, *Illicit Financial Flows from Developing*

introduction of the kind of serious criminal punishments for breach of trust that would meaningfully alleviate the principal–agent problem I have analysed.

I see the best prospects with regard to the second misalignment – though its mitigation alone can bring only limited relief. Progress here might involve two mutually reinforcing components: reductions in international inequality and improvements in the content and enforcement of (especially) international law. Reductions in international inequality have been gathering momentum as leading developing countries (India, Vietnam, Nigeria, Pakistan, Thailand, Indonesia, Malaysia, Argentina, Brazil) have joined China in growing their economies faster than the OECD countries. To be sure, growth in these countries has predominantly benefited their national elites: people who are internationally mobile and have a less-than-solid commitment to protecting the interests of the national population. But these elites do have their assets and power base in these developing countries and therefore do have an interest in bringing their countries' increasing economic strength to bear in favour of protecting the preconditions for continued solid economic growth in their respective countries.

The central message of my concluding thoughts, then, is that working through legal and moral discourses toward protecting humanity's future on this planet can be successful only insofar as we take careful account of the existing and evolving distribution of power and interests. It is not difficult at all to agree with Judge Weeramantry's Dissenting Opinion in the ICJ's Nuclear Weapons Advisory Opinion, which endorses 'the principle of intergenerational equity' and holds that the Court can and should recognise and protect the rights of future generations as these rights 'have woven themselves into international law through major treaties, through juristic opinion and through general principles of law recognised by civilised nations'.[15] Nor is it difficult to agree with the judgment of Simon Caney and the Human Rights Council of the United Nations that: 'climate change poses an immediate and far-reaching threat to people and communities around the world and has implications for the full enjoyment of human rights'.[16] But if such ideas

Countries 2000–2009: Update with a Focus on Asia (Global Financial Integrity, Washington DC, 2011).

[15] [1996] ICJ Rep 226, 17, discussed in Chapter 8 above by Tim Stephens.

[16] Human Rights Council, *Promotion and Protection of all Human Rights, Civil, Political, Economic, Social and Cultural Rights. Including the Right to Development*, 7th sess.,

were to give rise to judicial decisions that impose substantial costs or opportunity costs on powerful states, these would be far more likely to contribute to the irrelevance of the Court than to the compliance of the states that the Court's verdict sought to constrain. Law and its application must tread a difficult path here: they must smartly adjust themselves to existing geopolitical realities in order to gain the strength and prestige they need to increasingly assert themselves against such realities.

In the process of strengthening international law, it is especially important to find win–win reforms: new legal regimes or regime modifications that bring large collective gains that can be distributed so that the major players have prudential reasons to commit. One obvious idea in this direction is an internationally funded regime of rewards for green-technology innovations. Under such a regime, innovators would have the option of collecting rewards based on the environmental impact of their innovation on condition that they agree to license this innovation worldwide at zero cost.[17] Another obvious idea is an internationally funded regime designed to ensure that basic nutritional, educational and medical needs are securely met worldwide. Such a regime would bring large collective benefits today and would also, by greatly reducing total fertility rates among the currently poorest households and populations, result in a substantial reduction of the year 2100 human population, which in turn would greatly ease the ecological pressures this population would put on the environment and, indirectly, on itself and its descendants.[18]

I do not doubt that it is possible to shape moral and legal discourse and thereby to change the world. History provides inspiring examples of this, such as the struggle for the abolition of slavery and the struggle for the equal status of women – developments that cannot be explained by reference merely to strategic behaviour on the part of the persons and groups involved. Yet, moral reasons will, in the foreseeable future, be

Agenda Item 3, UN Doc. A/HRC/7/L.21/Rev.1 (26 March 2008), further discussed in Chapter 1 above by Peter Lawrence.

17 The idea is described in section VIII of Thomas Pogge, 'Keynote Address: Poverty, Climate Change, and Overpopulation' (2010) 38 *Georgia Journal of International and Comparative Law* 525. The idea is obviously modelled on the proposal of the Health Impact Fund, described in the second volume of this series. See Thomas Pogge, 'The Health Impact Fund: Better Pharmaceutical Innovations at Much Lower Prices' in Thomas Pogge, Matthew Rimmer and Kim Rubenstein (eds.), *Incentives for Global Public Health: Patent Law and Access to Essential Medicines* (Cambridge University Press, 2010) 135.

18 Ibid. ('Keynote') Section III.

able to command only minor forces in the grand contest over the future of national and international law. To be effective, these forces must then be used with vision, wisdom and strategic intelligence – to confound, co-opt and divert superior forces of self-interest that, for now, cannot be defeated in open confrontation. Profound change in human extraction, production and consumption patterns cannot be much delayed. To achieve it, we must conceive it and call for it, of course. But we must also master the political forces that can block or promote it: master them by way of intellectual analysis and, on this basis, also by way of practical engagement. To face the mighty challenge of preserving our planet, we need both discourse and strategy.

BIBLIOGRAPHY

Books, articles, monographs, reports

11th Central Committee of the Communist Party of China, *Resolution on Certain Questions in the History of our Party Since the Founding of the People's Republic of China* (6th Plenary Session, 27 June 1981)

16th Central Committee of the Communist Party of China, *The Outline of the Eleventh Five-Year Plan for National Economic and Social Development of the People's Republic of China* (5th Plenary Session, 11 October 2005)

Abbott, Carolyn, 'Environmental Command Regulation' in Ben Richardson and Stepan Wood (eds.), *Environmental Law for Sustainability* (Hart Publishing, Oxford, 2006) 64

Abbott, Chris, Rogers, Paul and Sloboda, John, *Global Responses to Global Threats: Sustainable Security for the 21st Century* (Oxford Research Group, Oxford, 2006)

Acheson, James, 'Institutional Failure in Resource Management' (2006) 35 *Annual Review of Anthropology* 117

Ackerman, Bruce and Stewart, Richard, 'Reforming Environmental Law' (1985) 37 *Stanford Law Review* 1333

Ackerman, Reuben, 'Japanese Whaling in the Pacific Ocean: Defiance of International Whaling Norms in the Name of "Scientific Research", Culture and Tradition' (2002) 25 *Boston College International and Comparative Law Review* 323

Adams, William, *Green Development: Environment and Sustainability in the Third World* (Routledge, London and New York, 2nd edn, 2001)

and Jeanrenaud, Sally, *Transition to Sustainability: Towards a Humane and Diverse World* (IUCN, Gland, 2008)

Adhiya, Jagat and Chisholm, Sallie, *Is Ocean Fertilization a Good Carbon Sequestration Option?* White Paper, Massachusetts Institute of Technology (2001)

Adler, Jonathan, 'Stand or Deliver: Citizen Suits, Standing, and Environmental Protection' (2001) 12 *Duke Environmental Law and Policy Forum* 39

Agius, Emanuel and Busuttil, Salvino, *Future Generations and International Law* (Earthscan, London, 1998)

Agrawala, Shardul and Andresen, Steinar, 'Indispensability and Indefensibility – The United States in the Climate Treaty Negotiations' (1999) 5(4) *Global Governance* 457

Agyeman, Julian, *Sustainable Communities and the Challenge of Environmental Justice* (New York University Press, 2005)

Bullard, Robert and Evans, Bob, 'Introduction: Joined-Up Thinking: Bringing Together Sustainability, Environmental Justice and Equity' in Julian Agyeman, Robert Bullard and Bob Evans (eds.), *Just Sustainabilities: Development in an Unequal World* (MIT Press, Cambridge, Mass., 2003) 1

Alagappa, Muthiah, 'Comprehensive Security: Interpretations in ASEAN Countries' in Robert A. Scalapino *et al.* (eds.), *Asian Security Issues: Regional and Global* (Institute of East Asian Studies, University of California, Berkeley, 1988) 50

Asian Security Practices: Material and Ideational Influences (Stanford University Press, 1998)

Albrecht, Eike, 'Transboundary Consultations in Strategic Environmental Assessment' (2008) 26 *Impact Assessment and Project Appraisal* 289

Alchian, Armen, *Pricing Society* (Institute of Economic Affairs, Leicester, 1967)

Alemanno, Alberto and Mahieu, Stephanie, 'The European Food Safety Authority before the European Courts' (2008) 5 *European Food and Feed Law Review* 320

Allen, Ross and Bergin, Anthony, 'Ocean Acidification: An Emerging Australian Environmental Security Challenge' (2009) 1(2) *Australian Journal of Maritime and Ocean Affairs* 49

Allison, Ian, *et al.*, *The Copenhagen Diagnosis: Updating the World on the Latest Climate Science* (The University of New South Wales Climate Change Research Centre, Sydney, 2009)

Aman, Alfred Jr, 'Administrative Law for a New Century' in Michael Taggart (ed.), *The Province of Administrative Law* (Hart Publishing, Oxford, 1997) 90

'Globalisation, Democracy and the Need for a New Administrative Law' in Michael Likosky (ed.), *Privatising Development: Transnational Law, Infrastructure and Human Rights* (Martinus Nijhoff Publishers, Leiden, 2005) 271

Anaya, S. James, *Indigenous Peoples in International Law* (Oxford University Press, New York, 2nd edn, 2004)

Anderson, Terry and Leal, Donald, 'Free Market Versus Political Environmentalism' (1992) 15 *Harvard Journal of Law and Public Policy* 297

Andre, Pierre, *et al.*, *Public Participation – International Best Practice Principles*, Special Publication Series No. 4 (International Association for Impact Assessment, Fargo, 2006)

Andresen, Steinar and Hey, Ellen, 'The Effectiveness and Legitimacy of International Environmental Institutions' (2005) 5 *International Environmental Agreements* 211

Angel, Jeff, *Green is Good* (ABC Books, Sydney, 2008)

Anghie, Anthony, *Imperialism, Sovereignty and the Making of International Law* (Cambridge University Press, 2004)

Arcuri, Alessandra, *The Case for a Procedural Version of the Precautionary Principle Erring on the Side of Environmental Preservation*, Global Law Working Paper No. 09/04 (2004)

Arrow, Kenneth, *Social Choice and Individual Values* (Yale University Press, New Haven, 1963)

Asia Pacific Forum of National Human Rights Institutions, *Human Rights and the Environment: Background Paper* (Asia Pacific Forum, Sydney, 2007)

Asia-Pacific Partnership on Clean Development and Climate, *Asia Pacific Partnership on Clean Development and Climate Brochure* (2008)

Asia-Pacific Partnership on Clean Development and Climate: Executive Summary of Task Force Action Plans (2006)

Auburn, F. M., *Antarctic Law and Politics* (C. Hurst, London, 1982)

Auditor-General of New South Wales, *Performance Audit Department of Land and Water Conservation, Regulating the Clearing of Native Vegetation* (2002)

Performance Audit Regulating the Clearing of Native Vegetation, Follow-Up of 2002 Performance Audit (2006)

Australian Conservation Foundation, *Rights and Responsibilities in Land and Water Management* (2002)

Australian Farm Institute, *Statutory Theft* (2001)

and Land and Water Resources Research and Development Corporation, *Developing a Good Regulatory Practice Model for Environmental Regulations Impacting on Farmers: Overview* (Australia Farm Institute, Sydney, 2007)

Australian Greenhouse Office, *Tracking to the Kyoto Target 2006* (2006)

Australia Institute, *A Poisoned Chalice: Australia and the Kyoto Protocol*, Background Paper No. 13 (1998)

Bäckstrand, Karin, 'Scientisation vs. Civic Expertise in Environmental Governance: Eco-Feminist, Eco-Modern and Post-Modern Responses' (2004) 13 *Environmental Politics* 695

Bakshi, Anita, 'Potential Adverse Health Effects of Genetically Modified Crops' (2003) 6 *Journal of Toxicology and Environmental Health, Part B Critical Reviews* 211

Baldock, David, *et al.*, *Growing Greener. Sustainable Agriculture in the UK* (Council for the Protection of Rural England, London, 1996)

Baldwin, Robert and Cave, Martin, *Understanding Regulation: Theory, Strategy, and Practice* (Oxford University Press, 1999)

Barnes, Richard, *Property Rights and Natural Resources* (Hart Publishing, Oxford and Portland, 2009)

Barry, Brian, 'Sustainability and Intergenerational Justice' in Andrew Dobson (ed.), *Fairness and Futurity: Essays on Environmental Sustainability and Social Justice* (Oxford University Press, 1999) 93

Bassett, Thomas, 'Introduction: The Land Question and Agricultural Transformation in Sub-Saharan Africa' in Thomas Bassett and Donald Crummy (eds.), *Land in African Agrarian Systems* (University of Wisconsin Press, Madison, 1993) 3

Bastmeijer, Kees and Koivurova, Timo 'Introduction' in Bastmeijer and Koivurova (eds.), *Theory and Practice of Transboundary Environmental Impact Assessment*, 3

(eds.), *Theory and Practice of Transboundary Environmental Impact Assessment* (Martinus Nijhoff, Leiden and Boston, 2008)

Bates, Gerard, *Environmental Law in Australia* (Butterworths, Sydney, 1st edn, 1983)

Environmental Law in Australia (LexisNexis Butterworths, Sydney, 5th edn, 2002)

Environmental Law in Australia (LexisNexis Butterworths, Sydney, 7th edn, 2010)

Baum, Lyman Frank, *The Wonderful Wizard of Oz* (Bibliolis, London, 2010 edn)

Beaumont, Joan, 'Contested Transnational Heritage: The Demolition of Changi Prison, Singapore' (2009) 15 *International Journal of Heritage Studies* 294

Beazley, Olwen and Deacon, Harriet, 'Safeguarding Intangible Heritage under the World Heritage Convention: Auschwitz, Hiroshima and Robben Island' in Janet Blake (ed.), *Safeguarding Intangible Cultural Heritage: Challenges and Approaches* (Institute of Art and Law, Builth Wells, 2007) 93

Beck, Ulrich, *Risk Society: Towards a New Modernity* (Sage Publications, London, 1992)

Beck-Gernsheim, Elizabeth, 'Life as a Planning Project' in Scott Lash *et al.*, *Risk, Environment and Modernity: Towards a New Ecology* (Sage Publications, London, 1996) 139

Beckerman, Wilfred, 'Sustainable Development and our Obligations to Future Generations', in Andrew Dobson (ed.), *Fairness and Futurity: Essays on Environmental Sustainability and Social Justice* (Oxford University Press, 1999) 71

Beckman, Ludvig, 'Do Global Climate Change and the Interests of Future Generations Have Implications for Democracy?' (2008) 17 *Environmental Politics* 610

Benvenisti, Eyal, 'The Interplay Between Actors as a Determinant of the Evolution of Administrative Law in International Institutions' (2005) 68 *Law and Contemporary Problems* 319

Bernauer, Thomas, *Genes, Trade and Regulation* (Princeton University Press, 2003)

Bickerstaff, Karen, *et al.*, 'Reframing Nuclear Power in the UK Energy Debate: Nuclear Power, Climate Change Mitigation and Radioactive Waste' (2008) 17 *Public Understanding of Science* 145

Biermann, Frank, *et al.*, 'The Fragmentation of Global Environmental Governance Architectures: A Framework for Analysis' (2009) 9(4) *Global Environmental Politics* 14

Billig, Michael, *Arguing and Thinking: A Rhetorical Approach to Social Psychology* (Cambridge University Press, New York, 1996)

Birnie, Patricia and Boyle, Alan, *International Law and the Environment* (Clarendon Press, Oxford, 1st edn, 1992)

Bix, Brian, 'Natural Law: The Modern Tradition' in Jules Coleman and Scott Shapiro (eds.), *The Oxford Handbook of Jurisprudence and Philosophy of Law* (Oxford University Press, 2002) 61

Blackstone, William, *The Commentaries on the Laws of England, Books 1 & 2* (Dawsons, London, 1966) (first published 1765–6)

Blake, Janet, *Commentary on the 2003 UNESCO Convention on the Safeguarding of the Intangible Cultural Heritage* (Institute of Art and Law, Leicester, 2006)

Blay, Sam, 'The Nature of International Law' in Sam Blay, Ryszard Piotrowicz and Martin Tsamenyi (eds.), *Public International Law: An Australian Perspective* (Oxford University Press, Melbourne, 2nd edn, 2005)

Block, Walter, 'Environmental Problems, Private Property Rights Solutions' in Walter Block (ed.), *Economics and the Environment: A Reconciliation* (The Frasier Institute, Vancouver, 1990) 281

Blomley, Nicholas, 'Law and the Local State: Enforcement in Action' (1988) 13(2) *Transactions of the Institute of British Geographers* 199

Boardman, John, *et al.*, 'Soil Erosion and Risk-Assessment for On- and Off-Farm Impacts: A Test Case Using the Midhurst Area, West Sussex, UK' (2009) 90 *Journal of Environmental Management* 2578

Bodansky, Daniel, 'Customary (and Not So Customary) International Environmental Law' (1995–6) 3 *Indiana Journal of Global Legal Studies* 105

'The Copenhagen Climate Change Conference – A Post-Mortem' (2010) 104 *American Journal of International Law* 9

'The Legitimacy of International Governance: A Coming Challenge for International Environmental Law' (1999) 93 *American Journal of International Law* 604

Boer, Ben, 'The Globalisation of Environmental Law: The Role of the United Nations' (1995–6) 20 *Melbourne University Law Review* 109

and Wiffen, Graeme, *Heritage Law in Australia* (Oxford University Press, Melbourne, 2006)

Bogdandy, Armin von, 'General Principles of International Public Authority: Sketching a Research Field' (2008) 9 *German Law Journal* 1909

Bogojević, Sanja, 'Ending the Honeymoon: Deconstructing Emissions Trading Discourses' (2009) 21 *Journal of Environmental Law* 443

'Litigating the NAP: Legal Challenges for the Emissions Trading Scheme of the European Union' (2010) 3 *Carbon and Climate Law Review* 217

'The EU ETS Directive Revised: Yet Another Stepping Stone' (2009) 11 *Environmental Law Review* 285

Bonny, Sylvie, 'Why Are Most Europeans Opposed to GMOs? Factors Explaining Rejection in France and Europe' (2003) 6(1) *Electronic Journal of Biotechnology* at www.ejbiotechnology.info/content/vol6/issue1/full/4/

Bonvoisin, Nick, 'Transboundary Issues in Strategic Environmental Assessment' in Barry Sadler *et al.* (eds.), *Handbook of Strategic Environmental Assessment* (Earthscan, London, 2011) 396

Bonyhady, Tim, *Colonial Earth* (Melbourne University Press, 2000)

Places Worth Keeping: Conservationists, Politics and Law (Allen & Unwin, Sydney, 1993)

and Macintosh, Andrew (eds.), *Mills, Mines and Other Controversies: The Environmental Assessment of Major Projects* (Federation Press, Sydney, 2010)

Bosselmann, Klaus, 'Ecological Justice and Law' in Benjamin Richardson and Stepan Wood (eds.), *Environmental Law for Sustainability: A Reader* (Hart Publishing, Oxford and Portland, 2006) 129

The Principle of Sustainability: Transforming Law and Governance (Ashgate, Aldershot, 2008)

Botterill, Linda and Fisher, Melanie (eds.), *Beyond Drought: People, Policy and Perspectives* (CSIRO Publishing, Melbourne, 2003)

Boulding, Kenneth, *et al.*, *Economics of Pollution* (New York University Press, 1971)

Bovins, Mark, *The Quest for Responsibility. Accountability and Citizenship in Complex Organisations* (Cambridge University Press, 1998)

Bowdler, Sandra, 'Repainting Australian Rock Art' (1988) 62 *Antiquity* 517

Boyle, Alan, 'Between Process and Substance: Sustainable Development in the Jurisprudence of International Courts and Tribunals', in Hans Christian Bugge and Christina Voigt (eds.), *Sustainable Development in International and National Law* (Europa Law Publishing, Groningen, 2008) ch. 2.2

and Chinkin, Christine, *The Making of International Law* (Oxford University Press, New York, 2007)

Brisbin, Richard and Hunter, Susan, 'The Transformation of Canadian Property Rights?' (2006) 21 *Canadian Journal of Law and Society* 135

Brown, Peter, 'Toward an Economics of Stewardship: The Case of Climate' (1998) 26 *Ecological Economics* 11

Brown Weiss, Edith, 'Opening the Door to the Environment and to Future Generations' in Laurence Boisson de Chazournes and Philippe Sands (eds.), *International Law, the International Court of Justice and Nuclear Weapons* (Cambridge University Press, 1999) 338

Brown Weiss, Edith, 'The Planetary Trust: Conservation and Intergenerational Equity' (1984) 11 *Ecology Law Quarterly* 495

In Fairness to Future Generations: International Law, Common Patrimony, and Intergenerational Equity (United Nations University, Tokyo, 1989)

Brubaker, Elizabeth, 'Property Rights: The Key to Environmental Protection' (2007) May *Fraser Forum* 19

Property Rights in the Defence of Nature (Earthscan, London, 1995)

Brunnée, Jutta, 'Climate Change, Global Environmental Justice and International Environmental Law' in Jonas Ebbesson and Phoebe Okowa (eds.), *Environmental Law and Justice in Context* (Cambridge University Press, 2009) 316

'COPing with Consent: Law-Making under Multilateral Environmental Agreements' (2002) 15 *Leiden Journal of International Law* 1

Bryman, Alan, *Social Research Methods* (Oxford University Press, 3rd edn, 2008)

Buchanan, James, and Tullock, Gordon, *The Calculus of Consent: Logical Foundations of Constitutional Democracy* (University of Michigan Press, Ann Arbor, 1965)

Buesseler, Ken, *et al.*, 'Ocean Iron Fertilization – Moving Forward in a Sea of Uncertainty' (2009) 319 *Science* 162

Bulkeley, Harriet, 'Discourse Coalitions and the Australian Climate Change Network' 18 (2000) *Environment and Planning C: Government and Policy* 727

Bullard, Robert *Dumping in Dixie: Race, Class, and Environmental Quality* (Westview, Boulder, 3rd edn, 2000)

(ed.), *Growing Smarter: Achieving Livable Communities, Environmental Justice, and Regional Equity* (MIT Press, Cambridge, Mass., 2007)

Burwell, Dollie and Cole, Luke, 'Environmental Justice Comes Full Circle: Warren County Before and After' (2007) 1 *Golden Gate University Environmental Law Journal* (2007) 9

Buzan, Barry, 'Human Security in International Perspective' in Mely Caballero-Anthony and Mohamed Jawhar Hassan (eds.), *The Asia Pacific in the New Millennium: Political and Security Challenges* (ISIS Malaysia, Kuala Lumpur, 2001) 583

Byers, Michael, *Custom, Power and the Power of Rules* (Cambridge University Press, 1999)

Who Owns the Arctic? (Douglas & McIntyre, Vancouver, 2009)

Byrne, Denis, Brayshaw, Helen and Ireland, Tracy, *Social Significance: A Discussion Paper* (NSW National Parks and Wildlife Service, Sydney, 2nd edn, 2003)

Byrne, John, Martinez, Cecilia and Glover, Leigh, 'A Brief on Environmental Justice' in John Byrne, Cecilia Martinez, and Leigh Glover (eds.), *Environmental Justice: Discourses in International Political Economy* (Transaction Publishers, New Brunswick, 2002) 3

(eds.), *Environmental Justice: Discourses in International Political Economy* (Transaction Publishers, New Brunswick, 2002)

Caballero-Anthony, Mely, 'Non-Traditional Security and Infectious Diseases in ASEAN: Going Beyond the Rhetoric of Securitisation to Deeper Institutionalization' (2008) 21 *The Pacific Review* 507

'Revisioning Human Security in Southeast Asia' (2004) 28(3) *Asian Perspective* 155

'The ASEAN Charter – An Opportunity Missed or One that Cannot Be Missed?' (2008) *Southeast Asian Affairs* 71

Caney, Simon, 'Cosmopolitan Justice, Responsibility, and Global Climate Change' (2005) 18 *Leiden Journal of International Law* 747

'Climate Change, Human Rights and Moral Thresholds' in Stephen Humphreys (ed.), *Human Rights and Climate Change* (Cambridge University Press, 2009) 69

'Climate Change and the Duties of the Advantaged' (2010) 13 *Critical Review of International Social and Political Philosophy* 203

Capeheart, Loretta and Milovanovic, Dragan, *Social Justice: Theories, Issues and Movements* (Rutgers University Press, New Brunswick and London, 2007)

Capie, David and Evans, Paul, *The Asia-Pacific Security Lexicon* (Institute of Southeast Asian Studies, Singapore, 2nd edn, 2007)

Capoor, Karan and Ambrosi, Philippe, *State and Trends of the Carbon Market 2009* (World Bank, Washington DC, 2009)

Carr, Anna, *Grass Roots and Green Tape: Principles and Practices of Environmental Stewardship* (Federation Press, Sydney, 2002)

Carson, Rachel, *Silent Spring* (Houghton-Mifflin, Boston, 1962)

Carter, Neil, *The Politics of the Environment: Ideas, Activism, Policy* (Cambridge University Press, 2007)

Cassese, Sabino, *et al.* (eds.), *Global Administrative Law: Cases, Materials, Issues* (Institute for International Law and Justice, New York, 2nd edn, 2008)

Charney, Jonathan, *The New Nationalism and the Use of Common Spaces* (Allenheld, Osmun, Totawa, 1982)

Chesterman, Simon, 'Globalisation and Public Law: A Global Administrative Law?' in Jeremy Farrell and Kim Rubenstein (eds.), *Sanctions, Accountability and Governance in a Globalised World* (Cambridge University Press, 2009) 75

Chilton, Paul, 'Metaphor, Euphemism and the Militarization of Language' (1987) 10 *Current Research on Peace and Violence* 7

Churchill, Robin R. and Lowe, A. Vaughan, *The Law of the Sea* (Manchester University Press, 1999)

and Ulfstein, Geir, 'Autonomous Institutional Arrangements in Multilateral Environmental Agreements: A Little Noticed Phenomenon in International Law' (2000) 94 *American Journal of International Law* 623

Cicin-Sain, Biliana (ed.), *Oceans and Climate Change: Issues and Recommendations for Policymakers and for the Climate Negotiations, Global Forum on Oceans, Coasts, and Islands* Draft Policy Briefs prepared for the World Ocean Conference, 11–15 May, 2009, Manado, Indonesia (2009)

Clapp, Jennifer and Dauvergne, Peter, *Paths to a Green World: The Political Economy of the Global Environment* (MIT Press, Cambridge, Mass., 2005)

Clogg, Jessica, 'British Columbia at a Crossroads: A Path to Sustainability or the Enclosure of the Commons?' (2004) 14 *Journal of Environmental Law and Practice* 189

Club of Rome, *Limits to Growth* (Universe Books, New York, 1972)

Coale, Kenneth, 'Preface' (1998) 45 *Deep Sea Research II* 915

Coase, Ronald, 'The Problem of Social Cost' (1960) 3 *Journal of Law and Economics* 1

Coates, Ken, *et al.* (eds.), *Arctic Front: Defending Canada in the Far North* (Thomas Allen, Toronto, 2008)

Colby, Bonnie, 'Regulation, Imperfect Markets and Transaction Costs: The Elusive Quest for Efficiency in Water Allocation' in Daniel Bromley (ed.), *The Handbook of Environmental Economics* (Blackwell Publishers, Oxford, 1995) 475

Cole, Luke and Foster, Sheila, *From the Ground Up: Environmental Racism and the Rise of the Environmental Justice Movement* (New York University Press, 2001)

Colley, Sarah, *Uncovering Australia: Archaeology, Indigenous People and the Public* (Allen & Unwin, Sydney, 2002)

Commonwealth of Australia, *Advancing the National Interest: Australia's Foreign and Trade Policy White Paper* (2003)

Carbon Pollution Reduction Scheme: Australia's Low Pollution Future (2008)

National Greenhouse Response Strategy (1992)

In the National Interest: Australia's Foreign and Trade Policy White Paper (1997)

Australia's Climate Change Policy: Our Economy, Our Environment, Our Future (2007)

Department of Climate Change, *Adapting to Climate Change in Australia: An Australian Government Position Paper* (Department of Climate Change, Canberra, 2010)

Department of Foreign Affairs and Trade, 'New Australian Government: Foreign Policy' (1996) 5 *Insight* 3

House of Representatives, Standing Committee on Environment and Heritage, *Public Good Conservation: Our Challenge for the 21st Century. Interim Report of the Inquiry into Effects Upon Landholders and Farmers of Public Good Conservation Measures Imposed by Australian Governments* (2001)

Human Rights and Equal Opportunity Commission, *Bringing Them Home: Report of the National Inquiry into the Separation of Aboriginal and Torres Strait Islander Children from their Families* (1997)

Industry Commission, *A Full Repairing Lease Inquiry into Ecologically Sustainable Land Management* (1998)

Prime Ministerial Task Group on Emissions Trading, *Report of the Task Group on Emissions Trading* (2007)

Productivity Commission, *Impacts of Native Vegetation and Biodiversity Regulations* (2004)

Connolly, William, *The Terms of Political Discourse* (Robertson, Oxford, 1983)

Cordonier Segger, Marie-Claire, 'Sustainable Development in International Law', in Hans Christian Bugge and Christina Voigt (eds.), *Sustainable Development in International and National Law* (Europa Law Publishing, Groningen, 2008) ch. 2.1

Costanza, Robert and Folke, Carl, 'The Structure and Function of Ecological Systems in Relation to Property-Rights Regimes' in Susan Hanna, Carl Folke and Karl-Goran Maler (eds.), *Rights to Nature: Ecological, Economic, Cultural, and Political Principles of Institutions for the Environment* (Island Press, Washington DC, 1996) 19

Cotgrove, Stephen and Duff, Andrew, 'Environmentalism, Middle-Class Radicalism and Politics' (1980) 28 *Sociological Review* 333

Cottier, Thomas, Nartova, Olga and Bigdeli, Sadeq Z. (eds.), *International Trade Regulation and the Mitigation of Climate Change* (Cambridge University Press, 2009)

Council for Security Cooperation in Asia Pacific, *CSCAP Memorandum No. 3: The Concepts of Comprehensive and Cooperative Security* (1995)

Cox, Dave, 'The Road from Rio: Multilateral Cooperation Gives Way to National Interest' in Richard Leaver and Dave Cox (eds.), *Middling, Meddling, Muddling: Issues in Australian Foreign Policy* (Allen & Unwin, Sydney, 1997) 215

Coyle, Sean and Morrow, Karen, *The Philosophical Foundations of Environmental Law: Property, Rights and Nature* (Hart Publishing, Oxford and Portland, 2004)

Craig, Paul, *Administrative Law* (Sweet & Maxwell, London, 3rd edn, 1994)

Administrative Law (Sweet & Maxwell, London, 6th edn, 2008)

EU Administrative Law (Oxford University Press, 2006)

Craik, Neil, *The International Law of Environmental Impact Assessment* (Cambridge University Press, 2008)

Critchley, W. Harriet, 'Polar Deployment of Soviet Submarines' (1984) 39 *International Journal* 828

Crowe, Beryl, 'The Tragedy of the Commons Revisited' (1969) 166 *Science* 1104

D'Amato, Anthony, 'Do We Owe a Duty to Future Generations to Preserve the Global Environment' (1990) 84 *American Journal of International Law* 190

Daley, John and Edis, Tristan, *Restructuring the Australian Economy to Emit Less Carbon*, Grattan Institute Report (2010)

Danchin, Peter, 'Whose Public? Which Law? Mapping the Internal/External Distinction in International Law' in Jeremy Farrell and Kim Rubenstein (eds.), *Sanctions, Accountability and Governance in a Globalised World* (Cambridge University Press, New York, 2009) 27

Darier, Éric, 'Foucault and the Environment: An Introduction' in Éric Darier (ed.), *Discourses of the Environment* (Blackwell, Oxford and Malden, 1999) 1

Davidson, Paul, 'The Role of International Law in the Governance of International Economic Relations in ASEAN' (2008) 12 *Singapore Yearbook of International Law* 213

Davies, Peter, 'Public Participation, the Aarhus Convention, and the European Community' in Donald Zillman, Alistair Lucas and George Pring (eds.), *Human Rights in Natural Resource Development: Public Participation in the Sustainable Development of Mining and Energy Resources* (Oxford University Press, 2002) 155

de Mulder, Jan, 'The Institutional Context for Transboundary Environmental Impact Assessment in Belgium: Multi Level Setting – A Matter of Smooth Governance?' (2008) 26 *Impact Assessment and Project Appraisal* 282

'Case Note' (2010) 19 *Review of European Community and International Environmental Law* 263

de Sadeleer, Nicolas, 'The Effect of Uncertainty on the Threshold Levels to which the Precautionary Principle Appears to be Subject' in Maurice Sheridan and Luc Lavrysen (eds.), *Environmental Law Principles in Practice* (Bruylant, Bruxelles, 2002) 32

Environmental Principles: From Political Slogans to Legal Rules (Oxford University Press, 2002)

Environmental Principles: From Political Slogans to Legal Rules (Oxford University Press, 2005 reprint)

de Soto, Hernando, *The Mystery of Capital: Why Capitalism Triumphs in the West and Fails Everywhere Else* (Basic Books, New York, 2000)

de Witt Wijnen, Rutger 'Emissions Trading under Article 17 of the Kyoto Protocol' in David Freestone and Charlotte Streck (eds.), *Legal Aspects of Implementing the Kyoto Protocol Mechanisms: Making Kyoto Work* (Oxford University Press, 2005) 40

del Castillo-Laborde, Lilian, 'Case Law on International Watercourses', in Joseph Dellapenna and Joyeeta Gupta (eds.), *The Evolution of the Law and Politics of Water* (Springer, Dordrecht, 2009) 319

Dembowski, Hans, *Taking the State to Court: Public Interest Litigation and the Public Sphere in Metropolitan India* (Asia House, Essen, 2001)

Demsetz, Harold, 'The Cost of Transacting' (1968) 82 *The Quarterly Journal of Economics* 33

Dennis, Richard, *Harder to Do Than to Say? The Failure of the CPRS to Reduce Emissions from Coal-Fired Power Stations*, The Australia Institute Policy Brief No. 5 (2009)

Des Jardins, Joseph, *Environmental Ethics* (Wadsworth Publishing Company, Belmont, Calif., 4th edn, 2006)

Desancker, Paul, 'The Kyoto Protocol and the CDM in Africa: A Good Idea But . . .' (2005) 56 *Unasylva* 24

Descartes, Rene, *Discourse on Method and the Meditations* (Penguin, Harmondsworth, 1978)

Deudney, Daniel, 'The Case Against Linking Environmental Degradation and National Security' (1990) 19 *Millennium* 461

Dietz, Thomas, Ostrom, Elinor and Stern, Paul, 'The Struggle to Govern the Commons' (2003) 302 *Science* 1907

Distefano, Michael, 'Managing Arctic Fish Stocks' (2008) 8(3) *Sustainable Development Law & Policy* 13

Diwasa, Tulasi, Bandhu, Chura Mani and Nepal, Bhim, *The Intangible Cultural Heritage of Nepal: Future Directions* (UNESCO, Kathmandu, 2007)

Dobson, Andrew, 'Environmental Sustainabilities: An Analysis and a Typology' (1996) 5 *Environmental Politics* 401

Citizenship and the Environment (Oxford University Press, 2003)

Justice and the Environment: Conceptions of Environmental Sustainability and Theories of Distributive Justice (Oxford University Press, 1998)

(ed.), *Fairness and Futurity: Essays on Environmental Sustainability and Social Justice* (Oxford University Press, 1999)

Douglas-Scott, Sionaidh, *Law After Modernity* (Edward Elgar, Cheltenham, forthcoming)

Dovers, Stephen,'Institutions for Sustainability' (2001) 7 *Tela* 18

Downs, Anthony, *An Economic Theory of Democracy* (Harper, New York, 1957)

Dragun, Andrew, *Environmental Institutional Design: Can Property Rights Theory Help*? (Department of Economics, University of Queensland, Brisbane, 1999)

Driesen, David, 'Sustainable Development and Market Liberalism's Shotgun Wedding: Emissions Trading under the Kyoto Protocol' (2008) 83 *Indiana Law Journal* 21

Dryzek, John, 'Paradigms and Discourses' in Daniel Bodansky, Jutta Brunnée and Ellen Hey (eds.), *The Oxford Handbook of International Environmental Law* (Oxford University Press, 2007) 44

'Transnational Democracy in an Insecure World' (2006) 27 *International Political Science Review* 101

Deliberative Global Politics: Discourse and Democracy in a Divided World (Polity Press, Cambridge, 2006)

Green Democracy, Occasional Paper 2/2010, The Academy of Social Sciences of Australia (2010)

Dryzek, John, *The Politics of the Earth: Environmental Discourses* (Oxford University Press, 1st edn, 1997)

The Politics of the Earth: Environmental Discourses (Oxford University Press, 2nd edn, 2005)

Dyzenhaus, David, 'The Rule of (Administrative) Law in International Law' (2005) 68 *Law and Contemporary Problems* 127

Eady, Veronica, 'Environmental Justice in State Policy Decisions' in Julian Agyeman, Robert Bullard and Bob Evans (eds.), *Just Sustainabilities: Development in an Unequal World* (MIT Press, Cambridge, Mass., 2003) 168

'Warren County and the Birth of a Movement: The Troubled Marriage Between Environmentalism and Civil Rights' (2007) 1 *Golden Gate University Environmental Law Journal* 41

Earth Charter International, *The Earth Charter: A Declaration of Fundamental Principles for Building a Just, Sustainable and Peaceful Society in the 21st Century* (2000)

Ebbesson, Jonas, 'Introduction: Dimensions of Justice in Environmental Law' in Jonas Ebbesson and Phoebe Okowa (eds.), *Environmental Law and Justice in Context* (Cambridge University Press, 2009) 1

Eckersley, Robyn, 'Markets, the State and the Environment: An Overview' in Robyn Eckersley (ed.), *Markets, the State, and the Environment: Towards Integration* (Macmillan Education Australia, Melbourne, 1995) 7

Ela, Jed, 'Law and Norms in Collective Action: Maximizing Social Influence to Minimize Carbon Emissions' (2009) 27 *UCLA Journal of Environmental Law and Policy* 93

Elgie, Stewart, 'Statutory Structure and Species Survival: How Constraints on Cabinet Discretion Affect Endangered Species Listing Outcomes' (2008) 19 *Journal of Environmental Law and Practice* 1

Ellerman, Denny and Joskow, Paul, *The European Union's Emissions Trading System in Perspective* (Pew Center on Global Climate Change, Arlington, 2008)

Elliott, Lorraine, 'Australia in World Environmental Affairs' in James Cotton and John Ravenhill (eds.), *The National Interest in a Global Era: Australia in World Affairs 1996–2000* (Oxford University Press and the Australian Institute of International Affairs, Melbourne, 2001) 235

Ellis, Geraint, 'Discourses of Objection: Towards an Understanding of Third-Party Rights in Planning' (2004) 36 *Environment and Planning A* 1549

Ellis, Jaye and FitzGerald, Alison, 'The Precautionary Principle in International Law: Lessons from Fuller's Internal Morality' (2004) 49(3) *McGill Law Journal* 779

Emmers, Ralf, Caballero-Anthony, Mely and Acharya, Amitav (eds.), *Studying Non-Traditional Security in Asia: Trends and Issues* (Marshall Cavendish Academic, London, 2006)

Engels, Anita, 'Market Creation and Transnational Rule-Making: The Case of CO_2 Emissions Trading' in Marie-Laure Djelic and Kerstin Sahlin-Andersson (eds.), *Transnational Governance: Institutional Dynamics of Regulation* (Cambridge University Press, 2006) 329

England, Philippa, 'Doing the Groundwork: State, Local and Judicial Contributions to Climate Change Law in Australia' (2008) 25 *Environmental and Planning Law Journal* 360

Epstein, Charlotte, *The Power of Words in International Relations: Birth of an Anti-Whaling Discourse* (MIT Press, Cambridge, Mass., 2008)

Esty, Daniel, 'Good Governance at the Supranational Scale: Globalizing Administrative Law' (2006) 115 *Yale Law Journal* 1490

European Group on Ethics in Science and New Technologies to the European Commission, *Ethics of Modern Developments in Agricultural Technologies*, Opinion No. 24, 17 December 2008

European Parliament Committee on the Environment, Public Health and Food Safety, *Draft Report on the Implementation of EU Legislation on GMOs, in Particular Directive 2001/18/EC and Regulations (EC) No. 1829/2003 and 1830/2003* (2008)

Evans, Gareth, 'Foreign Policy and the Environment' (1990) 61 *Australian Foreign Affairs and Trade: The Monthly Record* 112

'International Law and Australia's Interests' (1989) *Australian International Law News* 185

Making Australian Foreign Policy (Australian Fabian Society and Pluto Press, Sydney, 1989)

and Grant, Bruce, *Australia's Foreign Relations: In the World of the 1990s* (Melbourne University Press, 2nd edn, 1995)

Ewen, Stanley and Pusztai, Arpad, 'Effect of Diets Containing Genetically Modified Potatoes Expressing Galanthus Nivalis Lectin on Rat Small Intestine' (1999) 354 *The Lancet* 1353

Fairlie, Ian, 'New Information on Radiation Health Hazards' in David Elliott (ed.), *Nuclear or Not? Does Nuclear Power Have a Place in a Sustainable Energy Future?* (Palgrave Macmillan, Basingstoke, 2007) 101

Falkner, Robert, *Business Power and Conflict in International Environmental Politics* (Palgrave Macmillan, Basingstoke, 2008)

Farrajota, Maria Manuela, 'International Cooperation on Water Resources' in Joseph Dellapenna and Joyeeta Gupta (eds.), *The Evolution of the Law and Politics of Water* (Springer, Dordrecht, 2009) 337

Farrall, Jeremy and Rubenstein, Kim (eds.), *Sanctions, Accountability and Governance in a Globalised World* (Cambridge University Press, 2009)

Faure, Michael and Peeters, Marjan, *Climate Change and European Emissions Trading: Lessons for Theory and Practice* (Edward Elgar, Cheltenham, 2008)

Feigenblatt, Otto von, *ASEAN and Human Security: Challenges and Opportunities*, RACPS Working Paper No. 09–5 (2009)

Feinberg, Joel, 'Duties, Rights and Claims' (1966) 3 *American Philosophical Quarterly* 137

Fennell, Lee Anne, 'Adjusting Alienability' (2009) 122 *Harvard Law Review* 1403

Fiorino, Daniel, *The New Environmental Regulation* (MIT Press, Cambridge, Mass., 2006)

Fischer, Frank, 'Democratic Prospects in an Age of Expertise' in Frank Fischer (ed.), *Citizens, Experts and the Environment* (Duke University Press, Durham, NC, 2003) 5

Reframing Public Policy (Oxford University Press, 2003)

Fischer, Thomas, *The Theory and Practice of Strategic Environmental Assessment: Towards a More Systematic Approach* (Earthscan, London, 2007)

Fischer-Lescano, Andreas and Teubner, Gunther, 'Regime-Collisions: The Vain Search for Legal Unity in the Fragmentation of Global Law' (2004) 25 *Michigan Journal of International Law* 999

Fisher, Brian *et al.*, *Technological Development and Economic Growth*, ABARE Research Report 06.1 – Inaugural Ministerial Meeting of the Asia Pacific Partnership on Clean Development and Climate (2006)

Fisher, Douglas, *Australian Environmental Law* (Lawbook Co., Sydney, 1st edn, 2003)

Fisher, Elizabeth, 'Beyond the Science/Democracy Dichotomy: The World Trade Organization Sanitary and Phytosanitary Agreement and Administrative Constitutionalism' in Christian Joerges and Ernst-Ulrich Petersmann (eds.), *Constitutionalism, Multilevel Trade Governance and Social Regulation* (Hart Publishing, Oxford, 2006) 327

'Unpacking the Toolbox: Or Why the Public/Private Divide Is Important in EC Environmental Law' in Mark Freedland and Jean-Bernard Auby (eds.), *The Public Law/Private Law Divide: Une Entente Assez Cordiale? La Distinction du Droit Public et du Droit Privé: Regards Français et Britanniques* (Hart Publishing, Oxford, 2006) 215

Fisher, Roger, Ury, William and Paton, Bruce, *Getting to Yes: Negotiating Agreement Without Giving In* (Penguin Books, New York, 1991)

Fitzgerald, Brian, 'Port State Jurisdiction and Marine Pollution under UNCLOS III' (1995) 11 *Maritime Law Association of Australia and New Zealand Journal Part 1* 33

Fitzmaurice, Malgosia, 'Environmental Justice through International Complaint Procedures? Comparing the Aarhus Convention and the North American Agreement on Environmental Cooperation' in Jonas Ebbesson and Phoebe Okowa (eds.), *Environmental Law and Justice in Context* (Cambridge University Press, 2009) 211

Flachsland, Christian *et al.*, *Developing the International Carbon Market: Linking Options for the EU ETS* (Report to the Policy Planning Staff in the Federal Foreign Office, Potsdam Institute for Climate Impact Research, May 2008)

Flannery, Tim, 'Now or Never, A Sustainable Future for Australia?' (2008) 31 *Quarterly Essay*

Fleming, John, *The Law of Torts* (Lawbook, Sydney, 9th edn, 1998)

Flood, Josephine, *Archaeology of the Dreamtime: The Story of Prehistoric Australia and its People* (Collins, Sydney, 1989)

Rock Art of the Dreamtime (Angus & Robertson, Sydney, 1997)

Flood, Michael and Grove-White, Robin, *Nuclear Prospects: A Comment on the Individual, the State and Nuclear Power* (Friends of the Earth, London, 1976)

Fogel, Cathleen, 'The Local, the Global, and the Kyoto Protocol' in Sheila Jasanoff and Marybeth Long Martello (eds.), *Earthly Politics: Local and Global in Environmental Governance* (MIT Press, Cambridge, Mass., 2004) 103

Foucault, Michel, 'Chapter 5: 2 Lectures', in Colin Gordon (ed.), *Michel Foucault: Power/Knowledge: Selected Interviews and Other Writings, 1972–1977* (Pantheon Books, New York, 1980) 80

'What Is an Author?' in Gordon (ed.), *Michel Foucault: Power/Knowledge: Selected Interviews and Other Writings, 1972–1977*, 101

Discipline and Punish (trans. Alan Sheridan) (Vintage Books, New York, 1979)

The Archaeology of Knowledge (trans. Alan Sheridan Smith) (Pantheon Books, London, 1972)

The Foucault Effect: Studies in Governmentality (eds. Graham Burchell, Colin Gordon and Peter Miller) (University of Chicago Press, 1991)

The History of Sexuality (trans. Robert Hurley) (Vintage Books, New York, 1978)

Francioni, Francesco, 'Culture, Heritage and Human Rights: An Introduction' in Francesco Francioni and Martin Scheinin (eds.), *Cultural Human Rights* (Martinus Nijhoff Publishers, Leiden and Boston, 2008)

and Lenzerini, Federico, *The 1972 World Heritage Convention: A Commentary* (Oxford University Press, 2008)

Franck, Thomas, *Fairness in International Law and Institutions* (Oxford University Press/Clarendon Press, Oxford/New York, 1995)

Freeman, Jody and Kolstad, Charles, 'Prescriptive Environmental Regulations versus Market-Based Incentives' in Jody Freeman and Charles Kolstad (eds.), *Moving to Markets in Environmental Regulation: Lessons from Twenty Years of Experience* (Oxford University Press, 2007)

French, Duncan, *International Law and Policy of Sustainable Development* (Manchester University Press, 2005)

Freyfogle, Eric, 'Ethics, Community and Private Land' (1996) 23 *Ecology Law Quarterly* 631

Friends of the Earth, *Nuclear Power? No Thanks!* (Friends of the Earth, London, 1978)

Fritzsche, Alexander, 'Discretion, Scope of Judicial Review and Institutional Balance in European Law' (2010) 47 *Common Market Law Review* 361

Gardener, Stephen M., 'A Perfect Moral Storm: Climate Change, Intergenerational Equity, and the Problem of Moral Corruption' (2006) 15 *Environmental Values* 397

Gardner, Alex, 'The Duty of Care for Sustainable Land Management' (1998) 5 *The Australasian Journal of Natural Resources Law and Policy* 29

Garnaut, Ross, *The Garnaut Climate Change Review: Final Report* (Cambridge University Press, Melbourne, 2008)

Gianni, Matthew and Simpson, Walt, *The Changing Nature of High Seas Fishing. How Flags of Convenience Provide Cover for Illegal, Unreported and Unregulated Fishing* (Australian Department of Agriculture, Fisheries and Forestry, International Transport Workers' Federation, and WWF International, Canberra, London and Gland, 2005)

Gilbert, Martin, *Holocaust Journey: Travelling in Search of the Past* (Columbia University Press, New York, 1998)

Gillespie, Alexander, 'Environmental Impact Assessments in International Law' (2008) 17 *Review of European Community and International Environmental Law* 221

International Environmental Law, Policy and Ethics (Clarendon Press, Oxford, 1997)

Gilmore, Hankey and Kirke (GHK), Interim Report, *Evaluation of the EU Legislative Framework in the Field of Cultivation of GMOs under Directive 2001/18/EC and Regulation (EC) 1829/2003* (November 2009)

Glibert, Patricia *et al.* 'Ocean Urea Fertilization for Carbon Credits Poses High Ecological Risks' (2008) 56 *Marine Pollution Bulletin* 1049

Godard, Olivier, 'Le principe de précaution face au dilemme de la traduction juridique des demandes sociales, leçons de méthode tirées de l'affaire de la vache folle' in Charles Leben and Joe Verhoeven (eds.), *Le principe de précaution. Aspects de droit international et communautaire* (Panthéon-Assas, Paris, 2002) 29

Godden, Lee, 'Governing Common Resources: Environmental Markets and Property in Water' in Aileen McHarg *et al.* (eds.), *Property and the Law in Energy and Natural Resources* (Oxford University Press, 2010) 413

Goldie, L. F. E., 'Equity and the International Management of Transboundary Resources' in Albert E. Utton and Ludwik A. Teclaff (eds.), *Transboundary Resources Law* (Westview Press, Boulder, 1987) 103

Goldsworthy, David, 'Australia and Good International Citizenship' in Stephanie Lawson (ed.), *The New Agenda for Global Security: Cooperating for Peace and Beyond* (Allen & Unwin, Sydney, 1995) 171

Goodin, Robert E., *Protecting the Vulnerable, a Reanalysis of our Social Responsibilities* (University of Chicago Press, 1985)

Grafton, R. Quentin, *Too Few Fish and Too Many Boats*, Policy Briefs – Fishing Futures, Crawford School of Economics and Government, ANU (2006)

Graham, Nicole, *Lawscape: Property, Environment, Law* (Routledge, Abingdon, 2011)

Gran, H., 'On the Conditions for the Production of Plankton in the Sea' (1931) 75 *Rapports et Proces-Verbaux des Reunions Conseil International pour l'Exploration de la Mer* 37

Gray, John, 'The Rudd Essay and the Global Financial Crisis' (May 2009) *The Monthly* 45

False Dawn: The Delusions of Global Capitalism (Granta Publications, London, 2nd edn, 2002)

Gray, Kevin, 'International Environmental Impact Assessment: Potential for a Multilateral Environmental Agreement' (2000) 11 *Colorado Journal of International Environmental Law and Policy* 83

Grotius, Hugo, *On the Laws of War and Peace* (1st edn, 1625) at gallica.bnf.fr/ark:/12148/bpt6k580227.capture, last accessed 1 October 2009

Grove, Richard, *Ecology, Climate and Empire: Colonialism and Global Environmental History, 1400–1940* (White Horse Press, Isle of Harris, 1997)

Grove-White, Robin, 'Land Use Law and the Environment' in Robin Churchill, John Gibson and Lynda Warren (eds.), *Law, Policy and the Environment* (Blackwell, Oxford, 1991) 32

Gruber, Stefan, 'Human Displacement and Climate Change in the Asia Pacific Region (2011) 12(1) *Harvard Asia Pacific Review* (forthcoming)

'Protecting China's Cultural Heritage Sites in Times of Rapid Change: Current Developments, Practice and Law' (2007) 10 *Asia Pacific Journal of Environmental Law* 253

'The Impact of Climate Change on Cultural Heritage Sites: Environmental Law and Adaptation' (2011) 2 *Carbon & Climate Law Review* 209

'The Links between Poverty and the Loss of Cultural Heritage Sites' in Yves le Bouthillier *et al.* (eds.), *Poverty Alleviation and Environmental Protection* (Edward Elgar, Cheltenham, forthcoming)

Guerin, Kevin, *Encouraging Quality Regulations. Theories and Tools*, New Zealand Treasury Working Paper 03/24 (2003)

Gunningham, Neil, 'Environmental Law, Regulation and Governance: Shifting Architectures' (2009) 21 *Journal of Environmental Law* 179

and Sinclair, Darren, 'New Generation Environmental Policy: Environmental Management Systems and Regulatory Reform' (1998) 22 *Melbourne University Law Review* 592

Kagan, Robert and Thornton, Dorothy, *Social License and Environmental Protection: Why Businesses Go Beyond Compliance* (Centre for Analysis of

Risk and Regulation, London School of Economics and Political Science, London, 2002)

Guston, David, 'Boundary Organizations in Environmental Policy and Science: An Introduction' (2001) 26 *Science, Technology and Human Values* 399

Gyngell, Allan and Wesley, Michael, *Making Australian Foreign Policy* (Cambridge University Press, New York, 2nd edn, 2007)

Haas, Ernst, *When Knowledge Is Power: Three Models of Change in International Organizations* (University of California Press, Berkeley, 1990)

Habermas, Jurgen, *Between Facts and Norms: Contributions to a Discourse Theory of Law* (Polity Press, Cambridge, 1996)

Hajer, Maarten, 'Coalitions, Practices, and Meaning in Environmental Politics: From Acid Rain to BSE' in David Howarth and Jacob Torfing (eds.), *Discourse Theory in European Politics* (Palgrave Macmillan, Basingstoke, 2005) 297

'Discourse Coalitions and the Institutionalization of Practice: The Case of Acid Rain in Britain' in Frank Fischer and John Forester (eds.), *The Argumentative Turn in Policy Analysis and Planning* (Duke University Press, Durham, 1993) 43

The Politics of Environmental Discourse: Ecological Modernization and the Policy Process (Clarendon Press, Oxford, 1995)

and Laws, David, 'Ordering Through Discourse' in Michael Moran, Martin Rein and Robert Goodin (eds.), *The Oxford Handbook of Public Policy* (Oxford University Press, 2006) 249

and Wagenaar, Hendrik, *Deliberative Policy Analysis: Understanding Governance in the Network Society* (Cambridge University Press, 2003)

Hamilton, Clive, *Running from the Storm: The Development of Climate Change Policy in Australia* (UNSW Press, Sydney, 2001)

Hanemann, Michael, 'Cap-and-Trade: A Sufficient or Necessary Condition for Emission Reduction?' (2010) 26 *Oxford Review of Economic Policy* 225

Hanna, Susan and Jentoft, Svein, 'Human Use of the Natural Environment: An Overview of Social and Economic Dimensions' in Susan Hanna, Carl Folke and Karl-Goran Maler (eds.), *Rights to Nature: Ecological, Economic, Cultural, and Political Principles of Institutions for the Environment*, (Island Press, Washington DC, 1996) 35

Hansjürgen, Bern (ed.), *Emissions Trading for Climate Policy: US and European Perspectives* (Cambridge University Press, 2005)

Hardin, Garrett, 'The Tragedy of the Commons' (1968) 162 *Science* 1243

Hare, Bill and Meinshausen, Malte, 'How Much Warming Are We Committed to and How Much Can Be Avoided?' (2006) 75 *Climatic Change* 111

Harrison, D., *Ocean Nourishment in the Philippines – Proof of Concept Report for Sulu Sea* (Earth, Ocean & Space Pty Ltd, Sydney, 2007)

Hart, H. L. A., *The Concept of Law* (Clarendon Press, Oxford, 1994)

Harvey, David, 'The Environment of Justice' in Frank Fischer and Maarten Hajer (eds.), *Living with Nature: Environmental Politics as Cultural Discourse* (Oxford University Press, 1999) 153

A Brief History of Neoliberalism (Oxford University Press, New York, 2005)

Justice, Nature & the Geography of Difference (Wiley-Blackwell, Oxford, 2000)

Havini, Taloi, 'An Uncertain Future' (2008) (September to November) *Explore* 14

Hayden, Dolores, *The Power of Place: Urban Landscapes as Public History* (MIT Press, Cambridge, Mass., 1995)

Heckathorn, Douglas and Maser, Steven, 'Bargaining and the Sources of Transaction Costs: The Case of Government Regulation' (1987) 3 *Journal of Law, Economics and Organization* 69

Heinzerling, Lisa, 'The Environment' in Peter Cane and Mark Tushnet (eds.), *The Oxford Handbook of Legal Studies* (Oxford University Press, 2003)

Helfer, Lawrence, and Slaughter, Anne-Marie, 'Toward a Theory of Effective Supranational Adjudication' (1997) 107 *Yale Law Journal* 273

Hemmings, Alan and Stephens, Tim, 'The Extended Continental Shelves of Sub-Antarctic Islands: Implications for Antarctic Governance'(2010) 46 *Polar Record* 312

Henckels, Caroline, 'GMOS in the WTO: A Critique of the Panel's Legal Reasoning in EC–Biotech' (2006) 7 *Melbourne Journal of International Law* 278

Hepburn, Samantha, *Australian Property Law: Cases, Materials and Analysis* (LexisNexis Butterworths, Sydney, 2008)

Hervey, Tamara, 'Regulation of Genetically Modified Products in a Multi-Level System of Governance: Science or Citizens?' (2001) 10 *Review of European Community and International Environmental Law* 321

Hey, Ellen, 'Distributive Justice and Procedural Fairness in Global Water Law' in Jonas Ebbesson and Phoebe Okowa (eds.), *Environmental Law and Justice in Context* (Cambridge University Press, 2009) 351

Reflections on an International Environmental Court (Kluwer Law International, The Hague, 2002)

Holtorf, Cornelius, 'Is the Past a Non-Renewable Resource?' in Robert Layton, Peter Stone and Julian Thomas (eds.), *Destruction and Conservation of Cultural Property* (Routledge, London, 2001) 286

Holyfield, Ryan, 'Defining Environmental Justice and Environmental Racism' (2001) 22 *Urban Geography* 78

Horlick-Jones, Tom *et al.*, *A Deliberative Future? An Independent Evaluation of the GM Nation? Public Debate about the Possible Commercialisation of Transgenic Crops in Britain, 2003*, Understanding Risk Working Paper 04–02 (2004)

House, Kurt Zenz *et al.*, 'Permanent Carbon Dioxide Storage in Deep-Sea Sediments' (2006) 103(33) *Proceedings of the National Academy of Sciences of the United States of America* 12291

Howarth, William, *Wisdom's Law of Watercourses* (Shaw, Crayford, 5th edn, 1992)

Hüller, Thorsten and Leonhard Maier, Matthias, 'Fixing the Codex? Global Food-Safety Governance under Review' in Christian Joerges and Ernst-Ulrich Petersmann (eds.), *Constitutionalism, Multilevel Trade Governance and Social Regulation* (Hart Publishing, Oxford, 2006) 267

Hulme, Mike, *Why We Disagree About Climate Change* (Cambridge University Press, 2009)

Humphreys, David, 'Discourse as Ideology: Neoliberalism and the Limits of International Forest Policy' (2009) 11 *Forest Policy and Economics* 319

Hunt, Alan and Wickham, Gary, *Foucault and the Law: Towards a Sociology of Law as Governance* (Pluto Press, London, 1994)

Hunter, David, Salzman, James and Zaelke, Durwood, *International Environmental Law and Policy* (Foundation Press, New York, 2nd edn, 2002)

ILA Committee on the International Law on Sustainable Development, *Third Report* (2008)

Iles, Alastair, 'Mapping Environmental Justice in Technology Flows: Computer Waste Impacts in Asia' (2004) 4(4) *Global Environmental Politics* 76

In't Veld, Roel and de Wit, A., 'Clarifications' in Roel In't Veld (ed.), *Willingly and Knowingly: The Roles of Knowledge about Nature and the Environment in Policy Processes* (Lemma, Utrecht, 2000) 147

Intergovernmental Panel on Climate Change, *Climate Change 2007. Synthesis Report: Summary for Policy-Makers* (IPCC, Geneva, 2007)

Intergovernmental Panel on Climate Change Working Group I, *Climate Change 2007. The Physical Science Basis. Summary for Policy-Makers* (2007)

Intergovernmental Panel on Climate Change Working Group II, *Climate Change 2007. Impacts, Adaptation and Vulnerability* (Cambridge University Press, 2007)

International Alliance of Research Universities, *Synthesis Report from Climate Change: Global Risk, Challenges and Decisions* (2009)

International Commission on Intervention and State Sovereignty, *The Responsibility to Protect* (International Development Resource Centre, Ottawa, 2001)

International Law Commission , *Fragmentation of International Law: Difficulties Arising from the Diversification and Expansion of International Law: Conclusions* (A/CN.4/L.702) (2006)

Jacob, Bernard, 'Ancient Rhetoric, Modern Legal Thought, and Politics: A Review Essay on the Translation of Viehweg's "Topics and Law"' (1995) 89 *Northwestern University Law Review* 1622

Jacobs, Jack, 'A New Look at Environmental Impact Assessments: Using Customary Law to Prevent Domestic and Transboundary Environmental Damage' in Michael Faure and Song Ying (eds.), *China and International Environmental Liability* (Edward Elgar, Cheltenham, 2008) 225

Jacobs, Keith and Manzi, Tony, 'Discourse and Policy Change: The Significance of Language for Housing Research' (1996) 11 *Housing Studies* 543

Jacobs, Michael (ed.), *Greening the Millennium? The New Politics of the Environment* (Blackwell, Oxford, 1997)

Jaffee, Adam, Newell, Richard and Stavins, Robert, 'A Tale of Two Market Failures; Technology and Environmental Policy' (2005) 54 *Ecological Economics* 164

James, Tom and Fusaro, Peter, *Energy and Emissions Markets* (John Wiley and Sons, Chichester, 2006)

Jasanoff, Sheila, 'Heaven and Earth: The Politics of Environmental Images' in Sheila Jasanoff and Marybeth Long Martello (eds.), *Earthly Politics: Local and Global in Environmental Governance* (MIT Press, Cambridge, Mass., 2004) 31

Designs on Nature (Princeton University Press, 2005)

Jendroska, Jerzy and Stec, Stephen, 'The Aarhus Convention: Towards a New Era in Environmental Democracy' (2001) 9 *Environmental Liability* 140

Jessup, Brad, 'Investing the Law with an Environmental Ethic: Using an Environmental Justice Theory for Change' in Erika Techera (ed.), *Environmental Law, Ethics and Governance* (ID Press, Oxford, 2010) 21

'Plural and Hybrid Environmental Values: A Discourse Analysis of the Wind Energy Conflict in Australia and the United Kingdom' (2010) 19 *Environmental Politics* 21

Jessup, Philip C., and Taubenfeld, Howard, *Controls for Outer Space and the Antarctic Analogy* (Columbia University Press, New York, 1959)

Jorgensen, Marianne and Phillips, Louise, *Discourse Analysis as Theory and Method* (Sage Publications, London, 2002)

Joyner, Christopher, *Governing the Frozen Commons: The Antarctic Regime and Environmental Protection* (University of South Carolina Press, Columbia, 1998)

Jun Du, Shao *et al.*, 'Growth Enhancement in Transgenic Atlantic Salmon by the Use of an "All Fish" Chimeric Growth Hormone Gene Construct' (1992) 10 *Bio/Technology* 176

Kaiser, Jocelyn, 'Gulf's Dead Zone Worse in Recent Decades' (2005) 308 (5719) *Science* 195

Kant, Immanuel, *Critique of Pure Reason* (trans. Norman Smith) (Macmillan, London, 1933)

Kar, Dev and Curcio, Karly, *Illicit Financial Flows from Developing Countries 2000–2009: Update with a Focus on Asia* (Global Financial Integrity, Washington DC, 2011)

Kawaguchi, Yukiya, 'Covering Heritages, Erasing Locals: Passing on History to the Next Generation' in Kenji Yoshida and John Mack (eds.), *Preserving the Cultural Heritage of Africa: Crisis or Renaissance*? (James Curry/Unisa Press, Muckleneuk, 2008) 129

Kaye, Stuart, 'The Outer Continental Shelf in the Antarctic' in Alex Oude Elferink and Donald R. Rothwell (eds.), *The Law of the Sea and Polar Maritime Delimitation and Jurisdiction* (Martinus Nijhoff, The Hague, 2001) 125

Kemp, Ray, 'Planning, Public Hearings, and the Politics of Discourse' in John Forester (ed.), *Critical Theory and Public Life* (MIT Press, London and Cambridge, Mass., 1985) 102

Kemp, René, 'Why Not In My Backyard? A Radical Interpretation of Public Opposition to the Deep Disposal of Radioactive Waste in the United Kingdom' (1990) 22 *Environment and Planning* 1239

Keogh, Mick, *Property Rights and Farming in Australia. Defining Duty of Care for Farm Land* (NSW Farmers Federation, Sydney, 2002)

Keohane, Robert, Moravcsik, Andrew and Slaughter, Anne-Marie, 'Legalized Dispute Resolution: Interstate and Transnational' (2000) 54 *International Organization* 457

Kerr, Pauline, 'The Security Dialogue in the Asia-Pacific' (1994) 7 *The Pacific Review* 397

Kersten, Charles, 'Rethinking Transboundary Environmental Impact Assessment' (2009) 34 *Yale Journal of International Law* 173

Kindt, John, *Marine Pollution and the Law of the Sea* (W.S. Hein, Buffalo, 1986)

Kingsbury, Benedict, Krisch, Nico and Stewart, Richard, 'The Emergence of Global Administrative Law' (2005) 68 *Law and Contemporary Problems* 15

Kirk, Samuel Alexander, *Property Beyond Growth*, unpublished Ph.D. thesis, University of Melbourne (2011)

Kiss, Alexandre and Shelton, Dinah, *Guide to International Environmental Law* (Martinus Nijhoff, Leiden and Boston, 2007)

International Environmental Law (Transnational Publishers, Ardsley, 3rd edn, 2004)

Klijn, Anne-Marie, Gupta, Joyeeta and Nijboer, Anita, 'Privatizing Environmental Resources: The Need for Supervision of Clean Development Mechanism Contracts?' (2009) 18 *Review of European Community and International Environmental Law* 172

Knox, John, 'The Myth and Reality of Transboundary Environmental Impact Assessment' (2002) 96 *American Journal of International Law* 291

Koester, Veit, 'The Compliance Committee of the Aarhus Convention: An Overview of Procedures and Jurisprudence' (2005) 37 *Environmental Policy and Law* 83

Koh, Kheng-Lian, 'A Breakthrough in Solving the Indonesian Haze' in Sharelle Hart (ed.), *Shared Resources – Issues of Governance*, IUCN Environmental Policy and Law Paper No. 72 (2008) 225

'Animal Health, Biodiversity Conservation and Sustainable Development: A Case Study of Avian Influenza' (2005/6) *Environmental Law Programme Newsletter* 12

(ed.), *ASEAN Environmental Law, Policy and Governance: Vol. I* (World Scientific, New Jersey, 2009)

and Robinson, Nicholas, 'Strengthening Sustainable Development in Regional Inter-Governmental Governance: Lessons from the "ASEAN Way"' (2002) *Singapore Journal of International and Comparative Law* 640

Koivurova, Timo, 'Limits and Possibilities of the Arctic Council in a Rapidly Changing Scene of Arctic Governance' (2010) 46 *Polar Record* 146

'Transboundary Environmental Impact Assessment in International Law' in Simon Marsden and Timo Koivurova (eds.), *Transboundary Environmental Impact Assessment in the European Union: The Espoo Convention and its Kiev Protocol on Strategic Environmental Assessment* (Earthscan, London, 2011) 16

and Pölönen, Ismo, 'Transboundary Environmental Impact Assessment in the Case of the Baltic Gas Pipeline' (2010) 25 *The International Journal of Marine and Coastal Law* 151

and VanderZwaag, David, 'The Arctic Council at 10 Years: Retrospect and Prospects' (2007) 40 *University of British Columbia Law Review* 121

Kolodziej, Edward A., *Security and International Relations* (Cambridge University Press, 2005)

Kono, Toshiyuki (ed.), *Intangible Cultural Heritage and Intellectual Property: Communities, Cultural Diversity and Sustainable Development* (Intersentia, Antwerp, 2009)

Koskenniemi, Martti, 'Miserable Comforters: International Relations as the New Natural Law' (2009) 15 *European Journal of International Relations* 395

'Peaceful Settlement of Environmental Disputes' (1991) 60 *Nordic Journal of International Law* 73

Koyano, Mari, 'The Significance of the Convention on Environmental Impact Assessment in a Transboundary Context (Espoo Convention) in International Environmental Law: Examining the Implications of the Danube Delta Case' (2008) 26 *Impact Assessment and Project Appraisal* 299

Krämer, Ludwig, 'Environmental Justice in the European Court of Justice' in Jonas Ebbesson and Phoebe Okowa (eds.), *Environmental Law and Justice in Context* (Cambridge University Press, 2009) 195

Kratochwil, Friedrich, 'How Do Norms Matter?' in Michael Byers (ed.), *The Role of Law in International Politics: Essays in International Relations and International Law* (Oxford University Press, 2000) 34

Krisch, Nico and Kingsbury, Benedict, 'Introduction: Global Governance and Global Administrative Law in the International Legal Order' (2006) 17 *European Journal of International Law* 1

Kritikos, Mihail, 'Traditional Risk Analysis and Release of GMOs into the European Union: Space for Non-Scientific Factors?' (2009) 34 *European Law Review* 405

Krueger, Jonathan, 'Prior Informed Consent and the Basel Convention: The Hazards of What Isn't Known' (1998) 7 *Journal of Environment and Development* 115

Kütting, Gabriela, 'Environmental Justice' (2004) 4(1) *Global Environmental Politics* 115

Kwa, Eric, 'Climate Change and Indigenous People in the South Pacific: The Need for Regional and Local Strategies' in Ben J. Richardson *et al.* (eds.), *Climate Law and Developing Countries: Legal and Policy Challenges for the World Economy* (Edward Elgar, Cheltenham, 2009) 108

La Vina, Antonio, 'The Right to a Sound Environment in the Philippines: The Significance of the Minors Oposa Case' (1994) 3 *Review of European Community and International Environmental Law* 246

Lachapelle, Paul and McCool, Stephen, 'Exploring the Concept of "Ownership" in Natural Resource Planning' (2005) 18 *Society and Natural Resources* 279

Ladeur, Karl-Heinz, 'Coping with Uncertainty: Ecological Risks in the Proceduralization of Environmental Law' in Gunther Teubner, Lindsay Farmer and Declan Murphy (eds.), *Environmental Law and Ecological Responsibility: The Concept and Practice of Ecological Self-Organization* (Wiley, Chichester, 1994) 299

Lametti, David, 'The Concept of Property: Relations through Objects of Social Wealth' (2003) 53 *University of Toronto Law Journal* 325

Larner, Wendy, 'Neoliberalism: Policy, Ideology and Governmentality' (2000) 63 *Studies in Political Economy* 3

Larrère, Catherine, 'Le contexte philosophique du principe de précaution' in Charles Leben and Joe Verhoeven (eds.), *Le principe de précaution: Aspects de droit international et communautaire* (Panthéon-Assas, Paris, 2002) 15

Latour, Bruno, 'A Textbook Case Revisited – Knowledge as a Mode of Existence' in Edward J. Hackett *et al.* (eds.), *The Handbook of Science and Technology Studies* (MIT Press, Cambridge, Mass., 3rd edn, 2008) 83

We Have Never Been Modern (Harvard University Press, Cambridge, Mass., 1993)

Lawrence, Peter, 'Australian Climate Change Policy and the Asia Pacific Partnership on Clean Development and Climate. From Howard to Rudd: Continuity or Change?' (2009) 9 *International Environmental Agreements: Politics, Law, Economics* 281

Layton, Robert and Titchen, Sarah, 'Uluru: An Outstanding Australian Aboriginal Cultural Landscape' in Bernd von Droste, Harald Plachter and Mechtild Rössler (eds.), *Cultural Landscapes of Universal Value: Components of a Global Strategy* (Gustav Fischer Verlag, Jena, 1995) 174

Lazarus, Richard, *The Making of Environmental Law* (University of Chicago Press, 2004)

Leaver, Richard and Cox, Dave, 'Introduction: The World According to Gar' in Richard Leaver and Dave Cox (eds.), *Middling, Meddling, Muddling: Issues in Australian Foreign Policy* (Allen & Unwin, Sydney, 1997) 1

Lee, Maria, *EU Environmental Law: Challenges, Change and Decision-Making* (Hart Publishing, Oxford and Portland, 2005)

EU Regulation of GMOs (Edward Elgar, Cheltenham, 2008)

and Abbot, Carolyn, 'The Usual Suspects? Public Participation under the Aarhus Convention' (2003) 66 *Modern Law Review* 80

Lee, Simon and McBride, Stephen (eds.), *Market Liberalism, State Power and Global Governance* (Springer, Dordrecht, 2007)

Lefevere, Jürgen, 'Greenhouse Gas Emission Allowance Trading in the EU: A Background' (2004) *Yearbook of European Environmental Law* 149

'The EU ETS Linking Directive Explained' in Jos Delbeke (ed.), *EU Energy Law: The EU Greenhouse Gas Emissions Trading Scheme* (Claeys & Casteels, Leuven, 2006) 117

Lefèvre, Roger-Alexandre, *The Materials of Cultural Heritage in their Environment* (Edipuglia, Bari, 2006)

Lennon, Erika, 'A Tale of Two Poles: A Comparative Look at the Legal Regimes in the Arctic and the Antarctic' (2008) 8(3) *Sustainable Development Law & Policy* 32

Levidow, Les, 'The Transatlantic Agbiotech Conflict as a Problem and Opportunity for EU Regulatory Policies' in Robert Falkner (ed.), *The International Politics of Genetically Modified Food* (Palgrave Macmillan, Basingstoke, 2007) 134

Levi-Faur, David and Jordana, Jacint, 'Preface: The Making of a New Regulatory Order' (2005) 6 *Annals of the American Academy of Political and Social Science* 598

Lightfoot, Simon, 'A Good International Citizen? Australia at the World Summit on Sustainable Development' (2006) 60 *Australian Journal of International Affairs* 457

Lin, Jolene and Streck, Charlotte, 'Mobilising Finance for Climate Change Mitigation: Private Sector Involvement in International Carbon Finance Mechanism' (2009) 10 *Melbourne Journal of International Law* 70

Linn, Rob, *Battling the Land: 200 Years of Rural Australia* (Allen & Unwin, Sydney, 1999)

Litfin, Karen, 'Framing Science: Precautionary Discourse and the Ozone Treaties' (1995) 24 *Millennium: Journal of International Studies* 251

Ozone Discourses: Science and Politics in Global Environmental Cooperation (Columbia University Press, New York, 1994)

Liverman, Diana, 'Conventions of Climate Change: Constructions of Danger and the Dispossession of the Atmosphere' (2009) 35 *Journal of Historical Geography* 279

Locke, John, *Two Treatises of Government* (ed. Peter Laslett) (Cambridge University Press, 1988, first published 1689)

Logan, William and Reeves, Keir (eds.), *Places of Pain and Shame: Dealing with 'Difficult Heritage'* (Routledge, London, 2009)

Lohmann, Larry, 'Marketing and Making Carbon Dumps: Commodification, Calculation and Counterfactuals in Climate Change Mitigation' (2006) 14 *Science as Culture* 203

Lomberg, Bjorn, *The Skeptical Environmentalist's Guide to Global Warming* (Cyan-Marshall Cavendish, London, 2007)

Lovbrand, Eva, Rindefjall, Teresia and Nordqvist, Joakim, 'Closing the Legitimacy Gap in Global Environmental Governance? Lessons from the Emerging CDM Market' (2009) 9(2) *Global Environmental Politics* 74

Lovell, Heather, Bulkeley, Harriet and Owens, Susan, 'Converging Agendas? Energy and Climate Change Policies in the UK' (2009) 27 *Environment and Planning C: Government and Policy* 90

Lovelock, James, *Gaia: A New Look at Life on Earth* (Oxford University Press, rev. impr., 1987)

Low, Nicholas and Gleeson, Brendan, *Justice, Society, and Nature: An Exploration of Political Ecology* (Routledge, London and New York, 1998)

Lowe, A. Vaughan, 'Sustainable Development and Unsustainable Arguments' in Alan Boyle and David Freestone (eds.), *International Law and Sustainable Development: Past Achievements and Future Challenges* (Oxford University Press, 1999) 19

Lowe, Ian, *A Big Fix: Radical Solutions for Australia's Environmental Crisis* (Black Ink Press, Sydney, 2005)

One Earth: Social and Environmental Justice (Australian Conservation Foundation, Melbourne, 1999)

Lucy, William and Mitchell, Catherine, 'Replacing Private Property: The Case for Stewardship' (1996) 55 *Cambridge Law Journal* 566

Luhmann, Niklas, *A Sociological Theory of Law* (Routledge & Kegan Paul, London and Boston, 1985)

Luke, Timothy W., *Generating Green Governmentality: A Cultural Critique of Environmental Studies as a Power/Knowledge Formation*. Department of Political Science, Virginia Polytechnic Institute and State University Blacksburg (June 1996) at www.cddc.vt.edu/tim/tims/Tim514a.pdf, last accessed 8 May 2011

Luke, Timothy, 'Environmentality as Green Governmentality' in Eric Darier (ed.), *Discourses of the Environment* (Blackwell, Oxford, 1999) 121

Lunney, Mark and Oliphant, Ken, *Tort Law: Text and Materials* (Oxford University Press, 2nd edn, 2003)

Lynch-Wood, Gary and Williamson, David, 'The Social Licence as a Form of Regulation for Small and Medium Enterprises' (2007) 34 *Journal of Law and Society* 321

MacFarlane, S. Neil and Khong, Yuen Foong, *Human Security and the UN: A Critical History* (Indiana University Press, Bloomington, 1st edn, 2006)

MacFarquhar, Roderick and Schoenhals, Michael, *Mao's Last Revolution* (Harvard University Press, Cambridge, Mass., 2006)

Macintosh, Andrew and Denniss, Richard, *Property Rights and the Environment: Should Farmers Have a Right to Compensation?* The Australia Institute, Discussion Paper 74 (2004)

Mack, Andrew, *Human Security Report 2005: War and Peace in the 21st Century* (Oxford University Press, New York, 2005)

MacKenzie, Donald, *Material Markets: How Economic Agents Are Constructed* (Oxford University Press, 2009)

Macklin, Ruth, 'Can Future Generations Correctly Be Said to Have Rights?' in Ernest Partridge (ed.), *Responsibilities to Future Generations* (Prometheus Books, Buffalo, 1981) 151

Macpherson, Crawford (ed.), *Property: Mainstream and Critical Positions* (University of Toronto Press, 1978)

Maffi, Luisa and Woodley, Ellen, *Biocultural Diversity Conservation: A Global Sourcebook* (Earthscan, London, 2010)

Magraw, Daniel and Hawke, Lisa, 'Sustainable Development' in Daniel Bodansky, Jutta Brunnée and Ellen Hey (eds.), *The Oxford Handbook of International Environmental Law* (Oxford University Press, 2007) 613

Maguire, Steve and Ellis, Jaye, 'Redistributing the Burden of Scientific Uncertainty: Implications of the Precautionary Principle for State and Non-State Actors' (2005) 5 *Global Environmental Politics* 505

Malloy, Robin Paul, *Law in a Market Context* (Cambridge University Press, New York, 2004)

Mank, Bradford, 'Title VI and the Warren County Protests' (2007) 1 *Golden Gate University Environmental Law Journal* 73

Marong, Alhaji, 'From Rio to Johannesburg: Reflections on the Role of International Legal Norms in Sustainable Development' (2003–4) 16 *Georgetown International Environmental Law Review* 21

Marsden, Simon, 'Assessment of Transboundary Environmental Effects in the Pearl River Delta Region: Is there a Role for Strategic Environmental Assessment?' (2011) 31 *Environmental Impact Assessment Review* 593

'Enforcing Non-Discrimination in Transboundary Environmental Impact Assessment: Advantages for EU Citizens from the Transposition of the Espoo and Aarhus Conventions?' (2009) 6(4) *Journal for European Environmental and Planning Law* 437

'Introducing Strategic Environmental Assessment to the Antarctic Protocol: Lessons from International Experience' (2011) 1 *The Polar Journal* 36

'*MOX Plant* & the Espoo Convention: Can Member State Disputes Concerning Mixed Environmental Agreements Be Resolved outside EC Law?' (2009) 18 *Review of European Community and International Environmental Law* 312

'Transboundary Environmental Impact Assessment in European Law' in Simon Marsden and Timo Koivurova (eds.), *Transboundary Environmental*

Impact Assessment in the European Union: The Espoo Convention and its Kiev Protocol on Strategic Environmental Assessment (Earthscan, London, 2011)

Strategic Environmental Assessment in International and European Law (Earthscan, London, 2008)

and Koivurova, Timo (eds.), *Transboundary Environmental Impact Assessment in the European Union: The Espoo Convention and its Kiev Protocol on Strategic Environmental Assessment* (Earthscan, London, 2011)

Martin, John H., 'Glacial-Interglacial CO_2 Change: The Iron Hypothesis' (1990) 5 *Paleoceanography* 1

Fitzwater, Steve E. and Gordon, R. Michael, 'Iron Deficiency Limits Phytoplankton Growth in Antarctic Waters' (1990) 4(1) *Global Biogeochemical Cycles* 5

Martin, Paul, 'The Changing Role of Law in the Pursuit of Sustainability' in Michael Jeffrey, Jeremy Firestone and Karen Bubna-Litic (eds.), *Biodiversity Conservation, Law and Livelihoods: Bridging the North–South Divide* (Cambridge University Press, New York, 2008) 49

and Verbeek, Miriam, 'Property Rights and Property Responsibility' in Land & Water Australia (eds.), *Property: Rights and Responsibilities: Current Australian Thinking* (Land and Water Australia, Canberra, 2002) 1

Sustainability Strategy (Federation Press, Sydney, 2006)

Marx, Karl, 'The German Ideology: Part 1' in Robert C. Tucker (ed.), *The Marx–Engels Reader* (W. W. Norton & Co., New York, 1978) 146

Mashaw, Jerry, *Greed, Chaos, and Governance: Using Public Choice to Improve Public Law* (Yale University Press, New Haven, 1997)

'Public Law and Public Choice: Critique and Rapprochement' in Daniel Farber and Ann O'Connell (eds.), *Research Handbook on Public Choice and Public Law* (Edward Elgar, Cheltenham, 2010) 19

Mason, Michael, *Environmental Democracy* (Earthscan, London, 1999)

Mavrakis, Dimitrios, and Konidari, Popi, 'Classification of Emissions Trading Scheme Design Characteristics' (2003) 13 *European Environment* 48

Mayo-Ramsay, Julia, 'Taking a Precautionary Approach to Climate Mitigation Measures in the Southern Ocean' (2008) 12 *Antarctic & Southern Ocean Law & Policy Occasional Papers* 33

Mayor, Federico, *Memory of the Future* (UNESCO, Paris, 1995)

Mazoyer, Marcel and Roudart, Lawrence, *A History of World Agriculture from the Neolithic Age to the Current Crisis* (trans. James Membrez) (Earthscan, London, 2006)

McAllister, Sean, 'Human Rights and the Environment: The Convention on Access to Information, Public Participation in Decision Making, and Access to Justice in Environmental Matters' (1998) 9 *Colorado Journal of International Environmental Law Yearbook* 187

McAuslan, Patrick, 'The Ideologies of Planning Law' (1979) 2 *Urban Law and Policy* 1

McBarnet, Doreen and Whelan, Christopher, 'The Elusive Spirit of the Law: Formalism and the Struggle for Legal Control' (1991) 54 *The Modern Law Review* 848

McCaffrey, Stephen, *The Law of International Watercourses: Non-Navigational Uses* (Oxford University Press, 2nd edn, 2007)

McDonald, Matt, 'Fair Weather Friend? Ethics and Australia's Approach to Global Climate Change' (2005) 51 *Australian Journal of Politics and History* 216

McDorman, Ted, *Salt Water Neighbours* (Oxford University Press, New York, 2009)

McGarvin, Malcolm, 'Science, Precaution, Facts and Values' in Tim O'Riordan, James Cameron and Andrew Jordan (eds.), *Reinterpreting the Precautionary Principle* (Cameron May, London, 2001) 35

McGee, Jeffrey and Taplin, Ros, 'The Asia-Pacific Partnership and the United States' International Climate Change Policy' (2008) 19 *Colorado Journal on International Environmental Law and Policy* 179

'The Asia-Pacific Partnership on Clean Development and Climate: A Complement or Competitor to the Kyoto Protocol?' (2006) 18 *Global Change, Peace and Security* 173

'The Asia-Pacific Partnership on Clean Development and Climate: A Retreat from the Principle of Common but Differentiated Responsibilities?' (2009) 5 *McGill Journal of Sustainable Development Law and Policy* 11

McGrath, Chris, 'Australia's Draft Climate Laws' (2009) 26 *Environmental and Planning Law Journal* 26

McHoul, Alex and Grace, Wendy, *A Foucault Primer: Discourse, Power and the Subject* (New York University Press, 1997)

McIntyre, Owen, *Environmental Protection of International Watercourses under International Law* (Ashgate, Aldershot, 2007)

McIntyre-Tamwoy, Susan, 'Social Value, the Cultural Component in Natural Resource Management' (2004) 11 *Australasian Journal of Environmental Management* 289

McKibben, Bill, *The End of Nature* (Anchor Books, New York, rev. edn, 1999)

McLean, Janet, 'Divergent Legal Conceptions of the State: Implications for Global Administrative Law' (2005) 68 *Law and Contemporary Problems* 167

McNeil, Ben I., *et al.*, 'Anthropogenic CO_2 Uptake by the Ocean Based on the Global Chlorofluorocarbon Data Set' (2003) 299 *Science* 235

McPhee, Peter, 'The Misguided Greed of Peasants? Popular Attitudes to the Environment in the Revolution of 1789' (2001) 24 *French Historical Studies* 247

Meadowcroft, James, 'Sustainable Development: A New(ish) Idea for a New Century? (2000) 48 *Political Studies* 370

Meadows, Donella, *The Limits to Growth: A Report for the Club of Rome's Project on the Predicament of Mankind* (Universe Books, New York, 1974)

et al., *The Limits to Growth: The 30 Year Update* (Earthscan, London, 2005)

Metz, Bert, 'Ocean Storage' in Bert Metz *et al.*, *Carbon Dioxide Capture and Storage* (Cambridge University Press for the Intergovernmental Panel on Climate Change, 2005) 289

Metz, Bert *et al.*, *Carbon Dioxide Capture and Storage* (Cambridge University Press for the Intergovernmental Panel on Climate Change, 2005)

Meyer, Lukas, 'Intergenerational Justice' (2008) in *Stanford Encyclopedia of Philosophy* at plato.stanford.edu/entries/justice-intergenerational/, last accessed 21 August 2009

Mill, John Stuart, *On Liberty* (1859), repr. in John Stuart Mill, *Utilitarianism, On Liberty, Essay on Bentham* (Fontana, London, 1962) 126

Miller, Christopher, *Environmental Rights: Critical Perspectives* (Routledge, London and New York, 1998)

Mills, Alex and Stephens, Tim, 'Challenging the Role of Judges in Slaughter's Liberal Theory of International Law' (2005) 18 *Leiden Journal of International Law* 1

Misiolek, Walter and Elder, Harold, 'Exclusionary Manipulation of Markets for Pollution Rights' (1989) 16 *Journal of Environmental Economics and Management* 156

Mol, Arthur (ed.), *Globalization and Environmental Reform: The Ecological Modernization of the Global Economy* (MIT Press, Cambridge, Mass., 2001)

Moore, Lisa, 'Voluntary Carbon Offsets: A Legal Perspective' in Wayne Gumley and Trevor Daya-Winterbottom (eds.), *Climate Change Law: Comparative, Contractual & Regulatory Considerations* (Lawbook Co., Sydney, 2008) 159

Moore, Niamh and Whelan, Yvonne (eds.), *Heritage, Memory and the Politics of Identity* (Ashgate, Aldershot, 2007)

Morgan, Bronwen and Yeung, Karen, *An Introduction to Law and Regulation: Texts and Materials* (Cambridge University Press, 2007)

Morgenthau, Hans, *Politics Among Nations: The Struggle for Power and Peace* (Knopf, New York, 1948)

Morgera, Elisa, 'An Update on the Aarhus Convention and its Continued Global Relevance' (2005) 14 *Review of European Community and International Environmental Law* 138

Morrison, Wayne, *Jurisprudence from the Greeks to Post Modernism* (Cavendish Publishing, London, 1997)

Mulgan, Richard, 'AWB and Oil for Food: Some Issues of Accountability' in Jeremy Farrell and Kim Rubenstein (eds.), *Sanctions, Accountability and Governance in a Globalised World* (Cambridge University Press, 2009) 334

Muniesa, Fabian, Millo, Yuval and Callon, Michel, 'An Introduction to Market Devices' (2007) 55 *The Sociological Review* 1

Myhre, G., Alterskjær, K. and Lowe, D., 'A Fast Method for Updating Global Fossil Fuel Carbon Dioxide Emissions' (2009) 4 *Environmental Research Letters* 034012

Naim, Moises and Case, Dave, 'True Believer' (2001) (Mar/April) *Foreign Policy* 26

Nasu, Hitoshi, 'Who Guards the Guardian? Towards Regulation of the UN Security Council's Chapter VII Powers through Dialogue' in Jeremy Farrell and Kim Rubenstein (eds.), *Sanctions, Accountability and Governance in a Globalised World* (Cambridge University Press, 2009) 128

National Farmers Federation, *Policy on Sustainable Production, Land and Native Vegetation* (2004)

National Farmers Union, *Policy of the National Farmers Union* (2009)

Naumkin, Vitaly, 'Islam in the States of the Former USSR' (1992) 524 *Annals of the American Academy of Political and Social Science* 131

Neufeld, Mark, 'Interpretation and the "Science" of International Relations' (1993) 19 *Review of International Studies* 39

Neurath, Paul, *From Malthus to the Club of Rome and Back: Problems of Limits to Growth, Population Control, and Migrations* (M. E. Sharpe, Armonk, 1994)

Newell, Peter, 'The Political Economy of Global Environmental Governance' (2008) 34 *Review of International Studies* 507

'"What You Risk Reveals What You Value", and Other Dilemmas Encountered in the Legal Assaults on Risks' in David Freestone and Ellen Hey (eds.), *The Precautionary Principle and International Law: The Challenge of Implementation* (Kluwer Law International, The Hague and Boston, 1996) 73

Nollkaemper, André, 'Sovereignty and Environmental Justice in International Law' in Jonas Ebbesson and Phoebe Okowa (eds.), *Environmental Law and Justice in Context* (Cambridge University Press, 2009) 253

Note, 'The CITES Fort Lauderdale Criteria: The Uses and Limits of Science in International Conservation Decisionmaking' (2001) 114 *Harvard Law Review* 1769

Nussbaum, Martha, *Frontiers of Justice: Disability, Nationality, Species Membership* (Belknap Press, Cambridge, Mass., and London, 2006)

Ockenfels, Axel, 'Empfehlungen für das Auktionsdesign für Emissionsberechtigungen' (2009) 2 *Zeitschrift für Energiewirtschaft* 105

Oels, Angela, 'Rendering Climate Change Governable: From Biopower to Advanced Liberal Government?' (2005) 7 *Journal of Environmental Policy and Planning* 185

O'Faircheallaigh, Ciaran, 'Public Participation and Environmental Impact Assessment: Purposes, Implications and Lessons for Public Policy Making' (2010) 30 *Environmental Impact Assessment Review* 19

Office for the London Dumping Convention at the International Maritime Organization, *The London Convention: The First Decade and Beyond* (International Maritime Organization, London, 1991)

Okereke, Chukwumerije, *Global Justice and Neoliberal Environmental Governance: Ethics, Sustainable Development and International Cooperation* (Routledge, London and New York, 2008)

Olivetti, Alfred Jr and Worsham, Jeff, *This Land Is Your Land, This Land Is My Land: The Property Rights Movement and Regulatory Takings* (LFB Scholarly Publishing LLC, New York, 2003)

Oosterveer, Peter, 'Governing Global Fish Provisioning: Ownership and Management of Marine Resources' (2008) 51 *Ocean & Coastal Management* 797

O'Riordan, Tim, 'The Precautionary Principle and Civic Science' in Tim O'Riordan, James Cameron and Andrew Jordan (eds.), *Reinterpreting the Precautionary Principle* (Cameron May, London, 2001) 95

and Cameron, James (eds.), *Interpreting the Precautionary Principle* (Earthscan, London, 1994)

Orr, James C., *et al.*, 'Anthropogenic Ocean Acidification Over the Twenty-First Century and its Impact on Calcifying Organisms' (2005) 437 *Nature* 681

Ostrom, Elinor, *Governing the Commons: The Evolution of Institutions for Collective Action* (Cambridge University Press, New York, 1990)

Othman, Zarina, 'Human Security Concepts, Approaches and Debates in Southeast Asia' in Hans Günter Brauch *et al.* (eds.), *Facing Global Environmental Change – Environmental, Human, Energy, Food, Health and Water Security Concepts* (Springer, Berlin, 2009) 79

Outer Circle Policy Unit, *The Big Public Inquiry* (Outer Circle Policy Unit, London, 1979)

Owen, Dave, 'Law, Environmental Dynamism, Reliability: The Rise and Fall of CALFED' (2007) *Environmental Law* 1145

Owens, Susan, 'A Balanced Appraisal? Impact Assessment of European Commission Proposals' (2007) 1 *elni Review* 2

Ozawa, Connie, *Recasting Science: Consensual Procedures in Public Policy Making* (Westview Press, Boulder, 1991)

Page, Edward, *Climate Change, Justice and Future Generations* (Edward Elgar, Cheltenham, 2006)

Pallemaerts, Marc, 'An Introduction to the Sources, Principles and Regimes of International Environmental Law' in Marko Berglund (ed.), *International Environmental Law Making and Diplomacy* (University of Joensuu, Department of Law, 2004) 69

'International Environmental Law from Stockholm to Rio: Back to the Future?' in Philippe Sands (ed.), *Greening International Law* (Earthscan, London, 1993) 1

Palmer, Karen and Walls, Margaret, *Extended Product Responsibility: An Economic Assessment of Alternative Policies* (Resources for the Future, Washington DC, 1999)

Papadakis, Elim and Grant, Richard, 'The Politics of "Light-Handed Regulation": "New" Environmental Policy Instruments in Australia' (2003) 12 *Environmental Politics* 27

Parliament of Australia, Department of Parliamentary Services, Parliamentary Library, *Background Note: Climate Change Discussions and Negotiations: A Calendar*, 17 July 2009

Parry, Martin, 'Climate Change Is a Development Issue, and Only Sustainable Development Can Confront the Challenge' (2009) 1 *Climate and Development* 5

Partridge, Ernest, 'On the Rights of Future Generations' in Donald Sherer (ed.), *Upstream/Downstream: Issues in Environmental Ethics* (Temple University Press, Philadelphia, 1990) 40

Pearce, David, 'The Social Cost of Carbon and its Policy Implications' (2003) 19 (3) *Oxford Review of Economic Policy* 362

Pearsall, Judy and Trumble, Bill (eds.), *Oxford English Reference Dictionary* (Oxford University Press, 2nd rev. edn, 2001)

Pearse, Guy, *High and Dry: John Howard, Climate Change and the Selling of Australia's Future* (Penguin, Melbourne, 2007)

Pedersen, Ole, 'European Environmental Human Rights and Environmental Rights: A Long Time Coming?' (2008) 21 *Georgetown International Environmental Law Review* 73

Peel, Jacqueline, 'Climate Change Law: The Emergence of a New Legal Discipline' (2008) 32 *Melbourne University Law Review* 922

'Precaution – A Matter of Principle, Approach or Process?' (2004) 5 *Melbourne Journal of International Law* 483

'The Role of Climate Change Litigation in Australia's Response to Global Warming' (2007) 24 *Environmental and Planning Law Journal* 90

'When (Scientific) Rationality Rules: (Mis)Application of the Precautionary Principle in Australian Mobile Phone Tower Cases' (2007) 19 *Journal of Environmental Law* 103

The Precautionary Principle in Practice, Environmental Decision Making and Scientific Uncertainty (Federation Press, Sydney, 2005)

Pellow, David, *Resisting Global Toxics: Transnational Movements for Environmental Justice* (MIT Press, Cambridge, Mass., and London, 2007)

Pereira, Ravi Afonso, 'Why Would International Administrative Activity Be Any Less Legitimate? – A Study of the Codex Alimentarius Commission' (2008) 9 *German Law Journal* 1693

Perez, Oren, *Ecological Sensitivity and Global Legal Pluralism: Rethinking the Trade and Environment Conflict* (Hart Publishing, Oxford, 2004)

Peters, Robert, *A Critique for Ecology* (Cambridge University Press, Cambridge and New York, 1991)

Petersmann, Ernst-Ulrich, 'Introduction' in Christian Joerges and Ernst-Ulrich Petersmann (eds.), *Constitutionalism, Multilevel Trade Governance and Social Regulation* (Hart Publishing, Oxford, 2006) xxxviii

Petkova, Elena, and Veit, Peter, *Environmental Accountability Beyond the Nation State: The Implications of the Aarhus Convention* (World Resources Institute, Washington DC, 2000)

Pharad, Donat, *Canada's Arctic Waters in International Law* (Cambridge University Press, 1988)

Phillips, Louise and Jørgensen, Marianne, *Discourse Analysis as Theory and Method* (Sage Publications, London, 2002)

Pigou, Arthur, *Wealth and Welfare* (Macmillan, London, 1912)

Pletcher, Galen, 'The Rights of Future Generations' in Ernest Partridge (ed.), *Responsibilities to Future Generations* (Prometheus Books, Buffalo, 1981) 168

Pogge, Thomas, 'A Global Resource Dividend' in David Crocker and Toby Linden (eds.), *Ethics of Consumption* (Rowman and Littlefield, Oxford, 1999) 501

'Keynote Address: Poverty, Climate Change, and Overpopulation' (2010) 38 *Georgia Journal of International and Comparative Law* 525

'The Health Impact Fund: Better Pharmaceutical Innovations at Much Lower Prices' in Pogge, Rimmer and Rubenstein (eds.), *Incentives for Global Public Health: Patent Law and Access to Essential Medicines* 135

Rimmer, Matthew and Rubenstein, Kim (eds.), *Incentives for Global Public Health: Patent Law and Access to Essential Medicines* (Cambridge University Press, 2010)

Policy Commission on the Future of Farming and Food, *A Sustainable Future* (2002)

Pomar, Olga, 'Toxic Racism on a New Jersey Waterfront' in Robert Bullard (ed.), *The Quest for Environmental Justice: Human Rights and the Politics of Pollution* (Sierra Club Books, San Francisco, 2005) 125

Porras, Ileana, 'The Rio Declaration: A New Basis for International Cooperation' in Philippe Sands (ed.), *Greening International Law* (Earthscan, London, 1993) 20

Posner, Richard, 'Nobel Laureate: Ronald Coase and Methodology' (1993) 7 *Journal of Economic Perspectives* 195

Economic Analysis of Law (Little, Brown, Boston, 1972)

Proops, John, 'The (Non-) Economics of the Nuclear Fuel Cycle: An Historical and Discourse Analysis' (2001) 39 *Ecological Economics* 13

Prott, Lyndel (ed.), *Finishing the Interrupted Voyage: Papers of the UNESCO Asia-Pacific Workshop on the Protection of the Underwater Cultural Heritage* (Institute of Art and Law, Builth Wells, 2006)

and O'Keefe, Patrick, '"Cultural Heritage" or "Cultural Property"?' (1992) 1 *International Journal of Cultural Property* 311

Queensland Farmers Federation, *The Environmental Code of Practice for Agriculture* (1998)

Radaelli, Claudio, 'The Role of Knowledge in the Policy Process' (1995) 2 *Journal of European Public Policy* 159

Raff, Murray, 'Environmental Obligations and the Western Liberal Property Concept' (1998) 22 *Melbourne University Law Review* 657

'Toward an Ecologically Sustainable Property Concept' in Elizabeth Cooke (ed.), *Modern Studies in Property Law, Vol. III* (Hart Publishing, Oxford, 2005) 65

Rajamani, Lavanya, 'Public Interest Environmental Litigation in India: Exploring Issues of Access, Participation, Equity, Effectiveness and Sustainability' (2007) 19 *Journal of Environmental Law* 293

'The Principle of Common but Differentiated Responsibility and the Balance of Commitments under the Climate Regime' (2000) 9 *Review of European Community and International Environmental Law* 120

Raney, Terry and Pingali, Prahbu, 'Sowing a Gene Revolution' (2007) 297(3) *Scientific American* 104

Rawls, John, *A Theory of Justice* (Oxford University Press, 1972)

Rayfuse, Rosemary, 'Melting Moments: The Future of Polar Oceans Governance in a Warming World' (2007) 16 *Review of European Community and International Environmental Law* 196

Raz, Joseph, 'Right-Based Moralities' in Jeremy Waldron (ed.), *Theories of Rights* (Oxford University Press, 1984) 182

Razzaque, Jona, 'Participatory Rights in Natural Resource Management: The Role of Communities in South Asia' in Jonas Ebbesson and Phoebe Okowa (eds.), *Environmental Law and Justice in Context* (Cambridge University Press, 2009) 117

'Public Participation in Water Governance' in Joseph Dellapenna and Joyeeta Gupta (eds.), *The Evolution of the Law and Politics of Water* (Springer, Dordrecht, 2009)

Rechtschaffen, Clifford, 'Strategies for Implementing the Environmental Justice Vision' (2007) 1 *Golden Gate University Environmental Law Journal* 321

and Gauna, Eileen, *Environmental Justice: Law, Policy and Regulation* (Carolina Academic Press, Durham, 1st edn, 2003)

Regional Environmental Center for Central and Eastern Europe and United Nations Development Programme, *Benefits of an SEA* (2003)

Rehbinder, Eckard, 'Market Based Incentives for Environmental Protection' in Richard Revesz, Philippe Sands and Richard Stewart (eds.), *Environmental Law, the Economy and Sustainable Development* (Cambridge University Press, 2000) 245

Rehg, William, *Cogent Science in Context: The Science Wars, Argumentation Theory, and Habermas* (MIT Press, Cambridge, Mass., 2009)

Richardson, Benjamin, 'Environmental Law in Postcolonial Societies: Straddling the Local-Global Institutional Spectrum' (2000) 11 *Colorado Journal of International Environmental Law & Policy* 1

Richman, Barak, and Macher, Jeffrey, *Transaction Cost Economics: An Assessment of Empirical Research in the Social Sciences*, Duke Law School Legal Studies Research Paper Series, Research Paper No. 115 (2006)

Rittel, Horst and Webber, Melvin, 'Dilemmas in a General Theory of Planning' (1973) 4 *Policy Sciences* 155

Rodgers, Christopher, 'Agenda 2000, Land Use, and the Environment: Towards a Theory of "Environmental" Property Rights?' in Jane Holder and Carolyn Harrison (eds.), *Law and Geography Current Legal Issues 2002, Vol. V* (Oxford University Press, 2003) 239

Rogelj, Joeri, *et al.*, 'Copenhagen Accord Pledges Are Paltry' (2010) 464 *Nature* 1126

Rook, Deborah, *Property Law and Human Rights* (Blackstone Press, London, 2001)

Rose, Carol, 'Common Property, Regulatory Property, and Environmental Protection: Comparing Community-Based Management to Tradable Environmental Allowances' in Elinor Ostrom *et al.* (eds.), *The Drama of the Commons* (National Resource Council, Washington DC, 2003) 233

Rothwell, Donald R., 'International Law and the Protection of the Arctic Environment' (1995) 44 *International and Comparative Law Quarterly* 280

'The Arctic Environmental Protection Strategy and International Environmental Cooperation in the Far North' (1995) 6 *Yearbook of International Environmental Law* 65

'The Arctic in International Affairs: Time for a New Regime?' (2008) 15 *Brown Journal of World Affairs* 241

'Sovereignty and the Antarctic Treaty' (2010) 46 *Polar Record* 17

The Polar Regions and the Development of International Law (Cambridge University Press, 1996)

and Stephens, Tim, *The International Law of the Sea* (Hart Publishing, Oxford, 2010) ch. 13

Rudd, Kevin, 'The Global Financial Crisis' *The Monthly* 42, February 2009

Ruhl, J. B., 'Sustainable Development: A Five-Dimensional Algorithm for Environmental Law' (1999) 18 *Stanford Environmental Law Journal* 31

'Thinking of Environmental Law as a Complex Adaptive System: How to Clean UP the Environment by Making a Mess of Environmental Law' (1997) 4 *Houston Law Review* 101

Ryall, Aine, *Effective Judicial Protection and the Environmental Impact Assessment Directive in Ireland* (Hart Publishing, Oxford, 2009)

Rydin, Yvonne, *Conflict, Consensus and Rationality in Environmental Planning: An Institutional Discourse Approach* (Oxford University Press, 2003)

Sachs, Wolfgang, *Climate Change and Human Rights: WDEV Special Report 1/2007* (World Economy & Development, Luxembourg, 2007)

Sagoff, Mark, 'Controlling Global Climate: The Debate over Pollution Trading' in Verna Gehring and William Galston (eds.), *Philosophical Dimensions of Public Policy* (Transaction Publishers, New Brunswick, 2002) 311

The Economy of the Earth (Cambridge University Press, New York, 1988)

The Economy of the Earth: Philosophy, Law and the Environment (Cambridge University Press, 2nd edn, 2008)

Sahabat Alam Malaysia (ed.), *The Battle for Sarawak's Forests* (World Rainforest Movement/Sahabat Alam Malaysia, Penang, 2nd edn, 1990)

Salomon, Jean-Jacques, 'Science, Technology and Democracy' (2000) 38 *Minerva* 33

Sampford, Charles, 'Law, Institutions and the Public/Private Divide' (1991) 20 *Federal Law Review* 185

'The Potential for a Post-Westphalian Convergence of "Public Law" and "Public International Law"' in Jeremy Farrell and Kim Rubenstein (eds.), *Sanctions, Accountability and Governance in a Globalised World* (Cambridge University Press, 2009) 56

Sands, Philippe, 'International Environmental Litigation and its Future' (1999) 32 *University of Richmond Law Review* 1619

'International Law in the Field of Sustainable Development' (1994) LXV *British Yearbook of International Law* 303

Principles of International Environmental Law (Cambridge University Press, 2nd edn, 2003)

Sargent, John, 'The Economics of Energy and the Environment: The Potential Role of Market-Based Instruments' (2002) 28 *Canada–United States Law Journal* 499

Save the Ifugao Terraces Movement, *IMPACT: The Effects of Tourism on Culture and the Environment in Asia and the Pacific: Sustainable Tourism and the Preservation of the World Heritage Site of the Ifugao Rice Terraces, Philippines* (UNESCO Bangkok, Bangkok, 2008)

Savory, Allan with Butterfield, Judy, *Holistic Management: A New Framework for Decision Making* (Island Press, Washington DC, 2nd edn, 1999)

Saward, Michael, 'Representation' in Andrew Dobson and Robyn Eckersley (eds.), *Political Theory and the Ecological Challenge* (Cambridge University Press, Cambridge and New York, 2006) 183

'The Civil Nuclear Network in Britain' in David Marsh and Rod Rhodes (eds.), *Policy Networks in British Governance* (Clarendon Press, Oxford, 1992) 75

Sax, Joseph, 'Environmental Law Forty Years Later: Looking Back and Looking Ahead' in Michael Jeffery, Jeremy Firestone and Karen Bubna-Litic (eds.), *Biodiversity, Conservation, Law and Livelihoods: Bridging the North–South Divide* (Cambridge University Press, New York, 2008) 9

Schaaf, Thomas and Rössler, Mechtild, 'Sacred Natural Sites, Cultural Landscapes and UNESCO's Action' in Bas Verschuuren *et al.* (eds.), *Sacred Natural Sites Conserving Nature and Culture* (Earthscan, London, 2010) 161

Schlosberg, David, 'Reconceiving Environmental Justice: Global Movements and Political Theories' (2004) 13 *Environmental Politics* 517

Defining Environmental Justice: Theories, Movements and Nature (Oxford University Press, 2007)

Environmental Justice and the New Pluralism: The Challenge of Difference for Environmentalism (Oxford University Press, 1999)

Schmidt, Vivienne and Radaelli, Claudio, 'Policy Change and Discourse in Europe: Conceptual and Methodological Issues' (2004) 27 *West European Politics* 183

Scholtz, Werner, 'Equity as the Basis for Future Global Emission Reductions: Between Pragmatic Panacea and Idealistic Impediment. The Optimization of the CBDR Principle *via* Realism' (2009) 42(2) *The Comparative and International Law Journal of Southern Africa* 166

Schrage, Wiek 'The Convention on Environmental Impact Assessment in a Transboundary Context' in Kees Bastmeijer and Timo Koivurova (eds.), *Theory and Practice of Transboundary Environmental Impact Assessment* (Martinus Nijhoff, Leiden and Boston, 2008) 29

and Bonvoisin, Nick, 'Transboundary Impact Assessment: Frameworks, Experiences and Challenges' (2008) 26 *Impact Assessment and Project Appraisal* 234

Schroeder, Jeanne, 'Chix Nix Bundle-o-Stix: A Feminist Critique of the Disaggregation of Property' (1994) 93 *Michigan Law Review* 239

Schumacher, Eric, *Small Is Beautiful: A Study of Economics as if People Mattered* (Blond and Briggs, London, 1973)

Scott, Joanne, 'European Regulation of GMOs and the WTO' (2003) 9 *Columbia Journal of European Law* 213

European Regulation of GMOs: Thinking About Judicial Review in the WTO, Jean Monnet Working Paper 04/04, NYU School of Law (2004)

The WTO Agreement on Sanitary and Phytosanitary Measures: A Commentary (Oxford University Press, 2009)

Scott, Shirley, *The Political Interpretation of Multilateral Treaties* (Martinus Nijhoff Publishers, Leiden, 2004)

Scrase, Ivan and Ockwell, David, 'Energy Issues: Framing and Policy Change' in Ivan Scrase and Gordon MacKerron (eds.), *Energy for the Future. A New Agenda* (Palgrave Macmillan, Basingstoke, 2009) 35

Scurlock, Jonathan, 'A Concise History of the Nuclear Industry Worldwide' in David Elliott (ed.), *Nuclear or Not? Does Nuclear Power Have a Place in a Sustainable Energy Future*? (Palgrave Macmillan, Basingstoke, 2007) 24

Seibel, Brad and Walsh, Patrick, 'Biological Impacts of Deep-Sea Carbon Dioxide Injection Inferred from Indices of Physiological Performance' (2003) 206 *The Journal of Experimental Biology* 642

Sequeira, Gavin and Jones, Ian S. F., *Financial & Economic Modelling of the Sulu Sea Ocean Nourishment Project*, OTG Report No. 5/99, University of Sydney (1999)

Serdy, Andrew, 'Some Views Are More Equal than Others: Submissions to the Commission on the Limits of the Continental Shelf and the Strange Loss of Confidence in Article IV of the Antarctic Treaty' (2009) 28 *Australian Year Book of International Law* 181

Severino, Rodolfo, 'ASEAN Beyond Forty: Towards Political and Economic Integration' (2007) 23 *Contemporary Southeast Asia* 406

Shadian, Jessica and Tennberg, Monica (eds.), *Legacies and Change in Polar Sciences: Historical, Legal and Political Reflections on The International Polar Year* (Ashgate, Aldershot, 2009)

Shaikh, Anwar, 'The Economic Mythology of Neoliberalism' in Alfredo Saad-Filho (ed.), *Neo-Liberalism: A Critical Reader* (Pluto Press, London, 2004) 41

Shaw, Martin, *Theory of the Global State: Globality as an Unfinished Revolution* (Cambridge University Press, 2000)

Sheldon, Ian, 'Regulation of Biotechnology: Will We Ever "Freely" Trade GMOs?' (2002) 29 *European Review of Agricultural Economics* 155

Shelton, Dinah, 'Describing the Elephant: International Justice and Environmental Law' in Jonas Ebbesson and Phoebe Okowa (eds.), *Environmental Law and Justice in Context* (Cambridge University Press, 2009) 55

'Equity' in Daniel Bodansky, Jutta Brunnée and Ellen Hey (eds.), *The Oxford Handbook of International Environmental Law*, 639

'Rainforests and Regulation: New Directions in Brazilian Environmental Law and Legal Institutions: Environmental Rights and Brazil's Obligations in the Inter-American Human Rights System' (2009) 40 *George Washington International Law Review* 733

Sherman, Brad, 'Taxonomic Property' (2008) 67 *Cambridge Law Journal* 560

Shiva, Vandana, 'Epilogue: Beyond Reductionism' in Vandana Shiva and Ingunn Moser (eds.), *Biopolitics: A Feminist and Ecological Reader on Biotechnology* (Zed Books, London, 1995) 267

Simma, Bruno, 'Universality of International Law from the Perspective of a Practitioner' (2009) 20 *European Journal of International Law* 265

Sive, David, 'Some Thoughts of an Environmental Lawyer in the Wilderness of Administrative Law' (1970) 70 *Columbia Law Review* 612

'The Litigation Process in the Development of Environmental Law' (1995) 13 *Pace Environmental Law Review* 1

Skjærseth, Jon and Wettestad, Joergen, *EU Emissions Trading: Initiation, Decision-Making and Implementation* (Ashgate Publishing, Burlington, 2008)

Slaughter, Anne-Marie, *A New World Order* (Princeton University Press, 2004)

Smith, Laurajane, *Uses of Heritage* (Routledge, London, 2006)

(ed.), *Cultural Heritage: Critical Concepts in Media and Cultural Studies* (Routledge, London, 2007)

Smith, Mark and Pangsapa, Piya, *Environment and Citizenship: Integrating Justice, Responsibility and Civic Engagement* (Zed Books, London and New York, 2008)

Smith, Philip, *Cultural Theory: An Introduction* (Blackwell, Oxford, 2001)

Snape, William III, 'Overview: Radical Environmental Change in the Polar Regions Is the Globe's Wake-Up Call' (2008) 8(3) *Sustainable Development Law & Policy* 2

Sowers, Jeannie, 'The Many Injustices of Climate Change' (2007) 7(4) *Global Environmental Politics* 140

Spagnuolo, Francesca, 'Beyond Participation: Administrative-Law Type Mechanisms in Global Environmental Governance. Toward a New Basis of Legitimacy?' (2009) 15 *European Public Law* 49

Spiro, Peter, 'Non-Governmental Organisations and Civil Society' in Daniel Bodansky, Jutta Brunnée and Ellen Hey (eds.), *The Oxford Handbook of International Environmental Law*, 770

Stallworthy, Mark, *Sustainability, Land Use and Environment: A Legal Analysis* (Cavendish, London, 2002)

Stapleton, Jane, 'Duty of Care Factors: A Selection from the Judicial Menus' in Peter Cane and Jane Stapleton (eds.), *The Law of Obligations: Essays in Celebration of John Fleming* (Clarendon Press, Oxford, 1998) 59

Star, Susan Leigh and Griesemer, James, 'Institutional Ecology, "Translation" and Boundary Objects: Amateurs and Professionals in Berkeley's Museum of Vertebrate Zoology' (1989) 19 *Social Studies of Science* 387

State of Queensland Environment Protection Authority, *State of the Environment Queensland 2007* (2008)

Stec, Stephen, 'Environmental Justice Through Courts in Countries in Transition' in Jonas Ebbesson and Phoebe Okowa (eds.), *Environmental Law and Justice in Context* (Cambridge University Press, 2009) 158

Stephan, Paul, 'The New International Law – Legitimacy, Accountability, Authority, and Freedom in the New Global Order' (1999) 70 *University of Colorado Law Review* 1555

Stephens, Tim, 'Fishing-Led Development in the South Pacific: Charting a Pacific Way to a Sustainable Future' (2008) 39 *Ocean Development and International Law* 256

'Sustainability Discourses in International Courts: What Place for Global Justice?' in Duncan French (ed.), *Global Justice and Sustainable Development* (Martinus Nijhoff Publishers, Leiden, 2010) ch. 2

International Courts and Environmental Protection (Cambridge University Press, 2009)

and Rothwell, Donald R., 'Japanese Whaling in Antarctica: *Humane Society International Inc.* v. *Kyodo Senpaku Kaisha Ltd*' (2007) 16 *Review of European Community and International Environmental Law* 243

Stern, Nicholas, *The Economics of Climate Change: The Stern Review* (Cambridge University Press, 2007)

Stevenson, Christopher, 'Hans Off! The Struggle for Hans Island and the Potential Ramifications for International Border Dispute Resolution' (2007) 30 *Boston College International and Comparative Law Review* 263

Stirling, Andy, 'The Precautionary Principle in Science and Technology' in Tim O'Riordan, James Cameron and Andrew Jordan (eds.), *Reinterpreting the Precautionary Principle* (Cameron May, London, 2001) 61

Stone, Christopher, 'Ethics and International Environmental Law' in Daniel Bodansky, Jutta Brunnée and Ellen Hey (eds.), *The Oxford Handbook of International Environmental Law*, 291

'Should Trees Have Standing? Toward Legal Rights for Natural Objects' (1972) 45 *Southern California Law Review* 450

'Should Trees Have Standing? Revisited: How Far Will Law and Morals Reach? A Pluralist Perspective' (1985–6) 59 *Southern California Law Review* 1

Stone, Julius, *Legal System and Lawyers' Reasoning* (Stanford University Press, 1968)

Stott, Martin, Taylor, Peter and the Town and Country Planning Association, *The Nuclear Controversy* (Town and Country Planning Association, London, 1980)

Street, Paul, 'Constructing Risks, GMOs, Biosafety and Environmental Decision-Making' in Han Somsen (ed.), *The Regulatory Challenge of Biotechnology: Human Genetics, Food and Patents* (Edward Elgar, Cheltenham, 2007) 102

Sunstein, Cass, 'The Paradoxes of Regulation' (1990) 67 *University of Chicago Law Review* 408

Sutton, Peter, 'The Pulsating Heart: Large Scale Cultural and Demographic Processes in Aboriginal Australia' in Betty Meehan and Neville White (eds.), *Hunter-Gatherer Demography: Past and Present* (University of Sydney Press, 1990) 71

Szerszynski, Bronislaw, 'On Knowing What to Do: Environmentalism and the Modern Problematic', in Scott Lash *et al.* (eds.), *Risk, Environment and Modernity: Towards a New Ecology* (Sage Publications, London, 1996) 104

Takahashi, Taro, *et al.*, 'Global Sea-Air CO_2 Flux Based on Climatological Surface Ocean pCO_2, and Seasonal Biological and Temperature Effects' (2002) 49 *Deep-Sea Research Pt II* 1601

Tan, Andrew T. H. and Boutlin, J. D. Kenneth (eds.), *Non-Traditional Security Issues in Southeast Asia* (Select Publishing for Institute of Defence and Strategic Studies, Singapore, 2001)

Tannenwald, Nina, 'The Nuclear Taboo: The United States and the Normative Basis of Nuclear Non-Use' (1999) 53 *International Organization* 433

Taplin, Ros, 'International Co-operation on Climate Change and Australia's Role' (1995) 26 *Australian Geographer* 16

Targ, Nicholas and Bonorris, Steven, 'State Environmental Justice Programs and Related Authorities' in Michael Gerrard and Sheila Foster (eds.), *The Law of Environmental Justice: Theories and Procedures to Address Disproportionate Risks* (American Bar Association, Chicago, 2nd edn, 2008) 157

Tarlock, Dan, 'The Nonequilibrium Paradigm in Ecology and the Partial Unraveling of Environmental Law' (1994) 27 *Loyola of Los Angeles Law Review* 1121

Taverne, Dick, *The March of Unreason: Science, Democracy, and the New Fundamentalism* (Oxford University Press, New York, 2005)

Taylor, Simon, *Privatisation and Financial Collapse in the Nuclear Industry: The Origins and Causes of the British Energy Crisis of 2002* (Routledge, London, 2007)

Techera, Erika J., 'Synergies and Challenges for Legal Protection of Sacred Natural Sites in the South Pacific' in B. Verschuuren *et al.* (eds.), *Sacred Natural Sites Conserving Nature and Culture* (Earthscan, London, 2010) 170

Tennberg, Monica, *Arctic Environmental Cooperation: A Study in Governmentality* (Ashgate, Aldershot, 2001)

Teubner, Gunther, *Law as an Autopoietic System* (Blackwell, Oxford and Cambridge, Mass., 1993)

Thayyil, Naveen, 'Deliberative Turning from a Law-Science Cul-de-Sac: Speculations Regarding Community Transgenic Regulation' (2008) *Yearbook of European Environmental Law* 153

Thompson, Barton Jr, 'Markets for Nature' (2001) 25 *William and Mary Environmental Law and Policy Review* 261

Thompson, Erica, 'The World Heritage Convention and Climate Change: The Case for a Climate-Change Mitigation Strategy Beyond the Kyoto Protocol' in William Burns and Hari Osofsky (eds.), *Adjudicating Climate Change* (Cambridge University Press, 2009) 255.

Tietenberg, Tom, *Emissions Trading: Principles and Practice* (Resources for the Future, Washington DC, 2nd edn, 2006)

Torfing, Jacob, *New Theories of Discourse: Laclau, Mouffe and Žižek* (Blackwell, Oxford, 1999)

Treves, Tullio, *et al.* (eds.), *Non Compliance Procedures and Mechanisms and the Effectiveness of International Environmental Agreements* (TMC Asser Press, The Hague, 2009)

Triggs, Gillian, *International Law and Australian Sovereignty in Antarctica* (Legal Books, Sydney, 1986)

Trindade, Francis, Cane, Peter and Lunney, Mark, *The Law of Torts in Australia* (Oxford University Press, Melbourne, 4th edn, 2007)

Tromans, Stephen, *Nuclear Law: The Law Applying to Nuclear Installations and Radioactive Substances in its Historic Context* (Hart Publishing, Oxford, 2010)

Trouwborst, Arie, 'The Precautionary Principle in General International Law: Combating the Babylonian Confusion' (2007) 16 *Review of European Community and International Environmental Law* 185

Precautionary Rights and Duties of States (Martinus Nijhoff, Leiden and Boston, 2006)

Trull, Thomas, *et al.*, *Ocean Fertilisation: Science and Policy Issues*, Position Analysis 3 (Antarctic Climate & Ecosystems Cooperative Research Centre, Hobart, 2008)

Tsering, Thubten, 'The Status of Tibetan Language' in Karubaki Datta (ed.), *Essays on Tibetan Cultural Heritage* (Serials Publications, New Delhi, 2008) 80

Turner, Stephen, *A Substantive Environmental Right* (Wolters Kluwer Law & Business, Austin, 2009)

Tymchenko, Leonid, 'The Northern Sea Route: Russian Management and Jurisdiction over Navigation in Arctic Seas' in Alex Oude Elfernik and Donald R. Rothwell (eds.), *The Law of the Sea and Polar Maritime Delimitation and Jurisdiction* (Martinus Nijhoff, The Hague, 2001) 269

UNESCO World Heritage Centre, *Case Studies on Climate Change and World Heritage* (UNESCO World Heritage Centre, Paris, 2007)

Cultural Landscapes: The Challenges of Conservation (UNESCO World Heritage Centre, Paris, 2003)

United Kingdom, *A Programme of Nuclear Power*, Cmd 9389 (1955)

Meeting the Energy Challenge: A White Paper on Energy, Cm 7124 (2007)

Meeting the Energy Challenge: A White Paper on Nuclear Power, Cm 7296 (2008)

Our Energy Future – Creating a Low Carbon Economy, Cm 5761 (2003)

The Energy Challenge. Energy Review: A Report, Cm 6887 (2006)

Agriculture and Environment Biotechnology Commission, *GM Nation? The Findings of a Public Debate* (Department of Trade and Industry, London, 2003)

Department for Environment Food and Rural Affairs, *Controlling Soil Erosion: A Manual for the Assessment and Management of Agricultural Land at Risk of Water Erosion in Lowland England* (2005)

Her Majesty's Treasury, *The Stern Review on the Economics of Climate Change* (2006)

Performance and Innovation Unit, *The Energy Review* (2002)

Royal Commission on Environmental Pollution, *Sixth Report: Nuclear Power and the Environment*, Cmnd 6618 (1976)

Royal Commission on Environmental Pollution, *Twenty-Second Report: Energy – The Changing Climate*, Cm 4749 (2000)

Royal Commission on Environmental Pollution, *Sustainable Use of Soil* (1996)

Rural Development Service, *Entry Level Stewardship Handbook. Terms and Conditions and How to Apply* (2005)

Rural Payments Agency and Department for Environment, Food and Rural Affairs, *Single Payment Scheme. Cross Compliance Guidance for Soil Management* (2006)

Rural Payments Agency and Department for Environment, Food and Rural Affairs, *The Guide to Cross Compliance in England* (2009)

United Nations Commission on Human Security, *Human Security Now* (United Nations, New York, 2003)

United Nations Development Programme, *Human Development Report 1994* (Oxford University Press, New York, 1994)

Human Development Report 2007/2008 Fighting Climate Change: Human Solidarity in a Divided World (Palgrave Macmillan, New York, 2007)

United Nations Millennium Project, *Investing in Development. A Practical Plan to Achieve the Millennium Development Goals* (Earthscan, London, 2005)

United Nations Secretary-General's High-Level Panel on Threats, Challenges and Change, *A More Secure World: Our Shared Responsibility* (United Nations, New York, 2004)

Utaka, Yushi, 'The Hiroshima "Peace Memorial"' in William Logan and Keir Reeves (eds.), *Places of Pain and Shame: Dealing with 'Difficult Heritage'* (Routledge, London, 2009) 34

Van Asselt, Harro, 'Emissions Trading: The Enthusiastic Adoption of an "Alien" Instrument?' in Andrew Jordan *et al.* (eds.), *Climate Change Policy in the European Union* (Cambridge University Press, 2010) 125

Van der Sluijs, Jeroen and Turenburg, Wim, 'Climate Change and the Precautionary Principle' in Elizabeth Fisher, Judith Jones and René Von Scomberg (eds.), *Implementing the Precautionary Principle: Perspectives and Prospects* (Edward Elgar, Cheltenham, 2006) 254

Vanderheiden, Steve, *Atmospheric Justice: A Political Theory of Climate Change* (Oxford University Press, New York, 2008)

Vandervelde, Kenneth, 'The New Property of the Nineteenth Century: The Development of the Modern Concept of Property' (1980) 29 *Buffalo Law Review* 325

Vigni, Patrizia, 'Antarctic Maritime Claims: "Frozen Sovereignty and the Law of the Sea"' in Alex Oude Elferink and Donald R. Rothwell (eds.), *The Law of the Sea and Polar Maritime Delimitation and Jurisdiction* (Martinus Nijhoff, The Hague, 2001) 85

Vihma, Antto, 'Friendly Neighbour or Trojan Horse? Assessing the Interaction of Soft Law Initiatives and the UN Climate Regime' (2009) 9 *International Environmental Agreements: Politics, Law, Economics* 239

Voigt, Christina, *Sustainable Development as a Principle of International Law* (Martinus Nijhoff, Leiden, 2009)

Dann, Philipp and Goldmann, Matthias, 'Developing the Publicness of Public International Law: Towards a Legal Framework for Global Governance Activities' (2008) 9 *German Law Journal* 1375

Vrdoljak, Ana Filipa, *International Law: Museums and the Return of Cultural Objects* (Cambridge University Press, 2006)

Wallis, Ed, 'Fish Genes into Tomatoes: How the World Regulates Genetically Modified Foods' (2004) 80 *North Dakota Law Review* 421

Walt, Stephen, 'The Renaissance of Security Studies' (1991) 35 *International Studies Quarterly* 211

Wang, Yizhou, 'Defining Non-Traditional Security and its Implications for China' (2004) 12(5) *China & World Economy* 59

Wansborough, Tanya, 'On the Issue of Scientific Whaling: Does the Majority Rule?' (2004) 13 *Review of European and International Environmental Law* 333

Warren, Karen, 'The Power and Promise of Ecological Feminism' in Michael E. Zimmerman *et al.*, (eds.), *Environmental Philosophy: From Animal Rights to Radical Ecology* (Prentice-Hall, Englewood Cliffs, 1998) 325

Wates, Jeremy, 'The Aarhus Convention: A Driving Force for Environmental Democracy' (2005) 2 *Journal for European Environmental and Planning Law* 2

Watts, Arthur, *International Law and the Antarctic Treaty System* (Grotius, Cambridge, 1992)

Watts, Corey, *Getting on Track? A Discussion Paper on Australia's Progress Towards Ecologically Sustainable Management of our Rural Landscapes* (Australian Conservation Foundation, Melbourne, 2004)

Weinberg, Alvin, 'Science and Trans-Science' (1972) 10 *Minerva* 209

Weiss, Carol, 'Research for Policy's Sake: The Enlightenment Function of Social Research' (1977) 3 *Policy Analysis* 351

Weiss, Linda, *The Myth of the Powerless State: Governing the Economy in a Global Era* (Polity Press, Cambridge, 1998)

Welsh, Ian, 'The NIMBY Syndrome: Its Significance in the History of the Nuclear Debate in Britain' (1993) 26 *The Journal of the British Society for the History of Science* 15

Wentworth Group of Concerned Scientists, *A New Model for Landscape Conservation in New South Wales* (World Wide Fund for Nature, Sydney, 2003)

Wiersema, Annecoos, 'Adversaries or Partners? Science and the Precautionary Principle in International Wildlife Treaty Regimes' (2008) 11 *Journal of International Wildlife Law and Policy* 211

Willbanks, Thomas J., '"Sustainable Development" in Geographic Perspective' (1994) 84 *Annals of the Association of American Geographers* 541

Winickoff, David, *et al.*, 'Adjudicating the GM Food Wars: Science, Risk, and Democracy in World Trade Law' (2005) 30 *Yale Journal of International Law* 81

Wirth, David 'The Rio Declaration on Environment and Development: Two Steps Forward and One Back, or Vice Versa' (1995) 29 *Georgia Law Review* 599

Woolf, Lord, *The Pursuit of Justice* (Oxford University Press, 2008)

World Commission on Environment and Development, *Our Common Future* (Oxford University Press, 1987)

World Health Organization (WHO), *Right to Water* (WHO, Geneva, 2003)

Wouters, Jan, Nollkaemper, André and de Wet, Erika (eds.), *The Europeanisation of International Law: The Status of International Law in the EU and its Member States* (TMC Asser Press, The Hague, 2008)

WWF-Australia, *Native Vegetation Regulation: Financial Impact and Policy Issues* (2005)

Yamin, Farhana, 'The Kyoto Protocol: Origins, Assessment and Future Challenges' (1998) 7 *Review of European Community and International Environmental Law* 113

Young, Katie, 'Auschwitz-Birkenau: The Challenges of Heritage Management Following the Cold War' in William Logan and Keir Reeves (eds.), *Places of Pain and Shame: Dealing with 'Difficult Heritage'* (Routledge, London, 2009) 50

Young, Mike, Shi, Tian and Crosthwaite, Jim, *Duty of Care: An Instrument for Increasing the Effectiveness of Catchment Management* (Department of Sustainability and Environment, Melbourne, 2003)

Young, Saskia, 'Contemporary Issues of the Convention on International Trade in Endangered Species of Wild Fauna and Flora (CITES) and the Debate over Sustainable Use' (2003) 14(1) *Colorado Journal of International Environmental Law and Policy* 167

Zander, Joakim, *The Application of the Precautionary Principle in Practice: Comparative Dimension* (Cambridge University Press, 2010)

Zschiesche, Michael, 'The Aarhus Convention – More Citizens' Participation by Setting Out Environmental Standards?' (2002) 1 *Environmental Law Network International* 21

Judicial decisions

Arcelor Aquitaine et Lorraine and Others v. *Commission* (Case C-127/07) [2008] OJ C44/8

Bentley v. *BGP Properties Pty Ltd* (2006) 145 LGERA 234

Bering Sea Fur Seals Arbitration (Great Britain v. *United States)* (1893) 1 Moore International Arbitrations 755

Blue Wedges Inc. v. *Minister for Environment, Heritage and the Arts* (2008) 167 FCR 463

Blue Wedges Inc. v. *Minister for the Environment, Heritage and the Arts (No. 2)* [2008] FCA 1106 (15 July 2008)

Brown v. *Board of Education* 347 US 483 (1954)

Brown v. *Forestry Tasmania (No. 4)* (2006) 157 FCR 1

Case Concerning the Continental Shelf (Libya v. *Malta)* [1985] ICJ Rep [46]

Case Concerning Maritime Delimitation in the Black Sea (Romania v. *Ukraine)* Judgment of 3 February 2009

Case Concerning Pulp Mills on the Uruguay River (Argentina v. *Uruguay) (merits)* Judgment of 20 April 2010

Commission of the European Communities v. *Republic of Poland* (Case C-165/08) [2009] ECR I-6843

Corfu Channel (United Kingdom v. *Albania) (merits)* [1949] ICJ Rep 4

Dispute Concerning Japan's JARPA II Program of 'Scientific Whaling' (Australia v. *Japan)* (31 May 2010)

Diversion of Water from the River Meuse (Netherlands v. *Belgium)* [1937] PCIJ (Ser. A/B) No. 70

EnBW v. *Commission and Germany* (Case T-387/04 R) [2007] ECR II-1195

France v. *Commission* (Case T-257/07 R) [2007] ECR II-4153

Gabčíkovo-Nagymaros Project (Hungary v. *Slovakia)* [1997] ICJ Rep 7

Germany v. *Commission* (Case T-374/04) [2007] ECR II-4431

Greenpeace Limited v. *Secretary of State for Trade and Industry* (2007) EWHC 311

Humane Society International Inc. v. *Kyodo Senpaku Kaisha Ltd* (2004) 212 ALR 551

Humane Society International Inc. v. *Kyodo Senpaku Kaisha Ltd* [2005] FCA 664 (27 May 2005)

Humane Society International Inc. v. *Kyodo Senpaku Kaisha Ltd* (2006) 154 FCR 425

Humane Society International Inc. v. *Kyodo Senpaku Kaisha Ltd* (2008) 165 FCR 510

Lake Lanoux (France v. *Spain)* (1957) 12 UN Rep. Int. Arb. Awards

Latimer v. *AEC Ltd* [1953] AC 643

Legal Status of Eastern Greenland (Denmark v. *Norway)*, Judgment, PCIJ Reports, Ser. A/B, No. 53

Massachusetts v. *EPA* 549 US 497 (2007)

Minister for Planning v. *Walker* (2008) 161 LGERA 423

Minister of State for Immigration and Ethnic Affairs v. *Teoh* (1995) 183 CLR 273

Minors Oposa et al. v. *Secretary of the Environment and Natural Resources Fulgencio Factoran*, GR No. 101083, 30 July 1993, repr. (1994) 33 ILM 173

MOX Plant (Ireland v. *United Kingdom) (provisional measures)* [1997] ICJ Rep

MOX Plant (Ireland v. *United Kingdom) (suspension of proceedings on jurisdiction and merits and request for further provisional measures)* (order 3, of 24 June 2003) (2003) 42 ILM 1187

Newcrest Mining (WA) Limited v. *Commonwealth* (1997) 190 CLR 513

Nicholls v. *Director General National Parks and Wildlife Service* (1994) 84 LGERA 397

Nölle v. *Hauptzollamt Bremen-Freihafen* (Case C-16/90) [1991] ECR I-5163

North Sea Continental Shelf Cases (Germany v. *Denmark; Germany* v. *Netherlands)* [1969] ICJ Rep 3

Nuclear Tests (Australia v. *France) (merits)* [1974] ICJ Rep 253

Nuclear Tests (New Zealand v. *France) (merits)* [1974] ICJ Rep 457

Nuclear Tests, Request for an Examination of the Situation in Accordance with Paragraph 63 of the Court's Judgment of 20 December 1974 in the Nuclear Tests (New Zealand v. *France)* [1995] ICJ Rep 288

Nuclear Weapons Advisory Opinion [1996] ICJ Rep 226

Pfizer Animal Health SA v. *Council of the European Union* (Case T-13/99) [2002] ECR II-03305

Pulp Mills on the River Uruguay (Argentina v. *Uruguay) (request for provisional measures by Argentina)* (2006) 45 ILM 1025

Pulp Mills on the River Uruguay (Argentina v. *Uruguay) (request for provisional measures by Uruguay)* (2007) 46 ILM 311

Queensland Conservation Council Inc. v. *Xstrata Coal Queensland Pty Ltd* (2007) 155 LGERA 322

Request for an Examination of the Situation in Accordance with Paragraph 63 of the Court's Judgment of 20 December 1974 in the Nuclear Tests (New Zealand v. *France)* [1995] ICJ Rep 288

Re Xstrata Coal Queensland Pty Ltd [2007] QLRT 33

State of Connecticut v. *American Electric Power Co. Inc.* 582 F 3d 309 (2d Cir 2009)

Taralga Landscape Guardians Inc. v. *Minister for Planning and RES Southern Cross Pty Ltd* (2007) 161 LGERA 1

Telstra Corporation Limited v. *Hornsby Shire Council* (2006) 67 NSWLR 256

Territorial Jurisdiction of the International Commission of the River Oder [1929] PCIJ (Ser. A) No. 23

Top Performance Motors Pty Ltd v. *Ira Berk (Qld) Pty Ltd* (1975) 24 FLR 286

Trail Smelter (Canada v. *United States)* (1938 and 1941) 3 UN Rep. Int. Arb. Awards

United Kingdom v. *Commission* (Case T-178/05) [2005] ECR II-4807

Wyong Shire Council v. *Shirt* (1980) 146 CLR 40

Wyong Shire Council v. *Thomas Hughes Homes Pty Ltd* (2001) 115 LGERA 56

Legislation

Administrative Procedures Act, 5 USC (1946)

Antarctic Mining Prohibition Act 1991 (Cth)

Antarctic Treaty (Environment Protection) Act 1980 (Cth)
Arctic Waters Pollution Prevention Act, SC (1970)
Atomic Energy Authority Act 1954 (UK)
Australian Constitution
Carbon Pollution Reduction Scheme Bill 2009 (Cth)
Carbon Pollution Reduction Scheme (Consequential Amendments) Bill 2009 (Cth)
Catchment and Land Protection Act 1994 (Vic)
Clean Air Act, 42 USC § 7401 (1970)
Clean Energy Bill (2011) (Cth)
Climate Change and Sustainable Energy Act 2006 (UK)
Electricity Act 1957 (UK)
Energy Act 2004 (UK)
Energy Act 2008 (UK)
Environment Act 1995 (UK)
Environment Protection Act 1970 (Vic)
Environment Protection Act 1993 (SA)
Environment Protection (Sea Dumping) Act 1981 (Cth)
Environment Protection and Biodiversity Conservation Act 1999 (Cth)
Environmental Management and Pollution Control Act 1994 (Tas)
Environmental Protection Act 1990 (UK)
Environmental Protection Act 1994 (Qld)
Federal Actions to Address Environmental Justice in Minority Populations and Low-Income Populations US Executive Order 12898 of 11 February 1994
Federal Water Pollution Control Act, 33 USC § 1251 (1972)
Forest Practices Act 1985 (Tas)
Health Equity and Accountability Bill, House Bill 3090, 111th Congress of USA
Human Rights Act 1998 (UK)
Land Act 1994 (Qld)
National Environmental Policy Act, 42 USC (1969)
Native Vegetation Conservation Act 1997 (NSW)
Natural Resources Management Act 2004 (SA)
Offshore Petroleum and Greenhouse Gas Storage Act 2006 (Cth)
Pastoral Land Management and Conservation Act 1989 (SA)
Planning Act 2008 (UK)
Protection of the Environment Administration Act 1991 (NSW)
Protection of the Environment Operations Act 1997 (NSW)
River Murray Act 2003 (SA)
Seas and Submerged Lands Act 1973 (Cth)
Sustainable Energy Act 2003 (UK)
Trade Practices Act 1974 (Cth)

International and regional materials

Ad Hoc Group of Legal Experts on Dumping, *Report of the Fourth Meeting of the Ad Hoc Group of Legal Experts on Dumping*, LDC/LG 4/WP.2/Rev.1, 22–26 October 1990

African Charter on Human and People's Rights, opened for signature 27 June 1981, 1520 UNTS 217 (entered into force 21 October 1986)

African Convention on the Conservation of Nature and Natural Resources (Revised Version), opened for signature 11 July 2003 (not yet in force)

Agreement for the Implementation of the Provisions of the United Nations Convention on the Law of the Sea of 10 December 1982 relating to the Conservation and Management of Straddling Fish Stocks and Highly Migratory Fish Stocks, opened for signature 4 December 1995, 34 2167 UNTS 3 (entered into force 11 December 2001)

Agreement on Arctic Cooperation between Canada and the US, concluded on 11 January 1988 [1988] Canadian Treaty Series 29

Agreement on the Conservation of Polar Bears, opened for signature 15 November 1973, 13 ILM 13 (entered into force 26 May 1976)

Agreement on Technical Barriers to Trade, opened for signature 15 April 1994, 1868 UNTS 120 (entered into force 1 January 1995)

Annan, Kofi, *Report of the Secretary-General on the Work of the Organization*, UN GAOR, 55th session, Supp. No. 1, UN Doc. A/55/1 (30 August 2000)

'We the Peoples': The Role of the United Nations in the 20th Century: Report of the Secretary-General, 54th sess., Agenda Item 49(b), UN Doc. A/54/2000 (27 March 2000)

Antarctic Treaty, opened for signature 1 December 1959, [1961] ATS No. 12 (entered into force 23 June 1961)

Arctic Environmental Protection Strategy, concluded on 14 June 1991, 30 ILM 1624

ASEAN Agreement on the Conservation of Nature and Natural Resources, opened for signature 9 July 1985, 15 EPL 2 (not in force)

ASEAN Charter, opened for signature 18 November 2007 (entered into force 15 December 2008)

ASEAN Declaration on Environmental Sustainability, concluded 20 November 2007, Singapore

ASEAN Declaration on the 13th session of the Conference of the Parties (COP) to the United Nations Framework Convention on Climate Change (UNFCCC) and the 3rd session of the Conference of the Parties Serving as the Meeting of the Parties (CMP) to the Kyoto Protocol, concluded 20 November 2007, Singapore

ASEAN Foreign Ministers, *Acting Together to Cope with Global Challenges* Joint Communiqué of the 42nd ASEAN Foreign Ministers Meeting, 20 July 2009, Phuket, Thailand

ASEAN Joint Statement on Climate Change to the 15th session of the Conference of the Parties to the United Nations Framework Convention on Climate Change and the 5th session of the Conference Parties serving as the Meeting of Parties to the Kyoto Protocol, concluded 24 October 2009, Cha-am-Hua Hin, Thailand

ASEAN Leaders' Statement on Joint Response to Climate Change, concluded 9 April 2010, Ha Noi, Vietnam

ASEAN Political-Security Community Blueprint (2009)

Basel Convention on the Control of Transboundary Movements of Hazardous Wastes and Their Disposal, opened for signature 23 March 1989, 1673 UNTS 57 (entered into force 5 May 1992)

Basel Convention on the Transboundary Movement of Wastes, opened for signature 22 March 1989, 1673 UNTS 126 (entered into force 5 May 1992)

Cartagena Protocol to the Convention on Biological Diversity, opened for signature 15 May 2000, 222 UNTS 208 (entered into force 11 September 2003)

Charter of the Asia Pacific Partnership on Clean Development and Climate, concluded 13 January 2006, Sydney, Australia.

Consideration of the Report of the Scientific Group: Ocean Storage of Carbon Dioxide, at the Twenty-First Consultative Meeting of Contracting Parties to the Convention on the Prevention of Marine Pollution by Dumping of Wastes and Other Matter, LC 21/INF.2, 25 June 1999

Convention Concerning the Protection of the World Cultural and Natural Heritage, opened for signature 16 November 1972, 1037 UNTS 151 (entered into force 17 December 1975)

Convention for the Settlement of Difficulties Arising from the Operation of the Smelter at Trail between Great Britain and the United States, opened for signature 15 April 1935, 162 LNTS 73 (entered into force 14 January 1936)

Convention on Access to Information, Public Participation in Decision-Making and Access to Justice in Environmental Matters, opened for signature 25 June 1998, 2161 UNTS 447 (entered into force 30 October 2001)

Convention on Assistance in the Case of a Nuclear Accident or Radiological Emergency, opened for signature 26 September 1986, 1457 UNTS 134 (entered into force 26 February 1987)

Convention on Biological Diversity, opened for signature 5 June 1992, 1760 UNTS 79 (entered into force 29 December 1993)

Convention on the Conservation of Antarctic Marine Living Resources, opened for signature 20 May 1980, 1329 UNTS 47 (entered into force 7 April 1982)

Convention on Early Notification of a Nuclear Accident, opened for signature 26 September 1986, 1439 UNTS 276 (entered into force 27 October 1986)

Convention on Environmental Impact Assessment in a Transboundary Context, opened for signature 25 February 1991, 1989 UNTS 309 (entered into force 10 September 1997)

Convention on the Law of the Non-Navigational Uses of International Watercourses, opened for signature 21 May 1997, 36 ILM 700 (not yet in force)

Convention on Long Range Transboundary Air Pollution, opened for signature 13 November 1979, 335 UNTS 211 (entered into force 16 March 1983).

Convention on Nuclear Safety, opened for signature 20 September 1994, INFCIRC/449 (entered into force 24 October 1996)

Convention on the Prevention of Marine Pollution by Dumping of Wastes and Other Matter, opened for signature 29 December 1972, 1046 UNTS 138 (entered into force 30 August 1975)

Convention on the Protection and Promotion of the Diversity of Cultural Expressions, opened for signature 20 October 2005, 2440 UNTS 311 (entered into force 18 March 2007)

Convention on the Protection and Use of Transboundary Watercourses and International Lakes, opened for signature 17 March 1992, 1936 UNTS 269 (entered into force 6 October 1996)

Convention on the Protection of the Underwater Cultural Heritage, opened for signature 2 November 2001, 41 ILM 40 (entered into force 2 January 2009)

Convention on the Safeguarding of the Intangible Heritage, opened for signature 3 November 2003, 2368 UNTS 1 (entered into force 20 April 2006)

Convention on Wetlands of International Importance Especially as Waterfowl Habitat, opened for signature 2 February 1971, 996 UNTS 246 (entered into force 21 December 1975)

Decision III/2 of the Third Meeting of Parties to the Convention on Environmental Impact Assessment in a Transboundary Context, Doc. ECE/MP.EIA/6 annex II, 1–4 June 2004, Cavtat, Croatia

Decision III/8, *Guidance on Public Participation in Environmental Impact Assessment in a Transboundary Context*, of the Third Meeting of Parties to the Convention on Environmental Impact Assessment in a Transboundary Context, Doc. ECE/MP.EIA/6, annex VIII, 1–4 June 2004, Cavtat, Croatia

Declaration of ASEAN Concord II (Bali Concord II), concluded 7 October 2003, Bali, Indonesia

Declaration of ASEAN Concord 1976, concluded 24 February 1976, Bali, Indonesia

Declaration of Principles for the Preservation and Enhancement of the Human Environment, concluded 16 June 1972, Stockholm, Sweden

European Commission, *A Single Market for 21st Century Europe* (Communication) COM(2007) 724 final, 20 November 2007

Building a Global Carbon Market – Report Pursuant to Article 30 of Directive 2003/87/EC (Communication) COM(2006) 676 final, 13 November 2006

Guidance to Assist Member States in the Implementation of the Criteria Listed in Annex III to Council Directive (EC) 2003/87 (Communication) COM (2003) 830 final, 7 January 2004

European Council Decision No. 87/600/Euratom on Community arrangements for the early exchange of information in the event of a radiological emergency, 14 December 1987

European Council Regulation (EC) No. 178/2002 laying down the general principles and requirements of food law, establishing the European Food Safety Authority and laying down procedures in matters of food safety

European Council Regulation (EC) No. 1829/2003 on genetically modified food and feed

European Council Regulation (EC) No. 1367/2006 on the application of the provisions of the Aarhus Convention on Access to Information, Public Participation in Decision-Making and Access to Justice in Environmental Matters to Community institutions and bodies, 6 September 2006

European Council Regulation (EC) No. 73/2009 establishing common rules for direct support schemes for farmers under the common agricultural policy and establishing certain support schemes for farmers

European Decision 2002/623/EC establishing guidance notes supplementing Annex II to Directive 2001/18/EC of the European Parliament and of the Council on the deliberate release into the environment of genetically modified organisms and repealing Council Directive 90/220/EEC

European Directive 85/337/EEC on the assessment of the effects of certain public and private projects on the environment

European Directive 90/219/EEC on the contained use of genetically modified micro-organisms

European Directive 90/220/EEC on the deliberate release of genetically modified organisms

European Directive 90/679/EEC on the protection of workers from the risks related to exposure to biological agents at work

European Directive 2001/18/EC on the deliberate release into the environment of genetically modified organisms and repealing Directive 90/220/EEC

European Directive 2001/42/EC on the assessment of the effects of certain plans and programmes on the environment

European Directive 2003/87/EC establishing a scheme for greenhouse gas emission allowance trading within the Community and amending Directive 96/61/EC

European Directive 2009/29/EC amending Directive 2003/87/EC so as to improve and extend the greenhouse gas emission allowance trading system of the Community

Germany, Permanent Mission of Germany communication to the United Nations, Note No. 88/2005 (5 April 2005) at www.un.org/Depts/los/clcs_new/submissions_files/aus04/clcs_03_2004_los_deu.pdf, last accessed 4 January 2007

General Agreement on Tariffs and Trade 1994, opened for signature 15 April 1994, 55 UNTS 194, 1867 UNTS 187 (entered into force 1 January 1995)

Hague Declaration on the Environment, concluded 11 March 1989, The Hague, Netherlands, 28 ILM 1308.

Human Rights Council, *Promotion and Protection of All Human Rights, Civil, Political, Economic, Social and Cultural Rights. Including the Right to Development*, 7th sess., Agenda Item 3, UN Doc. A/HRC/7/L.21/Rev.1 (26 March 2008)

Ilulissat Declaration, Arctic Ocean Conference, 27–29 May 2008, Ilulissat, Greenland

Implementation Committee of the Convention on Environmental Impact Assessment in a Transboundary Context, *Opinions of the Implementation Committee 2001–2010*, 20th sess., Agenda Item 9, ECE/MP.EIA/IC/2001/INF.1 (13 January 2011)

International Convention for the Regulation of Whaling, opened for signature 2 December 1946, 161 UNTS 72 (entered into force 10 November 1948)

International Covenant on Civil and Political Rights, opened for signature 19 December 1966, 999 UNTS 171 (entered into force 23 March 1976)

International Covenant on Economic, Social and Cultural Rights, opened for signature 19 December 1966, 993 UNTS 3 (entered into force 3 January 1976)

International Maritime Organization, *Notification of Amendments to Annex 1 to the London Protocol 1996*, LC-LP.1/Circ.5, 27 November 2006

International Whaling Commission, Resolution 2007–1, 59th Annual Meeting, Anchorage, Alaska, 2007

Joint Declaration of ASEAN and China on Cooperation in the Field of Non-Traditional Security Issues (4 November 2002)

Joint Declaration of ASEAN Defence Ministers on Strengthening ASEAN Defence Establishments to meet the Challenges of Non-Traditional Security Threats (26 February 2009)

Kyoto Protocol to the United Nations Framework Convention on Climate Change, opened for signature 16 March 1998, 2303 UNTS 148 (entered into force 16 February 2005)

London Convention and London Protocol Circular, *Preparation for the Scientific and Legal Discussions in 2008 of Ocean Fertilization with a View to its Regulation under the London Convention and Protocol*, LC-LP.1 Circ.20, 29 January 2008

Statement of Concern Regarding Iron Fertilization of the Oceans to Sequester Carbon Dioxide, LC-LP.1/Circ.14, 13 July 2007

Montreal Protocol for Substances that Deplete the Ozone Layer, opened for signature 16 September 1987, 26 ILM 1550 (entered into force 1 January 1989)

Nordic Convention on the Protection of the Environment, opened for signature 19 February 1974, 13 ILM 511 (entered into force 5 October 1976)

Observer Status for the Association of Southeast Asian Nations in the General Assembly, GA Res. 61/44, 61st sess., 64th mtg, Agenda Item 153, UN Doc. A/RES/61/44 (4 December 2006)

Oslo-Paris (OSPAR) Convention for the Protection of the Marine Environment of the North East Atlantic, opened for signature 22 September 1992 (entered into force 25 March 1998)

OSPAR Commission for the Protection of the Marine Environment of the North-East Atlantic, *Placement of Carbon Dioxide in Sub-Sea Geological Structures', in Note by the Secretariat, 'Continuation of a Review of the Benefits of Carbon Dioxide Sequestration in Sub-Seabed Geological Structures and of New Information Relevant to the Protection of the Marine Environment*, concluded at the Meeting of the SG Intercessional Technical Working Group on Carbon Dioxide Sequestration, 3–6 April 2006, LC/SG-Carbon Dioxide.1/INF.2

Proposal by Sweden in 'List of Documents Issued in Connection with the First Meeting of the London Convention 1972 Amendment Group', London Convention 1972 Amendment Group (First Meeting), LC/AM 1/INF.2, 19–23 July 1993

Protocol on Environmental Protection to the Antarctic Treaty, opened for signature 4 October 1991, ATS No. 6 (entered into force 15 January 1998)

Protocol on Strategic Environmental Assessment to the Convention on Environmental Impact Assessment in a Transboundary Context, opened for signature 21 May 2003, [2010] ECE/MP.EIA/2003/2 (entered into force 11 July 2010).

Protocol to the Convention on the Prevention of Marine Pollution by Dumping of Wastes and Other Matter, opened for signature 7 November 1996, 36 ILM 1 (entered into force 24 March 2006)

Regulation of Ocean Fertilization, Res. LC-LP.1 (2008) of the Thirtieth Meeting of the Contracting Parties to the London Convention and the Third Meeting of the Contracting Parties to the London Protocol, LC 30/16, 31 October 2008

Report of the Conference of the Parties to the UNFCCC on its Fifteenth Session, Decision 2/CP 15, FCCC/CP/2009/11/Add1 (2009)

Report of the Conference of the Parties to the UNFCCC on its First Session, Decision 1/CP 1, FCCC/CP/1995/7/Add1 (1995)

Report of the Conference of the Parties to the UNFCCC on its Seventh Session, FCCC/CP/2001/13 (2002)

Report of the Conference of the Parties to the UNFCCC on its Thirteenth Session, Decision 1/CP 13, FCCC/CP/2007/6/Add1 (2007)

Report of the Fifteenth Consultative Meeting of Contracting Parties to the Convention on the Prevention of Marine Pollution by Dumping of Wastes and Other Matter, LC 15/16, 9–13 November 1992

Report of the International Law Commission, 53rd sess., 366, UN Doc. A/56/10 (2001)

Report of the Meeting of the CM Intercessional Legal and Related Issues Working Group on Sequestration, LC/CM-Carbon Dioxide 1/5, 10–12 April 2006

Report of the Meeting of the SG Intersessional Technical Working Group on Carbon Dioxide Sequestration, LC/SG-Carbon Dioxide 1/7, 3–7 April 2006

Report of the Seventeenth Consultative Meeting of Contracting Parties to the Convention on the Prevention of Marine Pollution by Dumping of Wastes and Other Matter, LC 17/14, 3–7 October 1994

Report of the Thirty-Second Consultative Meeting of Contracting Parties to the Convention on the Prevention of Marine Pollution by Dumping of Wastes and Other Matter, LC/SG 32/15, 11–15 October 2010

Report of the Twenty-Seventh Consultative Meeting of Contracting Parties to the Convention on the Prevention of Marine Pollution by Dumping of Wastes and Other Matter 1972, LC 27/6 Annex, 24–28 October 2005

Republic of Albania, Ministry of Environment, Forests and Water Administration, Progress Report for Implementation of Action Plan in Response to the Recommendations of the Compliance Committee of the Aarhus Convention, 31 December 2009

Res. LP.1(1) of the Twenty-Eighth Consultative Meeting of Contracting Parties to the 1972 Convention on the Prevention of Marine Pollution by Dumping of Wastes and Other Matter LC 28/15, October 2006 and 1st Meeting of Contracting Parties to the 1996 Protocol to the Convention on the Prevention of Marine Pollution by Dumping of Wastes and Other Matter 1972, LP 1/1, October–November 2006

Rio Declaration on Environment and Development, concluded 14 June 1992, Rio di Janeiro, Brazil

Sanitary and Phytosanitary Measures Agreement, opened for signature 15 April 1994, 1867 UNTS 493 (entered into force 1 January 1995)

Singapore Declaration of 1992, concluded 28 January 1992, Singapore

Singapore Declaration on Climate Change, Energy and the Environment, concluded 21 November 2007, Singapore

Statement of Australia to the Second Ministerial Meeting of the Asia Pacific Partnership on Clean Development and Climate, 15 October 2007

Statute of the River Uruguay, opened for signature 16 February 1975, 1295 UNTS 340 (entered into force 18 September 1976)

Submission by Australia (co-sponsored by France, Norway and the United Kingdom), 'Carbon Dioxide Sequestration in Sub-Seabed Formations: Consideration of Proposals to Amend Annex 1 to the London Protocol' to the First Meeting of Contracting Parties to the 1996 Protocol to the Convention on the Prevention of Marine

Pollution by Dumping of Wastes and Other Matter 1972, LP 1/6, 28 April 2006

Submission by the Netherlands, 'Explanatory Note Accompanying the Proposal for Restructuring and Amending the London Convention' in Note by the Secretariat, 'Inventory of Amendment Proposals' in Amendment Group – First Meeting, LC/AM 1/3, 10 June 1993, 42

Submission by the Netherlands, 'Future Work Programme Implementation and Review of the Long-Term Programme' to the Twenty-Fourth Consultative Meeting of Contracting Parties to the Convention on the Prevention of Marine Pollution by Dumping of Wastes and Other Matter, LC 24/14, 9 August 2002

Submission by the United Kingdom, 'Sequestration of Carbon Dioxide in Sub-Seabed Geological Structures', LP 1/6, 28 April 28 2006

Submission by the United States, 'Facilitation and/or Regulation of Carbon Dioxide Sequestration in Sub-Seabed Geological Structures: Options and Implications' at the Meeting of the CM Intersessional Legal and Related Issues Working Group on Carbon Dioxide Sequestration, LC/CM-Carbon Dioxide 1/3/1, 10–12 April 2006

Sydney Leaders Declaration on Climate Change, Energy Security and Clean Development, concluded 9 September 2007, APEC meeting, Sydney Australia

The Application of a Precautionary Approach in Environmental Protection within the Framework of the London Convention, Res. LDC.44(14) of the Fourteenth Consultative Meeting of Contracting Parties to the Convention on the Prevention of Marine Pollution by Dumping of Wastes and Other Matter, LC 14/16, 30 December 1991

Treaty Concerning the Construction and Operation of the Gabčíkovo-Nagymaros System of Locks, opened for signature 16 September 1977, 32 ILM 1247 (entered into force 30 June 1978)

Treaty of Lisbon amending the Treaty on European Union and the Treaty establishing the European Community on the Functioning of the European Union, opened for signature 13 December 2007 Lisbon (entered into force 1 December 2009)

UN SCOR, 62nd sess., 5663rd mtg, UN Doc. S/PV.5663 (17 April 2007)

UNESCO, *Records of the General Conference, 31st Session, Paris, 15 October to 3 November 2001, Vol. 1: Resolutions*, UNESCO Doc. 31C/Resolutions (2002, adopted 2 November 2001)

Records of the General Conference, 32nd Session, Paris, 29 September to 17 October 2003, Vol. 1: Resolutions, UNESCO Doc. 32C/Resolutions (2004, adopted 17 October 2003)

Summary Record of the Thirteenth General Assembly of States Parties to the Convention Concerning the Protection of the World Cultural and Natural

Heritage (UNESCO Headquarters, Paris, 30–31 October 2001), UNESCO Doc. WHC-2001/CONF.206/8 Rev. (29 July 2003)

UNFCCC, Copenhagen Accord, Decision 2/CP.15, FCCC/CP/2009/11/Add.1, 18 December 2009, Copenhagen, Denmark

Documentation to Facilitate Negotiations by Parties, FCCC/KP/AWG/2009/10/Add4/Rev2 (2009) 12–13

Ideas and Proposals on the Elements Contained in Paragraph 1 of the Bali Action Plan FCCC/AWGLCA/2009/MISC4 (Part I) (2009)

Ideas and Proposals on the Elements Contained in Paragraph 1 of the Bali Action Plan, FCCC/AWGLCA/2008/MISC5/Add2 (Part I) (2008)

Ideas and Proposals on the Elements Contained in Paragraph 1 of the Bali Action Plan, FCCC/AWGLCA/2008/MISC5/Add2 (Part II) (2008)

UNFCCC Ad Hoc Working Group on Long-Term Cooperative Action under the Convention, *Text to Facilitate Negotiations Among Parties, Tenth Session Bonn, 1–11 June 2010*, FCCC/AWGLCA/2010/6

United Nations Convention on the Law of the Sea, opened for signature 10 December 1982, 1833 UNTS 3 (entered into force 16 November 1994)

United Nations Declaration on the Rights of Indigenous Peoples, GA Res. 61/295, 62nd sess. (13 September 2007)

United Nations Economic and Social Council, *Communication concerning non-compliance by Belarus with the UN ECE Convention on Access to Information, Public Participation in Decision-Making and Access to Justice in Environmental Matters* (Communication ACCC/C/2009/37), 14 March 2009

Report of the Working Group on EIA on its 12th meeting, Geneva, 11–13 May 2009

United Nations Economic Commission for Europe, Working Group on Environmental Impact Assessment, *Inquiry Procedure – Review of the First Inquiry Procedure, Note by the Secretariat*, Tenth Meeting of the Parties to the Convention on Environmental Impact Assessment in a Transboundary Context, Geneva, 21–23 May 2007

United Nations Framework Convention on Climate Change, opened for signature 4 June 1992, 1771 UNTS 107 (entered into force 21 March 1994)

Universal Declaration of Human Rights, GA Res. 217A (III), UN GAOR, 3rd sess., 183 plen. mtg, UN Doc. A/810 (10 December 1948)

Vienna Declaration on Human Rights (Vienna Declaration and Programme of Action), UN Doc. A/CONF.157/23 (12 July 1993)

World Charter for Nature, GA Res. 37/7, 48th plenary mtg, UN Doc. A/RES/37/7 (28 October 1982)

World Heritage Committee, *Decisions Adopted by the 27th Session of the World Heritage Committee in 2003*, UNESCO Doc. WHC-03/27.COM/24 (Paris, 10 December 2003) Decision 27COM 7B.52

Decisions Adopted at the 28th Session of the World Heritage Committee (Suzhou, 2004), UNESCO Doc. WHC-04/28 COM/26 (Paris, 29 October 2004) Decisions 28 COM 14B.30, 28COM 15B.54

Decisions of the 29th Session of the World Heritage Committee (Durban, 2005), UNESCO Doc. WHC-05/29.COM/22 (Paris, 9 September 2005) Decision 29COM 7B.a

Final Decisions of the 33rd Session of the World Heritage Committee (Seville, 2009), UNESCO Doc. WHC-09/33.COM/20 (Seville, 20 July 2009) Decision 33COM 7A.26

Operational Guidelines for the Implementation of the World Heritage Convention, UNESCO Doc. WHC. 08/01 (January 2008)

Report of the 25th Session of the World Heritage Committee (Helsinki, Finland, 11–16 December 2001), UNESCO Doc. WHC-01/CONF.208/24 (Paris, 8 February 2002) VIII.111–120, Decision 25COM X.3

Report, World Heritage Committee, Twentieth Session, Merida, Yucatan, Mexico – 2–7 December 1996, UNESCO Doc. WHC-96/CONF.201/21 (10 March 1997)

State of Conservation of Properties Inscribed on the World Heritage List, UNESCO Doc. WHC-04/28.COM/15B (Paris, 15 June 2004)

World Trade Organization, *European Communities – Measures Affecting the Approval and Marketing of Biotech Products*, WTO Document, WT/DS 291 R, WT/DS 292 R, WT/DS 293 R (2006) Panel Report

Speeches and interviews

Abbott, Tony and Bishop, Julie, 'Transcript of Joint Doorstop Interview' (Canberra, 2 December 2009)

Bouchenaki, Mounir, 'The Interdependency of the Tangible and Intangible Cultural Heritage' (keynote address delivered at the ICOMOS 14th General Assembly and Scientific Symposium, Victoria Falls, 2003)

Caballero-Anthony, Mely, 'Non-Traditional Security and Infectious Diseases in Asia: The Need for a Global Approach for Health and Human Security' (Paper presented at the conference 'East Asia in Transition – Comprehensive Security in the Pacific Rim', Institute of East Asian Studies, University of California, Berkeley, 29 September 2006)

Delbeke, Jos, 'Environmental Policy in the Times of Economic Crisis – the Example of the EU ETS' (acceptance speech at the Smith Prize Award, Rotes Rathaus, Berlin, 20 May 2009)

'Putting the Emerging Global Carbon Market on a Solid Footing' (Deputy Director General, DG Environment, speech for opening of ICAP Global Carbon Market Forum, 19–20 May 2008, Brussels)

Dimas, Stavros, 'The EU and the Fight Against Climate Change' (speech to the European Commission, Responsible for Environment during a seminar on Climate Change organised by the Finnish Institute for International Affairs, Helsinki, 4 May 2006)

Climate Change, 'International and EU Actions' (speech, Prague, 31 October 2008)

Evans, Gareth, 'Foreign Policy and Good International Citizenship' (speech, Canberra, 6 March 1990)

Garnaut, Ross (keynote address to the Climate Change and Social Justice Conference, University of Melbourne, 3 April 2008)

Gotzen, Rudy, and Norer, Roland, 'Commission III Scientific and Practical Development of Agricultural Law in the EU, in Countries and in the WTO' (Congress Conclusions presented at the 25th European Congress and Colloquium of Agricultural Law, Cambridge, 23–26 September 2009)

Horn, Laura, 'Intra-Generational Equity' (Paper presented at the Australian Law Teachers Association Conference, Law and Public Policy: Taming the Unruly Horse? The University of Western Australia Perth, Australia, 23–26 September 2007)

Howard, John, Prime Minister of Australia (address to the Melbourne Press Club, Hyatt Hotel, Melbourne, 17 July 2007) www.pandora.nla.gov.au/pan/10052/20070823-1732/www.pm.gov.au/media/Speech/2007/Speech24445.html, last accessed 5 February 2009.

McClelland, Robert, 'Time to Repair our Reputation: The Rise and Fall of Australia as a Good International Citizen' (speech delivered at the Lowy Institute for International Policy, Sydney, 14 March 2007)

New South Wales, *Parliamentary Debates*, Legislative Assembly, 12 November 2003 (Craig Knowles, Minister for Natural Resources)

Parliamentary Debates, Legislative Assembly, 19 November 1997, 2075 (Kim Yeadon, Minister for Land and Water Conservation).

Philippines, *Parliamentary Debates*, 27 November 2007, Question of Privilege of Rep. Jaafar, Government Journal No. 40

Pitsuwan, Surin (keynote address at the 'Launch of the RSIS Centre for Non-Traditional Security Studies', 6 May 2008, Singapore)

Rudd, Kevin, 'Address by Prime Minister Kevin Rudd to the United Nations General Assembly' (speech delivered at the UN General Assembly, New York, 25 September 2008)

'Address to the 64th Session of the United Nations General Assembly' (speech delivered at the United Nations General Assembly, New York, 23 September 2009)

'Address to the High Level Segment of the 13th Conference of the Parties' (speech delivered at the High Level Segment of the 13th Conference of the Parties, UNFCCC, Bali, 12 December 2007)

'Address to the Lowy Institute' (speech delivered at the Lowy Institute, Sydney, 6 November 2009)

'An Action Agenda for Climate Change' (speech delivered at the Annual Fraser Lecture, Canberra, 30 May 2007)

'Formal Apology to the Stolen Generations' (speech delivered to the Parliament of Australia, Parliament House, Canberra, 12 February 2008)

Smith, Stephen, 'A New Era of Engagement with the World' (speech delivered at the Sydney Institute, Sydney, 19 August 2008)

Stavins, Robert, 'Linking Tradable Permit Systems: Opportunities, Challenges, and Implications' (Paper presented at the 7th Annual Workshop on Greenhouse Gas Emissions Trading, 9 October 2007, Paris, France)

Wallström, Margaret, 'Emissions Trading' (speech, Berlin, 8 November 2002)

Wettestad, Jorgen, 'Revising EU Emissions Trading: A "Requested Revolution"?' (Lecture given as part of the European Union and the Fight against Global Climate Change Lecture Series, 29 October 2008)

Wong, Penny, 'Australia's Contribution to a Global Agreement on Climate Change' (speech delivered at the Lowy Institute for International Policy, Sydney, 20 April 2009)

Internet materials

Albanese, Anthony, *Fact Sheet: What the Howard Government Has Said About Kyoto* (2009) at www.anthonyalbanese.com.au/file.php?file=/news/ZFYZABAMQVQJUKZLYOBILLHQ/index.html, last accessed 2 December 2009

Allsopp, Michelle, *et al.*, *Plastic Debris in the World's Oceans*, Greenpeace Online Report at oceans.greenpeace.org/en/documents-reports/plastic_ocean_report, last accessed 10 December 2009

ASEAN, *Annex for the ASEAN Security Community Plan of Action*, Official Website of the Association of Southeast Asian Nations (2009) www.aseansec.org/16829.htm, last accessed 21 April 2010

Asia-Pacific Partnership on Clean Development and Climate, *About the Asia-Pacific Partnership on Clean Development & Climate* (2009) www.asiapacificpartnership.org/english/about.aspx, last accessed 2 December 2009

Asia-Pacific Partnership – Organization at www.asiapacificpartnership.org/english/organization.aspx, last accessed 26 July 2009

Asia-Pacific Partnership Meetings and Events (2009) at www.asiapacificpartnership.org/english/meeting_events.aspx, last accessed 26 July 2009

Asia-Pacific Partnership on Clean Development and Climate (2009) at www.asiapacificpartnership.org/, last accessed 7 February 2009

Asia-Pacific Partnership Project Roster (2009) at www.asiapacificpartnership.org/english/project_roster.aspx, last accessed 29 July 2009

Asia-Pacific Partnership Public–Private Sector Task Forces at asiapacificpartnership.org/task_forces.aspx, last accessed 8 February 2009

Avoice (African American Voices in Congress), *Environmental Justice Timeline* at www.avoiceonline.org/environmental/timeline.html, last accessed 10 August 2009

Climos, *About Us* at www.climos.com/aboutus.php, last accessed 20 October 2010

How Does the Precautionary Principle Apply? at www.climos.com/faq.php#50, last accessed 20 October 2010

What Is Climos' Funding/Business Model? at www.climos.com/faq.php#9, last accessed 20 October 2010

Commonwealth of Australia, Department of Environment, Water, Heritage and the Arts, *Uluru-Kata Tjuta National Park* at www.environment.gov.au/parks/uluru/, last accessed 18 April 2011

Compliance Committee of the Aarhus Convention, *Implementation of Decisions of the Meeting of the Parties on Compliance by Individual Parties*, United Nations Economic Commission for Europe at www.unece.org/env/pp/CCimplementation.htm, last accessed 24 October 2010

European Commission, *Cheap Carbon Only Temporary in the EU ETS* (20 August 2009) Environment for Europeans at ec.europa.eu/environment/news/efe/climate/20090820_carbonets_en.htm, last accessed 21 May 2011

Friends of the Earth Australia, *Australia Isolates Itself at Climate Change Negotiations* (2006) at www.foe.org.au/media-releases/2006-media-releases/mr_14_11_06.htm, last accessed 2 December 2009

Genewatch UK, *Environmental Risks* at www.genewatch.org/sub-532322, last accessed 17 July 2010

Govtrack.US at wwwgovtrack.us, last accessed 10 August 2009

Guidance Document on Aarhus Convention Compliance Mechanism, Volume 11 (2008) at www.unece.org/env/pp/compliance/manualv8.doc, last accessed 21 May 2011

Hands Off Mother Earth, *Ocean Fertilization* at www.handsoffmotherearth.org/learn-more/what-is-geoengineering/ocean-fertilization/, last accessed 20 October 2010

Hofer, John, *et al.*, *Yield Potential and Response of Roundup Ready Soybean Varieties to Raptor or Pursuit Herbicides* (1998) Kansas State University at www.biotech-info.net/herb_resist_ksu.pdf, last accessed 21 May 2011

Independent Review of the Environment Protection and Biodiversity Conservation Act 1999 (Cth) at www.environment.gov.au/epbc/review/index.html, last accessed 21 January 2010

Institute for International Law and Justice, New York University School of Law, *Global Administrative Law Project – Background* at www.iilj.org/GAL/, last accessed 6 December 2010

International Institute for Sustainable Development, *COP-1 Report* (1995) Earth Negotiations Bulletin Vol. 12 No. 21 at www.iisd.ca/vol12/1221000e.html, last accessed 31 May 2011

COP 14 Highlights (2008) Earth Negotiations Bulletin Vol. 12 No. 388 at www.iisd.ca/vol12/enb12388e.html, last accessed 31 May 2011

Report of the Third Conference of the Parties to the United Nations Framework Convention on Climate Change: 1–11 December 1997 (1997) Earth Negotiations Bulletin Vol. 12 No. 76 at www.iisd.ca/vol12/enb1276e.html, last accessed 31 May 2011

Summary of the Copenhagen Climate Conference, 7–19 December 2009 (2009) Earth Negotiations Bulletin Vol. 12 No. 259 at www.iisd.ca/vol12/enb12459.html, last accessed 16 May 2010

Methane to Markets Partnership, *Partners* (2009) at www.methanetomarkets.org/partners/country/index.htm, last accessed 7 February 2009

Ocean Nourishment Corporation Pty Ltd, *Ocean Nourishment Corporation* at www.oceannourishment.com, last accessed 21 October 2010

Technology at www.oceannourishment.com/technology.asp, last accessed 20 October 2010

Parliament of Australia Parliamentary Library, *Montreal Protocol on Substances that Deplete the Ozone Layer* (2010) at www.aph.gov.au/library/pubs/ClimateChange/governance/international/montreal.htm, last accessed 17 January 2011

Petition to the Inter-American Commission on Human Rights Seeking Relief from Violations Resulting from Global Warming Caused by Acts and Omissions of the United States at www.ciel.org/Publications/ICC_Petition_7Dec05.pdf, last accessed 18 April 2011

Pew Center on Global Climate Change, *Summary of G8 Summit 2005 in Gleneagles Scotland* at www.pewclimate.org/policy_center/international_policy/summary_of_g8.cfm, last accessed 7 February 2009

Siegel, Bruce and Nolan, Lea, 'Leveling the Field: Ensuring Equity through National Health Care Reform' (2009) *The New England Journal of Medicine* Health Care Reform Centre at healthcarereform.nejm.org/?p=2461, last accessed 21 January 2010

UNFCCC, *Appendix I – Quantified Economy-Wide Emissions Targets for 2020* (2010) at unfccc.int/home/items/5264.php, last accessed 15 March 2010

Parties and Observers (2009) at http://unfccc.int/parties_and_observers/items/2704.php, last accessed 7 Febraury 2009

United Nations Climate Change Conference in Bali (2007) at http://unfccc.int/meetings/cop_13/items/4049.php, last accessed 7 February 2009

United Nations Food and Agriculture Organization, *General Situation of World Fish Stocks* at www.fao.org/newsroom/common/ecg/1000505/en/stocks.pdf, last accessed 1 November 2009

United States of America Department of State, *Asia-Pacific Partnership on Clean Development and Climate: Concluding Press Conference* (2006) at http://2001–2009.state.gov/g/oes/rls/or/2006/59213.htm, last accessed 2 August 2009

Bilateral and Regional Climate Partnerships (2009) at http://2001–2009.state.gov/g/oes/climate/c22820.htm, last accessed 7 February 2009

Intervention of the United States: Plenary Session of Ad Hoc Working Group on Long Term Cooperative Action under the Convention (2009) at www.state.gov/g/oes/rls/remarks/2009/120974.htm, last accessed 10 August 2010

Major Economies Process on Energy Security and Climate Change at http://2001–2009.state.gov/g/oes/climate/mem/index.htm, last accessed 7 February 2009

United States of America Government, *Asia Pacific Partnership on Clean Development and Climate Website; Program Office and Task Force Contacts* at http://2008–2009.app.gov/about/taskforce/index.htm#alum, last accessed 5 February 2009

US Involvement in the Asia-Pacific Partnership on Clean Development and Climate at http://2008–2009.app.gov/library/111306.htm, last accessed 8 February 2009

Washingtonwatch.com at www.washingtonwatch.com, last accessed 10 August 2009

Weier, John, *John Martin 1935–1993* (2001) NASA at http://earthobservatory.nasa.gov/Library/Giants/Martin/, last accessed 6 June 2009.

World Heritage Centre, *Uluṟu-Kata Tjuṯa National Park* at http://whc.unesco.org/en/list/447/documents/, last accessed 18 April 2011

Yale Forum on Climate Change & the Media at www.yaleclimatemediaforum.org, last accessed 22 November 2010

News

'After Tianjin, S'pore–Nanjing "Mini Eco-City" Mooted', *Straits Times* (Singapore), 24 April 2008

'ASEAN Agrees on Role of Human Rights Commission', *Straits Times* (Singapore), 21 July 2009

'ASEAN Needs Help to Tackle Haze: PM: International Expertise Needed to Help Nip Problem in the Bud', *Straits Times* (Singapore), 6 November 2006

'British Energy Goes into Meltdown', *ENDS Report* (London), October 2002, 28

'Chile and Argentina Unite Against UK Claim', *The Independent* (London) 8 March 2009, 36

'Climate Change Raises Spill Risks in Oil-Rich Arctic', *Calgary Herald* 26 July 2008, E5

'Haze on Line', *FIRE Information Bulletin* 3, 9 November 2006

'Jakarta Using Sand Ban to Put Pressure on S'pore', *Straits Times* (Singapore), 17 February 2007

'Monks on the March', *The Economist* (London), 15 March 2008

'Secretary of State Clinton Speaks on Joint Session of the Antarctic Treaty Consultative Meeting, The Arctic Council, 50th Anniversary of the Antarctic Treaty', *US Fed News*, 11 April 2009

Alford, Peter, 'Aussie Judgment Served on Whalers', *The Australian* (Sydney) 24 January 2008, 7

Annan, Kofi, 'Secretary-General Salutes International Workshop on Human Security in Mongolia' (Ulan Bator, press release, 8–10 May 2000)

'Two Concepts of Sovereignty', *The Economist* (London), 18 September 1999

Australian Broadcasting Corporation, 'China Unveils Plan to Limit Emissions' (2009) *ABC News* at www.abc.net.au/news/stories/2009/11/27/2754975.htm, last accessed 2 December 2009

'ETS Postponed by Rudd Government', *The 7.30 Report*, 27 April 2010

'Inuits Need Cash for Freezers in Warming Arctic', *ABC News*, 13 December 2009 at www.abc.net.au/news/stories/2009/12/13/2770156.htm, last accessed 18 April 2011

'Minister Defends Position on Greenhouse Gas Emissions', *Insiders*, 18 August 2002 at www.abc.net.au/insiders/content/2002/s651631.htm, last accessed 2 December 2009

'Record Heat Forces Closure of Canada Arctic Park', *ABC News*, 2 August 2008, at www.abc.net.au/news/stories/2008/08/02/2322340.htm, last accessed 2 August 2008

Australian Government, 'National Clean Energy Target' (press release, 23 September 2007)

Brown, D., 'James Watt's Land Rush', *Newsweek*, 29 June 1981, 24

Connor, Steve, 'Nuclear Power? Yes Please: Leading Greens Join Forces in a Major U-Turn', *The Independent* (London), 23 February 2009

Devan, Janadas, 'Haze: Why Jakarta Should Accept International Help', *Sunday Times* (Singapore), 4 November 2006

Farr, Malcolm, 'Clean Coal Powers Howard', *Herald Sun* (Melbourne), 14 November 2006

Human Rights Watch, 'China, India, Nepal: Free Tibetan Protesters' (News Release, 14 March 2008) at http://china.hrw.org/press/news_release/china_india_nepal_free_tibetan_protesters, last accessed 18 April 2011

Kelly, Paul, 'Internal Polling Tipped Gillard Over Line', *The Australian* (Sydney), 30 June 2010

Koh, Tommy, *et al.*, 'The ASEAN Charter', *PacNet Newsletter* 331 (7 September 2007)

Krugman, Paul, 'Building a Green Economy', *New York Times*, 5 April 2010

Ooi, Jeff, 'Haze: Balls on UN Table, Indonesia Upset', *Asian Correspondent.com*, 6 November 2006 at http://asiancorrespondent.com/6717/haze-balls-on-un-table-indonesia-upset/, last accessed 17 January 2011

Paulo, Derrick, 'Between the Sand and a Flooded Place', *Today* (Singapore), 13 February 2007

Phillips, Nicky, 'We're Dealing to Coal Addicts: Hansen', *Sydney Morning Herald*, 4 March 2010

President Truman, 'Policy of the United States with Respect to the Natural Resources of the Subsoil and Sea Bed of the Continental Shelf' (White House News Release, 28 September 1945)

Reuters, 'Germany Sticking to Ambitious CO_2 Target: Adviser', *Reuters*, 11 January 2010 at www.reuters.com/article/idUSTRE60A4D020100111, last accessed 15 February 2010

Rudd, Kevin, 'Carbon Pollution Reduction Scheme: Support in Managing the Impact of the Global Recession' (press release, 4 May 2009)

and Wong, Penny, 'Joint Press Conference with the Minister for Climate Change' (press conference, Copenhagen, 19 December 2009)

Tollefson, Jeff, 'UN Decision Puts Brakes on Ocean Fertilization' (2008) 453 *Nature News* at www.nature.com/news/2008/080604/full/ 453704b.html, last accessed 18 December 2009

Vidal, John, 'The Year the World Woke Up', *Society Guardian*, *The Guardian* (London and Manchester), 20 December 2006

Voice of America, 'Polar Bear Added to List of Threatened Species in US', *VOANews.com*, 16 May 2008, at www.voanews.com/english/news/science-technology/a-13–2008–05–16-voa27.html, last accessed 17 January 2011

Wong, Q., 'Study Estimates Vast Supplies of Arctic Oil and Gas', *Anchorage Daily News*, 24 July 2008, A6

INDEX